Environmental Law in Serbia

Environmental Law in Serbia

Fourth Edition

Vid Vukasović†
Dragoljub Todić

This book was originally published as a monograph in the International Encyclopaedia of Laws/Environmental Law.

Founding Editor: Roger Blanpain
General Editor: Frank Hendrickx
Volume Editor: Kurt Deketelaere

Wolters Kluwer

Published by:
Kluwer Law International B.V.
PO Box 316
2400 AH Alphen aan den Rijn
The Netherlands
E-mail: lrs-sales@wolterskluwer.com
Website: www.wolterskluwer.com/en/solutions/kluwerlawinternational

Sold and distributed by:
Wolters Kluwer Legal & Regulatory U.S.
920 Links Avenue
Landisville, PA 17538
United States of America
E-mail: customer.service@wolterskluwer.com

ISBN 978-94-035-3338-4

e-Book: ISBN 978-94-035-3348-3
web-PDF: ISBN 978-94-035-3358-2

This title is available on www.kluwerlawonline.com

The Authors

Dr Vid Vukasović completed studies at the Faculty of Law of the University of Belgrade and received his master's and PhD at the same University. He received his Diploma in Air and Space Law from McGill University (1968, Montreal, Canada).

From 1968 to 2006, he was a Research Fellow at the Institute of International Politics and Economics (Senior Research Staff from 1974), Belgrade. He was the Head of the International Law Department (1984–1987) and Chairman of the Scientific Council of the Institute (1984–1995 and 2000–2005).

He is a member of the International Council of Environmental Law (ICEL), the International Law Association (ILA), the Serbian International Law Association and the Serbian Association of Lawyers. He is also a member of other Yugoslavian and international organizations and other bodies dealing with international law, environmental protection and, air and space law.

He has participated in a number of important international conferences and projects, for example, in the work of the Intergovernmental Working Group of experts on natural resources shared by two or more States which drafted the principles concerning shared natural resources (Geneva 1976, Nairobi 1977); the Ad Hoc Meeting of Senior Government Officials Expert in Environmental Law (Geneva 1981 and Montevideo 1981) on which the System Wide Medium Term Environment Programme (SWMTEP) was drafted; the Mediterranean Action Plan (MAP) project 'Blue Book'; project concerning the interrelation between human rights and the development of science and technology commissioned by the United Nations University (Tokyo) in 1988–1990; various UNEP's working groups, sessions of the UNEP's Governing Council, a number of conferences dealing with the protection of the Mediterranean Sea, etc.

Dr Vukasović is a member of editing boards of various publications, including the main Yugoslav International Law Journal (*The Yugoslav International Law Review*) and International Problems and books: *International Law and the Development of Science and Technology* (in Serbian, with summaries in English and Russian), Belgrade 1978; *Protection and Improvement of the Environment-International Legal Regulation* (in Serbian with a summary in English), Belgrade, 1980; *Environmental Protection and the United Nations* (in Serbian, with a summary in English), Belgrade, 1985; (with D. Todić) *International Organizations in the Field of Environmental Protection* (in Serbian) 'Prometej', Novi Sad, 1999; edited (with D. Todić) *Pravo na adekvatnu zivotnu sredinu – pravo na informisanje i ucesce u odlucivanju prema Arhuskoj konvenciji (The Right to Adequate Environment – Right to Environmental Information and to Public Participation according to the Aarhus Convention and to Yugoslav legislation)*, Regional Environmental Centre for Central and Eastern Europe, Belgrade Office, Belgrade, 2001; edited (with D. Todić), *Zaštita životne sredine u međunarodnom i unutrašnjem pravu (Protection of the Environment in International and National Law)*, Uprava za zaštitu životne sredine Ministarstva zdravlja i životne sredine Republike Srbije, Belgrade, 2001; monograph (with D. Todić), *Serbia and Montenegro, Environmental Law, International Encyclopedia of Laws*, Supplement 37, Kluwer Law International, The Hague, London, New York, 2002; (with D. Todić) *Ekološka kriza u svetu i odgovor međunarodne zajednice (izbor najznačajnijih međunarodnih dokumenata i jugoslovenskih propisa)*, Savezni sekretarijat za rad, zdravstvo i socijalno staranje, Sektor za životnu sredinu i Institut za međunarodnu politiku i privredu, Belgrade, 2002; (one of the authors) *Enciklopedija – Životna sredina – Održivi razvoj*, published by ECOLIBRI, Beograd, Zavod za udžbenike i sredstva, Srpsko Sarajevo, 2003; (with D. Todić) *Zbirka propisa u oblasti životne sredine*, Megatrend univerzitet, Belgrade 2007.

Besides the mentioned books, he has published more than 300 articles and other shorter works in various periodicals. He has lectured in Serbia and abroad. For example, he has lectured at the Specialized Course in High Administration and Comparative Governance 2003–2004, the University of Bari and the Institute of International Politics and Economics, Bari and Belgrade and at the Specialized Course 'The Law of Energetic', Faculty of Law, Belgrade 2005 and 2006, etc.

Dr Dragoljub Todić earned his master's and PhD at the Faculty of Law, University of Belgrade and his bachelor's at the Faculty of Political Science, University of Belgrade. He was employed at the Institute of International Politics and Economics (Belgrade) (retired at the end of 2023). He served as a Professor at The Faculty of Geoeconomics and Faculty of Law from 2001 to 2012. His fields of interest include environmental law, international law, human rights protection, the EU environmental policy and law, sustainable development law, migration law, etc. He is a member of the International Law Association (ILA), the Serbian International Law Association (JUMP), and several environmental NGOs. Dr Todić has participated in a number of conferences in Serbia and abroad.

His published books are: Todić, D., Vukasović, V. 1999. Međunarodne organizacije i međunarodna saradnja u oblasti zaštite životne sredine [International Organizations and International Cooperation in the Field of the Environment]. 'Prometej', Novi Sad; Todić, D., Čok, V., Vukasović, V., Mijušković, O., Dabić, Lj., Pavličević, B. (Eds). 2000. Zakonodavstvo Evropske unije o životnoj sredini i zemlje u tranziciji [The EU Environmental Legislation and Countries in Transition]. Federal Ministry for Development, Science and the Environment, Belgrade; Todić, D., Vukasović, V. (Eds). 2001. Pravo na adekvatnu životnu sredinu – pravo na informisanje i ucesce u odlucivanju prema Arhuskoj konvenciji [The Right to Adequate Environment – Right to Environmental Information and to Public Participation According to the Aarhus Convention and to Yugoslav Legislation]. Regional Environmental Centre for Central and Eastern Europe, Belgrade Office, Belgrade; Todić, D., Vukasović, V. (Eds). 2021. Zaštita životne sredine u međunarodnom i unutrašnjem pravu [Protection of the Environment in International and National Law]. Uprava za zaštitu životne sredine Ministarstva zdravlja i životne sredine Republike Srbije, Beograd; Vukasović, V. Todić, D. 2002. Serbia and Montenegro, Environmental Law, International Encyclopaedia of Laws, Supplement 37, Kluwer Law International, The Hague, London, New York; Todić, D., Vukasović, V. 2003. Ekološka kriza u svetu i odgovor međunarodne zajednice (izbor najznačajnijih međunarodnih dokumenata i jugoslovenskih propisa) [Ecological crisis in the world and the response of the international community (selection of the most important international documents and Yugoslav regulations)]. Savezni sekretarijat za rad, zdravstvo i socijalno staranje, Institut za međunarodnu politiku i privredu, Beograd; Stevanović, B., Knežević, L., Čikarić, S., Ilić-Popov, G., Karaman, G., Nedović, B., Todić, D., Vukasović, V., et. al. 2003. Enciklopedija – Životna sredina – Održivi razvoj [Encyclopedia Environment and Sustainable Development: Book of Correct Answers]. Ecolibri, Beograd, Zavod za udžbenike i sredstva, Srpsko Sarajevo; Todić, D., Vukasović, V. 2007. Zbirka propisa u oblasti životne sredine [Collection of environmental regulations]. Megatrend univerzitet, Belgrade; Todić, D. 2008. Ekološki menadžment u uslovima globalizacije [Environmental Management in Circumstances of Globalization]. Megatrend, Beograd (Textbook); Todić, D. 2008. Savremena politika i pravo životne sredine [Contemporary Environmental Policy and Law]. Megatrend Univerzitet, Beograd (Textbook); Todić, D., Nikolić, M. (Eds) 2013. Strateški pravci razvoja i utvrđivanja položaja Srbije u savremenim međunarodnim odnosima [The Strategic Directions of Development and Determining the Position of Serbia in Contemporary International Relations]. Institut za međunarodnu politiku i privredu, Beograd; Grbić, V., Antevski, M., Todić, D. 2013. Finansiranje i zajedničke politike Evropske unije [Financing and Common Policies of the European Union], Institut za međunarodnu politiku i privredu, Beograd. Todić, D. 2014. Klimatske promene u pravu i reforma sistema upravljanja [Climate Change in Law and Reform of the Governance System]. Institut za međunarodnu politiku i privredu, Beograd; Todić, D., Grbić, V., Antevski, M. 2014. Pridruživanje Evropskoj uniji i održivi razvoj [EU Accession and Sustainable Development], Institut za međunarodnu politiku i privredu, Beograd; Grbić, V., Todić, D., Brnjas, Z. 2015. Savremene tendencije u poljoprivredi Evropske unije i problem navodnjavanja [Contemporary Tendencies in the Agriculture of the European Union and the Problem of Irrigation], Institut za ekonomiku poljoprivrede, Beograd; Todic, D. 2018. Environmental Law – Montenegro. International Encyclopaedia of Laws: Environmental Law, (ed.) Kurt Deketelaere, Kluwer Law International, Alphen aan den Rijn, The Netherlands; Todić, D. 2018. Ujedinjene nacije, međunarodni ugovori i životna sredina [United Nations, International Agreements and the Environment], Institut za međunarodnu politiku i privredu, Beograd; Todić D., Ignjatić M., Vukasović V. 2022. Environmental Law – Bosnia and Herzegovina, International Encyclopaedia of Laws: Environmental Law, (ed.) Kurt Deketelaere, Kluwer Law International, Alphen aan den Rijn, The Netherlands; Todić, D., Vučić, M. 2022. Prirodni resursi: između prava i konflikta [Natural resources: between law and conflict]. Institut za međunarodnu politiku i privredu, Beograd; Grečić, V., Vekarić, V., Todić, D. 2023. Migration Law in Serbia, Wolters Kluwer, Law & Business, Alphen aan den Rijn,

The Netherlands; Todić, D., Vučić, M. 2023. 'Montenegro', International Encyclopaedia of Law: Environmental Law, Kluwer Law International B.V. PO Box 316 2400 AH Alphen AAN DEN Run, The Netherlands.

Besides these, he has published more than 250 articles and other short works.

Table of Contents

List of Abbreviations

ABS	Accreditation Board of Serbia
AC	Aarhus Convention
AECQ	Answers to the European Commission's Questionnaire
AERS	Energy Agency of the Republic of Serbia
AP	Autonomous Province
APV	Autonomous Province of Vojvodina
BAT	Best Available Techniques
BPEO	Best Practical Environmental Options
CARDS	EU Community Assistance for Reconstruction, Development and Stabilization
CC	Constitutional Court
CDM	Clean Development Mechanism of the Kyoto Protocol
CIPIPDP	Commissioner for Information of Public Importance and Personal Data Protection
CITES	Convention on International Trade in Endangered Species of Wild Flora and Fauna
CLRTAP	Convention on Long-Range Transboundary Air Pollution
CSOs	Civil Society Organizations
EC	European Commission
EC 2016	Screening report Serbia, Chapter 27 – Environment
EC 2022	European Commission, Serbia 2022 Report, SWD(2022) 338 final, Brussels, 12.10.2022
EC 2023	European Commission, Serbia 2023 Report, SWD (2023) 695 final, Brussels, 8.11.2023
EEA	European Environment Agency
EIA	Environmental Impact Assessment
ELVs	Emission Limit Values
EMAS	Eco-Management and Audit Scheme
EMS	Environmental Management System
EPA	Environmental Protection Agency

List of Abbreviations

EPL	Environmental Protection Law (Law on Environmental Protection)
EU	European Union
FAO	Food and Agriculture Organization
FRY	Federal Republic of Yugoslavia
GMO	Genetically Modified Organisms
GOV RS	Government of the Republic of Serbia
IAEA	International Atomic Energy Agency
ICAO	International Civil Aviation Organization
ICJ	International Court of Justice
ICPDR	International Commission for the Protection of the Danube River
ICTY	UN International Criminal Tribunal for the former Yugoslavia
INECP	Integrated National Energy and Climate Plan (Draft)
IPA	Instrument for Pre-accession Assistance
IPPC	Integrated Pollution Prevention and Control
IRENA	International Renewable Energy Agency
LMO	Living Modified Organism
LSG	Local Self-Government
MAEP	Ministry of Agriculture and Environmental Protection
MAFWM	Ministry of Agriculture, Forestry and Water Management
MEA	Multilateral Environmental Agreement
MEDEP	Ministry of Energy, Development and Environmental Protection
MEI	Ministry of European Integration
MEMSP	Ministry of Environment, Mining and Spatial Planning
MEP	Ministry of Environmental Protection
MESP	Ministry of Environment and Spatial Planning
MME	Ministry of Mining and Energy
MOU	Memorandum of Understanding
NA	National Assembly
NAMAs	National Appropriate Mitigation Actions
NATO	North Atlantic Treaty Organization
NEPP	National Environmental Protection Programme
NGO	Non-governmental Organization
NPAA	National Programme for the Adoption of the EU Acquis, 2014
NPAA II	National Programme for the Adoption of the EU Acquis, Second Revision, 2016

NPAA III	National Programme for the Adoption of the EU Acquis, Third Revision, 2018
NPAA IV	National Programme for the Adoption of the EU Acquis, Fourth Revision, 2022
NPI	National Programme for Integration with the European Union
NSDS	National Sustainable Development Strategy
OJ	Official Journal
OJ – IT	Official Journal – International Treaties
OSCE	Organization for Security and Co-operation in Europe
PCBs	Polychlorinated Biphenyls
POPs	Persistent Organic Pollutants
PRTR	Pollution Release and Transfer Registers
REACH	EC Regulation on Registration, Evaluation, Authorization and Restriction of Chemicals
REC	Regional Environmental Centre
RES	Renewable Energy Sources
RHMS	Republic Hydrometeorological Service
RS	Republic of Serbia
S&M	Serbia and Moxsntenegro
SAA	Stabilization and Association Agreement
SAP	Stabilization and Association Process
SEA	Strategic Environmental Assessment
SFRY	Socialist Federal Republic of Yugoslavia
SRBATOM	Serbian Radiation and Nuclear Safety Directorate
SRS	Socialist Republic of Serbia
STAT. OFFICE RS.	Statistical Office of the Republic of Serbia
STAT.YEARB.SERB.	Statistical Yearbook of the Republic of Serbia
UN	United Nations
UNECE	United Nations Economic Commission for Europe
UNEP	United Nations Environment Programme
UNESCO	United Nations Educational, Scientific and Cultural Organization
UNHCR	Office of the United Nations High Commissioner for Refugees
UNMIK	The UN Interim Administration Mission in Kosovo
UNSC	United Nations Security Council
US	United States
WHO	World Health Organization

List of Abbreviations

Acknowledgements

The authors would like to thank Sean Bawden, Molly Grindley, John Lindsay, Carolyn Eliott Magwood and Anna Poliszot for research assistance in connection with the preparation of this volume.

The authors wish to thank Ms Mladenka Ignjatić (independent consultant, Belgrade) for her suggestions and contributions.

Acknowledgements

General Introduction

Chapter 1. General Information

§1. Geography and Population

1. The Republic of Serbia (RS) is located in southeastern Europe. Its total territory is 88.499 km^2.[1] The country lies between 41°53' (South) and 46°11' (North) northern geographical latitude and 18°49' (West) and 23°00' (East) eastern geographical longitude. Border countries are Albania, Bosnia and Herzegovina, Bulgaria, Croatia, Hungary, Macedonia, Montenegro and Romania. The total boundary is 2,361.7 km (total land boundary is 1,567.3 km; river boundary is 751.1 km; and lake boundary is 43.3 km).[2] It is important to add that some parts of the borders have not finally been demarcated yet.

2. The terrain varies extremely. There are rich fertile plains in the north (Vojvodina and Mačva) and some river valleys (the Sava Valley, the Morava Valley, etc.), while most of the other parts consist of mountains (the highest being Velika Rudoka Šar Planina – 2,660 m), high lands and hills.[3] There is 55% of arable land and 27% is forested. The main water resources are rivers. They belong to the basins of the Black, Adriatic and Aegean Seas. The Danube, Sava and Tisa are navigable. The longest river is the Danube, which flows through Serbia for 588 km along its 2,857 km long course.[4]

3. The climate is moderately continental with a gradual transition between seasons.[5] In the RS, 2022 was the second warmest year since 1951.[6] The most rainy

1. STAT. YEARB. SERB. 2023, 14. 'The land area (88 499 km^2) data relates to the territory of the Republic of Serbia and should be considered as provisional.' *Ibid.*, 13.
2. *Ibid.*, 14. Data on established State borders have been taken over from the border documentation available in the Borders Service of the Ministry of Foreign Affairs of the Republic of Serbia.
3. STAT. YEARB. SERB. 2023, 15. The RS 'has three major landforms – the plain areas in Vojvodina and the flood plains of the Danube, Sava, and Drina rivers; the Morava valley in its mainstream and two southern arms; and the mountainous areas that cover most of the country south of the Sava and Danube.' MAFWM. 2019. 17.
4. The Sava River Basin is a major drainage basin of Southeastern Europe, covering a total area of approximately 97,713.20 km^2, and represents one of the most significant sub-basins of the Danube River Basin, with a share of 12%. For additional information *see* MAFWM. 2019, 17.
5. 'Continental climate prevails in the mountainous regions of above 1,000 m altitude. The southwestern part of the country borders the Mediterranean, subtropical and continental climate.' MEP. 2023a, 2.

period is late spring and early summer. The annual precipitation during the 1961–1990 period averaged for the whole country is 896 mm.[7] The analysis of precipitation indices shows that, in addition to small (statistically nonsignificant) trends of change in accumulated annual precipitation, there is a change in precipitation pattern and a different redistribution by intensity.[8]

4. The estimated number of population in the RS (excluding Kosovo-Metohija)[9] in 2022 was 6,664,449.[10] In the period between the two last censuses (2002–2022), there was a decrease in total population of the RS which is primarily the result of a negative natural increase and emigration of our citizens abroad. Ethnically, the RS is a multinational community. Serbs make up 80.6% of the population. National minorities are: Hungarians 2.8%, Bosniaks 2.3%, Roma 2%, etc.[11] The population of Serbia is getting older. The average age in Serbia, as shown in Census 2022, is 43.9 years, thus ranking Serbia among countries with deep demographic age.

5. Thousands of Serbs and members of other ethnic groups moved during the war and crisis of the 1990s because of military actions and ethnic conflicts to Serbia from other parts of the former Yugoslavia (estimated number of refugees is more than half a million). At the same time, thousands, in most cases young and highly educated people, emigrated because of economic and political reasons, mainly to Western Europe and overseas countries. The impact of these migrations is still felt.

The registration of refugees residing in the RS, which was conducted from 27 November 2004 to 25 January 2005, counted 141,685 refugees. Out of this number, the refugee status of 104,246 persons was confirmed. Current number of refugees in the RS is *24.897* persons (17.074 from the Republic of Croatia and 7,823 from Bosnia and Herzegovina).[12]

In March 2000, in collaboration with the Office of the United Nations High Commissioner for Refugees (UNHCR), the Commissariat organized registration of internally displaced persons from Kosovo and Metohija, when 187,129 people were

6. EPA. 2023a, 136. 'The lowest temperature ever recorded since the instrumental measurements commenced on the territory of Serbia was -39,5°C in Karajukica Bunarima (near Sjenica) on January 29 1987 and the highest temperature ever measured was 44,9°C in Smederevska Palanka on July 24 2007.' Smailagić, J., et al. 2013, 2.
7. 'Dry areas with precipitation below 600 mm are situated in the north-eastern parts of the country, in the South Morava valley and part of Kosovo. Average annual precipitation at the Pester plateau and Mt. Kopaonik was much higher (up to 1,000 mm), and some mountainous summits in the south-west of Serbia had even heavier precipitation of over 1,000 mm.' EPA. 2007, 49.
8. Đurđević, V., et al., 2018, 12.
9. The AP of Kosovo-Metohija is, according to Resolution 1244 of the UN Security Council (1999), under the United Nations Interim Administration Mission (UNMIK), and is not covered in this Monograph. For text of the Resolution 1244, *see* UN, 1999. 'Census data from 1948 to 1981 refer to the whole territory of the Republic of Serbia, while censuses 1991. 2002 and 2011 and 2022 do not contain data for AP Kosovo and Metohija.' STAT. YEARB. SERB, 2023, 29.
10. The estimates are based on the results of the 2022 Census of Population, Households and Dwellings, and results of natural changes statistics and population internal migration. STAT. YEARB. SERB, 2023, 25.
11. STAT. YEARB. SERB. 2023. –), 30. *See also* the Official Website of the Government of RS, https://www.srbija.gov.rs/tekst/en/130129/people-language-and-religion.php (23.11.2023).
12. https://kirs.gov.rs/media/uploads/1statistika%202023.pdf (23.11.2023).

registered. In the period between 2000 and 2005, there were more than 20,000 newcomers from Kosovo, so at the end of 2005, the number of internally displaced persons in Serbia without Kosovo and Metohija was 209,021. Currently, this number is 201,047 persons.[13]

6. In 2015, RS became a significantly more frequent transit country for many migrants from Syria, Afghanistan, Iraq, Iran and Pakistan who want to go to the EU. The number of migrants who declared intention for asylum is in a significant increase. As of May 2015, the number of people who had expressed their intention to seek asylum in the RS suddenly began to grow.[14] 'The entire migration situation in 2021, both worldwide and in Serbia, was influenced by the fact that the COVID-19 pandemic is still ongoing.'[15]

7. The RS is an emigration country.[16] Nevertheless, according to the Economic Migration Strategy of RS, the RS is 'traditionally an emigration country, but also a country of immigration and transit migration. Historically, emigration was conditioned by economic and political factors'.[17]

8. The state of health of the population in Serbia was far from satisfactory at the end of the crisis in the 1990s. Certainly, one of the reasons for this was environmental pollution, but the more serious reason was overall poverty.[18] During the decade 1990–2000 of grave economic and political crisis, hundreds of thousands of refugees and wrong economic policy of the former regime caused further fall in living standards, what was, among other things, reflected in health. After the normalization in 2000, both standard of living and state of health have been steadily improving due to economic development and donations and investments from abroad.[19] The RS made significant progress in reducing poverty. Even though in the period 2013–2015, there was an increase in the at-risk-of-poverty rate, which is the basic indicator of financial poverty, its declining trend was observed since 2016 and the lowest rate ever since it was subject to measuring in Serbia was recorded in

---

13. https://kirs.gov.rs/eng/internally-displaced-persons/internally-displaced-persons (23.11.2023). *See also* GOV RS. 2015a. *See also* UN, 2020, points 17–23; UN, 2023, points 92–101.
14. *See* GOV RS. 2015b, 56.
15. GOV RS. 2022e, 5. 'In 2021, the highest number of immigrants came from China and Russia (21.4% and 14.8%, respectively).' *Ibid.*, 9.
16. 'According to the estimates of the UN, the total number of Serbian emigrants in 2019 was around 950,000, which accounts for about 14% of the resident population in the country (excluding Kosovo and Metohija)'. UNDP. 2022, 100.
17. GOV RS, 2020b, 5. Emigration processes in the second part of the 20th century have conditioned the depopulation of rural areas, due to internal rural-urban migration, predominantly of economic character. The qualified and most often highly educated population is mainly emigrating from the RS, therefore emigration has negative effects on the labour force supply and overall economic development. *Ibid.*, 6.
18. The Poverty Reduction Strategy paper (PRSp) for Serbia, GOV RS, 2003, 130. The Strategy was adopted in 2003, as a medium-term development framework directed at reducing key forms of poverty. https://kirs.gov.rs/media/uploads/Dokumenti-i-publikacije/Strategije/PRSP_Main_text.pdf (23.11.2023).
19. For more details, *see* S. Šolak. 2007; Slavnić. 2013.

2021.[20] 'The health of the Serbian population has improved over the last decade. Life expectancy at birth increased slightly in recent years, but it remains, for example, around 5 years below the average across European Union countries.'[21]

§2. Political History and Structure

9. Serbia was in the medieval centuries a kingdom and even for a while an empire (in the fourteenth century). The Ottoman Empire occupied it in the fifteenth century, and it was liberated in the nineteenth century, gaining full independence from the Ottoman Empire in 1878. Serbia was a principality until 1885 when it became a kingdom.[22] In 1918, it became a part of the Kingdom of Yugoslavia and, after the Second World War, a constituent Republic of the Socialist Federal Republic of Yugoslavia (SFRY).[23]

It must be added, however, that some parts of present Serbia were until 1918 a part of the Austro-Hungarian Empire (Vojvodina province). Some other territories also belonged, until 1912, to the Ottoman Empire (Kosovo-Metohija and some other parts of southern and southwestern Serbia).

10. One of the main characteristics of SFRY, from its establishment after the Second World War till its end in the 1990s, was the specific socialist model combined with self-management system in internal affairs and non-aligned policy on the international scene. After the disintegration of the Former SFRY, which consisted of six republics (Slovenia, Croatia, Serbia, Bosnia and Herzegovina, Montenegro and Macedonia), five new States appeared on the political map of Southeastern Europe. While other constituent republics proclaimed independence, Serbia and Montenegro remained, for a while, a federation (Federal Republic of Yugoslavia, proclaimed in 1992) sometimes called the Third Yugoslavia. It was transformed in 2003 into a loose semi-confederal State Union of Serbia and Montenegro which lasted till 2006 when Serbia and Montenegro became independent States.

It is important here to stress that the former Yugoslavia was different in many ways from the members of the Soviet Block. It was a non-aligned country that had a rather intensive international cooperation and an important role not only in the region but also in world politics (for instance, the former President of SFRY Tito was one of the founders of the non-aligned movement). Among other things, the country was more active than other socialist countries in environmental protection, taking an active part in important international conferences (for instance, the 1972 Stockholm Conference), environmental action plans (for instance, the Mediterranean Action Plan – MAP) and actively participating in the work of international

20. STAT. OFFICE RS. 2023b, 118. 'According to the Survey data, the at-risk-of-poverty rate was 21.2% in 2021, and compared to 2020, it was lower by 0.5 percentage points.' STAT. OFFICE RS. 2022b.
21. Bjegovic-Mikanovic, V, et al., 2019, xv; *See also*, STAT. OFFICE RS. 2021.
22. On this part of Serbian history, *see* Pavlović, 2004, 1–138.
23. About Serbian history in Yugoslavia, *see* Lj. Dimić, 2001.

organizations and other bodies (United Nations Environment Programme (UNEP), United Nations Economic Commission for Europe (UNECE), World Health Organization (WHO) etc.).

11. One of the Serbian Autonomous Provinces (APs), Kosovo-Metohija, has, after the 1999 North Atlantic Treaty Organization (NATO) intervention (24 March–10 June),[24] a special status according to the United Nations Security Council (UNSC) Resolution 1244. Under the UN Interim Administration Mission in Kosovo (UNMIK) governance, a whole new legal system has been formed with some UNMIK regulations concerning environmental protection as well.[25] Among other things, the Administrative Department of Environmental Protection was established.[26]

12. After the elections in September and December and the mass demonstration on 5 October 2000, Serbia has become a State of pluralistic and parliamentary democracy devoted to the promotion of the rule of law, market economy, social justice, human rights, equality and welfare of all citizens. Its position in the international community improved considerably after the United Nations (UN), European Union (EU) and United States (US) sanctions were lifted and its position in the UN and other key international organizations was normalized. In spite of that, it had many unresolved political, economic and other problems. Two main political problems were the future of the Federation and the status of Kosovo-Metohija. The first one was resolved when the Federation was first transformed into the State Union of Serbia and Montenegro and finally when the bond between the two republics was cut and they became two independent States.[27] The other problem (Kosovo-Metohija) is still one of the main political problems of Serbia.[28] 'Negotiations between Belgrade and Prishtina on issues of importance to the life of Serbs and other non-Albanian population in Kosovo-Metohija began in March 2011 in Brussels, with the mediation of the European Union.'[29] In the meantime, the 'Republic of Kosovo' has been recognized by some countries, although five EU States refuse to recognize it. The EU-facilitated Dialogue on the normalization of relations between Kosovo and Serbia continued. After months of intense negotiations, the

24. Several questions can be raised regarding the legality of the use of force and environmental protection in this case. For some open questions *see*, e.g., Gazzini. 2001, 409–434; *See also* Čavoški, 2020; Wheeler, 2001; Prosecutor's (ICTY) Report on the Nato Bombing Campaign, https://www.icty.org/en/press/prosecutors-report-nato-bombing-campaign (14.2.2024).
25. UNMIK Official Gazette, https://unmik.unmissions.org/sites/default/files/regulations/index.htm (4.1.2024).
26. UNMIK Regulation 032/2000.
27. *See* the Decision on the Declaration of the Independence of the Republic of Montenegro (OJ RM, No. 32/06) and the Decision on the Obligations of the State Bodies of the Republic of Serbia in Exercising the Competencies of the Republic of Serbia as a successor of the State Union of Serbia and Montenegro (OJ RS, No. 48/2006).
28. This is especially after 17 Feb. 2008, when the Assembly of Kosovo adopted 'Declaration of Independence'. *See also* GOV RS. 2008c.
29. *See* http://www.srbija.gov.rs/kosovo-metohija/index.php?id=43376 (4.1.2024). More on the Belgrade-Pristina negotiation process can be found here: https://www.kim.gov.rs/eng/pregovaracki-proces.php (13.2.2024).

Parties reached an Agreement on the Path to Normalization (in Brussels on 27 February 2023) and agreed on its Implementation Annex in Ohrid, North Macedonia (on 18 March 2023).[30] According to the EC, the overall pace of negotiations between Serbia and the EU will continue to depend, 'in particular, on the pace of rule of law reforms and on the normalization of Serbia's relations with Kosovo*'.[31]

13. In 2006, the new Serbian Constitution was adopted. Serbia is a republic with an elected President. The Prime Minister is elected by the Parliament. The Parliament has one house with 250 members. Parliamentary Elections (Elections for Members of Parliament of the RS) are held every four years. Early elections can be called as well when the National Assembly (NA) is dissolved by decree of the President of the Republic in cases stipulated by the Constitution. New elections were held on 17 December 2023. The formation of working bodies of the NA and the Government of the Republic of Serbia (GOV RS) is expected.[32]

14. The territorial organization of Serbia includes five regions (Belgrade region, Vojvodina region, Sumadija and western Serbia region, eastern and southern Serbia region and Kosovo-Metohija region). They include the city of Belgrade as a separate territorial unit established by the Constitution and law, and twenty-nine administrative areas, twenty-three cities, twenty-eight urban municipalities, 150 municipalities, 6,158 villages and 195 urban settlements.[33]

15. The RS made a formal application to join the EU on 22 December 2009. The Stabilization and Association Process (SAP) started in 2001. On 14 October 2004, the Serbian NA adopted the Resolution on EU Accession. The most crucial step on the path of accession so far was the signing of the Stabilization and Association Agreement (SAA) on 29 April 2008.[34] In March 2012, the country was granted EU candidate status. The European Council decided to open accession negotiations with Serbia in June 2013. The EU-Serbia SSA entered into force in September 2013. Accession negotiations were launched in January 2014. The first negotiating chapters were opened including Chapter 35 dealing with normalization of relations between Serbia and Kosovo[35] and the rule of law (Chapter 23 on judiciary and fundamental rights and Chapter 24 on justice, freedom and security).[36]

---

30. EC 2023, 3.
31. '* This designation is without prejudice to positions on status and is in line with UNSCR 1244/1999 and the ICJ Opinion on the Kosovo declaration of independence.' *Ibid.*
32. *See* https://www.rik.parlament.gov.rs/ (4.1.2024).
33. Law on Territorial Organizations of the Republic of Serbia (OJ RS, Nos 129/07, 18/16, 47/18 and 9/20 – other law).
34. At https://www.mei.gov.rs/eng/serbia-and-eu/history/ (4.1.2024).
35. 'This designation is without prejudice to positions on status, and is in line with UNSCR 1244/1999 and the ICJ Opinion on the Kosovo declaration of independence.'
36. The decision on the opening of negotiating Chs 5 (Public procurement) and 25 (Science and Research) was made at the Fourth Intergovernmental Conference in Brussels (13 Dec. 2016). The decision on the opening of negotiating Chs 20 (Enterprise and Industrial Policy) and 26 (Education and Culture) was made at the Fifth Intergovernmental Conference in Brussels (27 Feb. 2017). The decision on the opening of negotiating Ch. 4 (Free Movement of Capital) was made at the Eleventh

§3. ECONOMIC CHARACTERISTICS

16. Serbia is an agricultural-industrial country.[37] The economy was, generally speaking, after almost a decade of civil wars, UN, EU and US sanctions, NATO 1999 air raids and internal political crisis, in bad condition.[38] Lifting of the sanctions and the improvement of the international position of the country gave hope that the economy, with investments and donations from abroad and well-conceived economic policies, could be improved, after the shocks of the first phase of transition which began later than in any other former socialist country.

17. In comparison with other countries in transition, Serbia was late in starting reforms because of the situation in the 1990s of the previous century: internal conflicts in former Yugoslavia, international isolation, the 1999 NATO intervention, etc.

18. The 2001–2006 period was characterized by numerous reforms, establishment of macroeconomic stability and sustainable and stable economic development, restructuring of big systems, privatization of companies, and initiation of the process of accession to the EU, the process which includes adoption of numerous legal regulations in all domains of economy and society. After the changes in 2000, the Serbian economy *continued to accelerate growth.* 'In 2013, economic activity increased by 2.5%, primarily thanks to the recovery of agricultural and industrial production … .'[39] In 2016, real GDP growth of 2.8% was achieved, while positive trends in economic activity continued in 2017 as well.[40] 'After a strong rebound in 2021 from the contraction induced by COVID-19, the Serbian economy decelerated substantially in 2022, impacted by the economic fallout from Russia's war of aggression against Ukraine, in particular as regards rising inflation via soaring energy and food prices.'[41]

19. In 2022, foreign direct investment (FDI) inflow amounted to EUR 4.4 billion (net inflow EUR 4.3 billion). In eleven months of 2023, FDI inflow amounted to EUR 4.2 billion (net inflow EUR 3.9 billion), which still represents a higher amount compared to the same period last year, which was a record year when it comes to the inflow of FDI.[42] According to the last EC report, ' Public investment remained at a high level to address serious infrastructure gaps after years of underinvestment.'[43]

Intergovernmental Conference in Brussels (10 Dec. 2019). For more information, *see* https://www.mei.gov.rs/eng/serbia-and-eu/history/ (25.1.2024).

37. About socio-historical aspects of the industrial development of Serbia from 1815 to 1941, *see* Čalić, 2004.
38. For additional information, *see* Arsić, 2016.
39. For details, *see* GOV RS. 2014a, 69–72.
40. For details, *see* GOV RS. 2018, 142–149.
41. EC. 2023, 6–7; *See also*, MAFWM. 2023, 7.
42. NBS. 2024, 7. FDI inflow reached record levels of around 7% of GDP in 2021–2022.
43. EC. 2023, 7.

20. At the end of November 2023, the share of public debt in GDP amounted to 51.5% (general government public debt 51.9%).[44]

21. The first National Employment Strategy for the RS, which covers the period from 2005 through the end of the first decade of the twenty-first century, has been adopted. After that, the second National Employment Strategy for the RS was adopted in 2011 (OJ RS, No. 37/11). The currently valid strategy was adopted in 2021 and refers to the period 2021–2026 (OJ RS, Nos 18/21, 36/1 – corr). In 2022, the number of unemployed persons totalled 302 200, while the unemployment rate was 9.4%, i.e., by 1.6 percentage points lower than in 2021. This rate in women population was 9.8%, i.e., by 0.8 percentage points higher than the unemployment rate of men population (9.0%).[45]

22. One of the characteristics of economic development of Serbia is unbalanced development and great differences between regions. To solve this problem, the Government of Serbia adopted (2007) a special Strategy for the Regional Development of the RS for the period 2007–2012 (OJ RS, No. 21/07).[46]

§4. Social and Cultural Characteristics

23. According to Article 1 of the Constitution, RS is a State 'based on the rule of law and social justice, principles of civil democracy, human and minority rights and freedoms, and commitment to European principles and values'. One of the main strategic objectives in achieving social welfare in Serbia is, according to the National Sustainable Development Strategy (NSDS), promotion and development of sustainable lifestyles and promotion of 'values based on political liberalism and civic participation'.[47]

24. The official language in Serbia is Serbian (in former Yugoslavia, it was called Serbo-Croatian) and the script in official use is Cyrillic, while Latin script is also used. In areas where ethnic minorities live, their languages and scripts are in official use. The Constitution of the RS guarantees rights to minorities, in accordance with international standards.[48]

---

44. *See* NBS. 2024, 13. Considering the projected primary budget deficit of the RS for the period 2020–2024, including the volume of drawn loan instruments for project financing of budget beneficiaries, the effects of the foreign currency exchange rate of RSD against EUR and USD, the central government debt balance at the end of 2024 should amount to 52.7% of GDP. PDA. 2022, 80.
45. STAT. YEARB. SERB. 2023. 61.
46. At https://otvorenavlada.rs/strategija-regionalnog-razvoja177a-lat-doc/ (4.1.2024).
47. GOV RS. 2008b, 48.
48. 'The legal framework for respect for and protection of minorities and cultural rights is broadly in place and generally upheld, in line with the Council of Europe Framework Convention on National Minorities. Implementation of Serbia's "*Action plan for the realization of the rights of national minorities*" and relevant legislation needs to lead to a tangible improvement in the effective exercise of the rights of individuals belonging to national minorities throughout the country.' EC. 2023, 50).

25. The main religion of Serbia is Christian Orthodox (81.1%). Besides the Christian Orthodox, there are also other religious communities in Serbia: Islamic (4.2%), Roman Catholic (3.9%), Protestant, Jewish and others.[49]

26. Western European, Mediterranean, Oriental, Eastern European and other cultural influences mixed with each other on the territory of Serbia were producing in some cases original contributions (e.g., fresco paintings in Serbian medieval monasteries) to the European and world culture.

27. Cultural policy in the former Yugoslavia was more liberal than in other countries dominated by communists, although some intellectuals were persecuted for political reasons and, generally speaking, educational and cultural budgets were low and far from sufficient. During the crisis on the territory of former Yugoslavia, and especially due to the sanctions imposed by the UN, EU and US, the situation became even worse because culture was not regarded as one of the priority issues. After the introduction of the democratic regime in 2000, the situation is still not very satisfactory. Culture and education are still not a priority issue, but the country is now open to exchange, Non-Governmental Organization (NGO) activities and the inflow of various donations and/or internationally funded projects, some of which are even commercial in character. In 2021, the Government adopted the Strategic Priorities for the Development of Culture of the RS for the period from 2020 to 2025.[50]

28. Article 71 of the Constitution prescribes that everyone shall have the right to education. All citizens shall have access to higher education under equal conditions. The RS shall provide for free tertiary education to successful and talented students of lower property status in accordance with the law. Primary education is mandatory and free, while secondary education is free but not mandatory.[51]

In the period between the last two censuses (2011 and 2022), the share of illiterate persons in the population aged 10 and over decreased from 1.96% to 0.63%.[52]

---

49. https://www.srbija.gov.rs/tekst/en/130129/people-language-and-religion.php (13.2.2024).
50. https://www.kultura.gov.rs/extfile/sr/6132/Strate%C5%A1ki%20prioriteti%20razvoja%20kulture.pdf (14.2.2024). In addition, the Ministry of Culture prepared a draft of the Culture Development Strategy of the Republic of Serbia from 2020 to 2029. https://www.kultura.gov.rs/extfile/sr/3993/strategija-razvoja-kulture-od-2020--do-2029-godine.pdf (14.2.2024).
51. In this field, the Government adopted several strategic documents: Strategy for the development of education in the Republic of Serbia until 2030 (OJ RS, No. 63/2021), Strategy for the development of education in the Republic of Serbia until 2020 (OJ RS, No. 107/12), Adult Development Education Strategy (2006) and Vocational Education Development Strategy (2006), https://www.srbija.gov.rs/dokument/45678/strategije-programi-planovi-.php (4.1.2024). The latest strategic document in this area (Strategy for the development of education in the Republic of Serbia until 2030) was adopted in 2021 (OJ RS, No. 63/21). In addition, Action Plan for the period 2023–2026 was also adopted. *See*, https://www.srbija.gov.rs/dokument/45678/strategije-programi-planovi-.php (4.1.2024).
52. STAT. YEARB. SERB. 2023, 30. According to the results of the 2022 Census, less than 38,000 residents aged 10 and over are illiterate. The share of women in the total number of the illiterate is 71%.

§5. Main Environmental Problems

29. The state of the environment is the most threatened from the point of view of the quality of surface water, ambient air, and land.[53] However, 'ambient air quality has been one of the most topical issues … in recent years'.[54] 'Air pollution contributes significantly to the overall burden of disease and premature death in Serbia, which has higher estimates of premature death due to air pollution than most countries in the European Union.'[55] In addition, it could be said that the main environmental issues in Serbia are inadequate management of domestic, industrial and hazardous waste,[56] inefficient use of energy and air pollution from thermoelectric plants, water pollution from industrial wastes dumped into rivers, and[57] chemical pollution from chemicals used in agriculture (pesticides, herbicides, fertilizers, etc.). A significant part of the problem originates from obsolete technological processes in industries as well as weaknesses in public administration. There is also imported pollution, especially by inflow of rivers. Most of inflow rivers are already polluted and sometimes heavily (for instance, the pollution of the Tisza River in 2000 was caused by the discharge of dangerous substances from the Romanian gold mine, Baia Mare).[58]

30. A serious source of pollution was caused by the 1999 NATO intervention.[59] In some 35,000 air strikes, refineries and chemical plants were destroyed; also, depleted uranium (DU) ammunition, as well as other legally problematic weapons like cluster bombs and graphite bombs, were used. The bombing of Serbia had certainly, especially in some cases, characteristics of an ecological war, damaging not only man-made objects but also natural environment, including some areas of natural heritage (four national parks were bombed). Many animals and plants were destroyed or disturbed in their natural habitats, and some animals were forced to seek shelter in the areas outside Serbia. Several thousands of persons were killed and many wounded, and the environment was endangered not only locally but also to a certain extent in surrounding countries. The survey of the economic facilities destroyed or damaged in the NATO bombing of Serbia shows those that, among other civilian objects, were destroyed or badly damaged: 78 industrial plants, 43 installations for energy production, 115 objects in the field of transport, including most of the bridges and airports and, among many other objects even six installations for water management.[60]

---

53. EPA. 2019b, 96.
54. EPA. 2023a, 9. Ambient air quality in the Republic of Serbia is most affected by the presence of suspended particles PM10 and PM2.5, followed by sulfur dioxide and heavy metals in Bor, and nitrogen dioxide in Belgrade, Niš, and Novi Pazar. For additional information *see* EPA. 2023b.
55. WHO. 2019, 2, https://serbia.un.org/sites/default/files/2019-10/Health-impact-pollution-Serbia_0.pdf (4.1.2024).
56. For more information, *see*, EPA. 2023c; EPA. 2019c; NA. 2010; STAT. OFFICE RS. 2023a; GOV RS. 2010a; UNECE. 2015.
57. For additional information *see* EPA. 2023c.
58. *See* UNEP, OCHA. 2000.
59. Concerning the consequences of NATO bombing on the environment and the health of the population, after more than two decades, that issue is considered insufficiently researched. *See* Loets, 2012.
60. FMDSE. 2000, 65–70.

The whole damage done by the bombing has not been precisely estimated, but it is certainly enormous, and it certainly has had a negative impact on the environment in Serbia and, to a certain extent, on a wider area.[61] One of the main tasks after the change of regime in 2000 was cleaning so-called hotspots caused by the NATO bombing, cleaning debris from the Danube River and building new bridges and other infrastructure (especially in Novi Sad where all bridges were destroyed) with financial and other help of the EU and other international factors.

31. The main natural hazards are destructive earthquakes, especially in some seismically more active areas (like, for instance, southern Serbia), floods[62] and storms. 'Serbia in general has a very high risk of flooding. Among the 10 worst natural disasters (with respect to the number of affected people) in Serbia from 2006 to 2013 there have been six floods (in 2007, 2009 and twice in 2010 and in 2013) with 23,150 people affected.'[63] In 2018, there were 27,000 ha flooded area by surface and groundwater, of which 75.7% referred to utilized agricultural land. The area of eroded land in 2018 amounted to 3,834 km^2.[64]

32. It is a fact nowadays that the state of environment is closely linked to practically all human activities and due to that all phenomena in society have their environmental aspect.[65] In a society with so many problems, as is the case with Serbia, two issues deserve special attention: environmental aspect of development and the environmental aspect of human rights. Driving forces of negative environmental impacts include production and consumption in economic sectors (agriculture, energy, industry, transport), where renewable and non-renewable resources are exploited, energy is consumed, technology is applied, waste is landfilled, and land is used. Population, education level, and economic stability are also primary forces since the human community depends on the size of the population and development.[66]

33. Monitoring has been improved but needs further strengthening.[67] In the latest EC report, the need to strengthen monitoring is mentioned in the part related to air quality, waste management, water quality, chemicals, and climate change.[68]

34. The legal basis for an integrated environmental monitoring system was established by the 2004 *Law on Environmental Protection* (EPL). EPL prescribes that:

---

61. *See* generally, UNEP. 1999; UNEP. 2004; Bakrač, et al., 2018; Račić. 2019.
62. For additional information *see* GOV RS. 2019c.
63. UNECE. 2015, 117. A severe storm event hit the Balkans region strongly in May 2014, affecting Serbia mainly in the catchments of the Sava River and its tributaries. 'As a result of the flooding, 34 persons died – 13 by drowning – and over 30,000 were evacuated from their homes. Serious damage was also caused to coal mines, chemical plants, power plants and road infrastructure, which were entirely flooded, shut down or subject to landslides.' *Ibid.*, 140.
64. STAT. YEARB. SERB. *2019*, 247.
65. For general aspects, *see* GOV RS. 2008b, 19–32, 73–110. *See also*, GOV RS, 2019c.
66. EPA. 2019c, 10.
67. EC. 2019, 85. For more details, *see* UNECE. 2015, 81–89.
68. EC. 2023, 135–138.

Monitoring is carried out by systematic monitoring of indicator values, i.e., by monitoring of adverse impacts on the environment, the state of the environment, measures and activities to be taken in order to reduce negative impacts and increase the quality of the environment. The government sets the criteria for determining the number and distribution of measuring points, the network of measuring the points, extent and frequency of measurements, classification of occurrences that are monitored, work methodology and indicators of environmental pollution and their monitoring, deadlines and the way of delivering the data on the basis of special Laws (Article 70, paragraphs 1 and 2 of EPL).

The Law also provides for the establishment of an environmental information system (Article 74)[69] and a National and Local Register of polluters (Article 75).[70] This system is to be more specifically regulated by sectoral laws (Law on Water, Law on Waste Management, Law on Nature Protection, Law on Air Protection, Law on Statistical Research, etc.) which are also expected to be harmonized with relevant EU directives.

35. The state of the environment in the RS can be assessed in different ways depending on the segment of the environment (water, air, land, nature, etc.). Serbia produces its 'state of the environment report' annually. The last report was published in 2023 (for 2022).[71] It is difficult to give a general assessment. In a country in transition (like Serbia), there are many systemic issues which have to be solved as a precondition to solve environmental problems. However, it can be said that in the process of harmonization of national legislation with EU legislation, the elements of the system of environmental management and monitoring have been established.[72] The adoption of the relevant EU legislation, in particular their implementation, requires considerable investment in infrastructure over a long period of time. The total cost of the approximation was estimated at EUR 10.6 billion.[73]

According to the Screening Report (Chapter 27), 'overall, Serbia's legislation has a satisfactory level of alignment with the *acquis* …, but implementation and enforcement are at an early stage. There is a substantial amount of work to be undertaken as regards the implementation of legislation and the establishment of the necessary administrative and enforcement and control capacities required by the *acquis*'.[74]

The latest annual report of the European Commission (EC) notes that Serbia 'made some progress, including on last year's recommendations, in particular by

69. The information system shall be run by the environmental agency, and the Government shall prescribe more closely the contents and the manner of maintenance of information system, methodology, structure, common bases, categories and levels of data compilation, as well as the contents of information regulatory and obligatory released to public.
70. *See* Rulebook on the methodology of the national and local register of pollution sources, as well as the methodology related to types, methods and deadlines of data collection (OJ RS, Nos 91/10, 10/13, 98/16, and 72/23).
71. *See* EPA. 2023a.
72. For the overview of this process *see*, Todić, 2021.
73. GOV RS. 2011e, 12.
74. EC. 2016b, 17.

adopting the Low Carbon Development Strategy 2023–2030 and drafting its national energy and climate plan (NECP)'.[75] However, in the coming year, Serbia should, *inter alia*, '(1) modernize and simplify the overall sector structure and institutions to improve the efficiency and quality of the preparation, implementation, and quality control of investments including transparency of procedures; (2) align the Law on planning and construction with international standards; adopt other EU-compliant regulations; (3) implement the Action Plan for Administrative Capacity Development and the Programme of Air Protection; adopt the Industrial Emissions Directive; resume international cooperation on Transboundary Rivers; implement the Low Carbon Development Plan', etc.[76]

75. EC. 2023, 134.
76. *Ibid.*

Chapter 2. Basic Principles of Environmental Law

§1. Definitions and Notions

36. Although all basic laws contain provisions with definitions, the most important definitions in the field of environmental protection can be found in Article 3 of the EPL. Following definitions, out of a total of thirty-nine definitions included in the Article, deserve special attention:[77]

- *Environment*: a set of natural and man-made values whose complex mutual relations make up the environment, that is, area and conditions for life.
- *Environmental quality*: a state of environment in terms of physical, chemical, biological, aesthetic and other indicators.
- *Natural value*: natural wealth that comprises air, water, soil, forests, geological resources, plants and animal life.
- *Protected natural good*: a preserved part of nature with special values and characteristics (geodiversity, biodiversity, scenery, landscape, etc.), due to which they have permanent ecological, scientific, cultural, educational, health-recreational, tourist and other significance and therefore as a public good it enjoys special protection.
- *Public natural good*: a cultivated or uncultivated part of natural wealth, that is, air, water goods, water-fronts, underground goods, forests, sceneries or landscapes equally accessible to all.
- *Activity affecting the environment ('activity')*: any action (permanent or temporary) which changes or may change the status and conditions in the environment and relates to utilization of resources and natural goods; production and circulation processes; distribution and use of materials; emissions of pollution into water, air, or soil; waste and wastewater management; chemicals and harmful matters management; noise and vibrations; ionizing and no ionizing radiation; and accidents.
- *Polluter*: a legal or natural entity who by its activity or inactivity pollutes the environment.
- *Pollutants*: substances whose outflow into the environment affects or may affect its natural composition, properties and integrity.
- *Environmental pollution*: introduction of polluting matters or energy into the environment, caused either by human activities or natural processes, which has or may have adverse effects towards quality of the environment and human health.
- *Environmental capacity*: the ability of environment to accept a certain quantity of pollutants per unit of time and space so as to avoid irreparable damage towards the environment.

77. Other relevant definitions, if needed, are given in following text of this monograph.

- *Load to the environment*: individual or cumulative effect of activities to environment, which may be expressed as aggregate (several similar components), common (several heterogeneous components), permitted (within the permitted limit values), excessive (exceeding limit values) load.
- *Accident:* sudden and uncontrolled event that occurs with release, leakage or dispersion of dangerous substances, in the course of performing activities of production, utilization, processing, storage, disposal or long-term inadequate keeping (hereinafter 'the chemical accident').[78]
- *Degradation of environment*: a process of degradation of environment quality caused either by natural or human activity or it occurs as a consequence of non-performance of measures for elimination of causes of degradation of quality or damage towards the environment, natural or any man-made values.
- *Environment pollution sources:* location-wise specified and spatially limited point, line and area sources of pollutants and energy into the environment.
- *Responsible authority*: an authority responsible for implementing obligations within competences determined by this Law, in particular, the Ministry responsible for environment (hereinafter 'Ministry'); provincial authority responsible for environment; responsible authority of the Local Self-Governments (LSG) unit.
- *Operator:* any natural or legal person that, in accordance with regulations, manages the installation or an establishment or controls it or is authorized to make economic decisions in the field of technical functioning of an installation.
- *Seveso installation*, that is, installation where activities are performed in which dangerous substance is present or may be present in equal or higher quantities than prescribed (hereinafter 'the Seveso installation'): a technical unit within the establishment where dangerous substances are produced, utilized, stored or handled. Installation shall include all equipment, buildings, pipelines, machines, tools, internal tracks and warehouses, wharves, unloading ports for installations, piers, storehouses or similar structures, on water or land, which are necessary for the operation of installations.
- *Establishment:* the spatial unit under control of an operator where dangerous substances are present in one or several installations, including individual or common infrastructure or individual or common activities.
- *Requirements related to environmental quality:* a set of conditions and requirements that must be met at the specified time and in the specified area or in certain environmental media, in accordance with special regulations.

37. 'Public' has been defined in the same way in Law on Strategic Environmental Assessment (SEA), Law on Environmental Impact Assessment (EIA) and Law on Integrated Pollution Prevention and Control (IPPC), as one or several private or legal entities, their associations, organizations or groups.

78. Article 1 of the Law on Amendment of the Environment Protection Law (EPL) (OJ RS, 36/09). By this amendment several new definitions have been introduced. For example: operator, Seveso installation, requirements related to the environmental quality, etc. In addition, by the Art. 1 of the Amendment on the EPL (OJ RS, 14/16) several new definitions have been introduced. For example: dangerous substance, waste, sludge, public authorities, environmental information, etc.

The 'public concerned' is defined similarly in all three laws, and it includes:

- 'public affected or likely to be affected by the operation of the installation[79] and execution of activities, including non-governmental organizations dealing with environmental protection and being registered with the competent authority' (IPPC);
- 'public affected or public likely to be affected by the plan or programme and/or having interest in decisions related to environmental protection, including non-government organizations involved in environmental protection and registered with the competent authority' (SEA);
- 'public affected by or likely to be affected by the project, including non-governmental organizations that promote environmental protection and are registered with the competent authority' (EIA).[80]

§2. Constitutional Provisions

38. The Constitution of the RS (OJ RS, Nos 98/06, 115/21, 16/22) contains following six provisions dealing with the environment, *stricto sensu*: Article 74 (right to healthy environment), Article 83 (freedom of entrepreneurship), Article 88 (use of land), Article 97, point 9 (competences of the RS), Article 183, point 2 (competences of the APs) and Article 190, point 6 (competences of LSG).

I. Right to Healthy Environment

39. From the point of view of human rights protection,[81] the most important is provision of Article 74 of the Constitution. According to the first part of this Article, 'everyone shall have the right to healthy environment and the right to timely and full information about the state of environment' (paragraph 1).[82] But, it is also prescribed that 'everyone, especially the RS and autonomous provinces, shall be accountable for the protection of environment' and 'everyone shall be obliged to preserve and improve the environment'.[83]

79. 'Installation' is defined as a stationary technical unit where one or more activities are performed, for which special regulations have been determined and permit has been issued, as well as any other activity where there is a technical connection to the activities that are performed at the place and which, as a result, may cause emission and pollution (Art. 3, point 10 of the EPL).
80. Amendments of the EPL in Art. 1, para. 2 have introduced definitions of the 'public concerned': 'public which is affected or may be affected by decision-making of the responsible authority or which has an interest therein, including citizen associations and social organizations engaged in the environmental protection, that are recorded with the responsible authority'.
81. On this subject, *see* Pokuševski, 2022, 238–247.
82. In the legal system of the Republic of Serbia, the protection of this human right was established in 1974 within the framework of Art. 192 of the Constitution of the SFRY. The aforementioned article stands out in the literature 'as the very beginning of the constitutional regulation of subject law in the world.' Tintor, 2022, 328.
83. It is interesting to compare provisions of this Article with Art. 1 of the AC. For more information on human rights in the context of the Aarhus Convention, *see* Etinski. 2013a. It is clear that there is a

40. EPL proclaims that one of the basic principles of the system of environmental protection is the 'principle of protection of right to healthy environment and access to justice'.[84] Amendments to the EPL (from 2009) introduced a special provision entitled 'Right to Justice.' That provision reads as follows: 'The public concerned in the procedure of exercising the right to a healthy environment as a party shall be entitled to initiate the procedure of decision reviewing before the competent authority, i.e., court, in compliance with the law.' (Article 81a).[85]

II. Constitutional Competencies

41. The issue of competence for undertaking activities in the environmental field is regulated by the Constitution in a general way by defining competences of the Republic, APs and municipalities.[86]

A. Competencies of the Republic

42. It is prescribed by Article 97 that the RS organizes and provides for, *inter alia*:

(1) sovereignty, independence, territorial integrity and security of the RS, its international status and relations with other countries and international organizations;
(2) single market; legal status of business entities; system of performing particular economic and other activities; commodity reserves; monetary, banking, foreign exchange and customs system; international economic relations; system of foreign credit relations; fiscal system;

difference between the contents of the human right formulated in the Serbian Constitution and the AC. The difference is obvious at least in two elements. First, the AC stresses that the right belongs to both individuals of present and future generations. Second, the manner in which the right to sound environment is formulated in the Convention is more subtle. The right does not deal only with human health but also with human wellbeing in wider sense. Because of these important differences, it could be concluded that the formulations in the Serbian Constitution is narrower than in the Convention. It could be a problem when it comes to the implementation of the Convention, and especially its third column-access to justice.

84. According to Art. 9, point 11, 'a citizen or groups of citizens, their associations, professional and other organizations shall exercise their right to healthy environment before the competent authority, i.e., court, in compliance with the law'.

85. According to the explanation from the Draft Law, this was done to 'align with international regulations on public participation in environmental decision-making, i.e., the Aarhus Convention.' (Art. 47 of the Draft Law on Amendments). The connection with the Aarhus Convention is also indicated by the place where Art. 81a is found in the structure of the EPL. Namely, this provision is found in Ch. V of the Law, which is entitled 'Public Information and Participation.' Because of this, the question of the limits of the right to a healthy environment formulated in Art. 81a EPL could be considered open. There are numerous other specific issues (apart from the right to information and public participation) that can be grounds for reconsidering the respect for the right to a healthy environment.

86. This issue is regulated in detail by various laws.

(3) sustainable development; system of protection and improvement of environment; protection and improvement of flora and fauna; production, trade and transport of arms, poisonous, inflammable, explosive, radioactive and other hazardous substances;
(4) system in areas of healthcare, social security, protection of war veterans and the disabled, protection of children, education, culture and protection of cultural goods, sport, public information, system of public services;
(5) development of the RS, policy and measures for spurring balanced development of particular areas of the RS, including the development of underdeveloped areas; organization and utilization of space; scientific and technological development;
(6) regime and security in all areas of transport.

B. Competencies of the APs

43. APs shall, according to Article 183, 'in accordance with the Constitution and their Statutes, regulate the competences, election, organization and work of bodies and services they establish'.

APs shall, in accordance with the Law, regulate the matters of provincial interest in the following fields:

- urban planning and development;
- agriculture, water economy, forestry, hunting, fishery, tourism, catering;
- spas and health resorts, environmental protection, industry;
- craftsmanship, road, river and railway transport and road repairs;
- organizing fairs and other economic events;
- education, sport, culture, health care and social welfare and public; and
- informing at the provincial level.[87]

C. Competencies of the Municipality

44. The municipality shall, as prescribed by Article 190:

(1) regulate and provide for the performing and development of municipal activities;
(2) regulate and provide for the use of urban construction sites and business premises;
(3) be responsible for construction, reconstruction, maintenance and use of local network of roads and streets and other public facilities of municipal interest; regulate and provide for the local transport;

87. *See also*, Law on Establishing Competencies of the APV (OJ RS, Nos 99/09 and 67/12 CC, 18/20 – other law, and 111/21 – other law), and The Statute of The APV (OJ APV, No. 20/14), http://www.skupstinavojvodine.gov.rs/Strana.aspx?s=statut&j=EN (4.1.2024).

(4) be responsible for meeting the needs of citizens in the fields of education, culture, healthcare and social welfare, child welfare, sport and physical culture;
(5) be responsible for development and improvement of tourism, craftsmanship, catering and commerce;
(6) be responsible for environmental protection, protection against natural and other disasters; protection of cultural heritage of the municipal interest;
(7) protection, improvement and use of agricultural land;
(8) perform other duties specified by the Law.[88]

D. Other Relevant Constitutional Provisions

45. According to Article 83, 'entrepreneurship is permitted' but it can be restricted by the Law 'for the purpose of protection of people's health, environment and natural goods and security of the R S'.

46. In accordance with Article 87, natural resources, goods which are stipulated by the Law as goods of public interest, and assets used by the bodies of the R S shall be State assets. Natural and legal entities may obtain particular rights on particular goods in public use, under the terms and in a manner stipulated by the Law.[89] Natural resources shall be utilized under the terms and in a manner stipulated by the Law.

According to Article 88, 'utilization and management of agricultural land, forest-land and municipal building land on private assets shall be permitted'. The Law may restrict the models of utilization and management in order to eliminate the danger of causing damage to environment or prevent violation of rights and legal interests of other persons.

§3. Strategic Framework of National Environmental Policy and Environmental Law

47. The strategic framework of national environmental policy and environmental law has been defined in a number of strategic documents. The importance of these documents stems from their strategic character, from the point of view of general framework, goals, instruments, etc. They are guidelines for implementation of different activities. The mentioned activities include identification of the most important problems as well as projection of further development, drafting, adoption and implementation of relevant legal regulations.

48. Strategic planning in the environmental field is prescribed by the *EPL (2004)*. According to Article 12 of the Law:

88. *See also* Law on Self-Government (OJ RS, Nos 129/2007, 83/14 – other law, 101/16 – other law, and 47/18).
89. Foreigners may obtain a concession right for natural resources and goods, as well as other rights stipulated by the Law (Art. 85, para. 2).

> Sustainable usage and protection of natural values shall be provided for within the Strategy for spatial development of the Republic and within the National strategy of sustainable use of natural resources and goods. National strategy of sustainable utilization of natural resources and goods (hereinafter, National strategy) shall be enacted by the Government for the period of minimum ten years (para 2).[90]

49. The Action Plan is a short-term instrument for the implementation of the National Programme. The Action Plan elaborates on regulatory and institutional activities, monitoring activities, studies, preparation of project documentation, economic and financial instruments, information, education, management and capital investment (Article 65).

Serbia has adopted a number of basic strategic documents relevant to the environment, as for example, Biodiversity Strategy of the RS for the period 2011–2018 (2011), National Environmental Approximation Strategy for the RS (2011), National Strategy for Incorporation of the RS into Clean Development Mechanism (CDM) – Waste Management, Agriculture and Forestry Sector (2010),[91] National implementation plan for implementation of the Stockholm Convention (2010), Strategy on safety and health at work in the R S for the period 2009–2012 (2009), Strategy of introducing cleaner production in the RS (2009), National Strategy on Sustainable Development (2008), Spatial Plan (2011), National Waste Management Strategy for period 2010–2019 (2010), Water Management Strategy on the territory of the RSuntil 2034 (2016) (and the Action plan for the implementation of the Water Management Strategy on the territory of the RS for the period from 2021 to 2023), Agriculture and Rural Development Strategy of the RS for the period 2014–2024 (2014), Energy Development Strategy of the RS until 2025, with projection until 2030 (2015), Mineral Resources Management Strategy until 2030 (2015), Strategy of Safety and Health at Work for the period 2013–2017 (2013), Nuclear Safety and Security Programme (2014), Strategy for Development of Forestry (2006), Poverty Reduction Strategy (2003), Strategy for Development of Tourism (2006), Strategy for Official Statistics (2006), Public Administration Reform Strategy for the period from 2021 to 2030 (2021), Strategy on Science and Technology Development for the period 2021–2025 (2021), Strategy of sustainable urban development of the RS until 2030 (2019), National plan for reduction emissions of major pollutants from old large combustion plants (2020), etc.[92]

---

90. The National Strategy was adopted in 2012. For the text of the National Strategy, *see* OJ RS, No. 33/12. https://www.pravno-informacioni-sistem.rs/SlGlasnikPortal/eli/rep/sgrs/vlada/strategija/2012/
33/1/reg (28.1.2024). However, the Strategy ceased to be applied on the date of entry into force of the Decision on the cessation of application of certain public policy documents (OJ RS, No. 109/21), that is, on 27 Nov. 2021.
91. The strategy ceased to be applied on the date of entry into force of the Decision on the cessation of application of certain public policy documents (OJ RS, No. 109/2021), that is, on 27 Nov. 2021.
92. For the full list of strategies adopted by the Serbian Government, *see* http://www.srbija.gov.rs/vesti/dokumenti_sekcija.php?id=45678 (4.1.2024).

50. It should be added that the National Environmental Protection Programme (NEPP) has also been adopted (OJ RS No. 12/2010).[93] The environmental protection strategy of the RS, which is currently being drafted, structurally follows the five pillars of the Green Agenda ((1) climate action, including decarbonization, energy and mobility; (2) circular economy, addressing in particular waste, recycling, sustainable production and efficient use of resources; (3) biodiversity, aiming to protect and restore the natural wealth of the region; (4) fighting pollution of air, water and soil; and (5) sustainable food systems and rural areas) and should be a kind of umbrella strategy for reforms in this sector at the national level.[94]

51. Recently, the following key strategic documents were adopted: Programme of adaptation to changed climatic conditions for the period from 2023 to 2030 with Action plan (OJ RS, No. 119/2023);[95] Low-carbon development strategy of the RS for the period from 2023 to 2030 with projections until 2050 (OJ RS, No. 46/2023); Air protection programme in the RS for the period from 2022 to 2030 with Action plan;[96] Waste Management Program in the RS for the period from 2022 to 2031 (OJ RS, No. 12/22) with the Action plan for the period from 2022 to 2024.[97]

§4. Principles of the Environmental Protection in Serbia

52. Although it is not quite clear what concrete practical implications it should (or could) have,[98] the basic principles of environmental protection in Serbia have been formulated in several basic legal Acts and strategic documents. The principles are, for example, mentioned in the EPL, SEA, IPPC, Law on Waste Management, Water Law, Law on Nature Protection, as well as the National Environmental Strategy, the NSDS, the National Waste Management Strategy,[99] the Water Management

93. At https://www.pravno-informacioni-sistem.rs/SlGlasnikPortal/eli/rep/sgrs/vlada/odluka/2010/12/3/reg (4.1.2024). NEPP defines fundamental principles of environmental protection and sustainable development, as well as priorities for the institutional framework. One of the goals is development of a comprehensive legal environmental system, by adoption of and by improvement of law enforcement monitoring and of the judiciary system. *See* GOV RS. 2010a.
94. For more information *see*: https://www.ekologija.gov.rs/saopstenja/najave/obavestenje-o-pocetku-izrade-strategije-za-zastitu-zivotne-sredine-sa-akcionim-planom; https://www.euzatebe.rs/en/news/draft-environmental-protection-strategy-will-soon-be-open-for-public-discussion; https://www.bos.rs/rs/vesti/3/1568/strategija-zastite-zivotne-sredine--stizu-praznici-ali-ne-i-strategija.html (28.1.2024).
95. https://www.ekologija.gov.rs/saopstenja/vesti/usvojen-program-prilagodjavanja-na-izmenjene-klimatske-uslove-sa-akcionim-planom (4.1.2024).
96. https://www.ekologija.gov.rs/dokumenta/zastita-vazduha-i-ozonskog-omotaca/zakoni-0 (4.1.2024).
97. https://ekologija.gov.rs/saopstenja/vesti/usvojen-akcioni-plan-programa-upravljanja-otpadom-u-republici-srbiji-za-period-od-2022-do-2024-godine (4.1.2024).
98. On this subject, *see* Birnie & Boyle, 2002, 24–27. For more on this subject, *see* Todić, 2023b.
99. National Waste Management Strategy differentiates 'critical principles of waste management' and 'other principles'. Critical principles, which have to be considered during the definition and implementation of waste management planning, are Principle of Sustainable Development, Principle of Closeness, and Regional Approach to Waste Management, Principle of Precaution, Principle of 'The Polluter Pays', Principle of Waste Management Hierarchy, Principle of Implementation of the Most Practical Environmental Options, Principle of Producer's Liability. GOV RS. 2010b, 9–11. The implementation of environmental policy (according to the Waste Management Program in the RS

Strategy of the territory of the RS until 2034, the Mineral Resources Management Strategy of the RSuntil 2030, the Energy Development Strategy of the RS until 2025, with projection until 2030, etc.

53. It could be said that basic meanings have the principles defined in the EPL. In its Article 9 of the Law, the following eleven principles are mentioned:

(1) Integration principle.
(2) Principle of prevention and cautiousness.
(3) Principle of natural value preservation.
(4) Principle of sustainable development.
(5) Principle of polluters' and legal successors' liability.
(6) Principle of 'polluter pays'.
(7) Principle of 'user pays'.
(8) Principle of subsidiary liability.
(9) Principle of incentives.
(10) Principle of public information and participation.
(11) Principle of protection of right to healthy environment and access to justice.

54. The development and implementation of the NEPP is based on the following policy principles:

- Principle of sustainable development.
- Principle of preservation of natural values.
- Principle of cross-sectoral integration.
- 'Polluter pays' principle.
- 'User pays' principle.
- Incentives principle.
- Principle of shared responsibility.
- Subsidiarity principle.
- Prevention and precautionary principle.
- Awareness-raising principle.
- Access to information and public participation principle.
- Principle of liability of polluter or his/her legal successor.
- Principle of the right to a healthy environment and access to justice.
- Principle of the approximation with the EU environmental acquis.[100]

for the period from 2022 to 2031, OJ RS, No. 12/22) is based on the following principles: Sustainable development principle, Circular economy principle, Precautionary principle, Choosing the most optimal option for the environment principle, Self-sufficiency principle, Principle of proximity and regional approach to waste management, Principle of waste management hierarchy (prevention, preparation for reuse, recycling, other reuse operations, disposal), Principle of extended producer responsibility, and Polluter pays principle. GOV RS. 2022b, 60–63.

100. GOV RS. 2010a, 8–12.

55. The NSDS is based on the following principles:

- Inter- and intra-generations solidarity.
- Open and democratic society-public participation in decision-making.
- Knowledge as a factor of development.
- Inclusion in social processes.
- Integration of environmental issues in other sectoral policies.
- The precautionary principle.
- The polluter/user-pays principle, full inclusion of environmental costs in the product price.
- Sustainable production and consumption.[101]

56. The principle of sustainable development has become, under the influence of contemporary tendencies in environmental law, a leading principle included in all new legal regulations. In addition, the principle is often mentioned in various strategic documents, but it is not quite clear whether the content and the meaning of this principle are properly interpreted. The way in which principle of sustainable development is applied in practice can be discussed in various ways.

It is formulated in the EPL in the following way:

> the sustainable development is harmonized system of technical/technological, economic and social activities in the overall development, where the natural and acquired values of the republic are used in a cost efficient and reasonable manner, in order to preserve and enhance the quality of the environment for the present and future generations. The system of environmental protection shall be implemented through promulgation and implementation of decisions producing balance between the environmental protection and the interest of economic development (Article 9, paragraph 4).

57. Development of the new environmental legal regulation in Serbia is based on several principles of environmental protection with common economic incentives idea. *EPL* contains the 'polluter pays' principle, 'user pays' principle, principle of incentives, principle of polluters' and legal successors' liability, etc. The whole Part VI of the Law (Articles 83–101) is dedicated to economic instruments.[102]

A more radical novelty is also provisions concerning the formation of the Environmental Protection Fund (Articles 90–100).[103]

---

101. GOV RS. 2008b, 16–17.
102. Besides that, several other charges and taxes, relevant for environmental protection, have been prescribed by other legal regulations (in the fields of water, forestry, fishing, building, transport, etc.). In the framework of the Law on IPPC, it is planned that pollution charges for the 250 potential IPPC industrial installations will be progressively increased from 20% to 100% as of 2016.
103. Law on Amendment of the EPL (2009) have introduced new provisions related to the Fund. Besides that, it should be kept in mind that *EPL* Fund has been adopted (OJ RS, No. 72/09). This Law was repealed (25 Sep. 2012) by the Law on Repealing the Law on the Fund for Environmental Protection (OJ RS, No. 93/12). However, Green Fund of the Republic of Serbia is established as a budgetary fund for recording the funds intended for financing the preparation, implementation and

Chapter 3. Historical Background of Environmental Law

58. In a broader sense, some provisions regulating environmental protection, or at least elements of it, could be found in Serbia already in the Middle Ages. There were, for instance, some such provisions in Emperor Dushan's Code from the fourteenth century, as well as in legal Acts of some coastal cities (in the Middle Ages, Serbia was a maritime State).[104]

59. Research on biodiversity has a long tradition in Serbia. In a series of articles and monographs, a known Serbian scientist, Josip Pančić (1860, 1867, 1869, 1874 and 1883), initially described Serbian flora and fauna. His classical work, *Flora Principatus Serbiae*, initiated intensive floristic investigations. As a result of accumulated knowledge, the ten-volume edition of '(vascular) Flora of SR Serbia' was published (Josifović, 1970–1977; Sarić, 1986).[105]

60. The first legal Acts with some provisions concerning the environment (although the term 'environment' was, of course, not used at that time) were enacted in Serbia in the nineteenth century. These earlier regulations were actually linked with the management of public hygiene. For example, there is a provision in one decree from the year 1841 dealing with obligations to keep cleanliness in Belgrade.

61. Modernization of Belgrade was one of the main issues in this period of Serbian history. The first Serbian urbanist, Emilijan Josimovic, made a special contribution to this process (regulation of streets, connecting Kalemegdan fortress with the city centre, choosing a new site for the botanical garden, etc.). In this period, the first legal regulations, which according to modern methodology could be regarded as environmental regulations, were adopted. So, as examples, could be mentioned following by-laws:

- Regulation No. N. 561, C. 1098, from 22 July 1839 regarding inspection over timber cutting.
- Decision of the Council from 1 April 1840 concerning the above-mentioned regulation, signed by Serbian duke M.M. Obrenovic, by which fine was prescribed for those who cut timber without a permit.
- Order of M.M. Obrenovic, Duke of Serbia, No. 640 of 25 May 1840, concerning hunting regime of specific species of game: deer and does, rabbits, wild goats and certain species of birds.
- Regulation No. 1640 of 17 September 1840 on ban of use of poisons for fishing and punishment of offenders.
- The Law on Waters and Their Use from 26 December 1878.

---

development of programmes, projects and other activities in the field of conservation, sustainable use, protection and improvement of the environment – Law on Amendment of the EPL (19 Feb. 2016, OJ RS, No. 14/16). Green Fund is established for an indefinite period of time (Art. 90, paras 1 and 2).

104. *See* GOV RS. 2006a, 7.

105. EPA. 2007, 135. On this subject, *see also* Janković, 1996.

- The Law on Fruit Growing of 3 July 1878.
- The Law on Hunting of 16 July 1898.
- Regulation of Ministry of Interior Affairs No. 12.625 of 1 June 1901, on punishment of illegal hunters.
- The Law on Forestry of 23 March 1904.
- Rules on cutting and trading with timber No. S 23.638 of 30 September 1901.
- Regulation of the Ministry of Economy No. S 7107 from 4 April 1904 on supervision over forests and prosecution of offenders.
- Regulation of Ministry of Interior Affairs No. P 18630 from 13 July 1904 banning cutting monastery wood without permission.

62. Legal regulations of the environment were already developed to a certain extent in the new Kingdom of Serbs, Croats and Slovenes created in 1918 (which later became the Kingdom of Yugoslavia). The Kingdom of Yugoslavia had a number of legal sources concerning environment and related fields, as the following, for example:

- Regulations on supervision of drinking water (OJ of the Kingdom of Yugoslavia, No. 17-VI, 24 January 1931).
- The Law on Use of Hydro-energy (OJ of the Kingdom of Yugoslavia, No. 154-LI, 10 July 1931).
- The Law on Convention Regulating Definitive Status of the Danube River (OJ of the Kingdom of Yugoslavia, No. 180-LXI, 20 August 1931).
- The Law on Hunting (OJ of the Kingdom of Yugoslavia, No. 285-XCIII, 5 December 1931).
- The Law on Maritime Fishing (OJ of the Kingdom of Serbs, Croats and Slovenes, No. 243-XXXIII, 31 October 1922).
- The Law on Forestry (OJ of the Kingdom of Yugoslavia, No. 307-CXXXI, 31 December 1929).
- Regulations on forestation of deforested land therein and quick send (OJ of the Kingdom of Yugoslavia, No. 208-LXXII, 12 September 1930).
- Law on Control on Seeds of Cultivated Plants in Import and Internal Marketing (OJ of the Kingdom of Serbs, Croats and Slovenes, No. 125, 10 June 1922).
- The Law on the Protocol on the Ban of Use in War of Suffocating, Poisons and Similar Gases and Bacteriological Means, etc. (OJ of the Kingdom of Serbs, Croats and Slovenes, No. 117-L, 21 May 1929).
- Regulation on development of regulatory plans (OJ of the Kingdom of Yugoslavia, No. 152-LXIX, 16 July 1932).

63. It must be added, however, that the Northern part of Serbia (APV) was until 1918 a part of the Austro-Hungarian Empire, so the legislation concerning environmental protection (and closely related fields) which was until 1918 in force in the Empire was at that time in force in Vojvodina as well. Some other territories also belonged until 1912 to the Ottoman Empire and had special legal regulation in matters of environmental protection and related issues.

64. After the Second World War, the Federal People's Republic of Yugoslavia was formed (the name was later changed to SFRY). Its whole legal system was, in the beginning, more or less, based on the Soviet Marxist model, but later (from 1950), it evolved with the introduction of self-government and steadily rising autonomy of the Republics. The 1974 Constitution introduced practically elements of State sovereignty for all republics and transferred most of the Federal competencies, including those relevant to environmental protection, to the Republics, which had their own ministries or other bodies competent for environmental protection.

The same Constitution was, it should be added, one of the first Constitutions in the world to introduce provisions regarding the environment (for instance, Articles 87, 192, 193, etc.). The Federation had only certain competencies in the field of the environment (coordinated by the Committee of the Federal Government for the environment and spatial regulation). The SFRY had relatively developed environmental regulations on both federal and republican levels, was a contracting party to many international treaties, and was active in the UNEP and other organizations in the environmental field.

65. The FRY (Serbia and Montenegro) was proclaimed in 1992, after the disintegration of the former Yugoslavia. The competences in the field of the environment were divided between the Federation in which a Ministry for the Environment was formed (later merged with some other institutions into the Ministry for Development, Science and the Environment and later into the Ministry for Health and Social Politics), and the Republics.

The Serbian APs Kosovo-Metohija has, after the 1999 NATO intervention, a special status according to the UNSC Resolution 1244. There are many open issues and such a situation has an impact on the various environmental-related issues in Serbia and Kosovo.

66. The first Serbian Ministry for Environmental Protection was formed in accordance with the Law on Ministries (Article 22a, OJ RS, No. 44/91, 25 July 1991). The first specific law regulating environmental protection in contemporary sense of the word was adopted in 1991. That was the EPL (OJ RS, Nos 66/91, 83/92, 67/93, 48/94 and 53/95). The new EPL (OJ RS, Nos 135/04, 36/09 – other law and 72/09 – other law) was adopted on 21 December 2004 and significantly amended on 19 May 2009 (OJ RS, No. 36/09), amended on 22 February 2016 (OJ RS, No. 14/16), on 12 October 2018 (OJ RS, No. 76/18).

67. In 2003, the FRY was transformed into a semi-confederal State Union of Serbia and Montenegro which lasted until 2006 when Serbia and Montenegro became independent States.

Chapter 4. The Role of Governmental Institutions in the Shaping and Administration of Environmental Law and Policy

§1. The Governmental Institutions and Their Competences

68. A number of different institutions are involved in the shaping and administration of environmental law and policy in Serbia and one of the most serious problems is their cooperation and coordination. Depending on the issue and relevant legal regulations different institutions are competent in different cases. Short-term and long-term goals, key principles of activities of competent governmental institutions, and instruments for achieving goals are prescribed in a large number of strategic documents and action plans. Some directly relate to the field of the environment (as it is regulated by appropriate regulations), and some strategic documents have an indirect significance for the field of the environment, either by the fact that the solutions they contain affect (or can affect) the state of the environment, or by their implementation may depend on environmental activities.[106]

69. 'The institutional framework for public policy management was set up with the establishment of the Public Policy Secretariat (hereinafter: PPS),[107] and the regulatory framework was completed with the adoption of the Law on Planning System and by-laws for its implementation. Together, they represent the first ever coherent framework for development planning, public policy management and medium-term planning.'[108]

70. More detailed elaboration of the strategic objectives was done through a system of different regulations, among which the central place is occupied by the regulations prepared, adopted, and implemented by the bodies responsible for environmental affairs. In some situations, the competencies and activities of environmental authorities are more or less clearly defined, while in some circumstances, the intertwining of the competencies of different authorities is obvious and extremely complicated.[109]

71. Competence in the field of environment is divided vertically and horizontally among several different authorities (Assembly, Government, Ministries and

---

106. Some of these strategic documents will be discussed later in the text.
107. https://rsjp.gov.rs/en/ (1.2.2024).
108. GOV RS. 2021b. (Chapetr III: Public Policy Planning and Coordination, point 1: Situation Analysis). Nevertheless, 'the quality of strategic planning is still deemed to be poor, which means that the focus should be placed on an impact assessment of public policy documents and regulations, in particular the financial impact assessment and the monitoring of their implementation.' By the way, the Strategy for Public Administration Reform in the Republic of Serbia for the period 2021–2030 does not specifically mention 'environment'.
109. The issue of connections between different bodies (in terms of competence for environmental affairs) needs to be investigated in a special and detailed analysis. This especially concerns the relationship between bodies primarily responsible for environmental affairs and other bodies primarily responsible for other environmentally relevant affairs (energy, spatial planning, construction, agriculture, health, etc).

other Institutions). In addition, the responsibility for carrying out work in the field of environment is divided between the central authorities, the AP, and the LSG.

72. Provisions concerning the competence have been prescribed by the Constitution of the RS[110] and by the following legal Acts:

- Law on the National Assembly (OJ RS, No. 9/10).
- Law on Ministries (OJ RS, Nos 128/20, 116/22, 92/23 – other law).
- Law on State Administration (OJ RS, Nos 79/05, 101/07, 95/10, 99/14, 30/18 – other law and 47/18).
- Law on State Servants (OJ RS, Nos 79/05, 81/05 – corr., 83/05 – corr., 64/07, 67/07 – corr., 116/08, 104/09, 99/14, 94/17, 95/18, 157/20, and 142/22).
- Law on Government (OJ RS, Nos 55/05 and corr. 71/05, 101/07, 65/08, 16/11, 68/12 – CC, 72/12, 74/12 – corr. CC, 7/14 – CC, 44/14 and 30/18 – other law).
- Rules of Procedure of the Government (OJ RS, Nos 100/05, 61/06, 69/08, 88/09, 33/10, 69/10, 20/11, 37/11, 30/13, 76/14 and 8/19 – other regulation).
- Law on Planning System (OJ RS, No. 30/18).
- Law on Certain Competences of the AP (OJ RS, Nos 99/09, 67/12 – CC, and 18/20 – other law).
- Law on Local Self-Government (OJ RS, Nos 129/2007, 83/14 – other law, 101/16 – other law, 47/18, and 111/21 – other law).
- Law on Capital (OJ RS, Nos 128/07, 83/14 – other law, 101/16 – other law, 37/19, and 111/21 – other.
- Law on Inspection and Supervision (OJ RS. Nos 36/15, 44/18 – other law and 95/18).
- Law on General Administrative Procedure (OJ RS, Nos 18/16 and 95/18 – authentic interpretation, and 2/23 – CC).
- Law on Electronic Administration (OJ RS, No. 27/18), etc.

73. The highest legislative body in the RS is the NA.[111] It consists of 250 Members of Parliament (MPs), who are elected by free and secret ballot to a four-year term of office. The NA enacts laws and other general Acts within the competence of the RS in different areas, including the environment. It has nineteen standing committees, including the Committee for Environmental Protection.[112]

74. The President of the Republic[113] proposes to the NA the candidate for Prime Minister Elect, having heard the opinion of representatives of elected party lists.

---

110. *See* the part devoted to 'constitutional provisions'.
111. *See* Art. 98 of the Constitution of the RS. For more information, *see* http://www.parlament.gov.rs/national-assembly/role-and-mode-of-operation/jurisdiction.501.html (16.1.2024). *See also* Law on National Assembly (OJ RS, No. 9/10).
112. *See* Art. 46 of the Assembly's Rules of Procedure (OJ RS, No. 20/12), http://www.parlament.gov.rs/national-assembly/important-documents/rules-of-procedure/working-bodies-of-the-national-assembly.1355.html (16.1.2024).
113. *See* https://www.predsednik.rs/en (30.1.2024).

75. According to the Constitution, the Government's competences are required to do the following:

(1) define and pursue policies;
(2) enforce laws and other general Acts of the NA;
(3) adopt decrees and other general Acts in order to enforce laws;
(4) propose laws and other general Acts to the NA and provide opinions on them when another proponent submits them;
(5) direct and harmonize the work of ministries and other bodies of public administration and supervise their work; and
(6) perform other duties set forth by the Constitution and law. The Government[114] is accountable to the Parliament for the R S's policies, for law enforcement and for the work of public administration bodies.

76. The Government's term of office lasts until the end of term of the Parliament that elected it and starts from the day of taking oath before the Parliament. That means that the Government's term always ceases along with that of MPs who elected it – be it with the expiry of their term, that is, after four years or with the disbanding of the NA. Besides the above-mentioned, the Government's term can also cease before the end of the Parliament's term in cases of a no-confidence vote, Prime Minister's resignation and failure to vote confidence. No-confidence vote for the Government or an individual member can be requested by a minimum of sixty MPs. The NA accepts the proposal of no-confidence vote if more than half of the MPs vote for it.[115]

The Government, with the ceased term, until a new Government is elected, can perform only current and urgent duties set forth by law.[116]

77. The Prime Minister leads and guides the Government, takes care of unity of its political actions, harmonizes the work of its members, represents it and calls for and chairs its sessions. The Prime Minister can give mandatory directives and special assignments to other Government members, in accordance with the Government's programmes and policies. The Prime Minister takes decisions[117] and provides solutions.

78. A minister can submit to the Government proposals to regulate issues under the Government's and Parliament's jurisdiction and demand that the Government

---

114. The Government consists of the Prime Minister, one or more deputies and ministers. The Prime Minister leads and guides the Government's work, takes care of its even political activities, harmonizes the work of Government members and represents the Government. The ministers are accountable to the Prime Minister, Government and Parliament for their work and situation in the scope of their ministries' competences.
115. The Government can request vote on its confidence. The National Assembly accepts proposal of confidence vote if more than half of all MPs vote for it. If the National Assembly does not vote for confidence to the Government, the Government's term ceases. The Prime Minister can offer his/her resignation to the National Assembly. The Government's term ceases on the day of noting the Prime Minister's resignation.
116. A government member's term of office can cease before the time of its duration with noting of their resignation, no-confidence vote in the Parliament and relieving from office by the Parliament, at the Prime Minister's proposal.
117. Decisions taken by the Prime Minister are published in the 'Official Journal of the Republic of Serbia'.

take a stand on an issue from his/her competences. The minister is obliged to inform the Government of everything that will have a consequence for the Government's policy and decision-making. The minister is responsible for implementation of the Government's programme and policy, for decisions and actions that he/she has taken or failed to take and for the execution of mandatory directives and special assignments the Prime Minister allotted to him.

79. A government member cannot perform any other public function in a state body, or any authority of AP, local council, city, the city of Belgrade, nor can he/she deal with any activity unmatchable with the duty of government member, nor create a possibility of conflict between public and private interest.

80. According to the Law on Ministries (OJ RS, Nos 128/20, 116/22, 27/23 – other law),[118] the main ministry for environmental protection is the Ministry of Environmental Protection (MEP) (Article 6).[119] Article 6 of the Law on Ministries also describes the competencies of the Environmental Protection Agency (EPA). Apart from the MEP and EPA, the only body whose competence is 'environment', i.e., where the environment is explicitly mentioned in the description of the competencies, is the Ministry of Mining and Energy (MME).[120]

81. MEP has the following responsibilities:

– Basics of environmental protection.
– Environmental protection and improvement system.
– National parks.

118. By the 2016 EPL Amendment, definition of the 'organ of public authority' has been introduced. 'The organ of public authority is the authority responsible for the implementation of the obligations under authorizations under this Law, as follows: – the ministry responsible for the environment; – provincial authority responsible for environmental protection; – the competent authority of the local government; – other state body, territorial autonomy, local authorities and organizations entrusted with public authority; – natural or legal persons performing public functions and exercising public powers, including specific duties, activities or services in relation to the environment, as well as any other natural or legal persons performing public functions, or providing public services relating to the environment, and are under their control; – a legal entity established by the state authorities, territorial autonomy, local authorities and organizations entrusted with public authority, or which is funded in its entirety, or predominantly from the budget.' (Art. 3, point 29a) It seems that the inspiration for this definition is found in the provisions of the AC.

119. https://www.ekologija.gov.rs/organizacija/nadleznost (4.1.2024). In July 2017, on the basis of the Law on Ministries, an independent Ministry of Environmental Protection was formed. The Ministry of Environmental Protection is the leading institution for Ch. 27, while responsibilities for certain regulations have been assigned to the Ministry of Agriculture, Forestry and Water Management, while some regulations have remained within the competence of ministries in which they were previously (Ministry of Construction, Transport and Infrastructure, Ministry of Interior, Ministry of Mining and Energy, Ministry of Health, Ministry of Justice) (GOV RS. 2018, 1136).

120. It is prescribed that this body deals with 'state administration affairs related, *inter alia*, to: 'environmental protection, sustainable use of water resources and climate change in the field of energy' (Art. 8). This would mean that the relevance of other governmental bodies should be interpreted according to concrete circumstances and other criteria (eg. the definition of the term 'environment' from the LEP, the achievement of the goals of individual regulations in the field of the environment, and connections with goals in other areas, etc.).

- Inspection supervision in the field of environmental protection.
- Application of the results of scientific and technological research and development research in the field of environment.
- Implementation of the Convention on Access to Information, Public Participation in Decision-making and Access to Justice in Environmental Matters.
- Nature protection.
- Air protection.
- Ozone layer protection.
- Climate Changes.
- Transboundary air and water pollution.
- Protection of water from pollution in order to prevent deterioration of surface and groundwater quality.
- Determining the conditions for environmental protection in spatial planning and construction of facilities.
- Protection against major chemical accidents and participation in reacting in case of chemical accidents.
- Noise and vibration protection.
- Protection against ionizing and non-ionizing radiation.
- Management of chemicals and biocidal products.
- Implementation of the Chemical Weapons Convention in accordance with the law.
- Waste management, excluding radioactive waste.
- Creating conditions for access and implementation of projects within the scope of that Ministry which are financed from the pre-accession funds of the European Union, donations, and other forms of development assistance.
- Approval of transboundary movement of waste and protected plant and animal species, as well as other activities determined by law.

82. Another important body is the EPA,[121] established by Article 4 of the Law on Changes and Additions of the Law on Ministries (OJ RS, No. 19/04). According to the Article 6, paragraph 2 of the Lasw on Ministries (OJ RS, Nos 128/20, 116/22, 27/23 – other law) EPA, as an administrative body within the MEP, with the status of a legal entity, is competent for the following: development, harmonization and management of the national environmental information system (monitoring the state of environmental factors through environmental indicators, register of pollutants, etc.); implementation of state monitoring of air and water quality, including implementation of prescribed and harmonized programs for control of air, surface water and groundwater quality; management of the National Laboratory; collection and consolidation of environmental data, their processing and preparation of reports on the state of the environment and the implementation of environmental protection policy; development of procedures for processing environmental data and their assessment; keeping data on the best available techniques and practices and their application in the field of environmental protection; cooperation with the European Environment Agency (EEA) and the European Information and Observation Network (EIONET), as well as other tasks determined by law.

121. At http://www.sepa.gov.rs/index.php (4.1.2024).

83. The Environment Protection Fund has been established in accordance with Article 90 of the EPL (OJ RS, Nos 135/2004, 36/09 and 72/09) for the purposes of securing financial resources for encouragement of protection and improvement of environment in the RS. However, the Fund ceased to exist on 25 September 2012 (OJ RS, No. 93/12). Later, on 19 February 2016, the Green Fund of the RS as a budgetary fund was established – Amendments to EPL (OJ RS, No. 14/16). The budget fund is established for an indefinite period, following the law regulating the budget system. The budget fund is managed by the Ministry (Article 90, paragraphs 2 and 3 of the EPL).[122]

84. Due to the complexity of environmental problems, almost all ministries can be relevant for certain issues related to the environment. Without giving a complete list, here we only indicate some institutions whose jurisdiction covers various issues, among which there may be (at least partially) those that are important for conducting environmental policy, passing regulations in the environmental field, solving some specific problems in the field of environment, etc. These are the following ministries and other institutions:

- Ministry of Mining and Energy.[123]
- Ministry of Agriculture, Forest and Water Management.[124]
- Ministry of Construction, Transport and Infrastructure.[125]
- Ministry of Public Administration and LSG.[126]
- Ministry of Health.[127]
- Ministry of Economy.[128]
- Ministry of Labour, Employment, Veteran and Social Policy.[129]
- Ministry of Interior.[130]
- Ministry of Justice.[131]
- Ministry of Finance.[132]
- Ministry of European Integration.[133]
- Ministry for Public Investment.[134]
- Ministry of Culture.[135]
- Ministry of Education.[136]

122. EPL prescribes the method of allocating funds, the method of using funds, keeping records, etc. (Art. 90a-90g).
123. At https://www.mre.gov.rs/ (4.1.2024).
124. At http://www.minpolj.gov.rs (30.1.2024).
125. At https://www.mgsi.gov.rs/en (30.1.2024).
126. At http://mduls.gov.rs/en/home/ (4.1.2024).
127. At https://www.zdravlje.gov.rs/ (4.1.2024).
128. At https://privreda.gov.rs/ (4.1.2024).
129. At https://www.minrzs.gov.rs/srb-lat/ministarstvo (4.1.2024).
130. At http://www.mup.gov.rs/wps/portal/en/ministry (4.1.2024).
131. At https://www.mpravde.gov.rs/ (30.1.2024).
132. At https://www.mfin.gov.rs/en (30.1.2024).
133. At https://www.mei.gov.rs/eng/ (30.1.2024).
134. At https://www.obnova.gov.rs/english (30.1.2024).
135. At http://www.kultura.gov.rs/en/ (4.1.2024).
136. At https://prosveta.gov.rs/?lng=lat (4.1.2024).

– Customs Administration.[137]
– Republic Hydro Meteorological Service.[138]
– Institute for Nature Conservation.[139]
– Serbian Radiation and Nuclear Safety Directorate (SRBATOM).[140]
– Institute of Public Health of Serbia.[141]
– Statistical Office of the RS.[142]
– Institute of Soil, Belgrade.[143]
– Institute of Field and Vegetable Crops, Novi Sad.[144]
– Institute of Forestry.[145]
– Institute of Nuclear Sciences, Vinca.[146]
– Serbian Institute of Occupational Health,[147] etc.

85. The Directorate for Water[148] deserves special attention. It is a part of the MAFWM, and it is responsible for the development of water management policy, use of water resources, provision of water supply, flood protection, protection and rational consumption of water, monitoring and maintenance of national and trans-boundary water courses, as well as other tasks defined by law.

The public water management enterprise 'Srbijavode'[149] manages water resources in Serbia, and public water management enterprise 'Vode Vojvodine' has a similar role in the APV.[150]

86. An important role is also played by the Institute for Nature Protection,[151] which is responsible for protection of nature and protected areas (parks, nature reserves, wild flora and fauna habitats, etc.) and for supervision of these natural values. The Institute was established by a government decision (OJ RS, Nos 18/10, 9/17, and 65/22), and the Institute is an institution whose establishment, organization and work are subject to the regulations on public services (point 2 of the Decision).

87. The Chemicals Agency was founded in accordance with Article 5 of the Law on Chemicals (OJ RS, No. 36/09) as an independent, developmental, specialized

137. At https://www.carina.rs/en.html (4.1.2024).
138. At http://www.hidmet.gov.rs/index_eng.php (4.1.2024).
139. At http://www.zzps.rs/wp/?lang=en (28.8.2020).
140. At http://www.srbatom.gov.rs/srbatomm/?lang=en (4.1.2024).
141. At http://www.batut.org.rs/index.php?lang=2 (4.1.2024).
142. At https://www.stat.gov.rs/en-US/ (4.1.2024).
143. At http://www.soilinst.rs/ (4.1.2024).
144. At https://nsseme.com/en/home/ (4.1.2024).
145. At https://www.forest.org.rs/?sLang=en (4.1.2024).
146. At https://www.vin.bg.ac.rs/en/ (4.1.2024).
147. At http://www.imrs.rs/ (4.1.2024).
148. At https://rdvode.gov.rs/ (30.1.2024).
149. https://www.srbijavode.rs/ (4.1.2024).
150. https://vodevojvodine.com/en/ (4.1.2024).
151. https://zzps.rs/ (4.1.2024).

and regulatory organization that performs public authorizations with the aim to provide administrative capacities for quality, efficient and safe management of chemicals and biocidal products.[152]

88. Pursuant to Article 5 of the Law on Ionizing Radiation Protection and Nuclear Safety (Nos 36/09 and 93/12), the Serbian Agency for Ionizing Radiation Protection and Nuclear Safety was established as an independent regulatory body in compliance with the Law on Public Agencies (OJ RS, Nos 18/05 and 81/05 – corr., and 47/18). In accordance with Article 13 of the new Law on Radiation and Nuclear Safety and Security (OJ RS, Nos 95/18 and 10/19), the Serbian Radiation and Nuclear Safety and Security Directorate was established as a separate and independent regulatory authority conducting regulatory, professional and other related executive duties in the field of radiation and nuclear safety and security.[153]

89. Several other institutions responsible for environmental monitoring also deserve to be mentioned. They are as follows:

- The Public Health Institutes monitor local air quality in urban areas, surface water quality in urban areas, drinking water quality and noise.[154]
- The Public Forest Enterprises are responsible for the improvement and utilization of State-owned forests. The public management enterprise 'Serbia forest' manages forests in Serbia,[155] and public water management enterprise 'Vojvodina forest' has a similar role in the APV.[156]
- The Plant Protection Directorate,[157] as an administrative body within the MAFWM,[158] controls production, import, trade, storage and application of plant protection agents.
- Statistical Office of the RS collects and processes data relevant for the state of the environment (water, waste, air pollution, etc.).[159]

I. Autonomous Provinces

90. One of the key aspects of system of environmental policy in Serbia is the role of the AP and local authorities in environmental management. The role is prescribed by the Law on Definition of Competencies of the AP and by the Law on

152. The Chemicals Agency ceased to exist by the adoption of the Law amending the Law on chemicals, 25 Sep. 2012 (OJ RS, No. 93/12).
153. http://www.srbatom.gov.rs/srbatomm/?lang=en (4.1.2024).
154. *See, for example*, Institute of Public Health of Serbia, http://www.batut.org.rs/index.php?lang=2 (4.1.2024); City Institute for Public Health in Belgrade, https://www.zdravlje.org.rs/ (4.1.2024). There are 24 public health institutes in Serbia.
155. https://srbijasume.rs/en/ (4.1.2024).
156. http://www.vojvodinasume.rs/en/ (4.1.2024).
157. https://uzb.minpolj.gov.rs/en/ (4.1.2024).
158. The Veterinary Administration and the Forestry Administration have the same legal status. *See*: https://www.vet.minpolj.gov.rs/en/; https://upravazasume.gov.rs/ (31.1.2024).
159. https://www.stat.gov.rs/en-us/oblasti/zivotna-sredina/ (4.1.2024).

LSG. The competencies of the AP, according to the Law on Definition of Competencies of the AP (Article 25),[160] are as follows:

(1) to regulate, improve and ensure the environmental protection for the territory of APV;[161]
(2) to pass the act of putting under protection the natural goods, in accordance with the Law regulating nature protection;
(3) to enact the programme of environmental protection in its territory in compliance with the National Programme, the action and remediation plans and its interests and specificities;
(4) to enact plans and programmes for management of natural resources and goods, in accordance with the strategic documents;
(5) to control the use and protection of natural resources and goods in the territory of APV;
(6) to ensure continuous control and monitoring of the environmental situation and enact the monitoring programme for its territory which shall comply with the monitoring programme enacted by the Government for the period of two years;
(7) to ensure conditions for provision of measures and conditions of environmental protection, at the request of the body responsible for preparation and enactment of spatial and urban plans, based on the requirements and opinions of competent professional organizations;
(8) to participate in the process of preparation and enactment of spatial and urban plans and other plans;
(9) to enact the external plan for protection against accidents, the plan being an integral part of the response plan for emergency situations based on the competences under the regulation governing the field of protection and rescue;
(10) in case of an accident, declare the situation of environmental endangerment in the territory of APV, in accordance with the Law governing environmental protection;
(11) to establish the budget fund pursuant to the regulation governing the budget system, which shall be financed from the revenues collected in the territory of APV.[162]

160. Besides Art. 29 of the Law, a number of other Articles contain provisions concerning legal framework for competencies in different issues. For example, Art. 30 (Urban Planning), Art. 31 (Construction), Arts 36–40 (Mining and Power), Arts 41–49 (Agriculture), and so on.

161. *See also* Art. 13 of the Statute of APV ('The AP of Vojvodina shall provide conditions for environmental protection and improvement and undertake measures for prevention and elimination of detrimental effects which endanger environment and represent a threat to human life and health').

162. According to Art. 28 of the Law, APV, through its agencies shall perform the following tasks: (1) perform inspections in the field of environmental protection and take measures to prevent irregularities in the area, except for inspection control: in case of accident, in the field of ionizing radiation, in cross-border movement of goods, subject to jurisdiction of the Republican Inspectorate for Environmental Protection, and filled the conditions of the operator for permission to cross-border movement of goods (radioactivity, waste, poisons, substances that damage the ozone layer, protected plant and animal species), of certain facilities in the territory of AP Vojvodina, which will be defined by special Act; (2) give consent to the study on the assessment of environmental impacts for projects for which approval for the building issued by the competent provincial authority for

91. Based on the prescribed competencies, the Provincial Assembly adopted the Decision on the Environmental Protection Program of the Autonomous Province of Vojvodina for the period 2016–2025. (OJ APV, No. 10/2016).[163]

92. APV, through its agencies, shall establish the Provincial Institute for Nature Conservation of Vojvodina Province, to perform the tasks of nature protection and protection of natural resources that are entirely in the territory of Vojvodina (Article 26).[164]

93. According to Article 19 of the Statute of APV (OJ APV, No. 20/14), the APV through its bodies shall enact the following legal and other Acts: the Statute as the supreme legal Act of the APV Provincial Assembly decisions for issues which, under the Constitution, fall directly within the scope of competences of the APV, or are defined under the law as issues relevant to the Province; provincial decrees, decisions, declarations, resolutions, rules of procedure, books of regulations, directives, orders, rulings, recommendations, conclusions and other Acts.[165]

II. Local Self-Government

94. The Constitution of the RS establishes the right to LSG. Citizens exercise this right directly or through their freely elected representatives (Article 176, paragraph 1). The position and competence of LSG are regulated by several provisions of the Constitution, among which Articles 188–193 are especially important. The municipality, through its organs, *inter alia*: takes care of environmental protection and protection from natural and other disasters; takes care of protection of cultural assets of importance for the municipality; protects, improves, and uses agricultural land;

urban affairs; (3) approve the report on strategic assessment of environmental impact for the territory of the APV; (4) issue of integrated permits for installations and activities for which permission and approval for the construction and start work, or the performance or the conduct of activities, issued by other competent provincial authority; (5) give preliminary approval in the process of making foundation, plans and programs to protect and improve protected natural goods, flora and fauna, forests and water in the territory of the APV; (6) establish an information system for the protection and improvement of the environment as part of a unified information system of the Republic of Serbia; (7) consider complaints against the municipal or city government in the territory of the APV; (8) carry out inspection of the use and protection of natural assets and resources. Jobs in para. 1 of this Article shall be as committed.

163. The Report on the State of Environmental Quality for 2019 in the Autonomous Province of Vojvodina was also published. https://www.ekourbapv.vojvodina.gov.rs/wp-content/uploads/2021/01/izvestaj-o-stanju-zivotne-sredine-2019-APV.pdf (1.2.2024).

164. *See also*, Decision of the Provincial Assembly on the Establishment of the Provincial Institute for Nature Protection (OJ APV, Nos 2/2010, 23/2018) https://pzzp.rs/o-nama/ukratko-o-zavodu/dokumenta-pzzp.html (28.8.2020).

165. At http://www.skupstinavojvodine.gov.rs/Strana.aspx?s=statut&j=EN (4.1.2024).

arranges and ensures the performance and development of communal activities; arranges and ensures the use of construction land and business premises, etc. (Article 190, paragraph 1).[166]

95. According to the Public Administration Reform Strategy in the RS for the period 2021–2030 (2021), 'the preparation of the Programme for the Reform of the Local Self-Government System in the RS is underway, which should determine the objectives and measures for ensuring further decentralisation, more functional distribution of tasks and competences and more intensive development of local self-government positions and organisations in the public government system'.[167] The Law on LSG (OJ RS, Nos 129/07, 83/14 – other law, 101/16 – other law, 47/18, and 111/21 – other law) prescribes responsibilities of municipalities as follows: to enact development programmes, city plans, budget and an annual financial report; to organize and ensure performance and development of public services (urban sanitation, maintenance of deposit sites, etc.) as well as to ensure organizational, financial and other conditions for their realization; to take care of environmental protection; to adopt programmes for utilization and protection of natural values and environmental protection programmes, that is, local actions and sensitization plans in accordance with strategic documents and interests, define tax for environmental protection and improvement, etc. (Article 20).

III. Competencies of the AP and LSG According to the Environmental Laws

96. Different environmental laws transfer certain jurisdictions to the AP and LSG.[168] By adoption of the second set of environmental laws in May 2009, decentralization of competences was continued through competence shifts to provincial and local levels.

166. The Municipal Assembly shall, *inter alia*, pass general acts within its competences, adopt the budget and annual balance sheet, adopt the development plan and the municipal spatial plan, schedule the municipal referendum and perform other duties specified by the Law and the Statute (Art. 191, para. 2).
167. GOV RS. 2021b, Ch. VIII: Local Self-government system, point 1. Situation analysis. The specific objective is 'to build a modern, professional and efficient local self-government that is capable of providing quality public services to citizens and the economy, to apply the principles of good governance in its work and to improve the quality of life of citizens and contribute to the balanced development of the Republic of Serbia.'
168. In accordance with the Arts 4, 21 and 22 of the *Law on Local Self-Governments* (OJ RS, Nos 129/07, 83/14 – other law, 101/16 – other law, 47/18, and 111/21 – other law) the Republic of Serbia may entrust by a law to LSG particular matters within its competency, such as enforcement of laws and regulations, and LSGs are obliged and responsible to carry out these tasks as entrusted in a quality and efficient manner. Also, based on Art. 78, para. 2, bodies of the Republic supervise the legality of the work and acts of LSG bodies, in accordance with the Constitution and the law. *See also* Arts 4, 5, 45, 46, 48, 51–56, 59, 73, 75, 86 and 90 of the Law on State Administration (OJ RS, Nos 79/05, 101/07, 95/10, 99/14, 30/18 – other law, and 47/18); as well as Arts 4, para. 3; 12, para. 11; 44, para. 2, point 16; 50, para. 3; and 54, para. 1 of the Law on Inspection (OJ RS, No. 32/15).

The AP and LSG units are entrusted with activities based on environmental laws which pertain to several aspects including following: EIA, SEA, IPPC, air protection (local network of measurement stations, air quality plans and short-term action plans), water management, waste management (inert and non-hazardous one), nature protection, chemicals management, protection from non-ionizing radiation, protection and sustainable management of fish resources, protection against noise (acoustic zoning, development of strategic noise maps and action plans), spatial planning and building and so on.

A. Law on Environmental Protection

97. On the basis of Article 5 of EPL (OJ RS, Nos 135/04, 36/09, 72/09, 43/11 – CC, 14/16, 76/18 and 95/18 – other law), for the implementation of environmental protection system, among other subjects, the LSG is responsible for any activity that changes or can change the state of and conditions in the environment, that is, for not taking environmental protection measures, in accordance with the Law.[169]

98. According to Article 13, the AP and LSG, within the competencies prescribed in the present and specific law, shall issue their respective plans and programmes of natural resources and property management in accordance with the strategic documents referred to in Article 12 of this Law and their specific requirements.[170]

99. The measures and conditions of environmental protection shall be issued by the Ministry, the AP body or LSG at the request of the authority in charge of plan preparation and passing, on the basis of conditions and measures of competent authorities (Article 34). The LSG shall be obliged to obtain the prior consent of the Ministry for the proposal for an Act to determine the status of the endangered environment and priorities for rehabilitation and remediation for areas of local significance and for areas of local significance in the territory of the AP, the consent of the responsible authority of the AP (Article 43).

100. In the case of accident, depending on its scope, within or outside the plant and estimated consequences, which may cause direct or deferred threats towards human health and environment, the state of endangerment of environment shall be proclaimed, and the public shall be informed of the measures taken. The state of

169. On the basis of Art. 9, item 1 of EPL, bodies of LSG provide integration of protection and improvement of environment in all sectoral policies by implementation of mutually agreed plans and programmes and implementation of regulations through a system of permits, technical and other standards and regulations, by funding, stimulation and other measures of environmental protection.
170. Article 12 of the Law refers to the Strategy of spatial development of the Republic of Serbia and the National Strategy of sustainable use of natural resources and goods.

endangerment referred to in paragraph 1 of this Article shall be proclaimed by the Ministry, namely the authority of the AP and LSG (Article 62).

101. The AP and LSG shall promulgate the programme for environmental protection in their territory, namely local action and rehabilitation plans, in accordance with the national programme and plans referred to in Articles 65 and 66 of this Law and their interest and specificities (Article 68). The AP, namely LSG, shall adopt the programme of monitoring on its territory that must be in accordance with the programme referred to in paragraph 3 of this Article (Article 69).[171]

102. The AP and LSG shall be obliged to establish the budget fund in accordance with the law governing the budget system (Article 100) and shall perform inspection and supervision of the implementation of tasks delegated by this Law and regulations adopted based on this Law (Article 109).[172]

B. *Law on Environmental Impact Assessment*

103. According to Article 2 of the Law on EIA (OJ RS, Nos 135/04 and 36/09), 'competent authority' means the authority responsible for carrying out the EIA procedure within the functions set forth by this Law, that is, the Ministry responsible for environmental protection matters (the Ministry) – for those projects for which the permit for project implementation is under the responsibility of the Republic authority; the provincial authority responsible for environmental protection matters – for those projects for which the permit for project implementation is under the responsibility of the authority of the AP; the LSG authority responsible for environmental protection matters – for those projects for which the permit for project implementation is under the responsibility of the LSG authority.

C. *Law on Strategic Environmental Assessment*

104. Article 3 of the Law on SEA (OJ RS, Nos 135/04 and 88/10) prescribes that 'authorities and organizations concerned' are the authorities and organizations of the Republic, AP and LSG authorities having interest, in accordance with their responsibilities, in the decision-making process related to environmental protection (point 4).

---

171. The responsible authority of the AP and/or the responsible authority of the LSG shall submit data for preparation of the report, quarterly, to the EPA, in particular for the first, second and third quarter no later than two months after the elapse of the quarter, and for the last quarter by 31 January (Art. 76).

172. The responsible authority of the AP shall decide on the appeal against first instance decision of the responsible municipal, namely city authority from the territory of the AP, adopted in the course of performing delegated tasks (Art. 114).

D. Law on Integrated Pollution Prevention and Control

105. Pursuant to the Law on IPPC (OJ RS, Nos 135/04 and 25/15), the provincial authority responsible for environmental protection shall grant the permit in accordance with this Law for installations or activities for which permit or consent for construction and commencement of operation, or execution of activities were issued by other competent provincial authorities.[173]

106. The LSG authority responsible for environmental protection shall grant the permit in accordance with this Law for installations or activities for which permit or consent for construction and commencement of operation or execution of activities were issued by other competent LSG authorities.[174]

E. Law on Waste Management

107. According to Article 20 of the Law on Waste Management (OJ RS, Nos 36/09, 88/10, 14/16, 95/18 – other law, and 35/23), the LSG must perform the following tasks, *inter alia*: (1) adopt local plan for waste management (in accordance with Articles 13 and 14), provide conditions and care of its implementation; (2) regulate, provide, organize and implement municipal waste management (Article 43, paragraphs 5 and 7 and Article 55, paragraph 6 – waste vehicles), and non-hazardous or inert waste on its territory, in accordance with the Law; (3) regulate the procedure of services payment in the area of municipal, non-hazardous and inert waste management in accordance with the Law; (4) issue permits in accordance with Article 60, paragraphs 4 (for the city) and 5 (for the municipality); (5) give approvals and other documents pursuant to this Law; (6) keep records and submit data to the Ministry; (7) at the request of the Ministry or the competent body of the AP, provide opinion in the process of issuing permits in accordance with this Law; and (8) supervise and control measures of dealing with waste in accordance with this Law.[175]

108. The AP: (1) shall participate in the preparation of the Strategy and individual national waste management plans; (2) shall coordinate and perform waste management relevant to the AP and shall monitor performance;[176] (3) shall grant approval on

173. The AP is entrusted with the task of inspection, supervision over the installations and activities for which the permit is granted by the competent provincial authority in accordance with this Law.
174. The LSG unit is entrusted with the task of inspection, supervision over the installations and activities for which the permit is granted by the competent LSG authority in accordance with this Law.
175. Also, the LSG is obliged to determine by an Act the departments and bodies responsible for carrying out these tasks. Furthermore, based on Art. 97 Law on Waste Management, LSGs are obliged to draw up until May 2010 a list of unregulated landfills in their area which do not fulfil the requirements of this Law (Art. 97, item 1), i.e., until May 2011 to develop projects of remediation and recultivation of unregulated landfills, which is approved by the Ministry or AP (Art. 97, item 2).
176. In case of disagreement among LSGs regarding the location of the waste management facility, the location decision, on the proposal of the Ministry, that is, the competent authority of the AP shall be brought to the Government. In case of construction of the facility for treatment and hazardous

regional waste management plans on its territory; (4) shall issue permits, approvals, certificates and other Acts in accordance with this Law;[177] (5) shall supervise and control waste handling measures on its territory in accordance with this Law;[178] and (6) shall perform other activities prescribed by the Law (Article 19).[179]

109. The AP shall adopt the Waste Management Plan for certain waste types relevant to the AP in accordance with the Strategy and national plan referred to in paragraph 3 of this Article (Article 11).[180]

F. Law on Packaging and Packaging Waste

110. In accordance with the Law on Packaging and Packaging Waste (OJ RS, Nos 36/09 and 95/18 – other law), packaging waste from the RS is collected, transported, stored and treated under the terms and in the manner, prescribed by the Law which regulates waste management, by the law which regulates public utilities and by this Law.[181]

G. Law on Air Protection

111. The Law on Air Protection (OJ RS, Nos 36/09, 10/13, and 26/2021 – other law) entrusts the following tasks to the AP or LSG: within its competence established by law, monitor air quality (Article 9); for air quality monitoring the AP or LSG should establish a local network of measuring stations and/or measuring points; monitoring of air quality in the local network shall be conducted in accordance with the programme adopted by the competent authority of the AP or LSG for the respective territory, which must be in conformity with the programme referred to in Article 11, paragraph 3 of this Law (Article 15); monitor air quality through an authorized legal entity (Article 15); publicly announce and submit data

---

waste disposal, the Ministry shall decide on the location, in accordance with the law and upon obtaining the opinion of the LSG as well as of the AP regarding facilities constructed on its territory (Art. 34).

177. The AP shall be entrusted with issuance of permits for the collection, transportation, storage, treatment and disposal of waste for all activities performed on the territory of the AP and for all facilities for which the construction permit is issued by the competent authority of the AP (Art. 60).

178. The AP shall be entrusted with performance of inspection supervision over waste management activities completely carried out on the territory of the AP and over the operation of the waste management facility for which the competent authority of the AP issues a permit on the basis of this Law (Art. 84).

179. Once in two years the assembly of the AP shall consider the report on the implementation of regional and local plans on its territory (Art. 74).

180. The regional waste management plan may also be adopted in case of municipalities with less than 250,000 inhabitants in accordance with the previously drafted feasibility study on the adoption of the regional plan, for which the Ministry, that is, the competent authority of the AP, shall issue an approval (Art. 12).

181. The AP shall be in charge of controlling the supervision of the activities of packaging waste management on its territory. The inspection supervision shall be carried out by inspectors in charge of environmental protection in compliance with the Law on Waste Management and this Law (Art. 47).

on the results of air quality monitoring to the Agency by the fifteenth day in the month for the previous month, and annual report within sixty days after the end of the year for the previous year (Article 17); inform public, when concentration exceeds those established by law or exceed the concentration of certain pollutants hazardous to human health; provide air quality plan (Article 31); provide short-term action plans (Article 33); issue licences for work of stationary sources of pollution (Article 39); perform inspection over the implementation of measures for protection of air pollution in buildings for which the competent body of the AP or LSG issues approval for the construction or uses permit (Article 56); the AP shall be entrusted inspection and supervision of activities over the implementation of measures related to air protection against pollution in objects for which the AP competent authority has issued construction and occupancy permits (Article 74); and the first-degree appeal to be filed against a ruling issued by competent authority of municipality, that is, city in the territory of the AP, shall be decided upon by competent authority of AP (Article 78).

H. Law on Nature Protection

112. Law on Nature Protection (OJ RS, Nos 36/09, 88/10, 91/10 – corr.,14/16, 95/18 – other law, and 71/21) entrusts to the LSG the following tasks: initiate proclamation and proclaim protected areas, such as nature parks, nature monuments, as well as a region with exceptional features which are not of great cultural importance, and where the whole protected area is in the territory of the LSG; provide nature protection programme; submit report on the state of nature in its area; and perform inspections of the implementation of this Law in protected areas proclaimed by the competent body of the LSG.[182]

182. The habitat and landscape of exceptional characteristics inside of which there is no cultural good of exceptional significance, if the entire area is located within the territory of the AP; as well as a natural park with its entire area located in the territory of two or more LSG in the territory of the AP, is declared as protected area by the competent authority of the AP, according to the previously acquired consent by the Ministry and the previously acquired opinions of the competent ministries (Art. 41). The competent authority of environment protection in the AP, and/or LSG, give consent to the plan for managing the protected area, and the annual programme for the previous year and the annual management programme for the following year that has to be delivered before 15 December of the current year (Art. 54). The competent authority of environment protection in the AP and/or LSG gives consent to the rulebook on interior order and stewardship (Art. 56). The AP or LSG is obliged to pay the compensation for prohibition or restriction of usage rights (Art. 63). The competent authority of the AP and/or the competent authority of the LSG shall establish fulfilment of the conditions for manager's performance of operations of protection, improvement, promotion and sustainable development of protected natural asset in the manager selection procedure. The selection of the manager shall be carried out on the basis of a vacancy announcement, and if such selection is not possible, the manager shall be determined or appointed by the decision on the declaration (Art. 67). Financing of the protected area (Art. 69) and activities of the Provincial Institute for Nature Protection (Art. 103) are under competencies of the AP. The medium-term programme for protection of natural goods is to be approved by the Government, and the annual programme for protection of natural goods is to be approved by the Ministry, i.e., by the competent authority of AP (Art. 104). Nature protection organizations shall submit the report on implementation of medium-term and annual programmes for protection of natural goods to the Ministry, i.e.,

I. Law on Chemicals

113. Law on Chemicals (OJ RS, Nos 36/09, 88/2010, 92/2011, 93/2012 and 25/2015) entrusts to the LSG the following tasks: issue licences for conducting turnover activities, particularly for hazardous chemicals to dealer who is not an importer, manufacturer or future user, as well as grant permission for the use of particularly hazardous chemicals; and perform inspection of tasks entrusted by this Law (Article 67, paragraph 2).

J. Law on the Protection from Non-ionizing Radiation

114. According to the Law on the Protection from Non-ionizing Radiation (OJ RS, Nos 36/09 and 93/12), the programme of systematic testing of non-ionizing radiation levels is prepared by the Ministry in collaboration with the AP competent authority. The Republic or AP is obliged to provide funding for the implementation of the programme (Article 5).[183]

115. The AP competent authority, by decision, determines fulfilment of conditions for persons who may utilize the non-ionizing radiation sources of special interest (Article 6). The AP competent authority, by decision, determines fulfilment of conditions for persons who can perform testing of non-ionizing radiation sources of special interest and may also revoke the authorization (Article 10). The industrial company, the company and legal entity or entrepreneur, or the operator are obliged to inform the competent authority of the Republic, AP or LSG about the special event immediately and within twenty-four hours (Article 12). The testing of non-ionizing radiation exposure, on the request of the AP competent authority, shall be performed a special testing financed by the same authority, except in cases where determination is by measuring irregularities in the work or where the prescribed limits of broadcasting are exceeded, in which case the costs are paid by the owner of the radiation emitter (Article 13). Provincial inspection shall be performed for inspecting the non-ionizing radiation sources in the territory of AP, except for those for which approval for the construction and starting is issued by the competent authority of LSG, in which case LSG inspection is competent (Article 14).[184]

---

to the competent authority of AP (Art. 104). The competent authority of AP and LSG, in accordance with the Government Strategy on Nature and Natural Values Protection, should adopt the programmes on nature protection, for the period of ten years (Arts 111 and 113). The AP and/or LSG shall prepare nature performance reports for their territories, which shall be submitted to the Ministry (Art. 114). Competent authority of the AP supervises over legality of Provincial Nature Conservation Institute's work (Art. 118). The AP shall be entrusted with the performance of inspection supervision over the application of provisions contained in this Law in protected areas which are located on the AP territory (Art. 119).

183. Persons who carry out systematic testing, in the territory of the AP, are obliged to deliver to the AP competent authority an annual report on the results of testing, not later than 31 March of the current year for the previous year, and in case of extraordinary events, immediately (Art. 5).

184. On the basis of Art. 14, para. 4 of the Law on the Protection of Non-ionizing Radiation, the AP or LSG is entrusted with inspection tasks on the sources of radiation for which approval for the construction and beginning of work is issued by the competent body of AP or LSG.

K. Law on Protection Against Noise in the Environment

116. According to the Law on Protection against Noise in the Environment (OJ RS, No. 96/21), AP and/or LSG: (1) determines measures and conditions of sound protection in plans, programmes and projects, including those to which it gives consent in the process of strategic impact assessment, assessment of the impact of projects on the environment, or in the process of issuing an integrated permit for the operation of facilities and activities; (2) ensures the implementation and financing of noise monitoring in the environment on its territory; (3) performs supervision and control of the application of noise protection measures in the environment, for all facilities for which the construction permit is issued by the competent authority of the AP (Article 8, and Article 9. paragraph 1, points. 1, 4, and 5). In addition, the LSG Unit: carries out acoustic zoning, determines quiet zones, as well as prohibits and limits measures on its territory, by decision of the competent authority, in accordance with this law; regulates the measures and conditions of sound protection and the use of noise sources in residential and residential commercial buildings as well as in commercial buildings, in residential zones where activities that disturb the population in its territory are carried out, by decision of the competent authority in accordance with this law and other regulations (Article 9, paragraph 1, points 2, and 3).[185]

L. Law on the Protection and Sustainable Use of Fish Reserves

117. According to the Law on the Protection and Sustainable Use of Fish Reserves (OJ RS, Nos 128/14 and 95/18 – other law), AP carries out the tasks referred to in Articles 5, 6, 7, 8, 9, 17, 21, 31, 38, 44, 47, 49 and 52 of this Law as entrusted tasks.[186] The Ministry shall supervise the work of the competent authority of AP in the performance of the entrusted affairs (Article 53).

M. Law on Planning and Building

118. According to the Law on Planning and Building (OJ RS, Nos 72/09, 81/09 – corr., 64/10 CC, 24/11, 121/12, 42/13CC, 50/13CC, 98/13/CC, 132/14, 145/14, 83/18, 31/19, 37/19 – other law, 9/20, 52/21, and 62/23) APs are authorized, *inter alia*, for granting building permits for facilities specified in Article 133 of this Law which are built in whole on the community's territory (Article 134, paragraph 1). LSG units are authorized to grant building permits for facilities which are not specified in Article 133 of this Law (Article 134, paragraph 2).

185. The local self-government unit representing the agglomeration creates and revises strategic noise maps and submits them to the Agency, as well as agglomeration creates, revises and implements the action plan and submits it to the Ministry and the Agency (Art. 9, para. 2, and 3).

186. The fee for use of fishing areas in the territory of AP is the income for the AP's budget (Art. 7, para. 3). It ceased to be valid with the enactment of the Law on Fees for the Use of Public Goods (OJ RS, Nos 8/18 and 49/19) (Art. 258, para. 1, item 8).

Chapter 5. Sources of Environmental Law

§1. International Sources of Environmental Law

119. Despite the significant problems in achieving international cooperation during the last decade of the twentieth century and at the beginning of the twenty-first century, Serbia has significantly improved its position. This is usually explained as a result of legacy of the past, the crisis in the 1990s, international sanctions, etc. It took a significant amount of time to achieve the normalization of membership in international environmental agreements. However, besides formal participation in international treaties, the question of their interpretation and implementation is more important.[187]

120. International environmental cooperation of Serbia has been significantly improved after political changes in 2000 in all relevant fields. Besides the mentioned political changes, important factors which contributed to the process were strategic approaches of the Serbian Government and other relevant subjects, the present improved geopolitical position of Serbia in the region, economic interests and the transboundary character of pollution.[188]

121. The Serbian Constitution contains several provisions concerning international sources of environmental law and is relevant for international cooperation in the field of environment in general. The term 'cooperation' is also defined as a priority in the National Strategy of Environmental Protection.

Article 16 of the Constitution prescribes that 'generally accepted rules of international law and ratified international treaties shall be an integral part of the legal system in the RS and applied directly'.[189] The same Article states that foreign policy of Serbia is based on generally accepted principles and rules of international law.

122. Two general rules are prescribed by the Constitution, when relationship between international and national sources of law is defined:

- laws and other general Acts must be in compliance with the Constitution, generally accepted rules of the international law and ratified international treaties; and
- ratified international treaties must be in accordance with the Constitution (Article 16, paragraph 3).

187. *See* review of the state of implementation of the multilateral environmental agreements (MEAs) by the FR Yugoslavia in Todić, 2018b. For other States of the region, *see* Todić, 2019.

188. Especially important event was the Sixth Ministerial Conference 'Environment for Europe' held in Belgrade in October 2007 titled 'Building Bridges to the Future', *see* https://unece.org/belgrade-conference (4.1.2024).

189. For further information, *see* Etinski, 2013b.

123. It should be added that Article 194 of the Constitution prescribes that:

> Ratified international treaties and generally accepted rules of the international law shall be part of the legal system of the RS. Ratified international treaties may not be in non-compliance with the Constitution. Laws and other general acts enacted in the R S may not be in non-compliance with the ratified international treaties and generally accepted rules of the International Law.[190]

124. Procedure of ratification of international treaties is regulated by provisions of several legal Acts, from the Constitution to the Law on Government, the Law on Ministries, the Law on State Administration, Rules of Proceedings of Work of the Government and NA, etc.[191]

125. Serbia is the contracting party in a number of Multilateral Environmental Agreements (MEAs) and other agreements regulating the field of environment. This is partly due to succession from the former Yugoslavia and partly when it became a contacting party after FR Yugoslavia (Serbia and Montenegro) was proclaimed an independent State in 1992, and finally after Serbia became an independent State.[192] By 2007, Serbia became a member of the following MEAs:

- Convention Concerning the Use of the White Lead in Painting (1921).
- Agreement for the Establishment of a General Fisheries Council for the Mediterranean (1949).
- International Convention for the Protection of Birds (1950).
- Convention for the Establishment of the European and Mediterranean Plant Protection Organization (1951).
- International Plant Protection Convention (1952).
- International Convention for the Prevention of Pollution of the Sea by Oil (1954).
- Convention on Protection of Cultural Goods in Case of Armed Disputes (1954).
- European Agreement Concerning the International Carriage of Dangerous Goods by Road (ADR) (1957).
- Treaty on Fishery in the Danube River Waters between Government of FNRJ, People's Republic of Bulgaria, Romanian People's Republic and USSR (1958).
- Convention on the High Seas (1958).

---

190. In case when an interpretation is needed, the Constitutional Court (CC) decides (Art. 167 of the Constitution).
191. Formally speaking, the basic regulation relevant for concluding and implementation of international treaties, including those in the environmental field, is the Law on Conclusion and Implementation of International Agreements (OJ RS, No. 32/2013), and the Rules of Procedure of the Government (OJ RS, Nos 61/2006 – consolidated text, 69/2008, 88/2009, 33/2010, 69/2010, 20/2011, 37/2011, 30/2013, 76/14 and 8/19 – other rules). However, the lack of obligation to perform analysis of the effects resulting from the ratification law and the absence of the public debate in the process of preparation of the Law on Ratification of International Treaties could be considered as a major deficiency.
192. On this subject, *see* Todić, & Vukasović, 2002.

- Convention on Fishing and Conservation of the Living Resources of the High Seas (1958).
- Convention on the Territorial Sea and Contiguous Zone (1958).
- Convention on the Continental Shelf (1958).
- International Convention for the Safety of Life at Sea (1960).
- Vienna Convention on Civil Liability for Nuclear Damage (1963).
- Treaty Banning Nuclear Weapon Tests in the Atmosphere, in Outer Space and Under Water (1963).
- European Agreement Concerning the International Carriage of Dangerous Goods by Road (ADR); Annex A – Provisions Concerning Dangerous Substances and Articles; Annex B – Provisions Concerning Transport Equipment and Transport Operations (1967).
- European Convention for the Protection of Animals during International Transport (1968).
- European Convention on the Protection of Archaeological Heritage (1969).
- International Convention on Civil Liability for Oil Pollution Damage (1969).
- International Convention Relating to Intervention on the High Seas in Case of Oil Pollution Casualties (1969).
- Convention on Measures for Banning and Preventing Illegal Import, Export and Transfer of Properties of Cultural Goods (1970).
- Convention on Wetlands of International Importance Especially as Water Flow Habitat (1971).
- Treaty on the Prohibition of the Emplacement of Nuclear Weapons and other Weapons of Mass Destruction on the Sea-Bed and Ocean Floor and in the Subsoil Thereof (1971).
- Convention Concerning Protection Against Hazards of Poisoning Arising from Benzene (1971).
- International Convention for Compensation for Oil Pollution Damage (1971).
- Convention on Prohibition and Stockpiling of Bacteriological (Biological) and Toxin Weapons, and on Their Destruction (1972).
- International Convention on the International Regulations for Preventing Collision at Sea (1972).
- Convention Concerning the Protection of the World Cultural and Natural Heritage (1972).
- Convention on the Prevention of Marine Pollution by Dumping of Wastes and Other Matter (1972).
- International Convention for the Prevention of Pollution from Ships (1973).
- Protocol Relating to Intervention on the High Seas Cases of Marine Pollution by Substances other than Oil (1973).
- Yugoslav-Italian Treaty on Cooperation on Pollution Protection of the Adriatic Sea Waters and Coastal Areas (1974).
- Convention Concerning Prevention and Control of Occupational Hazards Caused by Carcinogenic Substances and Agents (1974).
- European Convention for the Protection of Animals Kept for Farming Purposes (1976).
- Convention for the Protection of the Mediterranean Sea against Pollution (1976).

- Protocol for the Prevention of Pollution of the Mediterranean Sea by Dumping from Ships and Aircraft (1976).
- Protocol Concerning Cooperation in Combating Pollution of Mediterranean Sea by Oil and Other Harmful Substances in Cases of Emergency (1976).
- Convention Concerning the Protection of Workers Against Occupational Hazards in the Working Environment due to Air Pollution, Noise and Vibration (1977).
- Protocol of 1978 Relating to the International Convention for the Prevention of Pollution from Ships (1978).
- European Convention for the Protection of Animals for Slaughter (1979).
- Convention on Long-Range Transboundary Air Pollution (CLRTAP) (1979).
- Convention on the Physical Protection of Nuclear Material (1979).
- Protocol for the Protection of the Mediterranean Sea against Pollution from Land-Based Sources (1980).
- Convention Concerning Occupational Safety and Health and the Working Environment (1981).
- Protocol Concerning Mediterranean Specially Protected Areas (1982).
- United Nations Convention on the Law of the Sea (1982).
- Protocol to the 1979 CLRTAP on Financing of the Cooperative Programme for Monitoring and Evaluation of the Long-Range Transmission of Air Pollutants in Europe (EMER) (1984).
- Vienna Convention for the Protection of the Ozone Layer (1985).
- Convention Concerning Occupational Health Services (1985).
- Convention for the Protection of the Architectural Heritage of Europe (1985).
- Treaty on Pollution Protection of the Tisza River Waters and Its Tributaries (1986).
- Convention Concerning Safety in Use of Asbestos (1986).
- Convention on Early Notification of a Nuclear Accident (1986).
- Convention on Assistance in the Case of a Nuclear Accident or Radiological Emergency (1986).
- Montreal Protocol on Substances that Deplete the Ozone Layer (1987).
- Basel Convention on the Control of Transboundary Movements of Hazardous Wastes and Their Disposal (1989).
- UN Framework Convention on Climate Change (1992).
- Convention on the Prohibition of the Development, Production, Stockpiling and Use of Chemical Weapons and on Their Destruction (1993).
- Treaty between the Federal Government of FRY and Government of the Russian Federation on Cooperation on Environmental Protection (1996).
- Treaty between the Federal Government of FRY and Government of the Russian Federation on Cooperation on Preventing Industrial Hazards, Natural Disasters and Remediation of their Consequences (1996).
- Convention on Biological Diversity (1992).
- Convention on International Trade in Endangered Species of Wild Flora and Fauna (CITES-1973).
- Convention on Cooperation for the Protection and Sustainable Use of the Danube River (Danube River Protection Convention).
- Amendments to the Montreal Protocol on Substances Depleting Ozone Layer.

- Framework Agreement on the Sava River Basin, Protocol on the Navigation Regime Additional to the Framework Agreement on the Sava River Basin and the Agreement Amending the Framework Agreement on the Sava River Basin and the Protocol on the Navigation Regime Additional to the Framework Agreement on the Sava River Basin.
- Treaty Establishing the Energy Community between the European Community and the Republic of Albania, Republic of Bulgaria, Bosnia & Herzegovina, Republic of Croatia, Former Yugoslav Republic of Macedonia, Republic of Montenegro, Romania, RS and the United Nations Interim Administration Mission in Kosovo Pursuant to the UNSC Resolution 1244.

126. In 2007, Serbia ratified the following multilateral environmental treaties:

- Kyoto protocol to the United Nations Framework Convention on Climate Change (1997).
- Framework Convention on the Protection and Sustainable Development of the Carpathians (2003).
- Convention on the Conservation of European Wildlife and Natural Habitats (1979) (ETS 104).
- Convention on the Conservation of Migratory Species of Wild Animals (1979).
- United Nations Convention to Combat Desertification in Countries Experiencing Serious Drought and/or Desertification, Particularly in Africa (1994).
- Convention on EIA in Transboundary Context (1991).

127. During the last phase, Serbia ratified the following international treaties:

- Convention on the Transboundary Effects of Industrial Accidents (1992), and Decision 2014/2 Amending Annex I to the Convention (2014).
- Amendment to the Montreal Protocol on Substances that Deplete the Ozone Layer (2016).
- Convention on the Protection and Use of Transboundary Watercourses and International Lakes (1992).
- Protocol on Water and Health to the Convention on the Protection and Use of Transboundary Watercourses and International Lakes and amendments to Articles 25 and 26 of the Convention on the Protection and Use of Transboundary Watercourses and International Lakes (1999).
- Convention on Access to Environmental Information, Public Participation in Decision-Making and Access to Justice in Environmental Matters (1998).
- Protocol on Pollutant Release and Transfer Registers to the Convention on Access to Information, Public Participation in Decision-making and Access to Justice in Environmental Matters (2003).
- Protocol on Heavy Metals to 1979 CLRTAP (1998).
- Protocol on Persistent Organic Pollutants (POPs) to 1979 CLRTAP (1998).
- Amendments to the Espoo Convention on Impact Assessment in Transboundary Context (2001 and 2004).
- Protocol on the prevention of water pollution caused by navigation to the Framework Agreement on the Sava River Basin (2009).

- Protocol on Flood Protection to the Framework Agreement on the Sava River Basin (2010).
- Protocol on Sediment Management to the Framework Agreement on the Sava River Basina (2015).
- Convention on the Prohibition of the Development, Production, Stockpiling and Use of Chemical Weapons and on their Destruction (1993).
- Stockholm Convention on POPs (2001).
- Rotterdam Convention on the Prior Informed Consent Procedure for Certain Hazardous Chemicals and Pesticides in International Trade (1998).
- Protocol on SEA to the Convention on EIA in a Transboundary Context (2003).
- Amendment to Annex B to the Kyoto Protocol (2006).
- Statute of the International Renewable Energy Agency (IRENA) (2009).
- Agreement Between RS and Regional Environmental Centre (REC) for Central and Eastern Europe on Legal Status of the REC in RS (2008).
- European Landscape Convention (2000) (ETS 176), and Protocol amending the European Landscape Convention (2016) (ETS 219).
- Convention on the European Forest Institute (2003).
- Convention on Nuclear Safety (1994).
- Joint Convention on the Safety of Spent Fuel Management and on the Safety of Radioactive Waste Management (1997).
- Hong Kong International Convention for the Safe and Environmentally Sound Recycling of Ships (2009).
- Multilateral Agreement among the countries of South-Eastern Europe for implementation of the Convention on EIA in Transboundary Context (2008).
- Agreement on the Conservation of African – Eurasian migratory waterbirds (AEWA) (1996).
- Agreement on the Conservation of Bats in Europe (1991).[193]

128. Following multilateral environmental treaties were in the process of preparation for ratification:

- Basel Protocol on Liability and Compensation for Damage Resulting from Transboundary Movements of Hazardous Wastes and their Disposal (1999).
- Convention on Civil Liability for Damage Resulting from Activities Dangerous to the Environment, Lugano (1993).
- Helsinki Protocol on the Reduction of Sulphur Emissions or their Transboundary Fluxes by at least 30% (1985).
- Sofia Protocol concerning the Control of Emissions of Nitrogen Oxides or their Transboundary Fluxes (1988).
- Geneva Protocol concerning the Control of Emissions of Volatile Organic Compounds or their Transboundary Fluxes (1991).
- The 1994 Oslo Protocol on Further Reduction of Sulphur Emissions.
- Protocol to Abate Acidification, Eutrophication and Ground-level Ozone, Gothenburg (1999).

193. For a list and text of ratified international environmental treaties, *see* http://www.pravno-informacioni-sistem.rs/reg-overview# (24.10.2022). *See also* Todić, 2018a, 362–371.

– Convention on the Law of the Non-navigational Uses of International Water Courses, New York (1997).[194]

129. Serbia is participating in bilateral cooperation in environmental protection with a number of countries, with an emphasis on cooperation with neighbouring countries[195] and receiving technical and other assistance from donor countries. In most cases, the effectiveness of cooperation depends less on the existence of formal agreements than on the availability of funds for joint programmes and projects, primarily in the context of regional cooperation. However, Serbia gives importance to the signing of such agreements and/or memorandums of understanding (MOUs). The following bilateral agreements on environmental cooperation have been ratified: with Azerbaijan (OJ RS – International Treaties (IT), No. 10/11); with Turkey (OJ RS – IT, No. 8/11); with Russian Federation (OJ FRY – IT, No. 6/96); with Croatia (OJ RS – IT, No. 13/18); and with Hungary (OJ RS – IT, No. 4/20). MOUs have been concluded with several countries including: People's Republic of Algeria (OJ RS – IT, No. 3/18), the Republic of Korea (OJ RS – IT, No. 13/18), Bulgaria (OJ RS – IT, No. 2/19), and Greece (OJ RS – IT, No. 6/19), etc.

§2. National Sources of Environmental Law

130. According to Article 99 of the Constitution, the NA, as the highest legislative body in the Republic, *inter alia*, adopts 'laws and other general acts within the competence of the Republic of Serbia' (point 7). Laws and other general Acts must be in compliance with the Constitution and with the ratified international treaties and generally accepted rules of the International Law (Article 195). It is also prescribed by the Constitution that 'laws and all other general acts shall be published prior to coming into force'.[196]

131. The right to propose laws, other regulations and general Acts belongs to every deputy, the Government, the assemblies of Aps, and at least 30,000 voters (Article 107). Procedure of adoption is defined, besides the constitutional provisions, also by the Law on NA, the Law on Government, the Law on State Administration, by Proceedings for the work of the Government and NA, etc. The New Law on Referendum and People's Initiative was adopted in 2001 (OJ RS, Nos 111/21, 119/21).[197]

194. GOV RS. 2011a, 83.
195. For more information on this subject *see* Todić, Todić, 2022.
196. Article 196 of the Constitution prescribes the obligation to publish laws and by-laws. They have to be published in the OJ of the Republic, i.e., of the AP (statutes, decisions and other general Acts of APs).
197. By a people's initiative, citizens propose the adoption, amendment, or repeal of the Constitution, laws, other regulations, and general acts within the competence of the National Assembly, and/or of the statute, other regulations, and general acts within the competence of the Assembly of the Autonomous Province and local self-government units, and submit other proposals following the Constitution and the law, and/or the statute of the autonomous province and local self-government unit (Art. 56). However, 'there has been no follow-up to a citizens' legislative initiative, with 38

132. In accordance with the Law on State Administration (OJ RS, Nos 79/05, 101/07, 95/2010, 99/14, 38/18 – other law and 47/18), State administration authorities (ministries and special organizations) may pass the following legislations:

- Regulations, orders and directives:
  - A Regulation prescribes in detail specific provisions of law and legislation of the Government.
  - An Order – order or prohibit action in one situation that is of general importance.
  - A Directive regulates ways in which State administration authorities and holders of public powers enforce certain provisions of law and other legislation.

All these sources of law must be published in the OJ RS (Article 15).[198]

133. Article 185 of the Law on State Administration regulates the right of APs to pass regulations as follows:

- The Statute shall be the supreme legal Act of the AP.
- The Statute of the APV shall be adopted by its Assembly, subject to prior approval of the NA.
- The AP shall enact other decisions and general Acts pertaining to matters within its competences.

Statutes, decisions and other general Acts of APs[199] and LSG units[200] must be in compliance with the Law. All general Acts of APs and LSG units must be in compliance with their statutes.

134. Municipal authorities are also authorized to pass legal Acts. The Statute of municipal authorities is the supreme legal Act of the municipality. The Statute has to be adopted by the Municipal Assembly. The Municipal Assembly shall pass general Acts within its competences, adopt the budget and annual balance sheet, adopt the development plan and the municipal spatial plan, schedule the municipal referendum and perform other duties specified by the Law and the Statute (Article 191).

---

000 signatures, on banning lithium mining, despite this being a legal obligation.' EC. 2023, 12. For more information about 'Jadar project' *see* Young Researchers of Serbia. 2022, 24–26.

198. According to Art. 16, Ministries and special organizations may only pass legislation when they are explicitly authorized by law or by the Government. Ministries and special organizations cannot by their legislation determine their or foreign competences, or rights and obligations of natural and legal persons that are not already prescribed by law.
199. According to Art. 185 of the Constitution, 'the autonomous province shall enact other decisions and general acts pertaining to matters within its competences'.
200. According to Art. 191 of the Constitution, 'the Municipal Assembly shall pass general Acts within its competences, adopt the budget and annual balance sheet, and adopt the development plan and the municipal spatial plan … '.

135. Belgrade has a special position as the capital city, and it has certain competences in the environmental field.[201] The basic legal Act of the City of Belgrade is a statute (Article 2). The Assembly of the City, in accordance with the Law, adopts Statute and Rule of Procedure, adopts development programmes, adopts urban plans and regulates utilization of the construction lands, adopts regulations and other general Acts, etc. (Article 12). In accordance with Article 33, city administration, *inter alia*, prepares drafts of the regulations and other Acts which have to be adopted by the Assembly of the City, Mayor or City Council.

136. The list of environmental legal regulations in Serbia is too voluminous to be cited here. Different criteria could be used for classification of numerous legal and sub-legal Acts regulating this field and/or closely related domains.[202] Relevant legal regulations will be mentioned in the proceeding text.

The framework for environmental protection consists, in Serbia, of the following four basic laws adopted in 2004 and later amended:

(1) *EPL* (OJ RS, Nos 135/2004, 36/2009 and 36/09 – other law, 72/2009 – other law, 43/11CC, 14/16, 76/18 and 95/18 – other law).[203]
(2) Law on Environmental Impact Assessment (OJ RS, Nos 135/2004 and 36/2009).
(3) Law on Strategic Environmental Impact Assessment (OJ RS, Nos 135/2004 and 88/2010).
(4) Law on Integrated Pollution Prevention and Control (OJ RS, Nos 135/2004, 25/2015, and 109/2021).

137. 'Since 2007, the legal framework has evolved in two main directions: (i) further extending the scope of environmental regulation; and (ii) improving instruments and procedures of compliance assurance.'[204] Group of environmental laws adopted in NA on 12 May 2009 includes the following:

– Law on Air Protection (OJ RS, Nos 36/09, 10/13, and 26/21).
– Law on Nature Protection (OJ RS, Nos 36/09, 88/10, 91/10 – corr.14/16, 95/18 – other law, and 71/21).

201. Special position of Belgrade has been regulated by the Law on the Capitol City (OJ RS, Nos 129/2007 and 83/14 – other law, 101/16 – other law, and 37/19).
202. *See* https://www.pravno-informacioni-sistem.rs/reg-overview# (6.1.2024) Part X – 'Goods of General Interest and the Environment'.
203. However, the following provisions of the EPL have ceased to apply: Art. 27 (paras 5–7), Art. 85, Art. 85a (paras 3 and 4), Arts 86 and 87 (except para. 3, point 3) and para. 6, and Art. 88 – on the day of the beginning of the application of the *Law on Fees for the Use of Public Goods* (OJ RS, No. 95/2018), i.e.,1 Jan. 2019 (*see* Art. 279 of the Law – 95/2018). The provisions of Art. 87, para. 3 (point 3) and para. 6, as well as Acts of local self-government units adopted on the basis of Art. 87 of the Law on Environmental Protection (OJ RS, Nos 135/04, 36/09, 36/09 – other law, 72/09 – other law, 43/11 – CC, 14/16 and 76/18) have ceased to be valid from 1 Mar. 2019 (*see* Art. 279 of the Law – 95/2018-267).
204. UNECE. 2015, 42.

- Law on Noise Protection (OJ RS, Nos 36/09 and 88/10).[205]
- Law on Non-ionizing Radiation Protection (OJ RS, No. 36/09).
- Law on Ionizing Radiation Protection and Nuclear Safety (OJ RS, Nos 36/09 and 93/12).[206]
- Law on Waste Management (OJ RS, Nos 36/09, 88/10, 14/16, 95/18 – other law, and 35/23).
- Law on Packaging and Packaging Waste (OJ RS, Nos 36/09 and 95/18 – other law).
- Law on Chemicals (OJ RS, Nos 36/09, 88/10, 92/11, 93/12 and 25/15).
- Law on Prohibition of Development, Production, Storage and Use of Chemical Weapons and their Destruction (OJ RS, No. 36/09).
- Law on Biocidal Products (OJ RS, Nos 36/09, 88/10, 92/11 and 25/15).[207]
- Law on Protection and Sustainable Use of Fish Resources (OJ RS, Nos 128/14 and 95/18 – other law).

The Law on Waters was adopted in 2010 (OJ RS, Nos 30/2010, 93/2012, 101/2016, 95/2018 and 95/2018 – other law).

The new Law on National Parks was adopted in 2015 (OJ RS, Nos 84/2015, 95/2018 – other law).

In 2018, a special Law on Fees for the Use of Public Goods was passed (OJ RS, Nos 95/2018 and 49/19), which regulated all fees of importance for the environment in one place.

In addition, the Law on Climate Change was adopted (OJ RS, No. 26/21).

Although there are still some open questions where these laws are concerned, the goal of their adoption was harmonization with EU regulations. Different level of compliance is achieved. In addition, there are some problems in implementation (capacity, coordination, financial resources, public awareness, etc.).[208] According to the EC 2022 Report Serbia made 'limited progress during the reporting period' and 'the adoption of important legislation and strategic documents is pending'.[209] Overall, 'Serbia made some progress, including on last year's recommendations'[210] (in particular by adopting the Low Carbon Development Strategy 2023–2030 and drafting its National Energy and Climate Plan (NECP), by continuing to increase environmental funding and investments in the waste management and water quality sectors). However, the adoption of important legislation and strategic documents is pending.

205. In the meantime, a new Law on Protection against Noise in Environment was adopted (OJ RS, No. 96/21).
206. This law has ceased to be valid. A new Law on Radiation and Nuclear Safety and Security has been adopted (OJ RS, Nos 95/18 and 10/19).
207. In the meantime, a new Law on Biocidal Products was adopted (OJ RS, No. 109/21).
208. For more information, *see* EC, Annual Reports of the European Commission,https://www.mei.gov.rs/srp/dokumenta/eu-dokumenta/godisnji-izvestaji-ek (24.10.2020); https://neighbourhood-enlargement.ec.europa.eu/enlargement-policy/serbia_en#key-documents (14.2.2024).
209. EC, Serbia 2022 Report, 120.
210. EC, Serbia 2023 Report, 134.

Part I. Pollution Control

Chapter 1. General Law

§1. Legislation

138. Pollution control is subject to regulation in many legal Acts of general as well as of specific character. Some of them primarily and directly regulate protection of the environment, while others regulate other issues that are important for protection of the environment and in some way related to it. During several recent years, a considerable number of systemic laws and other legal Acts have been adopted and/or drafted for adoption. It could be said that Serbia has, generally speaking, made significant progress in developing environmental legislation, although the implementation practice needs careful analysis of the progress made in different sub-fields.[211]

139. As mentioned above, most important general legal Acts that directly regulate environmental protection are as follows:

- *EPL* (OJ RS, Nos 135/04, 36/09 and 36/09 – other law, 72/09 – other law, 43/11CC, 14/16, 76/18 and 95/18 – other law).
- Law on Environmental Impact Assessment (OJ RS, Nos 135/04 and 36/09).
- Law on Strategic Environmental Impact Assessment (OJ RS, Nos 135/04 and 88/10).[212]
- Law on Integrated Prevention and Control of Environmental Pollution (OJ RS, Nos 135/04, 25/15, and 109/21).

I. Environmental Protection Law (EPL)

140. The basic framework legal Act which regulates environmental issues in Serbia is the EPL, adopted in 2004. Judging from a number of criteria and reasons, the EPL is a complex legal Act, which is even more obvious if we view it within

211. For more details concerning these issues, *see* S. Bogdanović, 2008.
212. There are proposals for new environmental laws in the parliamentary procedure. These are the Proposal of Law on Environmental Impact Assessment and the Proposal of Law on Strategic Environmental Impact Assessment. Also, the Proposal of Law on Controlling the Risk of Major Accidents Involving Dangerous Substances is in the process of adoption. *See* http://www.parlament.gov.rs/akti/zakoni-u-proceduri/zakoni-u-proceduri.1037.html (15.1.2024).

the context of political, economic, institutional, legal, international and other circumstances.[213] It is the basic legal Act regulating almost all important issues in the field and having functional relations with legal and sub-legal Acts in other fields, more or less related to the environment. Another reason for its complexity is the attempt of its creators to introduce novel solutions (in relation to the previous Law)[214] taken from contemporary European and wider world legal regulation.

141. According to Article 122, legal and private persons were obliged to harmonize their activities with the Law within a year from the day when this Law entered into force. This period has expired.

142. The EPL regulates 'the integral system[215] of environmental protection which shall ensure the human right to live and develop in a healthy environment as well as balanced economy growth and protection of the environment in the Republic' (Article 1). Provisions of the Law are divided into the following chapters:

(1) *General provisions*: subject of the environmental protection system, definitions, subject's liability, awareness raising, civil societies, cooperation, principles of environmental protection and special laws[216] (Articles 1–10).
(2) *Management of natural values*: planning and utilization of natural values – management of natural values, strategic documents, plans and programmes of the AP and LSG units (Articles 11–32).
(3) *Measures and conditions for environmental protection*: preventive measures, conditions for environmental protection, environmental quality standards and emission standards, environmental protection management system, products, processes and services standards, measures of protection from dangerous

213. For more information, *see* Petković, 2005; Todić, 2017b.
214. The EPL contains some radically new solutions, in comparison with the previous one, establishing a modern environmental management framework in line with the EU legislation, and introducing following novelties: introduction of development of strategies, establishment of the EPA, introduction of EMAS, the Environmental Protection Fund, introduction of economic instruments, introduction of higher level of decentralization, introduction of public participation in environmental procedure, establishment of legal basis and framework for Strategic Environmental Assessment and IPPC, eco label, etc. On the basis of this Law, many new by-laws and amendments of the existing ones have been adopted, for example, Rulebook on the form of legal identification card of inspector for environment protection (OJ RS, Nos 5/14 and 81/15 – other rulebook), Regulation on criteria for determining the status of endangered environment and priorities for rehabilitation and remediation (OJ RS, No. 22/10) and so on.
215. System of environmental protection in Serbia comprises the following elements: (1) sustainable management, preservation of nature balance, integrity, diversity and quality of natural values and conditions for survival of all living beings; and (2) prevention, control, reduction and rehabilitation of all kinds of environmental pollution (Art. 2).
216. Special laws and other regulations (sub-legal Acts and programme documents) include: (1) EIA of plans, programmes and projects; (2) integrated prevention and pollution control; (3) protection of nature; (4) protection of air, water, soil, forests, geological resources; (5) chemicals management; (6) waste management; (7) ionizing and non-ionizing radiation; and (8) protection against noise and vibrations; (8a) control of the major risks of accidents involving dangerous substances; (8b) transboundary movement and trade in wild species (Art. 10).

substances, production and placement on the market, handling dangerous substances, programmes and plans (Articles 33–68).

(4) *Environmental monitoring*: contents and mode of monitoring, authorized organization, polluter self-monitoring, data submission, information system, Integrated Polluter Cadastre, Environmental State Report (Articles 69–77).

(5) *Information and public participation*: access to information, data supply at request and rejecting request for data supply, participation of public in decision-making, limited participation of public in decision-making (Articles 78–84).

(6) *Economic instruments*: financing environmental protection, types of economic instruments, charges for use of natural resources, environmental pollution charges, types of incentives, etc. (Articles 83–90 and 100–101).

(7) *Liability for environmental pollution*: liability of legal and private entities, liability for pollution, liability for damage, insurance, reimbursement of damage (Articles 102–108).

(8) *Supervision*: administrative supervision, rights and duties of the inspector, powers of inspectors (Articles 109–115).

(9) *Penalty provisions*: commercial offences, offences (Articles 116–121).

(10) Transitional and final provisions (Articles 122–130).[217]

A. *Subjects of the Environmental Protection System*

143. Subjects of the environmental protection system in Serbia are as follows: (1) Republic; (2) AP; (3) municipality, that is, the city (hereinafter 'local self-governance body'); (4) companies, other domestic and foreign legal entities and entrepreneurs who use natural values in their economic and other activities, to endanger or pollute the environment (hereinafter 'legal and natural entities'); (5) scientific and expert organizations and other public services; (6) citizens, groups of citizens, their associations, professional and other organizations[218] (Article 4).

Besides the obligation 'to preserve and develop the environment' (Article 4, paragraph 2), all subjects have the general obligation to cooperate and provide for coordination and harmonization in decision-making and decision implementation. The Republic cooperates with other States and international organizations in the environmental field (Article 8).

217. When this Law entered into force, the following ceased to be in force: (1) Law on Bases of Environmental Protection (OJ FRY, Nos 24/98, 24/99 and 44/99); (2) *EPL* (OJ RS, Nos 66/91, 83/92, 53/93, 67/93, 48/94 and 53/95), apart from the provisions referring to protection of air, nature protection and protection from noise (Art. 129). Until the promulgation of regulations on the basis of authorizations from this Law, the regulations promulgated on the basis of the following shall be applied: (1) Law on Bases of Environmental Protection (OJ FRY, Nos 24/98, 24/99 and 44/99); (2) *EPL* (OJ RS, Nos 66/91, 83/92, 53/93, 67/93, 48/94 and 53/95) (Art. 128).

218. Article 7 of the EPL prescribes a general framework for activities of civil societies, established in the field of environmental protection as a subject of system of environmental protection. They are expected to prepare, promote and realize their protection programmes, protect their rights and interests concerning the environment, propose activities and measures conducive to protection, participate in the decision-making process in compliance with the law and help or directly disseminate information about the environment.

144. When the liability is concerned, Article 5 of the EPL prescribes that the Republic, AP, local self-governance body, legal and natural persons are responsible for every activity with which they change or may change environmental status and conditions, that is, by which they fail to implement environmental protection measures as regulated by the Law. In performing their activities, legal and natural persons are obliged to make rational use of natural resources, calculate environmental protection expenditures in their investment and running costs, and implement regulations, all according to the Law.

145. Article 6 imposes general obligation, where 'raising awareness' is concerned, on State authorities, scientific institutions, educational, information, cultural and other institutions, as well as other types of societies, that they should be in the field of their work, inspired to ensure better awareness concerning the importance of environmental protection.[219]

B. Management of Natural Values

146. 'Management of natural values' is one of the central parts of the EPL. It has been prescribed in general that natural values[220] management shall be carried out by planning sustainable utilization and preservation of their quality and versatility, in accordance with the conditions and measures of environmental protection set out in this and in special laws (Article 11). Strategic framework for the activities in the field of natural values management has been established by the Strategy for spatial development of the Republic and by the National Strategy of Sustainable Use of Natural Resources and Goods[221] (Article 12). The AP and local self-governance unit shall, besides that, issue their respective plans and programmes for natural resources and property management in accordance with the National Strategy.

147. Article 14 of the EPL prescribes that control over utilization and protection of natural resources and property is ensured by competent institutions of the Republic, AP and unit of self-governance, in accordance with the EPL and special laws, and in particular by the following:

219. Environmental awareness is imparted through education and upbringing system, scientific research and technological development, public information and popularization of environmental protection (Art. 6, para. 2).
220. Article 3, point 3 defines natural value as 'natural wealth which comprises air, water, soil, forests, geological resources, plants and animal life'. Article 11 prescribes that 'natural value' means: (1) natural resources as renewable or non-renewable geologic and biologic values, which are, directly or indirectly, usable or exploitable, and which have real or potential economic value; (2) protected natural goods; and (3) public natural goods.
221. Serbian National Assembly shall enact the National Strategy of Sustainable Utilization of Natural Resources and Goods for the period of minimum ten years. It shall be implemented through plans, programmes and principles on every individual resource or good enacted by the Government of the Republic of Serbia (Art. 12, paras 2 and 4).

(1) implementation of the National Strategy, plans, programmes and principles;
(2) application of standards, norms and regulations on utilization and protection of natural resources and goods;
(3) strategic impact assessment of plans, programmes, principles and other documents governing the utilization of natural values and environmental protection;
(4) EIA of projects at all levels of research and exploitation;
(5) integrated prevention and pollution control;
(6) harmonized system of licences, approvals and consents;
(7) maintenance of cadastre of utilization of natural resources and goods;
(8) organized monitoring of utilization of natural resources and goods and monitoring of the status of environment by means of compilation, integration and analysis of data and quantification of trends.

1. Consents

148. Articles 15 and 16 establish the basis for activities of the Ministry competent for the environment with regard to management of natural resources. According to Article 15, a competent authority may not issue approval for the use of natural resources without giving consent[222] to an environmental protection and rehabilitation project during and after the use of the natural resource (paragraph 1).[223]

149. Apart from that, a legal or natural person degrading the environment shall perform rehabilitation and remediation of the degraded environment, in accordance with a rehabilitation and remediation project (Article 16, paragraph 1).[224] When the person referred to in paragraph 1 of this Article does not perform rehabilitation and/or remediation of the degraded area, the Ministry shall, at the expense of the person referred to in paragraph 1 of this Article, perform the required actions in order to rehabilitate and/or remediate the degraded area (paragraph 6).[225] The minister shall prescribe in more detail the content of the rehabilitation and remediation project, procedure and conditions for provision of consent to the project, and the documentation that should be submitted with the application for provision of consent referred to in paragraph 2 of this Article (paragraph 9).

222. The consent to the project referred to in para. 1 of this Article is issued by the Ministry (para. 3). However, the consent referred to in para. 1 of this Article shall not be obtained for works and activities on the use of natural resources which are, in accordance with special law, subject to the EIA procedure and for which the environmental protection and rehabilitation measures during and after the use of the resources are laid down in the framework of the impact assessment procedure (para. 2).
223. The Minister responsible for environmental protection shall prescribe in more detail the content of the project referred to in para. 1 of this Article, as well as the procedure and conditions for the issuance of the consent to the project (para. 4).
224. The Ministry shall give consent to the rehabilitation and remediation project referred to in para. 1 of this Article, except for rehabilitation and remediation projects for mining facilities (para. 2).
225. In case of an initiated procedure of winding up or bankruptcy of the person referred to in para. 1 of this Article, the rehabilitation and remediation costs shall be covered from the bankruptcy estate (para. 7).

2. Protected Natural Goods

150. Where 'protected natural goods' are concerned, the EPL stipulates that they shall be used and developed in a manner that enables their permanent preservation and advancement in accordance with the Law on Nature Protection.[226] Activities threatening environmental capacity, natural balance, biodiversity, hydrographic, geomorphologic, geological, cultural and landscape values or which in any way degrade the quality and properties of natural goods shall not be allowed within a protected natural good (Article 17).[227]

151. Regarding 'public green areas in settlements and other places covered by spatial and urban plans', Article 20 stipulates that they shall be made and maintained in a way which shall enable preservation and development of natural and man-made values.[228] Assembly of the LSG unit shall adopt a special decision to regulate the general conditions of protection, the manner of establishment and maintenance, the rehabilitation of degraded public green areas as well as the keeping of records concerning public green areas (paragraph 3).

152. Protection of natural values (land and soil, water, air, forest, biodiversity, flora and fauna, waste, etc.)[229] is ensured by application of measures for their quality, quantity and reserves preservation, as well as their natural processes, interrelation and overall natural balance (Article 21).

C. Measures and Conditions for Environmental Protection

153. 'Measures and conditions for environmental protection' are prescribed in the third chapter of the EPL. The chapter consists of four subchapters. The first group of measures are preventive; the second group relates to 'conditions for environmental protection'; the third group relates to 'measures of protection from dangerous substances'; and the fourth group of measures relates to the 'plans and programmes'.

154. Preventive measures include measures regarding planning and construction (Article 33), spatial and urban planning (Article 34), SEA (Article 35), EIA (Article 36), IPPC (Article 37) and chemical accident protection (Article 38).

155. The Ministry, AP authority or local self-governance unit participates in preparation and planning of spatial planning, use of natural resources and goods

226. Only the general obligations of the competent subjects are mentioned here and 'protected natural goods' will be later elaborated in more detail.
227. Article 18 prescribes generally that public natural goods and goods of general interest shall be used in a way and under conditions that shall enable development and permanency of their natural, physical, health or aesthetic values in accordance with the regulations.
228. If a public green area has been destroyed, partially or totally, due to facility construction, it will be restored in a way determined by local self-governance unit.
229. Articles 22–32 have been devoted to these issues. This will be elaborated in the next chapters.

established by spatial and urban plans and other plans – plans of spatial arranging and agricultural land basis, forests, water system, hunting basis and programmes of enhancement of fishery in fishing areas as well as other plans – in a way established by law (Article 33, paragraph 2).

156. Article 34 prescribes that spatial and urban plans shall ensure measures and conditions of environmental protection[230] and that conditions for measures shall be issued by the Ministry, AP body or self-governance units, at request of the authority competent for plan preparation and adoption.

157. Conditions for environmental protection relate to: (1) environmental quality standards and emission standards (Limit Values (Article 39)),[231] Conditions for Facilities' Work and Activities (Article 40),[232] Limits to Enable Standards (Article 41),[233] Public Alerts (Article 42), Status of Endangered Environment (Article 43);[234] (2) Environmental Protection Management System (Articles 44–50); (3) Products, Processes and Services Standards (Technology, Process, Finished and Semi-products, Raw Materials (Article 51), Warning in the Declaration (Article 52), Ecological Label (Article 53), Awarding and Withdrawal of Ecological label (Article 54) and Appreciations and Awards (Article 55)).

158. Article 51 prescribes that domestic or imported technologies or processes can be applied, or products produced or offered on the market on the territory of

---

230. In particular: (1) to determine special regimes for preservation and use of the areas of protected natural goods, water springs, thermal and mineral springs, forests, agricultural land, public green areas, recreation areas and spas; (2) to determine areas of threatened parts of the environment (polluted areas, areas endangered with erosion and torrents, exploitation of mineral raw materials, flooded areas, etc.) and determination of measures for these areas rehabilitation; (2a) to determine measures of integrated protection and planning of landscape, aimed at regulating long-term conception, purpose and organization of landscape and harmonizing multipurpose utilization of space that threatens the landscape (agriculture, forestry, water management, mining, energy, transportation, habitation, recreation and other); (2b) to determine areas in which appropriate distances shall be maintained in long-term between facilities where one or more dangerous substances are present or may be present in quantities higher than prescribed and residential areas, public areas, as well as areas of special interest, for the purpose of protecting human life and health and the environment; and (3) to determine measures and conditions of environmental protection according to which space intended to be exploited for minerals shall be utilized, or according to which industrial and energetic plants shall be constructed, as well as facilities for waste storage, preparation for reuse, treatment and/or recovery and disposal, infrastructure and other facilities whose construction or utilization may threaten the environment.
231. The Government determines limit values of the emissions for pollutants at the place of their outflow into the environment and the levels of imissions for pollutants in the environment (Art. 39, para. 3).
232. Construction and other activities may proceed only if the set standards for emission and imission and equipment that reduce or prevent emission of pollutants or energy and provide for its conservation are fulfilled.
233. With the view to progressive implementation of standards for emission and imission and conservation of natural values, the Government may, for a period of time, limit the operations of installations and activities in certain area.
234. The Government determines criteria for the status of specially endangered environment, i.e., the status of endangered environment and for prioritization for rehabilitation and remediation (Art. 43, para. 3).

Serbia, if they meet the requirements related to the environment and/or product quality requirements or if technology, process, product, semi-finished product or raw material is not prohibited in the exporting country.[235] Producer or distributor is obliged to warn, of possible environmental pollution and damage to human health, which the product or its packaging causes or may cause, in the declaration of raw material, semi-finished or finished products.

159. Article 53 prescribes that the ecological label shall be established for products intended for general consumption, except foodstuffs, agricultural and other products obtained in accordance with regulations governing organic production, production of beverages, production of pharmaceutical products and medical equipment, if their production, marketing, consumption and disposal cause less environmental pollution compared with similar products, or if they are produced by waste recycling.

160. The Law also contains measures of protection from dangerous substances in following Articles: Import, Export and Transit of Waste (Article 57); Chemical accident protection – Obligations of Legal and Natural Entities (Article 58); Content of the Policy for Accident Prevention (Article 58a); Obligation to Submit Notification (Article 59); Content of the Report on Safety and Plan on Protection from Accident (Article 60); Submitting the Report on Safety and Plan on Protection from Accident (Article 60a); Submitting Information from the Plan on Protection from Accident (Article 60b); Public Availability, Presentation and Public Debate on the Report on Safety (Article 60c); Evidence in the Report on Safety (Article 60d); Evidence in the Plan on Protection from Accident (Article 60e); Consent on the Report on Safety and the Plan on Protection from Accident (Article 60f); Decision Prohibiting Operation or Start-Up of Seveso Installation (Article 60g); Appointment of the Special Working Group (Article 60h); Obligation of Keeping Records (Article 60i); Register of Installations and Register of Reported Accidents (Article 60j); Informing of the Accident (Article 60k); Obligations of Competent Authority (Article 61); Notification on Operators or Seveso Installations or Establishments of activities which may cause Chemical Accident with Transboundary Effects (Article 61a); Obligation to Submit Notification of the Responsible Authority of Other Country (Article 61b); Exceptions (Article 61c); Proclamation of the State of Endangerment (Article 62) and Rehabilitation Measures and Subsidiary Liability (Article 63).

161. The Fourth group of measures and conditions for environmental protection relate to 'programmes and plans' and includes the National Programme (Article

235. The Ministry may, in case of any doubts, request the evaluation of damaging effects of the technology, process, finished or semi-finished product or raw material, even if duly accompanied by regulated documents (Art. 51, para. 2). Production and trade of certain products and performance of certain activities may be prohibited for a specific period of time, or on a part of Republic territory, also by AP or local self-governance unit, in order to prevent danger for environment and human health (Art. 51, para. 4).

64);[236] Action Plan (Article 65); Rehabilitation Plan (Articles 66 and 67); Programmes and Plans of AP and Local Self-governance Unit (Article 68).[237]

D. Monitoring

162. Provisions concerning environmental monitoring are divided into three parts: Monitoring (Articles 69–73), Information System and Manner of Data Submission (Articles 74 and 75), and Environmental State Report (Articles 76 and 77).

EPL distinguishes between State monitoring carried out by the State authorities, AP, and LSGs and monitoring performed by polluters. State authorities have a duty to monitor the state of the environment, for example, air, water, soil, climate, and ozone layer, while the operator is obliged to monitor emissions.

163. The authorized organization may include monitoring, provided that it meets conditions concerning human resources, equipment and space, accreditation for the measurement of given parameters and SRPS standards in the domain of sampling, measurement, analysis and reliability of data in compliance with law (Article 71).

164. Article 72 of the EPL establishes legal basis for regulation of self-monitoring.[238] The operator of the installation or establishment that represents source of emissions and environmental pollution shall be obliged to, in accordance with law, through the responsible authority, authorized organization or independently, if it meets the conditions prescribed by law, perform monitoring, that is, to: (1) monitor the emission indicators and/or indicators of effect of its activities on the environment, indicators of efficiency of applied measures for prevention of occurrence or reduction of the level of pollution; (2) ensure meteorological measurements for big industrial establishments or facilities of special interest for the RS, AP or LSG unit (paragraph 1). The polluter shall prepare a plan for monitoring performance, duly keep records on monitoring and submit reports, in accordance with this Law (paragraph 2).[239]

---

236. *See* Introduction – Ch. 2. Basic Principles of Environmental Law, 'Strategic Framework of National Environmental Policy and Environmental Law'.

237. The AP and/or local government units shall adopt environmental protection programmes, action and/or rehabilitation plans referred to in Art. 68 of the *EPL* within a year from the date of entry into force of this Law (Art. 33 of the EPL Amendment, 2016).

238. Another legal Act relevant for self-monitoring is the Law on IPPC. It prescribes obligation for operators of installations being subject matter of this Law. The operator applying for the integrated permit must submit, among other documents, the monitoring plan (Art. 9, para. 1.3). The decision of the competent authority concerning application must contain requirements relating to the monitoring of emissions, specifying the following: monitoring methodology, time-scale for measurements, rules for interpreting measurement results and obligation for submitting data to the competent authority. The operator is obliged to carry out monitoring in accordance with the monitoring plan and requirements specified in the permit (Art. 16, para. 2.8). He/she is also obliged to send results of monitoring to the competent authority (Art. 17, paras 1.2 and 2).

239. The polluter shall plan and provide the financial resources for performing monitoring, as well as for other measurements and monitoring the effect of its activity on the environment (para. 4).

The Government shall determine types of activities and other occurrences which are subject to monitoring, work methodology, indicators, manner of recording data, deadlines for submission and data keeping, based on special laws (paragraph 3).

165. Article 74 of the EPL prescribes that an information system for environmental protection shall be established, for more efficient identification, classification, processing, monitoring and record keeping of natural values and environmental management. The information system shall be run by the EPA (paragraph 3).[240] National and local registers of sources of environmental pollution shall be maintained in accordance with this Law for the purpose of monitoring qualitative and quantitative changes in the environment and undertaking measures for the protection of the environment (Article 75, paragraph 1). National register of sources of environmental pollution shall be maintained by the EPA, and local register of sources of environmental pollution shall be maintained by the responsible authority of the LSG unit (paragraphs 2 and 3).[241]

166. The Government is obliged to report annually to the NA on state of the environment in the Republic (Article 76, paragraph 1).[242] The report shall contain following data: (1) state and changes of the state of environment based on data and information obtained through monitoring of relevant indicators; (2) implementation of strategy, National Programme and action plans; (3) rehabilitation plans and other measures undertaken; (4) financing the system of environment protection; and (5) other data which are relevant for management of natural values and environmental protection (Article 77).

E. Economic Instruments

167. Provisions concerning economic instruments could be divided into the following groups: Charges for Use of Natural Resources (Article 84), Environmental Pollution Charges (Articles 85–88),[243] Budgetary and International Financial Assistance Funds – Funds for Financing Environmental Protection (Article 89), Green

240. EPA shall establish and maintain the National Metaregister for Environmental Information (hereinafter 'National Metaregister'), which is a constituent part of the Information System (para. 5). In addition EPA shall establish and maintain the means for processing environmental information (para. 8).
241. EPA shall, on its own or in collaboration with a competent inspection, monitor data submission for the National Register of Pollution Sources and the accuracy of submitted data. The Agency shall initiate misdemeanour proceedings charges against persons who are obliged to report to the National Register of Pollution Sources and who have not submitted the required data or data were not submitted in the prescribed manner and within the statutory deadline and/or who have submitted inaccurate data (Art. 75a).
242. EPA shall draft the report referred to in para. 1 of this Article on the basis of collected and available data and information no later than 31 May of the current year (para. 2).
243. As already mentioned, the following provisions of the EPL have ceased to apply: Art. 27 (paras 5–7), Art. 85, Art. 85a (paras 3 and 4), Arts 86 and 87 (except para. 3, point 3) and para. 6, and Art. 88 – on the day of the beginning of the application of the *Law on Fees for the Use of Public Goods* (OJ RS, No. 95/2018), i.e.,1 Jan. 2019 (*see* Art. 279 of the Law – 95/2018). The provisions of Art.

Fund of the RS (Article 90–90g) and Economic Incentives (Article 101). Environmental funds can also be provided through donations, loans, international assistance funds, foreign investment funds intended for environmental protection, funds from instruments, programmes and funds of the EU, UN and international organizations (Article 83, paragraph 2).[244]

168. The following environmental taxes and charges were prescribed by the Law: pollution charges (emission taxes, industrial waste charges and product charges),[245] natural resource use charges, deposit refund schemes, subsidies, tax incentives and exemptions from charge payments and fines for non-compliance with environmental standards. Where ozone-depleting substances are concerned, their import is subject to an environmental tax.

169. Charges for the use of natural goods are prescribed by Article 84. The user of the natural values shall pay a charge for the utilization of natural values. He/she will also bear the cost of rehabilitation and recultivation of degraded area, in compliance with special law.[246]

170. In accordance with relevant regulations and depending on the kind of natural resource it refers to, the user of a natural resource is obliged to pay the charge for its use and bear expenses for the restoration and recultivation of degraded area. The Regulation on Control of Use and Trade of Wild Flora and Fauna (OJ RS, Nos 31/2005, 45/2005, 22/2007, 38/2008, 09/2010 and 69/2011) specifies details concerning the charge for commercial use of collected wild flora and fauna.

171. Article 85 prescribes 'charges for environmental pollution'. Paragraph 1 of Article 85 prescribes in a general way the duty 'of the polluter to pay charges for environmental pollution' and paragraph 2 defines the following criteria for assessment of the amount of charge:

(1) kind, quantity or characteristics of emissions from specific sources;
(2) kind, quantity or characteristics of emissions of produced or dumped waste; and

---

87, para. 3 (point 3) and para. 6, as well as Acts of local self-government units adopted on the basis of Art. 87 of the Law on Environmental Protection (OJ RS, Nos 135/04, 36/09, 36/09 – other law, 72/09 – other law, 43/11 – CC, 14/16 and 76/18), have ceased to be valid from 1 Mar. 2019 (*see* Art. 279 of the Law – 95/2018-267).

244. Total cumulative disbursements of development assistance for the sector 'environment protection' amounted to EUR 106 million during the period 2007–2013. Annual disbursements corresponded to some 0.05% of GDP. Some 95% of funds were provided in the form of grants; the remainder (some EUR 6 million) was concessional loans (UNECE. 2015, xxvi). For some information on the IPA programme results, *see* Ignjatić, Todić, 2014.

245. The Regulation on types of pollution, criteria for calculation of cost recovery for environmental pollution, and amount and calculation methods for fees (OJ RS, Nos 113/2005, 6/2007, 8/10, 102/10, 15/12 and 91/12) prescribes pollution charge rates and their calculation. The Regulation has ceased to apply (Art. 278, para. 1, item 24 of the Law on fees for the use of public goods).

246. Funds collected from the charge referred to in para. 1 of this Article shall be revenue of the Republic budget and budget of the AP and/or LSG unit, in accordance with special law (para. 2).

(3) contents of environmentally harmful substances in raw materials, semi-products and products.

172. The environmental charge payer is, according to the Law, 'every person who causes environmental pollution by emissions, waste or products, or who uses or puts on the market raw materials, semi-products and products containing environmentally harmful substances' (Article 85, paragraph 3).[247] According to paragraph 5 of this Article, 60% of the financial means obtained from the charges are allocated to the Republic budget and 40% to the budget of the local self-governance unit.

173. Pursuant to Article 85A, the Government shall determine areas of special State interest in the environmental protection area (upon proposal of the Ministry responsible for environmental issues) (paragraph 1). The amount and manner of payment of the charge for environment pollution in areas referred to in paragraph 1 of this Article shall be specified by the Government (paragraph 3).[248]

174. According to Article 87, the LSG unit may, within the scope of its rights and duties, prescribe the charge for protection and enhancement of the environment.[249]

175. The charge referred to in paragraph 1 of Article 87 shall be prescribed on the grounds of the following: (1) use of residential and commercial buildings, flats and business premises for residence or performing business activity, as well as for the use of land for performing the regular activity (hereinafter 'the real estate');[250] (2) performance of certain activities affecting the environment, which are specified by the Government;[251] (3) transport of oil and oil derivatives, as well as raw material, products and semi-finished products of chemical and other dangerous substances

247. The Government 'prescribe in more details' the following elements necessary for environmental charge payment: (1) kind of pollution; (2) criteria for charge assessment; (3) environmental charge payers; and (4) the amount of environmental charge and assessment procedure.
248. From the funds collected as the charge referred to in para. 3 of this Article, 80% shall be revenue of the budget of the Republic of Serbia, and 20% shall be revenue of the LSG unit and they shall be used for the protection and enhancement of the environment in accordance with programmes, namely action and rehabilitation plans that are adopted in accordance with this Law and special laws (Art. 85A, para. 4).
249. The charge shall be prescribed in the Act of the assembly of LSG unit (para. 2). The responsible authority of the LSG unit shall be obliged to obtain opinion of the Ministry on the proposal of Act (para. 9). The Government shall prescribe criteria for determining charge as well as the highest amount of such charge (para. 7). The LSG unit shall determine in accordance with the Act referred to in para. 2 of this Article the amount, deadlines, payers, manner of payment of the charge and relief for certain categories of payers, in accordance with the defined criteria referred to in para. 7 of this Article (para. 8).
250. Payers of the charge on the grounds referred to in para. 3 item 1 of this Article shall be holders of the property right for real estate, or lessees if the real estate is used based on the lease right, and the amount of charge shall be determined according to the area of the real estate, and it shall be paid monthly up to the amount that may not exceed the amount prescribed in accordance with this Law (para. 4).
251. Payers of the charge on the grounds referred to in para. 3 item 2 of this Article shall be legal persons and entrepreneurs which perform certain activities (para. 5).

from the industry or for the industry on the territory of LSG unit with the status of endangered environment on the area of importance for the R S (paragraph 3).[252]

176. The funds collected from the charge referred to in paragraph 1 of Article 87 shall be used, through the budget fund, for the protection and enhancement of the environment according to adopted programmes of budget fund use and/or local action and rehabilitation plans, in accordance with the strategic documents that are adopted based on this Law and special laws (paragraph 10).[253]

177. When incentive measures are concerned, the EPL in Article 101 stipulates that:

> for the legal and natural entities applying technologies, produce and place on the market the products environmentally more friendly than others, namely use RES (energy of the Sun, wind parks, biogas, etc.) plant and equipment directly protecting the environment, may have taxation, customs and other relief or exemption provided under the terms and conditions of special law.[254]

178. According to Article 90 of the EPL (2016),[255] the Green Fund of the RS shall be established as a budgetary fund designed to track the allocation of assets earmarked for financing the preparation, implementation and development of programmes, projects and other activities related to the protection, sustainable use and improvement of environment.[256]

179. Using the resources of the Green Fund of the RS shall be done in accordance with the law, the NEPP and strategic documents, as well as a list of priority

---

252. Payers of the charge on the grounds referred to in para. 3 item 3 of this Article shall be the owners of trucks and/or legal and natural persons engaged in transportation of oil and oil derivatives, as well as raw material, products and semi-finished products of chemical and other dangerous substances from industry or for the industry on the territory of the LSG unit with status of the endangered environment on the area of importance for the Republic of Serbia (para. 6). However, the provisions of Art. 87, para. 3, point 3 ceased to apply with the enactment of the Law on Fees for the Use of Public Goods (*see* Art. 278, para. 2).
253. The LSG unit may not prescribe charges that are prescribed based on Arts 84, 85 and 85a of this Law (para. 11).
254. For consumers who, in an organized manner, return used and non-used devices or parts thereof, products or their packaging, the producers of plastic carrier bags, operators of the facilities for reuse and/or recovery, collectors and other subjects in the waste management system, special incentives such as subsidies, deposits and their refund may be determined, under the terms and in the manner stipulated in this Law and special law (Art. 101, para. 2). For the purpose of assigning incentive payments, the Government shall determine the amount, criteria, conditions and manner of awarding the incentives as well as the classification of beneficiaries enjoying the incentives referred to in para. 2 of this Article, taking into account the classification of operators and other waste management entities stated in the law governing waste management (para. 3).
255. Fund for Environmental Protection ceased to work by adopting the law (OJ RS, No. 93/12 – 25 Sep. 2012).
256. Budgetary fund shall be established for an indefinite period of time in accordance with law governing budgetary system. Budgetary fund will be managed by the Ministry (Art. 90, paras 2 and 3). *See also* Decision on the establishment of the Green Fund of the Republic of Serbia (OJ RS, Nos 91/16, 78/17).

infrastructure projects in the field of environment, for the following: (1) protect, preserve and improve the quality of air, water, land and forests, as well as reducing the impact of climate change and to take adaptation measures, including protection of the ozone layer; (2) remediation of landfills, waste reduction, reuse, treatment, and recovery and disposal of waste; (3) the programmes, projects and other investment and operational activities in the field of waste management, in accordance with the Law governing waste management; (4) the introduction of cleaner production for the operation of facilities and activities, as well as to fulfil the requirements of environmental protection; (5) technologies and products that reduce stress and pollution of the environment; (6) protection and conservation of biodiversity, waste of injured, sick, seized or confiscated specimens of wild flora and fauna, including active protection measures such as reintroduction, repopulation and maintenance of habitats; (7) Promoting the use of renewable resources; (8) promoting environmentally friendly mode of transport; (9) promoting sustainable development, in addition to projects to improve energy efficiency, etc. The Ministry is obliged to keep records of taxpayers for paying all fees in the field of environmental protection (Article 90g).[257]

180. The AP and LSG shall be obliged to establish the budget fund in accordance with the law governing the budget system (Article 100). Charges shall be collected based on Articles 85, 85a and 87 of this Law (Article 100 paragraph 2). Budget fund resources shall be used for financing of environmental protection and improvement, for financing action and rehabilitation plans in accordance with the National Programme and/or for financing programmes and plans of AP and LSG unit referred to in Article 68 of this Law (Article 100 paragraph 3).[258]

181. When the results of implementation of this Law are assessed, it should be kept in mind that it is a framework legal Act.[259] Also, implementation of such a complex and systemic legal Act is influenced by many factors. There is no doubt that by adoption of such framework legal Act Serbia has acquired an Act which covers almost all important issues concerning the environment, as well as the fact that

257. ‘ In 2023, the Serbian national budget for environment and climate action was increased by 18% compared with 2022. ... Although Serbia is substantially increasing investment in environmental protection, it still lacks an effective institutional set-up and transparent procedures.’ (EC. 2023, 135)
258. Budget fund resources shall be used based on the defined programme of use of budget fund resources that is adopted by the responsible authority of the AP and the LSG unit. The responsible authority of the LSG unit shall obtain consent of the Ministry on the proposal of the programme of use of budget fund resources referred to in para. 1 of this Article (Art. 100, para. 3). The AP and local self-government unit shall submit to the Ministry a report on the use of the budgetary funds no later than 31 March of the current year for the previous year and/or at the request of the Ministry (para. 4).
259. The 2004 EPL outlines principles of environmental protection and sets the framework for the system of environmental protection. For most areas covered by the Law, detailed special laws and regulations have been adopted. For more information, *see* UNECE. 2015, 13, 25, 42, 52, 56, 59, 65, 93.

the Law has been adopted simultaneously with other systemic laws which regulate EIA, SEA and IPPC. Some issues are, however, still to be elaborated, as for example, the following:

- relationship between EPL and other relevant laws;
- overlaps in policy and implementation responsibilities;
- coordination between different subjects;
- capacities of various Government agencies (inspection, EPA, etc.) and other subjects;
- efficiency of use of the means of the Environment Protection Fund;
- state of environmental consciousness of public in general, professionals, scientific community, NGOs, etc.

II. Environmental Impact Assessment

A. *International Law*

182. Serbia is a contracting party of the Convention on EIA in a Transboundary Context, Espoo, 1991 (OJ RS, No. 102/07), Sofia (2001) and Cavtat (2004) amendments (OJ RS, No. 4/16). Besides that, Serbia has signed and ratified a multilateral agreement among the countries of Southeastern Europe for implementation of the Convention on EIA in a Transboundary Context, at the fourth meeting of the Parties (Bucharest, May 2008).[260] The Agreement contains detailed provisions concerning consultations, detailing appropriate means for providing information to authorities and to the public.[261]

B. *National Law*

183. EPL in Article 36, paragraph 3 stipulates that EIA shall be an integral part of the technical documents; without it, no project execution may start and it shall be realized in accordance with the procedure stipulated by special law.[262]

184. The Law on EIA was adopted in 2004 (OJ RS, Nos 135/2004 and 36/09). It contains forty-seven Articles divided into five chapters: Basic Provisions (Articles 1–5); Impact Assessment Procedure (Articles 6–34a); Supervision (Articles 35–39); Penalty Provisions (Articles 40–43); and Transitional and Final Provisions (Articles 44–47).

260. Participating countries are Albania, Bosnia and Herzegovina, Bulgaria, Croatia, Greece, Montenegro, Romania, Serbia and the former Yugoslav Republic of Macedonia.(OJ RS – IT, No. 12/18).

261. *See* https://unece.org/DAM/env/eia/documents/bucharest/SEE_multilateral_agreement_final.pdf (4.1.2024).

262. EIA has been introduced in legal system of Serbia by the previous EPL (1991) and by relevant by-laws.

185. According to Article 1 of this Law:

> regulates the impact assessment procedure for projects that may have significant effects on the environment, the contents of the Environmental Impact Assessment (EIA) Study, the participation of authorities and organizations concerned, the public participation, transboundary exchange of information for projects that may have significant impact on the environment of another state, supervision and other issues of relevance to impact assessment.[263]

186. EIA[264] is based on the elaboration of EIA study,[265] public consultation and participation and analyses of alternative measures, with the aim of collecting data, of foreseeing the harmful effects of certain projects on the environment and human health, flora and fauna, soil, water, air, climate and landscape, material and cultural resources and the interactive effects of these elements, and of determining and proposing measures that may be implemented in order to prevent, reduce or eliminate such harmful effects, having in mind the feasibility of these projects (Article 2, paragraph 5).

187. The impact assessment is applied to planned projects, projects which are being implemented, changes in technology, reconstruction, extension of capacity, termination of operations and termination of projects that may have a significant negative impact on the environment. Impact assessments are obligatory for projects in mining, energy production, transport, tourism, agriculture, forestry, water management, waste management and utility services, and all other projects in areas with protected natural resources of special value and in protected zones of cultural resources. It should be added that the law introduces screening, scoping and public participation in accordance with the EU Directive on EIA.

188. The project developer[266] has, according to Article 5, an obligation to obtain the impact assessment approval. Developer of a project for which impact assessment is mandatory and of a project for which need for impact assessment has been

---

263. The provisions of this Law do not apply to projects designated for national defence purposes (Art. 1).
264. EIA is a preventive measure of environmental protection, based on the elaboration of a study, public consultation and participation and analyses of alternative measures, with the aim of collecting data, of foreseeing the harmful effects of certain projects on the environment and human health, flora and fauna, soil, water, air, climate and landscape, material and cultural resources and the interactive effects of these elements, and of determining and proposing measures that may be implemented in order to prevent, reduce or eliminate such harmful effects, having in mind the feasibility of these projects (Art. 2, point 5).
265. 'Environmental impact assessment study' is defined as the document analysing and evaluating the qualitative elements of the environment and their sensitivity within certain areas, the interactive effects of the existing and planned activities, foreseeing the direct and indirect harmful effects of projects on elements of the environment, as well as measures and conditions for prevention, reduction and elimination of harmful effects on the environment and human health (EIA Study) (Art. 2, para. 6).
266. 'Project developer' means the applicant for a permit or an approval for construction or reconstruction of structures or for other interventions in nature and the environment (Art. 2, para. 3). The project developer shall cover the costs of the EIA Study elaboration, its modifying, amending and

established shall not start implementation and/or construction and realization of the project without the approval of the EIA Study from the competent authority (Article 5). In accordance with Article 18 of the Law on EIA, the EIA Study and approval of the EIA Study, that is, the decision that states that EIA shall not be needed, shall be an inseparable part of documentation that is submitted along with the application for construction permit or with the notification of the commencement of the project implementation (construction, workmanship, technology change, change in business activity and other activities).

189. The main stakeholders in the EIA procedure are as follows:

– Competent authorities (ministries, autonomous regions and local authorities).[267]
– Project developer (investor).
– Authorities and organizations concerned.[268]
– General public and public concerned.

1. EIA Procedure

190. Articles 6–34 of the Law on EIA prescribe environmental impact assessment. According to Article 6, the procedure in Serbia comprises the following steps:

(1) the decision on the need for an impact assessment of projects referred to in Article 4, paragraph 1, point 2 of this Law (Articles 8–11);
(2) the definition of the content and scope of an impact assessment (Articles 12–15); and
(3) the decision on the approval for an EIA Study (Articles 16–28).

191. Article 10 prescribes that the competent authority is obliged to inform the authorities, organizations and public concerned about the submitted application for a decision, concerning the need for an impact assessment, within ten days from the date of receipt of the complete application. The competent authority shall decide on the

---

updating, the costs of elaboration of the Study of the current status, and the costs related to the information and public participation proceedings in the impact assessment procedure and the work of the Technical Commission (Art. 33).

267. According to Art. 2 of the EIA Law 'competent authority' means the authority responsible for carrying out the EIA procedure within the functions set forth by this Law, i.e., the Ministry responsible for environmental protection – for those projects for which the permit for project implementation is under the responsibility of the Republic authority; the provincial authority responsible for environmental protection matters – for those projects for which the permit for project implementation is under the responsibility of the authority of the AP; the LSG authority responsible for environmental protection matters – for those projects for which the permit for project implementation is under the responsibility of the LSG authority.

268. 'Authorities and organizations concerned' means the authorities and organizations of the Republic, the AP, LSG and the companies granted the authority to set conditions and issue permits, authorizations and approvals for the construction of structures, for planning and spatial regulation, for environmental status monitoring and for the execution of activities for protection and use of natural and man-made resources (Art. 2, para. 8).

application within ten days, taking into account the opinions of the authorities, organizations and the public concerned (Article 14, paragraph 4).[269] The competent authority may determine scope and contents of the EIA Study through the decision establishing the need for EIA of a project. The decision establishing that EIA shall not be needed may contain minimal environmental protection requirements, as decided by the competent authority, in compliance with specific regulations. The competent authority shall submit the decision referred to in paragraph 4 of this Article to the project developer and shall inform stakeholders and organizations and public about it within three days of making such decision (Article 10, paragraphs 5–7).

192. The second phase starts with the application for a decision on the scope and content of the EIA Study (Article 12). The developer of a project that is subject to a mandatory impact assessment and of a project for which the competent authority has determined that an impact assessment is required shall submit the application. The competent authority shall inform the authorities, organizations, and the public concerned about the application within ten days from the date of receipt of the application for a decision on the scope and content of the EIA Study (Article 14, paragraph 1).[270]

193. The competent authority is obliged, within ten days from the expiry of the period anticipated for collection of opinions, to deliver the decision on the scope and content of the EIA Study, taking into account the opinions of the authorities, organizations and the public concerned (Article 14, paragraph 3). The competent authority is obliged to deliver this decision to the developer and inform the authorities, organizations and the public concerned about such decision, within three days from the date on which the decision was made (Article 14, paragraph 4).[271]

194. In the third phase, the project developer is obliged to submit to the competent authority the application for the EIA Study approval ('approval application') together with the EIA Study (Article 16). If the competent authority has decided on the scope and content of the EIA Study,[272] the project developer shall submit the application for approval within one year from the date of receipt of the final decision on the scope and content of the EIA Study.[273]

---

269. The project developer and the public concerned are entitled to file a complaint against the decision of the competent authority concerning the application for a decision on the need for an impact assessment (Art. 11, paras 1 and 2). The competent authority of the second instance shall decide on the complaint within thirty days from the date of receipt of the complaint (Art. 11, para. 3).
270. The authorities, organizations and the public concerned may submit their opinions on the application with regard to the application within twenty days from the date of receipt of notice referred to in Art. 14, para. 1.
271. The project developer and public concerned are entitled to file a complaint against the decision of the competent authority on the application for a decision on the scope and content of the EIA Study (Art. 15). The competent authority of the second instance shall decide on the complaint within thirty days from the date of receipt of the complaint (Art. 15, para. 3).
272. Article 17 prescribes obligatory elements of content of the EIA Study.
273. If the project developer submits the application for an approval after the expiry of the prescribed period, the competent authority shall decide on the application depending upon the circumstances of the individual case.

195. One of the obligations of the competent authority is to make the EIA Study available to public and to arrange a public presentation and debate on the Study (Article 20). Within seven days from the date of receipt of the application for the EIA Study approval, the competent authority is obliged to inform the project developer, the authorities, organizations and the public concerned about the time and venue for public consultation, presentation and debate on the EIA Study. Public debate may not be held sooner than twenty days from the date when the public was informed. The project developer is obliged to participate in the public presentation and debate on the EIA Study.

196. Technical Commission for the purpose of the EIA Study evaluation has to be established by the competent authority within at most ten days from the reception of the approval application as prescribed by Article 22.[274] The competent authority shall submit the EIA Study to the Technical Commission within three days of the establishment thereof. Upon the finalized public checking, that is, public presentation and consultations, the competent authority shall submit to the Technical Commission a report containing opinions from stakeholders and interested organizations and public (Article 22a). The commission has the task to evaluate the EIA Study, together with the systematized report on the consultations of the authorities, organizations and the public concerned and the report on the completed impact assessment procedure, and evaluate the suitability of the measures envisaged to prevent, reduce or eliminate the likely harmful effects of the project on the environment at the specific site and its vicinity during the construction and operation of the project, in cases of accidents, and upon the termination of the project operation (Article 23, paragraph 1). The competent authority as proposed by the Technical Commission may demand that the project developer make certain modifications and amendments to the submitted EIA Study within a certain time limit (Article 23, paragraph 3). If the project developer fails to act in full compliance with paragraph 3 of this Article, the competent authority may, as proposed by the Technical Commission, approve maximally one additional deadline for amendment of the EIA Study.[275]

197. The competent authority has the duty to adopt the decision granting the approval of the EIA Study, or to refuse the application for approval of the EIA

274. Members of the Technical Commission are persons with university education corresponding to the field and appointed by the following: (1) the employees or appointed persons of the competent authority; (2) the employees or appointed persons of the authorities and organizations concerned; (3) independent experts. Members of the Technical Commission shall not be the persons who: (1) have participated in the EIA Study elaboration that is the subject of evaluation; (2) are founders of a juridical person or entrepreneurs who carried out the EIA Study or employees of such persons; (3) are founders or employees of the project developer; (4) are spouses, blood relatives up to the fourth level of kinship and relatives of spouses up to the second level of kinship of persons listed in points (1) to (3) (Art. 22, paras 3 and 4).

275. The Commission is obliged to submit the report with the evaluation of the EIA Study and the proposed decision to the competent authority, within thirty days from the date of receipt of the EIA Study from the competent authority. This period shall not be in effect during the period granted to the project developer to make modifications and amendments to the EIA Study (Art. 23, paras 5 and 6).

Study, based on the completed EIA procedure and the report of the Technical Commission (Article 24).[276] Decision shall be submitted to the competent environmental inspector by the competent authority (Article 24, paragraph 3).

198. The competent authority is obliged, within ten days from the date of adoption of the decision, to inform the authorities, organizations and the public concerned about its decision to grant the approval for the EIA Study or to refuse the application for approval for the EIA Study (Article 25).[277]

199. The decision of the competent authority mentioned above is final, but the applicant and the public concerned are entitled to initiate the Administrative Court proceeding against the decision (Article 26).

2. Consultation in Transboundary Context

200. If the planned project could cause a significant impact on the environment of another State, or when another State in which the environment could be significantly threatened requests the information, the Ministry shall, within the shortest possible period, at the latest simultaneously notify its own public, submit to the State concerned with all relevant information.[278]

201. Basic provisions of the EIA Law have been further elaborated by adoption of the following sub-legal Acts:

(a) Regulation on the list of projects for which EIA is obligatory (List I) and the list of projects for which EIA may be required (List II) (OJ RS, No. 114/2008).
(b) Rulebook on the procedures of public access, presentation and public debate on study of the EIA (OJ RS, No. 69/2005).
(c) Rulebook on work of technical commission for assessment of the study of the EIA (OJ RS, No. 69/2005).
(d) Rulebook on contents of the study on EIA (OJ RS, No. 69/2005).
(e) Rulebook on contents, forms and method of keeping of public book on executed procedures and adopted decisions regarding EIA (OJ RS, No. 69/2005).
(f) Rulebook on contents of the application on needs for the impact assessment and contents of application for determination of size and contents of the study of the EIA (OJ RS, No. 69/2005).

276. The decision granting the approval of the EIA Study shall contain conditions and measures, that should be undertaken to prevent, reduce or eliminate adverse impacts on the environment.
277. It is prescribed that the notice must contain: (1) the content of the decision; (2) the main reasons for the decision; and (3) the most important measures that the project developer shall undertake in order to prevent, reduce or eliminate adverse effects.
278. Article 32 defines types of information that have to be submitted to another State in the process of transboundary consultation.

202. The EIA Directive 2011/92/EU is partially transposed by the Law on EIA, EPL and other implementing legislation. The amendments introduced by the Directive 2014/52/EU have not been transposed. Full transposition of EIA Directive 2011/92/EU as amended by Directive 2014/52/EU is planned to be achieved in 2017.[279] According to the last EC report, ' EIA implementation needs to be considerably strengthened.'[280]

III. Strategic Environmental Assessment

203. Article 35 of the EPL is devoted to the SEA. It is stipulated, *inter alia*, that 'strategic environmental impact assessment must be harmonized with other environmental impact assessments, as well as with the plans and programmes for the protection of environment and shall be made in keeping with the procedure set out in special law'.[281]

204. The Law on SEA has introduced strategic assessment of effects on the environment into the legal system of Serbia (OJ RS, Nos 135/2004 and 88/2010). The Law contains twenty-seven Articles divided into four chapters: Basic Provisions (Articles 1–4); Strategic Assessment Procedure (Articles 5–24); Penalty Provisions (Article 25); and Transitional and Final Provisions (Articles 26 and 27).

205. The Law on SEA prescribes that:

> the conditions, methods and procedure according to which the assessment of impact of certain plans and programmes on the environment shall be carried out in order to provide for the environmental protection and improvement of sustainable development through integration of basic principles of environmental protection into the procedure of preparation and adoption of plans and programmes (Article 1).

A. *Subjects of the SEA*

206. Article 5 of the Law prescribes that subjects of strategic assessment are plans, programmes, grounds and strategies[282] in the field of spatial and urban planning or land use, agriculture, forestry, fishing, hunting, energy, industry, transport,

279. EC. 2016b, 3. *See also* GOV RS. 2018, 1136.
280. EC. 2023, 135. For more information, *see* Drenovak – Ivanović – M. 2016. *See also*, Vučić, 2016.
281. AP or local self-governance units, within their rights and responsibilities, shall stipulate the types of plans and programmes subject to the strategic impact assessment.
282. '"Plans and programmes" are all development and other plans and programmes, bases, strategies, including their amendments, which are prepared and/or adopted by the authority at the Republic, provincial or local level, or which are prepared by the competent authority for the purpose of adoption in the appropriate procedure by the National Assembly or Government of the Republic of Serbia, or the assembly or the executive authority of the autonomous province or self-government units, as well as plans and programmes adopted pursuant to legislation' (Art. 3, point 1).

waste management, water management, telecommunication, tourism, protection of natural habitats and wild flora and fauna, by which the framework for obtaining a permit for future developmental projects is prescribed by regulations regarding EIA.[283]

207. The decision on the strategic impact assessment, in cases of plans and programmes which determine the use of smaller areas at the local level, or in cases of minor modifications to plans and programmes that do not require the formal adoption procedure, as well as of plans and programmes that are not listed in paragraph 1 of Article 5, is made by the competent planning authority if, according to the criteria[284] prescribed by this Law, it determines that there is a possibility of significant impact on the environment (Article 5, paragraph 2).[285]

208. The strategic EIA shall be carried out based on the plan or programme level, type, objectives, contents and scope (Article 7).[286]

B. Procedure

209. Articles 5–24 prescribe strategic assessment procedure, which is, in accordance with Article 8, composed of following three stages:

(1) The preparation stage includes:
  - the decision on the strategic assessment elaboration;
  - the selection of the strategic assessment developer;
  - the participation of authorities and organizations concerned.

(2) The strategic assessment report.

(3) The decision-making procedure includes:
  - the participation of authorities and organizations concerned;
  - the participation of the public concerned;
  - the report on the results of participation of authorities and organizations and public concerned;
  - the evaluation of the strategic assessment report;
  - the approval of the strategic assessment report.

---

283. Exempted are 'plans and programmes designated to the national defence purposes, plans of mitigation and elimination of consequences of natural disasters and financial and budget plans' (Art. 2).

284. Criteria for determining the possibilities of significant impact of plans and programmes on the environment and passing of the decision on elaboration of strategic assessment are listed in Annex I to this Law (Art. 6).

285. The Minister responsible for environmental protection shall closely determine the list of plans and programmes for which strategic EIA shall be mandatory and the list of plans and programmes for which strategic EIA may be required (Art. 5, para. 3).

286. If the plan or programme makes an inseparable part of certain hierarchy structure, the strategic EIA shall be carried out in compliance with guidelines for strategic EIA for plan or programme of higher hierarchy level (Art. 7, para. 2).

1. Preparation Stage

210. Competent planning authority, in accordance with the previously obtained opinion of the competent environmental protection authority and other authorities and organizations concerned, makes the decision on the strategic assessment elaboration (Article 9).[287] In accordance with the procedure set forth by the Law, the competent planning authority decides on selection of the strategic assessment report developer.[288]

211. The competent planning authority has an obligation to request, in preparation for the decision on strategic assessment elaboration or the decision on non-elaboration of the strategic assessment, the competent environmental protection authority and other authorities and organizations concerned, to submit their opinions (Article 11).[289]

2. Strategic Assessment Report

212. The strategic assessment report describes, evaluates and assesses the potential significant impact on the environment, which could result from implementation of plans and programmes.[290] It also defines measures for reduction of adverse effects on the environment (Article 12).

213. A strategic assessment report should include particularly the following: (1) the bases of the strategic assessment;[291] (2) the general and specific objectives of

287. However, the competent planning authority may decide not to elaborate the strategic assessment based on the previously obtained opinion of the competent environmental protection authority and other authorities and organizations concerned. According to the data of the Legal and Information System of the RS, from 2009 to the end of 2023, 177 decisions were made on the creation of SEA (spatial plans of special purpose areas, regional spatial plans, general principles of forest management, water management plans, etc.), or a decision to does not approach the creation of the SEA.

288. The strategic assessment report developer can be legal or natural person, inscribed in the corresponding Register as entitled to execute activities related to spatial planning and elaboration of plan documents, or town planning and elaboration of town plans (Art. 10, para. 2).

289. The submission deadline for opinions is fifteen days from the receipt of the request for opinion submission. If it is not submitted within this period, it shall be considered that no comments to the proposed content of the decision on strategic assessment elaboration, or the draft decision on non-elaboration of the strategic assessment, were submitted.

290. Article 3, point 3 defines 'strategic assessment report' as a part of documentation that is attached to plans or programmes and that includes the identification, description and assessment of potential significant effects on the environment caused by implementation of plans and programmes, as well as alternatives considered and adopted based on the objectives and area occupied by plans and programmes.

291. According to Art. 13, the background information in the strategic assessment shall include: (1) the short outline of the content and objectives of plans and programmes and relationship with other plans and programmes; (2) the outline of the current status and quality of the environment in the area that the report refers to; (3) the characteristics of the environment in areas likely to be exposed to significant impact; (4) the environmental protection issues and problems that have been considered in plans and programmes and the outline of reasons for omission of certain issues and problems out of the assessment procedure; (5) the outline of the prepared alternative solutions relating

the strategic assessment and selection of indicators; (3) the evaluation of likely impact with the description of measures planned for reduction of adverse effects on the environment; (4) the guidelines for elaboration of lower-level strategic assessments and assessments of environmental impact of projects; (5) the programme of monitoring of environmental status during the execution of plans and programmes (monitoring); (6) the outline of methodology applied and difficulties encountered during the strategic assessment elaboration; (7) the outline of decision-making methods, description of reasons vital for selection of the given plan and programme from the aspect of alternative solutions considered and the outline of methods in which the environmental issues have been included in plans and programmes; (8) the conclusions reached in the process of strategic assessment report elaboration presented in the way understandable for public; and (9) other data of relevance for the strategic assessment.[292]

214. Both general and specific objectives of the strategic assessment are defined on the basis of requests and objectives related to environmental protection in other plans and programmes, environmental protection objectives set at national and international levels, data collected on the status of environment and significant questions, problems and proposals related to environmental protection in plans or programmes (Article 14).[293]

215. The strategic assessment report includes the developed guidelines for plans and programmes at lower hierarchy levels that include the determination of the need for the strategic assessment elaboration and elaboration of assessment of impact of projects on the environment. They also define the environmental protection aspects and other questions of relevance for assessment of impact of lower hierarchy level plans and programmes on the environment.

216. The elements of assessment of possible impacts of plans and programmes on the environment are defined by Article 15. Among these elements are the data on air, water, soil, climate, ionizing and non-ionizing radiation, noise and vibrations, plant and animal life, etc.[294]

---

to the environmental protection in plans and programmes, including the zero alternative solution for plans and programmes and the most favourable solution from the aspect of environmental protection; and (6) the results of previous consultations with authorities and organizations concerned that are relevant from the aspect of objectives and evaluation of potential impact of the strategic assessment.

292. Obligation of the competent planning authority is to provide for participation of authorities and organizations and the public concerned in the procedure of granting the approval for the strategic assessment report in the way set forth by the Law (Art. 12, para. 3).

293. The appropriate indicators that shall be used in the strategic assessment are selected on the basis of defined objectives.

294. Criteria for assessment of possible characteristics of important impacts are defined in Annex I of the Law and criteria for the assessment of the strategic assessment report are given in Annex II.

3. The Decision-Making Procedure

217. First obligation of the competent planning authority in the decision-making procedure is submission of the strategic assessment report (referred to in Article 12) to the authorities and organizations concerned and requesting their opinion.

The competent planning authority must, prior to submission of application for granting the approval for the strategic assessment report, provide participation of the public.[295]

218. The competent planning authority is obliged to compile the report on participation of authorities and organizations and the public concerned (Article 20). The report shall include all opinions referred to in Article 18, paragraph 2, as well as the opinions submitted during the public insight and public debate on plans and programmes and the strategic assessment report referred to in Article 19.[296]

219. The competent planning authority must, after that, submit the strategic assessment report to the competent environmental protection authority for evaluation, with the report on participation of authorities and organizations and the public concerned (Article 21). The competent environmental protection authority shall evaluate the report, based on the criteria contained in Annex II. In accordance with that, the competent environmental protection authority shall approve or refuse the application (Article 22).

4. Exchange of Information on Transboundary Impacts

220. The Ministry responsible for environmental protection has an obligation to conduct the exchange of information on transboundary impact of plans and programmes on the environment (Article 23).[297] Besides that, the Ministry has also obligations:

(1) to inform the authorities and organizations and public concerned about the received information relating to transboundary impact of the proposed plans and programmes of another State in the way set forth in Article 19, paragraph 3 of this Law; and

295. The public shall consider the report, within the procedure of making the plans and programmes available for public insight and during the public debate, if it has not been otherwise provided for by the Law.

296. The report must be compiled within thirty days from the date of the public debate completion, and it shall include the rationale for all the accepted or rejected opinions.

297. In the period 2010–2012, Serbia participated in three transboundary SEAs (the National Energy Programme of Slovenia, the River Basin Management Plan of Croatia, and for the Energy Development Strategy of Montenegro). The only case where Serbia, as a party of origin, notified neighbouring States was in relation to the SEA for the new Energy Sector Development Strategy for the period until 2025 with projections to 2030 (2013). UNECE. 2015, 28.

(2) to take into account the results of consultations and obtained opinions of the authorities and organizations and public concerned when submitting the opinion to the competent authority of another State (Article 24).

221. National legislation is partially harmonized with the Directive 2001/42/EC.[298] Serbia has ratified the Espoo Convention on EIA in a Transboundary Context, the Protocol on the SEA to the Convention on the EIA in a Transboundary Context, and the Cavtat Amendment to the Convention. Serbia planned to achieve full transposition of the SEA Directive in 2017 by adopting amendments to the existing laws and the implementing legislation.[299]

IV. Integrated Pollution Prevention and Control and Risk Management

222. EPL prescribes only general obligations. According to Article 37 of the EPL, 'the operation of new and existent installations that may have negative impact on human health and environment shall require an integrated permit which shall secure the prevention and control on the environmental pollution'. Types of activities and installations, conditions and procedures of granting integrated permit, control and other issues relevant for IPPC shall be governed by special law.

223. The rules for issuance of integrated permits are prescribed by the Law on IPPC (OJ RS, Nos 135/2004, 25/2015, and 109/2021) which contains thirty-five Articles divided into six chapters: Basic Provisions (Articles 1–3); Integrated Permit (Articles 4–9); Permit Granting Procedure (Articles 10–25); Supervision (Articles 26–28); Penalty Provisions (Articles 29–32); and Transitional and Final Provisions (Articles 33–35).[300]

A. *Types of Activities and Installations*

224. Article 4 of the Law prescribes that:

> types of activities and installations, for which the integrated permit shall be granted, shall be sorted according to the level of pollution and risk that such activities may have to human health and the environment, including other technically similar activities that can cause emissions and environmental pollution.
>
> The types of activities and installations relate to both new and existing installations.[301]

298. GOV RS. 2018, 1139. On this subject, *see also* Josimović, Stefanović, Bezbradica, 2017.

299. EC. 2016b, 3. *See also* GOV RS. 2018, 1139.

300. The Law on IPPC regulates 'the conditions and procedure of granting of integrated permits for installations and activities that may have adverse effects on human health, environment or material resources, types of activities and installations, supervision and other issues that are of relevance for environmental pollution prevention and control' (Art. 1).

301. *See* the regulation on kinds of activities and installations for which the integrated permit is issued (OJ RS, No. 84/2005).

B. Competent Authorities

225. The following authorities are competent for granting the permit:

(1) the Ministry responsible for environmental protection (for installations or activities for which the permit or consent for construction and commencement of operation or execution of activities were issued by other competent Ministry);
(2) the provincial authority responsible for environmental protection (for installations or activities for which permit or consent for construction and commencement of operation or execution of activities were issued by other competent provincial authority); and
(3) the LSG authority responsible for environmental protection (for installations or activities for which permit or consent for construction and commencement of operation or execution of activities were issued by other competent LSG authority).

C. IPPC Permit

226. The IPPC permit is the key element of the system established by the Law on IPPC.[302] The operators[303] have an obligation to obtain the permit for the operation of installation and execution of activities from the competent authority (Article 7). They must submit relevant documents together with the permit granting application. According to the amendments to the Law (2021), the competent authority will issue a permit for existing facilities and activities no later than 31 December 2024 (Article 2 of the Law on Amendments to the Law on IPPC (OJ RS, No. 109/21).

227. Article 2, point 10 of the Law on IPPC describes 'integrated permit' as the decision of the competent authority adopted in the written form, approving the start-up of the whole or of a part of installation, or the execution of the activity, the integral part of which is the documentation containing the prescribed conditions which guarantee that such installation or activity is in compliance with the requirements prescribed by this Law. The competent authority keeps the register of the permits granted, as a part of the environmental information system, which is available to

302. Besides the IPPC permit, there are several other permits related to the environment: land-use permits, construction permits (accompanied by the EIA procedure), operation permits, water use permits and permits for the use of other natural resources (fish, medicinal herbs, timber, game, etc.). There is no emission permits for air pollution. Authorities competent for issuing permits are the respective ministries, APs, municipalities or appointed institutions.

303. Operator is defined as 'any natural or legal person which operates or controls the installation in accordance with the regulations, or to whom decisive economic power over the technical functioning of the installation has been delegated and onto the name of which the integrated permit is granted' (Art. 2, point 15).

public (Article 25). The Law regulating the general administrative procedure shall accordingly be applied in the case of the elements of the procedure not regulated by the Law on IPPC (Article 25a).

228. The application for permit issuance, which the operator submits to the competent authority, should contain data on emission sources and the nature and quantity of foreseen emissions to water, air or soil, originating from installations (Article 8 of the Law on IPPC).

229. Participation of organizations and the public regarding the process of permit issuance is regulated by Article 8 of the Law.[304] Competent authorities are obliged to inform authorities and organizations in various domains (agriculture, water management, forests, planning, building, transport, energy, mining, etc.), as well as authorities of local governments, on whose territory the activities are planned or the installations are situated. They are allowed to submit their opinions which have to be taken into account in the decision-making process.[305]

230. In the next phase, the competent authority is obliged to prepare the draft permit within forty-five days from the date of receipt of the complete permit granting application. During the drafting, the competent authority shall consider the opinions of other authorities and organizations and of the public concerned. Besides that, the competent authority is obliged to inform other authorities and organizations and the public concerned about the draft permit and possibilities of their insight into the enclosed documentation and to submit the draft permit to the above-mentioned parties, on their request, within five days from the date of receipt of such request (Article 12).

D. The Role of the Technical Commission

231. The Technical Commission, established by the decision of the competent authority, has to make assessment of conditions prescribed in the draft permit.[306] It includes the obligation to consider the operator's application and the attached documentation, draft permit, opinions of other authorities and organizations and of the public concerned, as well as the opinions obtained in the procedure of exchange of information and consultations on transboundary impact (Article 14).

232. The competent authority makes a decision on permit granting on the basis of the operator's application, the attached documentation, reports and evaluation of the Technical Commission, as well as on the basis of the obtained opinions of other

---

304. More precise provisions are prescribed by Art. 23, regarding the ways of informing other authorities, organizations and public which is explicitly related to Arts 11, 12 and 15.
305. Other authorities, organizations and representatives of public concerned may submit their opinions to the competent authority within fifteen days from the date of receipt of information.
306. The document on establishment of the Technical Commission defines its composition, tasks and other issues of relevance for the work of Technical Commission (Art. 13, para. 2).

authorities and organizations and the public concerned within 120 days from the date of receipt of complete permit granting application.[307] According to the provision of Article 15, paragraph 5, the competent authority shall refuse the permit granting application in cases where:

(1) the installation for execution of activities for which the permit is required does not satisfy the prescribed permit conditions;
(2) based on the data and documentation contained in the application, it concludes that conditions for implementation of the set environmental quality standards are not fulfilled; and when
(3) the application contains incorrect data that are of relevance for permit granting.

E. Conditions Determined by Permit

233. In accordance with Article 16, the permit shall prescribe conditions for operation of installations and execution of activities and operator's obligations, depending on the nature of activities and their impact on the environment.[308] The conditions include the following:

(1) implementation of the Best Available Techniques (BAT)[309] or other technical requirements and measures;
(2) measures contained in the EIA study or study of the current status;
(3) Emission Limit Values (ELVs) for pollutants determined for the relevant installation;
(4) measures necessary for air, water and soil protection;[310]
(5) measures relating to management of waste generated during the operation of the installation;

---

307. In exceptional cases, based on the operator's request or on the initiative of the competent authority, the period set in para. 1 of this Article may be extended, but not for more than 240 days from the date of receipt of the complete application (Art. 15, para. 2).
308. When environmental quality standards require stricter conditions than those achievable by the use of the BAT, the permit shall contain additional measures for implementation of these standards. At the same time, the Law prescribes that the permit may contain the temporary exemption from compliance with the prescribed conditions in case that the adopted programme of rehabilitation provides for implementation of measures leading to reduction of pollution and fulfilment of conditions (Art. 16, paras 3 and 5).
309. The notion BAT means the most effective and advanced stage in the development of activities and their methods of operation which enable more suitable implementation of particular techniques for compliance with the ELVs prescribed to prevent and, where that is not practicable, generally to reduce emissions and impact on the environment as a whole. Certain elements of the term 'BAT' shall have the following meanings: technique means the way in which the installation is designed, built, maintained, operated and decommissioned or closed, including the technology used; available means techniques that have been developed on a scale which allows the implementation in the relevant industry sector, under economically and technically acceptable conditions, including costs and benefits, as long as they are reasonably accessible to the operator; the best means the most effective in achieving a high general level of protection of the environment as a whole (Art. 2, point 14).
310. According to the provisions of Art. 33, the Government should define, in the period of six months after the IPPC comes in force, the thresholds values of emissions into air and water for the first five

(6) measures relating to reduction of noise and vibrations;
(7) measures relating to the efficient energy consumption;
(8) requirements relating to monitoring of emission;
(9) measures for prevention of accidents and elimination of their consequences;
(10) reduction of pollution including the transboundary pollution of the environment;
(11) measures planned for commencement of operation, for momentary stoppages in cases of disruption in functioning of the installations as well as for the termination of operations;
(12) undertaking measures of protection of the environment after the final termination of activities aimed at avoiding the risk of pollution and returning the site to a satisfactory status;
(13) method and frequency of reporting and scope of data contained in the report that shall be submitted to the competent authority in accordance with the regulations;
(14) results of the review of conditions and obligations set by the permit;
(15) other specific requirements.[311]

234. The validity period of the permit may be extended at the request of the operator, according to the provision in Article 21, but the issued permit is subject to reconsideration at least twice during its validity (Article 18).[312] The competent authority may amend the conditions set by the permit in cases of permit review by duty and in cases of planned changes to the installation or its operation that do not mean substantial changes in the sense of this Law (Article 20).[313]

F. Exchange of Information on Transboundary Impacts

235. In accordance with Article 24, the Ministry exchanges information on transboundary impact of operation of installations and activities on the environment. Consultations on transboundary impact shall be organized in the way and

---

years, of adaptation of certain branches of the economy to the provisions of this Law. Determination of ELVs still remains to be done and is in connection with adoption of new laws concerning air and water protection which are being drafted.

311. When defined conditions are concerned, operator has obligations prescribed in Art. 17 of the Law on IPPC, including the following: (1) to act in compliance with conditions set by the permit; (2) to submit the results of monitoring to the competent authority; (3) to inform the competent authority about all changes in operation, namely functioning of the installation or on accident, with possible visible effects on the environment or human health; (4) to submit to the competent authority the annual report on execution of activities that the permit was issued for; (5) to inform the competent authority on the planned change of operator; and (6) to undertake all measures that the competent authority set upon expiry of the permit validity.

312. The competent authority starts the review procedure officially or at the request of the operator (Art. 18, para. 2). In case that the competent authority initiates the permit reconsideration procedure, it shall inform the operator about the reasons for such action and request him to submit the data (Art. 18, para. 4).

313. The competent authority may request the operator to submit new application for permit granting, if too many changes aggravate the efficient control of activities (Art. 20, para. 2).

within periods set by arrangements between the competent State authorities based on the principles of reciprocity and equality.

236. There are two elements concerning the information exchange on transboundary impact:

(1) first, when the operation of certain installation is likely to have significant adverse effects on the environment in another State, or when the State likely to be significantly affected requests, the Ministry shall submit the information to another State, requesting its opinion; and
(2) second, the Ministry is obliged to inform another State, which has been consulted in the decision-making procedure, about the decision on the permit granting or the decision on refusal of application for its granting.[314]

237. Apart from the above-mentioned, two additional obligations of the Ministry have been established concerning the exchange of information on transboundary impact:

(1) to inform the public concerned on the received information on transboundary impact of installations and activities in another State in the way set forth in Article 23, paragraph 1 of this Law;[315]
(2) to take into consideration the results of consultations and the obtained opinions of the public concerned in giving its opinions to the competent authority of another State.

G. Sub-legal Acts

238. It should be added that, based on the IPPC, the following important sub-legal Acts have been adopted:

- Regulation on kinds of activities and installations for which the integrated permit is issued (OJ RS, No. 84/2005).
- Regulation on criteria for defining the BAT, for application of quality standards, as well as for defining threshold values of emissions in the integrated permit (OJ RS, No. 84/2005).

---

314. By means of submitting the information on the following: (1) the content of the decision on permit granting or decision to refuse the permit granting application and (2) the reasons that the decision has been based on, including the information on the public participation procedure (Art. 24, para. 3).

315. According to Art. 23, para. 1: 'The competent authority shall inform other authorities and organizations and public in cases referred to in Arts 11, 12 and 15 of this Law through the public media, publishing the information about them in at least one local newspaper published in the territory that will be affected by the impact of activities and installations and on the Internet.'

- Regulations on contents of programme of measures of adaptation of work of existing installation or activities according to the prescribed conditions (OJ RS, No. 84/2005).
- Regulation on determining the Programme on the timetable of filing applications for the issuance of integrated permits (OJ RS, No. 108/2008).
- Rulebook on content and method of keeping the Register of the issued permits (OJ RS, No. 69/2005).
- Rulebook on the content, appearance, and manner of submitting a request and issuing an integrated permit (OJ RS, Nos 30/06 and 32/16, 44/18 – other law, and 4/24).
- Rulebook on the integrated permit content and presentation (OJ RS, Nos 30/06 and 4/24).

V. Risk Management

239. Besides the Law on IPPC, several other regulations in the field of risk[316] management are relevant. First of all, the EPL contain provisions that are directly relevant for protection from chemical accidents (Articles 58–63).[317] According to Article 60j of the Law, the operator shall inform without delay the Ministry, LSG unit and authorities responsible for acting in emergency situations of the chemical accident,[318] in accordance with regulations governing protection and recovery, in particular of the following: the circumstances in connection with the chemical accident, present dangerous substances, available data for the assessment of consequences of the chemical accident for humans and the environment and of the undertaken urgent measures.[319] Apart from that, operator shall inform the responsible authorities of the subsequently collected data that affect the previously found

316. Risk is defined as 'a certain level of probability that certain activity, directly or indirectly, shall cause danger towards the environment, life and human health' (Art. 3, point 23 of the EPL).
317. However, provisions of Arts 58–61b (and Art. 38) of this Law shall not apply to the following: military installations; accidents caused by ionizing radiation; transportation of dangerous substances in road, rail, water, air and sea traffic, and transportation outside the establishments encompassed by this Law, including loading and unloading or transportation to and from other means of transportation on wharfs, piers or marshalling yards; transportation of dangerous substances by pipelines including pumping stations, outside the Seveso installation or establishment encompassed by this Law; accidents in the course of research and exploitation of mineral raw materials, except if raw materials are chemically or thermally processed or stored, and they contain dangerous substances in the prescribed quantities; locations of waste materials landfills, except active waste barren soil including artificial lakes and dams, which contain dangerous substances and in particular those that derive from chemical and thermal mineral processing (Art. 61v).
318. 'Accident' is a sudden and uncontrolled event or series of events which occur with uncontrolled release, leakage or dispersion of dangerous substances in the process of production, circulation, utilization, transport, processing, storage, disposal or long-term inadequate storage. This term shall not cover: military facilities; nuclear accidents; GMOs; transport of dangerous substances through pipe systems, including pump stations; accidents during the research and exploitation of mineral raw materials; damages to dams, with an exception of consequences from industrial accidents caused by such damages (Art. 3, point 24).
319. The Ministry shall conduct supervision and control of the fulfilment of obligations of operators (Art. 60j, para. 5).

facts and conclusions and shall inform the responsible authorities within a reasonable period of the planned measures for removing mid-term and long-term consequences of a chemical accident and for the prevention of reoccurrence of an accident (Article 60j, paragraphs 2 and 3).[320]

240. In the case of accident, depending upon its scope, within or outside the plant and estimated consequences, which may cause direct or deferred threats towards human health and environment, the site of endangerment of environment shall be proclaimed, and the public shall be informed of the measures taken.[321]

241. In order to prevent further spread of pollution caused by an accident, legal and natural person is obliged to immediately take, at his own cost, rehabilitation measures planned for protection. If the polluter, who is responsible for the accident, is determined subsequently, the authority that paid the cost of elimination of the consequences of environmental pollution shall claim the reimbursement (Article 63).

242. Pursuant to the EPL, Article 58, an operator of Seveso installation, that is, the complex where activities are performed that might include one or more dangerous matters, in quantities higher or equal to the prescribed, is obligated to submit to the Ministry of Environment, Mining and Spatial Planning (MEMSP) a notification and to create accident prevention policy or safety report and accident prevention plan, depending on the quantities of dangerous substances used for performance of the activities and to take measures for prevention of chemical accident and limiting of impact of the accident to human lives and health and environment.[322]

243. The operator that is obliged to prepare the Policy for Accident Prevention shall, prior to preparing the Policy for Accident Prevention, submit to the Ministry the notification on: (1) new Seveso installation or establishment at least three months before commencing operation; (2) existing Seveso installation or establishment six months from the day this Law comes into force at the latest; (3) existing Seveso installation or establishment the activities of which were such that the dangerous substances were present in quantities lower than prescribed, in case of increase in quantities of dangerous substances up to the quantities prescribed in Article 58 of this Law, within three months from the day of change at the latest; (4) the permanent termination of operation of Seveso installation or establishment, as

320. The operator shall be obliged to implement urgent mid-term and long-term measures for removing the consequences of the chemical accident, as well as to provide, following the analysis of all aspects of the chemical accident, recommendations for the future prevention measures (Art. 60j, para. 4).
321. State of endangerment shall be proclaimed by the Ministry, the authority of AP, or unit of local self-governance. For the accidents with transboundary effects, the state of the endangerment shall be proclaimed by the Government (Art. 62, paras 2 and 3).
322. The Minister shall prescribe list of dangerous substances and their quantities and criteria for determining types of documents prepared by the operator (Art. 58, para. 2) and content of the Policy for Accident Prevention (Art. 58a, para. 4).

well as in case of modification of Seveso installation or establishment, or any change that may affect the possibility of chemical accident occurrence (Article 59, paragraph 1).[323]

244. According to Article 60a, the operator referred to in Article 58 of this Law shall be obliged to prepare and submit to the Ministry the Report on Safety[324] and the Plan on Protection from Accident:[325] (1) for new Seveso installation or establishment at least three months before commencing operation; (2) for existing Seveso installation or establishment at the latest within eighteen months from the day this Law comes into force; (3) for existing Seveso installation or establishment the activities of which were such that the dangerous substances were present in quantities lower than prescribed, in case of increase of quantities of dangerous substances up to the quantities prescribed in Article 58 of this Law, within six months from the day of change at the latest.

245. The operator shall periodically review the Report on Safety and as needed update it: (1) at least every five years; (2) on its own initiative or upon request of the Ministry due to the new facts obtained based on the analysis of other chemical accidents or evaded accidents (Article 60a, paragraph 4).[326]

246. The operator referred to in Article 58 of this Law shall ensure that the information on safety measures and procedures in case of chemical accident from the Plan on Protection from Accident is submitted to all legal persons and public institutions (schools, hospitals, etc.), as well as to natural persons, that may be affected by the consequences of a chemical accident (Article 60b).[327]

323. The Minister shall prescribe content of the Notification referred to in para. 1 of this Article (Art. 59, para. 2).
324. Report on Safety shall contain, in particular, the following: information on the system of management and organization of operator for the purpose of preventing chemical accident; description of location of Seveso installation or establishment; description of Seveso installation or establishment; analysis of risk from chemical accident and manner of its prevention; protective measures and intervention measures for limiting consequences of chemical accident; listing of dangerous substances and other (Art. 60, para. 1).
325. The Plan on Protection from Accident shall contain in particular measures that are undertaken within the Seveso installation or establishment in case of chemical accident or in case circumstances arise which may cause chemical accident (Art. 60, para. 2).
326. In the event of modification of the work process, change of nature or quantity of dangerous substance or other changes that may affect the danger of occurrence of chemical accident, the operator must immediately enter changes in the Report on Safety and the Plan on Protection from Accident and submit them to the Ministry, and in the event the changes refer to the modification of installations or storehouses, prior to introducing such modifications. The operator shall be obliged to review, test and, if needed, update the Plan on Protection from Accident at least every three years (Art. 60a, paras 5 and 6).
327. Information referred to in para. 1 of this Article shall be updated every three years, and especially in case circumstances referred to in Art. 60a, para. 5 of this Law arise. Updated information referred to in para. 1 of this Article must be publicly available. The period between two regular submissions of information to the public may not be longer than five years (Art. 60b, paras 2–4).

247. The operator shall ensure that the Report on Safety and the list of dangerous substances that are present in the Seveso installation or establishment are publicly available.[328] The responsible authority shall ensure public availability, organize presentation and administer public debate regarding the Report on Safety in the procedure of deciding on providing consent on the Report on Safety (Article 60c, paragraphs 1 and 2). The responsible authority shall inform the person submitting the report, interested bodies and organizations and the public of the time and place for the public insight, public presentation and public debate on the Report on Safety within seven days from the date of the receipt of the Report on Safety (paragraph 4).[329]

248. Apart from the above-mentioned, EPL regulates following issues: Evidence in the Report on Safety (Article 60d); Evidence in the Plan on Protection from Accident (Article 60e); Consent on the Report on Safety and the Plan on Protection from Accident (Article 60f); Decision Prohibiting Operation or Start-Up of Seveso Installation (Article 60g); Appointment of the Special Working Group (Article 60h); Obligation of Keeping Records (Article 60i); Register of Installations and Register of Reported Accidents (Article 60k); Obligations of Responsible Authorities (Article 61); Notification on Operators or Seveso Installations or Establishments the Activities of Which May Cause Chemical Accident with Transboundary Effects (Article 61a); and Obligation to Submit Notification of the Responsible Authority of Other Country (Article 61b).

249. Following legal and sub-legal Acts also deserve mentioning:

- Law on Disaster Risk Reduction and Emergency Situation Management (OJ RS, No. 87/18).
- Law on Critical Infrastructure (OJ RS, No. 87/18).
- Law on Protection from Fire (OJ RS, Nos 111/2009, 20/15, 87/18 and 87/18 – other law).
- Regulation on the obligations of the subjects of the disaster risk reduction and emergency management system in the process of creating the Disaster Risk Register, the method of creating the Disaster Risk Register, and data entry (OJ RS, No. 122/20).
- Regulation on the content, manner of preparation and obligations of entities in connection with the preparation of disaster risk assessment and protection and rescue plans (OJ RS, No. 102/2020).
- Regulation on civil protection units, purpose, tasks, mobilization and manner of use (OJ RS, No. 84/2020).

---

328. The person submitting the Report on Safety may be allowed, upon approval of the responsible authority, not to provide for public availability and presentation of certain parts of the report due to protecting industrial, commercial and personal secret, public safety or defence of the country (Art. 60c, para. 3).
329. The regulation on the procedure of public availability, presentation and public debate regarding the study on EIA shall apply *mutatis mutandis* on the procedure of public availability, presentation and public debate concerning the Report on Safety (Art. 60c, para. 7).

– Regulation on the composition, manner and organization of the work of emergency headquarters (OJ RS, No. 27/2020).
– Regulation on the content and manner of drafting a disaster risk reduction plan (OJ RS, No. 21/2020).
– Rulebook on how to maintain shelters and adapt communal, traffic, and other underground facilities for sheltering the population (OJ RS, No. 4/24).
– Rulebook on the organization and working methods of fire-rescue units (OJ RS, No. 66/21).
– Rulebook on the method of training, training, curricula, and programs of subjects and forces of the disaster risk reduction and emergency management system (OJ RS, No. 128/20).
– Rulebook on the work of the Commissioner and Deputy Commissioner for Civil Protection and the criteria for their appointment (OJ RS, No. 102/2020).
– Rulebook on uniforms and insignia of civil protection, insignia of functions and specialties, and identity card of members of civil protection (OJ RS, Nos 32/20, 83/20).
– Rulebook on the manner of preparation and content of the Accident Protection Plan (OJ RS, No. 41/2019).
– Rulebook on the manner of keeping the Register of Companies and Legal Entities Handling Dangerous Substances (OJ RS, No. 34/2019).
– Rulebook on the type and quantity of hazardous substances on the basis of which the Accident Protection Plan is made (OJ RS, No. 34/2019).
– Rulebook on the content of the notice about new Seveso facility or complex, existing Seveso facility or complex and permanent cessation of Seveso facility or complex (OJ RS, No. 41/10).
– Rulebook on the content of accident prevention policy and the content and methodology of the Report on the safety and accident protection plan (OJ RS, No. 41/10).
– Rulebook on the list of hazardous substances and their amounts and criteria for determining the type of documents produced by the operator of the Seveso facility or complex (OJ RS, Nos 41/10, 51/15 and 50/18).
– Rulebook on the manner of notice, i.e., exchange of data on Seveso installation, i.e., establishment, whose activities may cause chemical accidents with cross-border effects (OJ RS, No. 26/13), etc.

250. Serbia ratified the UNECE Convention on the Transboundary Effects of Industrial Accidents on 31 July 2009.[330]

251. According to the EC report (2019) regarding industrial pollution and risk management, ‘ alignment with most of the EU *acquis* is at an early stage across industry, including as concerns the Industrial Emissions Directive’.[331] ‘ Inspection

330. *See* https://treaties.un.org/pages/ViewDetails.aspx?src=TREATY&mtdsg_no=XXVII-6&chapter=27&clang=_en (4.1.2024).
331. EC. 2023, 136. ‘The Kostolac B thermal power plant is Europe’s biggest sulphur dioxide polluter. Its desulphurisation plant started operating in January 2023.’

and law enforcement remain areas of concern.'[332] It was planned to achieve full harmonization with the Directive 2010/75/EU (IED) by 2018, by adopting amendments to the existing laws, adopting new laws and new by-laws.[333] The Seveso III Directive (Directive 2012/18/EU on the control of major accident hazards involving dangerous substances) is at an initial stage of transposition. Full legislative alignment is planned by 2025 through the adoption of a Law on the control of major accident hazards involving dangerous substances and several rulebooks transposing the relevant annexes.[334]

252. 'Serbia needs to increase its capacity for managing the integrated permitting processes. The quality of IPPC permits should be improved. Serbia should enforce the polluter pays principle in order to encourage industry to invest in green solutions.'[335]

§2. Access to Information and Public Participation in the Field of the Environment

I. International Law

253. A key issue when environmental protection is concerned is the right of the public to participate in decision-making in the field of the environment as well as the right to be informed.[336] These rights have been regulated at the international level by the 1998 Convention on Access to Environmental Information, Public Participation in Decision-making and Access to Justice in Environmental Matters, also known as the Aarhus Convention (AC).[337] Serbia ratified the AC on 31 July 2009 (OJ RS – International treaties, No. 38/09).[338]

Besides that, Serbia ratified the Convention's Protocol on Pollution Release and Transfer Registers (PRTR) – in force from 23 November 2011 (OJ RS – International treaties, No. 8/11).[339] Almaty amendment (2005) Serbia has not ratified.[340]

---

332. *Ibid.* ' Serbia has a good legal and policy framework for disaster risk management based on the Law on disaster risk reduction and emergency management. Revision of the law is planned in 2023 to address minor shortcomings and introduce new instruments to empower those involved at local level.' *Ibid.*, 137.
333. EC. 2016b, 11.
334. GOV RS. 2022f, 318.
335. EC. 2023, 136.
336. UNECE. 2007, 33.
337. For additional information *see*: Sharman. 2023; Tubić. 2012.
338. For the Serbian National Implementation Report (2017), *see* https://www.unece.org/env/pp/reports_trc_implementation_2017.html (4.1.2024). For the Serbian National Implementation Report (2021), *see* https://aarhusclearinghouse.unece.org/national-reports/reports?field_nr_report_language_aux_2_value=en&field_nr_report_language_aux_value=en&field_nr_party_target_id_verf%5B%5D=17621&combine= (4.1.2024).
339. Serbia started with the implementation of the PRTR Protocol and E-PRTR directive in 2008. Information system was developed in 2012, and GIS was developed in 2016. For additional information *see*: http://77.46.150.218/prtrportal/?lang=de (2.2.2024).
340. https://treaties.un.org/pages/ViewDetails.aspx?src=TREATY&mtdsg_no=XXVII-13-b&chapter=27&clang=_en (4.1.2024).

II. National Law

254. The public participation as well as access to information has been regulated on national level.[341] A number of legal and sub-legal Acts deserve mentioning.[342] In the first place, it is the Constitution of Serbia (2006) which declares that citizens have the right to be informed about the state of the environment apart from the right to a healthy environment. Two provisions of the Constitution specifically indicate this.[343]

255. Publicity of work of State authorities[344] is one of the basic principles of the work of State administration, according to the Law on State Administration (OJ RS, Nos 79/05, 101/07, 95/10, 99/14, 30/18 – other law, and 47/18). Article 11 of the Law prescribes that 'The work of state administration authorities shall be public. State administration authorities shall be obliged to enable the public to have access to their work in accordance with the law regulating free access to information of public importance.'[345] Public debate is subject of regulation of Article 77 of the Law. 'A ministry and a special organization shall be obliged to undertake public debate in the procedure of preparation of a law which essentially changes the legal regime in one field or which regulates issues of particular relevance for public.'

256. Article 8 of the Law on Civil Servants (OJ RS, Nos 79/05, 81/05 – correction, 83/05 – correction, 64/07, 67/07 – correction, 116/08, 104/09, 99/14, 94/17, 95/18, 157/20, and 142/22) prescribes that 'Information on work of civil servants shall be accessible to the public in accordance with the law that regulates the free access to information of public interest.'

257. Several other documents deserve mentioning: The 2004 Law on Free Access to Information of Public Interest (OJ. RS, Nos 120/2004, 54/2007, 104/2009, 36/2010, and 105/2021) and Instruction for the creation and publication of the Information Booklet on Public Authority Work (OJ RS, No. 68/2010). Both documents entitle citizens to enquire about the work of government bodies in general,

---

341. For more information on some open issues in administrative-judicial practice, *see* Lilić, Drenovak. 2009. Historically, citizen participation has been known in the practice of urban development planning in the Republic of Serbia since 1949, when the Basic Decree on the General Urban Plan (OJ FNRJ, No. 78/49) was adopted. GOV RS. 2019b, Ch. 4.1.3.2. Participation of citizens.

342. In addition, the general regulations governing the field of information and advertising include, *inter alia*, the following laws: Law on Electronic Media (OJ RS, No. 92/23), Law on Public Information and Media (OJ RS, No. 92/23), Law on Advertising (OJ RS, Nos 6/16, 52/19 – other law), Law on Public Media Services (OJ RS, Nos 83/14, 103/15, 108/16, 161/20, 129/21, 142/22, 92/23), etc.

343. 'Everyone shall have the right to be informed accurately, fully, and timely about issues of public importance. The media shall have the obligation to respect this right' (Art. 51, para. 1), and 'Everyone shall have the right to a healthy environment and the right to timely and full information about the state of the environment' (Art. 74, para. 1).

344. On this subject, *see* Ignjatović, J., & Đorđević, S. 2006.

345. Similar provision is also provided in Art. 76, by which it is prescribed that 'State administration authorities shall be obliged to inform the public about their work through means of public information or through other relevant means. Employees who are authorized to prepare information and data connected to informing the public shall be responsible for their accuracy and punctuality.'

including those in the environmental field. They can require such bodies to report to the public about their responsibilities, organizational structure, budget, services, public procedures, procedure for requesting information, and so on. Citizens are also given the possibility to voice their opinions about the Government's work and procedures.

258. In accordance with Article 5, 'everyone shall have the right to be informed whether a public authority holds specific information of public importance and/or whether such is otherwise accessible to him/her (paragraph 1)'.[346]

259. Information of public importance, within the meaning of this Law, is information held by a public authority body, created during or relating to the operation of a public authority body, which is contained in a document and concerns anything the public has a justified interest to know (Article 2, paragraph 1).[347] For information to be considered information of public importance, it shall be irrelevant whether the source of information is a public authority or another person, which medium carries the document containing the information (paper, tape, film, electronic media, etc.), on which date the information was created or in which way the information was obtained, nor shall any other similar properties of such information bear any relevance for this purpose (Article 2, paragraph 2).

260. A public authority shall, without delay, and within fifteen days of receipt of a request at the latest, inform an applicant whether it holds the requested information, grant him/her access to the document containing the requested information or issue or send to the applicant a copy of the document, as the case may be. A copy of a document shall be deemed to be sent to an applicant on the day it leaves the office of the public authority from which the information was requested (Article 16, paragraph 1).[348]

261. For the purpose of exercising the right of access to information of public importance held by public authorities, this Law shall provide for the establishment

346. Everyone shall have the right to access information of public importance by being allowed to examine a document containing information of public importance, by being entitled to make a copy of that document, and by being entitled to receive a copy of such document on request, by mail, fax, electronic mail or otherwise (Art. 5, para. 2).

347. Justified public interest to know within the meaning of Art. 2 of this Law shall be deemed to exist whenever information held by a public authority concerns a threat to, or protection of, *public health and the environment*, while with regard to other information held by a public authority, it shall be deemed that justified public interest to know within the meaning of Art. 2 of this Law exists unless the public authority concerned proves otherwise (Art. 4).

348. However, if a request relates to information which can reasonably be assumed to bear on the protection of a person's life or freedom and/or the protection of public health and *the environment*, a public authority must inform the applicant it holds such information, grant access to the document containing the requested information or issue a copy of the document to the applicant, as the case may be, within forty-eight hours of receipt of the request (Art. 16, para. 2).

of the institution of the Commissioner for Information of Public Importance (Commissioner: CIPIPDP)[349] as an autonomous government body independent in the exercise of its powers (Article 1, paragraph 2).[350] According to the Commissioner's report for 2022, ' the largest number of requests for information in 2022 concerned the budget (4625), followed by environmental protection (1141) and public health (1195), etc.'[351]

262. The basic law governing the protection of personal data is the Law on Personal Data Protection (OJ RS, Nos 97/2008, 104/2009, 68/12 CC and 107/12) which entered into force on 4 November 2008. Article 1, paragraph 3 of the Law prescribes that the affairs related to personal data protection are performed by the CIPIPDP as an autonomous State authority, independent in the performance of their duty. Every natural person shall be entitled to personal data protection regardless of their nationality and residence, race, age, gender, language, religion, political and other affiliations, ethnicity, social background and status, wealth, birth, education, social position or any other personal characteristic (Article 1, paragraph 2).[352]

263. Pursuant to Article 14, data shall be collected from data subjects and from public authorities authorized under the Law to collect such data. Data may also be collected from third parties if, *inter alia*, data are collected for the purpose of achieving or protecting the vital interests of a data subject, in particular his/her life, health and physical integrity (paragraph 2, point 5).[353]

264. Data Secrecy Law (OJ RS, No. 104/2009) regulate a single system of the classification and protection of secret data which are of interest for the national security and public safety, defence, internal and foreign affairs of the RS; protection of foreign classified data; access to classified data and their declassification; competence of authorities and oversight of the implementation of this Law; as well as

349. For more information, *see* https://www.poverenik.rs/en/data-protection/legal-framework.html (4.1.2024). *See also* Part V Juridical Actions of Individuals, Ch. 3 Other Forms of Juridical Actions of Individuals.

350. The number of complaints formally lodged with the Commissioner on the grounds of violation of freedom of information remains continually high, with an upward trend year-on-year. In 2022, the Commissioner received the highest number of complaints ever during one calendar year since its formation, namely 9,219 complaints, while 2,475 pending complaints had been carried forward from the preceding year. CIPIPDP. 2023, 75.

351. *Ibid.*, 73.

352. 'Personal data' means any information relating to a natural person, regardless of the form of its presentation or the medium used (paper, tape, film, electronic media, etc.), regardless on whose order, on whose behalf or for whose account such information is stored, regardless of the date of its creation or the place of its storage, regardless of the way in which such information is learned (directly, by listening, watching, etc. or indirectly, by accessing a document containing the information, etc.) and regardless of any other characteristic of such information (data) (Art. 3, point 1).

353. The right to notification, access and copy may be restricted in the following cases, *inter alia*, if the provision of such information would seriously prejudice privacy or a vital interest of the data subject, in particular his/her life, health and physical integrity (Art. 23, para. 1, point 8).

accountability for non-implementation of obligations arising from this Law, and other issues of importance for data secrecy protection (Article 1).[354]

A. The 2004 EPL

265. The 2004 EPL contains a number of provisions of systemic character relevant for access to environmental information and public participation (Articles 78, 80, 81, 81a and 82). First of all, Amendments to the EPL (2016) introduced the definitions of the following notions: 'environmental information',[355] 'information held for a public authority', 'applicant for environmental information', and 'information concerning environmental threats or environmental protection' (Article 3 points 33a, 33b, 33d and 33e).

Generally speaking, State authorities, authorities of the AP, authorities of LSG units and authorized and other organizations shall be obliged to regularly, timely, fully and objectively inform the public on the state of the environment, namely occurrences that are observed within the monitoring of the pollutant level and emission, as well as warning measures or development of the pollution which may pose a threat to human life and health, in accordance with this Law and other regulations

354. 'Classified data' means any data of interest for the Republic of Serbia, which have been classified and for which a level of secrecy has been determined by law, other regulations or decisions of a competent authority brought under law (Art. 2, point 2); 'Data of interest for the Republic of Serbia' means any data or documents in possession of a public authority, related to territorial integrity and sovereignty, protection of the constitutional order, human and minority rights and freedoms, national security and public safety, defence, internal affairs and foreign affairs (Art. 2, point 1); 'Foreign classified data' means any data delivered to the Republic of Serbia by another country or an international organization, committing the Republic of Serbia to keep them as classified data; as well as classified data arising from cooperation between the Republic of Serbia and other countries, international organizations and other international entities, under an international agreement concluded by the Republic of Serbia with another country, international organization or other international entity (Art. 2, point 3).

355. Similarly as it makes the Aarhus Convention, the EPL defines the notion of environmental information as follows: all information in written, visual, aural, electronic or other material form, held by or for a public authority, on: (1) the state of environmental factors such as air and atmosphere, water, land, soil, regions and natural areas, including swamp, inshore, river and lake areas, biodiversity and its components, geodiversity and geological inheritance, GMOs, and interaction of these factors; (2) factors such as substances, energy, noise, radiation or waste, including radioactive waste, emissions, discharges and other releases into the environment affecting or likely to affect the elements of the environment referred to in subpoint 1 of this point; (3) measures (including administrative measures) such as public policies, strategies, legislation, plans, programmes, environmental agreements, and activities affecting or likely to affect the elements and factors referred to in subpoints 1 and 2 of this point, and established measures or activities for the protection of these factors; (4) reports on the implementation of environmental legislation; (5) cost-benefit analysis, economic analysis and assumptions used within the framework of the measures and activities referred to in subpoint 3 of this point; (6) the state of human health and safety, including the threatened food webs, and, if necessary, conditions of human life, immovable cultural property and their protected environment, and construction facilities, in as much as they are or might be affected by the state of environmental factors referred to in subpoint 1 of this point, through such factors, the state of any factors referred to in subpoints 2 and 3 of this point (Art. 3, point 33a).

(Article 78, paragraph 1). However, access to environmental information shall be exercised in accordance with the Law on Free Access to Information of Public Importance (paragraph 2).[356]

266. Article 81 of the Law prescribes that:

> In accordance with law, public and the public concerned have the right to participate in the process of decision-making on: (1) Strategic EIA of plans and programmes; (2) Impact assessment of projects whose implementation may lead to the pollution of the environment or may present a risk for the environment and human health; (3) Approval of operations of new and/or existing installations; (4) Developing, amending, reviewing and adopting air quality plans, regional and local waste management plans, i.e., hazardous waste management plans, national waste management plan, waste prevention programmes, action plans for environmental noise prevention, and water pollution protection plan (paragraph 1):
>
>> Public participation regarding strategic impact assessment shall be ensured within the framework of the public presentation of a spatial and urban plan and/or other plan or programme referred to in Article 35 of this Law. Public participation in decision-making on environmental impact assessment of projects shall be enforced in the framework of public presentation of projects and public debate (paragraphs 2 and 3).[357]

B. The Law on Environmental Impact Assessment

267. The 2004 Law on EIA defines public participation, prescribing that the public should be informed at three different stages of the process and has the right to voice its opinion at each of these stages. The authorities must, if requested to do so, at all stages provide complete documentation, related to an EIA procedure. Specified confidential business or state information is an exception. According to Article 20 of the Law on EIA, the competent authority shall make the EIA Study available to public and arrange for a public presentation and debate on the Study. Within seven days from the date of receipt of the application for the EIA Study approval,

356. When application is related to information referred to in Art. 3, para. 1 point 33a subpoint 2 of this Law relating to measurement procedures, including analysis, sampling and sample pre-treatment, that were used for information gathering, public authority, with a notification about web page with available information, shall deliver to the applicant a notification on standard procedure used as well (para. 3).

357. Public participation in decision-making on commissioning new and/or existing facilities shall be enforced during the issue of new permits for IPPC (para. 4). The Government shall establish the public participation procedure in decision-making on developing, amending, reviewing and adopting plans and programmes referred to in para. 1, point 4 of this Article (para. 5). The interested public, in the process of exercising right to healthy environment, shall have the right, as a party, to initiate the decision-review procedure before the responsible authority or court, in accordance with the law (Art. 81a). In order to protect the interests of national security and defence, Serbian Government may 'limit participation of public in decision-making from Art. 81 of this Law' (Art. 82).

the competent authority shall inform the project developer, the authorities, organizations and the public concerned about the time and venue for public consultation, presentation and debate on the EIA Study. Public debate may not be held sooner than twenty days from the date when the public was informed. 'The project developer shall participate in the public presentation and debate on the EIA Study.'

C. The Law on Strategic Environmental Assessment

268. The 2004 Law on SEA prescribes that the public has the right to be informed about programmes in preparation and their impact on the environment. The authorities must inform and consult the public, before granting approval, about the content of the report. The Law also defines the procedure for public participation in the development and adoption of programmes and plans.

269. Article 19 of the Law on SEA prescribes that:

> the competent planning authority shall provide for public participation in the strategic assessment report consideration prior to submission of application for granting the approval for the strategic assessment report. The public referred to in paragraph 1 of this article shall consider the report within the procedure of making the plans and programmes available for public insight and during the public debate, if it has not been otherwise provided for by the Law. The competent planning authority shall inform the public referred to in paragraph 1 of this article about the method and deadlines for insight into the content of the report and submission of opinions, as well as about the time and venue of public debate organized in accordance with the Law regulating the procedure of adoption of plans and programmes.
>
> In accordance with this, the Law on Planning and Building (OJ RS, Nos 72/09, 81/09 – corr., 64/10-CC, 24/11, 121/12, 42/13-CC, 50/13-CC, 98/13-CC, 132/14, 145/14, 83/18, 31/19, 37/19 – other law, 9/20, 52/21, and 62/23) defines procedure for adoption of relevant urban and spatial plans.[358]

D. The Law on Integrated Pollution Prevention

270. The Law on IPPC prescribes public consultation in all phases, from preparation to adoption of integrated permits. The Register of permits is available to the public.

Article 11 prescribes that the competent authority 'shall inform competent authorities and organizations and public concerned on submission of application within five days from the date of receipt of a complete permit granting application'.

358. Presentation of the plan to the public is conducted, according to Arts 41–45, 45a, and 50–51.

271. The competent authority is also obliged to inform, in cases referred to in Articles 11, 12 and 15, other authorities and organizations and public, through the public media (including the Internet), publishing the information about them in at least one local newspaper published in the territory that will be affected by the impact of activities and installations (Article 23).

272. The Law on meteorological and hydrological activity (OJ RS, No. 88/10) also prescribes that the data and information on the weather, climate, water and quality of air and water obtained by performing meteorological and hydrological operations of interest to the RS are public, except those that represent an official or military secret (Article 30).

273. Certain issues concerning access to environmental information and public participation are regulated by sectoral regulations (e.g., water, GMOs, statistical research, ombudsman, consumer protection, etc.).

E. Role of NGO

274. Due to the fact that the basic direct beneficiary of rights from the AC is the citizen and/or organizations of citizens, implementation of the Convention is relevant to a vast number of Acts regulating position of citizens and their organizations. According to the data of the Agency for Business Registers, a total of 34,692 domestic and 72 representative offices of foreign associations were registered in the RS in 2020.[359] The Constitution of Serbia contains several provisions of importance for the work of NGOs and their relation to the public. It guarantees freedom of association (Article 55) and the CC is competent to pass judgment on 'whether are in accordance with Constitution and law general Acts of organizations entrusted with public authorities, political parties, trade unions, associations of citizens, and collective contracts' (Article 167, paragraphs 1, 5).

275. The EPL in Article 7 defines role of NGOs in a general way.[360] Article 7 prescribes that:

> civil societies, founded for the environmental protection shall prepare, promote and realize their protection programme, protect their rights and interest in the environmental protection, propose activities and measures conducive to protection, participate in the decision-making process in compliance with the law, help or directly disseminate information about the environment.

276. Article 81a of EPL envisages that the public concerned, in the process of exercising right to the healthy environment, shall, as a party, have the right to initiate the decision-review procedure before the responsible authority or court, in

359. GOV RS. 2022c. Ch. III. Civil society in Serbia: general data, 3.1. Status data of civil society organizations.

360. *See* part of the monograph devoted to the EPL (subject of the environmental protection system).

accordance with the Law. LEP, in Article 3, point 28, defines the term public concerned so that it presents the public affected or the one that can be affected by the decision made by the competent authority or which has some interest in it, including citizens' associations and community organizations engaged in environment protection and that are registered at the competent authority.[361]

277. The Law on Associations (OJ RS, Nos 51/2009, 92/11 – other law, and 44/18 – other law) regulates the establishment and legal status of associations, their entry and deletion from the Register, membership and bodies, associations' status changes and termination as well as any other issues of importance to their activities. The Law also regulates the status and operations of foreign associations.[362] According to the EC report (2023), 'the legal framework for cooperation between the government and civil society organizations (CSOs) is broadly in place; further efforts are needed to ensure systematic, genuine, and meaningful cooperation'.[363]

F. Institutional Aspect

278. Collection of information related to the environment and the obligation to make it public are in competence of a number of authorities and other institutions.

The EPA has the task of publishing reports about the environment. The websites of the EPA and the MEP provide key information about the state of the environment.[364] The Institute for Nature Protection also informs various stakeholders (schools, news media, etc.).[365] In the framework of Office for Cooperation with

361. Similar provisions are provided in Art. 2, items 1 and 7 of the Law on EIA (OJ RS, No. 135/04) which provides for that the public concerned that includes the public which is or can be affected by the plan or programme and/or which has interest in making decisions concerning environmental protection, including NGOs for environmental protection and which are registered with the competent authority, in Art. 2, points 16 and 17 of the Law on IPPC (OJ RS, Nos 135/04 and 25/15) and which provides for that public concerned includes the public affected by the work of installations and performing of activities or is likely to be affected by it, including NGOs for environmental protection registered within the competent authority.
362. Amendments to the Law on State Administration, Law on local self-government and the Law on the planning system introduced specific provisions aimed at improving public participation in policy development. However, the relationship between the government and CSOs is still marked by fragmented cooperation. EC. 2019, 10.
363. EC. 2023, 14, 15. An enabling environment for establishing, running, and financing CSOs needs to be strengthened. 'Verbal attacks and smear campaigns against CSOs continued, including by high-level officials. There was a significant increase in strategic lawsuits against public participation (SLAPP), notably launched by members of national and local authorities, against human rights defenders.' *Ibid.*, 15.
364. *See, for example*, EPA. 2023a. http://www.sepa.gov.rs/index.php?menu=5000&id=1304&akcija=showDocuments&godina=2022&Lang=Cyrillic# (4.1.2024). The national PRTR register is published online and included, in 2013, 277 facilities which were the most significant sources of pollution in Serbia. For the latest information, *see* http://77.46.150.218/prtrportal/lista-prtr-postrojenja-u-srbiji?lang=de (4.1.2024).
   Serbia also reports to E-PRTR on voluntary basis from 2011. UNECE. 2015, 3.
365. Other competent institutions in the field are the regional and local authorities, the five Aarhus Centres (Kragujevac, Subotica, Novi Sad, Nis and Belgrade) as well as the Administrative Court of Serbia, etc. *Ibid.*

Civil Society[366] activities during 2013, the Guidelines for participation of civil society in law-making procedures were elaborated (OJ RS, No. 90/14), although the real significance of this document in practice can be challenged.

279. The CIPIPDP has been established, as an independent State official, by the Law on the Free Access to Information of Public Importance (OJ RS, Nos 120/04, 54/07, 104/09, 36/10, and 105/21). He/she is autonomous in performing his/her duties, in order to provide realization of the right to free access to information of public importance.

There are significant results in the exercise and enforcement of the right of free access to information of public importance, but there is no doubt that the effects of implementation of the Law on Free Access to Information could be much better. The average of three to four thousand formally lodged complaints a year (in the past four years) is proof that information is still difficult to obtain from public authorities in many cases without the Commissioner's intervention and shows that citizens trust this independent State body when seeking protection of their rights.[367] During 2022, the Commissioner's work 'was marked primarily by a vast increase in the number of processed cases compared with all previous years'.[368]

280. Regarding the availability of environmental information, the vast array of environmental information and data in Serbia is available to the public and other stakeholders through Ecoregister (a sub-domain on the website of EPA).[369] Directive 2003/4/EC on public access to environmental information and Directive 2003/35/EC on public participation and access to justice are partly transposed. Full transposition had to be done by 2016 and implementation will be done by 2018.[370] According to the EC report, 'further progress has been made in transposing EU directives on public access to environmental information and public participation in environmental decision-making. Amongst others, Serbia has opened a fifth Aarhus centre in December 2015 in Belgrade. Additional efforts are required to further increase the effectiveness of public consultations'.[371] The report of the EC from 2016 is the last one in which an assessment of the compliance of internal regulations with EU regulations in the area of access to environmental information is given. Reports published after 2016 do not contain assessments regarding access to environmental information.[372]

---

366. The Office ceased to work following the adoption of the Law on Ministries (OJ RS, Nos 128/20, 116/22, and 92/23 – other law). The Ministry of Human and Minority Rights and Social Dialogue took over the affairs of the Office.
367. *See* Summary of the Report on implementation of the Law on Free Access to Information of Public Importance and the Law on Personal Data Protection for 2016, https://www.poverenik.rs/en/o-nama/annual-reports.html?start=6 (5.1.2024).
368. CIPIPDP. 2023, 6. In 2022 the Commissioner opened a total of 18,701 cases (12,221 in in 2021), including 13,285 cases in the field of freedom of information (7,244 in 2021), 4,116 cases in the field of personal data protection (3,366 in 2021) and 1,300 cases in both fields (1,611 in 2021). *Ibid.*
369. UNECE. 2015, 88.
370. EC. 2016b, p. 11.
371. EC. 2016a, 76.
372. Young Researchers of Serbia. 2023, 17.

§3. Environmental Management System (EMS) and Eco-Management and Audit Scheme (EMAS) in Serbia

281. Different legal and sub-legal Acts contain legal framework for introduction and application of standards of the Environmental Management System (EMS)[373] and eco-management and audit scheme (EMAS). Most important are the legal Acts by which issues of competences for certain activities in connection with standardization and the environment have been regulated as well as sub-legal Acts by which these two issues have been regulated in more detail.

I. Overview of the EMS/EMAS Legislation Competencies

282. The Serbian Constitution does not contain explicit provisions regarding standardization but contains several provisions dealing with the environment.[374] Article 97, point 6, of the Constitution, prescribes that the RS regulates and guaranties 'Common market; legal position of the business subjects; system of the undertaking of certain business and other activities ... '. Besides that, the Republic regulates the following:

- other economic and social relations of general interests (point 8);
- scientific and technological development (point 12);
- financing of implementation of the rights and duties of the RS, as prescribed by the Constitution and law (point 15);
- organization, competencies and work of the organs of the Republic (point 16); and
- other relations of the interests of the RS, in accordance with the Constitution (point 17).

283. According to Article 4 of the Law on Ministries (OJ RS, Nos 128/20, 116/ 22, 92/ 23 – other law), the Ministry of Economy is competent for standardization issues. Standardization is also in competence of the Serbian Institute for Standardization.[375] The rights, obligations and responsibilities of the Institute have been stipulated by the Law on Standardization.

284. Accreditation Body of Serbia (ATS)[376] is responsible for accreditation of conformity assessment organizations. ATS, as an independent non-profit

373. According to the ISO Survey at the end of 2006, companies from Serbia have eighty-four certifications for ISO 1401:2004. ISO Survey – 2006, 24. According to the data from the Survey for 2022, a total of 1,921 companies from Serbia have ISO 14001-2015 certificates.
https://www.iso.org/committee/54998.html?t=KomURwikWDLiuB1P1c7SjLMLEAgXOA7emZHKGWyn8f3KQUTU3m287NxnpA3DIuxm&view=documents#section-isodocuments-top (29.1.2024).

374. *See* chapter devoted to the 'constitutional provisions'.

375. *See* https://iss.rs/en/ (5.1.2024).

376. The Yugoslav Accreditation Body (JUAT), later to become the Accreditation Body of Serbia (ATS), was founded in 1998 by means of the Decree on the Establishment of the Yugoslav Accreditation

organization, has been established by the Government's decree (OJ RS, Nos 96/2006, 14/11 and 95/16), based on the Law on Accreditation (OJ RS, Nos 73/10, and 47/21), for the purposes of establishing the competency of organizations for performing the conformity assessment activities.

II. General Regulations in the Field of Standardization

285. Following are general legal Acts by which the field of standardization and EMS is regulated in Serbia:

- Law on Standardization (OJ RS, Nos 36/2009 and 46/15).
- Law on Accreditation (OJ RS, Nos 73/2010, 47/2021).
- Law on Technical Conditions for Products and for Testing of Products with Prescribed Requirements (OJRS, No. 36/2009).
- Law on Metrology (OJ RS, No. 15/16).

286. Of importance are also following sub-legal Acts:

- Decision on establishment of the Institute for Standardization of Serbia (OJ RS, Nos 88/2009, 93/15 and 27/16).
- Decision on the Establishment of the Serbian Accreditation Body (OJ RS, Nos 96/2006, 14/11, 95/16, and 79/21).
- Statute of the Accreditation Body of Serbia (OJ RS, Nos 97/11, 98/22).
- Regulation on the manner of recognition of foreign documents and marks of conformity (OJ RS, Nos 98/09 and 110/16).
- Regulation on manner of performing conformity assessment, content of the document of conformity, and shape, appearance and content of mark of conformity (OJ RS, Nos 98/09 and 23/17).
- Regulation on the manner of designation and authorization of conformity assessment bodies (OJ RS, No. 98/09).
- Regulation on legal units of measurement (OJ RS, No. 43/11).
- Regulation on manner of providing information and notification of technical regulations, conformity assessment and standards (OJ RS, No. 45/10).

Body. In the period between 1998 and 2000 JUAT performed its accreditation activities as a collegial public administration body of the Federal Republic of Yugoslavia within the Federal Ministry of Development, Science and Environment. From 2000 to 2003, JUAT was a separate organization, a collegial body detached from the Ministry, and from June 2003 to June 2006, it was a constituent part of the Ministry of Internal Economic Affairs of Serbia & Montenegro. It changed its name thereafter to the Accreditation Board of Serbia & Montenegro. By means of the 2006 Act on Establishment enacted by the Government of the Republic of Serbia ATS acquired the legal personality, and status of independent and non-profit body in accordance with the Law on Accreditation the implementation of which commenced on 1 Jan. 2006. *See* https://www.ats.rs/en/about-us/history (4.1.2024). The Decision on Amendments to the Act on Establishment of the Accreditation Board of Serbia entered into force on 24 Feb. 2011, whereby the existing English version of the name of the national accreditation body 'Accreditation Board of Serbia' was changed to 'Accreditation Body of Serbia'.

- Rulebook on manner of affixing marks of conformity on products and use of marks of conformity (OJ RS, No. 25/10).
- Rulebook on the establishment of a list of Serbian standards in the area of general product safety (OJ RS, No. 48/16).
- Rulebook on content and manner of keeping registers referring to technical regulations (OJ RS, No. 33/10).
- Rulebook on the noise emitted by equipment used in open space (OJ RS, No. 1/13), etc.[377]

III. Law on Standardization

287. The Law on Standardization governs the principles and objectives of standardization[378] in the RS, organization and activity of the national standardization body, and the adoption, publication and application of Serbian standards[379] and related documents (Article 1).[380]

288. Pursuant to Article 5 of the Law, the objectives of standardization in the RS shall include: (1) improvement of the protection of life, health and safety of humans, animals and plants, as well as the environment protection; (2) raising the quality of products, processes and services, their typification, compatibility and substitutability; (3) ensuring a unique technical basis; (4) developing and improving the production and circulation of products, construction works, namely provision of services through the development of internationally harmonized standards with the aim of efficient use of labour, material and energy; and (5) improvement of international trade, through the prevention and elimination of unnecessary technical barriers.[381]

---

377. For more information on legislation, *see* http://www.tehnis.privreda.gov.rs/en/Download.html (5.1.2024).
378. 'Standardization' shall mean a set of coordinated activities aimed at adoption of standards and related documents (Art. 3, point 1).
379. 'Standard' shall mean a publicly available document, defined by a consensus and adopted by a recognized body, which determines, for general and multiple use, the rules, requirements, characteristics, instructions, recommendations or guidelines for the activities or their results with the aim of achieving the optimal level of regulation in a specific area in relation to the current or potential problems (Art. 3, para. 1, point 2).
380. This Law shall apply to standards and related documents that are adopted and published by the national standardization body in the Republic of Serbia, as well as to international standards and related documents of the recognized international and European organizations for standardization referred to in Art. 3 items 12 and 13 of this Law which constitute the basis for adoption of Serbian standards (Art. 2).
381. Standardization in the Republic of Serbia shall be based on the following principles: (1) the right of all interested parties to voluntarily take part in adoption of Serbian standards; (2) consensus of interested parties; (3) prevention of the precedence of individual interests over the common interest of the interested parties; (4) transparency of the standardization procedure and public availability of Serbian standards and related documents; (5) mutual consistency of Serbian standards and related documents; (6) taking into account development of technology and rules of international and European organizations for standardization and relevant international agreements; and (7) non-discriminatory treatment of foreign products or services and same or similar domestic products or services, in accordance with ratified international agreements to which the Republic of Serbia is a signatory (Art. 4).

The Law also regulates establishment, activities, organs, membership and financing of the Institute of Standardization (Articles 6–11).

289. Article 7 (paragraph 1) of the Law prescribes that the Institute shall perform following tasks:

(1) adopt, publish, review and withdraw Serbian standards, in accordance with the rules of the Institute;
(2) provide the interpretation of Serbian standards, as well as interpretation of the application of Serbian standards, at the request of the interested parties;
(3) ensure the compliance of Serbian standards with international and European standards;
(4) keep the Register of adopted and withdrawn Serbian standards, in accordance with the rules of the Institute;
(5) participate in the preparation and review of international and European standards in the areas of interest for the RS;
(6) cooperate with the international and European organizations for standardization and national bodies for standardization of countries signatory of relevant agreements in the area of standardization;
(7) perform the standardization-related tasks, in accordance with the obligations arising from ratified international agreements to which the RS is a signatory;
(8) ensure the public availability of adopted and withdrawn Serbian standards and publications, as well as standards and publications of relevant international, European and national bodies for standardization, and carry out their sale;
(9) at the request of the State administration authority, provide the information on whether a relevant Serbian standard has been adopted in the area that is being regulated by a technical regulation or its adoption is pending, namely whether relevant international or European standard exists;
(10) act as an enquiry point for standards, for providing information and notifications related to standards, in accordance with the requirements provided for in the relevant international agreements and the obligations arising from the membership in relevant international and European organizations for standardization;[382]
(11) represent and act in the interest of the RS in the area of standardization in the international and European organizations for standardization;
(12) approve the use of national mark of conformity with the Serbian standards, in accordance with the rules of the Institute;
(13) issue the rules based on which Serbian standards are adopted, published, reviewed and withdrawn;
(14) delegate to the interested parties, in accordance with its rules, preparation of proposals of Serbian standards in specific areas;
(15) promote the application of Serbian standards; and

382. The manner of providing information and notifications referred to in para. 1 item 10 of this Article shall be governed by a regulation adopted by the Government (para. 4).

(16) perform other tasks in the area of standardization, in accordance with the law and articles of association.[383]

290. The Law regulates by its III and IV Chapters issues of adoption, publication and application of standards and related documents (Articles 12–19). So Article 12 prescribes following:

> Serbian standards shall be adopted and published in accordance with this Law and the rules of the Institute, which are harmonized with the rules of international and European organizations for standardization and the Code of Good Practice for the Preparation, Adoption and Application of Standards from the Agreement on Technical Barriers to Trade of the World Trade Organization (paragraph 1).[384]

IV. Law on Accreditation

291. The Law on Accreditation (OJ RS, Nos 73/10, and 47/21) regulates accreditation, status and operation of the national accreditation body in the RS and other issues relevant to the accreditation (Article 1).[385]

292. Article 3 prescribes that accreditation shall be used to determine the competence of conformity assessment bodies to carry out the following activities: (1) testing; (2) calibration; (3) inspection; (4) certification of products; (5) certification of management systems; and (6) certification of persons.[386]

293. In accordance with Article 5, the Accreditation Board of Serbia (ABS) is the sole accreditation body in the RS that is hereby entrusted to perform accreditation activities referred to in Articles 3 and 8[387] of this Law.[388] ABS shall be independent from the conformity assessment bodies it assesses. ABS must not: (1)

---

383. The Institute shall not perform tasks referred to in para. 1 of this Article with the aim of acquiring profit (para. 3).
384. As a rule, international standards and related documents shall be used as the basis for adoption of Serbian standards. In the event that international standard does not exist in particular area or the existing international standard is unsuitable, European or national standards and related documents of other countries may be used as a basis. The Institute shall publish in its OJ the notice on the instigation of procedure for adoption of a Serbian standard and, when it is necessary, for related document, as well as the notice on the placement of a standard or related document in the public discussion process (Art. 12, paras 2 and 3).
385. 'Accreditation' is an act of verification performed by the national accreditation body in order to confirm whether the conformity assessment bodies fulfil requirements of relevant Serbian and/or international and European standards and, where applicable, any additional requirements defined for specific fields, to carry out specific conformity assessment activities (Art. 2, point 1).
386. In addition to the competence to perform these activities accreditation shall be used to determine competence to perform other conformity assessment activities, in accordance with the specific law (para. 2). Accreditation is compulsory only if regulated by a specific law (Art. 4, para. 2).
387. It includes following activities: (1) set forth and publish the Rules of Accreditation based on the relevant Serbian, international and European standards, and on documents of international and European organizations for accreditation; (2) keep a public Register of Accredited Conformity

provide consultancy services to conformity assessment bodies; (2) perform activities or provide services provided by conformity assessment bodies; and (3) have proprietary and/or managerial rights or any other financial interests in conformity assessment bodies (Article 10).

V. Other Relevant Regulations

294. Law on Technical Requirements for Products and Conformity Assessment (OJ RS, No. 36/09) governs the manner of prescribing technical requirements for products and adoption of technical regulations, assessment of conformity of products with prescribed technical requirements (conformity assessment),[389] obligations of suppliers of products and owners of products in use, validity of foreign documents of conformity and conformity markings, notification of technical regulations and conformity assessment procedures and supervision of the implementation of this Law and regulations adopted based on this Law (Article 1).[390] Technical requirements for individual products or groups of products (technical requirements) shall be prescribed in a technical regulation directly, by specifying such requirements in the text of the regulation, or indirectly, by the reference in the technical regulation to the Serbian standard or technical specification (Article 4).[391]

295. Technical regulation shall mean any regulation which, for individual products or groups of products (the product)[392] governs at least one of the following elements: (1) technical requirements that must be met by a product being made available on the market; (2) conformity assessment procedures; (3) safety requirements for product throughout its lifecycle; (4) regular and extraordinary inspection of product throughout its lifecycle; (5) documents that accompany product when

Assessment Bodies; (3) participate in the work of international and European organizations for accreditation; and (4) perform other activities in accordance with the law, Establishment Act and Statute.

388. Founder of ABS is the Republic of Serbia, whereas the Government of the Republic of Serbia shall, under legal powers, exercise the rights of the Founder. ABS shall use Government property as means for performing its tasks and activities and ABS shall not operate on a profit-making basis (Art. 5, paras 2–4).

389. 'Conformity assessment' shall mean any activity whereby it is determined whether a product or production process is in compliance with the prescribed technical requirements (Art. 3, point 9).

390. If specific laws and regulations referred to in para. 1 of this Article do not govern matters related to the appointment and/or authorization of conformity assessment bodies and validity of foreign documents of conformity and conformity markings, the provisions of this Law shall apply to such matters. The provisions of this Law governing notification of appointed and authorized conformity assessment body, keeping of registers and notification of technical regulations shall also apply to the products for which technical requirements are governed by specific laws and regulations adopted based on such laws (Art. 1, paras 2 and 3).

391. In respect of ensuring market regulation in regard to safety of products for which there are no specific technical regulations, the Law on General Product Safety was adopted (OJ RS, Nos 41/09 and 77/19).

392. 'Product' shall mean any product which is, as the result of certain process, made or in any other manner obtained, regardless of the level of processing, if it is intended for placement on the market or making available on the market (Art. 3, point 1).

placed on the market or put to use; (6) marking and manner of marking the product; (7) requirements that must be met by the conformity assessment body; and (8) requirements with regard to packaging and labelling (Article 5, paragraph 1).[393]

296. The Law on Metrology (OJ RS, No. 15/16) regulates the organization of metrology activities, legal units of measurement, and measurement standards of the RS, placing on the market and use of measuring instruments, assessment of conformity of measuring instruments with prescribed requirements, pre-packaged products, the validity of documents and foreign conformity marks, supervision, and other metrology-related matters (Article 1). The purpose of this law is to ensure: (1) the use of measurement units compliant with the International Unit System; (2) unique measurement in the RS and confidence in the results of measurements applied for the protection of consumers, the life and health of humans and animals, environmental protection, general safety and protection of natural resources; (3) traceability of measurement standards of the RS to international standards and national standards of other countries; (4) free trade and prevention of unnecessary trade barriers; (5) support and development of appropriate metrology infrastructure that provides traceability of measurement results; (6) direction and funding of metrology research and development activities; (7) quick, accurate and easily understandable communication and exchange of information on metrological issues (Article 2).[394]

297. The metrology activities, in terms of this Law, in the RS are performed by: (1) the ministry responsible for metrology activities (hereinafter 'the Ministry'); (2) the administrative authority responsible for metrology activities, i.e., the Directorate for Measures and Precious Metals (hereinafter 'the Directorate'); (3) commercial entities and other legal persons authorized for performing measuring instruments verification (hereinafter 'authorized bodies');[395] (4) economic entities and other legal persons designated to perform the measuring instrument conformity assessment activities with the prescribed requirements (hereinafter 'the designated authorities'); (5) designated holders of national measurement standards (Article 6). The Directorate shall, *inter alia*: (1) be responsible of the system of legal units of measurement in the RS; (2) develop, realize, proclaim, keep, maintain and continuously improve measurement standards of the RS; (3) comply and supervise the work of designated holders of national measurement standards (4) provide metrological traceability; (5) conduct activities of research and development in metrological expertise; (6) conduct testing of pre-packaged products in order to check the fulfilment of metrological requirements; (7) perform metrological supervision; (8) authorize economic entities and other legal persons for performing the measuring instrument verification activities; (9) supervise the work of authorized bodies; (10)

393. Technical regulations and technical requirements contained therein shall be adopted for the purpose of protecting the safety, life and health of humans, protecting animals and plants, environment protection, protection of consumers and other users and protection of property (Art. 5, para. 2).

394. Provisions of this Law governing legal control of measuring instruments are applied to instruments used for measurement in the field of protection of health and general safety, environmental protection, control and safety of traffic, and trade in goods and services (Art. 3, para. 1).

395. Obligations of the authorized body are regulated by Arts 11–14 of the Law.

perform conformity assessment of measuring instruments; (11) make decisions in administrative proceedings in the field of metrology; (12) perform activities of metrological expertise; (13) keep registers of measuring instruments subject to legal control and other prescribed records; (14) provide metrological information and publish the Official Journal (Article 8, paragraph 1).

VI. Environmental Regulations Relevant for EMS/EMAS

298. The four systemic laws adopted at the end of 2004 are most important when regulations concerning the environment are regarded. They are as follows:

- Environmental Protection Law.
- Law on Environmental Impact Assessment (EIA).
- Law on Strategic Environmental Assessment (SEA).
- Law on Integrated Pollution Prevention and Control (IPPC).[396]

A. *Law on Environmental Protection*

299. EPL contains provisions directly related to the EMS and EMAS. The other three systematic laws are important primarily because they are systematic regulations by which certain environmental policy instruments important for the functioning of the system as a whole, have been introduced.

300. The legal basis for the system of EMAS has been formed by EPL. The Law contains a special section 2.2 devoted to the Environmental Protection Management System (Article 44).

301. Legal and natural person may certify the environmental protection management system according to SRPSISO 14001, in accordance with the law. Legal and natural person may register the certified environmental protection management system for the purpose of integration into the system of environmental protection management and control of the EU (the EMAS system), in accordance with this Law.[397]

302. Some other provisions of the EPL should also be mentioned and especially in provisions concerning the following:

- Rights and Duties of the Inspector (Article 110).
- Powers of Inspectors (Article 111).

396. All of them have been adopted on 21 Dec. 2004 (OJ RS, No. 135/2004).
397. The registration into the EMAS system shall be carried out on the basis of the request from legal and natural person submitted to the Ministry.

– Offences (Articles 117, 120 and 121).[398]

303. 'Voluntary initiatives, such as adoption of certified environmental management systems, continued to develop steadily but remained at a comparatively modest level.'[399]

Serbia had the intention to align its legislation by the end of 2015 with Regulation (EC) No. 1221/2009 on EMAS and Regulation (EC) No. 66/2010 on the EU Ecolabel.[400] In 2018, work was done to refine the Rulebook for EMAS in the RS with a guide for including companies in the system. The intention was to enable domestic organizations to join EMAS through the 'EMAS Global' and 'Third Country Registration' mechanisms.[401]

§4. Enforcement and Control

304. The environmental inspection is performed according to the Law on Inspection (OJ RS, Nos 36/2015, 44/18 – other law and 95/18),[402] EPL, and several other laws.

305. The Law on inspection shall govern the contents, types and forms, as well as the procedure of the inspection supervision, powers and obligations of the participants in the inspection supervision and other issues significant for the inspection supervision (Article 1).[403] Based on the Law on Inspection Supervision, a large number of by-laws were adopted.[404]

---

398. 'For the offence from Arts 117 and 118 of this Law, along with the penalty, a protective measure may be imposed by confiscating objects which have been used or intended to be used for an offence, or which have occurred or have been obtained in an offensive action.'
399. UNECE. 2015, 51.
400. EC. 2016b, p. 11.
401. To date, there is not a single EMAS-registered company in the Republic of Serbia, but three companies are prepared for EMAS registration. Full implementation is possible only from the moment when the Republic of Serbia becomes a full member of the EU. EPA. 2019b, 163. According to the information from EPA 2022d, the Ministry of Environmental Protection had prepared the 'Rulebook on the content and form of the request for issuing a certificate on the data on which official records are kept in the field of environmental protection for inclusion in the EMAS system, the documentation submitted with the request, the content and the confirmation form and content, the way of keeping and the appearance of the records'. *See*, EPA. 2022, 9. However, Rulebook has not been adopted. The adoption of Rulebook is not foreseen in the NPAA, IV.
402. Previously, the matter of inspection was regulated by the provisions of the Law on State Administration (OJ RS, Nos 20/92, 6/93 – CC, 48/93, 53/93, 67/93, 48/94 and 49/99 – other law, 79/05 – other law, 101/05 – other law and 87/11 – other law).
403. The inspection shall mean an authority within, an internal organizational unit or inspectors of the State administration authorities, i.e., authorities of the AP or local self-government unit or other entity holding public powers, which perform the inspection supervision (Art. 3, point 1).
404. This includes *inter alia*, the following: Regulation on common elements of risk assessment in inspection supervision (OJ RS, No. 81/15); Regulation on the layout of the form and the method of keeping records on inspection supervision (OJ RS, No. 81/15); Decision on the formation of the Coordination Commission (OJ RS, Nos 144/22, 71/23); Rulebook on the form and method of internal control in budget inspection (OJ RS, No. 6/23). Rulebook on the form and method of internal

306. According to Article 2 of the Law, the inspection supervision shall be the task of the State administration, the contents of which as well as the term have been specified by this Law, which governs the operation of the State administration, carried out by the State administration authorities, as well as the authorities of the AP and authorities of the LSG units, with the aim of taking preventive actions or imposing measures that secure legality and safety of operation and actions of the supervised entities, and thus prevent or remove the damaging consequences incurred to the goods, rights and interests protected by the law and other regulation.[405]

307. The intended purpose of the changes is to enhance coordination between the bodies charged with conducting inspection, determination of the inspector's competences, increase transparency in the operation of inspection, etc. The Law, *inter alia*, introduced a new term – 'unregistered entity'. An unregistered entity shall mean a supervised entity, which operates or performs activities and which is not registered with a relevant register maintained by the Business Registers Agency or other body or organization competent for the registration of incorporation of a legal entity and other entity (hereinafter 'the basic register'), when registration with this register has been specified as a requirement for operation or performance of activities (Article 3, point 4).[406]

308. Environmental inspection control is performed by the Ministry through its environmental inspectors.[407] Articles 109–115 of the EPL define position of

control in the tourist inspection (OJ RS, No. 68/22); Rulebook on special elements of risk assessment, criteria for risk assessment, special elements of the inspection plan, and the frequency of inspection by inspectors for drugs and medical devices (OJ RS, No. 9/22); Rulebook on special elements of risk assessment, the frequency of inspection supervision based on risk assessment, and special elements of the inspection supervision plan in the field of electric power (OJ RS, No. 106/18); Rulebook on special elements of risk assessment, frequency of inspection based on risk assessment, and special elements of the inspection plan in the field of geology and mining (OJ RS, No. 106/18); Rulebook on the form and method of internal control in health inspection, sanitary inspection, and inspection for drugs and medical devices, psychoactive controlled substances, and precursors (OJ RS, No. 94/18); Rulebook on special elements of risk assessment, special criteria for risk assessment, frequency of inspection based on risk assessment, and special elements of the inspection plan in the field of sanitary inspection (OJ RS, No. 94/18); Rulebook on special elements of risk assessment, frequency of inspection supervision in the field of the budget inspection (OJ RS, No. 90/18), etc.

405. Other forms of supervision and control shall comply with the inspection supervision, the performance of which shall examine the application of the law and other regulations, by direct insight into the operation and actions of the supervised entity, which shall be carried out by the authorities referred to in para. 1 of this Article as well as other entities holding public powers, in line with a special law (Art. 2, para. 2).
406. Inspection over 'unregistered entities' can be performed even when this was not anticipated in the inspection plan (Art. 33). In addition, such entities can be inspected without any prior notice or issuance of the inspection order, within the scope determined by the inspector. Immediately when it discovers an unregistered entity, the inspector will render a decision containing measures for elimination of irregularities and prohibiting the entity's further activities.
407. During 2021, the Environmental Protection Inspectorate dealt with a total of 3,912 cases. For more detailed information, *see* MEP. 2022, 35. In 2022, the Environmental Protection Inspectorate carried out 3,043 inspections: Regular (725), Extraordinary (1206), Mixed (34), Extraordinary (688), Supplementary (18), Control (313) and Emergency (59). MEP. 2023b, 34.

environmental inspection (rights and duties of inspectors, competencies of inspectors, etc.).

I. Rights and Duties of Inspectors

309. Rights and duties of inspectors in performing inspection control are prescribed by several provisions of the Law on inspection (Articles 21, 24, 25, 26, 27, 28, 29, etc.) and by provisions of Article 110 of the EPL.

310. According to Article 110 of the EPL, the inspector has the right and duty to determine, *inter alia*, the following: (1) whether the management, namely sustainable use and protection of natural resources and goods are carried out in line with strategic documents and conditions and measures; (2) whether collecting and placement on the market of wild flora and fauna and their developing forms and parts are carried out in accordance with prescribed conditions; (3) whether import, export and transit of endangered and protected species of wild flora and fauna and their developing forms and parts are carried out in compliance with prescribed conditions; (4) whether the measures and conditions of environmental protection in planning and constructing are being implemented; (5) whether the standards of environmental quality and emission are being applied; (6) whether the conditions for operation and activation of the installation have been fulfilled; (7) whether domestic or imported technologies or processes are being applied in compliance with prescribed norms of environmental protection; (8) whether prescribed prohibitions on production and trade with certain products and performance of certain activities are being implemented; (9) whether ecological label for products, processes or services is being used in a prescribed manner; (10) whether import and export of substances depleting ozone layer (and import, export and transit of waste) are being carried out in compliance with this Law; (11) whether dangerous substances in production, use, transport, trade, processing, storage and disposal are treated in accordance with prescribed measures; (12) whether monitoring of environmental state is being performed; (13) whether information system and integrated cadastre of polluters are being kept; (14) whether the Fund's finances are being earmarked; and (15) whether the obligations from ratified international agreements from the area of environmental protection are being implemented.

II. Authorization of the Inspector

311. Authorization of the inspector is prescribed by Article 26 of the Law on State Administration (generally) and by Article 111 of the EPL more precisely. According to Article 111 of the EPL, the inspector is authorized to:

(1) order the correction of irregularities in implementation of the measures of protection, reclamation and rehabilitation of the environment in the process of utilization of natural resources and goods, within a specified period;

(2) prohibit the use or utilization of natural resources and goods without approval or contrary to the approval and to instruct rehabilitation and/or undertaking of other appropriate protective measures;
(3) prohibit the introduction and growing of flora and fauna of foreign origin for the purpose of free habitation in nature, which could threaten autochthonic species and their spreading;
(4) prohibit destroying or damaging wild flora and fauna and their habitats;
(5) prohibit collecting or placing on the market wild flora and fauna, their developing forms and parts without licence;
(6) prohibit importation and exportation of endangered and protected species of wild flora and fauna, their developing forms and parts whose circulation is prohibited by international agreements;
(7) prohibit importation and exportation of endangered and protected species of wild flora and fauna, their developing forms and parts whose circulation is permitted if it is carried out without a licence;
(8) prohibit construction and use of installations or establishments and performance of activities if the prescribed requirements and norms regarding emissions and pollutant levels are not met, if they do not have appropriate and functioning equipment and devices which reduce or prevent the emission of pollutants or energy or if other measures and conditions of environmental protection have not been undertaken;
(9) prohibit production and circulation of means of transportation that do not meet the conditions regarding emission for mobile sources of pollution;
(10) prohibit release of polluting and dangerous substances, wastewaters or energy into air, water and soil in a manner and in quantities, namely concentrations or levels exceeding the prescribed ones;
(11) prohibit operation, use or utilization of technology, technological process that are not allowed according to the provisions of this Law;
(12) prohibit use or utilization of products, semi-finished products or raw material that are not allowed according to the provisions of this Law;
(13) instruct that, in case of doubt, certain technology, storing, technological process product, semi-finished product or raw material be examined with respect to potential harmful effect on the environment and to temporarily prohibit their use or utilization until the results of examination are presented;
(14) suspend operation of devices until the efficiency of devices for elimination or treatment of pollutants for which there are no prescribed limit values has been examined;
(15) prohibit placing on the market raw materials, semi-finished products or products which do not have a visible mark on the potential threat to the environment;
(16) prohibit use of ecological label contrary to the provisions of this Law;
(17) prohibit importation of hazardous waste of foreign origin;
(18) prohibit importation, exportation and transit of waste contrary to the provisions of this Law and order their return to the sender;

(19) prohibit operation of the Seveso installation or establishment when measures prescribed in the Policy on Accident Prevention or the Report on Safety or the Plan on Protection from Accident are not implemented or are insufficiently implemented;
(20) order preparation of the Policy on Accident Prevention or the Report on Safety or the Plan on Protection from Accident and undertaking of appropriate preventive and other measures for protection of the environment from dangerous substances, in accordance with this Law;
(21) prohibit operation of the Seveso installation or establishment if the Notification, Policy on Accident Prevention or the Report on Safety or the Plan on Protection from Accident have not been submitted within the specified period;
(22) in case of an accident, order undertaking of intervention measures and procedures for response to accidents, implementation of measures in accordance with the Plan on Protection from Accident, engaging of people, resources and undertaking of measures for rehabilitation and prevention of spread of pollution caused by the chemical accident;
(23) order the performance of monitoring in the prescribed manner;
(24) order implementation of measures of environmental protection, in accordance with this Law;
(25) prohibit use of funds from the account of a legal person, entrepreneur and natural person on the basis of an executive conclusion;
(26) take samples of soil, water, waste, and air through the authorized organization;
(27) in the procedure of enforced execution of a decision, carry out sealing of premises, installations or establishments, equipment or areas that have caused or might have caused polluting or damage to the environment, in accordance with law;
(28) carry out an order of other prescribed obligations within the specified period.

III. Cooperation Between Inspectors

312. Cooperation between inspectors from different domains is regulated by the Law on State Administration, and by provisions of specific laws which regulate certain domains. Especially important is provision of Article 27 of the Law of State Administration by which it is prescribed that inspector while performing his/her duties, cooperates with other inspectors, judicial organs, magistrates and other interested organs and organizations.[408]

408. Article 113 of the EPL prescribes general rules of cooperation of environmental inspectors with inspectors competent in other domains. It is prescribed by the Article that inspector is obliged 'to inform other competent authority aside from taking measures under his authorization', and that 'the other competent inspection authority shall inform the inspector of the measures taken'. In cases when inspector determines that a violation of law is also in the competence of other inspection authorities, he/she 'is obliged to inform the Minister thereof, without further delay, so that they could jointly perform inspection and take adequate measures'.

IV. Transferring Competence of Inspection

313. Certain activities concerning inspection control could be, by law, transferred to organs of counties, the city of Belgrade, other cities and APs (Article 22 of the Law on State Administration).

Chapter VII of the Law on State Administration regulates conflict of competencies between ministries, ministries and special organizations, between special organizations, organs of State administration and organs to whom duties of State administration were transferred, organs of State organizations and enterprises, institutions and other organizations, organs to whom are transferred duties of administration from the competencies of the Republic, between enterprises, institutions and other organizations when in performing administrative competencies make decision concerning specific rights and duties from the domain of rights and duties of Republic, etc. (Articles 72–74).

314. Article 109, paragraphs 3 and 4 of the EPL prescribes that the AP shall perform inspection supervision over the implementation of the activities given by this Law and regulations made on its basis. Local self-governance unit shall perform inspection supervision over the implementation of the activities given by this Law and regulations made on its basis.[409]

V. Other Legal Regulations Relevant for Environmental Inspection

315. Duties of environmental inspectors are also performed according to following environmental regulations:

- Law on National Parks (OJ RS, Nos 84/15, 95/18 – other law), Article 25 regulates supervision.
- Law on Nature Protection (OJ RS, Nos 36/09, 88/10, 91/10 – corr., 14/16, 95/18 – other law, and 71/21), Articles 118–124.
- Law on Soil Protection (OJ RS, No. 112/15), Articles 38–42.
- Law on Protection and Sustainable Use of Fish Reserves (OJ RS, Nos 128/14, and 95/18 – other law), Articles 53–57.
- Law on the Protection from Non-ionizing Radiation (OJ RS, No. 36/09), Articles 14–16.
- Law on Radiation and Nuclear Safety and Security (OJ RS, Nos 95/18 and 10/19), Articles 215–216.
- Law on prohibition of development, production, storage and use of chemical weapons and on their destruction (OJ RS, Nos 36/09 and 104/13), Articles 32–44.
- Law on Air Protection (OJ RS, Nos 36/09, 10/13 and 26/2021 – other law), Articles 73–77.

409. The Ministry shall supervise work of the EPA, authorities responsible for environmental protection in the AP and responsible authorities of the local self-governance unit, as well as authorized legal persons, in the performance of delegated tasks (Art. 109a).

- Law on Waters (OJ RS, Nos 30/10, 93/12, 101/16,95/18, and 95/18 – other law), Articles 196–208.
- Law on Environmental Impact Assessment (OJ RS, Nos 135/04 and 36/09), Articles 35–39.
- Law on Integrated Pollution Prevention and Control (OJ RS, Nos 135/04, 25/15, 109/21), Articles 26–28.
- Law on Chemicals (OJ RS, Nos 36/09, 88/10, 92/11, 93/12 and 25/15), Articles 86–96.
- Law on Biocidal Products (OJ RS, Nos 36/09, 88/10, 92/11 and 25/15), Articles 50–58.
- Law on Biocidal Products (OJ RS, No. 109/21), Articles 53–59.
- Law on Protection Protection against Noise in the Environment (OJ RS, No. 96/21), Articles 30–34.
- Law on Waste Management (OJ RS, Nos 36/09, 88/10, 14/16 and 95/18 – other law, and 35/23), Articles 83–86.
- Law on Packaging Waste (OJ RS, Nos 36/09 and 95/18 – other law), Articles 46–49.
- Law on Genetically Modified Organisms (OJ RS, No. 41/09), Articles 37–44, etc.

316. Besides that, there are a number of other legal Acts that could be relevant for the inspection, especially the following:

- Law on Ministries (OJ RS, Nos 128/20, 116/22, 92/23 – other law).
- Law on State Administration (OJ RS, Nos 79/05, 101/07, 95/10, 99/14, 30/18 – other law, 47/18).
- Law on Determining the Jurisdiction of the Autonomous Province of Vojvodina (OJ RS, Nos 99/2009, 67/12 CC and 18/20 – other law).
- Law on Local Self-Government (OJ RS, Nos 129/07 and 83/14 – other law, 101/16 – other law, 47/18, and 111/21 – other law).
- Law on the Capital (OJ RS, Nos 120/2007 and 83/14 – other law, 101/16 – other law and 37/19).
- Law on Communal Activities (OJ RS, Nos 88/11, 104/16 and 95/18).
- Law on communal militia (OJ RS, No. 49/19).
- Law on General Administrative Procedure (OJ RS, Nos 18/16 and 95/18 – authentic interpretation, 2/23 CC).
- Criminal Code (OJ RS, Nos 85/2005 and 88/2005 – corr., 107/2005 – corr., 72/09, 111/09, 121/12, 104/13, 108/14, 94/16 and 35/19).
- Law on Economic Offences (OJ SFRY, Nos 4/1977, 36/1977 – corr, 14/1985, 74/1987, 57/1989 and 3/1990, OJ FRY, Nos 27/1992, 16/03 – other law, 41/93 – other law, 50/93 – other law, 24/1994, 28/1996 and 64/2001, and OJ RS, No. 101/05 – other law).
- Law on Offences (OJ RS, Nos 65/13, 13/16, 98/16 CC, 91/19 – other law and 91/19, and 112/22 CC).
- Law on fees for the use of public goods (OJ RS, Nos 95/18, 49/2019, 86/2019 and 156/2020), etc.

VI. Other Relevant Inspections

317. There are several other inspections, besides environmental ones, relevant for environmental issues, for example, health inspection, sanitary inspection, forestry inspection, hunting inspection, agricultural inspection, phytosanitary inspection, veterinary inspection, water inspection, tourist inspection, market inspection, labour inspection, mining inspection, spatial planning inspection, building inspection, geodesic inspection, electro-energetic inspection, inspection for equipment under pressure, fire protection inspection, public roads inspection, administration inspection, communal inspection, etc.

318. In 2021, environmental protection inspectors submitted a total of fifty-eight requests for the initiation of misdemeanour proceedings, nineteen applications for the initiation of economic offence proceedings, and one criminal report.[410] In the EC report for 2023, inspection problems in two areas are particularly emphasized: in the area of waste management ('Serbia's inspection capacity in the waste sector remains insufficient') and inspections responsible for industrial pollution and risk management ('inspection and law enforcement remain areas of concern').[411]

319. In all reports of the EC, the issue of application of regulations is emphasized as being particularly important. '... implementation and enforcement need to be further improved, in particular by strengthening administrative capacity at central and local levels, including that of inspectorates and the judiciary. It will require the implementation of structural, cross-sectoral reforms'.[412]

§5. Legal Harmonization

320. To a certain extent, harmonization of the Serbian environmental law with the EU environmental *acquis* has already begun in the mid-nineties. A commission for harmonization of Yugoslav law with the EU law and the Council of Europe law was established in 1995 on the federal level, but due to the overall crisis and isolation of the country, it did not fulfil its task. After the political changes in 2000, the new federal Government formed an interdepartmental group with the assignment to coordinate activities concerning law harmonization. In Serbia, several expert groups were established and given the task of producing drafts of new legislation and/or amendments to the existing environmental legislation that should be harmonized with the relevant *acquis communautaire*. In November 2000, Serbia, as one of the two Republics of former FR Yugoslavia, became a part of the SAP.

410. MEP. 2020, 33. In 9 cases, the inspectors were called by the acting judicial authorities to the court to give statements as witnesses and 30 judgments were passed. The inspectors filed appeals against two verdicts.
411. EC. 2023, 136.
412. EC. 2023, 135. *See also*, EC. 2022, 120; EC. 2021, 114; EC. 2020, 105; EC. 2019, 85, etc.

321. Serbian NA adopted in 2004 a resolution on Serbia's European future,[413] and Serbian Government adopted in 2005 the National Strategy for Accession to the EU.[414] The document outlines, *inter alia*, activities which Serbia should undertake to harmonize its legal system (including the environmental field) to be able to become a member of the EU by 2012.

However, due to political reasons, the decision to start negotiations concerning conclusion of the SAA was not made until April 2005. By the decision of the EC, negotiations on SAP resumed in June 2007 and were successfully concluded by initialling the SAA on 7 November 2007.

It means that, in practice, all new draft legislation, including environmental legislation, must be submitted to the European Integration Office of the Government of Serbia. The Office is responsible for coordination of Government activities in the framework of the EU SAP, including analysis of compatibility of draft legislation with *acquis communautaire*. It should be stressed that Serbia has been, since 2006, also eligible for EU pre-accession financial assistance under the EU Community Assistance for Reconstruction, Development and Stabilization (CARDS) programme, and since 2007 under the Instrument for Pre-Accession Assistance (IPA).

322. The SAA was finally signed on 29 April 2008 and ratified by Serbia in September 2008 (OJ RS, No. 83/2008).[415] The SAA between Serbia and the EU entered into force in September 2013.

Signing of the SAA obliged Serbia to gradually harmonize its environmental legislation with environmental *acquis* and to implement it consistently. According to Article 72 of the SAA, it is under obligation, in agreement with the EC, to prepare a programme for the implementation of obligations arising from the SAA, which will be monitored by the EU.[416]

The European Council granted Serbia the status of a candidate country in 2012. Accession negotiations were launched in January 2014. The first four negotiating chapters are opened including Chapter 35 dealing with normalization of relations between Serbia and Kosovo[417] and the rule of law Chapters 23 and 24. 'Since the opening of Serbia's accession negotiations in January 2014, 22 out of 35 chapters have been opened, including … all chapters in Cluster 4 on the Green agenda and

413. *See* http://www.parlament.gov.rs/activities/european-integration/documents.611.html (5.1.2024).

414. The key goal of the Strategy is to provide an expert foundation for the decision-making in the European integration process, and to prepare a coordinated set of measures, policies and institutions necessary for the EU association, including the plan for the approximation of the domestic legislation with the *acquis communautaire* https://www.mei.gov.rs/srp/dokumenta/nacionalna-dokumenta/ (5.1.2024.

415. *See also* Council Decision (2008/213/EC) of 18 Feb. 2008 on the principles, priorities and conditions contained in the European Partnership with Serbia including Kosovo as defined by United Nations Security Council Resolution 1244 of 10 Jun. 1999 and repealing Decision 2006/56/EC, OJ L 080, 19 Mar. 2008 P. 0046-0070.

416. Article 72 prescribes that 'The Parties recognise the importance of the approximation of the existing legislation in Serbia to that of the Community and of its effective implementation. Serbia shall endeavour to ensure that its existing laws and future legislation will be gradually made compatible with the Community acquis. Serbia shall ensure that existing and future legislation will be properly implemented and enforced.'

417. This designation is without prejudice to positions on status and is in line with UNSCR 1244/1999 and the ICJ Opinion on the Kosovo declaration of independence.

sustainable connectivity.'[418] However, 'the overall pace of negotiations will continue to depend, in particular, on the pace of rule of law reforms and on the normalisation of Serbia's relations with Kosovo*'.[419]

323. The Government of Serbia adopted, in June 2008, the National Programme for integration with the EU that contains assessment of the state of harmonization of legal regulations and sets short- and long-term priorities in relevant domains.[420] While 'environment' is mentioned in several Articles of the SAA, Article 111 is completely devoted to it:

> The parties shall, in particular, establish cooperation with the aim of strengthening administrative structures and procedures to ensure strategic planning of environment issues and coordination between relevant actors and shall focus on the alignment of Serbia's legislation to the Community acquis. Cooperation could also centre on the development of strategies to significantly reduce local, regional and transboundary air and water pollution, to establish a framework for efficient, clean, sustainable and renewable production and consumption of energy, and to execute environmental impact assessment and strategic environmental assessment. Special attention shall be paid to the implementation of the Kyoto Protocol.

The National Plan for the Adoption of Acquis (NPAA) (2014–2018) has been adopted. The NPAA defines development and strategic goals on the one hand and policies, reforms and measures required for the realization of these goals on the other. It also establishes a detailed plan, time frame and priorities for the adoption of legislation and appoints bodies responsible for its implementation.[421] In the meantime, the second revision of the NPAA was adopted in November 2016,[422] and the third version of this document was adopted in 2018.[423] The fourth, latest revised NPAA was adopted on 21 July 2022.[424]

418. EC. 2023, 3. In June 2021, Serbia accepted the revised enlargement methodology.
419. '*This designation is without prejudice to positions on status and is in line with UNSCR 1244/1999 and the ICJ Opinion on the Kosovo Declaration of Independence.' *Ibid.*
420. *Short-term priorities* were, *inter alia*, 'to accelerate harmonization of Serbian legislature with the *acquis communautaire*; implement existing laws, in particular in the area of environmental protection, etc. *Mid-term priorities* were 'full implementation of legislation that has been harmonized with the *acquis communautaire*; implement relevant international conventions and the Kyoto Protocol; adopt and commence with the implementation of Air Pollution, Waste Management and Environmental Protection Strategy; fully implement the National Environmental Protection Strategy and Water Strategy; continue strengthening national- and local-level administrative capacities in charge of environmental issues; implement years-long environmental policy financing plan, including the investment plan for this area; complete the construction of facilities for hazardous waste disposal', GOV RS. 2008a, 619.
421. Full realization of the goals set in NPAA was envisaged to be completed by 31 Dec. 2018, with the exception of those obligations for which interim timeframes for adapting will be set during the course of the negotiations, after acquiring the EU membership. GOV RS. 2014a, 3.
422. GOV RS. 2016.
423. GOV RS. 2018.
424. https://www.mei.gov.rs/upload/documents/nacionalna_dokumenta/npaa/NPAA_2022-2025_EN.pdf (5.1.2024).

324. Explanatory and bilateral screenings on Chapter 27 – Environment and Climate Change were held from September to November 2014. 'Following the bilateral screening, the Negotiating Group 27 was required to prepare a Post-Screening Document which contains a detailed description of the transposition and implementation: the strategic framework for full transposition and implementation of directives, preliminary deadlines for full implementation of EU legislation regarding this chapter, particularly for heavy investment directives, as well as financial sources to fund the implementation, with the aim to demonstrate Serbia's preparedness in the accession process.'[425] The Government of the RS adopted (21 January 2020) a decision to submit, to the EC, the adopted Negotiating Position for Chapter 27 (environment and climate change).[426] Under the Negotiating Position (December 2019), the RS accepts the *acquis* of the EU in Chapter 27 – Environment and Climate Change and will be in a position to fully implement them until accession as they read on 1 June 2019, except the following EU legal acts: Directive 2007/2/EC (INSPIRE), Directive 2008/50/EC (Ambient air quality), Directive 2016/802/EC (Sulfur content), Directive 94/63/EC, and 2009/126/EC (VOC Petrol phase I and II), Directive 2008/98/EC (Waste), Directive 94/62/EC (Packaging and packaging waste), Directive 1999/31/EC (Landfills), Directive 2012/19/EU (Waste from electrical and electronic equipment), Directive 2006/66/EC (Waste batteries), Directive 2000/60/EC (Water Framework Directive), Directive 91/271/EEC (Municipal wastewater treatment), Directive 2008/105/EC (Environmental quality standards), Directive 2006/118/EC (Underground water), Directive 91/676/EEC (Protection of water from pollution caused by nitrates), Directive 98/83/EC (Quality of water intended for human use), Directive 2010/75/EU (Industrial emissions), Directive 2003/87/EC (EU ETS), and Directive 98/70/EC (Quality of oil and diesel fuel).[427]

325. In July 2017, on the basis of the Law on Ministries (OJ RS, Nos 44/14, 14/15, 54/15 and 96/15 – other law),[428] an independent MEP was formed. The MEP is the leading institution for Chapter 27, while responsibilities for certain regulations have been assigned to the Ministry of Agriculture, Forestry and Water Management (MAFWM), while some regulations have remained within the competence of ministries in which they were previously (Ministry of Construction, Transport and Infrastructure, Ministry of Interior, MME, Ministry of Health, Ministry of Justice).[429]

---

425. GOV RS. 2016, 1148. The Post-Screening Document entitled 'Transposition and Implementation of Environmental and Climate Change Acquis (Ch. 27): Status and Plans' was adopted on 4 Sep. 2015 and submitted to the EC. For more information on the activities of the negotiating group (Ch. 27), *see* https://www.pregovarackagrupa27.gov.rs/dokumenta/ (05/01/2024).
426. https://www.ekologija.gov.rs/lat/saopstenja/vesti/pregovaracka-pozicija-za-poglavlje-27---zivotna-sredina-i-klimatske-promene-stize-evropskoj-komisiji-u-brisel (10.2.2024). *See also*, https://www.mei.gov.rs/eng/documents/negotiations-with-the-eu/accession-negotiations-with-the-eu/negotiati
ng-positions/ (10.2.2024).
427. GOV RS. 2019a, 2,3. Transitional periods have been requested for these EU regulations.
428. *See also*, Law on Ministries (OJ RS, Nos 128/20, 116/22, and 92/23 – other law).
429. GOVR RS. 2018, 1136.

326. According to the last Report of the EC:

> 'Serbia has achieved some level of preparation in the area of environment and climate change. ... The adoption of important legislation and strategic documents is pending.'[430] For complete harmonization with EU regulations, the adoption of the new EIA law is required, as well as the Regulation on determining the list of projects for which an impact assessment is mandatory and a list of projects for which an environmental impact assessment may be required. In addition, it is necessary to adopt a new law on SEA.[431] Additional harmonization of the Law on Planning and Construction is also necessary, and the Directive on the protection of the environment through criminal law has been partially transposed into the national legislation.

§6. Critical Evaluation of the Efficiency of the Existing Serbian Environmental Law

327. A much more voluminous text would be needed for a detailed analysis of the evaluation of the efficiency of the Serbian legal provisions concerning environmental protection. The extent and the result of the analysis would also depend upon the chosen evaluation criteria and irregular and extremely difficult conditions under which the Serbian legal system in general and the environmental law, in particular, has been functioning. One of the most important facts is, without doubt, the fact that former FR Yugoslavia (Serbia and Montenegro) had been, between 1992 and 2000, practically excluded from all, or almost all, forms of international environmental relations. The crisis had grave consequences on the functioning of the legal system in general, as well as the legal regulation of environmental protection, including malfunctioning of the judiciary. A very important problem has been the corruption of the system,[432] including, in some cases, even corruption of judges. 'Corruption is prevalent in many areas and remains an issue of concern.'[433] Generally gloomy

430. EC 2023, 134. In the coming year, Serbia should, *inter alia*, improve the efficiency and quality of the preparation, implementation and quality control of investments as well as further improve strategic investment planning and management including transparency of procedures; align the Law on planning and building with international standards; adopt EU compliant EIA and SEA laws; align and adopt the Directive on Environmental Crime; implement the Action Plan for Administrative Capacity Development and the Programme of Air Protection; adopt the Industrial Emissions Directive; implement the Low Carbon Development Plan, etc. *Ibid.*

431. The proposals of both laws are in the parliamentary procedure. *See*: http://www.parlament.gov.rs/akti/zakoni-u-proceduri/zakoni-u-proceduri.1037.html (5.2.2024).

432. On this subject, *see* NA. 2005. After that, a new strategy for the fight against corruption was adopted for the period 2013–2018 with an action plan (*See* NA. 2013). During 2023, a special working group was formed to create a strategy for the period from 2023 to 2030. *See*, https://www.mpravde.gov.rs/sr/tekst/39384/nacionalna-strategija-za-borbu-protiv-korupcije-za-period-od-2023-2028-godine-.php (5.1.2024).

433. EC. 2023, 5; 31–37. For further information on environmental corruption, *See* Petković, 2014.

circumstances in Serbian society, including the pauperization of most of the population, and rising role of crime, caused in that time degradation of the legal system in general, including of course the environmental law, which is still felt to a certain extent today.

328. The state of environmental legislation is almost entirely determined by the process of EU integration. During the last decade, legislation of the RS is in the process of continuous monitoring and assessment of conformity with EU legislation. There is a detailed assessment of the level of compliance with all environmental regulations. However, generally speaking, it can be concluded that there are significant problems in the implementation of regulations in almost all areas (industrial pollution, waste management, water management, air protection, environmental protection, etc.). The capacity of the competent authorities is not satisfactory. The issue of coordination between different bodies (horizontal and vertical) can be significantly improved.[434] Financing in certain sectors is a serious problem, etc.

329. A considerable improvement has been achieved, especially since 2004. For instance, EIA has been the most efficient regulatory instrument since it was implemented in Serbia;[435] numerous international treaties have been ratified, much has been done in upgrading institutional structure, new laws and other legal Acts have been adopted and serious efforts have been made in the process of harmonization of Serbian environmental legislation with the EU standards. It should also take into account the elements of the positive impact of the EU integration process on international cooperation and the achievement of national goals in environmental policy.[436] The last phase is characterized by problems that are largely related to the practical application of certain regulations and the mutual harmonization of regulations from different areas. In the latest EC report, the need to amend both laws (EIA, SEA) was emphasized. Problems in the practice of implementing the Law on Planning and Construction were mentioned.[437]

330. According to the EC Progress Monitoring Report 2023, 'In the area of horizontal legislation, Serbia has a high level of alignment with the EU *acquis*. However, implementation and enforcement need to be further improved, in particular by strengthening administrative capacity at central and local levels, including that of inspectorates and the judiciary, which will require the implementation of structural,

434. Horizontal and vertical coordination mechanisms need to be improved. UNECE. 2015, 32–34.
435. UNECE. 2007, 91. However, capacity problems at the municipal level are significant, notably for EIA and IPPC. UNECE. 2015.
436. On details, *see* Todić, Dimitrijević, 2014,.
437. 'EIA implementation needs to be considerably strengthened. Serbia needs to carry out SEA for all plans and programs that fall under the framework for projects listed in the EIA Directive.' EC. 2023, 135.

cross-sectoral reforms.'[438] An inclusive stakeholder process started to support the development of a national Environmental Protection Strategy (Green Agenda for Serbia).

331. The issue of stakeholder participation in the process of harmonizing national regulations with EU regulations is not at a level that ensures the creation of quality regulations.[439] In the State administration rules governing this issue, there are gaps which create conditions for the adoption of regulations without the efficient participation of the public concerned. Public participation at local level is much more specific.[440] The results of research on the effectiveness of public participation in environmental decision-making show, *inter alia*, 'that the majority of associations of citizens report that information about opportunities for participation is not sufficiently available, requires considerable effort to collect, and is often incomplete and unclear'.[441] It is estimated that 'the role of participation is still mostly formal, i.e., reduced to providing legitimacy for making planning decisions. Despite all efforts to develop collaborative planning practice in the RS, the fair and equal treatment of pluralistic interests remains questionable, since there is no formal obligation to evaluate the success of participation'.[442] According to the EC, 'the quality of public consultations improved marginally during the reporting period. Serbia needs to ensure greater transparency about investments and their environmental effects as well as respect for freedom of expression and assembly in the environmental sector'.[443]

332. Regulatory impact assessment was introduced in the law preparation system (not by by-laws and international treaties) in 2005. There are certain results. However, the existing methodology of regulatory impact assessment – assessing costs of laws adoption and implementation that would affect the budget, citizens, the economy and other factors – cannot be taken as reliable. As a whole, it can be recognized that there is some unevenness present including the problems in providing necessary indicators for the assessment of state, anticipation of possible consequences and selection of alternative solutions.[444] The legal framework relevant for assessment of opportunities of the economy and the society for implementation of the national legislation harmonized with EU legislation has not been established in a satisfactory manner. The issue of administration capacities to assess the needs for transitional periods deserves more attention. To overcome this problem, the Law on

438. EC. 2023, 135. Legislative alignment on environmental liability and environmental crime acquis has not progressed. Transboundary cooperation did not improve during the reporting period, and Serbia is encouraged to pursue efforts to improve transboundary cooperation with neighbouring countries. *Ibid.*
439. 'While public consultations were conducted for all draft policy planning documents in 2022, this was the case for only 29% of draft laws and 30% of draft regulations. There is still no central body in charge of the quality control of public consultations, including on the e-consultations platform, established in December 2021.' EC. 2023, 17.
440. For details, *see* Bobić, Todić, 2015.
441. Young Researchers of Serbia. 2023, 12.
442. GOV RS. 2019b, Ch. 4.1.3.2. Participation of citizens.
443. EC. 2023, 135.
444. Todić, 2017a.

planning system (OJ RS, No. 30/18) was adopted by the parliament in April 2018.[445] In the meantime, based on this law, several by-laws were adopted.[446]

333. A part of problems concerning the state of environmental legislation in Serbia could be linked to the general situation in the Serbian judiciary which is still not efficient enough. However, 'Serbia has some level of preparation in the area of judiciary. … A number of steps have been taken to reduce the space for political influence on the judiciary. However, it is not yet possible to observe a consistent reduction of undue influence on judges and prosecutors in practice.'[447] This causes difficulties for citizens, enterprises and NGOs when they are subject to court procedures. It usually takes time for a court proceeding to result in a court order and an adequate sanction, which often are not imposed or are largely symbolic. 'There is a perception that the judiciary is ineffective when it comes to imposing sanctions for environmental offences. It can take some time for a court proceeding to result in a court order and an eventual sanction; then, in many cases, sanctions are not imposed or are largely symbolic.'[448]

334. Regarding environmental monitoring, the EPA plays a central role. The systematic monitoring of water and air quality, collection of data on waste generation and sources of water, air, and land pollution, and the collection of data on the endangerment of natural values, represent the tasks performed by the EPA. According to the EC report (2023), EPA's 'annual reports were frequently not published in a timely manner. Under the European Environment Information and Observation Network, Serbia's provisional scores for core data flows in 2022 dropped by 50% compared with 2021...'[449] In the report of Coalition 27, various issues are pointed out in several places in connection with the monitoring of air quality, water quality, waste management, noise, and climate change.[450]

---

445. EC. 2019, 82.
446. Regulation on the procedure for the preparation of the Draft Development Plan of the Republic of Serbia (OJ RS, No. 54/23). Regulation on mandatory elements of the development plan of autonomous provinces and local self-government units (OJ RS, No. 107/20). Regulation on the methodology of public policy management, analysis of the effects of public policies and regulations, and the content of individual public policy documents (OJ RS, No. 8/19). Regulation on the methodology for creating medium-term plans (OJ RS, No. 8/19).
447. EC. 2023, 21. 'Challenges and delays in implementation persist regarding the impartiality, accountability, efficiency and professionalism of the judiciary, access to justice, and high-quality training.' *Ibid.*
448. UNECE. 2015, 56.
449. EC. 2023, 135. The report points to 'monitoring' in several other parts: air quality ('Serbia needs to... improve air quality monitoring'); water quality (needs to 'strengthen administrative capacity in monitoring'); chemicals ('Serbia needs to boost its administrative capacity to... ensure proper monitoring of persistent organic pollutants'); climate change ('Full alignment of legislation on monitoring, reporting and verifying greenhouse gas emissions... is still pending').
450. For example, 'Each report issued by SEPA raises questions about the reliability and scope of air quality monitoring in Serbia'. Young Researchers of Serbia. 2023. 42, 'Current monitoring of surface waters is not appropriate in terms of its scope or fulfilment of the requirements of the Water Framework Directive.' *Ibid.*, 74.

335. In the field of environmental financing system, the medium-term 'reforms will require further strengthening of the environmental revenue collection, expanding the revenue base, fiscal decentralization, privatization and further increase of tariffs to achieve full cost recovery'.[451] 'The main source of financing environmental protection is the budget of the RS. Other sources include municipal budgets, revenues from charges and fees, and commercial sector funds. Funds can also be provided through donations, loans, international aid, instruments, programmes and funds from the EU, UN and other organizations.[452] For environmental protection, in 2019, approximately 0.3% of GDP was allocated, which is a similar amount to that in 2018.[453] In 2023, the Serbian national budget for environment and climate action was increased by 18% compared with 2022. However, 'it still lacks an effective institutional set-up and transparent procedures.'[454]

451. GOV RS. 2010a, 140.
452. EPA. 2021, 9. Economic instruments applied in the RS include charges and fees, as well as incentives and subsidies. *See* Art. 83 of the EPL.
453. EPA. 2021, 10.
454. EC. 2023, 135. 'All income generated from environmental fees should be earmarked for environmental purposes.'

Chapter 2. Air Pollution and Climate Change

336. During 2021, electricity and thermal energy production is the dominant source of *sulfur oxide* emissions (92%).[455] The sector of industry and heating plants of less than 50MW and individual furnaces participated with 4% and 2%, respectively, while other sources were negligible (up to 2%).[456] In the total emissions of *nitrogen oxides*, road traffic had the largest share (41%), and the electricity and thermal energy production sector was in second place with a slightly smaller contribution (39%).[457] The dominant share of *PM10 suspended particle* emissions came from heating plants with a capacity of less than 50MW and individual combustion plants (64%). In the RS, the road transport sector contributed 10% to national PM10 emissions, followed by agriculture and industry with 9% each, and all other sources contributed 8%. The influence of heating plants with a power of less than 50 MW and individual combustion plants on the total emissions of *suspended particles PM2.5* was extremely large and amounted to 80%.[458]

337. According to estimates from the Adaptation Program to Changed Climate Conditions, 'the Republic of Serbia is warming more and faster than the world average'.[459] Based on the results of the studies produced for the elaboration of RS's Third National Communication to UNFCCC, 'it was found that during the period from 1961 to 2017, the temperature increased by 0.36°C per decade, while in the period from 1981 to 2017, the recorded temperature increase was 0.60°C per decade'.[460]

§1. The Monitoring System

338. The national network for monitoring air quality is in competence of the EPA in accordance with the Law on Air Protection (OJ RS, Nos 36/09, 10/13, and 26/21 – other law).[461] The First Bi-annual Programme for Air Monitoring in Serbia

455. The list of combustion plants included in the National Plan for the reduction of emissions of major pollutants originating from old large combustion plants includes twelve plants such as Nikola Tesla Thermal Power Plant, Kostolac Thermal Power Plant, etc. GOV RS. 2020, Annex 1.
456. EPA 2023b, 13. The analysis of the spatial variation trends regarding accumulated annual and seasonal precipitation for both analysed periods (the one from 1998 to 2017 and the other from 2008 to 2017) shows an increase of precipitation up to 10%.
457. Emissions from the industrial sector represented 7% of the total emissions of this pollutant, off-road traffic 6%, heating power less than 50 MW and individual combustion plants 5%, and emissions from agriculture 2% of the total emissions.
458. The road transport sector was the second most important source of this pollutant with 9%, the industry sector contributed as a source with 5%, while all other sources contributed 6% of total PM2.5 emissions. *Ibid.*
459. GOV RS. 2023b. ('Introduction').
460. GOV RS. 2023a, Appendix 1. During the period 1998–2017, the number of days of heatwave increased by fifteen to twenty-five days concerning the larger part of the country's territory, while the warmest temperature peaks lasted over twenty-five days in eastern and western Serbia.
461. For more information, *see* http://www.sepa.gov.rs/index.php?menu=300&id=20028&akcija=showAll (5.1.2024).

dates from 1993 (OJ RS, No. 70/93). Air pollution monitoring is presently regulated by Articles 9–17 of the Law on Air Protection[462] and by the EPL (OJ RS, Nos 135/04, 36/09 – other law, 72/2009 – other law, 43/2011, 14/2016, 76/18 and 95/18 – other law). By Article 24 of the EPL, it is prescribed that 'measures of systematic air quality monitoring' should be undertaken, while Article 69 prescribes that 'The Republic, AP, and local self-governance unit, within their respective competencies under the law, shall provide for continual control and monitoring of the state of the environment.'

339. According to Article 70 of EPL, monitoring is carried out by systematic monitoring of indicator values, and monitoring of negative impacts on the environment, the state of environment, measures and actions to be taken in order to reduce negative impacts and improving the quality of the environment. The Government establishes the criteria for determining the number and distribution of measuring points, the network of measuring points, extent and frequency of measurements, classification of phenomena that are monitored, methodology and indicators of environmental pollution and its monitoring, deadlines and manner of submitting data.

340. Pursuant to Article 12 of the Law on Air Protection, the national network consists of stations for air quality monitoring in various areas and for different purposes: (1) regional and transboundary atmospheric transmission of polluting substances in air and aerosols within international obligations; (2) air quality in settlements, industrial and non-living areas; (3) air quality in protected natural areas and protected environment of immovable cultural goods; (4) air quality in areas under the influence of certain sources of pollution, including mobile sources; and (5) allergenic pollen.[463]

341. Automatic and systematic air quality monitoring in Serbia dates back to 2002 where first automatic monitoring in the RS started in Pančevo municipality and Belgrade PHI in 2002. Shortly after establishment of EPA in 2006, EPA monitoring stations were installed and put into operation.[464]

342. The state network for automatic air quality monitoring in the RS operated by EPA was expanding and was completed in 2009–2010 through an EU project. By the end of 2020, state network had 34 locations. Different locations measure different air quality parameters such as SO2, NO2, PM10, PM2.5, O3, CO, BTX (benzene, toluene, xylene), different heavy metals and PAHs.[465] During 2022, the EPA

462. Its provisions are specific with the following by-laws: Regulation for air quality monitoring and air quality requirements (OJ RS, Nos 11/10, 75/10 and 63/13), Regulation on the establishment of programmes for air quality control in national network (OJ RS, No. 58/11), and Regulation on the establishment of zones and agglomerations (OJ RS, Nos 58/11 and 98/12).
463. Following Art. 5 of the Law on Air Protection, the Regulation on the determination of zones and agglomerations (OJ RS, Nos 58/11 and 98/12) on the territory of the RS has determined three zones ('Srbija', 'Vojvodina', and 'Kosovo and Metohija'), and eight agglomerations. For additional details *see* EPA. 2023b, 9.
464. GOV RS. 2022a, 18.
465. *Ibid.*

carried out systematic measurements of air quality in the state network in accordance with the Regulation on the establishment of the Air Quality Control Program in the state network and collected and processed measurement results from all measurement points of the state network and from local networks of LSG units.[466]

343. In the RS, changes in climate conditions have been monitored for more than ten years, including observed climate changes and future changes until the end of the twenty-first century under different scenarios of greenhouse gas emissions (GHG).[467]

§2. State of Air Pollution and Climate Change

344. During 2022, as in previous years, suspended particles were the dominant pollutant in the RS.[468] Exceedances of the daily limit values (of 50 μg/m3) were at all measuring points and their number was from three days at the station Kamenicki Vis till the 178 days recorded at the station Valjevo ZZJZ. The highest daily concentrations of PM10 were measured on stations Beograd Ovca 516 μg/m3 and Zajecar 326 μg/m3. The exceeding of the annual limit value for PM2.5 (25 μg/m3) was recorded at the eighteen stations.[469]

345. The EPA air quality report for 2021 'listed an increased number of agglomerations with air pollution exceeding EU limits (20) compared with last year (19), meaning that around four million inhabitants are exposed to polluted air. The pollution caused by the Kostolac B thermal power plant needs to be addressed urgently'.[470]

346. By far, the highest impact on health is observed due to PM2.5, where for the modelling reference year 2015, the estimated premature deaths amount to 9773 premature deaths and more than 92 thousand life years lost. Considering the fact that ambient air quality has been deteriorating since 2015, the negative effects of air pollution are even higher.[471]

---

466. EPA 2023b, 4. For the list of stations *see* National Network of Automatic Stations for Air Qualtiy Monitoring: http://www.amskv.sepa.gov.rs/pregledstanica.php (12.1.2023).
467. GOV RS. 2023b, Ch. 3.1. (Overview of climate change monitoring in the RS).
468. EPA 2023b, 5.
469. Exceedances of *sulphur-dioxide* daily limit value (125 μg/m3) were registered at two stations (Bor Gradski park for four days at Bor Institut and Beograd Obrenovac IPHBGD for one day). Exceedances of the *nitrogen-dioxide* daily limit value, 85 μg/m3, were in Beograd at Despota Stefana IPHBGD twenty days and Mostar three days, in Novi Pazar and Nis O.S. 'Sveti Sava' one day. The results of measurements of *benzene* during 2022 show that there was no exceeding of the annual limit value. Exceedances of the target values for *ground-level ozone*, (120 μg/m3), more than twenty-five days were recorded at ten station. The results of measurements of *benzo(a)pyrene* show that target value (1 ng/m3) was exceeded in three stations. The results of measurements of *lead* show that daily limit value (1000 ng/m3) was exceeded at one station. During the activities of detection and quantification of pollen in ambient air *ambrosia pollen* was dominant. *Ibid.*
470. EC. 2023, 135.
471. GOV RS. 2022a, 23.

347. Current monitoring of climate change in the RS indicates the following characteristics of climate change in the RS: (a) rise in average temperature; (b) the change in average annual precipitation amounts is not significant; (c) increase in frequency and intensity/duration of heat waves; and (d) increasing frequency and intensity/duration of droughts.[472]

§3. LEGISLATION

I. International Treaties

348. Serbia has ratified following international treaties regulating air protection and air quality control:

- Convention on long-range transboundary air pollution (OJ SFRY – IT, No. 11/86).
- Protocol to the 1979 CLRTAP on Long-term Financing of the Cooperative Programme for Monitoring and Evaluation of the Long-Range Transmission of Air Pollutants in Europe, EMEP (OJ SFRY – IT, No. 2/87).[473]
- United Nations Framework Convention on Climate Change (OJ FRY – IT, No. 2/97).
- Kyoto Protocol to the United Nations Framework Convention on Climate Change (OJ RS – IT, No. 88/07).
- Amendment to Annex B to the Kyoto Protocol to the United Nations Framework Convention on Climate Change (OJ RS – IT, No. 38/09).
- Doha Amendment to Kyoto Protocol to the United Nations Framework Convention on Climate Change (OJ RS – IT, No. 2/17).
- Paris Agreement on Climate Change (OJ RS – IT, No. 4/17).
- Vienna Convention for the Protection of the Ozone Layer (OJ FRY – IT, No. 1/90).
- Montreal Protocol on Substances that Deplete the Ozone Layer (OJ FRY – IT, No. 16/90).
- Amendments to the Montreal Protocol: 1990 London Amendment, 1992 Copenhagen Amendment, 1997 Montreal Amendment and 1999 Beijing Amendment (OJ SM – IT, No. 24/04) – CLRTAP (OJ SFRY – IT, No. 11/86); Kigali Amendment (OJ RS – IT, No. 17/21).

II. National Legislation

349. In the last few years, several strategic planning documents in the field of climate change and air protection have been adopted in the RS: National plan to reduce emissions of major pollutants originating from old large combustion plants,

472. GOV RS. 2023b, Ch. 3.1. (Overview of climate change monitoring in the RS).
473. In addition, Serbia has ratified Protocol on Heavy Metals to 1979 CLRTAP (OJ RS – IT, No. 1/12) and Protocol on Persistent Organic Pollutants to 1979 CLRTAP (OJ RS – IT, No. 1/12).

Air Protection Program for the period 2022–2030 and an action plan, the low-carbon development strategy of the RS for the period from 2023 to 2030 with projections until 2050, Program for Adaptation to Changed Climate Conditions for the period from 2023 to 2030 with Action Plan. Serbia has yet to adopt its national integrated energy and climate plan and an energy strategy.

A. *Environmental Protection Law*

350. Provisions concerning air protection are contained in all four systemic environmental laws (EPL, Law on SEA, Law on EIA and Law on IPPC). They differ depending on the basic subjects of their regulations. However, the basic legal instrument is the Law on Air Protection adopted in 2009 (OJ RS, Nos 36/2009, 10/2013, and 26/2021 – other laws).

351. Certain provisions of the EPL (OJ RS, Nos 135/04, 36/09 – other law, 72/09 – other law, 43/11 CC, 14/16, 76/18 and 95/18 – other law) are relevant for air protection having in mind character of the air and possibilities for pollution.[474] 'Air' is defined as element of the 'natural value'[475] and 'public natural goods'.[476] Key issues concerning general air protection have been regulated by Article 24 which prescribes that 'measures of air protection[477] shall ensure overall atmosphere preservation with all the processes and climate characteristics thereof', aiming at 'Reducing air pollution to regulated limit values and below'.

352. According to Article 39, the Government is in charge of determining limit values of the emissions for pollutants at the place of their outflow into the environment and the levels of emissions for pollutants in the environment.[478] The Government is also obliged to determine criteria for the number and layout of measurement points, measurement point's network, scope and frequency of measurement, classification of phenomena monitored, methodology and indicators about the pollution of the environment and their monitoring, deadlines and manner of data submission has been stipulated according to Article 70, paragraph 2.

353. Action Plan for protection of air and atmosphere is anticipated to be prepared in accordance with Article 65 of the EPL.

474. 'Climate change' is mentioned in the EPL only in the part that refers to the use of resources from the Green Fund of the RS (Art. 90v).
475. Besides the water, soil, forests, geological resources, plants and animal life (Art. 3, point 3).
476. Besides the 'water goods, water-fronts, underground goods, forests, sceneries or landscapes' (Art. 3, point 5).
477. These are 'measures of systematic air quality monitoring, technical-technological and other necessary measures ... '.
478. Article 40 prescribes that pollutants and dangerous substances, wastewater or energy shall be released into air, water and soil in the manner prescribed and in the quantities, namely concentrations or levels not exceeding the prescribed limit values. The means of transportation made and placed on the market must comply with the conditions for emission from mobile pollution sources.

354. The use of funds of the Green Fund of the RS shall be carried out in accordance with the law, the NEPP and the strategic documents, as well as the list of priority infrastructure projects in the field of environment, for, *inter alia*, the protection, preservation and improvement of air, water, soil and forest quality, as well as the mitigation of climate change impacts and the adoption of adaptation measures, including the protection of the ozone layer (Article 90v, paragraph 1).

B. Law on Air Protection

355. The Law comprises the following chapters: I Basic provisions (Articles 1–4), II Controlling the air quality (Articles 5–17), III Air quality requirements (Articles 18–25), IV Strategy, plans and programmes (Articles 26–39), V Measures for air quality improvement (Articles 40–58), VI Measurement the emissions and level of the pollutants in the air (Articles 59–64), VII Informing and reporting (Articles 65–67), VIII Information system (Articles 68–70), IX Funding the protection and improvement of air quality (Articles 71–72), X Supervision (Articles 73–77), XI Competence for resolving upon the complaint (Article 78), XII Penal provisions (Articles 79–83), and Transitional and final provisions (Articles 84–90).

356. This Law regulates air quality management and establishes the measures, manners of organization and control of the protection implementation and improvement of the air quality as a natural value of a general interest that is especially protected.[479] (Article 1) The regulations of this Law are not to be implemented to address the pollution caused by radioactive matters, industrial accidents and natural disasters.

357. Pursuant to Article 4 of the Law, the protection and improvement of the air quality shall be performed by the RS, AP, LSG unit, business associations, entrepreneurs, as well as other legal and physical entities.[480] Monitoring both the air quality and emissions into the air is done by competent bodies of State administration and legal entities provided with the licence to perform these activities.

1. Controlling the Air Quality

358. The air quality is assessed in the RS regarding the level of the pollutants, depending on upper and lower assessment threshold, as follows: (1) in all the zones and agglomerations where the level of the pollutants exceeds the upper assessment

479. Air is the air in troposphere in the open space that does not include air in the closed space (Art. 3, part 1).

480. Business associations, other legal entities and entrepreneurs while performing their activities that affect or could affect the air quality must do the following: provide technical measures for preventing or decreasing the emission into the air; plan the costs of protecting the air against pollution within investment and manufacturing costs; monitor the effect of their activities to the air quality; provide other protection measures, in accordance with this Law and laws regarding environment protection (Art. 4, para. 2).

threshold for that matter, for assessing the air quality there are used the data obtained by fixed measurements, to which the data obtained by technical modelling and/or indicative measurements can be added; (2) in all the zones and agglomerations where the level of the pollutants is below the established upper assessment threshold for these pollutants, for assessing the air quality there can be used the combination of fixed measurements and technical modelling and/or indicative measurements; (3) in all the zones and agglomerations where the level of the pollutants is below the established lower threshold for these pollutants, for assessing the air quality there are used technical modelling and/or assessment techniques (Article 7).

359. Assessing the air quality is done mandatorily in terms of concentrations of sulphur dioxide, nitride dioxide and oxide nitrates, particulate matters (PM10, PM2.5), lead, benzene and carbon monoxide, ground ozone, arsenic, cadmium, nickel and benzo(a)pyrene (further on: pollutants), and can also be done for other pollutants, identified as such by relevant international regulations (Article 8).

360. With the aim of controlling, maintaining the State and/or improving the quality of the air, the Government identifies zones[481] and agglomerations in the RS territory.[482]

2. Licence for Measurement of the Emissions and Level of the Pollutants in the Air

361. Pursuant to Article 60, authorized legal entities can exercise the measurement after being issued a licence by the Ministry, if they meet the conditions in terms of staff, equipment and space, as well as if they are technically enabled according to the requirements of the standard SRPS ISO 17025.[483]

362. The operator exercising the air quality and/or emission measurement independently must obtain the agreement from the Ministry, provided that, within their registered activity, they independently exercise the tasks of measurement of the air quality and/or emission and that they are professionally and technically able according to the requirements of the standard SRPS ISO 17025 (Article 61).

481. The zone is the part of the Republic of Serbia territory with defined borders, specified with the aim of assessing and managing the air quality, being a characteristic functional whole from the point of controlling, maintaining and/or improving the state of the air quality. Agglomeration is the zone with more than 2,50,000 inhabitants. Agglomeration can also be a zone with fewer inhabitants, if the population density in that zone is higher than prescribed, so that justifies the need to assess and manage the air quality. The Government prescribes the population density for identifying agglomeration in event of number of inhabitants in the zone being fewer than 2,50,000 (Art. 5).

482. Zones and agglomerations are identified based on the air quality assessment, depending upon the identified upper and lower assessment limit (Art. 6, para. 1).

483. A complaint cannot be made upon the resolution by which the licence from para. 1 of this Article is issued or cancelled, but an administrative dispute can be initiated (Art. 60, para. 4).

3. Strategy, Plans and Programmes

363. Air Protection Policy and Planning instruments are as follows: (1) Air Protection Strategy; (2) air quality plans; (3) short-term action plans; (4) National Programme for gradual decrease of annual national emission ceilings of the pollutants; and (5) operator's plans for decreasing emissions from stationary installations (Article 26, paragraph 1).[484]

4. Air Protection Strategy

364. Air Protection Strategy (Strategy) is the basic document based on which the plans of air quality, short-term action plans and programmes for decreasing emissions of pollutants into the air are brought into action and need to be in consolidation with it.[485]

Strategy implementation is achieved by bringing the action plan for protecting the air and atmosphere and stopping climate change, which is its integral part and contains the following: (1) concrete measures taken in order to implement the Strategy's aims; (2) timelines for Strategy's aims achievement; and (3) activities' implementers. Ministry, in cooperation with other competent bodies, has the obligation to develop a plan (Article 29).

5. Air Quality Plans

365. In zones and agglomerations where the air quality category is 3, that is, when the air pollution exceeds the effects of the measures implemented, that is, when the environment capacity is endangered or there is permanent air pollution in the specific area, the competent body of AP and competent body of an LSG unit must bring the Air Quality Plan with the aim to reach appropriate limit values or target values identified by the Act from Article 18, paragraph 1 of this Law (Article 31).

6. Short-Term Action Plans

366. In accordance with Article 33, the competent body of AP, that is, the competent body of an LSG unit is due to bring in short-term action plans in the zone or agglomeration in their territory in events as follows: (1) if there is a danger that the levels of the pollutants in the air exceed one or more alert thresholds, determined

484. In February 2020, the Government adopted the National Plan for the reduction of emissions of the main pollutants originating from old large combustion plants (OJ RS, No. 10/20). In December 2022, following an extensive public consultation, Government adopted its first Air Protection Programme for the period 2022–2030 and an action plan. (OJ RS, No. 140/22).

485. The Ministry prepares draft Strategy that is brought into action by the Government for a six-year period (Art. 27).

by the Act from Article 18, paragraph 1 of this Law; (2) if there is a danger to exceed the alert threshold of the ground ozone, identified by an Act from Article 18, paragraph 1 of this Law, if the competent body makes an assessment, considering geographical, meteorological and economic conditions, that there is a significant potential to decrease the risk, duration and seriousness of such an exceedance. Short-term action plans can be, with the aim to protect people's health and/or environment as required, brought also in the case of a danger of exceeding one or more limits or target values for individual pollutants that are established by the Act from Article 18, paragraph 1 of this Law.

7. National Programme for Gradual Decrease of Annual National Pollutant Emission

367. National Programme for gradual decrease of annual national pollutant emission ceilings (henceforth, National Programme) is brought by the Government for a four-year period. National Programme contains the following: (1) data on the adopted instruments of air protection policy and measures for decreasing the pollutants emission from Article 26, paragraph 3 of this Law; (2) quantified assessment of policies and measures from point 1 of this paragraph regarding the pollutants emissions from the year 2000, which is taken as a reference; (3) approximate assessment of possible significant changes in geographical distribution of national emission ceilings; and (4) other data and documentation. National Programme needs to be available to the public and interested public (Article 37).[486]

8. Operator's Plan for Decreasing the Emissions from Stationary Installations

368. In the area in which air is assessed as the air quality category 3, the body competent for environmental matters orders the operator to develop a plan for decreasing emissions from stationary sources of air pollution and establishes the timeline for this plan's realization.[487] Operator is obliged to develop a plan for decreasing emissions from stationary air pollution sources in a timeline specified in paragraph 1 of this Article (Article 39).[488]

486. National plan for decreasing the emissions from the existing combustion installations is the part of the National Programme from Art. 37 of this Law. National plan for decreasing the emissions from the existing combustion installations specifically contains the following: (1) aims and defined target values in accordance with them; (2) measures and timelines for achieving the aims and target values; (3) procedure of monitoring this plan's implementation (Art. 38).

487. *Stationery pollution source* is a stationery technical unit, including the combustion installation, where one or more activities that can lead to the air pollution are performed, as well as any other activity technically connected with the activities performed at the location and that can produce emissions and pollution (Art. 3, para. 34).

488. Operator's plan for decreasing emissions from stationery sources of pollution contains the following: (1) description of an exceeded air pollution implications; (2) the zone where the operator is; (3) measures for achieving the air quality improvement; (4) description of selected technological

9. Air Quality Requirements

369. With the aim of monitoring the air quality, the Government, upon the Ministry's proposal, prescribes the air quality requirements.[489] The air quality requirements are numeric values of limit values of the pollutants level in the air, upper and lower threshold of air quality assessment, critical levels, margins of tolerance and tolerant values, target values and (national) long-term aims of the pollutants in the air, concentrations dangerous to human health and the concentrations to be reported to the public (Article 18).[490]

370. According to the pollution level, starting from the prescribed and limit and tolerant values and based on the measurement results, the following air quality categories are established: (1) Category 1 – pure or slightly polluted air where the limit values of none of the pollutants are exceeded; (2) Category 2 – moderately polluted air where limit values of one or more pollutants are exceeded, but tolerant values of none of the pollutants are not exceeded; and (3) Category 3 – too polluted air where tolerant values for one or more pollutants are exceeded (Article 21).[491] Special types of pollution are pollution from natural sources and exceedances because of sanding or salting of roads (Articles 24 and 25).

10. Measures for Air Quality Improvements

371. Pursuant to Article 40, measures for preventing and decreasing air pollution and improving air quality include the following: (1) prescribing the limit values of the pollutants emissions from the stationary pollution sources;[492] (2)

and other solutions; (5) cost assessment; (6) order of the planned activities' implementation; (7) timeline for the planned activities implementation; (8) resources for the plan's implementation; and (9) other data and documentation.

489. When the information threshold, in line with the Act from Art. 18 para. 1 from this Law, or the specific alert threshold, is exceeded, the Ministry, competent body of the AP and a competent body of an LSG unit is due to inform the public through radio, TV, daily newspapers, Internet and/or other appropriate manner (Art. 23).

490. The Act from para. 1 of this Article also prescribes timelines for reaching limit and/or target values, in events when they are exceeded.

491. In event of a pollutant not having a prescribed tolerance limit, its limit value shall be taken as the tolerant one. Air quality categories are established once a year for the previous calendar year. The list of air quality categories by zones and agglomerations at the Republic of Serbia territory is brought by the Government and published in 'The Official Journal of the Republic of Serbia', electronic media, as well as the websites of the Government and the Ministry (Art. 21, paras 2–3).

492. The Government prescribes the following: (1) limit values of the pollutants emissions into the air; (2) manner, procedure, frequency and methodology of measurement the pollutants emission; (3) criteria for establishing the measurement locations for measurement the emission; (4) procedure of evaluating the results of emission measurement and consolidation with the prescribed normatives; (5) content of the report on the taken emission measurement and emission result; and (6) manner of submitting the data on emissions for the needs of the information system and timelines for the data submission (Art. 41). Apart from that, the Government prescribes the ELVs of the pollutants from the existing combustion installations having in mind the type, capacity, age, planned working use of the installation and fuel used in it, as well as the methods, manner of measurement of the

prescribing the limit values of the pollutants emissions from the mobile pollution sources;[493] (3) consolidation with national emission ceilings after their establishment for individual pollutants;[494] (4) prescribing the allowed amounts of individual pollutants in specific products;[495] (5) decreasing the emission of greenhouse gases; (6) gradual decrease of the use of substances that deplete the ozone layer; and (7) other measures for pollution preventing and decreasing.

11. Licence for Work

372. A newly built or reconstructed stationary pollution source that has the obligation of issuing an integrated licence, that is, developing a study on the impact on the environment, and is not prescribed for can start working after obtaining the licence for work (Article 56).[496] The work of a newly built or reconstructed stationary air pollution source, as well as performance of other activities in an open space that can lead to the uncontrolled release of pollutants, is banned, until the licence for work from Article 56 paragraph 1 of this Law is obtained (Article 57).

373. The operator[497] must do the following: (1) submit the data on the stationary pollution source and its every change (reconstruction) to the Ministry, that is, Agency, competent AP body and competent LSG unit body; (2) enable regular emission monitoring and keep records on that; (3) enable permanent measurement of the emission when prescribed for specific pollutants and/or pollution sources, independently, through automatic machines for permanent measurement, with the Ministry agreement; (4) enable control measurements of the emission through an authorized

---

pollutants emission, criteria for selecting the measurement locations, manner of verifying the measurement accuracy (control measurement and calibration), manners of analysing the measurement results, manners and timelines for data submission and procedure of establishing total annual emission from the combustion installation (Art. 42).

493. Mobile pollution sources can be used and marketed if the pollutants in exhaust emissions from those sources do not exceed limit emission values established by technical provisions, in accordance with the Law. Mobile pollution sources emissions are controlled during regular, irregular and control technical examination, in accordance with an appropriate technical provision and the law regarding the traffic safety (Art. 46).

494. National emission ceilings are established for acidifying and eutrofying pollutants and ozone precursors, for the following: sulphur dioxides (SO_2), nitrate oxides (NO_x), volatile organic compounds and ammonia (NH_3), with the aim of improving and protecting the environment and people's health from the harm of acidification, eutrofication and ground ozone, and in order of achieving long-term aims including the maintenance of critical levels and population protection (Art. 47).

495. For fossil fuel (Art. 48), paints and polishes (Art. 49), emissions of greenhouse gases (Art. 50) and use of substances that deplete the ozone layer (Arts 51–54).

496. The licence from para. 1 of this Article is issued by the body competent for the matters of the environment protection in the form of resolution. A complaint can be stated upon the first instance resolution of the competent body of the AP and the competent body of an LSG unit from para. 2 of this Article. The Ministry's first instance resolution from para. 2 of this Article is final in the administrative procedure and an administrative dispute can be initiated against it (Art. 56, paras 2–4).

497. *Operator* is a business association, other legal entity or entrepreneur that manages the installation in accordance with the provisions, controls it or is authorized to make economic decisions in the field of installation's technical functioning (Art. 3, para. 24).

legal entity, if performing the measurement independently; (5) enable prescribed occasional emission measurements, through an authorized legal entity, twice a year, if not exercising a permanent measurement; (6) provide air quality monitoring upon the order of a competent inspection body, independently or through an authorized legal entity; (7) keep records on the exercised measurements with the data on measurement locations, results and frequency of measurements and submit the data in the prescribed written report form to the Ministry, that is, Agency, competent AP body and competent LSG body, for the following measurements: from paragraph 1 points 2 and 3 of this Article, once in three months within fifteen days after the trimester finishes, from paragraph 1 point 5 of this Article, within thirty days after the exercised measurement, for annual measurements in the form of annual report at the latest by 31 January of the running year for the previous calendar year; (8) keep records on type and quality of raw materials, fuel and waste in the combustion process; and (9) keep records on the work of installations for preventing or decreasing the pollutants emission, as well as measurement installations for emission measurement (Article 58).[498]

12. Public Information and Information System

374. According to Article 65 of the Law, competent body must inform the other bodies and organizations and public through electronic and printed media, at least in one local magazine in each official language, as well as through Internet about the following: (1) air quality; (2) plans of air quality and postponing the reaching of limit value for nitrate dioxide, benzene and particulate matter ten for a certain period of time; (3) plans for reaching limit values in zones and agglomerations with the exceedance of limit values; and (4) annual report on all pollutants included in this Law.[499]

375. Air quality information system for the RS is managed by the Agency (Article 68, paragraph 3).[500]

498. The operator must implement the measures for decreasing the pollutants, determined by the plan for its own stationery air pollution sources, at their own cost.
499. The competent body informs the public about the following: (1) air quality, in the form of annual report on the air quality condition, until 31 July of the current year for the previous one, and after 2012 until 28 February of the current for the previous year; (2) plans of air quality and postponing the reaching of limit value for nitrite dioxide, benzene and particulate matter ten for the certain period of time, within eight days after the adoption; and (3) plans for reaching limit values in zones and agglomerations with the exceedance of limit values, within eight days after the adoption (Art. 67).
500. State bodies and organizations, operators and authorized legal entities must timely and without charges submit the data from their competence, as well as the other data required for managing the air quality information system, to the Agency, with the aim of developing plans and reports, in accordance with this Law (Art. 68 para. 4).

376. The Ministry mediates and exchanges the data on air quality and emissions with international organizations and other countries in accordance with his/her confirmed international contracts (Article 70).[501]

C. Substances Depleting the Ozone Layer

377. Serbian legislation covering ozone-depleting substances is based on the provisions of the Montreal Protocol and the EC Regulation 2037/2000 of the European Parliament and of the Council on substances that deplete the ozone layer.[502] There is a ban on production of ozone-depleting substances in Serbia, pursuant to Article 53 paragraph 1 of the Law on Air Protection (OJ RS Nos 36/09, 10/2013, and 26/21 – other law) (below: the Law). There is a ban on consumption of substances listed in Annex A (Groups I and II), Annex B (Groups I, II and III), and Annex C (Groups II and III) in Serbia.[503]

378. With a view to implementing the Montreal Protocol, Articles 51–54 of the Law on Air Protection prescribe the management of ozone-depleting substances (phase-out of ozone-depleting substances, handling of these substances, handling of products and equipment that contain or have been manufactured using these substances, handling of ozone-depleting substances after the products and equipment containing them are no longer in use, ways of recovery, recycling and reclamation, consumption and final disposal of substances, placing on the market and calculation of costs for ozone-depleting substances reuse, and ways of labelling products and equipment containing ozone-depleting substances); handling of certain fluorinated greenhouse gases and products and equipment containing these gases; bans on and records of ozone-depleting substances and fluorinated greenhouse gases.[504]

379. According to Article 53 of the Law at the RS territory, the following actions are prohibited: (1) manufacturing the substances that deplete the ozone layer; (2) import and/or export of the substances that deplete the ozone layer that are assessed by the verified international contract, that is, products and equipment containing

---

501. The Agency mediates and exchanges the data with the European Agency for Environment Protection and European Network for Information and Monitoring (Art. 70 para. 2).

502. Republic of Serbia is an Art. 5 party of the Montreal Protocol (as developing country) with a delayed phase-out schedule until total elimination of consumption of controlled substances, considering that its annual calculated level of consumption of the controlled substances from Annex A is less than 0.3 kg per capita and of the controlled substances from Annex B is less than 0.2 kg per capita on the date of the entry into force of the Protocol following ratification, or at any time thereafter until 1 Jan. 1999. All activities relating to implementation of the Montreal Protocol in the Ministry are carried out and coordinated by the National Ozone Unit, established in December 2008 within the Sector for Protection of Natural Resources, Air Protection Unit. GOV RS. 2011a, p. 246.

503. Consumption of substances listed in Annex C, Group I (hydrochlorofluorocarbons) is allowed without limitations. Consumption of substances listed in Annex E, Group I (methyl bromide) is allowed, with the total annual quota of maximum 6.64 metric tons.

504. Pursuant to Art. 51 of the Law, the Ministry prepared the Regulation on ozone-depleting substances management as well as on conditions for licence issuance for import and export of such substances (OJ RS No. 22/10).

these substances, imported and/or exported from the countries into countries that are not the signing parties of that contract; (3) import and/or export and marketing without the permission of the substances that deplete the ozone layer and fluorinated greenhouse gases; (4) import and/or export and marketing of the new products and equipment containing the substances that are controlled, but that deplete the ozone layer, apart from chlorofluorohydrocarbons; (5) emission of the substances that deplete the ozone layer and fluorinated greenhouse gases; (6) loading the products and equipment containing fluorinated greenhouse gases with the substances that deplete the ozone layer; (7) washing out by substances that deplete the ozone layer; (8) retail marketing of the substances damaging ozone layer and fluorinated greenhouse gases; and (9) import and/or export and marketing the used products and equipment containing substances that deplete the ozone layer.

D. Climate Change: Policy and Legislation

380. The RS has been a member of the United Nations Framework Convention on Climate Change – UNFCCC since 10 June 2001. Kyoto Protocol entered into force in the RS on 17 January 2008. The RS, as a non-Annex I country (developing country), is not obligated to implement quantified GHG emission reduction in the first commitment period (2008–2012).[505]

381. Adoption of the Kyoto Protocol created the opportunity for the RS to contribute to global reduction of GHG emissions through reduction of 'local' environmental pollution through implementation of CDM of the Kyoto Protocol projects.[506] The National Strategy for incorporation of the RS into CDM for waste management, agriculture and forestry sectors was adopted on 11 February 2010 (OJ RS No. 8/2010). The MME developed Strategy for the implementation of CDM in energy sector in 2009.

382. The MEP is responsible for climate change issues. MEP is the national focal point for the implementation of the United Nations Framework Convention of the United Nations on Climate Change and its Kyoto Protocol. The EPA, established in 2004 within the MESP, is responsible, among other things, for data collection, processing and reporting on greenhouse gases.[507] The Law on Meteorological and Hydrological Activity (OJ RS, No. 88/10) defines the competences of the Republic Hydro Meteorological Service (RHMS) as a specific organization within the

505. Serbia also ratified Doha Amendment to the Kyoto Protocol (OJ RS – IT, No. 2/17), and Paris Agreement (OJ RS – IT, No. 4/17). For more information, *see* Todić, 2016.

506. Designated National Authority (DNA) for the implementation of CDM projects, a prerequisite for participation in this set of projects, has been fully operational since 21 Nov. 2008. So far, Serbia has realized seven CDP project. *See* https://www.klimatskepromene.rs/obaveze-prema-un/kjoto-protokol/cmd-projekti/ (5.1.2024).

507. Besides the MEP and EPA, ministries that have certain competences related to the climate change are: Ministry of Mining and Energy; Ministry of Economy; Ministry of Construction, Traffic and Infrastructure; Ministry of Finance and Ministry of Public Administration and LSG; Research is done by several universities and the Institute of Field and Vegetable Crops in Novi Sad.

Governmental system of the RS regarding the adoption and carrying out of multi-annual programmes of monitoring, research and forecasting climate changes, creating scenarios of regional and local climate change and participation in the programmes of multidisciplinary research of the impacts, vulnerability and adaptation options of certain economic sectors to climate change.

383. Initial National communication defines mitigation and adaptation-related programmes as well as plans for capacity building and awareness raising, scientific research and climatic observation.[508] The Second National Communication has also been prepared. Serbia submitted First Biennial Update Report[509] and Intended Nationally Determined Contribution.[510] The Government aimed at providing emission reduction of 9.8% by 2030 compared to 1990 levels. Serbia elaborated the National Appropriate Mitigation Actions (NAMAs) Development Guideline and submitted NAMAs to the registry.[511] In August 2022, Serbia submitted, with some delay, its updated nationally determined contribution to the Paris Agreement, committing to a 33.3% decrease in greenhouse gas emissions by 2030 compared with 1990 levels.[512] The low-carbon development strategy of the RS for the period from 2023 to 2030 with projections until 2050 was adopted in 2023 (OJ RS, No. 46/23).[513] In addition, the government adopted the Program for Adaptation to Changed Climate Conditions for the period from 2023 to 2030 with an Action Plan adopted in December 2023 (OJ RS, No. 119/23).

384. Certain national strategic documents consider the climate change issue as one of the key development issues. The NSDS and Action Plan for the Implementation of the NSDS for the period 2009–2017 (OJ RS, No. 22/09) put climate change issue as a key environmental risk factor and defines certain actions related to adaptation and mitigation.

385. Serbia has yet to adopt its national integrated energy and climate plan and an energy strategy.[514]

Law on Climate Change

508. *See* https://unfccc.int/resource/docs/natc/srbnc1.pdf (5.1.2024).
509. https://unfccc.int/files/national_reports/non-annex_i_parties/biennial_update_reports/application/pdf/serbur1e.pdf (5.1.2024).
510. At https://www4.unfccc.int/sites/ndcstaging/PublishedDocuments/Serbia%20First/Republic_of_Serbia.pdf (5.1.2024).
511. At https://unfccc.int/files/cooperation_support/nama/application/pdf/nama_development_guideline_en.pdf (5.1.2025).
512. https://unfccc.int/sites/default/files/NDC/2022-08/NDC%20Final_Serbia%20english.pdf (12.1.2024).
513. https://www.ekologija.gov.rs/saopstenja/vesti/vlada-republike-srbije-usvojila-strategiju-niskougljenicnog-razvoja-do-2030-godine (5.1.2024).
514. For Draft (English) version *see*: MME. 2023a. *See also*: https://www.mre.gov.rs/tekst/sr/1115/-integrisani-nacionalni-energetski-i-klimatski-plan-republike-srbije-za-period-do-2030-sa-vizijom-do-2050-godine.php (12.1.2024).

386. After a long period of preparation, the Law on climate change was adopted in March 2021 (OJ RS, No. 26/2021).[515] The law contains eighty-three articles divided into eleven chapters, namely: I Basic Provisions (Articles 1–5); II Strategies and plans (Articles 6–17); III Policies and measures to limit GHG emissions from sources (Articles 18–24);[516] IV Monitoring, reporting and verification of GHG emissions from facilities and aviation activities (Articles 25–56); V System for monitoring and reporting on national emissions (Articles 57–62); VI Projections of GHG emissions from sources and removal by sinks (Article 62); VII System for reporting on GHG policies, measures and projections (Articles 63–65); VII Administrative fees (Article 66); IX Supervision (Articles 67–69); X Penal provisions (Articles 70–74); and XI Transitional and final provisions (Articles 75–83).[517]

387. The law regulates the following issues: a system for limiting greenhouse gas emissions (hereinafter 'GHG')[518] and for adaptation to changed climate conditions, monitoring and reporting on the strategy of low-carbon development and its improvement, a programme for adaptation to changed climate conditions, adoption low-carbon development strategy and adaptation programme to changed climate conditions, issuing permits for GHG emissions to the plant operator, issuing approval for the aircraft operator's monitoring plan, monitoring, reporting, verification and accreditation of verifiers, administrative fees, supervision and other

515. For additional information on this subject, *see* Todić, 2023a.
516. In the part related to 'policies and measures to limit GHG emissions from sources', the Law regulates the possibility of using the clean development mechanism as well as the availability of data on the economy of fuel consumption and CO2 emissions in connection with the sale of new passenger vehicles.
517. According to the Explanation of the draft law, the adoption of this law and by-laws ensures harmonization of domestic legislation with the following legal acts of the EU: (1) Directive 2003/87/EC of the European Parliament and of the Council of 13 Sep. 2003 (establishment of a system of trading in emission units of greenhouse gases gardens); (2) Commission Regulation (EU) No. 600/2012 of 21 Jun. 2012 (verification of reports on greenhouse gas emissions and reports on ton kilometres and accreditation of verifiers in accordance with Directive 2003/87/EC); (3) Commission Regulation (EU) No. 601/2012 of 21 Jun. 2012 (monitoring and reporting on greenhouse gas emissions in accordance with Directive 2003/87/EC of the European Parliament and the Council. (CELEX 32012R0601); (4) Regulation (EU) No. 525/2013 of the European Parliament and the Council of 21 Mar. 2013 (mechanism for monitoring and reporting on greenhouse gas emissions and reporting on other information relevant to climate change); (5) Commission Delegated Regulation (EU) No. 666/2014 of 12 Mar. 2014 (establishing essential requirements for the inventory system of the European Union and taking into account changes in the potential of global warming and internationally agreed guidelines for inventories); (6) Commission Regulation (EU) on implementation No. 749/2014 of 30 Jun. 2014 (structure, format, submission procedures and review of information submitted by Member States); (7) Decision No. 406/2009/EC of the European Parliament and the Council of 23 Apr. 2013 (efforts undertaken by Member States to reduce greenhouse gas emissions in order to achieve Community goals; (8) Directive 1999/94/EC of the European Parliament and the Council of 13 Dec. 1999 (availability of information for consumers on the economy of fuel consumption and CO2 emissions in connection with the sale of new passenger vehicles).
518. The provisions of this law apply to GHG emissions caused by human activity and sectors and systems exposed to the effects of climate change (Art. 2, para. 1). GHG from para. 1 of this article are carbon dioxide (CO2), methane (CH4), nitrous oxide (N2O), hydrofluorocarbons (HFCs), perfluorocarbons (PFCs), and sulfur hexafluoride (SF6) and nitrogen trifluoride (NF3) (Art. 2, paras 1, and 2).

issues of importance for limiting GHG emissions and adaptation to changed climatic conditions (Article 1, paragraph 1).

388. Pursuant to Article 3, the aim of the Law is threefold and includes the following: (1) establishing a system to reduce GHG emissions in a cost-effective and economically efficient manner, which contributes to reaching the scientifically necessary levels of GHG emissions in order to avoid dangerous climate changes at the global level and adverse impacts of climate change; (2) reduction of GHG emissions and adaptation to changed climate conditions by adopting and implementing public policy documents; and (3) establishment of mechanisms for timely, transparent, accurate, consistent, comparable and complete reporting and verification of information on the fulfilment of obligations in accordance with international agreements.[519] In addition, to achieve the goals of this law, state bodies and organizations should adopt appropriate sectoral policies and measures within the scope of their competence (Article 4).

Strategies and plans

389. It is planned to adopt the following documents (strategies and plans): (1) low-carbon development strategy; (2) action plan for implementing the strategy;[520] (3) adaptation programme to changed climatic conditions (Article 6).[521] At the same time, the procedure for adopting these documents, their content, implementation of the Adaptation Program, public participation in the adoption process[522] and other relevant issues are prescribed. Public policy documents (sectoral strategies) must contain a quantitative assessment of the impact on the change in the level of GHG emissions from sources and removal by means of sinks calculated in accordance with accepted international methodology (Article 9).

390. Based on the Strategy and Action Plan, and following the obligations arising from the Convention and other international documents adopted for the implementation of the Convention, the Government prescribes the levels of GHG emissions: from sources at the national level, for facilities and aviation activities and

519. The following international agreements were explicitly mentioned: UN Framework Convention on Climate Change, with annexes (OJ FRY – International Treaties, No. 2/97), Kyoto Protocol (OJ RS – International Treaties, No. 88/07), Doha Amendment to the Kyoto Protocol with the Framework the United Nations Convention on Climate Change (OJ RS – International Agreements, No. 2/17) and the Paris Agreement (OJ RS – International Agreements, No. 4/17).

520. On the basis of the Strategy and Action Plan, and in accordance with the obligations arising from the Convention and other international documents adopted for the implementation of the Convention, the Government prescribes the levels of GHG emissions: from sources at the national level, for facilities and aviation activities and for GHG emissions from sectors and categories in which there is combustion of fuel and fugitive emissions from fuel, industrial processes and use of products, agriculture and waste (Art. 11).

521. *See*: Low-carbon development strategy of the RS for the period from 2023 to 2030 with projections until 2050 (OJ RS, No. 46/2023); and Program for Adaptation to Changed Climate Conditions for the period from 2023 to 2030 with an Action Plan (OJ RS, No. 119/2023).

522. The Ministry will inform the public about the draft of the Strategy, Action Plan, and Adaptation Program and enable the provision of opinions and objections, following the law that prescribes the drafting and adoption of public policy documents (Art. 16).

for GHG emissions from sectors and categories in which there is combustion of fuel and fugitive emissions from fuel, industrial processes and use of products, agriculture and waste (Article 11, paragraph 1).[523] The Ministry prepares an annual report on the achievement of GHG emissions following the act referred to in paragraph 1 of this article and in case of deviations, including permitted transfers under Article 12 of this law, prepares a proposal for the necessary corrective measures to achieve the GHG emissions from the source by 15 November of each year and submits it to the Government for adoption (Article 11, paragraph 4).[524]

391. The Ministry is preparing the Adaptation Program to Changed Climate Conditions (hereinafter 'Adaptation Program') with an Action Plan to identify the impact of climate change on sectors and systems and to determine adaptation measures to changed climate conditions (hereinafter 'Adaptation Measures') for those sectors and systems in which need to reduce adverse impacts (Article 13, paragraph 1).[525] The Law stipulates the mandatory content of the Adaptation Program, the method of its realization, and the participation of the public (Articles 14–16).[526]

392. This law establishes the National Council for Climate Change (hereinafter 'the Council') as an advisory body to the Government. Council members are appointed by the Government for five years with the possibility of re-election (Article 17, paragraph 1 and 2).[527] However, the Law does not prescribe the tasks and duties of the Council.

Policies and measures for limitation of GHG emissions from sources

523. The act referred to in para. 1 of this article stipulates in particular: (1) sectors, categories, and sources of emissions for which the levels of GHG emissions and the period to which they relate are determined; (2) method and methodology for determining the level of GHG emissions; (3) total levels of GHG emissions from sources concerning emissions in a given year; (4) annual levels of GHG emissions for facilities and aviation activities about emissions in a given year; (5) total levels of GHG emissions from sources concerning emissions in a given year, excluding emissions from point 4) of this paragraph. The act from para. 1 of this article prescribes GHG emissions for ten years and on an annual basis during this period (Art. 11, para. 2, and 3).
524. If the emissions from Art. 11, para. 2, point 5) of this law, in the prescribed period, in a certain year, are higher than the prescribed annual level of GHG emissions, it is allowed to carry over up to 5% of the annual amount from the following year. If the emissions from Art. 11, para. 2, item 5) of this law in the prescribed period, in a certain year, are less than the prescribed annual level of GHG emissions, this excess is allowed to be carried over to the following years in order to reach the annual levels of GHG emissions by the last year of that period (Art. 12).
525. The Adaptation Plan is adopted by the Government at the proposal of the Ministry and is published in the 'OJ RS' (paras 2, and 3).
526. The Ministry will inform the public about the draft of the Strategy, Action Plan and Adjustment Program and enable the provision of opinions and objections, in accordance with the law that prescribes the drafting and adoption of public policy documents (Art. 16).
527. The Council consists of representatives of the Ministry and other bodies and organizations, representatives of the scientific and professional public, as well as representatives of civil society, whose area of activity is important for determining and implementing activities in the field of climate change, as well as a representative of the Commissioner for the Protection of Equality (para. 3).

393. Measures to limit GHG emissions can be implemented through programs and projects within the CDM (Article 18, paragraph 1).[528]

394. The seller who puts a model of a new passenger vehicle on the market is obliged to place, at his own expense, a mark on the economy of fuel consumption and CO2 emissions of that vehicle in a visible manner at the point of sale or near the passenger vehicle (Article 20, paragraph 1).[529] Pursuant to Article 24 of the Law, it is forbidden to confuse potential buyers of new passenger cars by using signs, symbols, or inscriptions related to fuel consumption or the emission of CO2 and pollutants into the air on signs, in guides, on posters, or in promotional literature from Articles 20–23, of this law.

395. The supplier[530] must send the list of models of all new vehicles sold on the territory of the RS to the Agency for Traffic Safety in electronic form no later than 31 December of the current year with information on the prescribed form (Article 21, paragraph 1).[531]

396. The supplier and the seller are obliged to ensure that all promotional material contains data on the official fuel consumption and the official specific emissions of CO2 and polluting substances into the air of the model of the new passenger vehicle to which it refers (Article 23, paragraph 1).[532]

Monitoring, reporting and verification of GHG emissions from plants and aviation activities

528. The clean development mechanism is one of the three flexible mechanisms of the Kyoto Protocol and enables countries that have quantified obligations to reduce GHG emissions under the Kyoto Protocol to implement programs and projects that lead to the reduction of GHG emissions in developing countries, keeping the units of GHG emission reductions that are the result of project activity and which are expressed through SO2 equivalents (Art. 5, para. 1, point 17). The government prescribes the criteria and method of approving programs and projects implemented within the framework of the Clean Development Mechanism, with the exception of capital projects, in terms of the law regulating the budget system (para. 2).
529. The minister prescribes in more detail the content of the fuel consumption and CO2 emission label form from para. 1 of this article (para. 3).
530. The supplier is a manufacturer of passenger vehicles or its branch based in the Republic of Serbia. If the manufacturer or its branch does not have its seat in the Republic of Serbia, the supplier shall be considered an importer or a legal entity that puts a new passenger vehicle on the market of the Republic of Serbia for the first time for sale or leasing, as well as an entrepreneur who puts it on the market of the Republic of Serbia for the first time Serbia's new passenger vehicle for sale (Art. 5, para. 1, point 5).
531. The Agency for Traffic Safety publishes on its website: (1) a list of all models of new passenger vehicles sold in the Republic of Serbia during the year, compiled in alphabetical order of passenger vehicle brands with data from para. 1 of this article, and (2) a list of ten models of new passenger vehicles with the most economical fuel consumption, ordered according to increasing values of specific CO2 emissions for each type of fuel with data from para. 1 of this article (para. 2).
532. The minister prescribes the form and content of promotional material in more detail (para. 2).

397. In Part IV, which refers to monitoring, reporting and verification, the Law regulates in detail 'permits for GHG emissions to the facility operator',[533] approval of the monitoring plan, monitoring and reporting on GHG emissions from facilities and aviation activities, verification and accreditation, as well as submission and access information.

398. Before the start of the operation of the plant in which the activity leading to GHG emission is performed, the operator of the plant is obliged to obtain a permit for GHG emission (hereinafter 'permit') (Article 25, paragraph 1). Exceptionally, from paragraph 1 of this article, no permit is required for facilities or parts of facilities that are used for research, development, and testing of new products and processes, as well as for facilities that exclusively use biomass (paragraph 2).[534]

399. The Ministry, within five days from the date of receipt of the complete request for issuing a permit with a monitoring plan, submits it, together with the monitoring plan, to the EPA, evaluates the submitted monitoring plan, and within a maximum of two months from the date of receipt of the documents referred to in paragraph 1 of this article, submits to the Ministry a report containing an assessment of whether the monitoring plan was prepared following the regulations and whether the plant operator can provide monitoring and reporting on GHG emissions under this law.[535]

400. The Ministry issues a permit within a maximum of four months from the receipt of a complete request for the issuance of a permit, based on the Agency's positive assessment from Article 28 of this law (Article 29).[536] The operator of the plant informs the Ministry about any intended change in the type of activity, change in the capacity of existing plants and construction of new plants at the location, change of fuel, and main raw materials used in the plant (Article 31, paragraph 1).[537]

401. The termination of validity of the licence is regulated by Article 32. The Ministry issues a decision on the termination of validity of the licence if it receives

533. 'Operator' is a legal entity or an entrepreneur who, in accordance with regulations, manages the plant, controls it or is authorized to make economic decisions regarding the technical functioning of the plant (Art. 5, point 22).
534. The government prescribes the types of activities and gases from para. 1 of this article for which a permit must be obtained.
535. When evaluating the monitoring plan, the Agency may ask the applicant to provide it with additional information within a certain period that the applicant failed to provide in the monitoring plan, i.e., if some of the information provided in the monitoring plan is not listed, contradicts each other or is not sufficiently precise according to the requirements of the regulations from Art. 35, para. 7 of this law (Art. 28, para. 3).
536. Ex officio, the Ministry reviews the issued licence every five years and, if necessary, amends it (Art. 30). Conditions for the termination of validity of the licence are also prescribed (Art. 32).
537. The Ministry evaluates the changes referred to in para. 1 of this article and if it determines that the changes are such that they affect the permit, within thirty days from the date of receipt of the notification, it requires the operator of the plant to submit a request for a permit change within a certain period (para. 2).

a notification from the plant operator or learns in another way: (1) about the termination of validity of the integrated licence; (2) on the cessation of activities in the plant; (3) that plant operation is not possible for technical reasons; (4) that the plant is not working and its restart is not possible; (5) that no activity is carried out in the plant and the plant operator cannot guarantee that the plant will continue to operate within six months from the cessation of work, or within eighteen months in the case of cessation of work due to unforeseen circumstances that the operator cannot control affects (paragraph 1).[538]

402. The law also prescribes in detail the procedure for issuing approval for the GHG monitoring plan to the aircraft operator (Articles 33 and 34). An aircraft operator who has an operating licence under the law regulating air traffic is obliged to submit a monitoring plan to the Ministry no later than four months after the entry into force of the regulations from paragraph 3 of this article (Article 33, paragraph 1).[539] The Ministry, within five days from the date of receipt of the monitoring plan from Article 33, paragraphs 1 and 2 of this law, is submitted to the Directorate of Civil Aviation of the RS (hereinafter 'Directorate') (Article 34, paragraph 1).[540]

403. The operator of the plant and the operator of the aircraft ('operator') is obliged to monitor GHG emissions based on the approved monitoring plan that is an integral part of the permit, i.e., approved by the Ministry (Article 35, paragraph 1).[541] The operator is obliged to regularly check whether the monitoring plan reflects the nature and mode of operation of the facility or aircraft activities, as well as whether the GHG emission monitoring methodology can be improved, and to make changes to the monitoring plan based on this. The operator is obliged to inform the Ministry without delay about proposals for changes to the monitoring plan (Article 36, paragraphs 1 and 2).[542]

---

538. The provision from para. 1, item 5) of this article does not apply to plants in reserve or standby and to plants that perform their activities seasonally if: (1) the facility operator has a licence from Art. 29 of this law as well as an integrated licence if it is prescribed for that facility; (2) it is technically possible to start carrying out plant activities without physical changes to the plant; (3) the plant is regularly maintained.
539. An aircraft operator who is in the process of issuing an operating licence is obliged to submit a monitoring plan to the Ministry no later than two months before starting aviation activities based on the operating licence (para. 2). The government prescribes aviation activities and gases for which it is not necessary to submit a monitoring plan (para. 3).
540. The Directorate evaluates the submitted monitoring plan and, within a maximum of two months from the date of receipt of the documents referred to in para. 1 of this article, submits a report to the Ministry containing an assessment of whether the monitoring plan was prepared under the regulations and whether the aircraft operator can provide monitoring and reporting on GHG emissions in accordance with this law.
541. In the process of evaluating the monitoring plan, the Agency or the Directorate gives consent for the application of certain elements of the monitoring methodology, that is, certain written procedures or their parts (Art. 35, para. 5).
542. The plant operator who manages a plant with low GHG emissions can submit a request to the Ministry for approval of the use of a simplified monitoring plan (Art. 37, para. 1).

404. Monitoring of GHG emissions is carried out on the basis of the prescribed methodology (Article 39, paragraph 1).[543] If the plant operator claims that the application of a certain monitoring methodology is not technically feasible, the Agency evaluates the justification of this objection taking into account the technical and technological characteristics of that plant. Also, if the plant operator claims that the application of a certain monitoring methodology leads to unreasonably high costs, the Agency evaluates the justification of that objection, taking into account whether the costs of monitoring are greater than the benefits (Article 40, paragraphs 1 and 2).[544]

405. Obligations and rights of operators regarding data management and control, document and data storage, reporting, conservative assessment of GHG emissions, and reporting on improvements in monitoring methodology are regulated in detail in Articles 41–45 of the Law. The operator is obliged to submit a verified report on GHG emissions to the Agency or the Directorate by 31 March of the current year with a verification report for the previous calendar year, for facilities and from the air traffic sector (Article 43, paragraph 1). As an exception to paragraph 1 of this article, the report on GHG emissions submitted by an operator starting work for the first time in the first year after obtaining the permit from Article 29 of this law, i.e., the approval from Article 34 of this law, covers the period from the day of commencement of work to 31 December of that year (paragraph 2). The operator of a facility that has ceased operation, or in the case of bankruptcy, the bankruptcy administrator, is obliged to submit to the Agency or Directorate without delay a verified report on gas emissions for the period from 1 January of the current year to the day the facility ceases to operate (paragraph 3).[545]

406. The accredited verifier,[546] according to the prescribed procedure, verifies the report from Article 43 of this law and issues a verification report to the operator (Article 46, paragraph 1).[547] The provisions of the law governing accreditation and other general acts of the ABS, or the accreditation rules published by the ABS, apply to accreditation issues that are not specifically regulated by this law (Article 47).

543. The Minister prescribes the methodologies for monitoring GHG emissions from plants and the conditions for their application. The minister, with the approval of the minister responsible for transport affairs, prescribes the methodology for monitoring GHG emissions for aircraft operators (paras 2, and 3).

544. The method of assessing technical feasibility and unreasonably high costs is regulated in detail by a regulation issued by the minister (para. 3).

545. The Minister, and for aviation activities with the consent of the minister responsible for traffic affairs, prescribes the form and content of the report on emissions from para. 1–3 of this article, as well as the type and method of obtaining data on the historical level of activities and emissions from these activities (para. 5).

546. The verifier is a legal entity that performs verification activities following this law and the other relevant regulation and who is accredited by the Accreditation Body of Serbia (hereinafter 'ATS'), under the law regulating accreditation (Art. 5, para. 1, point 2).

547. The Minister prescribes the conditions that verifiers must fulfil, the procedure and verification criteria as well as the content of the verification report (para. 3).

407. The law prescribes in detail the rules related to the application for accreditation, evaluation of verifiers, evaluation team, obligations of verifiers, the programme of supervision over the work of verifiers, administrative measures, and notification of the scope of accreditation of verifiers, complaints against verifiers, delivery and access to information (Articles 48–56). The Ministry makes reports on gas emissions available to the public in accordance with the regulation regulating access to information of public importance (Article 56, paragraph 1).[548]

System for monitoring and reporting on national GHG emissions

408. The National GHG Inventory System is established, managed and constantly improved in order to ensure, in accordance with the requirements of the Convention, the assessment of GHG emissions from sources and removals through sinks, as well as the timeliness, transparency, accuracy, consistency, comparability and completeness of the GHG inventory (Article 57). The mandatory content of the inventory is prescribed (Article 58, paragraph 1), and the Minister prescribes the contents of the GHG Inventory and the GHG Inventory Report (paragraph 8). The Agency establishes and manages the GHG Inventory and prepares the GHG Inventory Report (paragraph 3).[549]

409. Authorities and organizations responsible for managing information systems and databases that contain data necessary for creating the GHG Inventory deliver data to the Agency, ensure data quality and conduct data quality control (Article 59, paragraph 1).[550] The Agency concludes an agreement with the bodies and organizations referred to in Article 59, paragraph 1 of this law, which determines the obligations of those bodies and organizations, especially the data, terms, form and method for their delivery to the Agency (Article 60).[551]

Projections of GHG emissions from sources and removals by sinks

410. The Ministry prepares projections of anthropogenic GHG emissions from sources and their removal using sinks (hereinafter 'projections') as a basis for determining and assessing the possibility of limiting GHG emissions, adopting policies and measures for economically profitable limitation of GHG emissions, as well as for monitoring the achievement of GHG emission limits (Article 62, paragraph 1). Projections are made for gases or groups of gases, as well as for sectors and categories, and are improved as needed.[552]

System for reporting on policies, measures and GHG projections

548. Data related to emissions, the state of the environment and possible negative impacts and consequences, monitoring results and inspection supervision cannot be marked as business secrets (para. 2).
549. The report on the GHG inventory is an integral part of the report on the state of the environment in the Republic of Serbia.
550. The government prescribes the bodies and organizations from para. 1 of this article and the type of data required for the preparation of the GHG Inventory.
551. In addition, the Agency creates and implements the Plan for quality assurance and data quality control for the purposes of creating and improving the quality of the GHG Inventory (Art. 61).
552. Projections for relevant sectors are made in cooperation with the relevant ministries (para. 3).

411. In order to ensure timeliness, transparency, accuracy, consistency, comparability and completeness of information on policies and measures and projections, a system for reporting on GHG policies and measures and projections is established, maintained and continuously improved (Article 63, paragraph 1).[553] Bodies and organizations, including bodies and organizations of LSGs responsible for environmental protection, are obliged to assess the effects of policies and measures on the level of GHG emissions within their jurisdiction and report them to the Ministry.[554]

412. The Ministry reports to the Government on the implementation of the Action Plan, the Adjustment Program, the implementation of policies and measures, projections and the achievement of quantitative goals from the Strategy (Article 64, paragraph 1).[555] The Government submits the reports from paragraph 1 of this article to the NA.

413. In accordance with the obligations arising from the Convention, the Ministry prepares the Biennial Report and the Report of the RS according to the UN Framework Convention on Climate Change (Article 65, paragraph 1). The reports from paragraph 1 of this article are adopted by the Government, and the Ministry makes them available to the public on its website.

Supervision

414. Supervision over the implementation of this law and the regulations adopted on its basis is carried out by the ministry responsible for environmental protection, the Directorate, and the ministry responsible for trade (Article 67, paragraph 1). The environmental protection inspector carries out inspection supervision over the application of the provisions of this law relating to the obligations of plant operators, the aviation inspector over the application of the provisions relating to the obligations of aircraft operators, and the market inspector over the application of the provisions of this law relating to the availability of information to consumers about the economy of fuel consumption and CO2 emissions from new passenger vehicles (paragraph 3).[556] The law prescribes the rights, duties and powers of inspectors (Articles 68 and 69).

Climate change bylaws

415. Following the adoption of the Law on climate change, Serbia so far has adopted six out of twelve pieces of implementing legislation. These are:

553. The system includes institutional, legal and procedural mechanisms for reporting on policies and measures and projections of anthropogenic GHG emissions from sources and removal by sinks.
554. The Government determines the list of bodies and organizations from para. 3 of this article, the content, form and deadlines for reporting to the Ministry (para. 4).
555. The government prescribes the form, content and deadlines for submitting the report from para. 1 of this article. The Ministry shall make the reports from para. 1 of this article as well as all relevant information, available to the public on its website.
556. The provisions of the law regulating inspection supervision are applied to the inspection supervision procedure unless otherwise prescribed by this law (Art. 87, para. 4).

- Regulation on types of data, bodies, organizations and other physical and legal entities that submit data for the creation of a national inventory of greenhouse gases (OJ RS, No. 43/2023).
- Regulation on types of activities and gases with a greenhouse effect (OJ RS, No. 13/2022).
- Rulebook on monitoring and reporting on greenhouse gas emissions (OJ RS, No. 118/2023).
- Rulebook on the content of the National Inventory of Greenhouse Gases and the National Report on the Inventory of Greenhouse Gases (OJ RS, No. 55/2023).
- Rulebook on data on fuel economy and CO2 emissions from new passenger vehicles (OJ RS, Nos 107/2022, 71/2023).
- Rulebook on verification and accreditation of verifiers of reports on greenhouse gas emissions (OJ RS, No. 107/2021).

E. Other Relevant Air Protection Legislation

416. Besides the above-mentioned laws, following legal Acts also regulate air protection in Serbia:

- Law on Meteorological and Hydrological Activities (OJ RS, No. 88/2010).[557]
- Law on Protection of Population from Exposure to Tobacco Smoke (OJ RS No. 30/2010).[558]
- Law on Transport of Dangerous Goods (OJ RS, Nos 104/16, 83/18, 95/18 – other law, and 10/19 – other law).
- Air Transport Law (OJ RS, Nos 73/2010, 57/2011, 93/2012, 45/2015, 66/2015 – other law, 83/18, 9/20, and 62/23).
- Regulation on determining the List of air quality categories by zones and agglomerations on the territory of the RS for 2022 (OJ RS, No. 93/23).
- Regulation on limit values of air pollutant emissions from stationary sources of pollution, except from combustion installations (OJ RS, Nos 111/15, and 83/21).
- Regulation on limit values of air pollutant emissions from combustion installations (OJ RS, Nos 06/16, and 67/21).
- Regulation on the methodology for the development of air pollutant emissions and projections inventory (OJ RS, No. 3/16).

---

557. The Law regulates meteorological and hydrological activities, organization and manner of performing meteorological and hydrological activities of interest for the Republic of Serbia and other meteorological and hydrological activities, meteorological and hydrological disasters early warning system, meteorological and hydrological data information fund, protection of Hydrological Information System, international cooperation, as well as other issues of importance for meteorological and hydrological activities.
558. New law completely bans smoking in health and social care facilities, educational, cultural, sport facilities, at meetings, in all public administration buildings, in facilities where drugs and food are prepared or stored, shopping centres, etc. Regarding restaurants and bars, completely smoke-free are only those which belong to buildings in which smoking is completely banned. Significant fines are imposed on owners and managers of buildings in which smoking is banned.

- Regulation on measurement of air pollutant emissions from stationary sources of pollution (OJ RS, No. 5/16).
- Regulation on handling fluorinated greenhouse gases and conditions for issuing import and export permits for these gases (OJ RS, Nos 120/13, 44/18 – other law).
- Regulation on the list of installations and activities, in which volatile organic compound (VOC) emissions shall be controlled, on VOC emission values at certain consumption of solvents and total allowed emissions, and schemes to reduce VOC emission (OJ RS, No. 100/11).
- Regulation on the methodology for data collection for the national inventory of unintentional emission of persistent organic pollutants (OJ RS, No. 76/2010).
- Regulation on determining the air quality control programme within the State network (OJ RS, No. 58/11).
- Regulation on handling ozone-depleting substances, as well as on conditions for the issuance of permits for import and export of such substances (OJ RS, Nos 114/13, 23/18, 44/18 – other law, and 95/18 – other law).
- Regulation on work method, criteria and timeframe for assessing and approving potential project on CDM by the National body for implementing CDM Projects under the Kyoto Protocol (OJ RS, No. 44/2010).
- Regulation on conditions for monitoring and requirements for air quality (OJ RS, Nos 11/2010, 75/10 and 63/13).
- Rulebook on the content of short-term action plans (OJ RS, No. 65/2010).
- Rulebook on the methods for exchanging information concerning measuring points within the State and local networks, on measuring techniques, as well as on the methods of exchanging data obtained by air quality monitoring in the State and local network (OJ RS, No. 84/2010).
- Rulebook on content of the plan for air quality (OJ RS, No. 21/2010).
- Rulebook on requirements of approvals for operators to measure air quality and/or emission from stationary pollution sources (OJ RS, No. 16/12).
- Rulebook on conditions for issuing air quality measurement permits and permits for measurement of emission from stationary pollution sources (OJ RS, No. 1/12).
- Rulebook on technical measures and requirements relating to the allowed volatile organic compound emissions resulting from storage and transport of petrol (OJ RS, Nos 1/12, 25/12, 48/12, 96/19, and 143/22).
- National emission reduction plan of major pollutants from the large combustion plants (OJ RS, No. 10/20).

F. Harmonization with the EU Legislation

417. In the field of air quality, ‘Serbia has a good level of alignment with the EU *acquis*, but implementation and enforcement should be further strengthened.’[559] Serbia has not yet aligned its legislation with the requirements of the EU acquis for

559. EC 2023, 135. Serbia needs to speed up implementation of air quality plans and further improve air quality monitoring.

national emission ceilings. Alignment with the EU acquis on volatile organic compound emissions needs to continue. Adequate staffing of the EPA needs to be ensured.[560]

418. Regarding climate change legislation, ' Serbia has some level of preparation..., but enforcement is at a very early stage.'[561] In addition, 'Serbia should set a coal phase-out date as an effective means to comply with Energy Community law and Serbia's Green Agenda commitments on reaching the EU target of climate neutrality. '[562]

560. *Ibid.*
561. EC 2023, 137.
562. *Ibid.*, 138 Full alignment of legislation on monitoring, reporting and verifying greenhouse gas emissions in line with the EU emissions trading system and the effort-sharing Regulation is still pending.

Chapter 3. Water Pollution

§1. Water Availability and Use

419. The available domestic waters (expressed through total precipitation) can be rated as 'moderately satisfactory.' At the same time, the exploitable quantities of surface and underground domestic waters are 'very modest' and it is necessary to make significant efforts to repair their regime, to meet the needs in the future.[563]

420. Most important international watercourse in Serbia is the Danube river that, with its vast basin and huge potential (both for navigational and non-navigational uses), deserves special attention and international cooperation concerning its protection and use in navigational and non-navigational purposes. Besides the Danube, there are many other rivers, some of which are international (for instance, Sava,[564] Tisza and Drina). The ten longest rivers are: Danube 588 km (total 2,783 km), Zapadna Morava 184 km (184 km), Juzna Morava 286 km (295 km), Ibar 238 km (272 km), Drina 220 km (346 km), Sava 206 km (945 km), Timok 202 km (202 km), Velika Morava 185 km (185 km), Tisa 168 km (966 km) and Nisava 151 km (218 km).[565]

The territory of the RS is poor in natural lakes.[566] There are also eleven areas inscribed in the list of Ramsar Areas (for instance, Gornje Podunavlje, Ludaško jezero, Obedska bara, Vlasina, Đerdap, etc). There are also some artificial lakes, the biggest and most important of which is the Iron Gate Lake.

421. Groundwater sources should also be mentioned. Groundwater resources in RS are relatively scarce and unevenly distributed. This resource is traditionally mostly used to supply water to settlements.[567] In terms of the density and variety of mineral and thermal mineral waters, the RS can be counted among the richest areas on the European continent. Nearly 1,200 occurrences of these waters have been registered in the RS; in AP Vojvodina, almost exclusively boreholes, and south of the Sava and Danube, mostly springs.[568] The use of water resources varies on a regional level. The use (specific consumption) of water in the household has a favourable

563. GOV RS. 2002. Domestic waters are relatively modest, slightly below 500 m3/s at the average annual level, or about 60 m3/s in the low-water period. Therefore, to meet the needs, it is necessary to count on the use of significant amounts of water that come to the territory of the RS (about 5,000 m3/s on an average annual level, or about 1,500 m3/s in a period of low water). GOV RS. 2017, 140.
564. The Sava river basin area is shared between five countries: the Republic of Slovenia (SI), Republic of Croatia (HR), Bosnia and Herzegovina (BA), Republic of Montenegro (ME), and Republic of Serbia (RS), while a negligible part of the basin area also extends to Republic of Albania (AL). MAFWM. 2019, 17.
565. STAT. YEARB. SERB. 2023, 16.
566. GOV RS. 2017, 14.
567. MCTI. 2021, 53. Groundwater for water supply is one of the most threatened mineral resources and strategically important resources for the existence of the population and sustainable development. *Ibid.*, 201.
568. GOV RS. 2017, 20.

(declining) trend in the period 2008–2017 years. The average specific water consumption in the same period was 151.8 (litre/user/day). The highest specific household water consumption in 2017 was in Niš (237) and the lowest in the Zaječar administrative district (oblast) (96) (litre/user/day).[569]

422. In 2019, the amount of water intake was about 670 million m3 per year. The losses are considerable and amount to 35% (about 235 million m3 per year). It is estimated that about 70% of water is extracted from groundwater, ranging from 55–100% per district. 30% originates from surface water, and part of it is captured from reservoirs.[570]

§2. Water Pollution Sources

423. The results of the analysis of a large number of samples (on average once a month in the period from 1998 to 2017) show that the worst condition is in the watercourses and canals of the catchment area of Vojvodina.[571] Wastewaters which discharged into the recipient without any kind of treatment (whether mechanical, biological, or chemical) are the key sources of water pollution in the RS. The total amount of wastewater discharged from settlements in 2018 decreased by 1.3% compared to 2017, out of which the amount of wastewater discharged into the public sewerage system decreased by 0.5% compared to the same period in 2017.[572]

424. International watercourses that enter Serbia are already polluted. The quality of water in most Serbian rivers is, according to the official water classification, between class II and class IV (class III prevails). So, for instance, the quality of the Danube water is usually class II or class III, and in the Tisza River, the quality is often class III and IV. Sometimes heavy accidental pollution occurs in the upstream countries. One of the most serious cases was heavy pollution (by cyanide and heavy metals) of the Tisza River in 2000 caused by a serious accident in a golden mine in Romania. In the recent period (from 1991 until today) in the RS (without AP Kosovo and Metohija), the percentage of the population connected to public water supply systems is about 81%.[573] At the same time, this percentage is the lowest in central Serbia (71%), while it is significantly higher in Belgrade (92%) and in AP

569. EPA. 2019b, 52.
570. GOV RS. 2023c,153.
571. EPA. 2019b, 96. From this territory, in relation to the total number of samples from the state monitoring network, 40% of the samples belong to the quality indicator 'bad' and 'very bad'. Even 79% of the samples belong to the very bad class. The best quality, in the 'excellent' category, was recorded in small watercourses in hilly and mountainous areas in eastern, southeastern and western Serbia. *Ibid.*
572. EPA. 2019c, 24. The percentage of polluted (untreated) wastewater had a favourable (declining) trend in the period 2008–2017. In 2017, it amounted to 87.9%, meaning that in 2017 the highest percentage of wastewater (12.1%) was treated in the mentioned period. *Ibid.*
573. GOV RS. 2017a, Ch. 2.2.1. It is noted that about 70% of the population of the RS is supplied with water from underground water resources. However, according to the EPA, the number of users connected to public water supply systems has a favourable (growing) trend and in 2017 reached a maximum of 6,104,004, which is 86.9% of the total population. EPA. 2019b, 52.

Vojvodina (91%). It is estimated that the population covered by the systems is predominantly concentrated in a smaller number of settlements (slightly more than a third of the total number of settlements) with a higher population density.[574]

425. Currently, about 150 public companies provide water supply and sewerage services. Seven large regional public communal companies (PUCs) supply about 30% of the population (including the Belgrade water supply with about 20%). The remaining 140 PUCs supply 45% of the population.[575]

426. Regular measurement of water quality is done by the competent hydrometeorological (hydrological, chemical, physical, biological and bacteriological characteristics) and health protection institutions (the quality of drinking water). The main institutions to be mentioned here are the RHMS, the Institute of Public Health and other specialized organizations and institutes.

It is important to add that Serbia is active in international cooperation in the field of water protection. A good example of such cooperation is its membership in the International Commission for the Protection of the Danube River (ICPDR), established according to the 1994 Convention on Cooperation for the Protection and Sustainable Use of the Danube River.

427. Water sector in Serbia is mostly under the competence of the MAFWM (i.e., under its Directorate for Water and two public water companies). The Directorate for Water is, according to the Law on Ministries, responsible for water resources management policy, multipurpose water usage, water regime, protection from water, water protection measures maintenance and other activities, as prescribed by the Law on Water.

The following ministries are also involved in the management and protection of water: Ministry of Construction, Transport and Infrastructure, Ministry of Environment, Ministry of Health, MME, Ministry of Public Administration and LSG, etc. Water sector is also managed by the Secretariat for Agriculture, Water Management, and Forestry of AP Vojvodina. Urban water and sanitation services are decentralized and delegated to the municipalities.

428. Following Article 196 of the Law on Waters, responsibilities for the enforcement of the Law on Waters are divided among three inspectorates: water, sanitary and environment. The water inspectorate (twenty people), which is part of the Water Directorate, checks compliance and enforces requirements related to the

574. GOV RS. 2017, *op. cit.* According to the STAT. OFFICE, in 2020, the proportion of the population using safely managed drinking water services was 75%. The share is slightly higher for the subpopulation from urban settlements (82%), while for the subpopulation of the population from other settlements it amounts to 67%. STAT. OFFICE RS. 2022a, 11.

575. GOV RS. 2023c, 173. For more information on the quality of surface water and of groundwater, *see* EPA, 2023c.

water use regime and quality of surface waters and groundwater, as well as to any activities that could affect water quality.[576]

§3. LEGISLATION

I. International Treaties

429. Serbia has ratified following international treaties relevant to use, management and protection of water resources:

- Convention on Cooperation for Protection and Sustainable Use of the Danube River (OJ S&M – IT, No. 2-2/2003).
- Framework Agreement on the Sava River Basin and Protocol on the Navigation Regime Additional to the Framework Agreement on the Sava River Basin (OJ S&M – IT, No. 12/2004).[577]
- Convention Regarding the Regime of Navigation on the Danube (1948) (OJ FPRY, No. 8/49; OJ FRY – IT, No. 6/98).
- Framework Convention on the Protection and Sustainable Development of the Carpathians (OJ RS – IT, No. 102/07).[578]

Serbia ratified the Helsinki Convention on the Protection and Use of Transboundary Watercourses and International Lakes, a treaty of key importance. (OJ RS – IT, No. 1/10), as well as the Protocol on Water and Health to this Convention (OJ RS – IT, No. 1/13.

430. Besides the above-mentioned multilateral treaties, Serbia is a contracting party of a number of bilateral agreements with neighbouring States which regulate cooperation in the field of waters. They are as follows: Agreement between the Government of FPRY and PR of Hungary on water management issues (1955), Agreement between the Government of FPRY and PR of Hungary on fishery in boundary waters (1957), Agreement between the Government of FPRY and PR of Hungary on water transport on River Tisza (1959), Agreement between the Government of FPRY and PR of Bulgaria on water management issues (1958), Agreement between the Government of FPRY and PR of Bulgaria on fishery in boundary waters (1962),

576. UNECE. 2015, 39. 'Responsibilities between water and environmental inspectorates are not entirely delineated and there are overlaps in the area of water quality, but, in practice, they find ways to overcome them and cooperation on the ground is good.' *Ibid.*, 40.

577. In addition Protocol on Flood Protection to the Framework Agreement on the Sava River Basin (OJ RS – IT No. 16/14), Protocol on the prevention of water pollution caused by navigation to the Framework Agreement on the Sava River Basin (OJ RS – IT No. 19/15), Protocol on sediment management to the Framework Agreement on the Sava River Basin (OJ RS – IT No. 20/15).

578. In addition, Protocol on Conservation and Sustainable Use of Biological and Landscape Diversity to the Framework Convention on the Protection and Sustainable Development of the Carpathians (OJ RS – IT No. 1/13), Protocol on Sustainable Forest Management to the Framework Convention on the Protection and Sustainable Development of the Carpathians (OJ RS – IT No. 5/15), Protocol on Sustainable Tourism to the Framework Convention on the Protection and Sustainable Development of the Carpathians (OJ RS – IT No. 5/15).

Agreement between the Government of FPRY and PR of Romania on hydroelectric questions on hydroelectric systems and water courses along the boundary or cut by boundary (1955), Agreement between the Government of FPRY and PR of Romania on fishery in boundary waters (1961), Agreement between the Government of FPRY and PR of Romania on building exploitation of the hydroelectric and navigation system Dzerdap (1963, 1964, 1967, 1976, 1977, 1987 and 1998).[579]

New bilateral agreements in water management field have been concluded with the following countries: Hungary (OJ RS – IT, No. 4/20), Turkey (OJ RS – IT, No. 4/20), Romania (OJ RS – IT, No. 4/20), as well as MOUs with Metito Utilities LTD. from the United Arab Emirates (OJ RS – IT, No. 3/19), Ministry of foreign trade and economic relations of Bosnia and Herzegovina (OJ RS – IT, No. 16/15), Ministry of agriculture, forest and water management of the Republic Serbska (OJ RS – IT, No. 17/14).[580]

II. National Legislation

A. Strategic Documents

431. Water Management Strategy in the RS for the period up to 2034 (OJ RS, No. 3/17) is a basic document adopted after preparations for several years.[581] It is 'a master planning document that will serve as a blueprint for the implementation of water sector reforms through the year 2034, aimed at achieving needed water management standards at the national, regional and local levels, and at fulfilling water management objectives. The Strategy also proposes the structural and non-structural measures required to achieve set objectives and outlines the needed funding, the implementation timetable, and the functions whose proper performance will govern the effective achievement of objectives. Additionally, the Strategy sets forth priority projects'.[582]

579. The current state of bilateral cooperation 'in the water sector is not satisfactory either in terms of quality or scope.' GOV RS. 2023c, 8. Only bilateral commissions with Romania and Hungary (which were formed based on the 1955 agreement) are active. Cooperation with Bulgaria has been suspended since 1982. To date, cooperation with neighbouring countries in the area of the former SFRY (Republic of Croatia, Bosnia and Herzegovina, Montenegro, and the Republic of North Macedonia) has not been regulated, although certain steps have been taken. There is trilateral cooperation in the area of defence against ice on the Danube (with Hungary and the Republic of Croatia). There is a need to create a legal basis for the establishment of trilateral cooperation with Hungary and Romania, as well as with the Republic of Croatia and Bosnia and Herzegovina. *Ibid.*

580. For more information on regional cooperation, *see* Todić, Zlatić,2018.

581. *See* http://www.rdvode.gov.rs/doc/Strategija_FINAL.pdf (5.1.2024). Furthermore, the River Basin Management Plan for the Danube River Basin in Serbia has been adopted. *See also*, Action plan for the implementation of the Water Management Strategy on the territory of the Republic of Serbia for the period from 2021 to 2023 (OJ RS, No. 79/21).

582. Executive Summary for the Water Management Strategy of the territory of the Republic of Serbia, MAEP, Belgrade, http://www.rdvode.gov.rs/doc/dokumenta/javne-rasprave/strategija/Strategija%20SUMMARY.pdf (5.1.2024).

B. Water Law

432. The water domain is regulated by numerous laws and regulations. The basic legal Act is the Water Law (OJRS, Nos 30/10, 93/12, 101/16 and 95/18).[583] *The Law on Waters* has entered into force on 15 May 2010. It has the following twelve parts: Part I – General Provisions (Articles 1–3), Part II – Water resources (Articles 4–12), Part III – Water facilities (Articles 13–23), Part IV – Integrated Water Management (Articles 24–112), Part V – Water Acts and water documentation (Articles 113–132), Part VI – Prohibitions, limitation of rights and obligations of owners and users of water land and water facilities (Articles 133–139), Part VII – Other water management subjects (Articles 140–146), Part VIII – Information and water information system (Articles 147–149), Part IX – Financing of water management (Articles 150–195), Part X – Supervision (Articles 196–208), XI – Penalties (Articles 209–215), Part XII – Transitional and final provisions (Articles 216–228). Independent Articles of the Amendments of the Water Law (2016) are Articles 106 (section 2)–116 (section 2).

According to Article 1, Water Law regulates the legal status of waters,[584] integrated water management, the management of water constructions and water land, sources of funding, supervision of the implementation of this Law, and other matters of importance to water management.

433. The provisions of this Law apply to all surface waters and groundwaters[585] within the territory of the RS, including thermal and mineral waters, but excluding groundwater from which useful mineral raw materials or geothermal energy can be extracted (Article 2, paragraph 1). Provisions of this Law also apply to watercourses that define or intersect the State border of the RS, as well as associated groundwater thereof, unless otherwise regulated by a specific Law (Article 2, paragraph 2). It also applies to the extraction of river deposits which do not contain admixtures of any other useful mineral raw materials (Article 2, paragraph 3).

1. Water Management Principles

434. Water management is founded on following principles: (1) *The principle of sustainable development* – water management must be conducted in a manner

583. The basic general goal of the amendments which were introduced in 2016 and 2018 is to achieve full compliance with EU legislation. Amendments to the Law on waters were adopted by the National Assembly in 2021. However, due to public opposition and protests, the President of the Republic did not sign the decree promulgating the law. For detailed information please refer to Young Researchers of Serbia. 2022, 75.

584. *Waters* means all flowing and standing waters on the ground surface, and all groundwaters (Art. 3, point 8).

585. *Groundwaters* means all water below the surface of the ground in the saturation zone and in direct contact with the ground or subsoil (Art. 3, point 44).

whereby satisfying the demands of the present generations does not compromise the ability of future generations to satisfy their own demands, that is, water use based on long-term protection of the quantity and quality of available water resources[586] must be ensured. (2) *The principle of holism* – natural processes of which water is a significant component, as well as the association and interdependency of aquatic ecosystems and riparian ecosystems must be respected. (3) *The principle of water-system*[587] *unity* – water management within a single water space must be conducted in harmony with the development of the RS, in order to maximize economic and social benefits equitably, and at the same time, international agreements must be respected. (4) *The principle of ensuring protection against the adverse effects of water* – the population and its property must be protected against water, while at the same time laws governing natural processes and the protection of natural treasures, as well as the economic viability of such protection must be respected. (5) *The 'user pays' principle* – anyone who uses a water asset, water construction or water system, as an asset of general interest, shall pay a realistic price for such use. (6) *The 'polluter pays' principle* – anyone whose activities result in water pollution shall pay the costs of any measures required for the elimination of such pollution. (7) *The principle of public participation* – the public has a right to information regarding the status of waters and the performance of competent authorities in the water sector, as well as to be involved in water management plan preparation, delivery and implementation supervision processes. (8) *The principle of recognizing best available techniques* – best known and best available techniques, which represent the most advanced achievements in respective fields, shall be applied in water management (Article 25, paragraph 1).

2. Integrated Water Management and Water Management Planning Documents

435. Integrated water management (water management), as contemplated herein, is a set of measures and activities aimed at preserving and improving the water regime,[588] providing the necessary amounts of water of required quality for different uses, protecting waters against pollution and ensuring protection against the adverse effects of water (Article 24, paragraph 1). Water management is under the jurisdiction of the RS (Article 24, paragraph 2). The RS shall realize water management via the Ministry and other competent ministries, the competent authority of the AP, the competent authority of the local self-governing unit and the public water management enterprise (Article 24, paragraph 3).

436. Article 29 of the Law defines strategic documents for water management, particularly: (1) Water Management Strategy for the territory of the RS; (2) Water

586. *Water resources* means all surface waters and groundwaters, in terms of quantity and quality (Art. 3, point 11).
587. *Water system* means all waters, water lands and water constructions in a particular area (Art. 3, point 12).
588. *Water regime* means the qualitative and/or quantitative status of groundwater and surface waters, resulting from natural or human activity, in a particular area and at a particular time (Art. 3, point 10).

Management Plan; (3) Annual Water Management Programme; (4) Plans Regulating Protection from adverse effects of water, particularly: flood risk management plan, general and operative plans for protection against floods and plans regulating water protection (plan for protection of water against pollution and monitoring programme). The Law also prescribes programme of measures for achievement of objectives of previously mentioned documents and active participation of public in passing of planning documents.

437. Water Management Strategy is a planning document which establishes long-term directions for water management (Article 30, paragraph 1). The Strategy shall be proposed by the Ministry and delivered by the Government for a period of at least ten years (Article 31, paragraph 1). The strategy is implemented through an action plan. Action plan is made by the Government (at the proposal of the Ministry) for a period of five years (Article 31a).

438. Water management plan of waters within a water district[589] shall be delivered, pursuant to the Strategy, for the Danube River Basin and for the water districts (Article 33, paragraph 1). According to Article 34, paragraph 1, the Water Management Plan for the Danube River Basin is to be prepared by the Ministry, which is to be updated every six years (Article 35, paragraph 1).

439. The annual water management programme (hereinafter 'the annual programme') is a planning document which identifies water constructions, types and scope of any works and/or actions funded during the time period for which the annual programme is delivered, the cost of such works and/or actions, the level of participation, and other matters pertaining to the construction, reconstruction, repair, rehabilitation and/or maintenance of water constructions, and for the undertaking of any actions which, as contemplated herein, are deemed to be actions of general interest (Article 42, paragraph 1). The annual programme is to be consistent with the Strategy and the Water Management Plan (Article 42, paragraph 2).[590]

440. Plans which address protection against the adverse effects of water include the Flood Risk Management Plan, the general Flood Defence Plan and the Operational Flood Defence Action Plan, as well as plans which address water protection (the water pollution protection plan and the monitoring programme) (Article 29, paragraph 1, point 4).[591]

---

589. *Water district* means the area made up of one or more neighbouring river basins and sub-basins or parts thereof within the territory of the Republic of Serbia, together with associated groundwaters, which is identified as the main unit for water management (Art. 3, point 13).

590. The Government, and on the territory of the AP authority of the AP, makes an annual programme (Art. 42, para. 3).

591. *See also* Arts 54 and 55.

3. Development of Watercourses and Protection Against the Adverse Effects of Water

441. Watercourse development, as contemplated herein, includes: (1) the erection and maintenance of water constructions for watercourse development; and (2) the undertaking of works in connection with the maintenance of bank stability or a watercourse channel and with the increase and/or maintenance of the water, ice and/or sediment conveyance capacity thereof (Article 44, paragraph 1). *Protection against the adverse effects of water* includes measures and works for river flood and internal flood protection, ice protection, protection from erosion and torrential streams and the elimination of resulting consequences (Article 45, paragraph 1).

442. The management of risks from the adverse effects of water shall include the preparation of a preliminary flood risk assessment;[592] the preparation and implementation of flood risk management plans;[593] the general flood defence plan;[594] and flood defence action plans;[595] the undertaking of ordinary and extraordinary flood defence; and protection from erosion and torrential streams (Article 45, paragraph 3).

---

592. A preliminary flood risk assessment shall be prepared by the Ministry for the territory of the Republic of Serbia and shall include, but not be limited to: (1) maps of water districts of suitable scale, identifying the boundaries of sub-basins and showing topography and land uses; (2) a description of past flood events which have resulted in significant harmful consequences to human health, the environment, cultural heritage and/or economic activity, and an indication of the likelihood of comparable events, which might have similar consequences, occurring in the future; and (3) an assessment of potential harmful consequences of future flood events to human health, the environment, cultural heritage and/or economic activity, considering the topographic, hydrologic and geological characteristics and the location of the watercourse, including flood-prone areas, the effectiveness of existing flood defences, the locations of populated areas and industrial zones, long-term development plans and climate change as relevant to flood events (Art. 47, para. 1).
593. The flood risk management plan shall ensure risk management through the reduction of potential harmful consequences of floods to human health, the environment, cultural heritage, and/or economic activity (Art. 49, para. 1). The flood risk management plan shall be delivered for the territory of the Republic of Serbia and for its water districts (Art. 49, para. 2). It shall be based on the flood hazard map and flood risk map (Art. 49, para. 3) and is to be delivered in the same manner and following the same procedure as for the water management plan (Art. 50). A flood hazard map and a flood risk map shall be prepared for flood-prone areas, where are presented or where might occur significant risks of flooding (Art. 48, para. 1). The flood risk map shall include information about any potential harmful consequences of floods to human health, the environment, cultural heritage, and/or economic activity, and other information relevant to flood risk management (Art. 48, para. 1).
594. A general flood defence plan (hereinafter 'the general plan') shall be delivered for first and second order waters and internal waters (Art. 54, para. 1). It should be prepared by the Ministry and delivered by the Government for a period of six years (Art. 54, para. 2).
595. A flood defence action plan (hereinafter 'the action plan') shall be delivered for (Art. 55, para. 1): (1) first order waters and internal waters; and (2) second order waters. The action plan referred to in para. 5 of this Article shall include, but not be limited to, information required for operational flood defence, criteria for the declaration of flood defence, names of flood defence managers and entities and warning and information dissemination methods (Art. 55, para. 6).

4. Water Development and Water Use

443. Water development, as contemplated herein, is a set of measures and works aimed at conserving and/or controlling water quantity in order to: (1) ensure the quantitative, spatial, and temporal distribution of waters for the provision of water supply to the population, industry, and other users; (2) ensure good status of aquatic and riparian ecosystems; (3) watercourses increase during periods of low flow; and (4) ensure conditions for special water use (Article 66).[596]

Any use of water which does not fall within the scope of general water use constitutes a special use of water (Article 68, paragraph 1). The right to special use of water shall be acquired on the basis of a water permit or, if special water use is exercised based on a concession agreement, pursuant to such agreement (Article 68, paragraph 2).

5. Protection of Water from Pollution

444. Protection of water, as contemplated herein, is a set of measures and activities by which surface water and groundwater quality is protected and improved, as well as protected from any impact of transboundary pollution, in order to: (1) preserve human life and health; (2) reduce pollution and prevent any deterioration of water status; (3) ensure harmless and unhindered use of water for different purposes; and (4) protect aquatic and riparian ecosystems, and achieve environmental quality standards pursuant to the regulation which addresses environmental protection and environmental objectives (Article 92, paragraph 1).

445. With the goal of preventing any deterioration of the quality of water and the environment, ELVs, as well as methods and conditions for the discharge of pollutants and the application of the ELVs, shall be specified for: (1) process wastewater prior to the discharge thereof into a public sewerage system; (2) process wastewater or other wastewater discharged directly into a recipient; (3) water discharged upon treatment from a public sewerage system into a recipient; and (4) wastewater discharged into a recipient from a septic or collection pit (Article 93, paragraph 1).

The Government, at the recommendation of the Minister and the minister responsible for environmental protection, determines the physical-chemical parameters and limit values for emissions of pollutants, methods and conditions of the discharge of pollutants, as well as the terms and conditions of application of the ELVs referred to in paragraph 1 of this Article, and deadlines to achieve them (Article 93, paragraph 2).[597]

596. General use of water is the use without any prior treatment, or without the use of special devices (pumps, vacuum units, etc.) or the erection of water constructions (Art. 67, para. 1).

597. A new Art. 93a has been introduced – relating to the standards of environmental quality and limit values for polluting substances.

446. Water protection shall be implemented pursuant to a water pollution protection plan[598] (Article 94, paragraph 1).

447. Any legal entity, entrepreneur or individual who discharges or disposes of any substance(s) which may pollute water, unless the natural person who uses water for drinking and sanitary needs of their own, shall, prior to the release thereof into a public sewerage system or recipient, partially or completely remove such substances and to purify wastewater pursuant to this Law and special laws which regulate environmental protection and/or regulations delivered based on these laws (Article 98, paragraph 1).[599]

6. Monitoring

448. Article 107 of the Law prescribes monitoring of surface and ground water for achievement of harmonized and comprehensive State overview. Monitoring is performed pursuant to annual monitoring programme that prescribes number and position of measuring points, manner and number of quantity and level measuring, for surface and ground water, manner and procedure of water quality testing, number and conditions of testing and contents of reports on determined water quality (Article 108). The authority responsible for conducting state-level water quality monitoring in cooperation with the republic organization responsible for hydrometeorological affairs performs monitoring and submits quarterly and annual reports to the competent institutions. Legal persons accredited by the A and with relevant references can perform water quality testing as well. These legal persons are obliged to submit data of the testing results to organization of the authority responsible for conducting state-level water quality monitoring (Article 109).

7. Classification of Surface Water and Groundwater Bodies

449. With the goal of protecting and improving the quality of surface and ground waters, bodies of surface and groundwater shall be classified depending on their quantitative and chemical status (Article 111, paragraphs 1 and 2). Classified bodies of surface water and classified bodies of groundwater shall be identified in the water management plan (Article 111, paragraph 4).[600]

---

598. The Ministry shall propose, and the Government shall deliver the water pollution protection plan for a period of six years (Art. 95, para. 1).

599. Wastewater treatment referred to in para. 1 of this Article is carried out to a level that corresponds to the ELVs or to a level that does not impair the quality standards of the environment of the recipient, in accordance with regulations governing the limits of pollutants into surface waters and groundwater, limit values priority, and other hazardous pollutants and regulation governing the limit values for emissions of pollutants into the water, taking more stringent criteria of these two (Art. 98, para. 2).

600. The Regulation on water classification (OJ SRS, No. 5/68), that regulates general classification of water into four classes according to the pollution level and purpose, prescribes water of the class II as suitable for bathing, recreation and water sports. The Regulation contains indicators and their

Article 133 prescribes activities which are to be prohibited in order to conserve and maintain bodies of surface water, bodies of groundwater, protective water constructions, and other water constructions, to prevent any deterioration of the water regime, to ensure the conveyance of high flows and the implementation of flood defence and to protect the environment.

8. Water Enactment, Water Documentation and Information Dissemination

450. Water enactments and water documentation are regulated in Chapter V of the Law. In order to ensure a single water regime and water management, in accordance with the Strategy, Water Management Plan and the relevant technical documentation, Water Acts are issued. The Water Acts are the following: (1) Water Conditions; (2) Water Consent; and (3) Water Permit. Water Act from paragraph 2 items (2) and (3) of this Article are administrative acts, which are adopted in accordance with the regulation governing the general administrative procedure (Article 113). The competence for issuing the mentioned water enactments is divided between the MAFWM – Republic Water Directorates, competent bodies of AP and LSG and a public water management company, depending on the type of structures and works (Article 114, paragraph 1).

451. The water permit is issued by an authority or a public water company responsible for issuing water conditions (Article 122, paragraph 3). The water permit is issued for a definite period of time, not longer than fifteen years (Article 122, paragraph 5).[601]

452. Water documentation shall include: (1) Water book[602] and (2) Water Register[603] (Article 129, paragraph 1).

453. The Ministry and the public water management enterprise shall ensure the transparency of their activities through information dissemination via public media outlets and formal releases (Article 147). A water information system shall be set up for purposes of water classification, water regime monitoring and improvement, watersystem development planning, and water management in the RS (Article 148, paragraph 1).

---

limit values for each of the classes. The Regulation is not complied with the Council Directive 2006/7 of 15 Feb. 2006 on water quality intended for recreation purposes.

601. The right granted on the basis of water permit cannot be transferred to other user without consent of the body that issued the water permit (Art. 125, para. 1).

602. A water book is a Register of water enactments which has been delivered (Art. 130, para. 1).

603. Water registers shall be maintained in order to ensure the availability of information required for water management, or water use, water protection and protection against the adverse effects of water (Art. 131, para. 1). Water registers include the following: (1) water asset register; (2) register of water constructions; (3) register of water uses; and (4) register of polluters (Art. 131, para. 2).

9. Funding of Water Management

454. Financing of water management is regulated in Chapter IX of the Law. The activities financed in line with this Law are given in Article 150. Issues related to basis for paying fees and defining fee payers and criteria for paying fees, in some cases exceptions to paying, etc., are regulated by Articles 153–177đ, 183 and 184 (However, the following provisions of the Law have ceased to apply: Article 90, paragraph 2, item 2, Articles 153–177, as well as Articles 191–195. – on the day of the beginning of the application of the Law on Fees for the Use of Public Goods (OJ RS, No. 95/2018), i.e.,1 January 2019 (*see* Article 279 of the Law).

455. Activities of general interest funded pursuant to this Law shall include: (1) watercourse development and protection against the adverse effects of water; (2) water development and water use; (3) water protection from pollution; (4) the construction, maintenance and management of reclamation systems – public ownership; (5) the construction, maintenance, and management of regional and multipurpose water systems; and (6) other activities of general interest (Article 150, paragraph 1). Funding for these activities shall be provided from: (1) the budget of the RS; (2) the budget of the AP; (3) water fees;[604] (4) concession fees; and (5) other sources (Article 151, paragraph 1).

456. A budgetary water fund of the RS (the National Fund) shall be established to earmark funds for activities of general interest which shall be financed pursuant to this Law within the territory of the RS, excluding the territory of the AP (Article 185, paragraph 1).[605] In addition, a budgetary water fund of the AP (hereinafter 'the Provincial Fund') shall be established to earmark funds for activities of general interest which shall be financed pursuant to this Law within the territory of the AP (Article 188, paragraph 1).

10. Inspection Supervision

457. The issue of inspection surveillance in the field of water is prescribed in Chapter X of the Law on Waters. Surveillance of implementation of this Law and regulations passed on the basis of it, other regulations and general Acts are performed by the inspector competent for water management activities (water management inspector), sanitary inspector and inspector for environmental protection, pursuant to competences prescribed by Law (Articles 196–208), by the Law on Determining the Jurisdiction of the Autonomous Province of Vojvodina (OJ RS, Nos 99/2009 and 67/2012 CC) and the Law on the Capital (OJ RS Nos 129/2007 and 83/14 – other law, 101/16 – other law) and other relevant laws.

---

604. Water fees include the following: (1) water use fee; (2) water discharge fee; (3) water pollution fee; (4) drainage fee; (5) water constructions and systems fee; and (6) fee for extracted river sediment (Art. 153). However, the provision of Art. 159 ceased to apply with the enactment of the Law on Fees for the Use of Public Goods (Art. 278, para. 1, item 7 of the Law).

605. *See also* Decision on the Water Budget Fund of the Republic of Serbia (OJ RS, No. 9/11).

458. Penalty system is laid down by Chapter XI of the Law on Waters.

C. Law on Environmental Protection

459. According to Article 23 of the EPL, waters may be used and burdened, and wastewater discharged into waters with the application of adequate treatment, in the manner and up to the level that shall not represent a threat to natural processes or to renewal of quality and quantity of water and which shall not reduce the possibility of their multipurpose utilization (paragraph 1).[606] Legal entity and/or entrepreneur who has a plant for wastewater treatment or needs to be built and which discharges its effluent into the recipient or the public sewerage system (except installations subject to integrated permitting), should adopt an action plan for the gradual establishment of ELVs pollutants in water, set deadlines for their gradual achievement, and to act in accordance with the action plan (paragraph 3). Protection of waters shall be achieved through undertaking systematic and control-monitoring measures of water quality, reducing pollution of waters with pollutants below the prescribed limit values and undertaking technical-technological and other measures necessary for their treatment, in order to avoid introduction of dangerous waste and other harmful substances in waters, as well as through monitoring the effect of polluted waters on the health of humans, animals and plants and the environment. Protection of waters shall include protection of waters from the impact of transboundary pollution, in a manner to ensure the overall preservation of waters (paragraph 7).

D. Other Regulations

460. In addition, a large number of other regulations apply in the field of water management. This includes, *inter alia*, the following:

- Regulation on determining the water management basis of the RS (OJ RS, No. 11/02).
- Regulation on establishing the Water Management Plan on the territory of the RS until 2027 (OJ RS, No. 33/23).
- Regulation on establishing the Water Management Program in 2023 (OJ RS, Nos 21/23, 58/23, 85/23, 103/23, and 112/23).
- Regulation on determining the General Plan for Flood Defense (OJ RS, No. 18/19).
- Regulation on leasing water land in public ownership (OJ RS, No. 50/19).

---

606. Protection and utilization of waters shall be realized within the integral water management through undertaking and implementation of measures for preservation of surface and underground waters and their reserves, quality and quantity, as well as through protection in accordance with special law (para. 2). For the purpose of protection and preservation of quantities and quality of underground water reserves, detailed research work shall be conducted, as well as preparation of balance of reserves of underground waters (para. 6).

- Order on determining of Operational Plan for flood defence for 2024 (OJ RS, No. 117/23).
- Regulation on Annual Water Status Monitoring Program in 2023 (OJ RS, No. 28/23).
- Regulation on limits of polluting substances emission in water and deadlines for implementation (OJ RS, Nos 67/11, 48/2 and 1/16).
- Regulation on limits of polluting substances in surface and subsurface waters and sediments and deadlines for implementation (OJ RS, No. 50/12).
- Regulation on limits of priority and priority hazardous substances polluting surface waters and deadlines for implementation (OJ RS, No. 24/2014).
- Regulation on categorization of watercourses (OJ RS, No. 5/68).
- Regulation on classification of water (OJ RS, No. 5/68).
- Rulebook on the determination of water bodies of surface and underground waters (OJ RS, No. 72/23).
- Rulebook on the method and criteria for determining the minimum sustainable flow (OJ RS, No. 96/23).
- Rulebook on determining the plan for extraction of river sediments (OJ RS, No. 112/ 23).
- Rulebook on conditions regarding technical-technological equipment and organizational and personnel qualifications for obtaining a licence to perform river sediment extraction activities, as well as on the manner of keeping records of issued and revoked licences (OJ RS, Nos 39/17 and 13/18).
- Rulebook on the content and manner of keeping registers of protected areas (OJ RS, No. 33/17).
- Rulebook on determining the criteria for determining protected areas (OJ RS, No. 13/17).
- Rulebook on determining the Methodology for drafting the risk map and flood risk map (OJ RS, No. 13/17).
- Rulebook on the content of the special water management plan (OJ RS, No. 9/17).
- Rulebook on conditions for distribution and use of funds of the Budget Fund for Waters of the RS and on the manner of distribution of those funds (OJ RS, Nos 13/17, 79/17, 40/18, 44/18 – other law, and 24/21).
- Rulebook on determining the cases in which it is necessary to obtain a water permit (OJ RS, Nos 30/17, and 27/23).
- Rulebook on the manner and conditions for measuring the quantities and examining the quality of wastewater and the content of reports on performed measurements (OJ RS, No. 33/16).
- Rulebook on the content and form of requests for the issuance of Water Acts, the content of opinions in the procedure of issuing water conditions and the content of reports in the procedure of issuing water permits (OJ RS, Nos 72/17,44/18 – other law), and 12/22.
- Rulebook on determining land reclamation areas and their boundaries (OJ RS, No. 90/18).
- Rulebook on determination of water units and their borders (OJ RS, No. 8/18).
- Rulebook on sub-basin boundaries (OJ RS, No. 54/11).

- Rulebook on the contents, keeping and form of water ledger (OJ RS, No. 86/2010).
- Rulebook on the contents and keeping of the cadastre of water facilities (OJ RS, No. 34/11).
- Rulebook on the contents and keeping of the water information system, methodology, structure, categories and levels of data collection as well as the contents of data public is being informed about (OJ RS, No. 54/2011).
- Rulebook on reference requirements for surface water types (OJ RS, No. 67/11).
- Rulebook on requirements related to technical-technological equipment and organizational and personnel capacities for exercising activities of general interest in the sphere of water management and the method of keeping a record of issued and revoked licences (OJ RS, Nos 23/12, 57/13, and 27/23).
- Rulebook on the parameters of ecological and chemical status of surface waters and parameters of chemical and quantitative status of subsurface waters (OJ RS, No. 74/11).
- Rulebook on dangerous matters in water (OJ RS, No. 31/82).
- Decision on determining the initial amount of rent according to which water land in public ownership can be leased (OJ RS, No. 40/19).
- Decision on water area boundaries (OJ RS, No. 92/17).
- Decision on establishment of the National Water Conference (OJ RS, No. 55/11), etc.

461. Besides mentioned, following legal Acts also deserve mentioning:

- Law on the Fees for the Use of Public Goods (OJ RS, Nos 95/18, 49/19, and 92/23).
- Law on Inspection (OJ RS, Nos 36/2015, 44/18 – other law and 95/18).
- Law on Meteorological and Hydrological Activities (OJ RS, No. 88/2010).
- Law on Local Self-Government (OJ RS, Nos 129/07, 83/14 – other law, 101/16 – other law, 47/18, and 111/21 – other law).
- Law on Communal Utilities (OJ RS, Nos 88/11, 104/16 and 95/18).
- Law on Public-Private Partnership and Concession (OJ RS, Nos 88/11, 15/16 and 104/16).
- Law on Planning and Building (OJ RS, Nos 72/09, 81/09 – corr., 64/10 – CC, 24/11, 121/12, 42/13 – CC, 50/13 – CC, 98/13 – CC, 132/14, 145/14, 83/18, 31/19, 37/19 – other law, 9/20, 52/21, and 62/23).
- Law on the Transport of Dangerous Goods (OJ RS, Nos 104/16, 83/18, 95/18 – other law and 10/19 – other law).
- Law on Navigation and Ports on Inland Waters (OJ RS, Nos 73/10, 121/12, 18/15, 96/15 – other law, 92/16, 104/16 – other law, 113/17 – other law, 41/18, 95/18 – other law, 37/19 – other law and 9/20).

E. Harmonization with the EU Legislation

462. According to the NSDS, problems in water sector relate to following: the lack of plan for implementation of the EU Water Framework Directive, insufficient institutional and other capacities, inadequate funding of water management, low price for water and services and lack of economic incentives, lack of harmonization in sectoral policies with other sectors, insufficient percentage of connection to public systems of water supply, lack of rational use of water and bad quality of water in certain areas, and bad quality of water in certain water courses and insufficient protection of water quality.[607]

463. The drafting of the new Law on Water was planned to be completed by the end of 2019, and the adoption of relevant by-laws by the end of 2020, which will completely transpose the water directives.[608] 'The level of alignment with the EU *acquis* on water quality is moderate.'[609] Non-compliance with water quality standards remains a serious concern and includes areas where arsenic is present. Belgrade, Niš and Novi Sad do not treat their wastewater. Serbia should address river pollution more rigorously and increase cooperation for transboundary rivers such as the Danube, Drina, Dragovištica and Pek rivers.[610]

607. GOV RS. 2008b, 66.
608. GOV RS. 2018, 1168.
609. EC 2023, 136.
610. *Ibid.* In addition, improving local governance, in particular for operating and maintaining water and wastewater facilities, remains a priority. Increased transparency on planning, selecting and managing environmental investments must be delivered to ensure better compliance with EU laws and standards in this sector and better value for money.

Chapter 4. Waste

464. Among the greatest pressures in the environment is the generation of all types of solid waste. The total amount of waste produced (approximately 11.5 million tons) was slightly reduced compared to the previous year.[611] According to the Report on the state of the environment for 2018, about 11.6 million tons of waste were produced in the RS. Of that, 92 thousand tons is hazardous waste. The largest producers of waste are thermal power plants.[612] Generated waste quantities, observed by sections and relative to the previous year, noted in 2019 the following trends: Agriculture, forestry and fishing – increase of 40.7%, Mining and quarrying – increase of 39.2%, Manufacturing – increase of 6.1%, Electricity, gas, steam and air conditioning supply – decrease of 0.1%, Water supply, sewerage, waste management and remediation activities – decrease of 14.8%, Construction – increase of 10.1% and Other service activities – increase of 0.5%.[613]

§1. Industrial Waste

465. There are a number of factors causing problems with industrial waste, for example, use of polluting technologies, inadequate organization, insufficient waste recycling, too slow introduction of sustainable industrial production, etc. The economic and financial crisis in Serbia, which lasted for almost a decade in the nineties, has also contributed to, among other things, problems with industrial waste. Most of the waste is generated by chemical industry and metallurgy, mining and energy production. Heavy industry in the RS is mostly connected to mining, and it includes processing industry, metallurgical and chemical industry, etc. Other industrial production includes cement and other construction materials, fertilizers, electrical equipment, wood processing, paper, leather and fur products, rubber, textile, and food products.[614]

It is estimated that safe deposition of ash is one of the biggest problems. Disposal sites cover an area of about 1,800 ha and contain about 170 million tons of ash, which is considered hazardous waste. It is often stored improperly and local water sources are at risk of contamination.[615]

611. EPA. 2023a, 12. In the course of the company's activity, approximately 77% of the generated waste is coal fly ash generated in thermal energy facilities. Approximately 1.30 million tons of waste were disposed of at 12 sanitary landfills, covering 42% of the population of the Republic of Serbia. For more information *see* EPA. 2023d.
612. EPA. 2019a, 174.
613. STAT. OFFICE RS. 2020.
614. GOV RS. 2010b, 23.
615. UNECE. 2007, 99. *See also* UNECE. 2015, 150 (Energy generation waste), 157, 176 (Recommendation 7.6).

§2. Municipal Waste

466. Municipal waste is separately collected household waste, including paper, cardboard, glass, metal, plastic, bio waste, wood, textiles, packaging, waste electrical and electronic equipment, waste batteries and accumulators, bulky waste, and mixed municipal waste and/or separately collected waste from other sources, if this waste is similar in nature and composition to household waste, but does not include waste from production, agriculture, forestry, fishing, and aquaculture, waste vehicles and waste from construction and demolition (Law on Waste Management, Article 5, paragraph 1, point 13).

Between 2006 and 2020, the generation of municipal waste per capita in Serbia fluctuated. It steadily increased until 2011, reaching a volume of 375 kg MSW per capita. This negative trend ended in 2015, after which MSW generation per capita started increasing again, reaching 427 kg in 2020.[616] In the RS, the largest part of municipal waste is deposited in landfills, which should be the last solution in the hierarchy of waste management, after prevention of waste generation, reuse of waste, recycling, and other types of waste utilization. The latest assessment of the EPA says that in the RS, about 15% (in 2022, 17.7%) of produced municipal waste is recycled and that LSG units participate in this with only up to 3%, while all other recycled quantities come from the informal sector.[617]

§3. Dangerous Waste

467. Most of the dangerous waste consists of oils and emulsions, but there are also various wastes from metal, plastic, paper, paint, etc. The mining industry is the biggest generating sector. Other major sources are chemical, petrochemical, metallurgical, paper, leather and textile industries.[618] In the first half of 2008, a database was formed containing dangerous substances located at the operators.[619] Companies that treat hazardous waste reported that they subjected 86,595 tons of hazardous waste to the treatment of reuse in 2022 through various operations. Of this, electrical and electronic equipment represents a significant amount of lead batteries and waste-containing oils.[620] During 2020, a total of 9.57 million tons of waste was generated in the RS, of which approximately 68,000 tons is hazardous waste.[621]

616. EEA. 2023, 3.
617. EPA. 2023d, 9.
618. During 2022, waste from thermal processes has the largest share in the amount of hazardous waste. Wastes from the gas treatment process that contain hazardous substances are the most represented, and the quantities of construction waste that are contaminated with dangerous substances are also represented to a significant extent. EPA. 2023d, 15. The reason for the differences in the amount of hazardous waste, which increased during 2022 compared to 2020 and 2021, is the recovery of economic activities after the Corona virus pandemic. *Ibid.*, 14
619. GOV RS. 2010a, 48.
620. EPA. 2023d, 17.
621. GOV RS. 2022b, Ch. 3.3.1.

468. There is no regular hazardous waste collection system in the territory of the RS. The hazardous waste collection system is primarily based on the economic value of waste.[622] In addition, there is no special legislation on the separate collection and management of hazardous waste from households in the RS.[623]

469. On the territory of the RS, there is still no national facility for the treatment of hazardous industrial waste, nor are there central regional warehouses for hazardous waste, although the design has been provided in the Spatial Plan of the RS since 2010.[624] A system for collecting hazardous waste from households has not been established so far.

The circulation of waste is subject to the permit system, in conformity with the Law on Ratification of the Basel Convention on the Control of Transboundary Movements of Hazardous Wastes and their Disposal as well as the EPL. Hazardous waste import is prohibited. Exceptionally, certain types of hazardous waste which are needed as secondary raw materials in the processing industry in the RS, in compliance with the national goals of that waste type processing, may be imported according to the permit (Article 71, paragraphs 5, and 6 of the Law on Waste Management).[625]

§4. Legislation

470. The three basic legal Acts concerning waste are the *EPL* (OJ RS, Nos 135/04, 36/09 and 36/09 – other law, 72/09 – other law, 43/11 CC, 14/16, 76/18 and 95/18 – other law),[626] the Law on Waste Management (OJ RS, Nos 36/09, 88/10,

622. For example, waste oil of a certain quality (high calorific value) or lead batteries are collected in any case because they can be sold to users in the formal or informal waste management sector. GOV RS. 2022b, Ch. 3.2.3. There is insufficient information on the collection of some hazardous waste streams without positive economic value (acids, chemical waste, oil-contaminated waste, sludge, etc.).
623. Certain hazardous household waste, such as waste electrical and electronic equipment and batteries, is collected under municipal supervision and in the context of special waste streams. For other hazardous household waste, e.g., waste oil, pharmaceutical waste (expired drugs), and chemical waste or varnishes, no regular collection system has been established in the Republic of Serbia so far.
624. In the private sector, several facilities treat hazardous waste and facilities that are planned for construction. Capacities for incineration of organic industrial and medical waste are lacking. GOV RS. 2022b, Ch. 3.2.3.
625. A total of 254,979 tons of waste were exported from the RS in 2022, of which 16,130 tons are hazardous and 238,849 tons are non-hazardous waste. More than half of the exported waste consists of metals of which the most represented are metals containing iron. Most of the waste was exported to the Republic of Croatia, the Republic of Bulgaria, the Republic of North Macedonia, the Republic of Slovenia, and Hungary. During the same year, 271,172 t of waste were imported, of which 8,163 t are hazardous and 263,009 t are non-hazardous. Waste paper and cardboard packaging and waste paper and cardboard make up 65% of the amount of imported waste. Most of the waste was imported from the Republic of Croatia, Hungary, Bosnia and Herzegovina, and the Republic of North Macedonia. Most hazardous waste was imported from Bosnia and Herzegovina, as well as from the Republic of Montenegro. EPA. 2023d, 19.
626. Apart from the EPL, several provisions of the Law on SEA (2004), Law on EIA (2004) and Law on IPPC (2004) are also relevant for waste management.

14/16, 95/18 – other law, and 35/23), and the Law on Packaging and Packaging Waste (OJ RS, Nos 36/09 and 95/18 – other law).

471. The Law on Waste Management (OJ RS, Nos 36/09, 88/10, 14/16, 95/18 – other law, and 35/23)[627] determines the entities competent for waste management, along with their defined obligations and responsibilities. The entities competent for waste management are: (1) RS; (2) AP; (3) LSG Unit; (4) EPA; (5) professional organizations for waste analysis; (6) NGOs, including consumer organizations; and (7) other bodies and organizations, pursuant to the Law (Article 17).

472. The RS oversees waste management on its territory through competent bodies and organizations. The EPA keeps and updates the waste management database in the environmental protection information system regulating environmental protection. Professional organizations and/or accredited laboratories perform testing of waste for transboundary shipment, treatment of waste and disposal of waste in accordance with their authority for testing waste. In the RS, there are six authorized laboratories for testing waste. NGOs, including organizations for the protection of consumers and other authorities and organizations (urban planning, nature protection, municipal services and internal affairs), submit their opinions to the LSG units in the process of issuing waste management permits.

I. Waste Management Program of the Republic Serbia

473. In early 2022, Serbia adopted the Waste management program 2022–2031 (OJ RS, No. 12/22) and the Action plan for 2022–2024 for the implementation of the Waste management program.[628] The Waste management program (hereinafter 'the Program') was preceded by the Waste Management Strategy for the period 2010–2019 (OJ RS, No. 29/10) (hereinafter 'the Strategy'), 'which set the conditions for the establishment and development of an integrated waste management system in the RS'.

474. The Program determines the strategic goals for the improvement of the waste management system and the basic principles that should guide all actors in waste management to achieve these goals in the RS for the period 2022–2031. The general objective is to develop a sustainable waste management system to conserve resources and the health of the people, as well as reduce negative environmental

627. With the latest amendments to the Law on Waste Management, additional harmonization has been made with the following secondary sources of EU law: Regulation (EC) No. 1013/2006 on shipment of waste, Directive 2010/75/EU on industrial emissions (integrated pollution prevention and control), Directive (EU) 2018/850 on the landfill of waste, Directive 2008/98/EC on waste, and Regulation (EU) 2017/852 he mercury.

628. https://www.ekologija.gov.rs/dokumenta/upravljanje-otpadom/program (22.1.2024). In addition, the Draft Sludge Management Program in the Republic of Serbia for the period 2023–2032 with an action plan for the period 2023–2027 has been prepared. https://www.ekologija.gov.rs/sites/default/files/2023-10/program_upravlana_mulem_2023-2032_sa_ar.pdf (22.1.2024).

impacts and space degradation. These include waste prevention, reduction of recyclable waste in landfills, reducing the share of biodegradable waste in municipal waste, reducing the negative impact of landfilled waste on the environment, climate, and human health, and waste management according to the principles of the circular economy.[629]

475. The implementation of environmental policy is based on the precautionary principle and the principle of prevention; namely, each activity must be planned and implemented in a way that causes the least possible change in the environment and poses the lowest risk to the environment and human health, reduce space and consumption of raw materials and energy in construction, production, distribution, and use.[630] The key principles that should be taken into account when establishing and implementing a waste management plan are the following principles: Sustainable development principle; Circular economy principle; Precautionary principle; Choosing the most optimal option for the environment principle; Self-sufficiency principle; Principle of proximity and regional approach to waste management; Principle of waste management hierarchy (Prevention, Preparation for reuse, Recycling, Other reuse operations, Disposal); Principle of extended producer responsibility, and Polluter pays principle.

476. The following four specific objectives are set to achieve the general objective of the Program: (1) Improved municipal waste management system through increased recycling rate, reduced disposal of biodegradable waste in landfills, and reduced disposal of waste in unsanitary landfills; (2) Sustainable hazardous and industrial waste management system in place; (3) Increased rate of collection, reuse, and recycling of special waste streams and more efficient use of resources; (4) Strengthened capacity of institutions in the field of waste management and regulations harmonized with EU regulations.

II. Law on Environmental Protection

477. A number of Articles of the EPL are related to waste management. Article 30 prescribes that:

> Waste[631] management shall be enforced according to regulated conditions and measures of waste treatment through system of collecting, transport, preparation for reuse, i.e. reuse of waste treatment and disposal, including supervision over those activities and concern for the facilities for waste treatment after their closure. The owner of the waste is obliged to undertake measures of waste

629. The progress made in achieving the overall objective of the Program will be monitored through the following indicators: (1) the level of municipal waste disposed of in non-sanitary landfills in relation to the total amount of waste generated by municipal waste (%), (2) degree of hazardous waste disposed of (%). GOV RS, 2022b, Ch. 5. General and Specific Objectives.
630. *Ibid.*
631. According to Art. 3, point 20 of the EPL, 'waste' is defined as any object or substance defined by the waste management law.

management in order to prevent or reduce waste generation, reuse and recycle; separation of secondary raw materials and use of waste as energents, that is, waste disposal.

III. Law on Waste Management

478. It has following fifteen parts: Part I – General Provisions (Articles 1–6), Part II – Types and Classification of Waste[632] (Articles 7 and 8), Part III – Waste Management Planning (Articles 9–16), Part IV – Waste Management Authorities (Articles 17–24), Part V – Responsibilities and Obligations in Waste Management (Articles 25–31), Part VI – Organization of Waste Management (Articles 32–46), Part VII – Specific Waste Streams Management (Articles 47–58), Part VIII – Waste Management Permits (Articles 59–70), Part IX – Transboundary Waste Movement (Articles 71–73), Part X – Reporting on Waste and Database (Articles 74–76), XI – Waste Management Financing (Articles 77–82), Part XII – Supervision (Articles 83–86), Part XIII – Competence for Settlement of Appeals (Article 87), Part XIV – Penalty Provisions (Articles 88–92), Part XV – Transitional and Final Provisions (Articles 93–105).[633]

479. According to Article 1, the Law on Waste regulates types and classifications of waste,[634] waste management planning, waste management entities, responsibilities and obligations in waste management,[635] waste management organization, managing of special waste flows, conditions and procedures for issuing of permits;

632. *Waste* is each substance or object to be rejected, intend to be reject or which is necessary to be rejected by holder (Art. 5, point 17). 'Construction and demolition waste' means waste generated in the execution of construction and other works on the construction and demolition of buildings, adaptations, renovations, reconstruction of residential, industrial, and other facilities, maintenance and replacement of infrastructure facilities, as well as excavations for residential, industrial and road infrastructure, and this includes non-hazardous and hazardous construction and demolition waste, namely: – Non-hazardous construction and demolition waste not containing hazardous materials, (recyclable, inert, etc.), – Hazardous construction and demolition waste requiring specific handling and/or having one or more hazardous characteristics making it hazardous waste (wastes containing asbestos, wastes with high heavy metal content, etc.) to which specific regulations apply (Art. 17a).

633. The provisions of this Law shall not apply to: (1) gases that are emitted into the atmosphere; (2) land (in situ) including unexcavated contaminated land and buildings permanently connected with land; (3) uncontaminated soil and other materials from nature, excavated during construction activities where it is certain that the material will be used in construction purposes in its natural form on the site where it was excavated; (4) radioactive waste; (5) deactivated explosives; (6) faeces, if they are not covered by para. 2, item 2) of this Article; (7) Straw and other natural non-hazardous agricultural or forest materials used in farming, forestry or for the production of energy from such biomass through processes or methods which do not threaten the environment or endanger human health; and (8) sludge from sewerage systems and septic tanks contents, other than plants from waste water treatment. (Art. 4, para. 1).

634. *Classification of waste* is the process of classifying of waste disposal to one or more waste lists which are regulated by special regulation, and according to its origin, composition and further purpose (Art. 5, point 10).

635. *Waste management* is the implementation of the prescribed measures for waste management including collection, transport, storage, treatment, i.e., reuse and waste disposal, including supervision of

transboundary movement of waste, reporting on waste and databases; financing of waste management; and supervision, as well as other issues relevant to waste management.

480. Article 2 prescribes that aim of this Law is to provide and ensure conditions for: (1) waste management in a way that does not endanger human health and the environment;[636] (2) prevention of waste, particularly through development of cleaner technologies and rational use of natural resources, as well as eliminating the risk of its harmful effects on human health and the environment; (3) reuse and recycling of waste, separation of secondary raw material from the waste and using waste as fuel; (4) development of procedures and methods for waste disposal;[637] (5) rehabilitation of unarranged landfills;[638] (6) monitoring of existing and newly created landfill; and (7) developing-raising awareness of waste management.

A. *Principles of Waste Management*

481. There are six generally accepted principles on which waste management is based (Article 6, paragraph 1): (1) *selection of the most optimal option for the environment* – application of the most optimal options for the environment establishes for the given objectives and circumstances, the option or combination of options that gives the greatest benefit or minimum damage to the environment as a whole, at an acceptable cost and profitability, in the long term, as well as in short term; (1a) *principle of self-sufficiency* – application of the principle of self-sufficiency means the establishment of integrated and adequate network of facilities for reuse and disposal of mixed municipal waste collected from households, including the collection of this type of waste generated by other waste producers, taking into account the BAT in accordance with this Law; (2) *proximity and regional approach to waste management* – the waste is treated or disposed as close as possible to their place of generation, that is, in the region of generation, with the aim to avoid negative effects to the environment during the transport. Regional waste management is provided by

---

these activities and taking care of waste management facilities after the closure of the activities undertaken by the trader and agent (Art. 5, point 36).

636. Waste management is performed in a way that provides the least risk to human life and health and to the environment, control and mitigation of (Art. 3, para. 1): (1) water, air and soil pollution; (2) threats to flora and fauna; (3) the threat of the emergence of an accident, explosion or fire; (4) negative impact on landscapes and natural goods of exceptional value; (5) the level of noise and unpleasant odour.

637. *Waste disposal* is any operation which is not reuse of waste, even when the operation has a secondary effect of the formation of substances or energy (D list) (Art. 5, point 16).

638. *Landfill* is a place for the final disposal of sanitary waste surface or below the surface of the earth including: internal disposal sites (landfill where the manufacturer is disposed their own waste at the source); permanent locations (more than one year) used for temporary storage of waste, but excluding warehouses where waste is unloaded for the purpose of preparation for further transport to the place for treatment, i.e., reutilization or disposal on other locations, and waste storage prior of treatment, i.e., reuse up to three years or waste storage before disposal up to one year) (Art. 5, point 5).

development and implementation of regional strategic plans based on European legislation and national policy; (3) *the principle of hierarchy of waste management* – the hierarchy of waste management is the order of priorities in waste management practices;[639] (4) *the principle of responsibility* – producers, importers, distributors and retailers of products affecting the growth of the waste are responsible for waste generated as a result of their activities. The producer is obliged to strive to reduce waste, developing products that are recyclable, as well as developing markets for reuse and recycling of their products; and (5) *polluter pays principle* – the polluter has to bear the full cost of expenses of their activities. Costs for waste generation, treatment and disposal must be included in the price of the product.

B. *Types and Classification of Waste*

482. According to Article 7, paragraph 1, types of waste are the following: (1) communal waste[640] (home waste);[641] (2) commercial waste;[642] and (3) industrial waste.[643]

483. Waste is classified according to the catalogue of waste (Article 8, paragraph 1). Catalogue of waste is a summary list of non-hazardous[644] and hazardous waste[645] according to the place of generation and composition (Article 8, paragraph

639. In terms of the implementation of the waste hierarchy to which the waste management hierarchy refers, actions shall be taken to initiate solutions to achieve the best overall result in terms of the environment, which in case of specific waste streams, may require deviations from the hierarchy where this shall be justified with the life cycle, taking into consideration total effects on such waste generation and management (para. 3). Development of the waste management legislation and policy shall be a fully transparent process, in accordance with applicable regulations on consultations and involvement of the citizens and all stakeholders (para. 4). In the implementation of the hierarchy principle, account shall be taken in to general principles of environmental protection, precaution and sustainability, technical feasibility and economic value, and protection of resources as well as of the overall effect on the environment, human health, and economic and social effects (para. 5).

640. *Communal waste* is separately collected household waste, including paper, cardboard, glass, metal, plastic, bio waste, wood, textiles, packaging, waste electrical and electronic equipment, waste batteries and accumulators, bulky waste and mixed municipal waste and/or separately collected waste from other sources, if this waste is similar in nature and composition to household waste, but does not include waste from production, agriculture, forestry, fishing and aquaculture, waste vehicles and waste from construction and demolition (Art. 5, point 13).

641. Depending upon hazardous characteristics that influence human health and the environment, communal waste can be (Art. 7, para. 2): (1) inert; (2) non-hazardous; and (3) hazardous.

642. *Commercial waste* is waste generated in enterprises and other institutions that are wholly or partly engaged in trade, services, office affairs, sport, recreation or entertainment, except household waste and industrial waste (Art. 5, point 11).

643. *Industrial waste* is waste from any industry or from the location of industry, except mullock and supporting mineral raw materials from mines and quarries (Art. 5, point 7).

644. *Non-hazardous waste* is waste that does not have characteristics of hazardous waste (Art. 5, point 15).

645. *Hazardous waste* is a waste which by its origin, composition or concentration of hazardous substances can cause danger to the environment and human health and has at least one of the hazardous characteristics defined by special regulations, including packaging in which hazardous waste was or is packed (Art. 5, point 18).

2). Hazardous waste is classified when necessary, according to limited values of dangerous substances concentration (Article 8, paragraph 3). The owner of the waste, that is, the operator,[646] is obliged to classify the waste in the prescribed manner, in accordance with this Law[647] (Article 8, paragraph 4).

484. The Minister in charge for environmental protection prescribes: (1) waste catalogue; (2) a list of categories of waste (Q list); (3) a list of categories of hazardous waste by the origin and composition (Y list); (4) a list of hazardous waste characteristics (H list); (5) a list of waste components for which it is considered hazardous waste (C list); (6) concentration limits of harmful components in the waste, on which characteristics of waste are determined; (7) a list of procedures and methods of disposal and reutilization of waste (List D & R List); (8) type, content and form of report on testing of waste; (9) types of parameters to determine the physical and chemical characteristics of hazardous waste to be used for physical-chemical treatment; (10) types of parameters for waste testing for thermal treatment purpose; (11) types of parameters for waste testing; and (12) manner and procedure for classification of waste (Article 8, paragraph 6).[648]

C. Planning, Responsibilities and Organizing of Waste Management

485. For planning of waste management, the following planning documents are adopted in the RS (Article 9, paragraph 1): (1) Waste Management Strategy (hereinafter 'Strategy'); (2) national plans for individual waste streams; (3) regional waste management plan; (4) local waste management plan; (5) waste management plan in the facility of which integrated permit is issued; and (6) work plan for waste management facilities.

486. Entities responsible for waste management are (Article 17, paragraph 1): (1) the RS; (2) AP; (3) LSG unit; (4) EPA; (5) professional organizations for the

---

646. *Operator* is any legal entity or entrepreneur who, in accordance with the regulations, manages the installation or controls it or is authorized to make economic decisions in the area of technical functioning of the facility and on whose name is issued a permit for waste management (Art. 5, point 19).

647. In order to determine the composition and characteristics of hazardous waste, the owner of the waste, i.e., operator is obliged to perform testing of hazardous waste, as well as waste which by the origin, composition and characteristics might be a hazardous waste (Art. 8, para. 5).

648. In the regulation referred to in para. 6 points 2, 3 and 5 of this Law, the Minister shall make a list of Serbian standards which shall contain technical requirements for waste categories and elements (para. 7). The inclusion of a substance or an object in the list referred to in para. 7 of this Article shall not mean that this shall be waste in all cases, but will be deemed waste only in so far it complies with the requirements in accordance with this Law (para. 8). The reclassification of hazardous waste as non-hazardous waste shall not be achieved by waste diluting or mixing so as to reduce the initial concentration of hazardous materials to the level below the limit values for the definition of hazardous waste (para. 9). Waste may be deemed non-hazardous waste in accordance with the waste catalogue referred to in para. 2 of this Article (para. 10). Amendments to the Law (2016) introduced also, *inter alia*, new provisions concerning the following issues: by-product, proving compliance with by-product related requirements and end of waste status (Art. 8a–8d).

examination of waste; (6) NGOs, including consumer organizations; and (7) other agencies and organizations, in accordance with the Law.

487. The producer of products is obliged to use technologies and develop production, ensuring rational use of natural resources, materials and energy, and also encourage reuse and recycling[649] of products and packaging and promote ecologically sustainable management of natural resources (Article 25, paragraph 1).

488. A producer or an importer whose product becomes hazardous waste is obliged, after use of such product, to take over that waste, without compensation costs and treat it in accordance with this Law and other regulations (Article 25, paragraph 2) or to authorize other legal entity to take over the products after use on his/her behalf (Article 25, paragraph 3).

489. The owner and/or other holder of waste shall bear all waste management costs (Article 27, paragraph 1). Disposal costs shall be borne by the owner and/or other holder and/or previous owner and/or other holder or the product producer who has produced the waste (Article 27, paragraph 3). The responsibility and obligations of the owner and/or other holder of waste is also the responsibility of a person who participates in the waste trade as an intermediate holder of waste but does not own the waste (Article 27, paragraph 4).[650]

490. Waste management is organized in a way that does not pose a threat to human health and the environment in accordance with the Law (Article 32, paragraph 1). The Minister may order additional measures for managing certain types of waste in case that: (1) the waste handling endangers or may endanger human health and the environment; (2) there are additional requirements for the implementation of provisions of international treaties binding on the RS (Article 32, paragraph 2).

491. A person[651] who collects or transports waste, collects waste from producers or owners, and/or other holders, and transports it to the waste management facilities, or to the collection centre, storage centre, transfer station or to the facility for treatment or reuse or disposal (Article 35, paragraph 1). Collected mixed waste can be accepted as recyclable material in a waste management facility if these materials are separated in the further process, in accordance with quality standards, i.e.,

649. *Recycling* means any operations (R2–R10 and R12) of reuse processing waste into a product, materials or substances, regardless of whether are used for the original or other purposes, including reprocessing of organic materials, except reuse for energy purposes, and reprocessing into materials that are intended for use as fuel or for landfill covering (Art. 5, point 27).

650. The obligations of other entities are also regulated: Obligations of Waste Carrier (Art. 28), Obligations of the Broker and Dealer (Art. 28a), Obligations of the Operator in the Waste Management Facility (Art. 29), Obligations of Waste Disposal Site Operator (Art. 30) and Qualified Person Responsible for Professional Activities (Art. 31).

651. *Waste collector* is a entrepreneur or legal entity who collects the waste (Art. 5, point 29). *Waste collection* is the collection of waste, including sorting and temporary storage at waste producers for the purposes of transportation to waste management facilities (Art. 5, point 28).

recycling (Article 35, paragraph 4). If pollution occurs during waste transportation, carrier is responsible for cleaning and removal of pollution (Article 35, paragraph 9). Hazardous waste is to be separately collected and transported (Article 35, paragraph 12).

492. The waste is stored in places that are technically equipped for temporary waste storage at the site of the manufacturer or of the owner and/or other waste holders in collection centres, transfer stations and other locations in accordance with this Law (Article 36, paragraph 1). Waste cannot be temporarily stored at the location of the producer, owner, and/or other holder of waste for longer than thirty-six months, after which the waste must be submitted for treatment, i.e., reuse or disposal (Article 36, paragraph 5).

493. Waste treatment is performed by applying the best available techniques and technologies in accordance with this Law (Article 37, paragraph 1). Facility and equipment for waste treatment can be stationary or mobile (Article 37, paragraph 2). The treatment of waste in stationary or mobile facilities shall be in accordance with a permit for treatment issued on the basis of this Law (Article 37, paragraph 3).

494. The competent authority for waste management takes necessary measures to ensure that the operations of waste reuse are carried out in accordance with Articles 3 and 6 of this Law (Article 38, paragraph 1). The Minister shall prescribe the conditions and manner of collection, transport, storage, treatment and recycling of wastes used as secondary raw materials or for energy production (Article 38, paragraph 10).

D. Management of Special Waste Streams

495. It is prohibited to transport batteries and accumulators containing more than 0.0005% mercury by weight, unless otherwise stipulated by this Law (Article 47, paragraph 1). It is prohibited to transport portable batteries and accumulators, including those that are built into devices, which contain more than 0.002% cadmium by weight, except those used in security and alarm systems, medical equipment or cordless electric tools, unless otherwise stipulated by this Law (Article 47, paragraph 3). The owner and/or other holder of waste batteries and accumulators, excluding households, is obliged to hand them over for treatment to a person who has permission to do so (Article 47, paragraph 7). The Minister is in charge of prescribing the content and appearance of markings on the batteries, button cells and accumulators according to the content of hazardous substances, manner and procedure for managing waste batteries and accumulators, as well as devices with built-in batteries and accumulators (Article 47, paragraph 9).

496. Where waste oil is concerned, the Law prohibits: (1) discharge or spill of waste oil into or onto land, surface and underground water and sewage system; (2)

disposal of waste oils and uncontrolled discharge of residues from the waste oil processing; (3) mixing of waste oil during collection and storage with Polychlorinated Biphenyl (PCB) and usage of PCB or halogenated substances and with substances that are not waste oil, or mixing with hazardous waste; (4) every kind of waste oil processing, which pollutes the air in concentrations above the prescribed limits (Article 48, paragraph 2).[652]

497. The entity that collects, transports, treats or disposes of waste tyres shall hold appropriate permit, maintain and keep records on quantities of collected and treated waste tyres and shall submit such data to the Agency.[653]

498. The waste originating from electrical and electronic products is not to be mixed with other types of waste. It is prohibited to dispose of electrical and electronic products' waste[654] without previous treatment (Article 50, paragraph 2). The components of electrical and electronic product waste that contain RSV must be separated and properly disposed of (Article 50, paragraph 4). The producer or importer of electrical or electronic products is required to identify there cyclable components of these products (Article 50, paragraph 5). When placed on the market, the use of new electrical and electronic equipment containing lead, mercury, cadmium, hexavalent chromium, polibromovanebiphenyls (PBB) and polibromovanediphenylethers (PBDE) maybe prohibited or restricted (Article 50, paragraph 9).

499. Waste fluorescent tubes containing mercury are collected separately (Article 51, paragraph 1). It is prohibited to dispose of such tubes without prior treatment (Article 51, paragraph 2). Also, the owner and/or other holder of waste fluorescent tubes containing mercury is obliged to hand them over for treatment to a person having permission to do so (Article 51, paragraph 3).

500. Waste containing PCB is to be collected separately (Article 52, paragraph 1). According to Article 52, points 1–6, it is prohibited to: (1) refill transformers with PCBs; (2) reuse PCB waste; (3) get PCB from PCB waste by recycling; (4) temporarily store PCBs, PCB waste and equipment containing PCB[655] for more than

652. Waste oil, for the purpose of this Law, are all mineral or synthetic oils or lubricants, which are useless for the purpose they were originally intended, such as hydraulic oils, engine oils, turbine oils or other lubricants, marine oil, oils or liquids for insulating or heat transfer, other mineral or synthetic oil, including oily residues from tanks, oil – water mixtures and emulsions (Art. 48, para. 1).

653. Waste tires, according to Art. 49, para. 1, are tires of motor vehicles (cars, buses, trucks, motorcycles, etc.), agricultural and construction machinery, trailers, towing machines, etc. after the end of their life cycle.

654. Electrical and electronic products waste cannot be mixed with other types of waste (Art. 50, para. 1). Waste liquids originating from electrical and electronic products must be separated and treated in an appropriate way (Art. 50, para. 3).

655. All equipment containing PCBs, as well as rooms or facilities in which they are located, including decontaminated equipment, must be marked (Art. 52, para. 10).

twenty-four months before securing their disposal or decontamination;[656] (5) incinerate PCB or PCB waste on ships; and (6) use equipment containing PCB in case they are not in working order or if they are leaking. An owner and/or other holder of equipment containing more than 5 dm^3 of PCB shall be obliged to report to the Ministry on such equipment, submit a replacement plan, i.e., equipment disposal and decontamination plan, ensure its disposal, i.e., decontamination, and inform the Ministry about all the changes in data pertaining to the equipment, within three months from the date of an occurred change (Article 52, paragraph 5).[657]

501. The owner of POP waste[658] and/or other holder is obliged to report to the Ministry the type and quantity of POP waste. The person performing treatment or disposal of POPs waste shall ensure that the remains after the treatment do not have characteristics of POPs substances (Article 53, paragraph 3).

502. The waste containing asbestos is separately collected, packed, stored and disposed of in a landfill in a visible marked place designated for the disposal of waste containing asbestos (Article 54, paragraph 1). The producer or owner and/or holder of waste containing asbestos is required to implement measures to prevent dispersion of asbestos fibres and dust in the environment (Article 54, paragraph 2). The owner of scrap cars (if known) is obliged to hand over the vehicle to the person who has permission for their collection or treatment (Article 55, paragraph 4).[659] A local government regulates the procedure of collection and delivery of vehicles and is entitled to charge the costs if the owner of scraped car is subsequently determined (Article 55, paragraph 6).

503. Producer of medical waste who produces more than 100 tons of non-hazardous medical waste and/or 200 kg of hazardous medical waste is obliged to prepare a medical waste management plan (Article 56, paragraph 1).

The Ministry responsible for public health with prior opinion of the Institute for Public Health, established for the territory of the RS, in cooperation with Ministry gives consent on the plan for medical waste management plan from health institutions and other forms of health services (hereinafter 'private practice'), other legal entities, i.e., Institutions that provide health care for people in accordance with the

656. *Decontamination* includes all operations that enable reuse, recycling or safe disposal of the equipment, objects or materials contaminated by hazardous materials, and may include the removal or replacement of hazardous materials by suitable less harmful material (Art. 5, point 4).

657. Entities that conduct PCB disposal shall be obliged to deliver to holders used PCBs and issue a confirmation in which they shall specify PCB properties and quantities. An owner and/or other holder of equipment containing PCBs shall be obliged to deliver PCB, PCB waste and/or equipment containing PCB to an entity that holds a permit in accordance with this Law, and take all the precaution measures in order to avoid a risk of fire, including keeping them away from flammable products. Equipment containing less than 5 dm^3 of PCBs, which are integral parts of other equipment, should be removed and separately collected, recycled or disposed, upon the termination of the use of the equipment of which they are integral parts (Art. 52, paras 6–8).

658. *POPs waste*, in accordance with this Law, is waste consisting of, containing or contaminated with Persistent Organic Pollutants (POPs) substances (Art. 53, para. 1).

659. If the owner of scraped vehicle is unknown, local government unit shall provide collection and delivery vehicles to a person who has permission for treatment (Art. 55, para. 5).

Law, as well as related medical, educational and scientific research activities that produce more than 500 kg of hazardous medical waste per year (Article 56, paragraph 2). Producer of medical waste provides, when possible, the reduction of quantities and/or hazardous characteristics of medical waste at the place of origin, as well as the reuse of waste (Article 56, paragraph 4). Producer of medical waste collects all waste at the place of origin and classify hazardous from non-hazardous waste, i.e., different types of hazardous medical waste and dispose of it in a suitable packaging adapted to its properties, quantity, the way of temporary disposal method, transport and treatment (Article 56, paragraph 5).[660]

504. Operations for disposal of titanium dioxide waste[661] cannot be made without permission of the Ministry[662] or the competent authorities of the AP (Article 57, paragraph 2).

505. The material used for packaging must be manufactured and designed in a way that during their life cycle are eligible for environmental protection, safety and human health, the health safety of packaged products, as well as conditions for product transportation and waste management (Article 58, paragraph 1).[663]

E. Permits

506. To perform one or more activities in the field of waste management, permits[664] shall be obtained as follows: (1) permits for waste collection, (2) permits for waste transport, (3) permits for waste storage, and (4) permits for waste treatment, specifically: – Storage permit; – Recovery permit; – Disposal permit (Article 59, paragraph 1).[665] The following documents are obtained (issued) for activities related

---

660. Amendments to the law (2016) introduced, also, new provisions related to the management of pharmaceutical waste (Art. 56a and 56b).
661. Waste from titaniumdioxide, according to this Law, are all types of waste originating from titaniumdioxide production, which the manufacturer is obliged to store in compliance with this Law, as well as the residual generated during the treatment of these type of wastes (Art. 57, para. 1).
662. The producer and owner and/or other holder of waste is obliged to have a licence, to keep and maintain records of quantities of this type of waste that is collected, stored, treated or disposed and shall submit information about that to the Agency (Art. 57, para. 3). The producer and owner and/or other holder of titaniumdioxide and waste from titaniumdioxide is obliged to implement measures for supervision of operations of the disposal, as well as controlling of land, water and air at the site where the waste from the titaniumdioxide has been used, stored or disposed of (Art. 57, para. 4).
663. Packaging and packaging of waste is managed in accordance with the special law (Art. 58, para. 2).
664. *Permit* is a decision of the competent authority to the legal entity or entrepreneur approving the collection, transport, import, export and transit, storage, treatment, and reuse or disposal of waste and sets out the conditions of waste management in a way that provides the lowest risk to human health and the environment (Art. 5, point 6).
665. The following permits were issued to operators until October 2021: 137 permits for collection; 178 transport permits, and 98 storage permits for the collection of municipal waste (household waste and similar commercial, industrial, and institutional waste), including separate collection of fractions (waste category 20) (Agency register on issued waste management permits). GOV RS. 2022b, Ch. 3.2.2.

to cross-border movement of waste: (1) permit for export of waste; (2) permit for import of waste; (3) waste transit permit; (4) confirmation of application for cross-border movement of waste.

507. To perform more activities, only one integral permit may be issued for one operator. Permission for collection and transport of hazardous waste shall be issued in accordance with this Law and other regulations (Article 59, paragraphs 3 and 4).[666]

508. The competencies in the field of permits are regulated by 2023 amendments.[667] Permits for collection, transport, storage, treatment, i.e., reuse and disposal of hazardous waste, permit for waste treatment by incineration, and permit for waste treatment in a mobile facility[668] are issued by the ministry and on the territory of the AP by the competent body of the AP (Article 60 paragraph 1).

509. Permits for regional landfills, i.e., landfills for the disposal of non-hazardous and inert waste for areas inhabited by more than 250,000 inhabitants, are issued by the ministry and on the territory of the AP by the competent body of the AP (Article 60, paragraph 2) (Article 60, paragraph 2).[669]

---

666. The permits referred to in paras 1 and 2 of this Article shall be issued for business activities in the field of waste management other than those for which, according to the IPPC-related regulations, the integrated permit is issued. By way of an exception, the permit referred to in paras 1 and 2 of this Article shall also be issued for new and existing waste management plants which are subject to the issue of the integrated permit, including the duration of the trial period, but no longer than 240 days from the completion of the trial period, as a temporary permit pending the issue of the integrated permit. An operator may lodge a complaint against a decision which serves as a basis for the issuance of the permit referred to in para. 4 of this Article, within fifteen days from the day of reception of the decision (paras 5–7).
667. Exceptions are prescribed in which no permit is issued. These are the following cases: (1) movement of waste within the location of the waste producer; (2) waste collection in containers or other household waste collection equipment in accordance with the law regulating communal activities; (3) the case of testing that is carried out in order to determine the technical and technological parameters of the treatment for the purpose of obtaining data in order to implement the procedure for the preparation of a study on impact assessment and/or equipment testing; (4) temporary storage of own waste to the waste producer; (5) use of waste for scientific research purposes; (6) the case of testing that is carried out in order to determine the technical and technological parameters of the reuse of waste for the purpose of obtaining data for the implementation of the procedure for the preparation of an impact assessment study; (7) disposal of one's own non-hazardous waste, to the waste producer at the place of its generation, except for waste that was created by waste treatment procedures (Art. 60, para. 1). For the case from para. 1, item 3), 5), 6) and 7) of this article, a certificate of exemption from the obligation to obtain a permit is issued (para. 2).
668. Mobile facility for waste management is mobile waste management facility is a mobile technical unit in which waste is treated (operations R1 to R12, D8, and D9) at the place of waste generation, i.e., at another location of the waste producer or at a location for which the operator of the mobile facility has a permit for its storage type of waste that is intended for treatment and that fulfils the conditions for the treatment of the waste in question, with the previously obtained consent of the local self-government unit (Art. 5, point 14).
669. The AP is entrusted with issuing permits for the collection and transportation of non-hazardous and inert waste on the territory of the AP, as well as for the storage, treatment, and disposal of waste if the construction permit is issued by the competent authority of the AP (para. 3).

510. The city of Belgrade is entrusted with issuing permits for the collection, transport, storage, treatment, or reuse and disposal of non-hazardous and inert waste for all activities in the territory of the city of Belgrade (Article 60, paragraph 4).[670]

511. The content of the request for the issuance of a permit is regulated by Article 62, the procedure for issuing a permit is regulated by Article 63, and the content of the permit by Article 64 of the Law.[671] In addition, the Law regulates in detail the conditions for rejection of requests for the issuance of a permit (Article 65), the validity period of permits (Article 66), revocation of permit (Article 67), amendment of permit (Article 68), and notification public (Article 69).

512. Permits for waste treatment, i.e., storage, reuse and disposal are issued for a period of ten years (Article 66, paragraph 1). The licence may be renewed at the request submitted 120 days before the expiration of the licence to ensure continuity of the licence (Article 66, paragraph 3).

513. A permit for the collection and/or transport of waste is issued to a company, entrepreneur, or other legal entity that meets the conditions prescribed by this law, as well as by the law governing transport in public transport and the law governing the transport of dangerous goods. (Article 70, paragraph 1).[672] Mandatory measures during collection and transportation of inert, non-hazardous and hazardous waste, in accordance with the provisions of this Law and other regulations, are prescribed in the permission (paragraph 7). The permit shall be issued for a period of five years and may be renewed (paragraph 8).

F. Reporting and Supervision

514. Report on Waste Management in the territory of the RS is an integral part of the Report on the state of the environment and shall be submitted annually to the NA (Article 74, paragraph 1).[673]

515. A producer, owner and/or other holder of waste, except households, shall maintain and keep daily records on waste and submit regular annual report to the Agency (Article 75, paragraph 1). Legal entities, i.e., entrepreneurs that participate in the trade of waste, shall be obliged to submit to the Agency data on the type and quantity of waste, including secondary raw materials that are placed on the market, in the prescribed manner (Article 75, paragraph 2).

---

670. The city, that is, the municipality, is entrusted with issuing a permit for the collection, transport, storage, treatment, i.e., reuse and disposal of inert and non-hazardous waste on their territory (para. 5).
671. The permit for the mobile facility for waste treatment contains operator's obligation to notify the Ministry about any change of location, i.e., the competent authority of the AP and submit approval for location (Art. 64, para. 5).
672. The Law prescribes the conditions under which a permit for the collection and/or transport of waste is not issued.
673. The producer owner and/or other waste holder, except households, is obliged to keep and maintain daily records on waste and submit regular annual report to the Agency (Art. 75, para. 1).

516. The Ministry shall supervise the work of the Agency, AP, local governments, as well as authorized legal entities in performing delegated tasks (Article 83).

G. Financing of Waste Management

517. Waste management costs are determined by the quantity and characteristics of waste in accordance with 'polluter pays' principle and include: (1) the cost of separate collection of waste;[674] (2) the cost of transportation of waste; (3) other costs of measures for waste management that are not covered by income generated by turnover of waste; (4) the costs for removal of waste which is left by an unknown person outside of the landfill;[675] and (5) costs for design and construction of facilities for storage, treatment and disposal of waste, facility costs, closing costs, its subsequent maintenance after termination of the work (Article 77, paragraph 1).

518. Households shall bear costs for waste management in compliance with regulations pertaining to utilities (Article 78, paragraph 3).[676]

519. Legal entity or entrepreneur performing the activity of collection, transport, treatment, and/or storage, recovery and disposal of waste shall charge for its services according to the price determined in compliance with the Law (Article 79, paragraph 1).[677] At the proposal of the ministry responsible for environmental affairs, the ministry responsible for economic affairs, and the ministry responsible for financial affairs, the government regulates in more detail the establishment, conditions, way of functioning, and organization of the organized waste market (paragraph 4).[678]

520. Operator shall bear costs for administrative fees, determined compliant with special regulations, for the following: (1) submission of a request for the issuance of a permit following this law; (2) issuance of a permit for hazardous waste management; (3) issuance of a permit for the management of non-hazardous waste; (4) issuance of a permit for cross-border movement of waste; (5) issuing a certificate for entry into the

674. Waste generator or owner and/or other holder shall bear costs for collection, transport, storage, treatment and disposal of waste, in compliance with this Law (Art. 78, para. 1). Legal entity or entrepreneur performing the activity of collection, transport, storage, treatment, reuse and disposal of waste shall charge for such services according to the price determined in compliance with law (Art. 79, para. 1).
675. Costs for removal of waste disposed of outside the landfill, origins of which cannot be established, i.e., its connection to the generator or to the person who disposed it cannot be established, shall be borne by LSG unit.
676. The price for the service of waste management, with pre-treatment included shall be determined depending upon the type, quantity, waste characteristics and frequency of services provided, as well as on length and conditions for transport of waste and other circumstances that affect price for organization of waste management (Art. 79, para. 2).
677. Price of waste landfilling service shall cover all costs of establishment and operation of the landfill, including financial guarantees or other equivalent instruments and estimated costs for closure and after-care for a period of at least thirty years, for all kinds of waste at the site (para. 3).
678. The government prescribes the type, amount, elements, conditions, and method of awarding incentives to operators who reuse and recycle waste to award incentives (para. 5).

register; (6) issuance of a certificate of exemption from the obligation to obtain a permit; (7) issuance of confirmation of application for cross-border movement of waste; (8) issuance of permit amendments. (Article 82, paragraph 1).

521. Funds for the financing of waste management in the RS are provided from: (1) the budget of the RS; (2) the budget of the AP and LSG; (3) EU funds and other international funds; (4) donations, gifts, contributions, assistance and similar sources for waste management; (5) loans from international financial institutions; and (6) other sources in accordance with the Law. The funds referred to in paragraph 1 of this Article may be used only for the purpose in the manner prescribed by this Law and in the way prescribed by the Law governing environmental protection (Article 80, paragraphs 1 and 2).[679]

IV. The Law on Packaging and Packaging Waste

522. The legal Act that regulates packaging and packaging waste in the RS is the Law on Packaging and Packaging Waste (OJ RS, Nos 36/2009 and 95/18 – other law). It has the following nine parts: Part I – General Provisions (Articles 1–6), Part II – Environmental conditions that packing must fulfil to be placed on the market (Articles 7–15), Part III – Management of packaging and packaging waste (Articles 16–37), Part IV – Reporting on packaging and packaging waste (Articles 38–42), Part V – Economic instruments (Articles 43–45), Part VI – Supervision (Articles 46–49), Part VII – Jurisdiction on complaint resolution (Article 50), Part VIII – Penal provisions (Articles 51–53) and Part IX – Transitional and final provisions (Articles 54–57).

523. This Law regulates the requirements for environmental protection that packaging[680] has to meet to be placed on the market, management of packaging and packaging waste,[681] reporting on packaging and packaging waste, economic instruments, as well as other issues important for the management of packaging and packaging waste (Article 1, paragraph 1).

---

679. The implementation of the Waste Management Program and plans, as well as the construction of facilities for treatment, i.e., storage, reuse, and disposal of waste from the jurisdiction of the Republic of Serbia, autonomous provinces, and local self-government units, is financed following the law (para. 3).

680. *Packaging* is a product made from materials with different properties, which is used for placing, storing, handling, delivery, presenting of the goods and the protection of its content. It includes items used as a supporting means for packaging, wrapping, binding, non-permeable closure, and preparing for shipment and labelling of goods. Packaging can be: *primary packaging* as the smallest packaging unit in which the product is sold to the final customer; *secondary packaging* as a packaging unit which includes multiple products in primary packaging intended that on point of sale enable grouping of certain number of units for sale, whether it is sold to the end user or it is used for supply at their tail stores. This package can be removed from the product without affecting its characteristics; *tertiary (transport) packaging* designed for safe transport and handling of products in the primary or secondary packaging. This package does not include containers for road, rail, water or air transport (Art. 5, point 1).

681. *Packaging waste* is any container or packaging material which cannot be used for its original purpose, except for residues resulting in the production process (Art. 5, point 5). *Packaging waste*

524. Provisions of this Law shall apply[682] to imported packaging, packaging that is produced or placed on the market, and all packaging waste resulting from business activities on territory of the RS,[683] regardless of its origin, use and used packaging material (Article 1, paragraph 2).

525. The aim of this Law is, in accordance with the principle of sustainable development, to provide (Article 3, paragraph 1): (1) conservation of natural resources; (2) protection of environmental and human health; (3) development of modern technologies for packaging production; (4) establishment of optimal system for management of packaging and packaging waste management in accordance with principle of shared responsibility; (5) functioning of the market in the RS; and (6) preventing of trade barriers creation, avoidance of disturbance and restrictions in the competition.

526. The basic principles for management of packaging and packaging waste are (Article 4, paragraph 1): (1) sharing responsibility of all business entities in accordance with 'polluter pays' principle during the product life cycle; (2) preventing or reducing the generation of packaging and packaging waste, as well as their harmfulness to the environment; (3) reuse[684] of packaging, recycling[685] and other forms of reutilization and reduce the final disposal of packaging waste; and (4) voluntary agreement on the management of packaging waste.

A. Packaging and Environment Protection

527. The packaging is compliant with the essential requirements for placing on the market if it complies with all specific requirements relating to (Article 8, paragraph 1): (1) packaging production,[686] (2) composition of packaging,[687] (3) reuse of

---

management is planning and organizing activities related to the collection, transport, storage, treatment and disposal of packaging waste, supervision of these activities and taking care of facilities for waste management after closure (Art. 5, point 8).

682. The provisions of this Law shall not apply to containers and big facilities for packaging – IBC used for road, rail, water or air international transport (Art. 2, para. 1).

683. *Subjects for management of packaging and packaging waste* are (Art. 5, point 21): producer; importer, packer/filler; supplier; collector, the end user, the end supplier, carrier, operator of packaging waste management system (hereinafter 'operator').

684. *Reuse* means any operation by which the packaging, planned and designed in the way to perform a minimum number of charging and discharging during usage (repeated use), and recharge or use for the same purpose for which it is planned, with or without supporting means presented in the market which enables recharging of packaging. Reused packaging becomes waste if it is not reused after a long time (Art. 5, point 10).

685. *Recycling of packaging waste* is the reprocessing of packaging waste in the production process for the original purpose or for other purposes, including organic recycling, but excluding utilization for energy purposes (Art. 5, point 17).

686. The requirements are applied on the entire packaging system (Art. 8, para. 2).

687. The requirements are applied on the component of packaging (Art. 8, para. 3).

packaging,[688] (4) packaging that is reusable by recycling[689] of materials, (5) packaging that is reusable by composting and biodegradation, and (6) packaging that is reusable in the form of energy.[690]

528. The producer and importer of packaging is required when placing packaging on the market or during its use to issue or provide a declaration on compliance of packaging with the requirements for placing on market in accordance with the Law[691] (Article 8, paragraph 5).

529. Packaging should be produced so that the total level of concentrations of lead, cadmium, mercury and hexavalentchromium in packaging or its components does not exceed the prescribed limit values[692] (Article 10, paragraph 1). Packaging should be manufactured so that concentrations of hazardous substances in emissions, ash and leachate are minimized (Article 10, paragraph 3).[693]

530. Physical and other characteristics of the packaging must ensure adequate quality of packaging and allow its reuse for the same purpose so that: (1) package design enables recharging or reloading, as well as certain number of charging or discharging cycles; (2) packaging may be enabled for reuse, taking into account the health and safety requirements; and (3) there is an available system on the market to achieve reuse (the collection of returnable packaging,[694] refilling or shipping)[695] (Article 11, paragraph 1).

---

688. Requirements for points 3–6 of this Article shall apply on the functional unit of packaging (Art. 8, para. 4).
689. The Minister in charge of environmental protection (hereinafter 'Minister') provides criteria for determining what can be the packaging, with examples for the application of criteria and determine a list of Serbian standards related to the basic requirements (hereinafter 'Serbian standards') (Art. 7, para. 2).
690. *Packaging waste utilization for energy purposes* is the use of packaging waste in direct incineration with or without the presence of other types of waste, with the primary goal of utilization of heat (Art. 5, point 18).
691. The packaging is compliant with certain specific request if it is made in accordance with the Serbian standard from the list of standards specified in Art. 7, para. 2 of this Law which applies to that specific request (Art. 8, para. 6). If the packaging is not produced in accordance with the Serbian standard, compliance of packaging with certain specific requirements may be proved with other appropriate means (technical specifications, technical documentation, with reports on examination, etc.) (Art. 8, para. 7).
692. Determination of concentration of heavy metals, depending upon the packaging material or its components, is done according to the methodology prescribed by the Serbian standard (Art. 10, para. 2). The Minister prescribes limit of total level concentration of lead, cadmium, mercury and hexavalentchromium in packaging or in its components, with the exception of application and deadline for limit values application (Art. 10, para. 6).
693. Identification of the presence of hazardous materials in the package or in its components and the possibility of their presence in emissions, ash and leachate from landfills is done in accordance with the Serbian standard (Art. 10, para. 4). If hazardous materials are identified in the package or in its components that can be released into the environment, packaging has to meet requirement for their minimization in the way determined by Serbian standards (Art. 10, para. 5).
694. *Returnable packaging* is packaging that, after returning from the consumer, is reusable for the same purpose (Art. 5, point 3).

531. Packaging that cannot be reused, or that cannot be reused through recycling,[696] biodegradation or controlled incineration, becomes packaging waste intended for disposal[697] in accordance with the Law (Article 11, paragraph 3).

532. Packaging that is reusable by composting[698] must be produced in the way that when it becomes packaging waste, that waste processed for composting purposes has such a natural biodegradable performance that it does not prevent the separate process of collecting, composting or activity that has begun with this process (Article 13, paragraph 1).

533. Packaging reusable for biodegradation must be manufactured so that when it becomes packaging waste, the waste should have such natural properties that can be subjected to physical, chemical, thermal or biological decomposition and that most of the finished compost is at the end decomposed into carbon dioxide, biomass and water (Article 13, paragraph 2). Packaging should be designed and manufactured in the way to meet thermodynamic requirements for allowed controlled burning of packaging waste with energy utilization (Article 14, paragraph 1).

B. Management of Packaging and Packaging Waste

534. National objectives for management of packaging and packaging waste are established by the Plan for reduction of packaging waste[699] (hereinafter 'Plan') (Article 16, paragraph 1). The Plan contains national objectives related to the collection of packaging and packaging waste, reuse[700] and recycling of packaging waste (Article 16, paragraph 1).

535. The producer, importer, packer/filler and supplier are obliged to take over the secondary or tertiary packaging waste, free of charge at the request of the end

---

695. Identifying the most appropriate reuse system for a particular type of packaging, taking into account the specific circumstances of its intended use is done according to the Serbian standard (Art. 11, para. 2).
696. The main criteria for packaging suitable for recycling, identified by Serbian standards, relate to: (1) design control, packaging composition and preparation process; (2) the existence of available recycling technologies; and (3) release to the environment as a result of the recycling process (Art. 12, para. 2).
697. *Disposal of packaging waste* is any process or method of handling the packaging waste when there are no possibilities for regeneration, recycling, processing, direct reuse or use as alternative energy sources, in accordance with the regulations governing waste management (Art. 5, point 20).
698. Packaging consisting of different components is considered suitable for composting or biodegradation if the components suitable for composting can be easily separated from components that are not suitable for composting or if all packaging materials are suitable for composting (Art. 13, para. 3).
699. The Government adopts plan on the proposal of Ministry responsible for environmental protection (hereinafter 'the Ministry') for a period of five years (Art. 16, para. 4).
700. *Reuse* is any procedure or method of utilization in terms of regulations governing the management of waste (Art. 5, point 16).

user[701] (Article 18, paragraph 1). It is also required to provide a space for taking over, collecting, sorting and temporary storage of packaging waste, that is, in accordance with Article 18 of this Law, taken or created during their activities, if the annual quantity of packaging waste exceeds the prescribed quantity[702] (Article 19, paragraph 1).

536. The end user is required to collect, store, put off or forward the communal packaging waste,[703] in accordance with the Law governing waste management and the Law governing communal activities (Article 20, paragraph 1). The end user must ensure that packaging and packaging waste which is not communal waste,[704] that is, forwarded or returned, is not contaminated with hazardous or other substances that are not contained in packed goods, which make the reuse or recycling impossible, or which make it feasible only at a disproportionately higher cost (Article 21, paragraph 2).

537. Producer, importer, packer/filler and supplier that provides its own packaging waste management is required to (Article 26, paragraph 1): (1) ensure that packaging waste taken or collected in any calendar year to be reused, recycled or disposed to the end of that calendar year, in order to achieve the national objectives; (2) bear the cost of reutilization, recycling or disposal of packaging waste which, despite the established collection system, appears in the collection system implemented by the operator; and (3) inform end users, by notice on the packaging placed on the market, about the possibility to leave packaging waste at place of purchase, or to return it later for free to the end supplier at designated place.

538. The operator cannot manage packaging waste without a permit from the Ministry (Article 31, paragraph 1). The permit is issued to the operator who is (Article 31, paragraph 2): (1) registered for performing activities of collecting, taking away, reuse, recycling or disposal in accordance with the Law governing the classification of activities; (2) alone or whose subcontractor has equipment, facilities and units that provide management of packaging waste in accordance with the Law; and (3) alone or whose subcontractor provides conditions for reuse, recycling or disposal of packaging waste in accordance with the Law.

---

701. Manufacturer, importer, packer/filler and the supplier is obliged, at the request of the end user, to take free of charge packaging waste that is not communal waste, and that comes from the primary packaging, if a specific way of taking over and collecting of such packaging is not prescribed (Art. 18, para. 4).

702. Minister prescribes the annual amount of packaging waste by the type of waste for which space for downloading, collecting, sorting and temporary storage is provided (Art. 19, para. 3).

703. *Communal packaging waste* is waste from primary and secondary packaging generated as waste in households (household waste) or in industry, craft activities, services or other activities (commercial waste), which is similar to waste from households in terms of its nature or composition and that is collected from a certain territorial unit, in accordance with the Law (Art. 5, point 6).

704. *Packaging waste which is not communal waste* is waste from primary, secondary or tertiary packaging generated as waste during production, retail, service and other activities that has not been collected through the collection system organized by a public utility company or other legal entity or entrepreneur (hereinafter 'utility') (Art. 5, point 7).

539. The operator is obliged to organize one or more centres for collection, sorting and temporary storage of collected packaging waste (Article 35, paragraph 1). The operator is obliged to arrange spaces for collection of packaging waste that is not communal waste, where the end user will bring the waste, if the taking over is not provided directly from the end user or from the end suppliers (Article 35, paragraph 2).

540. Reuse, recycling and disposal of packaging waste can be carried out in plants having permit for prescribed treatment and/or disposal, in accordance with the conditions stipulated by the Law governing waste management and by other regulations (Article 37, paragraph 1).

C. Economic Instruments

541. The supplier who packages or puts on the market a packaged product in the territory of the RS shall pay a fee (Article 43, paragraph 1).[705] Funds generated from the fee under paragraph 1 of this Article contribute to the budget of the RS and are used specifically for waste management through the Fund for the Environment, in accordance with the Law (Article 43, paragraph 3).[706]

542. The Government[707] may establish a deposit system for a disposable package when it is necessary to achieve the national objectives (Article 44, paragraph 1). The final supplier who places on the market the product packed in disposable packaging charges from the end user's deposit per unit of sales of packaging to establish a return system for used disposable packaging (Article 44, paragraph 2).

543. The producer or importer of a product packaged in returnable packaging shall establish a refund system (Article 44, paragraph 3). The final supplier[708] who puts on the market a product packaged in returnable packaging is required to collect a bail for this type of packaging from the end user (Article 44, paragraph 4). The

705. The fee referred to in para. 1 of this Article shall be determined depending upon the type, quantity, composition and purpose of packaging, on material from which the packaging is made, as well as in relation to national objectives (Art. 43, para. 2). The Government prescribes criteria for the calculation of fees and exemption from payment of fees, taxpayers, the amount of fee, as well as the method for calculation and payments of fee (Art. 43, para. 4).

706. However, provision of the Art. 43 of the Law on Packaging and Packaging Waste has ceased to be valid – on the day of the beginning of the application of *the Law on Fees for the Use of Public Goods* (OJ RS, No. 95/2018), i.e.,1 Jan. 2019 (*see* Art. 279, para. 1, point 13 of the Law – 95/2018).

707. The Government provides types of disposable packaging for which the deposit system is established, the mode of operation of the system and deposit amount and method of its collection (Art. 44, para. 7).

708. The end supplier is obliged to accept from the end user disposable packaging and returnable packaging (Art. 44, para. 5). After return of packaging, the end supplier is obliged to return the charged deposit, i.e., the bail to the end user (Art. 44, para. 6).

producer or importer[709] of certain chemicals is required to determine the amount of bail that consumer pays for a single packaging used for storing chemicals (Article 45, paragraph 1).

D. Reporting and Monitoring

544. The operator is obliged to inform the public and end users about the purpose, objectives, manner and place for packaging collection, as well as about possibilities for reuse and recycling of packaging waste (Article 38, paragraph 1).[710]

545. The Ministry establishes and maintains a Register of permits issued[711] in accordance with this Law (Article 42, paragraph 1). Agency draws up and publishes an annual report on the quantity of produced, imported and exported packaging and management of waste packaging in the RS and submits it to the Ministry (Article 42, paragraph 3).

546. The Ministry supervises the work of the Agency, an AP, local government units, as well as authorized legal entitities in performing delegated tasks, in accordance with the Law on Waste Management and this Law (Article 46, paragraph 1). The inspection supervision on implementation of provisions of this Law and regulations adopted for its implementation shall be performed by the Ministry, unless otherwise prescribed by the Law on Waste Management and by this Law (Article 47, paragraph 1).

547. In accordance with Article 101 of the Law on Waste Management, the Recycling Agency ceases its operation on the thirtieth day from the enactment of this Law.

V. Transboundary Movement of Waste

548. Transboundary movement of waste is regulated by the Basel Convention on the Control of Transboundary Movements of Hazardous Wastes and their Disposal (1989). The treaty was ratified by FR Yugoslavia in 1998 (OJ FRY – IT, No. 24/98).

549. The legal framework for controlling the transboundary movement of waste in RS consists of several laws and by-laws in this area.[712] EPL prescribes general

709. The Minister prescribes (Art. 45, para. 5): (1) for which chemical producer or importer is obliged to establish a bail for a single package used for storing of that chemical and (2) the amount of bail for certain types of packaging depending upon the type of packaging or chemical packed in.

710. The operator shall inform public of the city, city of Belgrade, i.e., municipality on the territory of which point of collection is located, through public media or internet, i.e., in usual local manner (Art. 38, para. 2).

711. The Minister prescribes the content and method for keeping records of issued permits, as well as the form of the report from Arts 39 and 40 of this Law (Art. 42, para. 4).

712. For further information, *see* Petković, 2021.

provisions on the import, export and transit of waste and its control. Import of hazardous waste to Serbia is prohibited by Article 57 of the EPL.[713]

550. Transboundary movement of waste is regulated by the Law on Waste Management (Chapter IX). This Law regulates, specifically: terms and mode of transboundary waste movement (Article 71), import, export and transit of waste (Articles 72 and 72a), prohibition of transboundary waste movement (Article 73),[714] as well as the basis for implementing legislation that defines in more detail the mode and procedure for transboundary waste shipments.[715]

551. Non-hazardous waste can be imported for the purpose of treatment, i.e., reuse, if there is a facility for the treatment of such waste (Article 71, paragraph 4). The import of waste for disposal and energy recovery purposes is prohibited (paragraph 5). The import of hazardous waste is prohibited (Article 71, paragraph 6). Exceptionally, certain types of hazardous waste that are required as secondary raw materials for the processing industry in the RS can be imported based on a permit issued by the Ministry (Article 71, paragraph 7). The import of hazardous waste can be permitted, provided that there is a facility for the treatment thereof, licensed to operate in accordance with the law (Article 71, paragraph 8).[716]

552. For the transbounary movement of waste, along with the request for the issuance of a permit, i.e., confirmation of the application, the documentation prescribed in Article 72, paragraph 3, is submitted to the ministry.[717] The obligations of exporters and importers of waste are regulated by the provisions of Article 72. The content of the permit, as well as the possibility of change, are regulated by Article 72a.

713. Licence for import, export or transit of waste shall be issued by the Ministry in accordance with law and other regulations. When applying for permit for import, export and transit the applicant shall submit the documentation whose contents is prescribed by the Ministry. The Minister shall prescribe the conditions that must be fulfilled by expert organizations for waste testing. The register of permits for cross-border movement of waste is being prepared. *See* http://www.sepa.gov.rs/index.php?menu=20174&id=20055&akcija=ShowExternal (5.1.2024).

714. Transboundary movement of waste is prohibited if: (1) all participating countries are not notified; (2) all participating countries have not issued a permit; (3) the issued licence is a forgery or was obtained by fraud; (4) is carried out contrary to the issued permit; (5) deliberate disposal of waste is carried out contrary to the provisions of this law and the general principles of international legislation on environmental protection (Art. 73, para. 1).

715. The government prescribes the following in more detail: (1) list of hazardous waste whose import is prohibited; (2) list of hazardous waste that can be imported as secondary raw material; (3) list of hazardous waste whose export and transit is permitted; (4) list of non-hazardous waste whose import, export and transit is allowed; (5) a list of non-hazardous waste for which no permit is issued, with documentation accompanying cross-border movement; (6) content, appearance and instructions for filling out the notification on cross-border movement of waste; (7) content, appearance and instructions for filling out the document on the transboundary movement of waste (Art. 72, para. 13).

716. Waste for which there are no environmentally sound and efficient treatment facilities and technical possibilities in the RS is exported (Art. 71, para. 3).

717. The Ministry decides on the request for approval of import, export, and transit of waste based on the facts contained in the documentation submitted with the request (para. 5).

553. With the adoption of the Regulation on lists of waste for cross-border movement, content and appearance of documents accompanying cross-border movement of waste with instructions for filling them in (OJ RS, No. 34/22),[718] the following regulations ceased to be valid:

– Regulation on lists of waste for cross-border movement, content and appearance of documents accompanying cross-border movement of waste with instructions for their completion (OJ RS, Nos 60/09 and 36/21); Regulation on determining certain types of hazardous waste that can be imported as secondary raw materials (OJ RS, No. 60/09); and Regulation on the List of non-hazardous waste for which no permit is issued, with documentation accompanying cross-border movement (OJ RS, Nos 102/10 and 36/21).

VI. Other Relevant Waste Management Legislation

554. Besides the mentioned, the following legal Acts, *inter alia*, are also relevant when waste is concerned:

– Regulation on technical and technological conditions for the design, construction, equipment, and operation of plants and types of waste for the thermal treatment of waste, limit values of emissions, and their monitoring (OJ RS, No. 103/23).
– Regulation on the manner and procedure of sludge management from municipal wastewater treatment plants (OJ RS, No. 103/23).
– Regulation on the type of financial guarantees and equivalent insurance that ensures the performance of waste management activities (OJ RS, No. 103/23).
– Regulation on the manner and procedure of construction and demolition waste management (OJ RS, Nos 93/23, 94/23 – correction).
– Rulebook on the content and appearance of the permit for waste management (OJ RS, No. 118/23).
– Rulebook on the content of the request for the issuance of a certificate of exemption from the obligation to obtain a permit and the content of the certificate of exemption from the obligation to obtain a permit (OJ RS, No. 116/23).
– Rulebook on the methodology for collecting data on the composition and quantities of municipal waste on the territory of the local self-government unit (OJ RS, No. 14/20).
– Decision on joint implementation of waste management (OJ RS, No. 45/18).
– Regulation on disposal of waste in landfills (OJ RS, No. 92/10).

718. This regulation specifies the list of hazardous waste whose importation is prohibited; list of hazardous waste that can be imported as a secondary raw material; list of hazardous waste whose export and transit is permitted; list of non-hazardous waste whose import, export, and transit is allowed; list of non-hazardous waste for which a permit is not issued with documentation accompanying cross-border movement; content, appearance and instructions for filling out the Notice on the transboundary movement of waste; content, appearance and instructions for filling out the Document on the transboundary movement of waste (Art. 1).

- Rulebook on the list of plants for incineration and co-incineration whose nominal capacity does not exceed two tons per hour (OJ RS, No. 7/2019).
- Rulebook on types of waste that can be treated in mobile plants and types of mobile plants for which a waste treatment permit is issued (OJ RS, Nos 93/2019, 95-/22).
- Rulebook on technical requirements and other special criteria for certain types of waste that cease to be waste (OJ RS, No. 78/19).
- Rulebook on the content of the request for entry in the Register of by-products and the Register of waste that has ceased to be waste (OJ RS, Nos 76/19, 95/22).
- Rulebook on the list of waste prevention measures (OJ RS, No. 7/2019).
- Rulebook on the application form for the issuance of a permit for treatment, i.e., storage, reuse and disposal of waste (OJ RS, No. 38/2018).
- Rulebook on the manner of keeping and appearance of records of landfills and dumps in the area of the local self-government unit (OJ RS, No. 18/18).
- Rulebook on the list of electrical and electronic products, measures of prohibition and restrictions on the use of electrical and electronic equipment containing hazardous substances (OJ RS, No. 99/10).
- Rulebook on the procedure for end-of-life vehicle management (OJ RS, No. 98/10).
- Rulebook on conditions and manner of collection, transport, storage and treatment of waste that is used as a secondary raw material or for energy production (OJ RS, No. 98/10).
- Rulebook on the procedure for the management of waste fluorescent tubes containing mercury (OJ RS, No. 97/10).
- Rulebook on the contents, manner and appearance of the Register of issued permits for waste management (OJ RS, No. 95/10).
- Rulebook on the forms of daily records and annual reports on waste with instructions to complete it (OJ RS, Nos 7/20, 79/21).
- Rulebook on the manner of storage, packaging and labelling of hazardous waste (OJ RS, Nos 92/10, 77/21).
- Rulebook on the procedure for management of waste batteries and accumulators (OJ RS, No. 86/10).
- Rulebook on medical waste management (OJ RS, No. 48/19).
- Rulebook on pharmaceutical waste management (OJ RS, No. 49/19).
- Rulebook on the manner and procedure of waste tire management (OJ RS, Nos 104/9 and 81/10).
- Rulebook on disposal of waste containing asbestos (OJ RS, No. 75/10).
- Rulebook on conditions, methods and procedure of waste oil management (OJ RS, No. 72/10).
- Rulebook on the content of the certificate of exemption from the obligation of obtaining a permit to store inert and non-hazardous waste (OJ RS, No. 73/10).
- Rulebook on categories, testing and classification of waste (OJ RS, Nos 56/10, 93/19, 39/21).
- Rulebook on the list of POPs substances, manner and procedure for the management of POPs waste and limit values of concentrations of POPs substances related to the disposal of waste containing or contaminated with POPs substances (OJ RS, Nos 65/11 and 17/17).

555. In the field of packaging and packaging waste management, several by-laws have been adopted. The most significant are the following:

- Regulation on determining the Packaging Waste Reduction Plan for the period from 2020 to 2024 (OJ RS, Nos 81/20, 93/23).
- Rulebook on chemicals for which the producers or importers are obligated to establish a deposit for an individual packaging containing chemicals (OJ RS, No. 99/10).
- Rulebook on form of the report on packaging management and packaging waste (OJ RS, Nos 21/10, 10/13 and 44/18 – other law).
- Rulebook on the contents and methods for keeping the Register of licences issued for packaging waste management (OJ RS, No. 76/09).
- Rulebook on the criteria for determining whether something is package, with examples for the application of criteria and the list of Serbian standards regarding basic conditions which a package must fulfil to be placed on the market (OJ RS, No. 70/09).
- Rulebook on the annual quantity of packaging waste according to types which must be provided space for the takeover, collection, classification and temporary storage (OJ RS, No. 70/09).
- Rulebook on the manner of numbering, abbreviations and symbols on which the system of identification and marking of packaging materials is based (OJ RS, No. 70/09).
- Rulebook on the type and annual quantity of packaging used for the packaged product placed on the market, for which the producer, importer, packer/filler and the supplier are not obliged to ensure packaging waste management (OJ RS, No. 70/09).
- Rulebook on the types of durable packaging (OJ RS, No. 70/09).
- Rulebook on the limit value of the total level of concentration of lead, cadmium, mercury and 6-valent chromium in the package or its components, exemptions from application and the deadline for limit value application (OJ RS, No. 70/09).
- Rulebook on the form of Document on the movement of waste with the filling instructions (OJ RS, No. 114/13).
- Rulebook on the form of the Document on the movement of hazardous waste, the form of prior notification, the manner of its delivery and instructions for their completion (OJ RS, No. 17/17).

VII. Harmonization with EU Legislation

556. 'Regarding waste management, Serbia has a good level of alignment with the EU *acquis*, but implementation should be further strengthened.'[719] In April 2023, Serbia amended the Law on waste management. The programme for the development of the circular economy was adopted in December 2022. Serbia's inspection capacity in the waste sector remains insufficient.[720]

---

719. EC 2023, 136.
720. *Ibid.*

Chapter 5. Soil Pollution

§1. The State of Soil Pollution

557. The greatest pressures on soil in the RS are erosion, the occurrence of landslides, reduction of organic matter, pollution, and change in land use. Climate change can worsen land degradation and cause further desertification.[721] Based on the first data published by the EPA, 'in 2007, 375 sites were identified in the territory of the RS, where soil pollution was confirmed by laboratory analyses of soil and groundwater near localized pollution sources, and where pollution had been present for a longer period'.[722]

According to data from the Strategy of Agriculture and Rural Development of the RS (2014–2024), the main threats to soil quality, presented by intensity, are soil compaction, organic matter decline, soil acidification, soil pollution, and erosion. Approximately 88% of the total land area in the RS is subject to water erosion, while wind erosion affects approximately 25% of the territory of the RS. Much of the arable land is acidic (more than a quarter of the total area) as a result of uncontrolled use of chemicals, while parts of the AP Vojvodina are saline (14%).[723]

Another cause of soil degradation is chemicals, especially pesticides, as well as the use of fertilizers containing some polluting substances (cadmium, nitrogen, etc.).[724] Finally, soil degradation was caused, on some sites, by armed conflicts and especially by the 1999 NATO bombing.[725]

558. With the adoption of the Law on Land Protection (December 2015), a legal basis was obtained for the establishment of systematic monitoring of land at the state and local levels. 'This will enable more adequate monitoring of the condition and pressures on the land, reporting at the national and international level, but also the planning of rehabilitation and protection measures.'[726]

721. EPA. 2020, 4. 'Over the last several decades Serbia has faced increased frequency of drought and drought severity. This trend is especially noticeable after 2000.' Djurdjević. 2020, 4.
722. EPA. 2019c, 32. 'In the territory of the RS 709 potential contaminated and contaminated sites were identified in 2017.' *Ibid.*
723. GOV RS. 2014b, Ch. 2.2. State of resources and environment (2.2.1. Land a) Extent, structure, and quality of land resources). For erosion data *see also* EPA data at: http://indicator.sepa.gov.rs/pretrazivanje-indikatora/indikatorilat/allfindp/610114eb2fe04dec8e4d7793c191045d (23.2.2024). According to the Stat. Office in 2022, 4,292 km2 were affected by erosion. STAT. YEARB. SERB. 2023, 273. (Eroded land is land covered, threatened, worn, and damaged by erosion due to the destructive effect of atmospheric water, wind, or glaciers where the fertile layer of land has been partly or completely removed, so its use for crop production is considerably reduced or completely disabled. *Ibid.*, 264).
724. Detected concentrations of pesticides in sediment samples of several river basins, for the period 2012–2016 years indicates their continuous use. EPA. 2019b, 121.
725. According to NATO data, 112 locations in Kosovo and Metohija Province were contaminated with DU. The NATO claims that 31,000 30 mm projectiles were used (equivalent to 10 tons of DU), but according to Serbian military data at least 50,000 projectiles were fired, equivalent to 15 tons of DU. Outside Kosovo, 3,000–5,000 projectiles were fired too, mostly in southern Serbia, EPA. 2007, 117.
726. EPA. 2020, 4.

559. Several ministries and other bodies share competence concerning soil protection – the MEP, including EPA, the MAFWM, the MME, the MC, TI, relevant institutions in AP, LSG, etc. The Statistical Office of the RS also plays an important role. It collects statistical data on the land area, by types of use, areas used and types of crops and areas for other cropped land, fallow land, etc.

§2. LEGISLATION

560. Article 88 of the Constitution of Serbia prescribes that utilization and management of agricultural land, forestland and municipal building land on private assets shall be permitted.[727] Terms of utilization and management could be prescribed by Law, in order to eliminate the danger to environment or prevent violation of rights and legally based interests of other persons. The municipality shall, through its bodies and in accordance with the Law, *inter alia*, regulate protection, improvement and use of agricultural land (Article 190).

561. It is prescribed, by Article 22 of EPL (OJ RS, Nos 135/04, 36/09 and 36/09 – other law, 72/09 – other law, 43/11 CC, 14/16, 76/18 and 95/18 – other law), that:

> Protection of land area (land) and its sustainable use shall be achieved through the measures of systematic monitoring of land quality, monitoring of indicators for the assessment of risk of land degradation, as well as through the implementation of remediation programs for removing consequences of land contamination and degradation, regardless if they occur naturally or are caused by human activities. Upon change of the holder of the right to utilize land, the land user whose right to utilization ends, and whose activity has affected or could have affected or impeded natural functions of land, shall be obliged to prepare a report on the state of land.[728] Program of systematic monitoring of land quality, indicators for assessment of risk of land degradation and methodology for preparation of remediation programs referred to in paragraph 1 of this Article shall be prescribed by the Government.
>
> Article 34, paragraph 2 of the same Law prescribes that the conditions for measures, for environmental protection in spatial and urban plans, 'shall be issued by the Ministry, AP body or self-governance units at request of the

727. In accordance with Art. 86 private, cooperative and public ownership are guaranteed. Public property is a State-owned property of the Republic of Serbia, the property owned by the AP, and property of the units of local government. All forms of ownership have equal legal protection, while public property is turned into private or State-owned property under the conditions, in a manner and within time limits prescribed by the Law. Subject of privatization may be the land entered in a relevant real estate rights registry as social, mixed or property of the subject to be privatized. The subject of privatization may not be natural resources, goods in general use, goods of general interest, as well as cultural assets under public ownership entered in the register of cultural heritage, which shall be conducted in accordance with the law governing cultural property (Art. 5. paras 2 and 3, Law on Privatisation, OJ RS, Nos 83/14, 46/15, 112/15 and 20/16). However, only domestic legal or natural person may be the buyer of agricultural land (Art. 121, para. 1).
728. The Minister shall prescribe the content and methodology for preparation of report on the state of land (Art. 22, para. 4).

authority in charge of plan preparation and its passing in, and on the basis of conditions and measures of competent authorities'.

I. The Law on Soil Protection

562. The basic legal Act regulating Soil protection in the RS is the Law on Soil Protection (OJ RS, No. 112/15). It has the following nine parts: Part I – General Provisions (Articles 1–7), Part II – Preventive measures of soil protection (Articles 8–11), Part III – Soil Protection (Articles 12–27), Part IV – Programme of systematic monitoring of soil state and quality (Articles 28–34), Part V – Access to the information (Articles 35), Part VI – Financing of soil protection (Articles 36 and 37), Part VII – Supervision (Articles 38–42), Part VIII – Penalties (Articles 43–47), and Part IX – Transitional and final provisions (Articles 48–54).

According to Article 1, The Law on Soil Protection regulates the protection of soil, systematic monitoring of the soil quality, measures of remediation, reclamation, inspection and other issues of importance for the protection and preservation of soil as a natural resource of national importance.[729]

563. The purpose of this Law is to preserve areas and functions of the soil as a natural resource and to prevent or eliminate harmful changes in the soil that can occur as a result of: (1) erosion;[730] (2) reducing the content of organic matters in the soil; (3) inappropriate agricultural and forest production (inadequate and uncontrolled agro-technical measures and meliorative, deforestation, etc.); (4) uncontrolled change of use, management and use of soil; (5) unplanned urbanization, construction and development of infrastructure; (6) acidic (acidification), salinity (salinization) and alkalization; (7) the soil compaction, landslides and avalanches; (8) fires and chemical accidents; (9) contamination[731] (resulting from waste management, the discharge of waste water, emissions from point and diffuse sources, chemical contamination, etc.); (10) exploitation of mineral and organic materials; (11) exploitation of gravel, sand and rock; and (12) illegal archaeological excavations and research, etc. (Article 3, paragraph 1).

564. The principles of soil protection: The following principles of soil protection are in use in the RS: Preserving of natural values of soil principle, Integrity in soil protection principle, Polluter pays principle, User pays principle, Principle of subsidiary responsibility, Information of public and public participation and Protecting the right to preserve the natural values of the soil (Article 5).

---

729. The provisions of this Law shall apply to all types of soil in the Republic of Serbia as a natural resource, regardless of the form of ownership, its purpose and use (Art. 2).

730. *Erosion* is the process of destruction and removal of the soil caused by occurrence of natural and anthropogenic factors (Art. 4, para. 1, point 7).

731. *Soil pollution* is a process of disposal and the introduction of hazardous and harmful substances on the surface of the soil and in the soil caused by human activities or natural processes (Art. 4, para. 1, point 8).

565. Subjects of the soil protection: Soil protection within their responsibilities and duties is provided by the Republic, AP, LSG, legal entities, entrepreneurs and owners and users of soil that in carrying out activities threaten, degrade or pollute the soil (Article 6, paragraph 1).

566. Soil protection: Soil protection is provided for under this Law that makes the implementation of strategy, planning and documentation for soil protection. Soil protection is achieved by implementation of measures and activities in the process of planning, management, use, monitoring and protection from pollution and soil degradation in order to preserve its natural characteristics and functions (Article 12, paragraphs 1–2).[732]

567. Financing of the soil protection and supervision: Financing of protection and improvement of soil quality is ensured from: (1) the budget of the Republic, the APs and LSG units budget; (2) revenues from charges in accordance with Law; (3) proceeds in accordance with international cooperation programmes and projects; (4) the donation of domestic and foreign legal and natural persons; and (5) other sources in accordance to the Law (Article 36).[733]

II. Law on Planning and Building

568. Land in Serbia is divided into three categories: construction land, agricultural land and forestland.

Construction land is the land on which structures have been built, as well as the land that serves for regular use of these structures, or the land designated by the urban plan for construction and regular use of structures. Construction land is divided into urban construction land and construction land outside the perimeter of urban construction land (Article 84 of the Law on Planning and Building (OJ RS, Nos 72/09, 81/09 – corr., 64/10 CC, 24/11, 121/12, 42/13 – CC, 50/13 CC, 98/13 CC, 132/14, 145/14, 83/18, 31/19, 37/19 – other law, 9/20, 52/21, and 62/23).

III. Law on Agricultural Land

569. The key legal instrument for the protection of agricultural land is the Law on Agricultural Land (OJ RS, Nos 62/06, 65/08 – other law, 41/09, 112/2015, 80/17, 95/18 – other law). The Law has the following chapters: Basic Provisions (Articles 1–4); Planning of Protection, Organization and Utilization of Agricultural Land (Articles 5–14); Protection of Agricultural Land (Articles 15–29); Organization of the Agricultural Land (Articles 30–58); Utilization of Agricultural Land (Articles

---

732. In order to protect soil on the territory of the Republic, the following documents for soil protection are adopted: (1) Soil Protection Plan; (2) the Annual Program of soil protection and (3) Soil Program Monitoring (Art. 14, para. 1).

733. The Ministry supervises the work of the competent authority of the AP, the competent authority of local governments and agencies in the performance of duties in accordance to this Law, as well as the work of authorized legal persons in performing of soil monitoring (Art. 38, para. 1).

59–75); Information System of Agricultural Land (Articles 76 and 77); Administration for Agricultural Land (Articles 77a and 77b);[734] Authorization for Adoption Sub-legal Acts (Article 80); Supervision (Articles 81–84); Penal provisions (Articles 85–87); and Transitional provisions (Articles 88–96).

570. The Law defines agricultural land soil used for agricultural production (fields, gardens, orchards, vineyards, meadows, pastures, fish ponds and wet lands) and the land planned to be used for agricultural production (Article 2, point 1). It regulates planning, protection, management and utilization of agricultural land, supervision and other issues relevant for protection and utilization of agricultural land as a good of general interest (Article 1). The Law stipulates that a foreign natural person or a corporation cannot own agricultural land (Article 1, paragraph 4).

571. A special part (Articles 15–29) of the Law is devoted to the protection of agricultural land (Articles 15–29). These provisions include the following:

- ban of emission and dumping of dangerous and harmful substances, finding the existence of dangerous and harmful substances in agricultural land and in irrigation water;
- measures against erosion;
- control of fertility of agricultural cultivable land and the quantity of used mineral fertilizers and pesticides;
- ban of use of agricultural cultivable land for non-agricultural purposes;
- permission for change of use of agricultural cultivable land; and
- protection of agricultural land against frost, hail, fire, etc.

IV. Law on Forest

572. The Law on Forest (OJ RS, Nos 30/10, 93/12, 89/15 and 95/18 – other law) prescribes that forestland means the land on which a forest is cultivated, the land on which, because of its natural characteristics, it is more rational to grow forest, as well as the land covered with the features intended for forest and game management and for multiple forest functions, and which cannot be used for other purposes, except in cases and under the conditions laid down by this Law (Article 5, paragraph 5). Pursuant to Article 7 of the Forest Law, forest owner, that is, forest user, has to implement the measures of forest protection, to protect forests and forestlands against degradation and erosion, execute forest management plans, and perform other measures stipulated by this Law and regulations passed based on the Law.[735]

734. Administration for agricultural land has been established in accordance with Art. 77a. It performs different activities including managing agricultural land owned by the State, carrying inspections and other activities in the field of agricultural land, establishing an information system, etc.

735. Change in land-use form of forestlands (and forest) can be carried out only in compliance with provisions of Art. 10 of the Law. Legal person shall be fined RSD 300,000–RSD 3,000,000 for the

573. Forest owner and forest user have to monitor the effects of biotic and abiotic factors on forest health and undertake timely measures for the protection of forests and forestlands. The user or owner of forest that manages forest in accordance with the base is required to monitor the impact of biotic and abiotic factors on the health of forests and timely take measures for the protection of forests and forestlands (Article 42, paragraph 1).[736]

574. It shall be forbidden to dispose of garbage, toxic substances and other dangerous waste in the forest and on forestland at a distance less than 200 m from the forest boundary and to construct the improvements for the storage, conversion or destruction of garbage, toxic substances and other dangerous waste (Article 49, paragraph 1).[737] Forest owner, that is, forest user shall prevent the disposal of garbage, toxic substances and other dangerous waste and, without delay, notify the Ministry and on the territory of the AP, the competent organ of the AP (Article 49, paragraph 2).

575. The compensation for the utilization of forestlands (and forest) shall be paid by the forest user, that is, owner (Article 85, paragraph 1).[738]

576. Forestlands (as well as State forests) shall not be alienated, except in cases of redistribution and consolidation and in the cases stipulated by this Law (Article 98, paragraph 1).[739] However, a part of a State forestland (or State forest), in which rational management cannot be organized, can be sold by forest user, with the Government's approval, under market conditions, or exchanged for a private forest or forestland if such forests are isolated, that is, if they are enclaves or semi-enclaves in the complexes of State forests (Article 98, paragraph 2).[740]

---

following economic offences, *inter alia*, land-use change of forestlands (and forest) contrary to Art. 10, para. 1 of this Law (Art. 111, para. 1 point 7). A physical person shall be fined in accordance with provisions of Art. 113, paras 1 and 2.

736. If a forest owner or forest user does not act in accordance with the provision under para. 1 of this Article, the Ministry, and on the territory of the AP, the competent organ of the AP, shall ensure the execution of the obligation at the expense of the forest owner, i.e., user (Art. 42, para. 2). Legal person shall be fined RSD 300,000–RSD 3,000,000 for the following economic offences, *inter alia*, failing to monitor the effects of biotic and abiotic factors on forest health and undertake timely measures for the protection of forests and forestlands (Art. 111, para. 1, point 24).

737. Forest owner, i.e., forest user shall prevent the activities under para. 1 of this Article, remove the garbage, toxic substances and other dangerous waste, and undertake all measures to restore the damaged forest (Art. 49, para. 3). Legal person shall be fined RSD 100,000–RSD 1,000,000 for the following offences, *inter alia*, disposing garbage, toxic substances and other waste, and constructing the improvements for their storage, conversion or destruction, in the forest and on forestland at a distance less than 200 m from the forest (Art. 112, para. 1, point 14). A physical person shall be fined in accordance with provisions of Art. 113, paras 1 and 2.

738. The basis for the calculation of the compensation consists of the total annual income of the forest user realized by forest management (Art. 85, para. 2).

739. State-owned forestlands can be leased prior to the reinstatement determined by forest management plans. The purpose of this land cannot be changed for the duration of the lease (Art. 99, paras 2 and 3).

740. The funds realized by virtue of para. 2 of this Article are the revenue of the Budget of the Republic of Serbia, i.e., Budget of the AP, and shall be used for special purposes through the Budget Funds

V. Law on Waters

577. Pursuant to Article 8, water land is the land on which water is permanently or intermittently present and thus creates special hydrological, geomorphological and biological interactions that reflect on aquatic and riparian ecosystems (paragraph 1).[741] Riparian land, as contemplated herein, is the belt of land adjacent to the major channel of a water course, which serves to maintain protective constructions and the major channel and which is used for other activities pertaining to water management (Article 9, paragraph 1). Water land is managed by a public water management company established to carry out water activities in a given territory (Article 9a, paragraph 2).

578. The boundaries of water land, with respect to first order waters, shall be designated by the Ministry and the competent authority of the AP within the territory of the AP (Article 11, paragraph 1).[742]

579. Water land is intended for the maintenance and improvement of the water regime in accordance with this Law and the Acts based on this law, and in particular for:

(1) construction, reconstruction and rehabilitation of water facilities;
(2) maintenance of watercourses and water facilities; and
(3) implementation of measures related to water management and protection against harmful effects of water, water management, and water management and protection.

In addition, water land may be, in accordance with this Law and the Acts based on this law, used for the following:

(1) construction and maintenance of line infrastructure facilities;
(2) construction and maintenance of facilities intended for State defence;

---

under Arts 81 and 83 of this Law, primarily for the procurement of forests or forestlands, in the aim of enlargement and consolidation of holdings in State ownership (Art. 98, para. 3).

741. Water land holding flowing waters includes the major channel and the riparian land (para. 2); water land holding standing waters includes the channel and the belt of land adjacent to the standing-water channel, up to the highest water level on record (para. 3). Water land also includes any abandoned channel, sandbar or pointbar, which water intermittently, inundates, and land flooded by water due to interventions works (damming of flowing water, extraction of mineral raw materials and the like) (para. 4).

742. The water land referred to in para. 1 of this Article shall be entered into public records of real estate and the rights conferred thereon (Art. 11, para. 2). The Minister shall stipulate the method to be used for the designation of water land boundaries (Art. 11, para. 4). Public owned waters and water lands are public water assets (Art. 5, para. 2). A public water asset is unalienable (Art. 5, para. 3). Public water assets shall be used in a manner that does not result in any adverse effects on water or the riparian ecosystem and that does not restrict the rights of others (Art. 5, para. 4). The right to use a public water asset may be acquired under the conditions set forth in this Law and a special law. On water land, public ownership may be acquired right to lease (Art. 5, para. 5).

(3) construction and maintenance of shipyards, as well as ports, docks, waterways and other facilities in accordance with the law regulating navigation;
(4) construction and maintenance of facilities for the use of natural baths and for the implementation of protective measures on natural baths;
(5) construction and maintenance of facilities for electricity generation; and
(6) performing economic activity, etc. (Article 10).

580. Prohibitions and restrictions on rights and obligations of owner and users of water land and water constructions are prescribed in Articles 133–139 (Chapter VI).[743]

VI. Other Legislation

581. Serbia is a member of the United Nations Convention to Combat Desertification in those Countries Experiencing Serious Drought and/or Desertification, Particularly in Africa (1994) (OJ RS – IT, No. 102/07). Serbia submitted its last report in 2023.[744]

582. In addition to the aforementioned laws, several laws contain provisions that could be of importance for land protection. This group includes the following laws:

– Law on the Spatial Plan of the RS (OJ RS, No. 88/10).
– Law on Mining and Geological Explorations (OJ RS, Nos 101/15, 95/18 – other law, and 40/21).[745]

743. In order to conserve and maintain surface water bodies, bodies of groundwater, protective water constructions and other water constructions, to prevent any deterioration of the water regime, to ensure the conveyance of high flows and the implementation of flood defence, and to protect the environment, the following shall be prohibited on water land: (i) to erect any constructions which reduce the conveyance capacity of a channel; (ii) to dispose of solid waste, hazardous material or harmful material; (iii) to store wood or other solid material in such a way that it interferes with the conveyance of high flows; (iv) to plant trees on any flood control dike, within the floodplain belt which is at least 10 m wide from the unprotected bottom of the dike on the water side, or in the protected zone contrary to the issued-water criteria; (v) to wash cars and other machines; (vi) to undertake other actions, except in the event of: (1) construction of public infrastructures pursuant to this Law or a special law; (2) implementation of any measures for the conservation, enhancement or presentation of natural treasures; (3) erection of any constructions for water use, watercourse development, assurance of navigation or implementation of protection measures in natural bathing areas, pursuant to this Law; (4) erection of any constructions for water protection from pollution; (5) erection of any constructions dedicated to national defence; (6) creation of any temporary sand or gravel dumpsites, such that they do not interfere with the conveyance of high flows, at a distance which shall not be less than 30 m from the unprotected bottom of the dike; (7) undertaking of any action aimed at protecting people, animals and/or property; and (8) extraction of any mineral raw materials pursuant to this Law and special law.

744. https://www.unccd.int/our-work-impact/country-profiles/serbia (23.2.2024).

745. For more information, *see* chapter on subsoil.

– Law on Public-Private Partnership and Concession (OJ RS, Nos 88/11, 15/16 and 104/16).[746]
– Law on the Basis of Property Relations (OJ SFRY, Nos 6/80 and 36/90, OJ FRY, No. 29/96, OJ RS, No. 115/05 – other law).[747]
– Law on Privatization (OJ RS, Nos 83/14, 46/15, 112/15 and 20/16 – authentic interpretation).

583. Following legal Acts are also relevant for soil use and protection in Serbia:

– Law on Plant Protection Products (OJ FRY, No. 41/09).
– Law on Chemicals (OJ RS, Nos 36/09, 88/2010, 92/2011, 93/2012 and 25/2015).
– Law on Biocidal Production (OJ RS, No. 109/21).
– Law on Organic Production (OJ RS, Nos 30/10 and 17/19 – other law).[748]
– Law on Fees for the Use of Public Goods (OJ RS, Nos 95/2018 and 49/19).

584. The list of by-laws relevant to soil protection includes the following:

– Rulebook on the list of activities that can be the cause of land pollution and degradation, the procedure, data content, deadlines, and other requirements for land monitoring (OJ RS, No. 102/20).
– Rulebook on the conditions that a legal entity must meet to perform land monitoring activities, as well as the documentation submitted with the request for authorization for land monitoring (OJ RS, No. 58/19).
– Rulebook on the content and method of maintaining the Cadastre of contaminated locations, type, content, forms, method, and deadlines for data submission (OJ RS, No. 58/19).
– Rulebook on the contents of remediation and recultivation projects (OJ RS, No. 35/19).
– Regulation on limit values of polluting, harmful and dangerous substances in soil (OJ RS, Nos 30/18, 64/2019).
– Rulebook on the methodology for creating rehabilitation and remediation projects (OJ RS, No. 74/15).
– Regulation on establishing criteria for determining the status of the endangered environment and priorities for rehabilitation and remediation (OJ RS, No. 22/10), etc.

---

746. The law regulates, *inter alia*, the scope of concessions, protection of the rights of parties participating in the procedure, the authorities and parties in charge of the concession approval procedure, the termination of concessions, the conditions and manner for preparing, proposing and approving project proposals for public-private partnership, public bodies and parties in charge of proposing and implementing public-private partnership projects, the rights and obligations of public and private partners, public-private partnership contracts with or without concession elements, the establishment and the competences of the Commission, and other relevant issues.
747. This Law is still applied in Serbia for regulation property relations. It, however, does not specify quantitative limitations in property rights concerning the agricultural land.
748. For the list of by-laws in the field of organic agriculture, chemicals, biocide products, etc. *see* the relevant parts of the this monograph.

585. Efficiency of implementation of legal regulation concerning the use and protection of soil should be viewed within the entire context of all environmental problems. Serbia adopted the Law on soil protection, but the enforcement of the law requires changes in the system and a certain period of time. Regarding the possibility of ownership of agricultural land, the Law on agricultural and rural development 'still does not provide EU citizens and Serbian citizens with the same conditions in terms of acquiring agricultural land'.[749]

749. EC. 2023, 102. Amendments to the Law on the Basics of Property Relations, 'which will aim at providing EU citizens with the same treatment as Serbian nationals regarding the acquisition of real estate, are still being drafted. Against this background, Serbia is not complying with its obligations under the SAA.' *Ibid.*

Chapter 6. Noise and Vibrations

586. Causes of environmental noise are all types of transport (road, railway and air), as well as operation of industrial facilities. Various local sources cause noise, such as catering services and craft workshops, and similar facilities.[750]

According to reports for the year 2022, noise data was submitted from five agglomerations of the RS, namely: Belgrade, Niš, Novi Sad, Kragujevac, and Subotica with 61 measuring points, as well as from 46 LSG units that had measured values at a total of 457 measuring points' places. The highest percentage of the total noise indicator in the territory of agglomerations as well as in the territories of other LSG units, Lden, is in the range of 60–64 dB, while the highest percentage of the night noise indicator, Lnight, is in the range of 55–60 dB. Exceeding the threshold values of total and night noise had minimal deviations concerning the permitted value.[751]

587. Noise protection in Serbia is in competence of the MEP, the EPA, and the Ministry of Construction, Transport and Infrastructure, the Civil Aviation Directorate. The Agency's responsibility is to monitor and register environmental noise. The noise monitoring data management falls within the general scope of environmental protection informational system (various polluters, cadastre, etc.). The Ministry of Infrastructure is responsible for outdoor equipment, such as lawn mowers and other outdoor machinery-produced noise. The Traffic Safety Department takes care of vehicle noise. The Civil Aviation Directorate is responsible for compliance with the rules and standards for using air space, including issuing certificates on aircraft noise levels.

It should be added that certain environmental responsibilities were, in 2002, delegated to the AP, including protection from noise and LSG.[752]

§1. Legislation

588. Two basic legal Acts concerning protection from noise are the Law on Protection from the Noise in the Environment (OJ RS, No. 96/21) and the EPL (OJ RS, Nos 135/04, 36/09 – other law, 72/09 – other law, 43/11 – CC, 14/16, 76/18 and 95/18 – other law).

I. The Law on Protection from Noise in the Environment

589. The Law on Protection from Noise in the Environment is divided into following nine chapters: I Basic provisions (Articles 1–4), II Subjects of protection

750. GOV R. 2010a, 56.
751. EPA. 2023a, 19.
752. According to the Law on Noise Protection (OJ RS, Nos 36/09 and 88/10), the RS entrusts to the AP and/or LSG the key tasks in this field.The new Law on Protection against Noise in the Environment (2021) also entrusts certain tasks to AP and LSG.

from noise in the environment (Articles 5–11), III Measures and conditions of protection from noise in the environment and sound protection (Articles 12–22), IV Measuring noise in the environment (Articles 23–27), V Access to information on noise (Articles 28 and 29),[753] VI Supervision (Articles 30–34), VII Competence for solving complaints (Article 35); VIII Penal provisions (Articles 36–39), and IX Transitional and final provisions (Articles 40–44). The provisions of this law refer to noise in the environment to which people are exposed, especially in built-up areas, public parks or other quiet zones in agglomerations, in quiet zones outside settlements, near schools, hospitals and other facilities, noise-sensitive zones, which originates from the operation of noise sources in the sense of this law (Article 1, paragraph 2).[754]

590. Pursuant to Article 5, Subjects of environmental protection against noise on the territory of the RS, within the framework of their powers, are: (1) RS; (2) AP; (3) municipality, city, or the city of Belgrade (hereinafter 'local self-government unit'); (4) legal entities and entrepreneurs, who emit noise in the course of economic activity, as well as owners, managers (of main roads, main railways and main airports) and concessionaires (of main roads, main railways and main airports) of noise sources (hereinafter 'legal entities'); (5) scientific and professional organizations and other public services, associations, citizens and other legal entities (Articles 6–11).[755] In addition, subjects of environmental protection against noise are obliged to cooperate with each other in making decisions and implementing measures, in accordance with this law and special laws regulating environmental protection (Article 11, paragraph 1).

753. Environmental noise protection subjects are obliged to provide public access to information and data from strategic environmental noise maps and action plans, in accordance with this law and the law governing environmental protection. Information and data from para. 1 of this article must be communicated to the public in a clear, comprehensible and accessible manner, with the use of the most suitable information technologies, and are available on the Agency's website (Art. 28). Data on noise in the environment are an integral part of the report on the state of environmental protection in the Republic of Serbia (Art. 29).

754. However, the Provisions of this law do not apply to noise: (1) which occurs at the workplace and in the working environment; (2) which occurs in the means of transport; (3) originating from military activities and activities to protect against natural disasters, natural and other disasters; (4) from activities in the household or noise from the neighbouring household from the apartment or other space used for these purposes; (5) to which those who create it are exposed; (6) from domestic and wild animals. In addition, the provisions of this law do not apply to noise originating from sound announcements by bells or electroacoustic devices from religious buildings, as well as to noise from aircraft to the extent that protection against noise from aircraft is regulated by other special laws and regulations in the field of aviation traffic (Art. 2).

755. Subjects of environmental protection against noise from Art. 5 of this law are responsible for any activity that causes exposure to noise above the limit values or for failure to take prescribed measures to protect against noise in the environment, in accordance with the law (Art. 10, para. 1). Legal entities that, by performing their activities, affect or may affect exposure to noise above threshold values are required to ensure: participation in the costs of noise protection in the environment as part of investment, current and production costs; monitoring the impact of your activity on noise; implementation of appropriate noise protection measures, i.e., sound protection in accordance with this law and the law regulating environmental protection (para. 2).

II. Measures and Conditions for Protection from Noise in the Environment and Sound Protection

591. Preventive measures for protection from noise are related primarily to planning and construction.[756] Plans and programs to which the regulations governing the strategic EIA procedure are applied contain an assessment of the noise level and noise protection measures in the environment (Article 12, paragraph 2).[757] In the process of assessing the impact of projects on the environment, the EIA study determines the conditions and measures by which the harmful effects of noise can be prevented, reduced, or eliminated following the law regulating EIA (Article 13, paragraph 1).[758] In the process of technical inspection and issuance of a use permit for buildings, projects for which an EIA is not required and projects for which an EIA study has been prepared, the fulfilment of sound protection measures is determined in accordance with technical regulations and standards (Article 14, paragraph 3).

592. Noise indicators are used to determine the level of noise in the environment, assess and predict the level of noise and its effects, create strategic noise maps and plan noise protection measures (Article 15, paragraph 1). The value of noise indicators in the environment is determined by applying methods of measurement, calculation or assessment, in accordance with the special regulation regulating noise indicators and this law.[759] Limit values are indicated by noise indicators in accordance with this law (Article 16, paragraph 2).[760]

593. The person responsible for creating spatial and urban plans carries out acoustic zoning by entering data on acoustic zones in existing reference maps and graphic representations of spatial and urban plans, that is, by determining acoustic zones (Article 17, paragraph 2).[761]

---

756. Spatial and urban planning measures and conditions for noise protection are provided, in particular: (1) mutual spatial distribution of infrastructure, industrial, residential, recreational and other zones and facilities; (2) traffic system design, traffic planning, noise reduction, sound protection measures and control of noise sources; (3) acoustic zoning (Art. 12, para. 1).
757. Spatial and urban planning and implementation of projects referred to in Art. 12, para. 2 of this law also include sound protection measures that are provided through planning of the dedicated use of space, traffic planning, noise reduction with sound protection measures and control of noise sources (Art. 14, para. 1).
758. The conditions for the operation of facilities and activities for which an integrated permit is issued contain noise protection measures under the law governing the integrated prevention and control of environmental pollution (para. 2).
759. Calculation methods are used to predict the value of the noise indicator (para. 3).
760. The Minister responsible for environmental protection (hereinafter 'the Minister') prescribes noise indicators, limit values, methods for evaluating noise indicators, disturbance and harmful effects of noise in the environment and on human health, types and methods of data collection necessary for their assessment (para. 3).
761. Acoustic zoning is carried out based on the purpose of the space, that is, reference maps of spatial and urban plans, and following a special regulation regulating the methodology for determining acoustic zones. The decision to limit the use of noise sources is made by the local self-government unit, based on specific acoustic zones. The Minister prescribes the methodology for determining acoustic zones

594. The legal entity that is the owner or user of the noise source is obliged to provide the first noise measurement at the location before putting the noise source into use, i.e., after reconstruction or replacement of technical capacities, obtain a report from an authorized professional organization on noise measurement, bear the costs of these measurements and necessary to implement sound protection measures following this law (Article 18).[762]

595. A catering facility in which music is broadcast or an entertainment programme is performed is obliged to provide the prescribed conditions and sound protection measures prescribed by this law and the regulations governing the field of catering (Article 19, paragraph 1). It is foreseen that the control and measurement of the noise level from the catering facilities will be carried out by the municipal police officer with a noise measuring device.[763]

596. Strategic noise maps must be prepared for all agglomerations, main roads, main railways, and main airports, following this law (Article 21, paragraph 1). Strategic noise maps for agglomerations are prepared by the LSG unit in cooperation with other environmental protection entities.[764]

597. Strategic noise maps for main roads, main railways, and main airports on the territory of the RS are prepared by legal entities that are owners and concessionaires of main roads, main railways, and main airports in cooperation with other environmental protection entities (Article 21, paragraph 4). The prepared strategic noise maps are submitted to the Agency. Strategic noise maps are reviewed and, if necessary, revised every five years.[765]

598. Environmental noise protection action plans are drawn up for all areas for which strategic noise maps are drawn up (Article 22, paragraph 1). The action plan for agglomerations is drawn up by the LSG unit in cooperation with other protection entities. The action plan for main roads, main railways, and main airports, i.e.,

762. The Minister prescribes noise measurement methods, content, and scope of noise measurement reports (para. 2).
763. The local self-government unit can, by special act, regulate the conditions for arranging and equipping the hospitality facility referred to in para. 1 of this article, which protects against noise, as well as the way to control the noise level (Art. 19, para. 3). In addition, local self-government units decide on the holding of public gatherings, entertainment and sports events, and other outdoor and indoor activities that may lead to exceeding the prescribed noise limit values. The law stipulates that public gatherings and other outdoor or indoor activities must be announced twenty days in advance (Art. 20).
764. The competent authority of local self-government units adopts strategic noise maps for the agglomeration (Art. 21, para. 3).
765. Strategic noise maps are used as a basis for creating action plans and as a means of informing the public about the level of noise in the environment and the harmful effects of noise (Art. 21, para. 6).

the area near them, is drawn up by legal entities that are owners and concessionaires of main roads, main railways, and main airports in cooperation with other protection entities.[766]

III. Measurement of Noise in the Environment

599. The measurement of noise in the environment is regulated by Articles 23–27 of the Law. The following issues are regulated: Noise measurement of individual noise sources, Noise monitoring, Authorized professional organizations for noise measurement, Noise measurement from catering facilities and Information system.

600. The owner, that is, the user of the noise source, performs a regular periodic measurement of the noise level in the environment once every three years. The measurement of noise from individual sources is carried out in the manner prescribed by the by-law (Article 23). Noise monitoring is carried out by systematic monitoring of noise indicators, and it is provided by the RS, APs and LSG units (Article 24).[767]

601. The measurement of noise in the environment is performed by an authorized legal entity if it meets the prescribed conditions following this law (Article 25).[768] The Minister prescribes in more detail the conditions that the professional organization must meet for measuring noise in the environment, the necessary documentation, the authorization procedure, the content of the authorization decision, as well as the content, scope, and validity period of the report on noise measurement (Article 25, paragraph 12).

602. The measurement of noise originating from catering establishments can be carried out by the communal militiaman of the LSG unit, with calibrated noise measuring devices under the special regulation regulating the methodology of noise measurement, and by the decision of the LSG unit body (Article 26).[769]

766. Adopted action plans are submitted to the Agency. Action plans are reviewed and, if necessary, revised in case of significant changes affecting the noise level, at least every five years. The minister and the minister in charge of traffic affairs regulate the content and methods of creating the strategic noise map and the action plan, as well as the way they are created and presented to the public (Art. 22, paras 5–8).

767. The Republic of Serbia, an autonomous province, or a unit of local self-government, legal entities that manage main roads, main railways, and main airports provide noise monitoring, and continuous monitoring of noise in the environment (Art. 24, para. 2).

768. The legal entity submits the request for authorization for the tasks referred to in para. 1 of this article to the Ministry (para. 2).

769. The body of the local self-government unit in which the communal militiaman from para. 1 of this article is employed must also have accreditation, following a special law. The minister prescribes in more detail the conditions that the municipal militiaman must meet to be able to carry out noise measurement tasks (paras 2 and 3).

603. Data from noise monitoring, strategic noise maps, and action plans are part of a unique environmental information system following the law regulating environmental protection. The Agency submits data from strategic noise maps and the content of action plans to the EC. The Minister prescribes in more detail the methodology for creating and managing the noise information system (Article 27).

IV. Supervision and Penal Provisions

604. The Ministry supervises the work of the Agency, APs, and LSG units in the performance of entrusted tasks (Article 30). Inspection supervision over the implementation of the provisions of this law and the regulations adopted for its execution is carried out by the Ministry unless otherwise prescribed by this law.[770]

605. The AP carries out inspection supervision over the execution of tasks entrusted by this law through inspectors. The LSG unit carries out inspection supervision over the execution of tasks entrusted by this law through inspectors (Article 31).

606. Article 32 of the Law prescribes the powers of the municipal militia. The municipal militia, in addition to the powers prescribed by the law regulating the affairs and powers of the municipal militia, is also specially authorized to measure noise levels originating from catering facilities. Articles 33 and 34 of the law prescribe the rights and duties of inspectors, as well as the powers in performing inspection supervision.

607. Penal provisions (Articles 36–39) provide sanctions for misdemeanours for legal entities, as well as for responsible persons in administrative bodies, local governments, or organizations that exercise public powers, for violating the provisions of this law. The amount of sanctions is harmonized with the provisions of the Law on Misdemeanors.[771]

V. Law on Environmental Protection

608. The EPL (OJ RS, Nos 135/04, 36/09, 72/09, 43/11 CC, 14/16, 76/18 and 95/18 – other law) contains some general provisions about noise. Besides the provisions of Article 3, point 9 (definitions),[772] the Law prescribes the following in Article 31: ‘The user of a noise source may place on the market and may use noise sources according to regulated conditions and by applying regulated measures of

770. The inspection supervision is carried out by the environmental protection inspector within the scope established by this law.

771. In addition to the imposed fine for a misdemeanour, a protective measure of confiscation of objects that were used or intended for the commission of a misdemeanour, or that were created by the commission of a misdemeanour, may be imposed on a legal entity.

772. Article 3 (point 9) prescribes that ‘activity affecting the environment ... is any action (permanent or temporary) which changes or may change the status and conditions in the environment and

protection by which noise emissions, that is, the use of facilities, devices, machines, transport means and gadgets that produce noise shall be abated.'

609. Vibrations have not yet been regulated and there are no regulations adopted within environmental protection area which regulate this area.[773] Protection from vibrations shall be enforced by undertaking measures by which threat towards the environment from effects of mechanical, periodical and individual vibrations caused by human activity shall be prevented and eliminated. Article 39, point 2 of the EPL defines obligation to establish integral norms 'in order to: control the quality of air, water and soil, procedures with waste and chemicals, wastewater treatment, industrial pollution and risk management, level of noise and vibrations, etc.' Article 65 of the same Law prescribes obligations regarding adoption of action plans: 'Action plans shall be made for, among other things, ... 12) protection from noise and vibrations' ... and, finally, Article 70 prescribes that 'State monitoring shall be carried out by systematic measurement, examination and rating of indicators of the status and pollution of environment, including the noise.'

VI. Other Legislation and Harmonization with EU Legislation

610. Another legal Act containing provisions on noise is the Air Transport Law (OJ RS, Nos 73/2010, 57/11, 93/12, 45/15, 66/15 – other law, 83/18 and 9/20). Articles 200–203 (Chapter IX) of the Law on Air Transportation (OJ RS, No. 73/2010) regulate issues related to protection against noise and exhaust gas emissions. The Law lays down that aviation entities shall be obliged to take measures for protection of environment against aircraft noise and other noise-related external factors that result from the operation or provision of services in civil aviation (Article 200 of the Law). An aerodrome operator shall be obliged to ensure the implementation of environment protection measures when airport is in use, in accordance with the Air Transport Law and the regulations that govern environment protection (Article 201 of the Law).

611. Article 202 of the Law prescribes that noise and gas emissions at airports and in the vicinity of the airports shall not be higher than prescribed limit values.[774]

---

relates to: utilization of resources and natural goods; production and circulation processes; distribution and use of materials; emissions of pollution into water, air or soil; waste and wastewater management; chemicals and harmful substances management; noise and vibrations; ionizing and non-ionizing radiation; accidents.'

773. GOV RS. 2010a, 57.

774. The Minister competent for transport affairs, with the consent of the Minister competent for environment protection affairs, prescribes allowed noise levels at airports, allowed gas emission levels at airports, methods of emission monitoring and operative restrictions at certain airport points, as well as the measures for the reduction of aircraft emission.

Aircraft operators shall pay the charge for environment protection against aircraft noise and aircraft gas emissions (Article 202, paragraph 3).[775]

612. Pursuant to Article 203 of the mentioned Law, the operators of general purpose airports and airports used for commercial air transport that, during the previous year, had more than 50,000 take-offs and landings, as well as the operator of the combined airport open for operations of military and jet aircraft, shall provide continual measuring of noise generated at airport and its vicinity as a result of aircraft take-offs and landings. The results received by noise measuring are used for development of strategic noise maps and action plans for environmental protection against noise and vibrations in air transport and for designation of noise-protected areas where aircraft noise exceeds allowed level.[776]

613. Pursuant to Article 10 of the *Law on Railway* (OJ RS, No. 41/18), the manager of public railway infrastructure is obligated to, when performing his/her duties, take care of environment protection and energy efficiency in accordance with Law and other regulations (paragraph 2).

614. In the field of *road vehicles*, in the RS, international UN/ECE – Agreement Concerning the Adoption of Uniform Technical Prescriptions for Wheeled Vehicles, Equipment and Parts which can be fitted and/or be used on Wheeled Vehicles and Conditions for Reciprocal Recognition of Approvals Granted on the Basic of these Prescriptions is applied. The Road Traffic Safety Agency is responsible for implementation of the 1958 Agreement and for the relevant UN/ECE Regulations.[777]

615. Based on the new Law on Protection from Noise in the Environment (2021), several by-laws were adopted. These are following:

- Rulebook on the content and methods of creating a strategic noise map and action plan, the way they are created and presented to the public, as well as their forms (OJ RS, No. 90/23).

775. The Minister competent for transport affairs, with the consent of the Minister competent for environment protection affairs, prescribes the amount of the charge for the environmental protection against aircraft noise and gas emission.
776. The Minister competent for traffic affairs, with the consent of the Minister competent for environment protection affairs, prescribes the method of noise measuring at airports.
777. Uniform provisions concerning the approval of category L2, L4 and L5 vehicles with regard to noise (UN/ECE R. 9) (OJ SFRJ – IT, No. 16/72) (corresponding to the EU Directive/Regulation with relevant amendments and modifications: 97/24); Uniform provisions concerning the approval of motor cycles with regard to noise (UN/ECE R.41) (OJ SFRJ, No. 60/86) (corresponding to the EU Directive/Regulation with relevant amendments and modifications: 97/24); Uniform provisions concerning the approval of motor vehicles having at least four wheels with regard to their noise emissions (UN/ECE R. 51) (OJ SFRJ, Nos 48/84 and 1/87) (corresponding to the EU Directive/Regulation with relevant amendments and modifications:70/157); Uniform provisions concerning the approval of replacement silencing systems (UN/ECE R. 59) (OJ SFRJ, No. 43/92) (corresponding to the EU Directive/Regulation with relevant amendments and modifications: 70/157 and 81/334); Uniform provisions concerning the approval of two-wheeled mopeds with regard to noise (UN/ECE R. 63) (OJ SFRJ, No. 73/87) (corresponding to the EU Directive/Regulation with relevant amendments and modifications: 97/24).

- Rulebook on conditions that must be met by an expert organization for noise measurement in the environment, necessary documentation, authorization procedure, content of authorization decision, as well as content, scope, and validity period of noise measurement report (OJ RS, No. 139/22).
- Rulebook on noise measurement methods, content, and scope of reports on noise measurement in the environment (OJ RS, No. 39/22).
- Rulebook on the conditions to be met by the municipal police officer to be able to measure noise from catering establishments (OJ RS, No. 132/21).

Regulations adopted in accordance with the Law on Protection from Noise in the Environment (OJ RS, Nos 36/09, 88/10) which are applied until the adoption of by-laws based on authorization from the Law on Protection from Noise in the Environment (OJ RS, No. 96/21) are as follows:

- Regulation on noise indicators, limit values, methods for assessing indicators of noise, disturbance and harmful effects of noise on the environment and public health, as well as types and manner for collecting data necessary for their assessment (OJ RS No. 75/10).
- Rulebook on methodology for determining acoustic zones (OJ RS No. 72/10).

616. The basic goal of passing the new Law on Environmental Noise Protection is to fully harmonize this area with Directive 2002/49/EC. The draft law has been harmonized with Directive 2002/49/EC (32002L0049) relating to the assessment and management of environmental noise. According to the EC assessment for 2022 'alignment with the EU rules on noise increased through the adoption of a new Law on environmental noise protection … Implementation remains at an early stage. Serbia needs to improve administrative capacity for preparing noise maps and action plans and for enforcing noise legislation'.[778] The situation was assessed in the same way in the report for 2023.[779]

778. EC 2022, 123.
779. EC 2023, 137.

Chapter 7. Radiation

§1. Levels of Radioactivity in Serbia

617. According to the overall results of measuring the radioactivity of the environment in the territory of the RS in 2019, it can be concluded that the activity of both natural radionuclides and long-lived radionuclides of artificial origin (mainly from Chernobyl precipitation), in different types of samples (air, precipitation), was at low levels.[780] The results of measuring radionuclide activity on the territory of the RS in 2022 are in accordance with the results of measurements from previous years at the same locations.[781]

618. Continuous monitoring of the dose of gamma radiation on the territory of the RS is made possible by the early warning system for nuclear or radiological accidents. This system consists of nine networked stations on which detectors of the ambient equivalent dose of gamma radiation in the air are placed, from which data are collected every half hour. The stations are located in Palić, Novi Sad, Belgrade, Vinča, Kladovo, Zlatibor, Niš, Vranje and Kosovska Mitrovica.[782] Of the nine stations, seven are equipped with Geiger-Miller counters (Figure 1.2) and two with ionization chambers. The measuring station in Belgrade and the measuring station in Kosovska Mitrovica were not in operation in 2022.[783]

619. During the NATO intervention in 1999, ammunition with DU was used, polluting a number of sites in Kosovo-Metohija, southern Serbia and Montenegro. Currently, three metal containers containing about 300 depleted uranium bullets, two metal containers with aluminium bullet shells contaminated with depleted uranium, seven metal containers with a mixture of bullets and shells and 15 200 litre drums with soil contaminated with depleted uranium are stored in hangar H2.[784]

Potential danger for Serbia is nuclear installations functioning in the region. There are, namely, thirty-nine reactors (mainly used for the production of electricity) in neighbouring countries, some of which are already relatively old.

620. In RS, radioactive waste is currently generated in medical, industrial and research activities. Besides operating storage facilities, radioactive waste can be kept by legal entity that generated this waste for no longer than one year according to Article 35 of the Law 2009. After this period, radioactive waste must be transferred to licensed operating radioactive waste storage facilities.[785]

---

780. SRBATOM. 2020, 20.
781. SRBATOM, 2023,19.
782. GOV RS. 2011b, 77. *See also*, SRBATOM. 2023, 5.
783. *Ibid.*
784. SRBATOM. 2018, 38. Waste was collected during decontamination activities on sites contaminated due to NATO bombing of territory of RS and RM with the ammunition with depleted uranium in 1999.
785. There is no spent nuclear fuel on territory of Republic of Serbia. The only nuclear fuel existing at the time of writing this Report in the Republic of Serbia is natural metal uranium rods placed in dry storage in reactor hall and LEU fuel elements TVR-S type in the core of the reactor RB. The

621. Solid radioactive waste including spent sealed radioactive sources is stored in four storage facilities namely hangars H0, H1, H2 and H3 and Secure Storage for sealed radioactive sources. Liquid waste is stored in four underground liquid waste tanks namely VR1, VR2, VR3 and VR4.[786]

622. Most of radioactive waste has been deposited in, as already mentioned, the Institute of Nuclear Sciences 'Vinca' situated in Vinca, a village near Belgrade. The main sources of the waste are research reactors in the Vinca Nuclear Institute (which contributed to about 4% of the total radioactive waste), remnants of isotopes used in medicine, industry, etc. radioactive materials used in medicine, radioactive waste from the industry of fertilizers especially phosphates, radioactive lightning rods, etc. A project of nuclear fuel transportation from Vinca to the Russian Federation has been started, with collaboration of the International Atomic Energy Agency (IAEA). The contract on repacking and transportation to the Russian Federation, where it will be reprocessed, was signed between the IAEA, the Institute of Nuclear Sciences 'Vinca' and consortium of three Russian companies.[787]

623. Protection from ionized radiation and nuclear safety is in the competence of the MME, the Ministry of Education, Science and Technological Development, according to the provisions of the Law on Ministries (Articles 7 and 14). The Ministry in charge of environmental protection and other ministries participate in the implementation of certain activities (e.g., development of strategic documents, etc.).[788]

Systematic monitoring of ionizing radiation, as prescribed by the decision on systematic testing of content of radionuclides in the environment, is performed in the Serbian Institute of Occupational Health 'Dr Dragomir Karajovic'.[789]

Border control of radioactivity (dosimetric control and gamma-spectrometric measurement) of imported and exported goods, as well as the goods in transit, is performed in accordance with the Rulebook on control of radioactivity of goods during import, export and transit (OJ RS, No. 86/19).

For the purpose of providing the conditions for professional and efficient performance of regulatory control over the practices regulated by the Law on Radiation and Nuclear Safety and Security, the Serbian Radiation and Nuclear Safety and Security Directorate was established as a separate and independent regulatory authority conducting regulatory, professional and other related executive duties in the field of radiation and nuclear safety and security, by law.[790]

---

burn-up level of fuel is very low due to low power. Once permanently removed from the reactor RB this fuel can be stored in Secure Storage. In 2010 all spent fuel from the research reactor RA was repatriated to the Russian Federation in the context of IAEA Russian research Reactors Fuel Return Programme. Republic of Serbia. *Ibid.*, 17.

786. *Ibid.*

787. IAEA. 2007, 28; *see also* GOV RS. 2008a, 403.

788. Nevertheless, several different bodies are involved in carrying out activities related to radiation and nuclear safety. One of the problems relates to coordination within different ministries and other organizations (science, environment, health, defence, interior affairs, etc.).

789. http://www.imrs.rs/index.php?id=72 (5.1.2024).

790. http://www.srbatom.gov.rs/srbatomm/about-us/?lang=en (5.1.2024).

Pursuant to Article 48a of the Law on Ionising Radiation Protection and Nuclear Safety (OJ RS, Nos 36/2009 and 93/12), Public Company Nuclear Facilities of Serbia[791] was established to manage nuclear facilities listed in Governmental Decision on Establishment of public company for nuclear facility management (OJ RS, No. 50/09). 'These facilities are two research reactors RA and RB, radioactive waste storage facilities H0, H1, H2, H3 and Secure Storage, liquid radioactive waste storage tanks VR1-VR4, Waste Processing Facility and so-called Radium Bunker, all previously managed by Vinča Institute, and hydrometallurgical plant in Gabrovnica near Kalna (Eastern Serbia, Stara Planina Mountain), previously managed by Institute for Technology of Nuclear and Other Mineral Raw Materials.'[792]

§2. Legislation

624. The EPL contains only general provisions concerning radiation. Article 32 prescribes that protection from radiation shall be enforced by implementing measures by which threat towards the environment and human health from the effects of radiation from ionizing and non-ionizing sources shall be prevented and by which the consequences of emissions from those sources shall be prevented. Legal and natural persons may produce, circulate or use sources of ionizing and non-ionizing radiation according to existing legal regulations. Using the resources of the Green Fund of the RS shall be done in accordance with the Law, the NEPP and strategic documents, as well as a list of priority infrastructure projects in the field of environment, *inter alia*, the removal of sources of ionizing radiation from radioactive lightning rods and disposal of abandoned sources of ionizing radiation of unknown owners or users; the improvement and construction of infrastructure for protection from ionizing and non-ionizing radiation (Article 90в, paragraph 1, points 17 and 18).

I. Law on Radiation and Nuclear Safety and Security

625. The legal Act that regulates ionizing radiation protection and nuclear safety in the RS is the Law on Radiation and Nuclear Safety and Security (OJ RS, Nos 95/18 and 10/19). It has the following sixteen parts: Part I – General Provisions (Articles 1–5); Part II – Radiation and Nuclear Safety and Security Strategies (Articles 6–12); Part III – Serbian Radiation and Nuclear Safety Directorate (Articles 13–28); Part IV – Fundamental Principle of Ionizing Radiation Protection (Article 29); Part V – Exemption from Notification Requirement, Notifications and Authorizations (Articles 30–65); Part VI – Radiation and Nuclear Safety (Articles 66–181); Part VII – Records and Control of Nuclear Material, Activities, Special Equipment, and Non-nuclear Material Associated with Nuclear Fuel Cycle (Articles 182–184); Part VIII – Radiation and Nuclear Security (Articles 185–191); Part IX – Preparedness and Response in Case of Nuclear or Radiological Emergency

791. http://www.nuklearniobjekti.rs/ (5.1.2024).
792. SRBATOM. 2018, 8.

(Articles 192–195); Part X – Trade in Radiation Sources (Articles 196–202); Part XI – Transport of Dangerous Goods Class 7 ADR/RID/ADN (Radioactive Material) (Articles 203–205); Part XII – Public Information and Transparency (Article 206); Part XIII – Liability of a Licensee for Nuclear Damage (Articles 207–210); Part XIV – Inspectional Supervision (Articles 211–222); Part XV – Criminal Provisions (Articles 233–236); Part XVI – Transitional and Final Provisions (Articles 237–250).

626. The Law regulates the measures of radiation and nuclear safety and security, conditions for conducting practices with radiation sources, response in case of planned, existing and emergency exposure to ionizing radiation, and aims at ensuring proper protection of members of the public, the public and the environment from the harmful effect of ionizing radiation, now and in the future. The Law provides for the establishment of the Serbian Radiation and Nuclear Safety and Security Directorate (hereinafter 'the Directorate') with the aim of exercising regulatory control over the practices regulated by the Law (Article 1).

627. The Law shall apply to all practices involving peaceful use of nuclear energy and ionizing radiation conducted in the territory or under the jurisdiction or control of the RS. In addition, the Law shall apply to any planned, existing or emergency exposure situations involving the risk of exposure to ionizing radiation that cannot be disregarded from a radiation protection of a member of the public, the public and the environment point of view (Article 2). The Law shall apply in particular to: (1) manufacture, production, processing, handling, disposal, use, storage, holding, transport, and trade of radioactive material in the RS; (2) siting, designing, construction, trial run, operation and decommissioning of nuclear facilities, and closure of radioactive waste disposal facilities; (3) manufacture and operation of electrical equipment emitting ionizing radiation and containing components operating at a potential difference of more than 5 kilovolt (kV); (4) human activities involving the presence of natural radiation sources resulting in a significant increase in the exposure of workers or other members of the public, in cases of: (a) the operation of aircraft, in view of the exposure of crews; (b) the processing of materials with naturally-occurring radionuclides; (5) exposure of workers or other individuals to indoor radon, external exposure to ionizing radiation from building materials, and exposure resulting from an emergency or a past human activity; (6) preparedness for, response plan, and management in case of emergency exposure situations and nuclear and radiological emergencies that are deemed to warrant health protection measures of the workers and other members of the public.[793]

793. However, the Law shall not apply to: (1) exposure to the natural background level of radiation, such as radionuclides contained in the human body and cosmic radiation prevailing at ground level; (2) exposure of workers or other individuals other than aircraft crew to cosmic radiation in flight or in space; (3) above ground exposure to radionuclides present in the undisturbed crust of the earth (Art. 3).

A. Radiation and Nuclear Safety and Security Strategies

628. In order to provide for the implementation of the policies in the area of radiation and nuclear safety and security and the policies of spent fuel and radioactive waste management in the RS, the following strategic documents shall be passed: (1) Radiation and Nuclear Safety Strategy; (2) Spent Fuel and Radioactive Waste Management Strategy; (3) Radiation and Nuclear Security Strategy; (4) Existing Exposure Situation Management Strategy (Article 6, paragraph 1).[794]

629. The Directorate, in cooperation with the ministries responsible for environmental protection, health, science, defence, emergency situations and other interested bodies and organizations, shall prepare and propose the Strategies under paragraph 1 hereof (Article 6, paragraph 4).[795]

B. Serbian Radiation and Nuclear Safety and Security Directorate

630. For the purpose of providing the environment for professional and efficient regulatory control of practices regulated by the Law, the Serbian Radiation and Nuclear Safety and Security Directorate shall be established by law as an independent and separate regulatory body with regulatory, expert and associated executive functions in the area of radiation and nuclear safety and security (Article 13).[796,797]

Fundamental principles of radiation protection are: (1) *Justification*: Decisions introducing a practice shall be justified in the sense that such decisions shall be taken with the intent to ensure that the individual or societal benefit resulting from the practice outweighs the health detriment that it may cause. Decisions introducing or altering an exposure pathway for existing and emergency exposure situations shall be justified in the sense that they should do more good than harm. (2) *Optimization*: Radiation protection measures of individuals subject to public or occupational exposure shall be optimized with the aim of keeping the magnitude of individual doses, the likelihood of exposure and the number of individuals exposed as low as reasonably achievable taking into account the current state of technical knowledge and economic and societal factors. The optimization of the protection of individuals subject to medical exposure shall apply to the magnitude of individual doses and be consistent with the medical purpose of the exposure. (3) *Dose limitation*: In planned exposure situations, the sum of doses to an individual shall not

794. The Strategies under para. 1 hereof determine long-term strategic direction and policies in the area of radiation and nuclear safety and security, and determine the measures to enhance spent nuclear fuel and radioactive waste management commensurate with the international standards and principles in this area as well as assumed international commitments (Art. 6, para. 2).

795. The Directorate shall prepare and submit to the Government, at least once a year, the report on the implementation of the Strategies (Art. 6, para. 6).

796. http://www.srbatom.gov.rs/srbatomm/?lang=en (5.1.2024).

797. With respect to the performance of functions within its competence, the Directorate shall be responsible to the Government of the Republic of Serbia. The Directorate is a legal entity. The head office of the Directorate is in Belgrade (Art. 14, paras 1–3).

exceed the dose limits laid down for occupational exposure or public exposure. Dose limits shall not apply to medical exposures (Article 29).

C. Environmental Radioactivity Monitoring and Reporting

631. Pursuant to Article 91 of the Law on Radiation and Nuclear Safety and Security, the purpose of environmental radioactivity monitoring[798] is to determine the presence of radionuclides in the environment and to assess the levels of exposure of the public to ionizing radiation in normal circumstances, in case of a suspicion of an emergency, and during a nuclear or radiological emergency (paragraph 1).[799]

632. Environmental Radioactivity Monitoring Programme serves to establish the locations, time intervals and the manner of control of radioactivity in the environment (paragraph 3). Only a person with the approval to carry out the tasks of radiation protection, that is, radioactivity monitoring or individual monitoring tests, can conduct environmental radioactivity monitoring (paragraph 4).

633. The approved radiation protection officer conducting the environmental radioactivity monitoring shall submit the Environmental Radioactivity Monitoring Report to the Directorate not later than 31 March of the current year for the previous year, or immediately in case of a nuclear or radiological emergency, or at the request of the Directorate (Article 92, paragraph 1). Environmental radioactivity monitoring results serve the Directorate to observe the level of public exposure to ionizing radiation, to assess the doses received by the public and, in case of increased radioactivity, to make arrangements for and order urgent and other protection measures to be taken (paragraph 2).

634. The Directorate shall publish the annual report on the levels of public exposure to ionizing radiation in the RS not later than 31 May of the current year for the previous year (Article 92, paragraph 3).[800]

635. Closure of radioactive waste disposal facility shall include the activities of decontamination, dissembling and demolishing of structures, systems and components and bringing the facility to a state that ensures long-term safety of disposed

798. Environmental radioactivity monitoring means the measurement of external dose rates due to radioactive substances in the environment or of concentrations of radionuclides in environmental media (Art. 5, point 34).

799. The environmental radioactivity monitoring under para. 1 hereof shall be implemented in accordance with the Environmental Radioactivity Monitoring Programme, which is passed by the Directorate (para. 2). The Directorate shall specify the manner of conducting radioactivity monitoring under para. 1 hereof, the content and the schedule of adopting the Environmental Radioactivity Monitoring Programme, as well as the requirements for its modification (para. 5).

800. Financial arrangements for the environmental radioactivity monitoring and the assessment of the public exposure level shall be provided from the budget of the Republic of Serbia (Art. 92, para. 4).

radioactive waste (Article 147, paragraph 1).[801] The measures of control particularly include, *inter alia*, environmental radioactivity monitoring and surveillance of the closed disposal facility site (paragraph 3).

636. Workplace monitoring shall comprise the measurement of external dose rates, the measurement of radionuclide-specific activity concentration in air and surface density of contaminating radionuclides (Article 77, paragraph 1).[802]

D. Dose Constraints for Occupational Exposure, Public Exposure and Medical Exposure

637. Authorization holder shall specify the dose constraint for occupational exposure, as well as the exposure of outside workers (Article 67, paragraph 1). Dose constraint in case of public exposure is determined for a single dose that a member of the public receives in the event of planned exposure (paragraph 2). Dose constraint in case of medical exposure shall pertain only regarding the protection of carers, comforters and volunteers taking part in medical and biomedical research (paragraph 3).[803]

638. Individual exposure for non-medical imaging purposes shall be conducted only with the previously obtained consent form the Directorate (Article 69, paragraph 1).[804] Preliminary to the introduction of a new class of radiation practice, the Directorate shall give consent to the use thereof in terms of exposure to ionizing radiation as justified based on the information submitted by the legal entity or entrepreneur (Article 70, paragraph 1).

639. Workplaces shall be classified as controlled areas and supervised areas (Article 72, paragraph 1). Classification under paragraph 1 hereof shall be made with regard to the expected annual doses and the probability and magnitude of potential exposures (paragraph 2). The authorization holder shall classify the workplaces in accordance with paragraphs 1 and 2 hereof.[805]

640. Medical surveillance of the exposed workers shall be based on the principles governing health protection (Article 74, paragraph 1). Medical examination

---

801. The licensee for the closure of radioactive waste disposal facility shall establish and implement measures of control at the site of closed radioactive waste disposal facility (para. 2).

802. The Directorate shall specify the requirements and the method of conducting the workplace monitoring under para. 1 hereof.

803. Dose constraints under paras 1, 2 and 3 hereof shall be established only in terms of an individual effective or equivalent dose during the specified period. The Directorate shall specify the manner of determining and constraining the doses under paras 1, 2 and 3 hereof (Art. 67, paras 4 and 5).

804. The Directorate shall evaluate the justification of the exposure for non-medical imagining purposes based on the submitted application. The Directorate shall specify, together with the Ministry responsible for health, the criteria for non-medical imaging exposure and the list of justified practices (paras 2 and 3).

805. The Directorate shall specify the conditions of the classification under para. 1 hereof (Art. 72, para. 4).

of the exposed workers shall be performed prior to employment, during employment, following an emergency, and, if necessary, after cessation of work (paragraph 2). The authorization holder shall conduct medical surveillance of the exposed workers in accordance with paragraphs 1 and 2 hereof.[806]

641. The authorization holder shall be responsible for the ionizing radiation protection of the outside workers, hired either directly or through contractual agreements with their employer to carry out certain work (Article 79, paragraph 1). The authorization holder shall ensure that the system for individual radiological monitoring affords the outside workers equivalent protection to that for the exposed workers employed on a permanent basis.[807]

642. The Directorate may decide, in exceptional circumstances, to evaluate case by case, excluding emergencies, and where a specific operation so requires, to authorize individual occupational exposures of identified workers exceeding the dose limits (Article 80, paragraph 1).[808] The Directorate shall specify the requirements for the permission of the exposures under paragraph 1 hereof (paragraph 3).

643. In order to ensure the protection of individuals from the harmful effects of ionizing radiation, the licensee shall, in the facilities where the practices are performed, implement radiation and nuclear safety and security measures with particular regard to: (1) Examination and approval of the proposed siting and design of the facility from a radiation protection point of view, taking into account relevant demographic, meteorological, geological, hydrological and ecological conditions, as well as environmental protection conditions; (2) Acceptance into service of the facility subject to the requirement of adequate protection against radiation exposure or radioactive contamination; (3) Examination and approval of plans for the discharge of radioactive effluents; (4) Measures to control the access of members of the public to the facility (Article 86, paragraph 1).[809] In case of practices subject to registration, the Directorate shall specify the requirements for health protection of the members of the public under normal circumstances (paragraph 3).

644. Prior to obtaining relevant authorization, a legal entity or entrepreneur shall ensure that in the course of practice performance and commensurate with radiation exposure risk all arrangements are made for the estimation of doses for a representative person and a member of the public (Article 87, paragraph 1).[810] The authorization holder shall obtain the consent form the Directorate for every instance of deliberate discharge of radioactive effluents into the environment (Article 88, paragraph 1).

806. Ministries responsible for health and labour shall specify the scope and the schedule of the medical surveillance under para. 2 hereof (Art. 74, para. 4).
807. The outside workers shall make their own contributions to adhere to all radiation protection measures the authorization holder requires (para. 3).
808. The exposures under para. 1 hereof are limited in time, confined to certain working areas and within the maximum exposure levels that the Directorate defines for a particular case (para. 2).
809. The Directorate shall specify the conditions under para.1 hereof (para. 2).
810. The Directorate shall specify, proportionately to the risk involved, the practices requiring the evaluation of doses under para. 1 hereof and the manner of evaluating the dose (para. 2).

645. Medical exposure shall show a sufficient net benefit, weighing the total potential diagnostic or therapeutic benefits it produces, including the direct benefits to health of an individual and the benefits to society, against the individual detriment that the exposure might cause, taking into account the efficacy, benefits and risks of available alternative techniques having the same objective but involving no or less exposure to ionizing radiation (Article 81, paragraph 1).[811]

Any medical exposure shall take place under the clinical responsibility of a practitioner competent for medical exposure (Article 83, paragraph 1).[812]

E. Authorization for Performing Operations of Radiation Protection

646. A legal entity or an entrepreneur shall submit to the Directorate the application for a licence for moderate-risk radiation practice, high-risk radiation practice or a nuclear activity (Article 42, paragraph 1). In addition to the application under paragraph 1 hereof, the applicant shall submit: (1) confirmation that the general and particular conditions under Article 39 hereof have been fulfilled and (2) confirmation that radiation and nuclear safety and security measures have been implemented (paragraph 2).[813] In case of high-risk radiation practice, it is necessary to obtain consent from the Directorate for the initial Safety Analysis Report (paragraph 4).[814]

647. The Directorate shall bring a decision on issuing *the licence*[815] *for moderate-risk radiation practice performance* after affirming that all requirements under Article 42 hereof have been fulfilled (Article 47, paragraph 1).[816] In addition

811. Medical exposure shall be such that all doses are kept as low as reasonably achievable consistent with the required medical information, taking into account economic and societal factors (Art. 82, para. 1).
812. In terms of medical practices and pursuant to the fundamental principles of radiation protection under Art. 29 hereof, the Directorate shall specify the following: (1) protection measures for persons using radiation sources in medicine; (2) protection measures for patients including justification and optimization of exposure; (3) the type and the scope of procedures necessary to perform a radiation practice in medicine; (4) training and education of persons taking part in medical exposure; (5) criteria for technical specifications and functionality of radiation generators or devices with integrated radioactive sources; (6) protection measures for particularly important groups; (7) measures relating to accidental and unintended medical exposures; (8) method of evaluating the level of medical exposure; (9) radiation safety and security measures in medicine; (10) special measures necessary for medical radiation practice performance (Art. 85).
813. The implementation of radiation and nuclear safety and security measures shall be confirmed based on the Safety Analysis Report, Radiation Protection Programme and other documentation specified by the Directorate (para. 3).
814. The licensee shall report to the Directorate, without undue delay, and within eight days the latest, any change in data on the fulfilment of conditions that served as the basis for licence issuance (para. 5).
815. *Licence* means permission granted in a document by the competent authority to carry out a practice in accordance with specific conditions laid down in that document (Art. 5, point 44).
816. The Directorate shall issue the decision under para. 1 hereof within sixty days of duly submitted application (para. 2). The licence under para. 1 hereof shall enter into force on the day of delivery (para. 5). The licensee under para. 1 hereof, sixty days prior to the termination of the licence at the latest, shall submit to the Directorate the application for its extension (para. 6).

to the licence to perform a moderate-risk radiation practice, the Directorate shall issue a decision on the use of radiation sources (paragraph 3).[817]

648. The Directorate shall bring a decision on issuing *the licence for a high-risk radiation practice performance* after affirming that all requirements stipulated by Article 42 hereof have been fulfilled (Article 48, paragraph 1). The applicant for the performance of a high-risk radiation practice shall establish, maintain and implement the integrated system of management.[818] The Directorate shall issue a decision within ninety days of the day of duly submitting the application (paragraph 5).[819]

649. In addition to the licence to perform a high-risk radiation practice, the Directorate shall issue the decision on the use of radiation sources (paragraph 8).[820] The licensee for the performance of a high-risk radiation practice shall submit to the Directorate the application for the extension of the licence within ninety days prior to its termination at the latest (Article 48, paragraph 9).[821]

650. The Directorate shall bring a decision on issuing *the licence for the performance of a nuclear activity* after affirming that all requirements under Article 42 hereof have been fulfilled (Article 49, paragraph 1). The applicant for nuclear activity performance shall establish, maintain and implement the integrated system of management.[822] The decision under paragraph 1 hereof shall be issued within 180 days of duly submitted application (paragraph 4).

In addition to the application for the licence for a nuclear activity, the applicant shall submit the consent to the assessment of the environmental effect of the project

817. The licence for a moderate-risk radiation practice shall be issued for the period of ten years except the licence for a moderate-risk radiation practice – trade in radiation sources and transport of dangerous goods Class 7 ADR/RID/ADN (radioactive material) which is issued for the period of three years (para. 4).
818. In addition to verifying that the requirements under paras 1 and 2 hereof have been met, a legal entity or an entrepreneur shall submit the consent from the Ministry of Interior to the Security Plan, pursuant to this Law (para. 3). Provisions under para. 3 hereof shall not pertain to the applicants for the licence for practices associated with radiation source generators (para. 4).
819. The licence for the performance of a high-risk radiation practice shall be issued for the period of five years, except the licence for high-risk radiation practices of trade in radiation sources and transport of dangerous goods Class 7 ADR/RID/ADN (radioactive material) which is issued for the period of three years (para. 6). The licence under para. 1 hereof enters into force on the day of delivery (para. 7).
820. The decision to issue the licence for the performance of a high-risk radiation practice shall be published in the Official Gazette of the Republic of Serbia (para. 9).
821. The licence for the performance of a high-risk radiation practice with unsealed sources and sources of categories I and II shall expire, *inter alia*, on the day of issuing the licence for a radiation facility decommission (para. 10).
822. In addition to verifying that the requirements under paras 1 and 2 hereof have been met, a legal entity or an entrepreneur, pursuant to this Law, shall submit the consent from the Ministry of Interior to the Security Plan (para. 3). The licence under para. 1 hereof enters into force on the day of delivery (para. 8).

from the Ministry responsible for environmental protection pursuant to a special law (paragraph 5).[823]

F. Obligations of the Licence Owner Towards Occupationally Exposed Persons

651. Authorization holder shall bear prime responsibility for radiation and nuclear safety and security. Authorization holders shall be responsible for all activities conducted by legal entities, physical entities and entrepreneurs they engage and whose practices can affect radiation and nuclear safety and security (Article 34, paragraphs 1 and 2).[824] Authorization holder shall ensure that radiation doses for exposed workers, apprentices, students and the public, as well as the impact of radiation on the environment, are, in terms of social and economic factors, as low as reasonably practicable (paragraph 4).[825]

652. The obligations of the Authorization holder are prescribed by Article 36 of the Law. Authorization holder is obliged to: (1) apply the fundamental principles of radiation and nuclear safety; (2) take all necessary steps to protect people's health and the environment from the harmful effect of ionizing radiation, now and in future, by keeping the exposure level below the specified limits, and take all reasonable steps to minimize, now and in future, the harmful effect on the public; (3) plan and implement technical and organizational measures necessary to ensure the adequate level of radiation and nuclear safety and security; (4) prepare and implement the plan in case of emergency in accordance with the Law; (5) keep relevant records and report to the Directorate on emergency events in accordance with the Law; (6) ensure compliance with the prescribed dose limits and monitor the exposure of workers to ionizing radiation; (7) obtain adequate financial and human resources with adequate qualifications and competences necessary to conduct the prescribed radiation and nuclear safety and security measures when conducting practices; (8) ensure that their subcontractors, whose activities can affect radiation and nuclear safety and security, throughout the practice performance provide for required staffing with appropriate qualifications and competences necessary to carry out their activities; (9) provide for continuous education and training of persons participating in the practice performance; (10) provide for adequate financial resources to handle disused radiation sources, radioactive waste management, decommissioning and liability in case of radiological or nuclear damage; (11) enable the inspectors of the Directorate to carry out their work without impediment and to have

823. The decision that serves as the basis for issuing the licence for a nuclear activity shall be published in the Official Journal of the Republic of Serbia (para. 6). The licence for a nuclear activity performance shall be issued for the period of ten years except the licence for the nuclear activity – trial run of a nuclear facility that shall be issued for the period of two years (para. 7). The licensee for a nuclear activity performance shall submit to the Directorate the application for the extension of the licence within 180 days prior to its termination at the latest (para. 9).

824. The responsibilities under paras 1 and 2 hereof cannot be delegated (para. 3).

825. Authorization holder shall be responsible for the safety and security of the facility where the practice is performed even if the authorization has expired, as long as the facility, the site, and the parts thereof are not released from the regulatory control (para. 5).

access to the facilities and sites where the practice is conducted; (12) not modify the manner of the performance of the authorized practices in a way that could affect the protection of workers, the public or the environment without previously notifying and obtaining the appropriate authorization from the Directorate, and; (13) provide, upon the request of the Directorate or in line with the requirements, all information regarding the practice performance that the Directorate deems necessary or relevant for radiation and nuclear safety and security (paragraph 1).[826]

653. Pursuant to the Article 78, in the course of practice, the authorization holder shall provide for the exposed workers, persons engaged in emergency response, persons engaged in remediation activities, students and apprentices, and workers exposed to radon at their workplace, the following: (1) prior evaluation to identify ionizing radiation risk; (2) optimization of radiation protection in all working conditions, including occupational exposures as a consequence of practices involving medical exposures; (3) classification of exposed workers into different categories; (4) monitoring relating to the different areas and working conditions, including, where necessary, individual monitoring; (5) medical surveillance; (6) education and training; (7) the undertaking to inform the exposed workers on: (1) the radiation health risks involved in their work; (2) the general radiation protection procedures and precautions to be taken; (3) the radiation protection procedures and precautions connected with the operational and working conditions of both the practice in general and each type of workstation or work to which they may be assigned; (4) the relevant parts of the emergency response plans and procedures; (5) the importance of complying with the technical, medical and administrative requirements; (6) the obligation timely to inform the employer on pregnancy or breastfeeding; (7) availability of the results of the individual monitoring (Article 78, paragraph 1).[827]

654. According to Article 90 of the Law, in the course of practice performance and for the purpose of ensuring the control of the exposure of the members of the public and the public, the authorization holder shall carry out the following tasks: (1) achieve and maintain an optimal level of protection of members of the public; (2) accept into service the adequate equipment and procedures for measuring and assessing the exposure of the members of the public and radioactive contamination of the environment; (3) regularly check the efficiency and maintenance of the equipment under item 2) and ensure regular calibration of measuring instruments; (4) seek advice from a radiation protection expert in the performance of the tasks under items (1), (2) and (3), if necessary.[828]

655. Systematic X-ray survey of the population shall be prohibited, except in exceptional cases, when the Ministry in charge of health care prescribes such

826. The Directorate shall specify the requirements under para. 1 hereof (para. 2).
827. Responsibilities of the authorization holder under para. 1 hereof are duly applied to the protection of volunteers as well (para. 2).
828. The Directorate shall specify the authorization holder's tasks in terms of ionizing radiation protection for the public (Art. 90, para. 2).

measure, with the approval of the Agency on the fulfilment of protection measures concerning systematic x-ray survey of the population (Article 45, paragraph 1).

G. Radiation and Nuclear Safety

656. In this chapter, Law regulates following issues: fundamental principles of radiation and nuclear safety (Article 66); (1) Radiation Safety (Articles 67–71); Professional Exposure (Articles 72–80); Medical Exposure (Articles 81–85); Public Exposures (Articles 86–98); Services and Experts (Articles 99–104); Radioactive Sources (Articles 105–111); (2) Nuclear Safety, including construction of nuclear facility, nuclear facility operation, decommissioning (Articles 112–137); (3) Remediation (Articles 155–158); (4) Safety of Radioactive Waste And Spent Nuclear Fuel Management (Articles 159–176); and (5) Control of Transboundary Shipments of Radioactive Waste and Spent Nuclear Fuel (177–181).

The Government, based on previously obtained consent from the NA, shall decide on the construction of a nuclear facility, except for a mobile radioactive waste processing unit (Article 124, paragraph 1). The applicant for the decision on a nuclear facility construction shall obtain and submit to the Government, together with the application, the following: (1) consent to the intention to construct a nuclear facility under Article 116 hereof;[829] (2) licence for a nuclear facility design under Article 120 hereof;[830] (3) consent for the reports on a nuclear facility site selection and a nuclear facility design under Articles 119[831] and 120 hereof.[832]

657. Design of a nuclear facility, except mobile radioactive waste processing unit, shall be performed only with the previously obtained consent from the Directorate to the report on the nuclear facility site selection under Article 119, paragraph 2 hereof (Article 121, paragraph 1).[833] The Directorate shall specify the requirements for a nuclear facility design, and the scope and the content of a nuclear facility design (paragraph 6).

658. The licensee for a nuclear activity shall implement and maintain an integrated system of management. The licensee for a nuclear activity performance shall

829. The Government of the Republic of Serbia shall give its consent for the intention to change the purpose of the existing facility into a nuclear facility (Art. 116, para. 2).

830. The licensee for a nuclear facility siting, prior to a nuclear facility design, shall obtain the licence for a nuclear facility design pursuant to Art. 42 hereof (Art. 120, para. 1).

831. The licensee for performing a nuclear facility siting shall obtain the consent from the Directorate on the report on the nuclear facility site selection after conducting the analyses under Art. 118, para. 1 hereof. The Directorate shall issue the consent under para. 1 hereof within sixty days of the day of the duly submitted application (Art. 119, paras 1 and 2).

832. The licensee for a nuclear facility siting, prior to a nuclear facility design, shall obtain the licence for a nuclear facility design pursuant to Art. 42 hereof (Art. 120, para. 1).

833. The licensee for a nuclear facility design shall draft the initial decommissioning plan during the design stage for all nuclear facilities, i.e., the initial closure plan for radioactive waste disposal facilities pursuant to this Law. Design of a nuclear facility, except a mobile radioactive waste processing unit, shall be in line with the regulations governing planning and construction of facilities (paras 4 and 5).

take measures to improve and develop nuclear safety and nuclear security culture by implementing the integrated system of management (Article 115, paragraphs 1 and 2).[834]

659. Nuclear facility, except mobile radioactive waste processing unit, can be constructed only on the site with a spatial and urbanistic plan, issued construction permit and other documentation pursuant to the laws governing urban planning and construction and the assessment of the environmental effect. Nuclear facility has to be constructed in a manner so that its decommissioning can be conducted in a safe and secure manner (Article 127, paragraphs 1 and 2).[835]

660. The licensee for a nuclear facility construction, prior to the nuclear facility commissioning, shall obtain the licence for trial run of a nuclear facility in accordance with Article 42 hereof.[836] The applicant for the licence for trial run of a nuclear facility shall submit to the Directorate, together with the application, the Trial Run Programme (Article 128, paragraphs 1 and 2).[837]

661. Trial run of a nuclear facility consists of two stages: (1) non-nuclear testing (before the introduction of nuclear or certain types of radioactive material) and (2) nuclear testing (after the introduction of nuclear or certain types of radioactive material) (Article 129, paragraphs 1 and 2).[838]

662. Nuclear facilities which are recommissioned after cessation or reconstructions and modifications due to changes in operational technology are subject to Articles 128, 129, 130 and 131 hereof (Article 132).

834. The Directorate shall specify the measures and requirements for the establishment of the integrated system of management (Art. 115, para. 3).
835. The licensee for nuclear facility construction shall ensure that all structures, systems and components are constructed, installed, reviewed and tested in accordance with the applicable standards and regulations throughout all stages of construction. The Directorate shall specify the requirements for a nuclear facility construction (paras 3 and 4).
836. A legal entity or an entrepreneur shall submit to the Directorate the application for a licence for moderate-risk radiation practice, high-risk radiation practice or a nuclear activity. In addition to the application under para. 1 hereof, the applicant shall submit: (1) confirmation that the general and particular conditions under Art. 39 hereof have been fulfilled; and (2) confirmation that radiation and nuclear safety and security measures have been implemented. The implementation of radiation and nuclear safety and security measures shall be confirmed based on the Safety Analysis Report, Radiation Protection Programme and other documentation specified by the Directorate. In case of high-risk radiation practice, it is necessary first to obtain the consent from the Directorate to the initial Safety Analysis Report. The licensee shall report to the Directorate, without undue delay, and within eight days the latest, any change in data on the fulfilment of conditions that served as the basis for licence issuance (Art. 42).
837. The licence for a nuclear facility trial run shall be terminated, *inter alia*, with the issuance of the licence for a nuclear facility operation (para. 3).
838. The licensee for a nuclear facility trial run shall make use of the trial run period to confirm the quality of completed and installed systems, structures and components relevant for the safety and security (Art. 129, para. 3). The Directorate shall specify the requirements for trial run of a nuclear facility (para. 6).

663. The licensee for a nuclear facility trial run shall obtain the licence for a nuclear facility operation pursuant to Article 42 hereof. Before nuclear facility operation is licensed, the Directorate shall carry out the inspection, review and assessment of: (1) implementation of radiation and nuclear safety and security measures; (2) results of trial run tests; (3) operational conditions an limits; (4) operating instructions and procedures; (5) human resources ensuring safe and secure performance of the activities; (6) arrangements for emergency preparedness and response (Article 132, paragraphs 1 and 2).[839]

664. The licensee for a nuclear facility operation shall ensure that: (1) nuclear facility is operated within the operational limits and conditions established by the Safety Analysis Report; (2) in-service inspection, surveillance and testing of structures, systems and components relevant for safe operation of the facility are established and implemented; (3) the maintenance programme for the structures, systems and components relevant for safe operation of the facility is established and implemented; (4) review and analysis of any changes in the procedures and the integrated system of management, and changes in the structures, systems and components important for the safety of the facility are implemented before submitting the application for modification of the decision on the issuance of the licence to the Directorate and pursuant to this Law; (5) the adequate number of duly competent and trained staff have been engaged and the training programme has been in place; (6) the safety and physical protection measures have been implemented and maintained during nuclear facility operation (Article 134, paragraph 1). In addition, the licensee for nuclear facility operation shall, during the operation of a nuclear facility, periodically review and update the radioactive waste management plan, the initial decommissioning plan for all nuclear facilities except for the radioactive waste disposal facility, i.e., the initial closure plan for a radioactive waste disposal facility in accordance with the Law (paragraph 2).[840]

665. Nuclear facility, except mobile radioactive waste processing unit, can be temporarily shut down due to any justified reason that was not devised by the Safety Analysis Report for a nuclear facility operation (Article 135, paragraph 1). The licensee shall ensure safe and secure management of a nuclear facility during temporary shut-down, particularly in terms of radioactive waste, spent fuel and radiation sources management, and fire protection and suppression.[841] The licensee for a nuclear facility operation shall obtain from the Directorate a consent to the nuclear facility's temporary shut-down (Article 136, paragraph 1).

839. The licence for nuclear facility operation shall be terminated, *inter alia*, on the day of the issuance of the licence for nuclear facility decommissioning (para. 3).

840. Mobile radioactive waste processing unit shall be operated only on the site that meets all requirements for safe and secure practice performance, which are determined by the analysis under Art. 118, para. 1 hereof. The Directorate shall specify the requirements for nuclear facility operation (paras 3 and 4).

841. Pursuant to the Law, the Directorate may require the licensee to submit the application for the licence for a nuclear facility trial run after its temporary shut-down. The Directorate shall specify the requirements for a temporary shut-down of a nuclear facility (paras 3 and 4).

H. Decommissioning

666. Pursuant to Article 137, the Government shall make the decision on the end state of a nuclear facility decommissioning,[842] except in case of a mobile radioactive waste processing unit at the request of the licensee for a nuclear facility decommissioning. In addition to the application, the applicant under paragraph 1 hereof shall submit to the Government a document verifying the selected end state of decommissioning as justified, and the licence for a nuclear facility decommissioning (paragraphs 1 and 2).[843]

667. Nuclear facility decommissioning serves to reduce radiation risk and to release the nuclear facility or a part thereof from regulatory control. Nuclear facility decommissioning consists of the preparation stage and actual decommissioning activities (Article 139, paragraphs 1 and 2).[844]

668. The licensee for nuclear activity, pursuant to the Law and prior to the commencement of a nuclear facility construction, shall provide for financial arrangements that will be available for decommissioning, including the management of radioactive waste arising from decommissioning activities and for the closure of a disposal facility (Article 152, paragraph 1).[845]

669. The licensee for a nuclear activity shall perform environmental radioactivity monitoring in the vicinity of the nuclear facility that the Directorate consents to (Article 153, paragraph 1). The Directorate shall specify the manner and the requirements for environmental radioactivity monitoring under paragraph 1 hereof.[846]

I. Accident Response

670. The Government of the RS shall adopt the Response Plan in case of a nuclear or radiological emergency inside or outside the territory of the RS with the objective of protecting the lives and health of the people and the environment (Article 193, paragraph 1). The Directorate, in cooperation with other competent State authorities and organizations, shall prepare the draft of the Response Plan in case of a nuclear or radiological emergency.[847]

---

842. *Decommissioning* means administrative and technical actions taken to allow the removal of some or all of the regulatory controls from a facility (Art. 5, point 11).
843. The end state of the facility can be: (1) use of the nuclear facility, site and the parts thereof without limitations; (2) limited use of the nuclear facility, site and the parts thereof; (3) limited access to the nuclear facility, site and the parts thereof (para. 3).
844. The Directorate shall specify the requirements for a nuclear facility decommissioning.
845. In case of the existing nuclear facilities, the Government shall provide for financial means to cover decommissioning costs, including the management of the resulting radioactive waste (paras 1 and 2).
846. The licensee for a nuclear activity shall provide for the financial arrangements for the radioactivity monitoring under para. 1 hereof (Art. 153, para. 3).
847. The Directorate shall specify categorization of facilities, practices and activities with radiation sources based on threat assessment and possible consequences resulting from the practices and

671. The decision to declare emergency in one part or entire territory of the RS, which results from a nuclear or radiological emergency situation, shall be made in accordance with the regulations governing emergency situations (Article 193, paragraph 4).[848]

672. According to Article 195, in compliance with the ratified international conventions and agreements, the Directorate shall inform the IAEA and the competent authorities in other countries in case of a nuclear or radiological emergency that poses a risk of radioactive contamination spreading beyond the borders of the RS, as well as in case of theft, sabotage, loss or discovery of radiation sources that could have adverse effect on the other countries.[849]

673. Pursuant to Article 192, the authorization holder shall keep, as appropriate, a recording and analysis system of emergency events involving or potentially involving accidental or unintended exposures.[850] The authorization holder shall promptly notify the Directorate of the occurrence of any significant event in connection with the performed practice and immediately take all necessary actions to eliminate or mitigate the consequences, including the initial assessment of circumstances and the effects of an emergency event and the assistance that can be provided during the implementation of protection measures.[851]

J. Radioactive Waste Management

674. Pursuant to Article 4 of the Law, 'imports of radioactive waste[852] and spent nuclear fuel of foreign origin into the territory of the RS shall be prohibited' (paragraph 5). In addition, deliberate dilution of radioactive waste in order to fulfil the criteria for the release from regulatory control shall be prohibited, too (paragraph 10).[853]

---

activities performed at these facilities including transport, loss or theft, discovery of sources outside regulatory control, radioactive contamination of unknown origin etc. The Directorate shall specify the content of the plans under para. 6 hereof. (Art. 193, paras 7 and 8).

848. Radiological or nuclear emergency management is conducted in accordance with the law governing emergency situations (para. 5).

849. The Government shall bring a decision on seeking assistance from other countries or the International Atomic Energy Agency and on providing assistance to other countries in case of a nuclear and radiological emergency (Art. 195, para. 2).

850. The authorization holder shall prepare a contingency plan in case of an emergency for facilities where radiation practices and nuclear activities are performed and the sites thereof (Art. 194, para. 1).

851. The Directorate shall specify the requirements for the system of record keeping and analysis under para. 1 hereof (Art. 192, para. 3).

852. Radioactive waste processing means chemical or physical operations on radioactive material to benefit safety and/or economy by changing the characteristics of the waste by volume reduction, removal of radionuclides from the waste and change of composition (Art. 5, point 110).

853. Control of transboundary shipments of radioactive waste and spent nuclear fuel is regulated by the provisions of Arts 177–181 of the Law.

675. Spent Fuel and Radioactive Waste Management Strategy shall be passed with the aim of planning for the implementation of the principles of responsible and safe management of spent fuel and radioactive waste (Article 10).[854]

676. General principles governing safe management of radioactive waste and spent nuclear fuel in the RS are: (1) the generation of radioactive waste shall be kept to the minimum which is reasonably practicable, both in terms of activity and volume, by means of appropriate design measures and of operating and decommissioning practices, including the recycling and reuse of materials; (2) the interdependencies between all steps in spent fuel and radioactive waste generation and management shall be taken into account; (3) radioactive waste and spent nuclear fuel shall be safely managed, including in the long-term with passive safety features; (4) implementation of radiation and nuclear safety and security measures shall follow a graded approach; (5) the costs for the management of spent fuel and radioactive waste shall be borne by those who generated such materials; (6) an evidence based and documented decision-making process shall be applied with regard to all stages of the management of spent fuel and radioactive waste (Article 159).[855]

677. The authorization holder whose practices give rise to radioactive waste or spent nuclear fuel[856] shall bear prime responsibility for safe and secure radioactive

---

854. The Strategy shall include the following: (1) review, analysis and assessment of spent fuel and radioactive waste management conditions; (2) fundamental safety principles in respect of spent fuel and radioactive waste management in accordance with the law; (3) general statutory objectives and fundamental principles in respect of spent fuel and radioactive waste management; (4) significant milestones and clear timeframes for the achievement thereof in the light of over-arching national strategy objectives; (5) inventory of all spent fuel and radioactive waste and estimates for their future quantities, including those from decommissioning, which serve to clearly indicate the location and the amount of radioactive waste and spent fuel in accordance with the appropriate radioactive waste classification; (6) concepts and technical solutions for radioactive waste and spent fuel management from generation to disposal; (7) concepts or plans for the post-closure period of a disposal facility's lifetime, including the period during which appropriate controls and the means to be employed to preserve knowledge of that facility in the longer term are retained; (8) research, development and demonstration activities that are needed in order to implement solutions for the management of spent fuel and radioactive waste; (9) responsibility for the implementation of the national programme and the key performance indicators to monitor progress towards implementation; (10) assessment of the national programme costs and the underlying basis and hypotheses for that assessment, which must include a profile over time; (11) financing scheme and programme of the strategy; (12) means and measures for making necessary information available to workers and the public so as to provide their full participation in the decision-making process; (13) agreements concluded with other States, if any, on spent fuel and radioactive waste management, including those on the use of radioactive waste disposal facilities; (14) manner and schedule in respect of reporting on Strategy realization.

855. The Republic of Serbia shall provide for safe and secure storing of radioactive waste, disused radiation sources and spent nuclear fuel in the centralized storage. The Republic of Serbia shall make arrangements for the safe and secure disposal of radioactive waste, disused radiation sources and spent nuclear fuel (paras 2 and 3).

856. Stages of radioactive waste and spent nuclear fuel management are as follows: (1) generation and collection; (2) characterization; (3) keeping; (4) radioactive waste processing or spent nuclear fuel reprocessing; (5) storing; (6) disposing (Art. 162, para. 1). The Directorate shall specify the requirements for radioactive waste and spent nuclear fuel management, the type of packaging and markings (Art. 162, para. 4).

waste and spent nuclear fuel management until its delivery to the centralized storage, processing or reprocessing facility, or radioactive waste or spent nuclear fuel disposal facility (Article 161, paragraph 1).[857]

678. In accordance with Article 163 of the Law, the authorization holder shall: (1) collect, record and keep radioactive waste and spent nuclear fuel in an appropriate way and in accordance with the requirements and deliver it to the licensee for the operation of the nuclear facility for processing or reprocessing, storage or disposal of radioactive waste and spent nuclear fuel; (2) ensure that the facilities and premises where the radioactive waste and spent nuclear fuel is collected, recorded and kept fulfil all technical requirements, and radiation and nuclear safety and security measures; (3) implement the measures to prevent the radioactive waste and spent nuclear fuel from contaminating the environment.[858]

K. Transport of Dangerous Goods Class 7 ADR/RID/ADN (Radioactive Material)

679. The transport of dangerous goods class 7 ADR/RID/ADN (radioactive material) in the RS shall be conducted in accordance with the Law, the regulations governing the transport of dangerous goods, and ratified international conventions and agreements (Article 203).[859]

680. Transport of dangerous goods Class 7 ADR/RID/ADN (radioactive material) in the RS shall be conducted with the previously obtained permit for transport that is issued by the Directorate (Article 205, paragraph 1).[860]

681. The Directorate shall issue the permit for transport of dangerous goods under paragraph 1 hereof at the request of the consignor or the consignee, i.e., the

857. The licensee for the operation of facility for storage, processing or reprocessing and disposal of radioactive waste and spent nuclear fuel shall bear prime responsibility for the safe and secure management of stored, processed, reprocessed and disposed radioactive waste or spent nuclear fuel (Art. 161, para. 2).

858. Other obligations are also prescribed, which include the following: Generation and Collection of Radioactive Waste and Spent Nuclear Fuel (Art. 164), Temporary Keeping of Radioactive Waste and Spent Nuclear Fuel (Art. 165), Characterization of Radioactive Waste and Spent Nuclear Fuel (Art. 166), Classification of Radioactive Waste (Art. 167), Processing of Radioactive Waste (Art. 168), Reprocessing of Spent Nuclear Fuel (Art. 169), Storage of Radioactive Waste and Spent Nuclear Fuel (Art. 170), Disposal of Radioactive Waste or Spent Nuclear Fuel (Art. 171), Radioactive Waste and Spent Nuclear Fuel Acceptance Criteria (Art. 172), Release of Radioactive Waste from Regulatory Control (Art. 173), Radioactive Waste and Spent Nuclear Fuel Management Plan (Art. 174), Financial Arrangements for Radioactive Waste and Spent Nuclear Fuel Management (Art. 175) and Record Keeping of Radioactive Waste and Spent Nuclear Fuel (Art. 176).

859. Authorization for Transport of Dangerous Goods Class 7 ADR/RID/ADN (radioactive material) is regulated by Art. 204 of the Law.

860. The permit for transport of dangerous goods under para. 1 hereof shall be issued for a single or multiple transport (Art. 205, para. 2). The Directorate shall issue the permit for transport under para. 2 hereof based on fulfilment of the requirements and in accordance with the provisions of ratified international agreements (Art. 205, para. 5).

organizer of the transport having the authorization for the transport of dangerous goods under Article 204, paragraph 3 hereof[861] (Article 205, paragraph 3).[862]

682. The permit under paragraph 5 hereof shall contain: (1) Information on the manufacturer, consignor, carrier and consignee; (2) UN number of dangerous goods, data and certificates prescribed by ADR/RID/ADN; (3) Information on the type, volume, chemical and physical features of dangerous goods, as well as the type of packaging, portable pressure vessels or tanks for the transport of dangerous goods; (4) Tachograph; (5) Point of upload and unload of goods; (6) Point of start and anticipated end of transport; (7) Information about the vehicle and the driver of dangerous goods in road transport; (8) Time and place intended for rest; (9) Authorization from the competent authority in the neighbouring country allowing import or transit; (10) The name of exit and entry border crossings (Article 205, paragraph 6).[863]

L. Liability of a Licensee for Nuclear Damage

683. In accordance with The Law on Ratification of Vienna Convention on Civil Liability for Nuclear Damage (the Law on Vienna Convention) and in accordance with this Law, the licensee for a nuclear activity performance shall be liable for nuclear damage arising from a nuclear emergency event, based on the evidence that such damage occurred in the nuclear facility of the licensee (Article 207, paragraph 1).[864] In addition, the Law regulates the following issues: Insurance Coverage for Nuclear Damage (Article 208), Nuclear Damage Compensation Period (Article 209), and Claim for Nuclear Damages and Court Jurisdiction (Article 210).

684. Regulatory inspectional supervision over the implementation of provisions of the Law and pertaining subsidiary legislation shall be performed by the Directorate through the inspector for radiation and nuclear safety and security (hereinafter 'the inspector'), within the remit established by the Law (Article 211, paragraph 1).[865]

---

861. The Directorate shall issue the decision on registration, i.e., licence for the practice of transport of dangerous goods Class 7 ADR/RID/ADN (radioactive material) upon confirmation that all prescribed conditions under Arts 39 and 42 hereof have been fulfilled (Art. 204, para. 3).
862. Further to the application under para. 3 hereof, the authorization holder for the transport of dangerous goods shall submit to the Directorate all prescribed documentation as well (Art. 205, para. 4).
863. If the application is submitted for multiple transport permits, it is not necessary to provide data under para. 6, items 9 and 10 hereof (para. 7). The Directorate shall specify the documentation required for the issuance of the permit under para. 6 hereof (para. 8).
864. Liability of the licensee under para. 1 hereof shall be limited to the amount of USD 5 million for each nuclear accident and shall not include interests or expenses awarded by the court in nuclear damage liability lawsuits (para. 2). Liability for nuclear damage caused by nuclear material that has been stolen, lost, jettisoned or abandoned shall rest on the licensee that last exercised the control of such material (para. 3).
865. Unless this Law states otherwise, inspectional supervision is subject to a special law governing inspectional supervision (Art. 211, para. 2). Inspectional supervision is conducted according to the

II. Law on Prohibiting Construction of Nuclear Power Plants

685. Another law that should be mentioned is the Law on Prohibiting Construction of Nuclear Power Plants in FRY (OJ FRY, No. 12/95, OJ RS, No. 85/05) now in Serbia. It is a very concise legal Act containing only five Articles, which forbids construction of nuclear power plants, installations for production of nuclear fuel and installations for treatment of used nuclear fuel (Article 1). It does not forbid scientific and research activities, mining and geological research, geological seismic research and educational activities (Article 2).[866]

III. Other Relevant Legislation

686. Based on the Law on Radiation and Nuclear Safety and Security (OJ RS, Nos 95/18 and 10/19)., the following by-laws were adopted:

- Statute of the Directorate for Radiation and Nuclear Safety and Security of Serbia (OJ RS, Nos 9/19, 127/21, 30/22).
- Rulebook on the decommissioning of nuclear facilities (OJ RS, Nos 30/22, 81/23).
- Rulebook on notification of intention and issuance of authorization for radiation activities (OJ RS, Nos 30/22, 81/23).
- Rulebook on the management of radioactive waste and spent nuclear fuel (OJ RS, No. 127/21).
- Rulebook on the method and procedure of selection, the right and amount of compensation, and the terms and methods of work of the members of the Commission for determining the justification of new radiation activity (OJ RS, No. 127/21).
- Rulebook on the issuance of authorizations for the performance of protection against ionizing radiation (OJ RS, Nos 127/21, 81/23, 97/23 – correction).
- Rulebook on conditions for categorization of radiation activities (OJ RS, Nos 94/19, 133/21, 30/22, 113/22, 81/23).

687. In line with the Law on Ionized Radiation Protection and Nuclear Safety, the Rulebook on the Programme for Systematic Examination of Radioactivity in Environment (OJ RS, No. 100/2010 of 28 December 2010) has been adopted.[867]

Annual Inspectional Supervision Plan that shall be published on the website of the Directorate until 31 December of the current year for the following year (Art. 211, para. 3).

866. The criminal law provisions contained in Art. 3 of the Law have ceased to apply (*see* Art. 431, para. 2 of the Criminal Code – 85/2005).

867. Regulations adopted on the basis of the previously valid Law on Ionizing Radiation Protection and Nuclear Safety (OJ RS, Nos 36/2009 and 93/2012) shall be applied until the adoption of regulations on the basis of new Law (Art. 240 of the Law on Radiation and Nuclear Safety and Security, OJ RS, Nos 95/18 and 10/19).

688. Following by-laws are adopted on the base of the Law on Ionized Radiation Protection and on Nuclear Safety (OJ RS, Nos 36/09 and 93/12), and they are applied until the adoption of regulations on the basis of new law:

- Regulation on establishing the Action Plan in the event of an accident (OJ RS, No. 30/18).
- Regulation on determining the Programme of Nuclear Safety and Security (OJ RS, No. 39/14).
- Regulation on the security measures of nuclear facilities and nuclear materials (OJ RS, No. 39/14).
- Decision on the establishment of the Agency for Protection against Ionizing Radiation and Nuclear Safety of Serbia (OJ RS, Nos 76/09, 113/13, 62/18).
- Rulebook on the control of radioactivity of goods during import, export, and transit (OJ RS, Nos 86/19, 90/19 – correction, 55/23).
- Rulebook on the limits of radionuclide content in drinking water, foodstuffs, animal feed, medicines, items of general use, construction materials, and other goods placed on the market (OJ RS, No. 36/18).
- Rulebook on the form and appearance of the official identification of inspectors for protection against ionizing radiation: (OJ RS, Nos 44/14, 81/15 – other rulebooks).
- Rulebook on the use of ionizing radiation sources in medicine (OJ RS, No. 1/12).
- Rulebook on Notification and Registration of Radiation Sources (OJ RS, Nos 25/11, 50/18).
- Rulebook on procedure of keeping records of nuclear materials (OJ RS, No. 27/11).
- Rulebook for Establishing Programme of Additional Training and Specialized Education of Occupationally Exposed Persons and Persons Responsible for Implementation of Radiation Protection Measures (OJ RS, No. 31/11).
- Rulebook on the performance of nuclear activities (OJ RS, No. 37/11).
- Rulebook on conditions for obtaining licence to perform nuclear activity (OJ RS, No. 37/11).
- Rulebook on Limits of Radioactive Contamination of People, Working and Living Environment and Ways of Performing Decontamination (OJ RS, No. 38/11).
- Rulebook on Limits of Exposure to Ionizing Radiation and Measurements for Assessment of the Exposure Levels (OJ RS, Nos 86/11, 50/18).
- Rulebook on Radioactivity Control of Goods During the Import, Export and Transit (OJ RS, Nos 44/11, 86/19-other rulebook, 90/19 – correction of other rulebook).
- Rulebook on radioactive water management (OJ RS, No. 60/11).
- Rulebook on Conditions for Obtaining Licence to Perform Radiation Practices (OJ RS, Nos 61/11, 101/16, 44/18 – other law, 50/18, 30–22-other rulebook).
- Rulebook for Establishing Programme for Early Warning of Emergency (OJ RS, No. 70/11).
- Rulebook on the Records of Radiation Sources, Professionally Exposed Persons, Patients Exposure to Ionizing Radiation and Radioactive Waste (OJ RS, Nos 97/11, 127/21-other rulebook).

- Rulebook on Radioactivity Monitoring (OJ RS, No. 97/11).
- Rulebook on the amount of fees for issuing licences, permits, decisions, registration certificates, and certificates (OJ RS, No. 100/10).[868]

IV. International Conventions

689. Serbia is a contracting party to the following international conventions in the field of nuclear safety:

- Statute of the International Atomic Energy Agency (OJ FPRY – IT, No. 1/1958).
- Treaty banning experiments with nuclear weapons in the atmosphere of the cosmos and underwater (OJ SFRY – IT, No. 11/63).
- Treaty banning the deployment of nuclear and other weapons of mass destruction at the bottom of the sea and oceans and into their subsoil (OJ SFRY, No. 33/73).
- Vienna Convention on Civil Liability for Nuclear Damage (1963) (OJ SFRY – IT, No. 5/77).
- Convention on the Physical Protection of Nuclear Material (1979) (OJ SFRY – IT, Nos 9/85 and 4/2016).
- Convention on Early Notification of a Nuclear Accident (1986) (OJ SFRY – IT, No. 15/89).
- Treaty on the Non-Proliferation of Nuclear Weapons, (OJ SFRY, No. 10/70).
- Statute of the IAEA (OJ SFRY, No. 01/58).
- Convention on Assistance in the Case of a Nuclear Accident or Radiological Emergency, (OJ SFRY – IT, No. 04/91).
- Comprehensive Nuclear Test Ban with Protocol CTBT (OJ SM – IT, No. 4/04).
- International Convention for the Prevention of Nuclear Terrorism (OJ SCG – IT, No. 2/2006).
- Agreement between the Government of the Republic of Serbia and the Government of the Russian Federation Concerning Cooperation on the Import of Irradiated Nuclear Fuel from a Research Reactor into the Russian Federation (OJ RS – IT, No. 105/09).
- Agreement between the Government of Hungary and the Government of the Republic of Serbia for the Early Exchange of Information in the Event of Radiological Emergency (OJ RS – IT, No. 19/15).
- Convention on the Safety of Spent Fuel Management and on the Management of Radioactive Waste Management (OJ RS – IT, No. 10/2017).

868. In addition, regulations adopted based on previously valid federal laws in the field of protection against ionizing radiation, which has not been legally repealed are the following: Decision on the application of foreign standards when testing the effectiveness of molecular and organic iodine retention on impregnated activated carbon for special purpose filters (OJ RS, Nos 9/1986, 34/1986); Rulebook on intervention and derived intervention levels and measures for the protection of the population, domestic animals, and agriculture (veterinary, plant production, and water management) in an extraordinary event (OJ SRJ, No. 18/1992).

- Nuclear Safety Convention (OJ RS – IT, No. 10/2017).
- Additional Protocol between the Republic of Serbia and the International Atomic Energy Agency with the Agreement between the Socialist Federal Republic of Yugoslavia and the International Atomic Energy Agency on the application of guarantees regarding the Non-Proliferation Treaty (OJ RS – IT, No. 10/2018).[869]

690. 'On nuclear energy, nuclear security and radiation protection, Serbia's legislation is partially in line with the *acquis*. ... The Serbian public utility 'Nuclear Objects' has yet to finalize the licensing of two old storage facilities, which expired in November 2019, two nuclear research reactors, and an abandoned uranium mine. The new radioactive waste processing facility received the trail run license.'[870]

V. Non-ionizing Radiation

A. The Law on Protection from Non-ionizing Radiation

691. The Law on Protection from Non-ionizing Radiation (OJ RS, No. 36/09) contains twenty-three Articles divided into the following parts: Basic Provisions (Articles 1 and 2), Principles (Article 3), Measures of Protection from Non-ionizing Radiation[871] (Articles 4–13), Supervision (Articles 14–16), Competence for Complaints Resolving (Article 17), Penal Provisions (Articles 18–20), and Transitional and Final Provisions (Articles 21–23). The Law regulates conditions and measures for protection of human health and the environment from harmful impact of non-ionizing radiation. Protection from professional exposition to sources of non-ionizing radiation is not regulated by this Law (Article 1).[872]

---

869. *See* http://www.srbatom.gov.rs/srbatomm/international-contracts/?lang=en (5.1.2024).
870. EC. 2023, 132. ' The Serbian Radiation and Nuclear Safety and Security Directorate will need to increase its number of employees to fulfil its future obligations.' *Ibid.*
871. *Non-ionizing radiations* are electromagnetic radiations that have photon energy below 12.4 eV. They include: ultraviolet radiation (wavelength 100–400 nm), visible radiation (wavelength 400–780 nm), infrared radiation (wavelength 780–1 mm), radiofrequency radiation (frequency 10 kHz–300 GHz), electromagnetic fields of low frequencies (frequency 0–10 kHz) and laser radiation. Non-ionizing radiation also includes ultrasound and sound that has frequency higher than 20 kHz (Art. 2, point 1).
872. Based on the Law on Protection from Non-ionizing Radiation several by-laws have been adopted. These are following: Regulation on determining the programme of systematic examination of the levels of non-ionizing radiation for the period 2017–2018 (OJ RS, No. 02/17), Rulebook on condition to be fulfilled by legal entities performing tasks of systematic examination of the levels of non-ionizing radiation, and the manner and methods of systematic examination in the environment (OJ RS, No. 104/09), Rulebook on the sources of non-ionizing radiation of special interest, types, sources, manner and period of their examination (OJ RS, No. 104/09), Rulebook on the contents of records of the sources of non-ionizing radiation of special interest (OJ RS, No. 104/09), Rulebook on the limits of exposure to non-ionizing radiation (OJ RS, No. 104/09), Rulebook on the content and appearance of the form of the report on systematic examination of the levels of non-ionizing radiation in the environment (OJ RS, No. 104/09), and Rulebook on the conditions to be fulfilled by legal entities performing tasks of examination of the levels of sources of non-ionizing radiation in the environment (OJ RS, No. 104/09).

B. Principles

692. Non-ionizing radiation protection is based on the following fundamental principles:

(1) *principle of prohibition* – exposition to non-ionizing radiation above prescribed limit and every unnecessary exposition are not allowed;
(2) *principle of proportionality* – conditions and permissibility of use of sources of non-ionizing radiation of special interest are determined and rated according to the benefit their use represents for the society, in relation to potential risks of harmful impact caused by their use, and taking into account the level and duration of exposition of population in each specific case, age and state of health of exposed population, method, time and place of use of such source, presence of other sources with different frequencies, as well as other relevant circumstances of each specific case;
(3) *principle of publicity* – data on non-ionizing radiation are accessible to the public (Article 3).

C. Measures of Protection from Non-ionizing Radiation

693. During the process of protection from non-ionizing radiation, the following measures are undertaken:

(1) regulation of limits of exposition to non-ionizing radiation;
(2) detection and measurement of levels of exposition to non-ionizing radiation;
(3) determination of conditions for use of sources of non-ionizing radiation of special interest;[873]
(4) realization of organizational, technical, financial and other conditions for implementation of protection from non-ionizing radiation;
(5) keeping evidence of sources of non-ionizing radiation of special interest;
(6) labelling sources of non-ionizing radiation of special interest and zones of dangerous radiation in the prescribed way;
(7) implementation of control and assurance of quality of sources of non-ionizing radiation of special interest in the prescribed way;
(8) application of means and equipment for protection from non-ionizing radiation;
(9) control of levels of exposition to non-ionizing radiation in the environment and control of undertaken measures of protection from non-ionizing radiation;
(10) providing material, technical and other conditions for systematic testing and monitoring of levels of non-ionizing radiation in the environment;
(11) education and professional training of staff in the field of protection from non-ionizing radiation in the environment;

873. There are 11,269 radio base stations on the territory of the Republic of Serbia, of which 266 have been declared sources of *special interest*. In 2018, 28 permits were issued for the use of non-ionizing radiation sources of *special interest*. EPA. 2019, 174.

(12) informing population about impact on health of exposition to non-ionizing radiation and measures of protection and informing on level of exposition to non-ionizing radiation in the environment (Article 4).

694. Systematic testing of levels of non-ionizing radiation in the environment is performed, aimed at detecting presence, detecting danger, informing and undertaking measures of protection from non-ionizing radiation (Article 5).[874]

695. Systematic testing of levels of non-ionizing radiation in the environment can be performed by commercial society, enterprise and other legal person if they fulfil conditions regarding staff, equipment and space.

Persons who perform systematic testing of levels of non-ionizing radiation in the environment are obliged to submit to the Ministry (and for territory of AP to the competent organ of AP) annual report on results of testing, at the latest till 31 March of the current year for previous year, and in the case of exceptional event immediately (Article 5).[875]

696. Commercial society, enterprise, other legal person and entrepreneur can use sources of non-ionizing radiation of special interest if they fulfil the following conditions: (1) if they have for the sources of non-ionizing radiation an estimate of their impact on the environment, in accordance with this Law; (2) if the level of exposition of the population does not exceed prescribed limits (Article 6, paragraph 1).[876] The entities referred to in paragraph 1 of this Article must not start the use of non-ionizing radiation source of special interest before they receive the Act on compliance with all the conditions for their use.[877]

697. Also, commercial entity, enterprise or other legal entity can execute detection of the level of non-ionizing radiation sources of special interest in the environment if they comply with the conditions regarding personnel, equipment and space

874. The Government adopts the programme systematic testing of levels of non-ionizing radiation in the environment for a period of two years (Art. 5, para. 2).

875. The Minister prescribes in detail conditions that must be fulfilled by persons who perform systematic testing of levels of non-ionizing radiation, as well as ways and methods of systematic testing of levels of non-ionizing radiation in the environment (Art. 5, para. 8).

876. Compliance with the conditions of para. 1 of this Article shall be authorized by the Minister by issuing the decision, and for the territory of the AP the competent authority of the AP (Art. 2, para. 2). However, it should be mentioned that provisions of Art. 6 of this Law do not apply to sources of non-ionizing radiation of special interest registered by the Ministry competent for defence and the Ministry of Internal Affairs. Exceptionally, provisions of Art. 6 of this Law do not apply to: (1) sources of non-ionizing radiation that are transported by railway, motor vehicles, aeroplane or by water transport, if they are technically secured so that they cannot be used nor they can generate non-ionizing radiation; and (2) sources of non-ionizing radiation that are stored or that are used for selling or in other purposes in such a state that they are not possible to be put in working function or used in a way which could represent potential danger (Art. 7).

877. The Minister prescribes: (1) limits of exposition to non-ionizing radiation and (2) sources that are regarded as sources of non-ionizing radiation of special interest, as well as the method of their testing (Art. 6, para. 6).

(Article 10). Compliance with paragraph 1 of this Article shall be determined by the Minister by issuing the decision and for the territory of the AP, the competent authority of the AP.[878]

D. Obligations of Commercial Society, Enterprise, Other Legal Person and Entrepreneur Who Use Sources of Non-ionizing Radiation of Special Interest

698. Commercial society, enterprise, other legal person and entrepreneur who use sources of non-ionizing radiation of special interest are obliged to do the following:[879]

– to keep record on these sources and to designate a person responsible for protection from non-ionizing radiation (Article 8, paragraph 1);[880]
– to organize testing of levels of their radiation in the environment (Article 9, paragraph 1);[881]
– to organize first testing of radiation of sources from paragraph 1 of this Article, before the commencement of their use, in case of increase of their number, or in case of change of conditions of their use, or in case of reconstruction of objects with sources of non-ionizing radiation.

699. Periodically, the detection of the level of the non-ionizing radiation source referred to in paragraph 1 of this Article shall be executed in the specified period of time (Article 9, paragraph 3).[882]

700. In addition to the above-mentioned commercial society, enterprise, other legal person and entrepreneur who use sources of non-ionizing radiation of special interest are obliged to keep evidence and documentation on testing of sources of non-ionizing radiation (Article 11).[883]

701. Commercial society, enterprise, other legal person and entrepreneur, that is, operator or manager, is obliged immediately, and at the latest in hours, to inform

878. The Minister shall determine other conditions that entities referred to in para. 1 of this Article shall have to comply with. The Minister, or the competent authority of the AP, shall detract the licence for detection of non-ionizing radiation sources referred to in para. 2 of this Article, if it is subsequently determined that the commercial entity, enterprise or other legal entity does not comply with the formal conditions or if it is determined that the decision is issued based on untrue or inaccurate data (Art. 10, paras 4 and 5).
879. Commercial entity, enterprise and other legal entity or entrepreneur that use the non-ionizing radiation sources are obligated to coordinate their operations with the provisions of this Law within three years of its coming into force (Art. 22).
880. The Minister shall determine in detail the contents of the record (Art. 8, para. 3).
881. Costs of the detection of the sources referred to in para. 1 of this Article shall be borne by the user of the source.
882. The Minister shall determine the types of non-ionizing radiation sources of special interest for which the detection of the level of non-ionizing radiation is obligatory, as well as the period of time for their detection (Art. 9, para. 5).
883. Public has the right to access information in accordance with this Law (Art. 11, para. 2).

the Ministry about the extraordinary event, and for the territory of AP competent organ of AP, or organ of the unit of LSG competent for activities concerning protection of the environment (Article 12).[884]

E. Supervision

702. Supervision over application of provisions of this Law and regulations adopted on the basis of this Law is performed by the Ministry. The AP performs inspectoral supervision over sources of non-ionizing radiation on the territory of AP, in accordance with this Law. The unit of LSG performs inspectoral supervision over sources of non-ionizing radiation for which the permit for construction and commencement of work has been issued by the competent organ of the unit of LSG (Article 14).[885]

---

884. The notice referred to in para. 1 of this Article shall contain particularly information on circumstances of the emergency, place, time, direct danger for human health and the short description of undertaken measures (Art. 12, para. 2).

885. EPA maintains records and prepares a database of sources of non-ionizing radiation of particular interest. *See*: http://www.sepa.gov.rs/index.php?menu=2085&id=20077&akcija=ShowAll (19.2.2024).

Chapter 8. Other Sectors

§1. Noxious Substances

703. Use and production of potentially dangerous chemicals in Serbia is one of the main hazards for the environment. The lack of financial means for renewal of technology and environmental protection, obsolete technologies and other reasons have made some installations in this sector of industry become sources of pollution. It should be added that the situation became especially bad during the UN sanctions and the 1999 NATO intervention. A number of potentially dangerous installations were bombed (especially Pancevo and Novi Sad refineries) and heavy pollution was caused, impact of which is still felt.

In 2008, 761 companies were engaged in the manufacture of chemicals and chemical products in the RS, which is 0.9% of total number of companies in non-financial business economy. The number of persons employed in this field was 24,849, which is 2.3% of persons employed in non-financial business economy. Turnover in manufacture of chemicals and chemical products in 2008 was RSD 177,124 million (EUR 1,999 million), which is a 3.0% turnover in non-financial business economy.[886]

704. In order to identify locations which present highest potential chemical risks, a Preliminary List of Seveso II Establishments was developed in 2008, including first and second-tier establishments, containing 132 companies which are obligated to develop Safety Report and Contingency Plan, that is, that are obligated to develop accident prevention policy.[887]

705. In accordance with Article 5 of the Law on Chemicals (2009), the Government established the Chemical Agency 'as an independent, developing, professional and regulatory organization performing public competences in compliance with the Law, in order to ensure administrative conditions for quality, efficient and

886. GOV RS. 2011a, p. 235. 'Export of chemicals and chemical products from the Republic of Serbia into European Union in 2008 amounted to EUR 396.1 million, in 2009 EUR 163.1 million, and in the first ten months of 2010 EUR 253.9 million. Export of chemicals and chemical products from the Republic of Serbia into EFTA in 2008 amounted to EUR 1.5 million, in 2009 EUR 1.2 million, and in the first ten months of 2010 EUR 2.8 million. Number of products (at the level 10 digit of Serbia's custom tariff) exported to European Union countries in 2009 was 389, and into EFTA countries 38.' *Ibid.*, 236.

887. These are the companies which perform different industrial activities and which may have certain types of dangerous substances in their locations in quantities that exceed the prescribed ones. Some of them are: NIS a.d. Novi Sad, organizational parts Oil Refinery in Pancevo and Oil Refinery in Novi Sad (HIP Azotara – artificial fertilizers, HIP Petrohemija – petrochemical products – Bor (Mining and Smelter Complex Bor)), Sabac (HI Zorka – artificial fertilizers, PVC, pesticides), Sremska Mitrovica ('Matroz' – pulp and paper production), Belgrade (Prva iskra Baric – basic chemicals, TPP 'Nikola Tesla' A and B), Subotica (Zorka Holding – artificial fertilizers, inorganic acids; Azotara – nitrogen and complex fertilizers), Loznica (production of pulp, synthetic fibres and plastic materials), GOV RS. 2010a, 54. The preliminary list of Seveso plants in 2022 contained a total of 112 Seveso plants, namely: 47 plants of a higher order and 65 plants of a lower order. MEP. 2023b, 14.

sound chemicals and biocidal products management'.[888] However, Agency stopped working on the adoption of Amendments to the Law on Chemicals on 25 September 2012 (OJ RS, No. 93/12). The rights and obligations of the Chemicals Agency, established by the Decision on the Establishment of the Chemicals Agency (OJ RS, No. 78/09), as well as employees, objects, equipment, archives, and registries, have been transferred to the Ministry of Energy, Development and Environmental Protection (MEDEP) (Article 17).[889]

I. Legal Regulation

706. EPL contains general provisions concerning dangerous substances.[890] Article 10 of the Law prescribes that 'sustainable management of natural values as well as the protection of the environment shall be governed by this Law, special laws and other regulations, governing', *inter alia*, 'chemicals management'.[891] Management of dangerous substances shall be carried out under the conditions and in a manner that ensures reduction of risk from their properties dangerous to the

888. Pursuant to Art. 6 of the Law on Chemicals (2009) the Chemical Agency shall be responsible for: (1) enacting of sub-legal Acts for the implementation of the Law on Chemicals and Law on Biocidal Products; (2) adopting of a list of classified substances; (3) issuing of a ruling on entry of a chemical into the Chemicals Registry and keeping that Registry; (4) keeping the integrated Chemicals Registry; (5) publishing the list of substances of very high concern; (6) conducting of notification procedure and the prior informed consent procedure for import and export of certain hazardous chemicals; (7) issuing of permits for distribution and use of particularly hazardous chemicals; (8) issuing of an approval for use of surfactants in detergents; (9) preparation and implementation of the projects for monitoring if chemicals are placed on the market and used in such a way that they do not have adverse effects on human health, environment and property; (10) publishing of the lists of active substances in biocidal products; (11) issuing of ruling on the entry of biocidal product in temporary list for delivery of Technical Dossier; (12) issuing of the authorization for placing the biocidal product on the market; (13) assessment of Technical Dossier for the biocidal product; (14) preparation of annual declarations on production, processing and use of chemicals from the lists given by the law which regulates the prohibition of the development, production, stockpiling and use of chemical weapons and their destruction, as well as annual declarations on production of discreet organic substances and conducts other tasks pursuant to that Law; (15) providing professional and administrative – technical assistance for the Joint Body for the Integrated Chemicals Management; (16) providing information and professional instructions to the economic operators, LSG units and inspectors, for the purpose of implementation of this Law and other laws under the competence of the Agency, as well as to provide professional assessment on properties and intended use of certain chemicals; (17) carrying out cooperation with the European Chemicals Agency, other countries Agencies and Secretariats of International Conventions which regulate chemical management and other international organizations dealing with different aspects of chemicals management; (18) carrying out activities of awareness raising on the effects of chemicals on human health and environment, risk reduction measures and sound use of chemicals; and (19) carrying out other activities set out in this Law, Law on Biocidal products and other laws.
889. Dismantling of the functional Chemicals Agency (and of the Green Fund) remain issues of concern, especially in relation to the overall capacity of these institutions to ensure effective implementation and enforcement of the *acquis*. EC. 2016b, p. 18.
890. Dangerous substances are 'chemicals or other substances with harmful or hazardous intrinsic properties' (Art. 3, point 21). The definition is closely linked to the definition of 'accident'. *See* Part 1 (Ch. 1 General Law IV – Integrated Pollution Prevention and Control and Risk Management).
891. Similarly, as in case of Art. 65 which stipulate that Action plans shall be made for, *inter alia*, chemicals management.

environment and human health in the process of production, storage, utilization and disposal (Article 29). Legal or natural persons managing dangerous substances are obliged to plan, organize and undertake all the necessary preventive, protective, safety and rehabilitation measures by which the risk towards the environment and human health shall be reduced to the least possible level.

707. There are a number of other provisions of the EPL that are relevant to dangerous substance issues. These provisions relate to the following: Accident Risk Management and Obligation of Natural and Legal Entities (Article 38); Conditions for Facilities' Work and Activities (Article 40); Ecological Label (Article 53); Protection from the Chemical Accident – Obligations of Operators (Article 58);[892] Content of the Policy for Accident Prevention (Article 58a); Obligation to Submit Notification (Article 59); Content of the Report of the Safety and Plan on Protection from Accident (Article 60); Submitting the Report on Safety and Plan on Protection from Accident (Article 60a); Submitting Information from the Plan on Protection from Accident (Article 60b); Public Availability, Presentation and Public Debate on the Report on Safety (Article 60c); Evidence in the Report on Safety (Article 60d); Evidence in the Plan on Protection from Accident (Article 60e);Consent on the Report on Safety and the Plan on Protection from Accident (Article 60f); Decision Prohibiting Operation or Start-Up of Seveso Installation (Article 60g); Appointment of the Special Working Group (Article 60h); Obligation of Keeping Records (Article 60i); Register of Installations and Register of Reported Accidents (Article 60j); Informing of the Accident (Article 60k); Obligations of Responsible Authorities (Article 61); Notification on Operators or Seveso Installations or Establishments the Activities of Which May Cause Chemical Accident with Transboundary Effects (Article 61a); Obligation to Submit Notification of the Responsible Authority of Other Country (Article 61b); Exceptions (Article 61c); Proclamation of the State of Endangerment (Article 62); Rehabilitation Measures and Subsidiary Liability (Article 63); Rehabilitation Plan (Article 66); and Rights and Duties of the Inspector (Article 110) and Commercial Offences (Article 116).

II. Specific Legislation

A. *Law on Chemicals*

708. The Law on Chemicals (OJ of RS, Nos 36/2009, 88/2010, 92/2011, 93/2012 and 25/2015) is the basic legal Act regulating the use of chemicals as products.

892. Legal or natural person producing, transporting, placing on the market, use, processing, storing or disposing dangerous substances is obliged to: (1) make the plan for accident prevention and update or review the same every three years, at least, in compliance with the changes in the operations of the plant, applying technology or operations, including the check-up readiness for its implementation; (2) implement preventive and other measures management of risk from accident from the plan of accident prevention; and (3) make the report on safety state which shall be available to public and, at least once in five years, like in case of changes in operation and activities of a plant, to review the report on safety state (Art. 58, para. 2).

It contains 108 Articles grouped into following groups: basic provisions (Articles 1–4); competencies of the Ministry (Articles 5 and 6); integrated management of chemicals (Articles 7 and 8); classification, packing, labelling and storage of chemicals (Articles 9–33); counsellor for chemicals (Articles 34–37); integrated Register of chemicals (Articles 38–48); limits and prohibitions of production, marketing and use of chemicals (Articles 49 and 50); import and export of certain dangerous chemicals (Articles 51–62); permits for marketing and use of extra dangerous chemicals (Articles 63–72); detergents (Articles 73–81); taxes (Article 81a); systematic detection of chemicals (Articles 82 and 83); availability of data (Articles 84 and 85); supervision (Articles 86–96); penal provisions (Articles 97–101); and transitional and final provisions (Articles 102–108).

709. This Law is regulates integrated management of chemicals[893] classification, packing, and labelling of chemicals, integrated Register of chemicals and Register of chemicals on the market, limits and prohibitions of production, marketing and use of chemicals, import and export of certain dangerous chemicals, permits for marketing and use of extra dangerous chemicals, marketing of detergents, systematic detection of chemicals, availability of data, supervision and other issues of importance for management of chemicals (Article 1).[894] The Law is based on the principle of prevention and principle that the producer, importer or further user, produces, puts in the market and uses chemicals in such a way as to avoid harmful consequences to human health and the environment (Article 2).

---

893. 'Chemical' means a substance and mixture (Art. 3, point 20).

894. Provisions of the Law do not apply to: (1) radioactive chemicals; (2) chemicals in transit; (3) transport of dangerous chemicals (Art. 4, para. 1) and the following:(1) chemicals that are regarded as waste according to provisions of the Law that regulate waste management; and (2) chemicals that are under duty supervision in the duty storage or in free zones with intent to be exported again or sent into transit, if they are not pre-fabricated on the spot (Art. 4, para. 2). Provisions of the Law that regulate recording of chemicals in the Register of Chemicals and recording of substances that arise worry in the Register of Chemicals, do not apply to chemicals which are put on the market in their final form as: (1) biocide products; (2) means for plant protection; (3) medicines and medical supplies used in human and veterinary medicine; (4) cosmetic products; (5) food, food additives and aromas; (6) animal food and animal food additives (Art. 4, para. 2). Provisions of the Law that regulate classification, packing and labelling of chemicals do not apply to chemicals:(1) that are used for scientific research and development and which are not on the market and which are kept under controlled conditions and low exposition; and (2) which are put on the market in their final form as medicines and medical supplies used in human and veterinary medicine; cosmetic products; food, food additives and aromas; animal food and animal food additives (Art. 4, para. 3). Provisions of the Law from Ch. VIII (that regulate import and export of certain dangerous chemicals) do not apply to: (1) chemical weapons and precursors for chemical weapons; (2) precursors of narcotics and psychotropic substances; (3) food and food additives; (4) animal food and additives for that food; (5) medicines and medical supplies used in human and veterinary medicine; (6) chemicals used for scientific research and development in quantity which does not have harmful impact on human health and environment, and does not exceed 10 kg for each chemical in one import (Art. 4, para. 5).

1. Competencies of the Ministry Responsible for Environmental Protection

710. The Ministry provides conditions for quality, efficient, and safe management of chemicals and biocidal products (Article 5).

Some of the responsibilities of the Ministry are the following: (1) adopt the by-laws for implementation of the Law on Chemicals and Law on Biocidal Products; (2) adopt the list of classified substances; (3) issues a decision on registration of chemicals in the Register of chemicals and water that register; (4) keeps integrated register of chemicals; (5) publish the list of substances of very high concern; (6) issues permits for performing activities of transport particularly hazardous chemicals; (7) issues licences for the use of surfactants in detergents; (8) develops and implements projects to monitor whether chemicals are placed on the market and used in such a way that they have no harmful effect on human health, the environment and property; (9) announces the list of the active substances in the biocide product; (10) adopt the decision on inclusion of the biocidal product into the Temporary List for the submission of the technical dossier; and (11) issue approvals for placing on the market of biocidal products, etc. (Article 6, paragraph 1).

2. Integrated Management of Chemicals

711. With intention to realize principles of strategic approach to the management of chemicals, to apply adequate management of chemicals in all stages of life cycle of chemicals, from production to import and dumping, as well as to contribute to sustainable development of the RS, the minister competent for the environment (minister), in accordance with regulations concerning State administration, with his/her decision establishes the joint body for integrated management of chemicals (Joint body) (Article 7, paragraph 1).[895]

712. Task of the Joint body is to prepare the integrated programme of management of chemicals and action plans for implementation of that programme, as well as implementation of programmes and action plans and coordination of activities in connection with secure management of chemicals (Article 7, paragraph 4).[896]

3. Classification, Packing, Labelling and Storage of Chemicals

713. Producer, importer or final user that puts chemicals and certain products on the market is obliged to classify them, and supplier of chemicals to label and pack

895. The Joint body is composed of representatives of State organs, in the field of the chemical management, industry, scientific research organizations and NGOs (Art. 7, para. 2).

896. The integrated programme of management of chemicals is adopted by the Government (Art. 7, para. 5).

them in accordance with this Law and regulations adopted on basis of it (Article 9, paragraph 1).[897]

714. Classification of chemicals and certain products is done on the basis of evaluation of their physical and chemical characteristics, characteristics that influence human life and health, characteristics that have an impact on the environment, as well as the established criteria of classification of different classes of danger (Article 10, paragraph 1).[898] Dangerous chemicals can be further classified in different ways depending on the impact they have on people or on the environment or on the base of the nature of the chemical effects (Article 10, paragraph 3).[899]

715. Supplier is obliged to keep evidence (record) about chemicals, especially concerning data on their identity, distributors, final users and quantity of distributed chemicals, as well as of total quantity of chemicals distributed to users during a calendar year (Article 19).[900] Apart from this, supplier is obliged to produce a safety data sheet when he/she puts on the market a dangerous chemical, chemical which contains substances identified as persistent – bio cumulative – toxic (PBT) or very persistent – very bio cumulative (vPvB) and other chemicals having characteristics described in Article 43, paragraph 3 of this Law, or to any other distributor or final user in the supply chain without charge, in Serbian language in printed or electronic form (Article 20, paragraph 1). Exporter of chemicals is obliged to present to the importer a safety data sheet, and if possible, the safety data sheet should be in the language of the importing country (Article 20, paragraph 2).[901] If the report on security of chemicals and scenario of exposition is prepared, information in safety data sheet must correspond to information from the report on security of chemicals and scenario of exposition must be enclosed in the annexe of the safety data sheet (Article 20, paragraph 4).

4. Chemicals Adviser

716. Supplier of dangerous chemicals is obliged to provide a person whose duty is to take care of correct management of chemicals (chemicals adviser) (Article 34, paragraph 1). Exceptionally, certain suppliers of dangerous chemicals are not

897. Exporter is obliged to label and pack chemicals in accordance with this Law and regulations adopted on basis of it, except in case when it is needed to label and pack chemicals in a different way, in accordance with international standards, and if the importing country wants so (Art. 9, para. 2).
898. A dangerous chemical is a chemical that belongs to at least one class of danger (Art. 10, para. 2).
899. The Ministry regulates in detail the method of classification of chemicals and certain products (Art. 10, para. 4); the list of classified substances (Art. 11, para. 3); methods of testing dangerous characteristics of chemicals (Art. 15); method of packing and labelling of chemicals and certain products (Art. 16); method of advertising chemicals (Art. 17), etc.
900. The Ministry prescribes method of evidence (record) keeping (Art. 19, para. 5).
901. Safety data sheet contains identification of chemicals, data of their characteristics, method of use, preventive measures, and measures for lessening of risk and data about the supplier of chemicals (Art. 20, para. 3). The Ministry prescribes criteria for identification of substances as PBT or vPvB, as well as precise contents of the safety data sheet (Art. 20, para. 5).

obliged to provide a chemical adviser (Article 34, paragraph 2).[902] Chemicals adviser must have appropriate professional qualification and have passed the examination for chemical adviser. Knowledge of the chemical adviser shall be tested every six years (Article 35, paragraphs 1–2).[903]

5. Integrated Register of Chemicals

717. Integrated Register of chemicals on the market of RS includes the Register of chemicals and the Register of biocide products, as well as data concerning means for herbal protection (Article 38, paragraph 1).[904]

718. In order to ensure risk control and replacement of certain substances with suitable, safer alternative substances, the Ministry shall publish the list of substances of very high concern (Article 43, paragraph 1).[905]

6. Bans and Restrictions of the Manufacturing, Placing on the Market and Use of the Chemicals

719. The Ministry prescribes, for chemicals that represent unacceptable risk for human health and the environment, limitations and prohibitions of their production, marketing and use (limitations and prohibitions) (Article 49, paragraph 1).[906]

7. Import and Export of Certain Dangerous Chemicals

720. With an intent of improving, sharing responsibility and cooperation in international trade of dangerous chemicals, in accordance with the Rotterdam Convention, concerning the procedure of giving consent on the basis of preliminary

902. The Ministry prescribes kind, sector and field of supplier's activity (Art. 34, para. 3).
903. The Ministry shall lay down the professional qualification, the training programme and the type of examination for the chemicals adviser (Art. 35, para. 3).
904. For the purpose of data exchange and integrated chemicals management, the Ministry shall keep the Integrated Chemicals Registry as an electronic database (Art. 38, para. 4). Any chemical manufactured or imported on the market of the Republic of Serbia shall be entered into the Chemicals Registry (Art. 39, para. 1).
905. The list of substances of very high concern shall consist of substances which meet the criteria for classification as carcinogenic categories 1 and 2, mutagenic categories 1 and 2, reproductive toxic categories 1 and 2, as well as of substances identified as PBT or vPvB (Art. 43, para. 2). The list of substances of very high concern shall also consist of substances which may lead to disturbance of endocrine system or have the PBT or vPvB properties, but do not meet the criteria for identification as PBT or vPvB, and it is scientifically proved that they cause significant damage to human health and to the environment (Art. 43, para. 3).
906. Regulation referred to in para. 1 of this Article shall consist of banned, i.e., allowed uses, as well as other conditions for manufacturing, placing on the market and use of substance, mixture and Article (Art. 49, para. 2).

information for certain dangerous chemicals and pesticides in international trade (Rotterdam Convention) for import and export of certain substances for which were introduced limitations and prohibitions of production, marketing and use, as well as certain combination of products that contain this substance, applied is procedure of preliminary information that is, procedure of giving consent on the basis of preliminary information (PIC procedure) (Article 51, paragraph 1). Procedure of preliminary information is applied to chemicals from the list of chemicals for procedure of preliminary information, and the PIC procedure is applied to chemicals from the list of chemicals for the PIC procedure (Article 51, paragraph 3).[907]

721. Procedure of preliminary information for export is applied by the Ministry. It sends to the competent organ of the country of import information on export of chemicals from the list of chemicals for procedure of preliminary information, that is, chemical that contains a substance from this list in such concentration that it could be, according to this Law, regarded as dangerous, as well as information on export of products which contain chemicals from the list of chemicals for PIC procedure (Article 53, paragraph 1). Exporter of chemicals and products is obliged, before the export, to lodge an application to the Ministry to undertake procedure of preliminary information, and with the application to supply information containing especially identity of chemicals, data about exporter and importer of chemicals or products, as well as data on characteristics of chemicals and on measures for minimizing of risk (Article 53, paragraph 2).

722. On the basis of information from the application of exporter of chemicals, the Ministry prepares information for importing country and applies the procedure of preliminary information. The Ministry is obliged to issue to the exporter a certificate that the procedure of preliminary information has been undertaken (Article 53, paragraph 4).[908]

723. Procedure of preliminary information for import has to be undertaken for chemicals for which production, marketing and use are prohibited or limited by regulations of the country of export. The Ministry, after receiving information on export from the competent organ of the country of export, is obliged to inform that organ that it received the information (Article 54).

907. The list of chemicals for procedure of preliminary information especially contains names of chemicals, identification numbers of chemicals, tariff number and subcategory of chemicals. The list of chemicals for PIC procedure especially contains names of chemicals, identification numbers of chemicals, tariff number and category of chemicals. The list of chemicals for procedure of preliminary information contains certain chemicals from the list of chemicals for PIC procedure. The list of chemicals for PIC procedure contains chemicals from the list of Rotterdam Convention (Art. 51, paras 4–7).

908. The Ministry prescribes procedure and time limits for procedure of preliminary information, cases when procedure of preliminary information is not needed, contents of information on export, as well as documents needed for the procedure (Art. 53, para. 5).

8. PIC Procedure

724. PIC procedure has to be undertaken for import or export of chemicals from the list of chemicals for PIC procedure or chemical that contains substance from this list in such concentration that, according to this Law, it should be labelled as dangerous (Article 55, paragraph 1). The Ministry is obliged to send to the Secretariat of the Rotterdam Convention information concerning every chemical from the list of the Rotterdam Convention. Apart from that, the Ministry is obliged to take action concerning the import of chemicals that are not on the list of the Rotterdam Convention, by asking the competent organ of the country of export, if the country prescribes preliminary concord according to the PIC procedure (Article 55, paragraphs 2–3).[909]

The exporter shall, for the chemical from the list of chemicals subject to the PIC procedure, that is, for chemical containing the substance from this list in such concentration that is labelled as hazardous pursuant to this Law, submit a request to conduct the PIC procedure to the Ministry (Article 56).[910]

The Ministry shall lay down detailed conditions and deadlines regarding the PIC procedure and content of the request for conducting the PIC procedure (Article 57).

9. Other Provisions Regarding Export and Import of Chemicals

725. Exporter of chemicals from the list of chemicals for procedure of preliminary information, or for chemicals containing substances from that list, as well as for chemicals from the list of Chemicals for PIC procedure, or for chemicals containing substances from that list, is obliged to inform the Ministry by 31 March of the current year, on quantities of exported chemicals or products during the previous year, as well as on data of the importer and on the country of import (Article 58, paragraph 1).

Importer of chemicals from the list of chemicals for procedure of preliminary information, or for chemicals containing substances from that list, as well as for chemicals from the list of chemicals for PIC procedure, or for chemicals containing substances from that list, is obliged to inform the Ministry by 31 March of the current year, on data for previous year as prescribed in Article 42, p. 1 of this Law, as well as data about the country of export (Article 58, paragraph 2). Importer of products containing chemicals from the list of chemicals for PIC procedure is obliged to

909. Response from paras 2 and 3 of this Article may be consent, consent under certain conditions or no consent, and shall be made based on the bans and restrictions set out in Art. 49 of this Law or pursuant to the Act which allows placing on the market of the chemical in accordance with the legislation regulating plant protection products or biocidal products (Art. 55, para. 4). The response referred to in paras 2 and 3 of this Article, for plant protection products, shall be made by the Ministry in cooperation with the competent authority in charge of plant protection, and for chemicals with pesticide effect with the authority in charge of those chemicals (Art. 55, para. 5).

910. By the way of derogation from para. 1 of this Article, the exporter is not obliged to submit the request for conduction of the PIC procedure for the chemicals from Rotterdam Convention List, where the Party of the Rotterdam Convention delivered its response related to that chemical to the Secretariat of that Convention (Art. 56, para. 2).

inform the Ministry by 31 March of the current year of data for previous year about the imported quantities, as well as data about the country of export.[911]

726. Exporter is obliged to inform the Ministry about the request by the competent organ of a country member of the Rotterdam Convention, for transit of chemicals from the list of Rotterdam Convention, via the territory of that country at least thirty days before the first transit occurs or eight days prior any following transit (Article 59, paragraph 1).[912]

727. Certain dangerous chemicals and products are prohibited for use and cannot be exported. The Ministry prescribes the list of dangerous chemicals and products that are prohibited for export (Article 60, paragraphs 1 and 4).[913]

728. Customs authority shall examine whether the notification procedure and/or PIC procedure has been conducted (Article 62).

10. Permits for Activities Concerning Marketing of Chemicals and for Use of Very Dangerous Chemicals

729. Marketing of certain dangerous chemicals (very dangerous chemicals) can be done only by legal persons or entrepreneurs who have permit for marketing such chemicals (Article 63, paragraph 1). Permit for marketing of very dangerous chemicals is issued to legal persons or entrepreneurs who have provided such storage of very dangerous chemicals in such a way as not to be attainable to persons who could use them in illegal purposes and who have undertaken preventive measures for secure keeping and storage of very dangerous chemicals (Article 63, paragraph 2).[914]

730. Physical persons who use very dangerous chemicals must have a permit for their use (Article 64, paragraph 1).[915]

---

911. The Ministry on the basis of data from paras 1, 2 and 3 of Art. 58 keeps evidence, in the form of electronic data basis, of imported and exported chemicals or products according to the procedure of preliminary information and PIC procedure (Art. 58, para. 4).
912. The Ministry shall forward the information on transit of the chemical to designated national authority of the Party to the Rotterdam Convention referred to in para. 1 of this Article no later than fifteen days before the first transit or prior to any subsequent transit (Art. 59, para. 2). The Ministry shall lay down the list of parties to the Rotterdam Convention requiring information concerning transit movements of chemicals and the content of this information (Art. 59, para. 3).
913. The Ministry responsible for the environment shall lay down the list of hazardous chemicals and articles subject to export ban (Art. 60, para. 4).
914. The Ministry prescribes for which very dangerous chemicals are needed permits, and for which very dangerous chemicals they are not needed (Art. 63, para. 3).
915. Permit for use of very dangerous chemicals is issued to physical person who uses them in artistic, scientific and other specific purposes, if instead of these chemicals other alternative chemicals cannot be used, if they are used and kept in a secure way, and if the person has not been sentenced to jail longer than six months (Art. 64, para. 2).

731. Permit for marketing of very dangerous chemicals to importer, producer or final user is issued by the Ministry (Article 67, paragraph 1).[916]

732. The Ministry, or the organ of a self-government unit, can withdraw permit if correct data were not given during the procedure of issuance or if other conditions for permit issuance were not fulfilled. The decision can be lodged as a complaint to the Minister. However, the Minister's decision is final and against it is possible to start an administrative court procedure (Article 70, paragraphs 1–3).

11. Detergents

733. Producer of detergents[917] can put detergent on the market if surfactant contained in the detergent fulfils criteria of complete aerobic biodegrading and if chemicals and surfactants contained in the detergent fulfil other conditions prescribed by this Law (Article 73, paragraph 1). Exceptionally, detergent that contains surfactant which does not fulfil criteria of complete aerobic biodegrading can be put on the market if the Ministry has issued permit for the use of that surfactant in detergent or if use of the surfactant in detergents is allowed in the EU (Article 73, paragraph 3). In this case, producer of detergent is obliged to send to the Ministry an officially certified copy of the EU regulation legalizing the use of surfactant.[918]

734. The list of surfactants for which permits have been issued or for which there exists an EU regulation allowing use of the surfactant in detergent, as well as the list of surfactants for which permits were refused or which are forbidden in the EU, is published in 'OJRS' (Article 79).

735. Laboratory testing biodegrading surfactant must be accredited for adequate method of testing or its work must be harmonized with principles of good laboratory practice (Article 80).

736. Producer of detergent is obliged to keep results of testing, which prove that criterion of complete aerobic biodegrading of surfactants is fulfilled, and to send the data to the Ministry if it demands so (Article 81, paragraph 1). Besides the obligations from this Law regarding classification, packing and labelling, producer of

916. Permit for marketing of very dangerous chemicals to distributor who is not importer, producer or final user, is issued by the competent organ of the self-government unit (Art. 67, para. 2). Scientific research institutions, persons engaged in cultural activities, organs of State administration, public agencies and organs of self-government units which need very dangerous chemicals for their work, as well as legal and physical persons who have permit for production and marketing of medicines in accordance with the law which regulates medicines, do not need permit for marketing of very dangerous chemicals (Art. 71).

917. Producer of detergents is a legal person or entrepreneur who puts detergent or surfactant on the market, and who imports these products, labels and packs them (Art. 73, para. 2).

918. The Ministry prescribes criteria and method of testing biodegrading surfactant (Art. 73, para. 5).

detergent is obliged to label detergent in accordance with regulations on labelling adopted on the basis of this Law. Producer of detergent intended for general use is obliged to make a list of ingredients of the detergent and to keep the list for five years, as well as to make accessible to the public on his/her internet site certain data from the list (Article 81, paragraphs 2–3).[919]

12. Systematic Monitoring of Chemicals

737. The Ministry prepares and implements projects for monitoring of placing on the market and use of chemicals, monitoring of their metabolites and pathway of chemicals in the environment and living organisms in order to monitor risk that those chemicals pose on human health and environment, that is, control the intended use of the substances of very serious concern and enforces the bans and restrictions of the manufacturing, placing on the market and use of chemicals (Article 82).[920]

738. The Poison Control Centre shall provide the Ministry with data obtained in accordance with the Law regulating health protection (Article 83, paragraph 1). The Ministry provides the Poison Control Centre information on chemicals and properties of chemicals it possesses, and which are necessary for work of that Centre (Article 83, paragraph 3).[921] The Poison Control Centre and other medical workers and/or associates may use obtained information for medical purposes only, that is, for the purpose of preventive and medical treatment measures, especially in emergency situations and may not be used for any other purposes (Article 83, paragraph 5).

13. Data Availability

739. Data submitted to the Ministry in the process of entering chemicals into the Chemicals Registry, as well as other data placed at the Ministry responsible for environment disposal, shall be made available to public and, in particular, as follows: (1) chemical name according to the IUPAC nomenclature of hazardous substance contained in the chemical; (2) trade name of the chemical; (3) classification and labelling of the chemical; (4) data on physical and chemical properties of the chemical; (5) data concerning the pathways of the substance and its environmental fate; (6) the results of toxicological and ecotoxicological studies; (7) no-effect level;

919. The Ministry prescribes specific method of labelling detergents, contents of the list of ingredients of the detergent, as well as data from that list which must be made accessible to the public (Art. 81, para. 4).

920. For the implementation of the projects referred to in para. 1 of this Article, the Ministry may engage scientific research institutions (Art. 82, para. 3).

921. The Ministry may use data referred to in para. 1 of this Article only for control of risk which some chemicals pose to human health and the environment (Art. 83, para. 2).

(8) the guidance on safe handling; and (9) analytical methods for identification of a hazardous substance when released into the environment and for determination of the direct exposure of humans (Article 84, paragraph 1).[922] In emergency cases, where necessary for the purpose of safety and protection of human health and environment, the Ministry may make available data referred to in paragraph 3 of this Article (Article 84, paragraph 4).

740. Any person may submit the request to access data from the Ministry responsible for environmental disposal (Article 85, paragraph 2).[923]

B. The Law on Biocidal Products

741. The legal Act that regulates biocidal products[924] in the RS is the Law on Biocidal Products (OJ RS, No. 109/21). It has the following fifteen parts: Part I – General provisions (Articles 1–4); Part II – Active substances in biocidal products (Articles 5–7); Part III – Procedures for adoption of Acts based on which biocidal products are made available on the market and used (Articles 8– 36); Part IV – Research and development (Article 37–38); Part V – Clasification, packaging, advertising and safety data sheet of biocidal product (Article 39); Part VI – Import of biocidal products (Articles 40); Part VII – Safe use of biocidal product (Article 41); Part VIII – Treated product (Article 42); Part IX – Professional assistance to the Ministry (Articles 43); Part X – Data availability (Articles 44–49); Part XI – Records (Article 50–51); Part XII – Register of biocidal products (Articles 52); Part XIII – Supervision (Articles 53–59); Part XIV – Penal provisions (Articles 60–64), Part XV – Transitional and final provisions (Articles 65– 69).

---

922. Besides the data referred to in para. 1 of this Article, data from notification referred to in Art. 53 of this Law shall also be available to public (Art. 84, para. 2). The Ministry shall consider the following data as professional secrecy and shall not be available to public: (1) data on full composition of mixture; (2) precise intended use and application of the substance; (3) relations between the manufacturer, importer and downstream user in the supply chain; (4) precise quantity of the chemicals manufactured or placed on the market (Art. 84, para. 3).
923. The Ministry shall deny access to data considered as confidential to the person referred to in para. 2 of this Article, if it assesses that it is necessary to restrict the access to this data in accordance with this Law and the law regulating free access to information of public importance, and shall issue Ruling on this deny (Art. 85, para. 3).
924. *The biocidal* product is: (1) a substance or mixture that consists of, contains or creates one or more active substances, prepared in the form in which it is supplied to the user, with the purpose of destroying, deterring, rendering harmless, preventing the action of or otherwise controlling a harmful organism, in any way except by purely physical or mechanical action, (2) a substance or mixture that is created from substances or mixtures that do not fall under sub-point (1) of this point, and which is used with the intention of destroying, deterring, rendering harmless, preventing action or otherwise controlling harmful organism, by any means other than purely physical or mechanical action, (3) a treated product that has a primary biocidal function; (Art. 4, para. 1, point 1).

742. This Law regulates[925] the list of active substances, procedures for passing acts based on which biocidal products are made available on the market[926] and used; research and development; classification, packaging, labelling, advertising, and safety data sheet of the biocidal product; Register of biocidal products; safe use of biocidal products; placing on the market and marking of treated products; supervision and other issues of importance for the safe making available on the market and use of biocidal products and treated products. (Article 1).

1. Active Substances in Biocidal Products

743. The Law distinguishes between two lists: List I and List II. Active substances are entered in List I – List of approved active substances (hereinafter 'List I') and List Ia – List of active substances that may contain biocidal products that are approved under a simplified procedure (hereinafter 'List Ia') which were published in the European Union (hereinafter 'EU') (Article 5, paragraph 1).[927] Active substances for which entry in the lists referred to in paragraph 1 of this article for a given type of biocidal product has been refused are entered in List II – List of active substances for which entry in List I or List Ia has been refused (hereinafter 'List II')[928] (Article 5, paragraph 4).[929]

---

925. The provisions of this law do not apply to: (1) medicated feed for animals; (2) active implantable medical devices, in vitro diagnostic medical devices and medical devices; (3) veterinary drugs and drugs for use in human medicine; (4) supplements for animal feed; (5) food hygiene (food products) and food hygiene of animal origin; (6) food additives; (7) flavors and other ingredients with aromatic properties for use in food; (8) food for animals; (9) plant protection products; (10) cosmetic products; (11) toys; (12) detergents and surfactants in detergents to which the law governing chemicals applies, and which do not have a biocidal effect; (13) food or animal feed used as repellents or attractants and biocidal products used as aids in the production of food or animal feed (Art. 3, para. 1). Exceptionally from para. 1 of this article, the provisions of this law apply to biocidal products and treated products that are used for purposes that are not covered by the regulations governing the areas from para. 1 of this article. The provisions of this law relating to the classification, packaging, and labelling of biocidal products do not apply to the transport of biocidal products. In addition, the provisions of this law relating to placing on the market do not apply to treated products that are biocidal, as well as to products that have been treated only by fumigation or disinfection of rooms or containers used for storage or transport and where there are no residues after such treatment. labelling of treated products (paras 2–4).

926. *Placing on the market* is the first making available on the market of a biocidal product or treated product, whereby import is also considered placing on the market (Art. 4, para. 1, point 8).

927. List I specifies in particular: the name of the active substance; the minimum level of purity of the active substance; the type of biocidal product in which that substance can be used; the conditions under which an act can be adopted based on which the biocidal product is made available on the market and used; the conditions for using the active substance in the treated product, as well as an indication of whether the active substance is a candidate for replacement, i.e., a nanomaterial (Art. 5, para. 2).

928. List II specifies in particular: the name of the active substance and the type of biocidal product in which that substance cannot be used (Art. 5, para. 5).

929. Active substances that are under review in the EU for use in a biocidal product are entered in the Program of active substances for registration in List I or List Ia (hereinafter 'Program for registration') (Art. 5, para. 7).

2. Procedures for Passing Acts Based on Which Biocidal Products are Made Available on the Market and Used

744. The basic principle is that a biocidal product must be approved before it is made available on the market or used.[930] The basic act based on which biocidal products are made available on the market and used is approval. This law took over the provisions of the Regulation (EU) 528/2012 on Biocidal Products, which regulate the documentation attached to the request for approval, as well as the procedure carried out by the Ministry when deciding on the request for approval, that is, on the request for the implementation of a simplified procedure for approval.

745. Biocidal products shall be classified into product types[931] according to their purpose, i.e., the harmful organism on which they act (Article 8, paragraph 1).

746. According to Article 9, a biocidal product is made available on the market or used if the manufacturer, importer, distributor, or user: (1) has approval for making it available on the market and for use; (2) has a decision on registration in the List of biocidal products that can be made available on the market and used until approval from point 1) of this article is issued; (3) has a decision on recognition of approval for making available on the market and use made under the EU regulation by the competent body of the EU Member State or by the EC (paragraph 1).[932]

747. The procedure for approving the use of a biocidal product and the method of making it available on the market are regulated in detail in Articles 10–20 of the Law. An application for approval to make it available on the market and use a biocidal product (hereinafter 'approval') is submitted to the Ministry (Article 10, paragraph 1).[933]

748. An application can be submitted to the Ministry for a simplified procedure for approving making available on the market and using a biocidal product: (1) whose active substances are all listed in List Ia and comply with the restrictions specified in that list; (2) which does not contain a substance of concern; (3) which does not contain nanomaterials; (4) which is efficient enough; (5) whose handling

930. Within this chapter, the following issues are regulated: (1) Approval for Making Available On the Market and Use of the Biocidal Product; (2) Registration of a Biocidal Product in the List of Biocidal Products That May be Made Available on the Market and Used; (3) Recognition of Approval for Making Biocidal Product Available on the Market and Use Adopted in Line with EU Regulations by Competent Authority of EU Member State or by the European Commission; (4) Extension, Termination and Amendment of Acts Based on Which the Biocidal Product is Made Available on the Market and Used; (5) Temporary Permit.

931. Minister shall lay down the biocidal products types (Art. 8, para. 2).

932. The provisions of the law regulating the general administrative procedure are applied to matters of procedure that are not otherwise regulated by this law (para. 2).

933. The Minister prescribes the content of the request, the scope and content of the file for the biocidal product and the conditions for adjusting the request for data from the file (Art. 10. para. 10).

and intended use do not require personal protective equipment (Article 11, paragraph 1).[934] The Ministry within thirty days from the date of receipt of the application from Articles 10 and 11 of this law performs a formal evaluation of the documentation submitted with the request (Article 15, paragraph 1). The Ministry evaluates a biocidal product[935] or a group of biocidal products based on the submitted documentation and, in accordance with the guidelines for evaluating a biocidal product, prepares a report on the assessment of the biocidal product and issues an approval within one year from the date of receipt of the complete documentation from Article 10 of this law, i.e., within ninety days from the date of receipt of complete documentation from Article 11 of this law (paragraph 3).[936]

749. To obtain data for the dossier for the biocidal product, it is necessary to carry out tests of the active substance and the biocidal product. The provisions of Articles 12–14 of this law prescribe that the methods established by the regulations regulating chemicals or other scientifically appropriate or internationally recognized methods are used during testing. It is emphasized that to obtain data on the efficiency of the biocidal product, the EU guidelines for efficiency testing or other test methods or relevant data from the field are applied. Given that the EU pays special attention to the welfare of animals, it is an obligation to reduce animal testing to a minimum; that is, it can only be carried out if the necessary data cannot be obtained in any other way.

750. The provision of Article 15 of this law prescribes the procedure to be carried out by the Ministry when deciding on the request for approval, as well as on the request for the implementation of a simplified procedure for the approval. The first step in this procedure is the formal assessment of the submitted documentation. The Ministry within thirty days from the date of receipt of the request performs a formal evaluation of the documentation submitted with the request (Article 15, paragraph 1).[937]

751. The second step is the very essence of this procedure, i.e., the assessment of the biocidal product based on the data from the file, i.e., whether the biocidal product poses an acceptable risk to human health, animal health, and the environment when used in the intended way and whether it can be approved to make it available on the market and safely used. Due to the complicated evaluation procedure, the Regulation on Biocidal Products establishes common principles for the

934. The minister prescribes the content of the request from para. 1 of this article (para. 4).
935. The Minister prescribes guidelines for the evaluation of the biocidal product (Art. 15, para. 8).
936. The approval from para. 3 of this article can be appealed to the Government (para. 6).
937. The deadlines prescribed for the completion of incomplete documentation differ from the deadlines established by the law regulating the general administrative procedure for the reason that the documentation submitted in this procedure is obtained after extensive tests and is contained in several thousand pages (biocidal product file), and therefore, it requires a longer deadline for assessing the completeness of the documentation submitted with the request for approval, but also a longer deadline for the actions of business entities, i.e., the submission of additional information. In addition, these deadlines follow the deadlines prescribed for this procedure in the Regulation on Biocidal Products.

evaluation of the biocidal product, which will be adhered to by all competent authorities when implementing this procedure to ensure a harmonized approach when evaluating the biocidal product.[938] There is an obligation to pay a fee for the formal assessment of the documentation and the assessment of the biocidal product or group of biocidal products (Article 15, paragraph 5).

752. The provision of Article 16 of this law regulates the essence of the law itself. It defines the conditions that must be met for the biocidal product to be approved to make it available on the market and for use. It is necessary to ensure that the biocidal product, when properly used for its intended purpose, is sufficiently effective and that it does not have unacceptable effects on human health, animal health, or the environment, i.e., that it does not have unacceptable effects on target organisms, such as resistance, i.e., those vertebrates do not cause unnecessary suffering and pain. If these requirements are not met, the biocidal product is not approved.[939]

753. Article 18 of the Law prescribes an exception in the case when the use of such a biocidal product is justified because otherwise, it would cause a disproportionately greater negative impact on society compared to the risks arising from its use. To facilitate the making available on the market and the use of biocidal products that have the same active substances, similar composition with certain deviations, similar ways of use, and similar levels of risk or effectiveness, according to Article 19 of this law, it is possible to authorize making available on market and the use of this group of biocidal products.[940]

754. Concerning the complicated and demanding approval procedure, both in terms of financial and human capacities, this law prescribes an alternative procedure that is simpler and more time and financially acceptable to domestic economic entities on the one hand and the other hand ensures that the biocidal products that are available on the market and used in the territory of the RS are sufficiently safe, but also efficient. With this procedure, the biocidal product is entered in the List of biocidal products that can be made available on the market and used until approval is granted for making the biocidal product available on the market and using it (hereinafter 'Provisional list') (Articles 21–24).

938. These guidelines are given in Annex VI of the Regulation on Biocidal Products and will be taken over by a by-law issued by the minister based on the authorization given in this article.

939. Certain biocidal products may pose a certain risk if they are used by the population. Therefore, in Art. 17 of this law, it is prescribed that these biocidal products cannot be approved for use for general use, that is, when necessary, these biocidal products can be used by trained persons, i.e., professional or industrial users.

940. The approval is valid for a maximum of ten years, and if the biocidal product contains an active substance that is a candidate for replacement, the approval is valid for a maximum of five years (Art. 20, para. 3).

3. Recognition of Approval for Making Available on the Market and Use of a Biocidal Product Adopted Based on EU Regulations by the Competent Authority of an EU Member State or by the European Commission

755. A biocidal product that, based on EU regulations, has already received the approval of the competent authority of an EU Member State or the approval of the EC cannot be entered in the Provisional List, but a new procedure is established for making it available on the market and for use on the territory of the RS – the recognition of that approval (Articles 25–28). The process of recognition of approval is not the usual taking over of an act issued by the competent authority of an EU Member State, that is, the EC. Namely, in this procedure, the Ministry assesses whether the conditions under which the biocidal product is made available on the market and used in the EU Member State that issued the approval, i.e., at the EU level, are in accordance with the conditions under which the product would be made available on the market and used in the RS or need to be adapted.[941]

756. In this procedure, it is envisaged that the competent authority will issue a decision on the recognition of approval within 120 days from the date of submission of complete documentation (Article 28, paragraph 3).[942] The validity period of the decision on the recognition of the approval must be the same as the validity period of the approval made following the EU regulation by the competent body of the EU Member State or by the EC (Article 28, paragraph 4).[943]

4. Extension, Termination of Validity, and Amendment of the Act Based on Which the Biocidal Product is Made Available on the Market and Used

757. The validity periods of the approval or the decision on the recognition of the approval can be extended. The request for extending the validity of the approval is submitted no later than 550 days before the expiration of its validity period (Article 29, paragraph 2), and the request for the extension of the validity of the decision on the recognition of the approval is submitted no later than 180 days before the expiration of the validity period of that decision (paragraph 3).

758. The holder of the approval, the holder of the decision on the entry of the biocidal product in the Provisional List, and the holder of the decision on the recognition of the approval are obliged to monitor the effects and circumstances related

941. This means that in the act of recognition of approval, the competent authority determines the conditions for making available on the market and use of the biocidal product in the territory of the Republic of Serbia, and may refuse to recognize approval if it considers it necessary to protect: the environment; public policy and public security; health and life of people, especially sensitive groups; animals or plants; national treasures of artistic, historical or archaeological value; if the target organisms are not present in harmful amounts or if the active substance is a candidate for replacement; as well as for animal welfare.
942. The decision from para. 3 of this article can be appealed to the Government (para. 6).
943. There is a prescribed obligation to pay a fee for the assessment of documentation to pass a decision on the recognition of approval (Art. 28, para. 5).

to the biocidal product that may hurt human health, animal health, and the environment, as well as to monitor the effectiveness of the biocidal product (Article 30, paragraph 1).[944]

759. In the procedure for extending the validity of the approval or decision on the recognition of the approval, the Ministry may: (1) amend the act based on which the biocidal product is made available on the market and used; (2) issue a decision on the termination of the validity of the act based on which the biocidal product is made available on the market and used (Article 31, paragraph 2). The Ministry issues a decision on the termination of the validity of the act based on which the biocidal product is made available on the market and used if the active substance in that biocidal product is entered in List II for the relevant type of biocidal product or when it is requested by the holder of the approval, the holder of the registration decision of the biocidal product in the Provisional List and holder of the decision on recognition of approval (Article 33).[945]

5. Temporary Permit

760. This law, as in the previous one, provides a special instrument that, in certain cases, a temporary licence can be issued to make available on the market or use a biocidal product. In the event of an unforeseen occurrence of harmful organisms that cannot be controlled by other means or a biocidal product for which an act has been passed based on which the biocidal product is made available on the market and used, a temporary permit for making it available on the market or using the biocidal product can be issued (in hereinafter 'temporary permit') (Article 35, paragraph 1).[946] If the request referred to in paragraph 2 of this article is submitted by a producer who is not based in the RS, the request can be submitted through a representative, that is, a representative who is based in the RS and who is responsible for fulfilling all obligations prescribed by this law (paragraph 3).[947]

---

944. In this regard, they are obliged to inform the Ministry of new findings, which, based on this information, can issue a decision amending the conditions for making biocidal products available on the market and using them, or can issue a decision on the termination of the validity of these acts.
945. In the act from Art. Arts 31 and 33 of this law determine the period in which the biocidal product can be made available on the market and the period of use of existing stocks. The period referred to in para. 1 of this article cannot be longer than 180 days for making the biocidal product available on the market and an additional 180 days for the use of existing stocks of the biocidal product (Art. 34, paras 1, and 2). As an exception to para. 1 of this article, the Ministry may order the immediate withdrawal of a biocidal product if further making it available on the market or using that biocidal product would pose an unacceptable risk to human health, animal health, or the environment (Art. 34, para. 3).
946. For the issuance of a temporary permit, the manufacturer, importer, or user of the biocidal product applies to the Ministry (para. 2). The minister prescribes the content of the request in para. 2 of this article (para. 6).
947. The representative of the manufacturer referred to in para. 3 of this article must have a contract of representation, which specifically determines and ensures responsibility for any damage caused by the use of the biocidal product on the territory of the Republic of Serbia (para. 4). At the request of the Ministry, the applicant for a temporary licence is obliged to submit a sample of the biocidal product (para. 5).

761. Along with the request for a temporary permit, the following shall be submitted: data on the identity of the active substance and the biocidal product; data on the manufacturer of the active substance and biocidal product; type of biocidal product; full composition of the biocidal product; data on the intended use; data on classification, labelling and packaging; data on the efficiency of the biocidal product; data on the required quantities and on the persons who will use the biocidal product, as well as a proposal for systematic monitoring of the use of that biocidal product (Article 36, paragraph 1).[948]

762. Based on the evaluation of the data from paragraph 1 of this article, the Ministry issues a temporary permit within thirty days from the day of receipt of complete documentation. The temporary licence specifies the conditions for limited and controlled use of the biocidal product, namely: quantities; day of start of use; field of use; method of use; method of systematic monitoring of usage; the name of the person who will use it and the term of use (Article 36, paragraphs 3, and 4).[949]

6. Research and Development

763. These provisions (Articles 37, 38) stipulate that a biocidal product for which an act has not been adopted based on which the biocidal product is made available on the market and used can only be made available on the market for use in an experiment or test based on confirmation. The purpose of this institute is to enable the import of these biocidal products, as well as for the competent authority to have insight into the use of biocidal products for which the standard procedure for making them available on the market and their use has not been implemented.[950]

764. A permit for an experiment or test must be obtained only if the use of the biocidal product may lead to its release into the environment (Article 38). If an experiment or test can have immediate or delayed adverse effects on the health of people, especially sensitive groups or animals, or unacceptable side effects on people, animals, or the environment, the Ministry can prohibit the experiment or test or prescribe conditions in the permit (e.g., the amount of biocidal of the product that can be used, the size of the area to be treated) under which the experiment or test will be carried out (Article 38, paragraph 5).[951]

---

948. Data on the effectiveness of the biocidal product referred to in para. 1 of this article shall be submitted to the Ministry in Serbian or English (para. 2). A fee shall be paid for the evaluation of the data referred to in para. 1 of this article (para. 6).
949. The term of validity of the temporary permit cannot be longer than 180 days. The act from para. 3 of this article can be appealed to the Government (Art. 36, paras 5, and 7).
950. The payment of a fee is also prescribed for the assessment of data submitted to issue a permit for an experiment or test.
951. The act from para. 4 of this article can be appealed to the Government (Art. 38, para. 8).

7. Classification, Packaging, Labelling, Advertising, and Safety Data Sheet of the Biocidal Product

765. Correct and complete hazard assessment and classification of the biocidal product is the first and most important step in the primary goal of protecting human health, animal health, and the environment. Starting from this step, the next necessary step is the correct labelling of the biocidal product. The holder of the approval, the holder of the decision on the entry of the biocidal product in the Provisional List, the holder of the decision on the recognition of the approval, and the holder of the temporary licence are obliged to classify, package, label and advertise the biocidal product following the regulations governing the classification, packaging, labelling, and advertising of chemicals, as well as under the specific requirements for packaging, labelling, and advertising of the biocidal product (Article 39, paragraph 1).[952]

8. Import of Biocidal Products

766. The customs authority will allow the import of a biocidal product for which an approval or a decision on the entry of a biocidal product in the Temporary List or a decision on the recognition of an approval or a temporary permit or certificate has been made (Article 40, paragraph 1). In the event of a need for clarification or doubt as to whether the provisions of this law are applied to the product that is the subject of the customs import procedure, the customs authority will contact the Ministry for expert assistance (paragraph 2).[953]

9. Safe Use of Biocidal Products

767. These provisions stipulate that the biocidal product must be used following the conditions established in the act based on which the biocidal product is made available on the market and uses and prescribed requirements for labelling and packaging, taking into account the rational application of a combination of physical, biological, chemical and other measures, as well as to minimize its use (Article 41, paragraph 1). The correct use of a biocidal product includes the rational application of a combination of physical, biological, chemical, or other measures, if necessary, which limits the use of biocidal products to the smallest possible extent, and appropriate precautions are taken (paragraph 2).

---

952. The Minister prescribes specific requirements for the packaging, labelling, and advertising of the biocidal product (Art. 39, para. 3).
953. At the request of the Ministry, the customs body is obliged to submit a report on the realized import of biocidal products in the previous year by 31 March of the current year (para. 3).

768. The biocidal product referred to in Article 18 of this law[954] must be used in such a way that the exposure of people and the environment to that biocidal product is minimized (Article 41, paragraph 3).

10. Treated Product

769. The novelty introduced by this Law refers to the placing of 'treated products' on the market. [955] To protect human health, animal health, and the environment, products can be treated with a biocidal product that contains only approved active substances, i.e., active substances that are listed in List I or List Ia or active substances that are listed in the Registration Program or active substances that are entered in the List for inclusion in the Enrollment Program.

770. Placing a treated product on the market can only be done if that product has been treated with a biocidal product or contains a biocidal product whose active substance is listed in List I for the relevant type of biocidal product or in List Ia and meets specific conditions or restrictions from those lists or is listed in Program for enrollment or in the List for inclusion in the Program for the relevant type of biocidal product (Article 42, paragraph 1). The label of the treated product must be visible, easy to read, and durable enough. The label is printed in Serbian on the packaging, on the instructions for use, or on the warranty, when necessary due to the size or function of the treated product (paragraph 3).[956]

11. Professional Assistance to the Ministry

771. To provide expert assistance in the most complex tasks (e.g., evaluation of data for granting approval and making a decision on recognition of approval), the Ministry can hire a legal or natural person who meets the requirements for professional training and specific knowledge needed to perform these tasks (Article 43, paragraph 1).[957] The persons referred to in paragraph 1 of this article must sign a statement in the absence of a conflict of interest (paragraph 3).

---

954. Article 18 of the Law prescribes an exception in the case when the use of such a biocidal product is justified because otherwise, it would cause a disproportionately greater negative impact on society compared to the risks arising from its use.
955. 'A treated product' is a substance, mixture, or product that has been treated with one or more biocidal products or intentionally contains them (Art. 4, para. 1, point 10).
956. The person who places the treated product on the market is obliged to provide information on the biocidal treatment of the treated product free of charge within forty-five days at the consumer's request (para. 5).
957. The persons referred to in para. 1 of this article may not be persons who produce or make biocidal products available on the market, persons who participate in the creation and assessment of biocidal product dossiers, as well as spouses, blood relatives up to the fourth degree of consanguinity and relatives by in-laws up to of the second degree of kinship of those persons (Art. 43, para. 2).

12. Data Availability

772. From the date of adoption of the act on the basis of which the biocidal product is made available on the market and used, the Ministry makes the following information publicly available free of charge: (1) conditions from the act on the basis of which the biocidal product is made available on the market and used; (2) summary of the characteristics of the biocidal product (Article 49). Anyone can submit a request to be made available to the data available to the Ministry (Article 45, paragraph 1). However, the Ministry will not allow access to data marked as confidential if it judges that access to that data needs to be restricted in accordance with this law and the law regulating free access to information of public importance and issues a decision on this (paragraph 2).[958]

773. The applicant for approval, the applicant for the entry of a biocidal product in the Provisional List, the applicant for a decision on the recognition of approval, or the applicant for the issuance of a temporary permit may mark certain information as confidential, with a written explanation that the disclosure of this information could affect his business or privacy or security (Article 44, paragraph 1). The ministry or the person referred to in Article 43[959] will not make certain types of data (information on the full composition of the biocidal product, the precise amount of the active substance or biocidal product produced or made available on the market, the relationship between the manufacturer of the active substance and the person who places the biocidal product on the market or the connection between the person who places the biocidal product on the market and the distributor of the biocidal product, as well as information on the name and address of the person involved in testing on vertebrates) available to the public.[960]

774. Certain data cannot be declared confidential (Article 46, paragraph 1).[961] Employees of the Ministry, as well as other persons who have access to confidential information in the course of their work, are obliged to preserve it even after the completion of their work (Article 47).

958. The decision from para. 2 of this article can be appealed to the Government (para. 3).

959. This is a person who provides professional assistance to the ministry.

960. However, in urgent cases, when it is necessary for the protection of human health, animal health, security or environmental protection, or other reasons of public importance, the Ministry can also make available the data referred to in para. 2 of this article (para. 3).

961. (1) name and address of the holder of the act on the basis of which the biocidal product is made available on the market and used; (2) name and address of the manufacturer of the biocidal product; (3) name and address of the manufacturer of the active substance; (4) the content of the active substance in the biocidal product and the name of the biocidal product; (5) data on the physical and chemical properties of the biocidal product; (6) methods for converting the active substance or biocidal product into less dangerous ones; (7) a summary of the results of testing the effectiveness of the biocidal product and its effects on humans, animals and the environment and, if necessary, data on its ability to contribute to the development of resistance; (8) recommended methods and precautionary measures for reducing hazards during handling, transport and use, as well as in case of fire or other hazards; (9) safety sheet; (10) test methods used to obtain data on the chemical identity, quantity and technical equivalence of active substances in the biocidal product and, if necessary, impurities and other substances that are significant and relevant due to toxicological and

775. Data submitted in the process of adopting acts based on which the biocidal product is made available on the market and used by the Ministry cannot be used in another process of adopting these acts, unless the period of protection of such data has passed (Article 48, paragraph 1). The period of protection of data that was submitted in the process of adopting acts based on which the biocidal product is made available on the market and used expires ten years from the first day of the month following the adoption of the first act (paragraph 2).[962]

13. Records

776. The holder of the approval, the holder of the decision on the entry of the biocidal product in the Provisional List, and the holder of the decision on the recognition of the approval are obliged to keep records of placing the biocidal product on the market (Article 50, paragraph 1).[963] The person referred to in paragraph 1 of this article is obliged to keep the data from the biocidal product records for at least ten years from the day the biocidal product was placed on the market, i.e., for ten years from the date of cancellation or expiration of the act based on which the biocidal product was placed on the market, and used, depending on which is earlier, as well as to deliver them to the Ministry at its request.[964]

777. In addition to the records from Article 50, paragraph 1 of this law, the producer of a biocidal product placed on the market is obliged to keep records on the production process that are relevant to the quality and safety of the biocidal product placed on the market, as well as to store samples of production batches (Article 51, paragraph 1).[965]

---

ecotoxicological properties, as well as data on their residues which are significant due to toxicological properties or for the environment, and which originate from the way of use that is approved; (11) method of disposal of the biocidal product and its packaging; (12) procedures to be implemented and measures to be taken in case of spillage or leakage; (13) the manner in which first aid and medical advice should be provided in case of injuries.

962. The period of protection of data submitted in the process of extension or amendment of acts based on which the biocidal product is made available on the market and used expires five years from the first day of the month following the adoption of the act. Data whose protection period has expired cannot be protected again (paras 3, and 4).

963. The minister prescribes the detailed content and method of keeping records from para. 1 of this article (para. 4).

964. If the person referred to in para. 1 of this article has transferred his work or part of his work to a third party, the obligation to keep data is transferred to that person, and if he has ceased to work, the responsible person of the holder of the act based on which the biocidal product is made available on the market and used properly is to submit that information to the Ministry immediately after the termination of work (Art. 50, para. 3).

965. The minister prescribes the detailed content and method of keeping records from para. 1 of this article (para. 3).

14. Register of Biocidal Products

778. The Ministry, based on data submitted in the process of passing the act based on which the biocidal product is made available on the market and used, as well as based on data from Article 36, paragraph 1, Article 37, paragraph 3, and Article 38, paragraph 3 of this of the law maintains the Register of Biocidal Products, which is an integral part of the Integral Register of Chemicals, established by regulations governing chemicals (Article 52, paragraph 1). Once a year, the Ministry publishes in the 'OJRS' the following information from the Register of Biocidal Products: name and seat of the holder of the approval, holder of the decision on the entry of the biocidal product in the Provisional List or holder of the decision on the recognition of the approval; name of the biocidal product; number, date of adoption and term of validity of those acts (paragraph 3).[966]

15. Supervision

779. Supervision over the implementation of this law and the regulations adopted on its basis is carried out by the ministry responsible for environmental protection (Article 53, paragraph 1). Inspection supervision is carried out by the ministry responsible for environmental protection through environmental protection inspectors, the ministry responsible for health through sanitary inspectors, and the ministry responsible for veterinary affairs through veterinary inspectors (paragraph 2).[967]

780. The environmental protection inspector, sanitary inspector, and veterinary inspector may carry out sampling of the biocidal product or treated product to determine whether the conditions for making it available on the market or for the use of the biocidal product or treated product are met (Article 54, paragraph 1).[968] If the inspector finds that other laws and regulations have been violated during the inspection, the violation of which may have an impact on the health of people, animals, or the environment, i.e., safety at work, he is obliged to immediately inform the competent authority, perform the inspection together with him and take appropriate measures (Article 59).[969]

---

966. The Minister prescribes the detailed content and manner of maintaining the Register of Biocidal Products, as well as the method of submitting data to the Register of Biocidal Products (para. 4).
967. The inspections referred to in para. 2 of this article cooperate, that is, inform each other about the measures taken, exchange information, provide immediate assistance, and undertake joint measures and activities significant for the implementation of supervision (para. 6).
968. The costs of sampling and testing the biocidal product or treated product shall be borne by the legal or natural person or entrepreneur from whom the sample was taken, if it is determined in the final procedure that it does not meet the prescribed conditions for making it available on the market, i.e., for using the biocidal product or treated product (para. 3).
969. Every legal entity, entrepreneur, and natural person is obliged to enable the inspector to carry out the inspection, to make available to him without delay the necessary documentation and other evidence, and to state the facts that are important for the inspection (Art. 58).

C. Transport of Dangerous Goods

781. Transport of dangerous goods by road, railway, waterway and air is regulated by the Law on Transport of Dangerous Goods (OJ RS, Nos 104/16, 83/18, 95/18 – other law, 10/19 – other law). The Law regulates the conditions for performing internal and international transport of dangerous goods on road, rail and inland water transport as regards the territory of the RS. This law does not apply to, *inter alia*, maritime transport, transport of dangerous goods performed by means of transport belonging to the ministry in charge of defence, the ministry in charge of internal affairs, the Serbian Army, as well as military forces of other States and organizations that use the transport infrastructure of the RS, etc. (Article 2). The Law is divided into seven Chapters and eighty-one articles.[970] This Law sets the requirements in relation to packaging, mobile equipment, and administrative issues necessary for the safe and controlled transport and transit of potentially dangerous (for environment, human and animal health) goods and substances. In addition, the Law defines the methods for examination and inspection; competent State authorities and organizations in the transport of dangerous goods; conditions and obligations that should be meet by all participants in the above-mentioned activity; and offences and related penalties.

782. The Authority responsible for the transport issues in the RS is the Ministry of Construction, Transport and Infrastructure. Functioning of each Transport Sectors is regulated by separate Laws: Law on Transport in Road Traffic (OJ RS, Nos 68/15, 41/18), Law on Transport in International Road Traffic (OJ FRY, Nos 60/98, 5/99 – corr., 44/99, 74/99, 4/00 – corr., OJ RS, Nos 101/05 – other law, 18/10 and 68/15 – other law), Law on Railway (OJ RS, No. 41/18), Law on Railway Traffic Safety (OJ RS, No. 41/18), Law on Contracts on Transport in Railway Traffic (OJ RS, No. 38/15), Law on Air Transport (OJ RS, Nos 73/10, 57/11, 93/12, 45/15, 66/15 – other law, 83/18 and 9/20), Law on Navigation and Ports in Inland Waters (OJ RS, Nos 73/10, 121/12, 18/15, 96/15, 92/16, 104/16 – other law, 113/17 – other law, 41/18, 95/18 – other law, 37/19 – other law and 9/20), and Law on Maritime Navigation (OJ RS, Nos 87/11, 104/13, 18/15, 113/17 – other law and 83/18).

Some of the by-laws enacted in accordance with the Law on Transport of Dangerous Goods are in force, as follows: Regulation on mobile equipment under pressure (OJ RS, No. 120/17), Regulation on the criteria for the classification of violations of regulations according to the category of danger from the occurrence of consequences in the transport of dangerous goods (OJ RS, No. 82/17), Rulebook on the manner and procedure of issuing ADR vehicle approval certificates (OJ RS, No. 23/18), Rulebook on the content and form of certificates of specialist knowledge in the field of ADN and the Register of issued certificates of specialist knowledge in the field of ADN (OJ RS, No. 66/17), Rulebook on the conditions for issuing and revoking the designation for conformity assessment of the type of packaging or tank

970. The chapters are: (1) Introductory provisions; (2) Basic rules for transport of dangerous goods; (3) Authorities and obligations of authorities and organizations, and participants in transport of dangerous goods; (4) Special provisions for transport of dangerous goods by road; (5) Supervisions; (6) Penalty provisions; (7) Transitional and final provisions.

for the transport of dangerous goods (OJ RS, No. 89/20), Rulebook on the manner and conditions for determining routes for the transport of dangerous goods by road and the manner of locating and monitoring vehicles (OJ RS No. 59/19), etc.

783. The following ratified international agreements on transport of dangerous goods are implemented, *inter alia*:

(1) European Agreement concerning the International Carriage of Dangerous Goods by Road (ADR) (OJ RS – IT, No. 22/15).
(2) Agreement on Acceptance of Uniformed Conditions for Homologation and Mutual Recognition of Equipment and Motor Vehicle Parts Homologation (OJ FPRY – IT, No. 5/62).
(3) Convention on International Convention concerning Carriage by Rail (COTIF) – Regulations concerning the International Carriage of Dangerous Goods (RID) (OJ RS – IT, No. 17/15).
(4) Annex 18 to the Convention on International Civil Aviation Organization (ICAO) – the Safe Transport of Dangerous Goods by Air and ICAO Doc. 9284 AN/905 – Technical Instructions for the Safe Transport of Dangerous Goods by Air.
(5) European Agreement concerning the International Carriage of Dangerous Goods by Inland Waterways (ADN) (OJ RS – IT, Nos 3/10, 7/15).
(6) Convention on the Physical Protection of Nuclear Material (OJ SFRY – IT, No. 9/85), etc.

D. Other Relevant Regulations

784. Other legal and sub-legal Acts to be mentioned are following:

- Law on Medicines and Medical Devices (OJ RS, Nos 30/10, 107/12, 105/17 – other law and 113/17 – other law).
- Law on the Prohibition of the Development, Production, Stockpiling and Use of Chemical Weapons and on their Destruction (OJ RS, Nos 36/09 and 104/13).
- List of poisons whose production, marketing and use is forbidden (OJ RS, No. 72/2006).
- List of active substances in biocidal products (OJ RS, No. 7/19).
- List of surfactants for which approval was issued or an Act adopted approving the use of surfactants in detergent in the EU and List of surfactants for which application for approval was denied and surfactants which are prohibited in EU (OJ RS, No. 94/10).
- List of substances of concern (OJ RS, Nos 94/13, 101/16 and 22/18).
- List of substances candidates for the List of substances of concern (OJ RS, Nos 58/16 and 22/18).
- List of biocidal products registered in the Register of Biocidal Products in 2018 (OJ RS, No. 45/19).
- Rulebook on Chemicals Registry (OJ RS, Nos 16/16, 6/17, 117/17, 44/18 – other law, 7/19 and 93/19).

- Rulebook on the method of keeping the Register on biocidal products (OJ RS, No. 28/11).
- Rulebook on Advisor for Chemicals (OJ RS, Nos 13/11, 28/11 and 47/12).
- Rulebook on the List of Classified Substances (OJ RS, No. 22/20).
- Rulebook on the List of Classified Substances (OJ RS, No. 19/19).
- Rulebook on permits for the performance of traffic activities or permits for the use of particularly hazardous chemicals (OJ RS, Nos 6/17 and 29/18).
- Rulebook on criteria for identification of substances such as PBT and vPvB (OJ RS, No. 23/2010).
- Rulebook on certain dangerous biocidal products that cannot be placed on the market for general use (OJ RS, No. 37/11).
- Rulebook on the content of basic information on a biocidal product and the active substance in that biocidal product (OJ RS, No. 64/17).
- Rulebook on types of biocidal products (OJ RS, No. 23/2010).
- Rulebook on detergents (OJ RS, No. 25/15).
- Rulebook on specific requirements for packaging, labelling and advertising of biocidal products (OJ RS, Nos 59/2010 and 26/11).
- Rulebook on classification, packaging, labelling and advertising of chemicals and certain products (OJ RS, Nos 59/2010, 25/11 and 5/12).
- Rulebook on classification, packaging, labelling and advertising of chemical and certain article in accordance with the UN Globally Harmonized System for Classification and Labeling (OJ RS, Nos 105/13, 52/17 and 27/19).
- Rulebook on volume and content of the technical dossier for biocidal product, that is, low-risk biocidal product (OJ RS, No. 97/10).
- Rulebook on import and export of certain hazardous chemicals (OJ RS, Nos 89/10, 15/13 and 114/14).
- Rulebook on restrictions and bans on the manufacture, placing on the market and use of chemicals (OJ RS, Nos 90/13, 25/15, 2/16, 44/17, 36/18 and 9/20).
- Rulebook on guidelines for assessing biocidal products on the basis of technical dossier (OJ RS, No. 28/11).
- Decree on the amount of tax, the payers, as well as the manner of payment of tax for assessment and verification of data on biocidal products (OJ RS, No. 90/15).

III. International Treaties and Harmonization with EU Legislation

785. Serbia has ratified the Rotterdam Convention on the prior informed consent procedure for certain hazardous chemicals and pesticides in the international trade (OJ RS-Int. treaties, No. 38/09) and Stockholm Convention on POPs (OJ RS-Int. treaties, No. 42/09).

786. 'Serbia has a high level of alignment with the EU *acquis* on chemicals.'[971] However, developments in several fields (the EC Regulation on Registration, Evaluation, Authorization and Restriction of Chemicals (REACH) Regulation and the Classification, Labelling and Packaging Regulation, and on animal experiments and

971. EC 2023, 137.

asbestos legislation) 'continued to be slow.' Serbia needs to boost its administrative capacity to implement legislation in these areas and ensure proper monitoring of POPs.[972]

§2. Rational Use of Energy

787. The strategic determination of the RS to implement the energy efficiency policy is one of the basic prerequisites for a successful energy transition towards a safe, reliable, and environmentally acceptable form of energy and energy supply. Within the framework of energy efficiency, special attention is paid to the use of biomass.[973]

788. According to the Energy Strategy, 'the energy future of the country shall largely depend on the amount and manner of consumption of energy. Existing indicators of energy consumption compared to the value of GDP have values comparable to countries in the region, but significantly above average values for EU countries, even though the consumption of energy per capita is lower than average in EU'.[974] According to official estimates, the RS has significant potential for Renewable Energy Sources (RES) (wind energy, solar energy) for the production of electricity and thermal energy, as well as for use in traffic.[975] 'The RES share in Serbia's electricity production has been stable over the past decade. More specifically, the RES share in electricity production for 2019 is 30.1%, which is 4.5% lower than the EU 27.'[976]

789. Main institutions competent for rational use of energy are: MME and MEP; the Energy Efficiency Agency ceased to exist on 25 September 2012 with the adoption of the Law on Amendments to the Law on Energy (OJ RS, No. 93/12). Rights, obligations, objects, equipment, archives, employees and appointed officials in the Energy Efficiency Agency, as at the date of entry into force of this law, take over the MEDEP (Article 19 of the Law).

972. *Ibid.*

973. MME. 2023b, 112.

974. NA. 2015, Ch. 5.7: Efficient Energy Use. In industry, reduction of energy consumption is possible by 15–25%, compared to the reference scenario, in the period up to 2025 based on the improvement of combustion processes, by use of waste heat from energy facilities and production processes, by replacement of the existing electric motors, etc. Improvement of energy efficiency in transport partly refers to the renewal of vehicle fleets in all sectors, an increase of energy efficiency in rail transport, highway traffic, and air traffic, improvement of public transportation, etc. *Ibid.*

975. MME. 2023b, 39.

976. MME. 2023a, 9. In comparison to the other countries, Serbia has a higher share only from Bulgaria and North Macedonia, whereas the remaining countries have a significantly higher share due to their installed capacity mix. *Ibid.* As for the year 2023, in the structure of the planned total domestic production of primary energy for the year 2023, renewable energy sources participate with 26%, while the estimated value for the year 2022 is 25%. GOV RS. 2022d. (Ch. 2.6. Renewable Energy Sources). Nevertheless, according to the Energy Balance for 2024 (OJ RS, No. 8/24), in the structure of the planned total domestic production of primary energy for the year 2024, RES participates with 30%.

I. Legal Regulation

A. National Regulations

790. The legal framework of the RS in the field of energy efficiency consists of all the regulations 'that directly or indirectly regulate the field of efficient use of energy. The RS introduced the concept of energy efficiency into its legislation, establishing in the Law on Energy (2004), the legal basis for the establishment of the Agency for Energy Efficiency as a special organization'.[977] However, when legal regulation of the energy sector in Serbia is concerned, the first deserve to be mentioned are programmatic Acts:

- Energy Development Strategy of the RS until 2025, with projection until 2030 (OJ RS, No. 111/15).
- Regulation on Establishment of Implementation Program of the Energy sector Development Strategy of the RS for the period to 2025 year with projections to 2030, the year of the period 2017 to 2023 year (OJ RS, No. 104/17).
- Energy Balance of the RS for 2024 (OJ RS, No. 8/24).
- National Action Plan for Energy Efficiency (OJ RS, 1/2017).
- Regulation on approval of the Programme for financing of activities and measures for the improvement of energy efficiency in 2023 (OJ RS, No. 29/23).
- National Renewable Energy Action Plan (OJ RS, No. 53/2013).

1. Environmental Protection Law

791. There are several provisions of the EPL concerning the energy and energy sector. Most of them have a general character, but some are very relevant and have practical implication for energy sector (Spatial and urban planning, Article 34, point 3; SEA, Article 35; EIA, Article 36; Limit values, Article 39; Requirements for operating the plant and performing the activities, Article 40; Ecological sign, Article 53; Registers of sources of environmental pollution, Article 75; Types of incentive measures, Articles 101, etc.).

792. Funds of the Green Fund of the RS shall be carried out in accordance with the law, the NEPP and the strategic documents, as well as the list of priority infrastructure projects in the field of environment, for, *inter alia*, encouraging the use of renewable resources; encouraging sustainable development, apart from energy efficiency improvement projects, etc. (Article 90v).

793. Technologies and more environmentally friendly products than others due to the use of RES (energy of the Sun, wind parks, biogas, etc.) plant and equipment directly protecting the environment may have taxation, customs and other relief or exemption provided under the terms and conditions of special Law (Article 101).

977. For detailed information, *see* Lepotić Kovačević, 2021, 268.

794. While performing their activity, legal and natural persons shall be obliged to ensure environmental protection by, *inter alia*, sustainable use of natural resources, goods and energy by introducing energy efficient technologies and use of renewable natural resources (Article 102).

2. Energy Law

795. Basic legal Act regulating the field of energy in the R S is the Energy Law (hereinafter 'The Law') (OJ RS, Nos 145/14, 95/18 – other law, 40/21, 35/23 – other law, and 62/23), adopted in 2014. It has the following fourteen parts: Part I – General Provisions (Articles 1 and 2); Part II – Energy policy and energy development planning (Articles 3–15); Part III – Energy activities, licences and energy permits (Articles 16–37); Part IV – Energy agency of the R S (AERS) (Articles 38–64); Part V – Renewable energy sources (Articles 65–87); Part VI – Prices of Energy, energy commodities and services (Articles 88–93); Part VII – Electricity (Articles 94–219); Part VIII – Natural gas (Articles 220–323); Part IX – Oil and oil derivatives (Articles 324–344); Part X – Energy reserves (Articles 345–353); Part XI – Heat energy (Articles 354–366); Part XII – Supervision (Articles 367–388); Part XIII – Penalties (Articles 389–391); and Part XIV – Transitory and final provisions (Articles 392–434).

796. The Law regulates the following: energy policy objectives and methods of their implementation; conditions for reliable, secure and quality energy[978] and energy commodities delivery; conditions for safe supply to the customers; protection of consumers of energy and energy commodities; conditions and manner for performing energy-related activities; conditions for constructing new energy facilities; rights and duties of governmental bodies and Energy Agency of the Republic of Serbia (AERS) (hereinafter 'Agency'); usage of RES, incentives and guaranty of origin; manner of organizing and functioning of the electricity, natural gas and oil and oil derivatives market; rights and obligations of market participants; establishment of ownership of networks of operators of the system, as well as supervision over the implementation of this Law. This Law regulates the production, distribution and supply of heat energy as well as energy-related activities (Article 1).

797. The energy policy of the RS shall include measures and activities taken to achieve following long-term objectives: (1) reliable, safe and quality supply of energy and energy sources;[979] (2) creating conditions for safe and reliable energy systems operation and sustainable development; (3) energy market competition based on the principles of non-discrimination, publicity and transparency; (4) providing conditions for promoting energy efficiency in carrying out energy activities

978. *Energy* means electricity and heat energy (Art. 2, point 24).

979. *Energy sources* are coal, natural gas, oil, oil derivatives, oil shale, renewable and other energy sources (Art. 2, point 20).

and energy consumption; (5) creating economic, commercial and financial conditions for generating energy from RES and combined heat and electricity generation;[980] (6) creating regulatory, economic and commercial conditions for the improvement of efficiency in power system management, particularly having in mind the development of distributed electricity generation, development of distributed electricity storage capacities, introduction of a consumption management system, and introduction of the advanced network concept; (7) creating conditions for the use of new energy sources; (8) *improvement of environmental protection in all energy-related areas*; (9) creating conditions for investments into the energy sector; (10) protection of energy and energy sources' customers; (11) connecting the energy system of the RS with the energy systems of other countries; and (12) electricity and natural gas market development and their relation with the regional and internal market of the EU (Article 3, paragraph 1).

798. Energy activity can be carried out by a public company, a company, and/or another legal entity or an entrepreneur, possessing licence for carrying out energy activity, unless otherwise prescribed by this Law (Article 17, paragraph 1).[981] Energy entity can begin performing energy activity on the basis of a licence issued by the Agency, unless otherwise regulated by this Law (Article 20, paragraph 1).

a. Energy Agency of the RS

799. The Agency is a regulatory body for energy sector established to improve and direct electricity and natural gas market development on the basis of principles

980. *Electricity generation* means production in hydropower plants, thermal power plants, CHP plants and other plants using RES (hereinafter 'power plants') (Art. 94, para. 1).

981. According to Art. 16 of the Law energy-related activities include the following: (1) electricity generation; (2) combined generation of electricity and thermal energy; (3) electricity transmission and electricity transmission system management; (4) electricity distribution and electricity distribution system management; (5) electricity distribution and closed distribution system management; (6) electricity supply; (7) wholesale electricity supply; (8) organized electricity market management; (9) natural gas transport and natural gas transport system management; (10) natural gas storage and natural gas storage facility management; (11) natural gas distribution and natural gas distribution system management; (12) natural gas supply; (13) public natural gas supply; (14) production of oil derivatives; (15) oil transport via oil pipelines; (16) oil derivatives transport via oil derivatives pipelines; (17) transport of oil, oil derivatives and biofuels by other transport modes; (18) oil, oil derivatives and biofuel storage; (19) trade in oil, oil derivatives, biofuels and compressed natural gas; (20) trade in fuels outside supply stations for vehicles; (21) filling of containers for liquid petroleum gas, compressed and liquefied natural gas; (22) trade in motor and other fuels at supply stations for vehicles; (23) trade in vessel fuels; (24) thermal energy generation; (25) thermal energy distribution; (26) thermal energy supply; (27) biofuel production; (28) bioliquid production; (29) blending of biofuels with fuels of oil origin. Energy-related activities under para. 1, items (1), (2), (6), 7), (8), (12), (14), (17), (18), (19), (20), (21), (22), 23), (27) and (29) of this Article shall be performed in accordance with market principles. Energy-related activities under para. 1, items (3), (4), (9), (10), (11), (13), (15), (16), (24), (25) and (26) of this Article are activities of general interest, pursuant to a separate law. Energy-related activity under para. 1, item 5 of this Article shall be performed in accordance with the provisions of this Law.

of non-discrimination and efficient competition, by creating a stable regulatory framework, as well as for performing other activities defined by this Law (Article 38, paragraph 1).[982]

In performing regulatory operations stipulated by this Law, the Agency shall take measures to achieve or contribute to the achievement of the following objectives: (1) ensuring safe supply of energy to the customers through efficient functioning and sustainable development of energy systems, in accordance with the energy policy of the RS, including environmental protection and development of RES; (2) development of the electricity market in the RS and its integration into the regional and Pan-European electricity market; (3) ensuring a stable, transparent and non-discriminatory regulatory framework for energy customers, system users and investors; (4) stimulating efficient functioning of energy systems; and (5) ensuring high standards of service in electricity and natural gas supply with the protection of energy vulnerable customers (Article 48).[983]

800. The Agency shall be financed by means of fees paid for licences for performing energy activities, a part of the price for system access determined by the methodologies referred to in Article 50, paragraph 1, items 1, 2, 6, 7, 8 and 10 of this Law, as well as other revenues made in performing operations within its competency in accordance with the Law (Article 62, paragraph 1).[984]

b. Energy from Renewable Energy Sources (RES)

801. The use of energy from renewable sources is in the interest of the RS. At the Ministry's proposal, the Government shall adopt the National Action Plan for RES usage (hereinafter 'National Action Plan')[985] which ensures that the share of RES will be in line with confirmed international agreements (Article 65, paragraphs 1 and 2).[986] The Ministry shall monitor implementation of the National Action Plan and submit every second year report[987] on its implementation to the Government (Article 66, paragraph 1).

982. The Agency is an autonomous legal entity and functionally independent from executive authority in carrying out its activities, as well as from other State authorities and organizations, legal entities and individuals engaged in energy activities (Art. 38, para. 2).

983. The Agency shall issue licences for performing energy-related activities and adopt an act of licence withdrawal, under conditions stipulated hereof, and shall keep registries of issued and withdrawn licences (Art. 49).

984. The Agency may be funded by donations, except from donations of energy entities or entities related in any way to those entities (Art. 62, para. 2).

985. Content of the National Action Plan is prescribed in Art. 65, para. 4.

986. The objectives of the National Action Plan shall be established based on energy needs, economic potential and obligations of the Republic of Serbia undertaken by ratified international agreements (Art. 65, para. 3). National Action Plan must be harmonized with regulations governing energy efficiency and reduction emission of gases causing greenhouse effect (Art. 65, para. 5).

987. Content of the Report is prescribed in Art. 66, para. 2.

802. A guarantee of origin[988] is issued by the transmission system operator at the request of producers of electricity from RES and is responsible for its accuracy, reliability and protection from abuse (Article 82, paragraph 1). A guarantee of origin is valid for a period of one year, starting from the last day of production period that is issued (Article 82, paragraph 7).[989]

c. Privileged Electricity and Heat Producers

803. Energy entities may, in accordance with this Law, acquire the status of a privileged producer of electricity (hereinafter 'privileged producer') for power plant, i.e., part of power plant upon meeting the following conditions: (1) using RES in the process of electricity generation and meets the requirements in terms of installed capacity: in hydroelectric power plant up to 30 MW, hydropower plant on the existing infrastructure up to 30 MW, biomass power plant, the biogas, wind, power plant on solar energy, geothermal and waste power plant and in other power plant in accordance with the Act from Article 74 of this Law; (2) was built and fit for use in accordance with the law governing construction of buildings; (3) has a special measuring, separated from the measurement in other technological processes, in which measures are taken and handed over electricity, i.e., thermal energy in the system; (4) produces electricity in newly constructed or reconstructed facilities in which the unused equipment is installed; (5) is licensed to conduct activities in accordance with this Law; (6) use the wind and solar energy, and has installed capacity less than the free capacity determined by the Act from Article 74 of this Law; (7) fulfil other conditions in accordance with the Act from Article 74 of this Law (Article 70, paragraph 1).

Energy entity may acquire the status of a privileged producer of electricity also for power plant, i.e., power plant that produce energy from high combined production of electricity and heat energy (conditions are prescribed in Article 70, paragraph 2). Energy entity may acquire status of producer of electricity for RES under conditions prescribed in Article 70, paragraph 3.[990]

988. *Guarantee of origin* is an electronic document with a sole function of proving to the final customer that a given share or quantity of energy was produced from RES, as well as from combined electricity and heat production with high energy conversion efficiency (Art. 2, point 12).

989. The procedure for issuing, transfer, utilization and termination of the guarantee of origin shall be based on the principles of objectivity, transparency and non-discrimination (para. 12).

990. The status of privileged producer, temporary status of privileged producers and status of producer from renewable sources can acquire a physical person generating electricity from renewable sources only for one power plant installed power of 30 kW under the conditions set out in paras 1–3 of this Article. The energy entity and physical person referred to in para. 5 of this Article may not at the same time have the status of energy producer from renewable sources and the status of privileged producer for the same power plant (Art. 70, para. 4–5). The energy entity or physical person referred to in Art. 70, para. 5 of this Law may, before acquiring the status of privileged producer, acquired a temporary status of privileged power producers for a period of three years (hereinafter 'temporary privileged producer') under the conditions stipulated in Art. 71, para. 1.

804. The Ministry shall establish the status of privileged producer, temporary privileged producer, and producer from renewable sources within thirty days of the request (Article 72, paragraph 1).[991]

d. Incentive Measures

805. Incentive measures, in accordance with this Law, shall include: (1) the obligation to purchase electricity from a privileged producer; (2) prices of the energy; (3) the period of validity of the obligation to purchase electric energy; (4) taking over balance liability; and (5) other incentive measures prescribed by the Act (Article 76, paragraph 1).[992]

806. A temporary privileged producer shall be entitled to incentive measures by the conclusion of an agreement on electricity purchase with a guaranteed supplier, under suspensive conditions, to acquire the status of a privileged producer pursuant to this law and regulations passed on the basis hereof (Article 77, paragraph 1).[993]

807. Privileged heat energy producers are the producers using RES in the process of heat energy production and fulfilling the conditions in terms of energy efficiency (Article 365).[994]

The LSG unit shall keep the registry of privileged heat energy producers, which shall particularly comprise data on thermal energy production plants, their location, installed power of the heating plant, the time envisaged for exploitation, conditions of construction and exploitation for that plant, the type of primary source used, and entities performing the energy-related activity of heat energy production in those facilities (Article 366, paragraph 1).

991. The request for obtaining the status under para. 1 of this Article shall be submitted in the form of contents which shall be determined in accordance with the Act under Art. 74 hereof. Enclosed with the request, the applicant shall submit the evidence of the fulfilment of conditions under Art. 70 hereof, as well as other evidence pursuant to this Law and regulations passed on the basis hereof. The decision under para. 1 of this Article may be appealed to the Government within fifteen days as of the decision receipt date.

992. Privileged energy entity shall be entitled to use incentive purchase price (Art. 76, para. 2).

993. Upon a request of a temporary privileged producer, the guaranteed supplier shall conclude an agreement on electricity purchase within thirty days as of the request submission date (para. 2). A temporary privileged producer that has acquired the status of a privileged producer pursuant to this Law shall be entitled only to incentive measures applicable on the date of submission of the request for obtaining the status of a temporary privileged producer (para. 3). The Government shall prescribe in more details the categories of privileged electricity producers, incentive measures for electricity generation from renewable sources and from highly efficient combined generation of electricity and thermal energy, the conditions for their acquisition, the method for determining and the duration of the incentive period, rights and obligations arising from such measures of privileged electricity producers and other energy entities, and other matters in accordance with the law.

994. The local self-government unit shall prescribe incentive measures and conditions for acquiring the status of a privileged thermal energy producer and the criteria for the fulfilment of those conditions, and shall determine the manner and procedure for acquiring such status.

808. Upon a proposal of the Ministry, the Government shall prescribe in more detail the share of biofuels in the market, reporting entities of the system for placing biofuels on the market and their obligations, incentives, measures and manner of placing biofuels on the market, reporting in the system for placing biofuels on the market, registry of reporting entities of the system for placing biofuels on the market and their reports, as well as other elements of the system for placing biofuels on the market (Article 340, paragraph 1).[995]

3. Law on the Use of Renewable Energy Sources

809. The Law on the Use of RES (OJ RS, Nos 40/21, and 35/23) regulates the use of energy from renewable sources,[996] the method for determining the share of RES of the RS in the gross final energy consumption, the integration of energy from renewable sources to the market, the incentive system for producing electricity from renewable sources, guarantees of origin for electricity, the production of electricity from renewable sources for own consumption, the use of RES in the field of thermal energy and the field of transport, special procedures related to the construction and connection of energy facilities that use RES, the bases of cooperation mechanisms with other states in the field of RES, monitoring the implementation of this Law, and other matters of relevance for RES (Article 1, paragraph 1).[997]

810. The provisions of the law are classified into the following twenty-one chapters: I Introductory provisions (Articles 1–8),[998] II Systems of incentives for electricity production from renewable sources (Articles 9–13), III Market premium system (Article 14–32), IV Fid-In tariff system (Articles 33–45), V Agreement on purchase of electricity from renewable sources (Article 46),[999] VI Guarantee of origin

995. Upon a proposal of the Ministry, the Government shall prescribe in more detail the payers of biofuel fee. The funds which are used as an incentive for the system for placing biofuels on the market shall be provided from the budget of the Republic of Serbia, in an amount to be determined for each year by the Budget Law of the Republic of Serbia within the Ministry's compartments in accordance with the defined limits in the fiscal strategy for the current year, with projections for the following two years (Art. 341, paras 1 and 2).

996. 'RES' are non-fossil sources of energy such as watercourses, biomass, wind, sun, renewable hydrogen, biogas, landfill gas, gas from sewage water treatment plants, geothermal energy sources, and other RES (Art. 4, para. 1, point 28),

997. The law pertaining to energy shall apply to all energy matters relating to RES which are not regulated by this Law (para. 2).

998. The use of energy from renewable sources is in the public interest of the Republic of Serbia and of particular significance for the Republic of Serbia (Art. 2, para. 1). Aiming to achieve the public interest as per para. 1 of this Article, the Republic of Serbia, the Autonomous Province and local self-government units shall adopt strategic and other documents, programmes and plans for achieving the objectives set out by this Law and provide funds in their budgets for complying with the obligations set out by this Law and strategic documents.

999. Power producers from RES may conclude a power purchase agreement for electricity generated from RES with the end-buyer, according to the market principle (Art. 46, para. 1). Power producers from renewable sources from para. 1 of this Article shall have a licence for electricity supply, following the law governing energy.

(Articles 47–55), VII Register of status (Article 56),[1000] VIII Incentive funds (Article 57),[1001] IX Production of electricity from renewable sources for own consumption (Articles 58–61), X Communities of RES (Articles 62–66), XI Duties of transmission, distribution and closed distribution system operators (Articles 67–69), XI Use of RES in the field of thermal energy (Articles 70–74), XII Use of RES in traffic (Articles 75–78), XIII Sustainability criteria and saving of greenhouse gas emissions for of biofuels, bioliquids and fuels from biomass (Articles 79–82), XIV Innovative technologies (Article 83),[1002] XVI Measures and activities for the achievement of public interest (Articles 84–91), XVII Implementation of the auction procedure and procedures related to the status of temporary privileged producer, the status of privileged producer and the status of producer from renewable sources (Articles 92–99), XVIII Mechanisms of cooperation (Article 100),[1003] XIX Supervision (Articles 101–105), XX Penal provisions (Articles 106–107), and XXI Transitional and final provisions (Articles 108–123).

Objectives of the Law, the share of energy from renewable sources and the ban on the construction of hydropower plants.

811. Article 3 of the law prescribes the objectives of the law. Regulation of the use of energy from renewable sources includes measures and activities undertaken to achieve eleven long-term goals, namely: (1) Decrease in the use of fossil fuels and increase in the use of RES with the aim of environmental protection; (2) Long-term decrease in the dependence on fuel imports; (3) Creation of jobs and development of entrepreneurship; (4) Incentives for research, innovation, and competitiveness in the field of using RES; (5) Digitalization, simplicity, cost-effectiveness, and efficiency of procedures in the field of RES; (6) Integration of electricity from renewable sources into the electrical energy market; (7) Ensuring

---

1000. The Ministry shall maintain a public and electronic register that contains data on the following: (1) producers that hold the status of privileged producer, (2) producers that hold the status of temporary privileged producer, (3) producers that hold the status of the producer from renewable sources, and (4) producers for whom the status from items 1), 2) and 3) of this paragraph has ceased to be in effect (Art. 56).

1001. The Government shall prescribe the method of calculation, payment and allocation of funds on the basis of the fee for the incentives to privileged producers and the method of calculation, payment, collection and allocation of additional incentive funds, the purpose and method of allocation of funds obtained on the basis of negative market premium, as well as monitoring and reporting regarding the incentive funds and funds obtained on the basis of negative market premium (Art. 57, para. 4)

1002. Incentives may be given to technologies under early development using new renewable sources, such as green hydrogen and other fuels, to increase the use of energy from renewable sources (Art. 83, para. 1). Renewable hydrogen may be used in the field of thermal energy, transport, and natural gas following the provisions of this Law and the law governing energy. The Government, upon a proposal by the Ministry, shall determine incentive measures for the production, transport, storage, and use of renewable hydrogen following para. 2 of this Article.

1003. Mechanisms of cooperation are forms of cooperation between states that cover the following: joint projects, statistical transfers from the energy balances of states, joint support schemes and other forms of cooperation that provide for a reduction in the costs of states for achieving their total share of RES in the gross final consumption of energy. The Republic of Serbia may agree on mechanisms of cooperation with other states, to achieve a share of energy from renewable sources in the gross final consumption of energy, in accordance with confirmed international agreements (Art. 100, paras 2, and 1).

the stability of the electrical energy market; (8) Regional development of the use of RES; (9) Stability of the system of incentives and use of operational state aid in the form of market premiums, except for small plants and demonstration projects; (10) Awarding incentives through auctions in a public, transparent, competitive, and cost-effective manner, without discrimination, ensuring a high degree of project implementation, except in the case of small plants and demonstration projects where incentives need not be awarded through auctions; (11) Sustainable and independent development through maximized utilization of national scientific research, technological-developmental and human capacities in the process of planning the increase of the use of RES.[1004]

812. The share of energy from RES in the gross final consumption of energy and final energy consumption in transport, as well as the share of RES in the electricity sector and thermal energy sector, shall be determined in the Integrated National Energy and Climate Plan (INECP) following the law governing energy (Article 6).[1005]

813. In addition, the Law prescribes which types of power plants are considered power plants from RES and establishes a ban on the construction of hydroelectric power plants in protected areas (Article 5). Article 5, paragraph 3 stipulates that the construction of hydropower plants in protected areas shall be prohibited. However, exceptions are prescribed when the construction of hydropower plants is allowed. Pursuant to Article 5, the government may, at the proposal of the Ministry, based on a previously obtained opinion of the ministry responsible for environmental protection, allow works and activities or projects for the construction of a hydropower plant in a protected area, in case these projects are of public and general interest, that is, on projects of special or national importance for the RS (paragraph 4).[1006]

1004. According to the explanation from the Draft Law, the goal of this law is to create a legal framework that will create an encouraging business environment for more dynamic investment in the field of RES to achieve goals in the field of RES that are defined by public policy documents. For this reason, the law with secondary legal acts should create legal certainty for investment in three key energy sectors that are important for the area of RES: the power sector, the heating and cooling sector, and the transport sector. The law should solve the problem of insufficient increase in the share of RES by removing the main causes that prevent their growth, but also achieve other goals in this area.

1005. The monitoring and reporting on achieving the share of energy from RES in the gross final consumption of energy and transport shall apply special rules for the calculation of the share from RES (Art. 7, para. 1).

1006. It shall be considered that the conditions referred to in para. 4 of this Article are met particularly in the case when the construction of a hydropower plant contributes to the safety of the electricity system, that is, it provides for new production capacities for the production of electricity from renewable sources that are necessary to achieve the planned growth rate of electricity production from RES, then to achieve national targets defined by the Integrated National Energy and Climate Plans, or when new production capacities for electricity production from RES are needed to achieve the targets of energy transition or fulfil international obligations (para. 5). It is quite obvious, that the broadly formulated norm on exceptions creates conditions that make it difficult to apply the rule prohibiting the construction of hydroelectric power plants.

Systems of incentives for electricity production from renewable sources[1007]

814. Within this chapter (Articles 9–13), the following issues are regulated: Types of Incentive Systems, Undertaking Balancing Responsibility, Rights and Obligations of the Guaranteed Supplier and Privileged Producer in the Market Premium System, Reimbursement of Costs of the Guaranteed Supplier, Right to Priority Access to the Transmission, and/or Distribution System or Closed Distribution System,[1008] Power Plants which are the Subject of Incentives,[1009] Informing the Public on the Incentive System and Evaluation of System Efficiency.

815. Incentives for the production of electricity from renewable sources shall be implemented in a certain incentive period through the system of market premiums and the system of feed-in tariffs related to the price of electricity, taking over balancing responsibility, the right to priority access to the system, and other incentives prescribed by law (Article 9. paragraph 1).[1010]

816. A guaranteed supplier shall assume balance responsibility for privileged producers[1011] who are in the market premium system (Article 10, paragraph 1).[1012] Guaranteed supplier shall be entitled to reimbursement of costs due to the undertaking of balance responsibility for privileged producers within the market premium system (Article 10b, paragraph 1).

Market premium system[1013]

817. The market premium shall be paid monthly for electricity that a power plant delivers into the electricity system (Article 14, paragraph 5). Article 15 of the

1007. *An incentive system* is a set of incentive measures related to a given technology for producing energy from renewable sources, used to achieve national goals regarding the use of RES (Art. 4, para. 1, point 42).

1008. A transmission, distribution, or closed distribution system operator shall receive, as a priority, electricity from renewable sources in demonstration projects, in power plants whose approved power is lower than 400 kW, i.e., for power plants that connect to the network after 1 Jan. 2026, and whose approved power is lower than 200 kW, regardless of whether it is a part of the incentive system or not, except in the case when the safety of the operation of the transmission or distribution system is endangered (Art. 11, para. 1).

1009. Incentive measures may be acquired for the following power plants using RES: (1) hydropower plant with installed power of 30 MW, (2) hydro power plant in an existing infrastructure with installed power up to 30 MW, (3) biomass power plant, (4) biogas power plant, (5) wind power plant, (6) solar power plant, (7) geothermal power plant, (8) biodegradable waste power plant, (9) landfill gas power plant, (10) power plant using gas from urban wastewater treatment plants, and (11) power plant using other RES (Art. 12, para. 1).

1010. Privileged producers are entitled to only one incentive system for the same power plant (para. 2).

1011. A privileged power producer from RES (hereinafter 'privileged producer') is a legal person or entrepreneur producing electricity from renewable sources and achieving the right to a feed-in tariff or market premium following this Law (Art. 4, para. 1, point 36).

1012. The privileged producer shall have the right to transfer balance responsibility to another balance responsible party following the law governing the field of energy and market operation rules (para. 2).

1013. A market premium is a type of operational state aid that represents an addition to the market price of electricity delivered to the market by the premium beneficiaries, determined in euro cent per kWh in the auction process (Art. 14, para. 1).

law prescribes the methodology for determining the market premium. The auction procedure for awarding the market premium as well as other related issues is regulated by Article 16.[1014] The status of a temporary privileged producer in the auction system, the basis for the adoption of a by-law that more closely regulates the conditions for application in the qualification phase, and other relevant issues are regulated by Articles 23–32.

Fid-In tariff system[1015]

818. This part of the law is dedicated to regulating the system of feed-in tariffs, auctions for feed-in tariffs, the status of a temporary privileged producer, the agreement on a feed-in tariff, the obligations of a guaranteed supplier, the duration and extension of the status of a temporary privileged producer, the obligations of a temporary privileged producer, conditions for cancellation of the status of temporary privileged producer, conditions for acquiring the status of the privileged producer. In addition, the obligations of the privileged producer, the conditions for withdrawing the status of the privileged producer, the duration of the incentive period, etc., are prescribed (Articles 33–46).

819. A feed-in tariff may be acquired for small plants and demonstration projects, in accordance with this Law and the by-law adopted on the basis of this Law. Feed-in tariffs shall be calculated and paid on a monthly basis. A feed-in tariff can be acquired for the entire or part of an electric power plant capacity (Article 33, paragraphs 2–4).[1016]

Guarantee of origin

820. This chapter of the Law prescribes producers from RES, obligations of producers from RES, conditions for cancelling the status of producers from RES, guarantees of origin, recognition of guarantees of origin issued in other countries, transfer of guarantees of origin, contents of guarantees of origin, register of guarantees origin, as well as the calculation of the share of all types of energy sources in the sold electricity (Articles 47–55). A producer from renewable electrical energy sources is an energy entity producing electricity from renewable sources that does not have the status of Temporary Privileged Producer or Privileged Producer (hereinafter producer from RES).[1017] Producer from RES is entitled to guarantees of origin (Article 47, paragraphs 1 and 2).

1014. Articles 17–22 prescribe the conditions for starting auctions, the method of starting the auction procedure, qualifications, bidding, the adoption of a ranking list and the method of filling the quota, as well as the method of selecting the best offers and exercising the right to legal protection in auction procedures.

1015. A feed-in tariff is a type of operational state aid awarded in the form of an incentive purchase price guaranteed per kWh for electricity delivered to the electrical power system during the incentive period (Art. 33, para. 1).

1016. The Ministry shall assign the right to a feed-in tariff under the auction procedure based on the available quotas prescribed by the Government (para. 5).

1017. As an exception from para. 1 of this Article, if the temporary privileged producer or privileged producer has acquired that status only for a part of the capacity of the power plant, they may acquire the status of a power producer from renewable sources for the remaining part of the capacity of the power plant which is outside of the incentive system (para. 3).

821. Power producer from renewable sources from paragraph 1 of this Article may acquire the status of the producer from renewable sources if: (1) they utilize RES in the process of electricity production, (2) a use permit was obtained for the power plant following the law regulating the construction of facilities, (3) they have secured separate measurement, distinct from measurement in other technological processes, measuring the received and transmitted electrical, and/or thermal energy into the system, (4) they hold a licence for performing the activity following the law regulating the field of energy, (5) that it is connected to the electricity transmission, distribution, and/or closed distribution system (paragraph 4).[1018]

Production of electricity from renewable sources for own consumption

822. The law regulates the following issues: the position of the prosumer,[1019] the relationship between a prosumer and a supplier, the right to priority access of a prosumer, and the Prosumer's Register and assessment of their production (Articles 58–61). Prosumer is entitled to, independently or through an aggregator: (1) produce electricity for their consumption, (2) store electricity for their own needs, (3) deliver the excess produced electricity into the electricity transmission, distribution, and/or closed distribution system, (4) and other rights and obligations following this Law and the law governing energy (Article 58, paragraph 1).[1020]

823. An operator of a transmission, distribution, or closed distribution system shall receive, as a priority, electricity from the prosumer, except in the case when the safety of the system operation is in danger (Article 60, paragraph 1).[1021]

824. An operator of a transmission, distribution, or closed distribution system shall establish a register of prosumers connected to the transmission, distribution, or closed distribution system (Article 61, paragraph 1).[1022]

Communities of RES

825. This part of the law prescribes the legal position of the community of RES,[1023] its goals, as well as its rights and obligations (Articles 62–66). The primary goal of establishing a Community is the use of RES to meet the energy needs

1018. The Ministry shall decide on the request for acquiring the status of producer from renewable sources by decision under an administrative procedure within fifteen days of the date of submission of the request (para. 5).

1019. *The prosumer* is an end-buyer who has connected their facility for generating electricity from RES to the internal installations, where the generated electricity is used for own consumption, and the surplus generated electricity is delivered to the transmission system, distribution system, or closed distribution system (Art. 4, para. 1, point 22).

1020. Prosumer from para. 1 of this Article may not use incentive measures in the form of a market premium and feed-in tariff, nor may they have the right to guarantees of origin (para. 2).

1021. An operator of a transmission, distribution, or closed distribution system shall instal a meter, at the place of the handover of electricity of a prosumer, which would enable a separate measurement of the delivered and received electricity, following the law governing energy and this Law.

1022. The Ministry shall further prescribe the manner of maintaining the Register from para. 1 of this Article and the assessment methodology from para. 2 of this Article (para. 3).

1023. A RES Community (hereinafter 'Community') is a legal person established according to the principle of open and voluntary participation of its members, following this Law, which is controlled

of members of the community in a sustainable manner that covers environmental, economic, or social benefits for members, as well as the local community and society (Article 64, paragraph 1). To achieve the primary goal, a Community shall develop, invest, and implement RES and energy efficiency projects.

Duties of transmission, distribution, and closed distribution system operators

826. This part of the Act prescribes the duties of transmission and distribution system operators (Articles 67–69). This includes the obligations and rights of the 'transmission system operator' and 'distribution, i.e., closed distribution system operator'. The issue of taking measures to simplify connections and inform the public is also regulated.[1024]

827. Transmission system operator shall maintain an electronic, centralized, and publicly available register of all connected power plants that use RES and shall contain the following: name of electricity producer, name of the power plant, power plant capacity, power plant location, trial operation year and the year of permanent connection of the power plant (Article 67, paragraph 1).[1025] In addition, in the course of the preparation of the transmission system development plan following the law governing the field of energy, the transmission system operator shall present (in its analysis of the adequacy of production and the transmission system) the following: (1) the list of connection projects for which the agreement on the preparation of the study of the facility connection was concluded with the transmission system operator, i.e., for which the design requirements and connection of the power plant have been issued by the distribution system operator or closed distribution system operator and whose connection may not be postponed following paragraph 2 hereof and Article 68b of this Law; (2) overview of historical data on the contracted and provided reserve for system balancing for the relevant period; (3) methodology for the assessments of available and required reserves for system balancing; (4) assessment of the required reserve for system balancing in the control area; (5) assessment of currently available reserve for system balancing in the control area; (6) assessment whether and how much reserves for system balancing are lacking in the case of connection of all power plants that are in the process of connecting and which use variable RES; (7) indicators of production system adequacy to meet the consumption, obtained based on calculation; (8) conclusion on the risks for the safe

by its members whose residence or registered office is in the vicinity of the location of the renewable energy power plants which is owned or developed by this legal person (Art. 62).

1024. The Transmission System Operator, Distribution System Operator or Closed Distribution System Operator shall undertake active measures to simplify the connection procedure for power plants producing electricity from renewable sources (Art. 69, para. 1). The Transmission System Operator, Distribution System Operator or Closed Distribution System Operator shall inform the public on the measures undertaken from para. 1 of this Article appropriately through their website (para. 2).

1025. The transmission system operator shall publish a list of all requests submitted under the connection procedure which shall contain the following: name of the applicant, power plant location, data on the required power of the power plant, and the phase of connection procedure (para. 2).

operation of the power system and the need to postpone the connection of power plants that use variableRES, except for the power plants from item 1) hereof (Article 67a, paragraph 1).

828. The Distribution System Operator or Closed Distribution System Operator shall, *inter alia*, maintain an electronic, centralized, and publicly available register of all connected power plants that use RES, which shall contain the following: name of the electricity producer, power of the power plant, location of the power plant and the year of permanent connection (Article 68, paragraph 1).[1026]

Use of RES in the field of thermal energy and use of RES in traffic

829. In these two chapters of the law, the availability of information on the share of RES in thermal energy,[1027] incentive measures, the connection of an independent producer to the distribution system of thermal energy, the procedure and conditions for the connection of an independent producer, the right to subsidies (Articles 70–74) are attributed. In addition, the use of RES in traffic, the share of RES in the final energy consumption in traffic,[1028] incentives for the production of biofuels, placing biofuels on the market, as well as the basis for the adoption of a by-law in the transport sector are prescribed (Articles 75–78).[1029]

Sustainability criteria and saving of greenhouse gas emissions for biofuels, bioliquids, and fuels from biomass

830. This part of the Law prescribes sustainability criteria and saving greenhouse gas emissions for biofuels, bioliquids, and biomass fuels, verification of sustainability criteria, and a by-law regulating sustainability criteria in more detail (Articles 79–82). Biofuels, bioliquids, and fuels from biomass placed on the market must comply with the criteria for sustainability and achieve savings in greenhouse gas emissions (Article 79, paragraph 1). The energy produced from biofuels, bioliquids, and fuels from biomass will be: (1) taken into consideration for calculating the planned share of energy from renewable sources in the gross final energy consumption and final energy consumption used in all forms of transport, (2) the

1026. The Distribution System Operator or Closed Distribution System Operator shall publish a list of all requests submitted under the connection procedure, which shall contain the following: name of the applicant, location of the power plant, data on the required power of the power plant, and the phase of connection procedure (para. 2).

1027. Local self-government units shall ensure that the thermal energy suppliers make available information on the share of RES to the end consumers on the website of the thermal energy supplier, along with the bill, at the request of the end consumers or in another suitable manner (Art. 70).

1028. Fuel suppliers shall ensure that part of the RES in the final consumption of energy in transport by 2030 follows the national goal for the use of renewable sources in transport established by the Integrated National Plan for Climate and Energy (Art. 75, para. 1). The determination of the national goal from para. 1 of this Article shall take into consideration renewable liquid and gaseous fuels of non-biological origin intended for use in transport when used as an intermediate product for the production of conventional fuels, and fuels from recycled carbon may also be taken into consideration.

1029. The Government, upon a proposal by the Ministry, shall further prescribe incentives and measures for achieving the share of RES in the sector of transport, obligations of the fuel supplier regarding the achievement of the share of RES in the sector of transport, method, and criteria for granting incentives, the manner of fulfilling that obligation, etc (Art. 78, para. 1).

subject of financial incentives to increase the use of biofuels, bioliquids and fuels from biomass, and (3) calculated in the fulfilment of obligations of fuel suppliers to achieve the share of RES which are placed on the market in transport (paragraph 2).[1030]

Measures and activities for the achievement of public interest

831. This part of the Law prescribes measures and activities for the realization of public interest, benefits for investors who introduce energy from RES in the construction of buildings, conditions for appointing a strategic partner, decision-making method, and decision elements for choosing a strategic partner, procedure and method of choosing a strategic partner, public invitation for the selection of a strategic partner, the possibility of determining the project of the strategic partner as a project of importance for the RS, the possibility of determining public interest for the needs of expropriation for the construction of a power plant within the project that is being developed with the strategic partner, as well as the measures of the LSG unit (Articles 84–92).

832. Aiming to achieve the public interest as per paragraph 2 of this Article, the RS, AP, and LSG units,[1031] through strategic and other documents, programs, and plans, shall envisage measures and activities prepared to meet the goals set out by this Law (Article 84, paragraph 1).[1032]

833. Upon a proposal of the minister in charge of energy matters, the Government may decide to implement the strategic partner selection process for the execution of a construction project with or without management and maintenance of a power plant that uses RES or an energy facility important for the integration of electricity from variable RES into the system (Article 87, paragraph 1).[1033]

1030. The Government shall further prescribe the criteria for sustainability, greenhouse gas emissions savings and method of their calculation, method of verification and subjects of verification, reporting on compliance with the criteria for sustainability and greenhouse gas emissions savings, independent audit of information submitted under the reporting procedure, manner of keeping the register of subjects of verification and verifiers, etc. (Art. 82, para. 1).

1031. A local self-government unit may determine, by decision, the criteria, amount, and procedure for reducing contributions for the regulation of construction land, special decreases in the amount of contributions for missing infrastructure, and other benefits for investors that, during the construction of a new building, as well as during the reconstruction, adaptation, recovery or energy recovery of an existing building, envisage alternative provision of electrical or thermal energy from the domain of RES (Art. 85, para. 1).

1032. When planning the measures and activities from para. 1 of this Article, the Republic of Serbia, Autonomous Province, and local self-government units shall pay particular attention that the planned measures are contributing to the energy security of the Republic of Serbia, sustainable and uniform regional and local economic development, ensuring and improving the energy needs of the population, and preserving and protecting the environment (para. 2).

1033. Upon a proposal of the minister in charge of energy matters, the Government may determine that the power plant from Art. 87, para. 1 of this Law shall be a project of importance for the Republic of Serbia within the meaning of the law governing the construction of facilities, except for power plants, which cover a protected area or an ecological network area, according to special laws (Art. 90). In addition, the Government may, by a special decision, determine the public interest for

Implmentation of the auction procedure and procedures related to the status of temporary privileged producer, the status of privileged producer and the status of producer from renewable sources

834. In this chapter, the law prescribes the auction procedure and procedures related to the status of a temporary privileged producer, the status of a privileged producer, and the status of a producer from renewable sources, then the processing of the request, the method of delivery, the form of the documents to be submitted, the delivery of the decision, the delivery confirmation and the electronic notice board (Articles 92–99).[1034]

835. During the implementation of the auction procedures and procedures concerning the status of the Temporary Privileged Producer, the status of the Privileged Producer, and the status of the Producer from RES, the competent body shall solely conduct a check of compliance with the formal conditions for action and shall not engage in assessments of the technical documentation, nor test the authenticity of documents obtained under such procedures (Article 92, paragraph 1).[1035]

Supervision

836. Monitoring over the implementation of the provisions of this Law and regulations adopted based on this Law shall be conducted by the Ministry unless prescribed otherwise by this Law (Article 101, paragraph 1).[1036]

837. Inspection shall be performed by the Ministry through the energy inspector (hereinafter 'inspector') within the scope established by this Law (Article 102, paragraph 1). However, supervision over the implementation of the provisions of this Law and regulations adopted based on this Law, related to the quality of biofuels

expropriation, administrative transfer, and/or incomplete expropriation of immovables to construct a power plant from Art. 87, para. 1 of this Law, as well as facilities for its purposes and connections to the electric power system, following applicable planning documents (Art. 91).

1034. The law regulating the general administrative procedure shall apply to issues related to the auction procedure and procedures related to the status of temporary privileged producer, the status of privileged producer, and the status of producers from RES, which are not specifically regulated by this Law (Art. 99).

1035. The Ministry shall solely test compliance with the following formal conditions: (1) competence to act upon the request; (2) whether the party submitting the request is a person that, under this Law, may submit a request; (3) whether the request contains all the prescribed data; (4) whether all of the documentation prescribed by this Law and by-laws adopted based on this Law is submitted with the request; (5) whether evidence of the payment of the prescribed fee has been supplied with the request; (6) whether the conditions prescribed by this Law and the by-laws adopted based on it for the adoption of the request have been met (para. 2).

1036. Energy subjects, the Autonomous Province, local self-government units, and other legal persons and entrepreneurs whose rights and obligations are prescribed by this Law, shall submit all required data for performing the tasks from the scope of work of the Ministry upon request by the Ministry (Art. 101, para. 2).

placed on the market, shall be performed by the ministry competent for trade affairs through market inspectors following the law regulating trade (paragraph 2).[1037]

By-laws in the field of RES

838. Based on the Law on the Use of RES (OJ RS, No. 40/2021), several by-laws have been enacted, including the following:

- Regulation on sustainability criteria for biofuels, bioliquids, and fuels from biomass (OJ RS, No. 96/23).
- Regulation on the selection of a strategic partner for the implementation of the construction project without management and maintenance of large-capacity self-balanced solar power plants with battery systems for electricity storage in the RS (OJ RS, No. 58/2023).
- Decision on the selection of a strategic partner (OJ RS, No. 93/2023).
- Regulation on the assumption of balance responsibility and the model agreement on the assumption of balance responsibility (OJ RS, No. 45/2023).
- Regulation on the quota in the market premium system for solar power plants (OJ RS, No. 45/2023).
- Regulation on market premium and FID tariff (OJ RS, No. 45/2023).
- Regulation on the amount of special compensation for the incentive of privileged electricity producers in 2023 (OJ RS, No. 3/2023).
- Regulation on the model contract on the market premium (OJ RS, No. 112/2021).
- Regulation on market premium and feed-in tariff (OJ RS, Nos 112/2021, 45/2023 – other regulation).
- Decree on the quota in the market premium system for wind power plants (OJ RS, No. 107/2021); Decree on the criteria, conditions, and method of calculating claims and obligations between the customer – manufacturer, and supplier (OJ RS, Nos 83/2021, 74/2022).
- Decision on the maximum offered price for electricity for auctions in the market premium system (OJ RS, No. 45/2023).
- Decision on implementation of the procedure for the selection of a strategic partner: (OJ RS, Nos 37/2023 71/2023).
- Rulebook on the method of proving the fulfilment of the conditions by which the postponement of connection to the transmission, distribution, or closed distribution system is not applied to power plants that use variable energy sources (OJ RS, No. 76/2023).

1037. Supervision the implementation of the provisions of this Law and other regulations related to the requirements to be met by power plants regarding the issuing of integrated permits, waste management permits, and the use of waste and other requirements prescribed by the law and following the regulations in the field of environmental protection shall be performed by the ministry competent for environmental protection affairs through the environmental protection inspector following the regulations regulating environmental protection (para. 3). Supervision over the implementation of the provisions of this Law and other regulations related to the requirements to be met by hydropower plants regarding the issuing of water permits shall be performed by the ministry competent for water management affairs through water inspectors under the regulations on the issuing of water permits (para. 4).

– Rulebook on the method of calculation and presentation of the share of all types of energy sources in the sold electricity (OJ RS, No. 2/2023).
– Ordinance on the budget for the share of RES (OJ RS, No. 2/2023).
– Rulebook on the manner of keeping the Register of customers – producers connected to the transmission, distribution, or closed distribution system and the methodology for evaluating the produced electricity in the production facility of the customer-producer (OJ RS, No. 33/2022).

4. Law on Energy Efficiency and Rational Use of Energy

839. The basic legal Act regulating the field of efficient use of energy in the RS is the Law on Energy Efficiency and Rational Use of Energy (OJ RS, No. 40/2021), adopted in 2021. It has the following seventeen parts: Part I – General Provisions (Articles 1–3); Part II – Policy of efficient energy usage (Articles 4–9); Part III – The Energy Management System and Energy Audit (Articles 10–34); Part IV – Energy Efficiency of Buildings (Articles 35–37); Part V – Control of the Heating/Air-Conditioning System in the Building (Articles 38–42); Part VI – Energy Services (Articles 43–47); Part VII – Energy Efficiency of Energy Activities and Final Customers (Articles 48–53); Part VIII – Energy Efficiency of Energy Facilities (Articles 54–58); Part IX – Obligations of Beneficiaries of Public Funds (Articles 59–61); Part X – Energy Savings in Road Transport (Articles 62); Part XI – Energy Labelling and Ecodesign Requirements (Articles 63–67); Part XII – Financing, incentives and other measures of efficient energy usage (Articles 68–77); Part XIII – Incentives for Highly Efficient Cogeneration and Individual Participants in the Energy Market (Acticles 78–117); Part XIV – Implementation of Auction Procedures and Procedures Relating to the Status of the Temporary Privileged Electricity Producer and the Status of the Privileged Electricity Producer (Articles 118–125); Part XV – Supervision (Articles 126–135); Part XVI – Penalties (Articles 136–151);and Part XVII – Transitory and final provisions (Articles 152–168).

840. This law regulates the conditions and method of efficient use of energy[1038] and energy sources (hereinafter ‘energy’); policy of efficient energy use; energy management system; energy efficiency policy measures: energy use in buildings, energy activities and end customers, for energy facilities and energy services; energy labelling and eco-design requirements; financing, incentives and other measures in this area; the establishment and operations of the Directorate for Financing and Encouraging Energy Efficiency (hereinafter ‘the Directorate’), as well as other matters of importance for the rights and obligations of natural and legal persons in connection with the efficient use of energy (Article 1).

841. The goal of the Law is defined in Article 2 as creating conditions for efficient use of energy and improvement of energy efficiency. In this way, it contributes

1038. *Efficient use of energy* is the use of energy for quality performance of appropriate activities and provision of services in a way that achieves minimum energy consumption, within the technical capabilities of modern plants, equipment, and devices (Art. 3, para. 1, point 20).

to achieving energy savings, security of energy supply, reducing the impact of the energy sector on the environment and climate change, sustainable use of natural and other resources, increasing the competitiveness of the economy, improving conditions for economic development, and reducing energy poverty.[1039] Energy efficiency goals are determined by strategic and planning acts from Article 5, paragraph 1 (Article 5, paragraph 3).

a. Policy of Efficient Energy Use

842. According to Article 5 of the Law, the basic acts that determine the energy efficiency policy are: (1) the Energy Development Strategy of the RS, which is adopted following the law governing the field of energy (hereinafter 'Strategy'); (2) Programme that determines the conditions, method, dynamics, and measures for the implementation of the Strategy, which is adopted under the law governing the field of energy; (3) INCEP,[1040] which is adopted following the law governing the field of energy (paragraph 1).[1041]

b. Energy Management System

843. Subjects of the energy management system are the Government, Ministry, obligees of the energy management system,[1042] energy managers, and energy consultants (Article 10). The Government, as a subject of the energy management system, adopts regulations in the field of energy efficiency and rational use of energy, at the proposal of the Ministry, following the provisions of this law (Article 11). The Ministry regulates, organizes, implements, and monitors the functioning of the energy management system and the realization of its goals (Article 12).

1039. Energy efficiency and rational use of energy are in the public interest of the Republic of Serbia. They are of special importance for the Republic of Serbia, except when it comes to protected areas and ecological network areas (Art. 4).

1040. NEKP, in the part related to energy efficiency, especially contains an indicative energy efficiency goal, a cumulative energy savings goal, measures to achieve them, as well as an energy efficiency goal for central government buildings (para. 4).

1041. Strategic and planning documents of the republic's bodies, which are not listed in para. 1 of this article, and which contribute to the implementation of the energy efficiency policy, are adopted with the consent of the ministry responsible for energy affairs (hereinafter 'the Ministry') and the ministry responsible for environmental protection affairs, when strategic and planning documents refer to the protected area and the area of the ecological network (para. 2).

1042. Obligors of the energy management system are: (1) companies and public enterprises whose main activity is in the production sector, if they have an annual energy consumption greater than the amount prescribed by the Government; (2) economic companies and public enterprises whose main activity is in the trade and services sector, if they have an annual energy consumption greater than the amount prescribed by the Government; (3) local self-government unit and city municipality with more than 20,000 inhabitants according to the last population census; (4) state administration bodies, other bodies and organizations of the Republic of Serbia, bodies and organizations of autonomous provinces and organizations for mandatory social insurance (Art. 13, para. 1).

844. The provisions of Articles 20–34 regulate issues related to the energy manager[1043] and energy consultant[1044] and the performance of an energy audit. Article 20 defines who can be an energy manager and what tasks he performs.

c. The Objectives of Energy Savings and Limit Values of Spending

845. The Government, on the proposal of the Ministry, determines the annual energy-saving goals for the System Obligers following the acts referred to in Article 5, paragraph 1, point. 1)–3) of this law and the threshold value of annual energy consumption based on which it is determined which companies and public enterprises are liable for the system (Article 15, paragraph 1).[1045]

d. Financing of Efficient Use of Energy

846. The Law in Chapter XII (under the title Financing, incentives and other measures of efficient energy use) includes Articles 67–76 and has the following two sections: 1. Financing of efficient energy use (sections 67–70),[1046] and 2. Administration for financing and encouraging energy efficiency (Articles 71–76).[1047] Funds for financing the efficient use of energy are provided from: (1) the budget of the RS; (2) the budget of the AP and LSG units; (3) funds of the European Union, multilateral and other funds for the fight against climate change and other international funds; (4) donations, gifts, contributions, assistance and the like; (5) loans from international financial institutions; (6) other sources following the law (Article 69).

847. For the performance of executive and professional tasks related to the financing of efficient energy use operations following this law, the regulations

1043. An energy manager is a natural person who has an energy manager's licence, issued following this law, and who is appointed by the System Obligor. The energy manager performs the following tasks for the System Obligor: (1) collects and analyses data on the way energy is used; (2) organizes and participates in the preparation of energy efficiency programs and plans; (3) proposes energy efficiency measures and participates in their implementation; (4) preparing the Annual Report; (5) undertakes other activities and energy efficiency measures (Art. 20, paras 1, and 2).

1044. An energy consultant is a natural person who has an energy consultant's licence (Art. 22, para. 1). The energy consultant can conduct energy audits.

1045. The Minister prescribes the method of calculating annual energy consumption from para. 1 of this article (para. 2).

1046. In s. 1, the following issues are regulated: financing, incentives, and other measures of efficient energy use; the subject of financing, means of financing at the state level, at the level of autonomous provinces and local self-government units, as well as tax, customs and other benefits.

1047. Section 2 regulates the establishment and work of the Directorate for Financing and Encouraging Energy Efficiency; tasks, resources for work, distribution of funds, use of funds, and cooperation with other domestic and international bodies of the Administration are prescribed. Article 73 refers to the sources of funds for the work of the Administration, and Art. 74 refers to the distribution, that is, the allocation of funds to beneficiaries. Art. 74 also defines the beneficiaries who can receive funds allocated by the Administration. The Minister prescribes in more detail the conditions for the distribution and use of the funds of the Administration. The use of funds must be strictly intended, otherwise the user of the funds is responsible for the non-intended use of funds (Art. 75). Article 76 provides for the possibility and manner of cooperation of the Administration with other domestic and international bodies.

adopted based on this law and the application of energy efficiency measures, the Administration is formed as an administrative body within the Ministry, and its jurisdiction is determined (Article 72, paragraph 1).[1048]

848. The competent body of the AP or LSG unit can by its act determine special financial and other incentives, the establishment of budget funds as well as the use of funds from existing funds for the implementation of projects and other activities for the efficient use of energy in its territory, following the law and regulations that regulate the work of these organs (Article 70, paragraph 1).[1049]

e. By-laws in the Field of Energy Efficiency

849. Based on the new Law on Efficient Use of Energy (OJ RS, Nos 40/21, and 35/23), several by-laws have been enacted, including the following:

- Regulation on establishing the Program for financing activities and measures to improve energy efficiency in 2023 (OJ RS, No. 29/2023).
- Regulation on the content of the guarantee of origin and the method of keeping the register for electricity produced in high-efficiency cogeneration (OJ RS, No. 89/2023).
- Regulation on the model contract on the feed-in tariff for the sale of electricity produced in a micro-cogeneration unit or small cogeneration (OJ RS, No. 43/2023).
- Regulation on energy labelling of products that affect energy consumption (OJ RS, Nos 21/2023, 34/2023). Regulation on energy management system payers (OJ RS, No. 59/2022).
- Regulation on minimum energy efficiency requirements that new and reconstructed energy buildings must meet (OJ RS, No. 44/2022).
- Regulation on the obligations of the Guaranteed Supplier and on the obligations of the Authorized Contracting Party regarding financial incentives for high-efficiency cogeneration (OJ RS, No. 30/2022).
- Rulebook on requirements regarding staff training, technical equipment and space to be fulfilled by the organization for carrying out the training of energy managers and energy advisors (OJ RS, No. 89/2023).
- Rulebook on control of building heating systems (OJ RS, No. 80/2023).
- Rulebook on the content of the report on the conducted energy audit (OJ RS, No. 63/2023).
- Rulebook on the methodological framework for determining the technical feasibility and cost justification of equipping a building that is to be energy-renovated in detail with devices for regulation and devices for measuring the delivered amount of thermal energy (OJ RS, No. 60/2023).

1048. The headquarters of the Administration is in Belgrade. The management has the capacity of a legal entity. The administration is managed by a director, who is appointed by the Government for five years, at the proposal of the minister, according to the law regulating the position of civil servants and officials.

1049. The competent authority of the autonomous province and local self-government unit is obliged to inform the Ministry about the activities carried out in the sense of para. 1 of this article (para. 2).

– Rulebook on the minimum criteria for conducting an energy audit (OJ RS, No. 45/2023).
– Rulebook on the methodology for calculating energy savings that are the result of implemented energy efficiency measures (OJ RS, No. 20/2023).
– Rulebook on the type of data on implemented energy efficiency measures and achieved energy savings submitted by users of public funds (OJ RS, No. 19/2023); Rulebook on the ISEM information system (OJ RS, No. 18/2023).
– Rulebook on the type of testing for determining the degree of usefulness from reports on thermo technical testing for energy facilities for energy production (OJ RS, No. 14/2023).
– Rulebook on control of building air conditioning systems (OJ RS, No. 14/2023).
– Rulebook on the methodological framework for determining the technical feasibility and cost justification of equipping technical systems for heating and air conditioning of non-residential buildings with automatic regulation and control systems (OJ RS, No. 8/2023).
– Rulebook on closer conditions for the appointment of energy managers (OJ RS, No. 137/2022).
– Rulebook on the content of the study on the energy efficiency of an energy facility and techno-economic analysis in the case of combined production of heat and electricity in an energy facility (OJ RS, No. 137/2022).
– Rulebook on the methodological framework for determining the technical feasibility and cost justification of the installation of devices for measuring the thermal energy transferred to parts of the building and the heat distributor on each heating element in buildings connected to the district heating system (OJ RS, Nos 117/2022, and 137/2022- 93 – correction).
– Rulebook on training and examination for energy manager (OJ RS, No. 117/ 2022).
– Rulebook on closer conditions regarding the energy efficiency of buildings under which the supply of thermal energy can be contracted for users of public funds (OJ RS, No. 84/2022).
– Rulebook on energy service contracts (OJ RS, No. 82/2022).
– Rulebook on the number and corresponding license of energy consultants who conduct energy audits depending on the category of energy audit (OJ RS, No. 70/2022).
– Rulebook on the method of budgeting annual energy consumption on the basis of which it is determined which economic companies and public enterprises are liable for the energy management system (OJ RS, Nos 68/2022, 60/2023), etc.[1050]

1050. In addition, it should be borne in mind that some regulations adopted on the basis of the old Law on Efficient Use of Energy (OJ RS, No. 25/13) are still in force. These are the following by-laws: Rulebook on energy efficiency labeling of cooling devices (OJ RS, No. 43/21); Ordinance on energy efficiency labeling of household washing machines and household washing and drying machines (OJ RS, No. 43/21); Rulebook on energy efficiency labeling of household dishwashers (OJ RS, No. 43/21); Rulebook on marking the energy efficiency of water heaters, hot water tanks and sets of water heaters and solar devices (OJ RS, No. 67/18); Rulebook on energy efficiency labeling of space heaters, combined heaters, sets of space heaters, temperature regulation equipment and solar devices and sets of combined heaters, temperature regulation equipment and solar

Several regulations concerning eco-design have been adopted.[1051]

5. Other Legal Regulation

850. In addition to these laws, the area of energy efficiency in the building sector is regulated by the Law on Planning and Building (OJ RS, Nos 72/2009, 81/09 – corr., 64/10 – CC, 24/11, 121/12, 42/13 – CC, 50/13 – CC, 98/13 – CC, 132/14, 145/14, 83/18, 31/19, 37/19 – other law, 9/20, 52/21, and 62/23) and related Delegated legislation: Rulebook on energy efficiency of building construction (OJ RS, No. 61/2011) and the Rulebook on the conditions, content and manner of issuing certificates of energy performance of buildings (OJ RS, Nos 69/12, 44/18 – other law, and 111/22).

851. The Law on Mining Geological Explorations (OJ RS, Nos 101/15, 95/18 – other law, and 40/21) regulates geological exploration, exploitation of mineral raw materials, revenue generation by the State, establishment of the Mining Agency, as well as other relevant matters.[1052]

852. The Law on Excises (OJ RS, Nos 22/01, 73/01, 80/02 – other law, 43/03, 72/03, 43/04, 55/04, 135/04, 46/05, 101/05 – other law, 61/07, 5/09, 31/09, 101/10, 43/11, 101/11, 6/12, 43/12, 76/12, 93/12, 119/12, 8/13, 47/13, 4/14, 68/14 – other law, 142/14, 4/15, 55/15, 103/15, 5/16, 108/16, 30/18, 153/20, 53/21, and 75/23) proscribes, *inter alia*, excises for oil derivatives.

853. Law on Pipeline Transportation of Gaseous and Liquid Hydrocarbons and Distribution of Gaseous Hydrocarbons (OJ RS, No. 104/09) regulates the requirements for safe and undisturbed pipeline transport of gaseous and liquid hydrocarbons

---

devices (OJ RS, No. 17/18); Rulebook on energy efficiency labeling of tumble dryers for households (OJ RS, No. 24/17); Rulebook on energy efficiency labeling of household ovens and hoods (OJ RS, No. 19/17); Rulebook on energy efficiency labeling of air conditioning devices (OJ RS, No. 24/14); Rulebook on marking the energy efficiency of televisions (OJ RS, No. 24/14); Ordinance on marking the energy efficiency of household refrigerating appliances (OJ RS, Nos 17/14, 43/21 – other bylaw).

1051. Regulation on eco-design of products that affect energy consumption (OJ RS, No. 132/21); Rulebook on eco-design requirements for solid fuel boilers (OJ RS, No. 120/23); Rulebook on eco-design requirements for solid fuel local space heaters (OJ RS, No. 117/23); Rulebook on eco-design requirements for simple set top box devices (OJ RS, No. 65/23); Rulebook on eco-design requirements with regard to electricity consumption in standby mode, switched off mode and networked standby mode for electrical and electronic devices in the household and office equipment 65/23); Rulebook on eco-design requirements for household washing machines and household washing and drying machines (OJ RS, No. 45/23); Rulebook on eco-design requirements for household dishwashers (OJ RS, No. 45/23); Rulebook on eco-design requirements for electronic screens (OJ RS, No. 111/22); Rulebook on eco-design requirements for cooling devices (OJ RS, No. 111/22).

1052. For more details, *see* chapter devoted to subsoil and minerals.

and distribution of gaseous hydrocarbons, design, construction and maintenance and use of pipelines, and indoor gas installations (Article 1).[1053]

854. Following by-laws, *inter alia*, regulate oil and oil derivatives market:

- Regulation on operational reserves of oil derivatives, coal, and other energy sources (OJ RS, No. 79/21).
- Rulebook on deadlines, content, and method of submitting data on the procurement and sale of oil, oil derivatives, biofuels, bioliquids, compressed natural gas, liquefied natural gas, and hydrogen (OJ RS, No. 72/21).
- Rulebook on consent for storage and supply of oil, oil derivatives, and biofuels for own needs (OJ RS, Nos 12/16, 44/18 – other law, 65/18 and 79/21).
- Regulation on technical conditions for unhindered and safe transportation of oil (OJ RS, No. 37/13).
- Regulation on labelling (marking) of petroleum products (OJ RS, Nos 51/15, 5/17, 115/22).
- Regulation on monitoring the quality of oil derivatives and biofuels (OJ RS, Nos 97/15, 5/17, 8/17 – corr., 119/17 and 102/18).
- Regulation on the amount, method of calculation, payment and charge for establishing mandatory reserves of oil and oil derivatives (OJ RS, No. 108/14).[1054]

855. The main authority in the energy field in Serbia is the MME, which performs activities concerning mining and energy. The other body is the AERS, established in 2005, which is competent for protection of customers, as well as improvement and guide of energy market development (price regulation, issuing licences for energy activities, etc.)[1055] and implementation of international treaties.

B. International Legal Regulation and Harmonization with EU Legislation

856. Serbia has ratified the Treaty establishing the Energy Community between the European Community and the Republic of Albania, the Republic of Bulgaria, Bosnia and Herzegovina, the Republic of Croatia, the former Yugoslav Republic of Macedonia, the Republic of Montenegro, Romania, the RS and United Nations

1053. 'Pipeline transport' – transport of gaseous and liquid hydrocarbons via oil pipelines, oil product pipelines and gas pipelines having operating pressure greater than sixteen bar; 'Distribution' – transfer of gaseous hydrocarbons from transport gas pipeline to customer via gas pipelines having operating pressure sixteen bar or lower (Art. 2, points 1 and 2).

1054. For more information about legislation, *see* https://www.mre.gov.rs/sektori/sr/81/4/0/0 (4.1.2024).

1055. The AERS has, among other things, elaborated tariff systems, http://www.aers.rs/Index.asp?l=2&a=92 (4.1.2024). According to the Law on Rational Use of Energy (OJ RS, No. 25/13) the jurisdiction in this area lies with the Government, Ministry in charge of energy issues and local self-government. However, the increase in energy efficiency would also contribute to a more efficient implementation of other energy policy measures which are important for the activities within the Agency's jurisdiction (above all, of those related to households as energy customers). *See* https://www.aers.rs/Index.asp?l=2&a=127&ted=&ed=&id_ed=&tp=&id=&idag=&tvid=&lid=&sid=1 (4.1.2023).

Interim Administration Mission in Kosovo, according to the Security Council Regulation 1244 (OJ RS, No. 62/2006). The Treaty established the legal and institutional framework for electricity and natural gas trade in Southeastern Europe. It is completely harmonized with the relevant EU regulations, including regulations concerning environmental protection.

In 2007, Serbia also ratified the Kyoto Protocol, a Non-Annex 1 country. That means that Serbia has the opportunity to use the CDM for financing projects in the energy efficiency and RES fields.

857. In addition, the RS signed several agreements/conventions in the field of energy with non-Member States of the EU. These are, *inter alia*, the following international agreements:

(1) Agreement between the Federal Government of the FRY and the Government of the Russian Federation on Cooperation on the construction of the Gas Pipeline on the Territory of FRY (OJ FRY – IT, No. 4/96).
(2) Agreement between the Serbian Government and the Government of the Russian Federation on Cooperation in the Oil and Gas Sector (OJ RS – IT, No. 83/08).
(3) Agreement on Economic and Technical Cooperation in the Field of Infrastructure Between the Government of the Republic of Serbia and the Government of the People's Republic of China (OJ RS – IT, No. 90/09).
(4) Agreement Between the Government of the Republic of Serbia and the Government of the Swiss Confederation Concerning of the Granting of the Financial Assistance for the Project 'Modernization of the Monitoring and Control System of NikolaTesla Thermal Power Plant B' of 6 May 2009.
(5) Statute of the IRENA (OJ RS – IT, No. 105/09).
(6) Agreement between the Government of the Republic of Serbia and the Government of the Republic of Italy on cooperation in the field of energy, signed in Rome on 25 October 2011 (OJ RS – IT, No. 7/12). Agreement between the Government of the Republic of Serbia and the Government of Japan on the Project of construction of the desulphurization facility for the thermo-power plant 'Nikola Tesla' (OJ RS – IT, No. 1/12). Agreement between the Government of the Republic of Serbia and the Government of Russian Federation on Natural Gas Supply from Russian Federation to the Republic of Serbia (OJ RS – IT, No. 3/13).
(7) Memorandum of Understanding between the Government of the Republic of Serbia and the Government of the State of Kuwait on Cooperation in the Field of Oil and Gas (OJ RS – IT, No. 10/17).
(8) Agreement between the Government of the Republic of Serbia and the Government of the Russian Federation on cooperation in the field of the use of nuclear energy for peacetime purposes on the basis of proven and innovative technologies (OJ RS – IT, No. 2/2019).
(9) Agreement between the Government of the Republic of Serbia and the Government of Hungary on cooperation with regard to the construction, operation, maintenance, reconstruction, and breakdown recovery of natural gas transmission pipeline crossing the state border (OJ RS – IT, No. (4/20).

858. It could be concluded that the development and promotion of the use of RES, with the aim to reduce the consumption of fossil fuels, reduce import dependency and produce electrical and heat energy with reduced adverse environmental effects, remains an important goal to be attained by Serbia.[1056]

859. Regarding RES, 'Serbia made some progress on further alignment with the EU acquis. In April 2023, Serbia amended the 2021 Law on RES, paving the way to launch the delayed first RES auctions.'[1057] For full transposition of the Renewable Energy Directive (RED II, Directive (EU) 2018/2001), Serbia should ensure a simplified and swift permit granting process by designating one or more contact points to guide applicants.[1058]

860. In the area of energy efficiency, 'Serbia continued to progress in aligning with the EU acquis... by adopting 22 acts of implementing legislation under the new Law on energy efficiency and rational use of energy, these focused on energy savings, eco-design, and energy labeling frameworks.'[1059] Only 'limited progress was made in aligning with the Energy Performance of Buildings Directive (Directive (EU) 2018/844) and setting up an implementing legislation framework for the renovation of building stock.'[1060]

1056. GOV RS. 2008b, 101.

1057. EC. 2023, 131. ' In June 2023, the Government approved a three-year auction plan 2023–2025 with a total capacity of 1,300 MW. The first auctions for producers of electricity from renewable energy sources were conducted in July 2023 and results were published.' *Ibid.*

1058. Serbia made no progress in introducing a national scheme to verify the sustainability criteria for biofuels, bioliquids, and biomass fuels. *Ibid.*, 132.

1059. *Ibid.*, 132.

1060. ' The human resource capacity in the Energy Efficiency Administration 'needs to increase, its institutional role must be strengthened, and energy efficiency financing must be increased to take the sector decisively towards the 'energy efficiency first principle.' *Ibid.*

Part II. Nature Conservation and Management

861. In accordance with Article 87 of the Constitution of Serbia, 'natural resources, goods which are stipulated by the Law as goods of public interest and assets used by the bodies of the RS shall be the State assets. State assets shall include other things and rights, according to the Law'. Natural resources shall be utilized under the terms and in a manner stipulated by the Law. Natural and legal entities may obtain particular rights on particular goods in public use, under the terms and in a manner stipulated by the Law.

862. Provisions directly relevant for nature conservation and management are contained in the EPL (2004). Complete Part II of the 2004 EPL is devoted to the 'management of natural values' (Articles 11–32).[1061] This part of the EPL is divided into two chapters: (1) Planning and Utilization of Natural Values (Articles 11–20); and (2) Protection of Natural Values (Articles 21–32).

863. The Law prescribes in general that sustainable management of natural values and environmental protection shall be realized in accordance 'with this Law' (Article 2, paragraph 2). The system of environmental protection shall comprise measures, conditions and instruments for, *inter alia*, sustainable management, preservation of nature balance, integrity, diversity and quality of natural values and conditions for survival of all living beings. General interest is the basic element of the notion 'protected natural good'.[1062] However, EPL also defined the notion 'public natural good'.[1063]

864. The Law on Nature Protection (OJ RS, Nos 36/2009, 88/2010, 91/2010 – corr., 14/2016, 95/2018 – other law, and 71/2021) regulates the protection and conservation of nature, as well as biological, geological and landscape diversity as part

1061. Notion of 'natural value' is defined very widely. It is 'natural wealth which comprises air, water, soil, forests, geological resources, plants and animal life' (Art. 3, point 3).
1062. 'Protected natural good' is a preserved part of nature with special values and characteristics (geodiversity, biodiversity, scenery, landscape, etc.), due to which they have permanent ecological, scientific, cultural, educational, health-recreational, tourist and other significance and therefore as a public good it enjoys special protection (Art. 3, point 4).
1063. Public natural good is defined as a cultivated or uncultivated part of natural wealth (i.e., air, water goods, water-fronts, underground goods, forests, sceneries or landscapes equally accessible to all) (Art. 3, point 5).

of the environment. According to this Law and to special laws, nature as a resource of common interest to the RS shall enjoy special protection (Article 1).

865. The Law on Nature Protection consists of XVII chapters. Basic provisions of the Law are given in Chapter I consisting of six Articles (Articles 1–6). Provisions for Nature Protection are given in Chapter II (Articles 7–26) which is divided into two subchapters – Subchapter 1– Planning, regulation and space usage, natural resources, protected areas and ecological network (Articles 8–13) and Subchapter 2 – Subjects of protection (Articles 14–26). Chapter III – Protected natural goods (Articles 27–40) consists of following three subchapters: (1) Protected areas (Articles 28–35); (2) Protected species (Article 36); and (3) Mobile protected natural documents (Articles 37–40). Procedure for declaration of protected natural goods is given in Chapter IV (Articles 41–50). Chapter IV also consists of three subchapters: (1) Categorization of protected areas (Articles 41–47); (2) Strictly protected and protected wild spaces (Article 48); and (3) Mobile protected natural documents (Articles 49 and 50). Provisions for management and use of protected areas are given in Chapter V (Articles 51–70).[1064] Regulations about protection and conservation of wild species are given in Chapter VI (Articles 71–96). Chapter VII prescribes measures for protection of mobile-protected natural documents (Articles 97–100). Organization of nature protection is prescribed in Chapter VIII (Articles 101–104). Chapter IX – Nature protection sign consists of two Articles 105 and 106, as well as Chapter XI – Guarding of protected areas (Articles 109 and 110). Nature protection documents are prescribed in Chapter XII (Articles 111–114), while access to information and public participation are prescribed in Chapter XIII (Articles 115–117). Supervision is regulated by Chapter XIV (Articles 118–123). Chapter XV – Competence for settlement of complaints consists of only one Article (Article 124). Penalty provisions are prescribed in Chapter XVI (Articles 125–129), while the final Chapter XVII prescribes transitional and final provisions (Articles 130–135).[1065]

1064. However, provision of Art. 68, para. 1, point 11, Art. 70, and Art. 127, para. 1, point 9 of the Law on Nature Protection has ceased to apply – on the day of the beginning of the application of the Law on Fees for the Use of Public Goods (OJ RS, No. 95/2018), i.e., 1 Jan. 2019 (*see* Art. 278 of the Law - 95/2018).

1065. Nature protection is also regulated, *inter alia*, by the Law on Forests (OJ RS, Nos 30/10, 93/12, 89/15 and 95/18 – other law), the Law on Game and Hunting (OJ RS, Nos 18/10, 95/18 – other law, and 92/23 – other law), and relevant implementing legislation adopted based on these laws, as well as Spatial Plan for the period 2010–2020 (OJ RS, No. 88/10).

Chapter 1. Monuments and Landscapes

866. In Serbian legislation, protection and conservation of monuments and landscapes could be divided into two closely related subgroups of regulation (monuments and landscapes), with less attention paid to landscapes.

§1. MONUMENTS

867. Due to the geographical position and the fact that various cultures and religions have throughout history been here intermixing with each other, the territory of Serbia is exceptionally rich in cultural monuments from various historical periods. Some of the most valuable have been put on the United Nations Educational, Scientific and Cultural Organization (UNESCO) List of World Cultural Heritage (the Medieval Serbian capital Ras, Sopocani Monastery, Studenica Monastery, etc.).
There are several categories of cultural monuments in Serbia. They include the following types (census 1994): archaeological finds (197); area and architectural wholes (eighty-one); residential architecture (508); public architecture (230); religious architecture (721); military architecture (65); economic purposes' architecture (204); memorial architecture (341), etc.[1066]

868. State of the monuments differs. It is estimated that less than two-thirds of them are preserved. The most important factors that contribute to their degradation are inadequate location of industrial plants, tourist activities, transport, electric energy production, uncontrolled growth of cities and other settlements, etc. The 1999 NATO intervention, as well as attacks of ethnic Albanians against Serbs and Serbian cultural monuments in March 2004 in Kosovo-Metohija,[1067] caused destruction and serious damage to many monuments in Serbia.

869. In accordance with Article 22 of the Law on Ministries (OJ RS, Nos 128/20, 116/22, 92/23– other law), the Ministry of Culture[1068] performs public administrative tasks which relate to, *inter alia*, the development and promotion of culture and artistic creativity; protection of cultural property; endowments, foundations and funds; cooperation in the field of cultural heritage protection, etc. The Sector for Heritage Protection does work related to the monitoring and analysis of the heritage protection situation, the recommendation of measures for their improvement and the monitoring of proceedings in the area of protection of monuments and artefacts, etc.

1066. STAT. YEARB. SERB, 2007, 379.
1067. *See* Cultural Heritage in South-East Europe, Kosovo Protection and Conservation, A Multi-ethnic Heritage in Danger, Mission Report 26–30 Apr. 2004, http://www.unesco-paris.mfa.gov.rs/odrzavanje/uploads/Citati+slike_unesko_final.pdf (5.1.2024).
1068. *See* https://www.kultura.gov.rs/tekst/54/o-nama.php (5.1.2024); *see also* Institute for protection of monuments of culture, http://www.heritage.gov.rs/english/ (4.1.2024).

Article 90 of the Law on the Cultural Heritage (OJ RS, No. 129/21) prescribes, *inter alia*, that the 'central protection institutions in the RS are the Republic Institute for the Protection of Cultural Monuments, the National Museum of Serbia, the State Archives of Serbia, the National Library of Serbia and the Yugoslav Cinematheque'.[1069]

§2. Legal Regulation

870. There are numerous legal and sub-legal Acts relevant for protection of monuments. Article 89 of the Serbian Constitution (protection of heritage) prescribes that 'everyone shall be obliged to protect natural rarities and scientific, cultural and historical heritage, as well as goods of public interest in accordance with the Law. The RS, APs and LSG units shall be held particularly accountable for the protection of heritage'.

871. According to the Spatial Plan of Serbia (OJ RS, No. 88/10), 'the basic goal' in the field of protection and sustainable use of cultural heritage is to articulate cultural heritage as a development resource, protect, develop and use it in a manner which will contribute to the establishment of regional and local identity in accordance with European standards of protection.[1070]

I. Law on Environmental Protection

872. The EPL (OJ RS, Nos 135/04, 36/09, 72/09, 43/11CC, 14/16, 76/18 and 95/18 – other law) contains several basic provisions relevant to the protection of monuments linking them to protection of the environment. The notion of 'protected natural good' is defined in such a way that it is linked to nature. Article 3, point 4 prescribes that 'preserved part of nature with special values and characteristics (geodiversity,[1071] biodiversity,[1072] scenery, landscape, etc.), due to which they have permanent ecological, scientific, cultural, educational, health recreational, tourist and other significance and therefore as a public good it enjoys special protection'.

1069. *See also*, Art. 3, para. 1, point 16. Institutions for the protection and preservation of cultural heritage are institutions carrying out the activity of protection and preservation of cultural heritage in accordance with the provisions of this Law and the provisions of special laws governing individual areas of protection of cultural heritage (Art. 3, para. 1, point 14).

1070. NA. 2010.(point 3 'basic goals').

1071. Article 3, point 6 of the EPL defines 'geodiversity (geological diversity)' as a presence or dispersion of different elements and features of geological texture, geological structure and processes, geochronological units, rocks and minerals of different composition and genesis types and different paleoecosystems which have been changed in space under influence of internal or external geodynamic components in the course of geological time.

1072. Article 3, point 6 of the EPL defines 'biodiversity (biological diversity)' as a diversity of organisms within specie, among the species and ecosystems and it covers full genetic diversity, species and ecosystems diversity at local, national, regional and global level.

873. General obligations have been stipulated in Article 17 of the Law. According to the Article, natural goods are to be used and developed in a manner that enables their permanent preservation and advancement in accordance with the Law on Nature Protection. The 'activities which threaten environmental capacity, natural balance, biodiversity, hydrographic, geomorphologic, geological, cultural and landscape values, or which in any way degrade the quality and properties of the natural good shall not be allowed within a protected natural good'.

874. Cultural goods have been included in Strategic EIA (Article 35) and EIA (Article 36). The strategic EIA shall be made for certain plans, programmes and principles in the domain of, *inter alia*, protection of natural and culture goods, flora and fauna and their habitats, etc. and shall be an integral part of the plan, programme or principle. In the same way, EIA shall cover 'all the projects planned on the protected natural goods and in the protected environment of non-movable culture good' as well as projects in industry, mining, energy, traffic, tourism, agriculture, forestry, water management and communal activities.

875. The environmental protection organization may decide to temporarily prohibit ongoing activities.[1073] If the Act, by which a natural resource is placed under protection, is not adopted, the temporary ban concerning the execution of work is lifted. A complaint on the decision does not suspend its implementation.

II. Law on Planning and Building

876. 'Culture' and 'cultural asset and values' are part of the provisions of the Law on Planning and Building (OJ RS, Nos 72/2009, 81/2009 – corr., 64/2010 – CC, 24/2011, 121/2012, 42/2013 – CC, 50/2013 – CC, 98/2013 – CC, 132/2014, 145/2014, 83/18, 31/19, 37/19 – other law, 9/20, 52/21, and 62/23) because culture and cultural asset and values must be taken into account in space planning.

877. The development and use of space is, *inter alia,* based on the following principles: sustainable development; the encouragement of even regional development; reconciliation of social development, economic and energy efficiency and the protection and revitalization of the environment and building heritage, *natural, cultural and historic values*, etc. (Article 3 paragraph 1).[1074]

878. According to Article 15, the Spatial Plan of the RS[1075] particularly includes the following, *inter alia*: goals and principles of spatial planning; principles and

---

1073. A decision concerning a temporary prohibition concerning the execution of work is submitted to the investor, the contractor and to the competent body which issued the building permit or the permit to carry out other type of work and to the body competent for placing the natural within a three-month period.

1074. The principles also include the instruments for implementation (Art. 3, para. 5).

1075. The Spatial Plan of the Republic of Serbia is passed for the territory of the Republic of Serbia and constitutes the basic planning document of spatial planning and development in the Republic. Other planning documents must comply with the Spatial Plan. It has a strategic-developmental

proposals for the protection, landscaping and development of nature and natural systems; measures of protection, landscaping and improving natural and cultural property; and measures of environmental protection (Article 15 points 9 and 10).

879. The General Regulation Plan[1076] particularly includes the following: (1) rules of landscaping and rules of construction by zones and wholes; (2) zones for which the drawing up of a Detailed Regulation Plan is mandatory; (3) locations for which an Urban Design Project is in progress; (4) deadlines for the production of detailed regulation with mandatory prohibition of building new facilities and reconstruction[1077] of existing facilities (construction of facilities or execution of works which alter the state in the space), until the adoption of the Plan; (5) measures of protection of *cultural and historic monuments, and protected natural wholes*; (6) engineering and geological conditions; (7) measures of energy efficiency in construction, etc. (Article 26).

880. A Detailed Regulation Plan is drawn up for undeveloped parts of a populated locality, bringing in order informal settlements, zones of urban renewal, infrastructural corridors and facilities, construction of facilities or populated localities on buildable land outside of populated localities, as well as in protected surroundings of *immobile cultural property* (Article 27).[1078]

881. In accordance with Article 117, the general project contains particularly the data about the macro location of the facility, general disposition of the facility, technical and technological concept of the facility, the method of providing the infrastructure, the possible options for the spatial and technical solutions, from the point of fitting into the space, the natural conditions, the effect on the environment, geological engineering and technical characteristics of the land from the aspect of determining the general concept and justifiability of construction of the facility, investigation work made for the preparation of the preliminary project, and *the protection of natural and immovable cultural property*, the functionality and rationality of the project.

---

and general regulatory function, and it is adopted for a period of at least ten years, and a maximum of twenty-five years. However, it can be changed even before the expiration of the deadline for which it was drawn up (Art. 14).

1076. The General Regulation Plan is mandatory for a populated settlement which is the seat of a unit of local administration and can also be drawn up for other populated settlements in the territory of a municipality, i.e., the city of Belgrade, when this is provided for in the spatial plan of the unit of local administration. It is mandatory for units of local administration for which a General Urban Plan is being drawn up following this Law, that the General Regulation Plans are drawn up for the whole buildable area of the inhabited settlement, by parts of the inhabited settlement (Art. 25).

1077. '*Reconstruction*' is the execution of construction and other works on an existing facility, by which the stability and safety of the facility are affected; structural elements are replaced or the technological process changed; the exterior elevation of the facility is altered; the number of functional units is increased; influence is exerted on the safety of adjacent facilities, traffic fire fighting and environmental protection; the regime of waters is changed; and *the protection of natural or immobile cultural property* is affected, along with its protected surroundings (Art. 2, point 32).

1078. A Detailed Regulation Plan particularly includes, *inter alia*, rules of landscaping and rules of construction by wholes and zones (Art. 28, point (5)).

882. The preliminary project contains the situational solution and the data about the micro location of the facility, the functional, construction and representational properties of the facility, the technical and technological and exploitation characteristics of the facility, the geological engineering and technical properties of the terrain and soil with preliminary calculations of stability and safety of the facility, the decision about the founding of the facility, the technical, technological and organizational elements of construction of the facility, the measures for the prevention or reduction of negative influences on the environment, the preliminary project of the infrastructure, comparative analysis of alternative technical solutions in view of the properties of the soil, functionality, stability, and estimate of the influence on the environment, *natural and immovable cultural property*, rationality of the construction, costs of construction, transport, maintenance, energy provision and other costs (Article 118).

883. Technical documentation necessary for taking measures of technical protection on *immoveable cultural property* can be prepared by the organization which performs the activity of protection of cultural property (Article 127, paragraph 4).[1079]

884. Article 133 prescribes that the building permit for the construction of a facility is issued by the Ministry authorized for the tasks in construction (Ministry), if it is not otherwise determined by this Law.[1080] The Ministry issues the building permit for following facilities: *cultural property of exceptional importance* and their protected surroundings with clearly determined borders of land registry lot; cultural property entered in the World List of Cultural and Natural Heritage and facilities in protected areas in accordance with the Act on protection of cultural property (except the transformation of common premises into a flat, or business premise in the protected surroundings of cultural property of exceptional importance and cultural property entered into the World List of Cultural Heritage) as well as facilities within national parks and facilities within a protected natural property of exceptional importance (except residential facilities, agricultural and economic facilities and infrastructure facilities which are important for them and which are built-in villages), in accordance with the Law.

1079. The technical documentation for the construction of a facility can be prepared by a company or other legal entity, or a contractor which are entered into the appropriate Register for the preparation of technical documentation (Art. 126, para. 1). The person employed in a company, other legal entity or contractor firm who is authorized to determine any of the conditions on the basis of which the technical documentation is prepared cannot participate in the preparation of the technical documentation (Art. 127, para. 1). The person who carries out the supervision over the application of the provisions of this Law cannot participate in the preparation in the technical documentation (Art. 127, para. 2). The legal entity performing communal activities or activities of general interest can prepare the technical documentation for the construction of facilities which it will use for the performance of its activity under the conditions prescribed by this Law (Art. 127, para. 3).

1080. The issue of the building permit is entrusted to the AP for the construction of facilities determined by Art. 133 of this Law, which is completely built on the territory of the AP. The issue of the building permit is entrusted to the local government units for the construction of facilities which are not determined in Art. 133 of this Law (Art. 134).

885. According to Article 145, the construction of facilities referred to in Article 2, paragraph 1, items 24[1081] and 25[1082] of this Law, execution of works on capital maintenance of facilities and removal of obstruction for persons with invalidity, adaptation, repair and change of the purpose of facilities are made based on the decision which approves execution of this work, or change of purpose of these facilities, which is issued by the agency authorized for issuing building permits (paragraph 1).

886. For the works mentioned in paragraph 1 of Article 145 on *facilities of cultural and historic importance* and facilities for which before renewal (restoration, conservation, revitalization)[1083] or adaptation must be issued conservation conditions, the agreement of the agency or organization authorized for tasks of *protection of cultural property* about the preliminary or main project must be submitted (Article 145 paragraph 3).[1084]

887. Removal of a facility, or part thereof, except in the case of execution of a decision by the inspection, can be carried out only based on the permission for the removal of the facility or part thereof (Article 168 paragraph 1). Together with the request for permission for the removal of the facility, or part thereof, it is also necessary to submit, *inter alia*, special conditions, in case of a facility whose removal would endanger the public interest (protection of existing and other infrastructure, *protection of cultural goods, protection of the environment*, etc.) (Article 168 paragraph 2).[1085]

1081. 'An auxiliary facility' is a facility which is linked to the primary facility and is built on the same lot as the primary residential, business, or facility of public use (garage parking, storage, septic tank, wells, cisterns, etc.).

1082. 'A special type of facility for which building permits are not issued' are anti-hail facilities; type encasements of basic stations on appropriate supports, aerial supports with antennas, except parabolic antennas of radio stations whose diameter is not larger than 2.5 m (except aerial systems of ground antenna stations), containers holding telecommunication equipment and devices, typical lockers for interior and exterior fitting for holding telecommunication equipment, micro-ditches for optical and other cables, etc. single electric power distribution on transmission poles, part of the low voltage grid which includes a 10 kV or 20 kV line, typical 10/04 kV or 20/04 kV transformer stations and the part of the electric power distribution grid from the 10/04 kV or 20/04 kV transformer station to the connection point on the facility of the client (1 kV); connections to a completed gas distribution grid; typical hot water connections; fitting of interior installations (gas, electric power, water, heating, etc.) in an existing facility.

1083. 'Restoration, conservation and revitalization works on cultural property' are works carried out on *immobile cultural property* and their protected surrounding, in compliance with this and special laws (Art. 2, point 37).

1084. Exceptionally, in reference to the provisions of para. 1 of this Article, requests for the issue of decisions for approval of execution of works on construction, or execution of works on construction of facilities mentioned in Art. 2, item 24 of this Law, as well as for the adaptation and repair of facilities within boundaries of national parks and facilities within boundaries of *protection of cultural property of exceptional importance*, as well as for execution of work on capital maintenance, adaptation and repair in the protected *surroundings of cultural property of exceptional importance* entered in the world list of cultural heritage, are solved by the authorized agency of the local government unit on whose territory are the subject facilities (Art. 145, para. 4).

1085. The permission for the removal of the facility, or part thereof, is issued within fifteen days from submission of adequate documentation. An appeal can be submitted against the resolution referred to in para. 3 of this Article within fifteen days from delivery of the resolution (Art. 168, paras 3 and 4).

888. The construction permit cannot be issued later for facilities which are constructed, or reconstructed, or enlarged, without construction permit, if the facility has been constructed, or reconstructed, in the *zone of protection of natural and cultural goods* (Article 187, point 4).[1086]

III. Specific Legislation

889. Besides the mentioned general legislation, following specific legal instruments in the field of culture and protection of monuments are in force:

- Law on Cultural Heritage (OJ RS, No. 129/21).
- Law on Cultural Properties (OJ RS, Nos 71/94, 52/11 – other law, 99/11, other law, 6/20- other law, 35/21 – other law, 76/23 – other law).[1087]
- Law on Culture (OJ RS, Nos 72/09, 13/16 and 30/16 – corr., 6/20, 47/21, 78/21, and 76/23).
- Law on Library and Information Sector (OJ RS, Nos 52/11, 78/21).
- Law on Old and Rare Library Materials (OJ RS, No. 52/11).
- Law on the preservation of the cultural and historical heritage of the Holy Hilandar Monastery (OJ RS, No. 94/21).
- The Law on Protection of Freedoms and Rights of National Minorities (OJ FRY, No. 11/2002, OJ S&M, No. 1/2003, OJ RS, No. 72/2009 – other law 79/13 CC, 47/18).
- Law on Deposit of Publication (OJ RS, Nos 52/11 and 13/16).
- Copyright Law (OJ RS, Nos 104/09, 99/11, 119/12, 29/16 CC, and 66/19).
- Law on reconstruction of cultural and historical heritage and development support of Sremski Karlovci (OJ RS, No. 52/01).
- Law on Endowments and Foundations (OJ RS, Nos 88/10, 99/11 – other law, and 44/18).

1086. Legalization, according to this Law, is the later date issue of construction and usage licences for a facility, or parts of a facility, which is constructed, or reconstructed without the construction permit. The construction permit, referred to in para. 1 of this Article, will be issued for all constructed, reconstructed or enlarged facilities without construction permit up to the date when this Law became effective (Art. 185, paras 1 and 2).

1087. The provisions of Arts 42–45 have ceased to be valid on the date of commencement of the Law on Mandatory Copies of Publications (OJ RS, No. 52/11), that is, on 24 Oct. 2011 (*see* Art. 18 of the Law – 52/11). The provisions relating to old and rare books ceased to be valid on the day the Law on Old and Rare Library Material (OJ RS, No. 52/11) came into effect, that is, on 24 Jan. 2012 (*see* Arts 62 and 63 of the Law – 52/11). The provisions of Art. 46 and Art. 130, para. 1, point 17) ceased to apply, on the date of commencement of the Law on Cinematography (OJ RS, No. 99/11), that is, on 5 Jul. 2012 (*see* Art. 40 of the Act – 99/11). Several provisions of the Law cease to be valid on the day of application of the Law on Archival Materials and Archival Activity (OJ RS, 6/20), that is, on 1 Feb. 2021 (*see* Art. 74 of the Law – 6/20). Several provisions of the Law cease to be valid on the date of commencement of the Law on Museum Activities (OJ RS, 35/21), i.e., on 16 Oct. 2021. (*See* Art. 92 of the Law – 35/21). Some provisions of the Law cease to be valid on the date of commencement of the implementation of the Law on Cultural Heritage (OJ RS, 129/21) (*see* Art. 137 of the Law – 129/21). Some provisions of the Law cease to be valid at the beginning of the application of the Law on Film and Other Audiovisual Heritage (OJ RS, 76)/23), that is, on 16 Sep. 2024 (*see* Art. 79 of the Law – 76/23).

- Law on Establishment of the Museum of Genocide Victims (OJ RS, Nos 49/92, 53/93 – other law, 67/93 – other law, 48/94 – other law, 101/2005 – other law, and 49/21).
- Law on Matica Srpska (OJ RS, No. 49/92).
- Law on Cinematography (OJ RS, Nos 99/11, 2/12 – corr., 46/14 CC, 76/23 – other law).
- Publishing Law (OJ RS, Nos 37/91, 53/93 – other law, 67/93 – other law, 48/94 – other law, 135/2004 and 101/2005 – other law).
- Law on the Serbian Literary Cooperative (OJ RS, Nos 20/97, and 10/19), etc.

890. The Law on Cultural Heritage (OJ RS, No. 129/21) shall regulate the system of protection and preservation of cultural heritage (Article 1). The aim of this Law shall be to establish a legally regulated and organized system for protection and preservation of cultural heritage[1088] through the discovery, collection, research, documentation, study, evaluation, protection, preservation, presentation, interpretation, use and management of cultural heritage (Article 2). Cultural heritage may be both tangible cultural heritage[1089] and intangible cultural heritage.[1090]

891. The provisions of the Law are grouped into the following fifteen chapters: I Basic provisions (Articles 1–12), II Tangible and intangible cultural heritage (Articles 13–25), III Valuation of cultural heritage (Articles 26–40), IV Determination of cultural heritage (Articles 41–54), V Registration and maintenance of the register of cultural goods, intangible cultural heritage and records of goods under prior protection (Articles 55–68), VI General protection measures (Articles 69–71), VII Protection activities and preservation of cultural heritage (Articles 72–97), VIII Support for scientific research and educational activities for the protection and preservation of cultural heritage (Article 98), IX Rights and obligations of owners and holders of cultural goods and goods under prior protection (Articles 99–102), X Traffic, commercial use and expropriation of cultural goods (Articles 103–106), XI Import, destruction, export and export, return (Articles 107–113), XII Return of cultural objects illegally removed from the territory of the Member States of the European Union Union (Articles 114–129), XIII Penal provisions (Article 130), XIV Supervision over implementation (Articles 131–133), and XV Transitional and final provisions (Articles 134–138).

1088. Cultural heritage is 'a set of resources, tangible and intangible, inherited from the past, recognized as a reflection and expression of continuously evolving values, beliefs, knowledge and traditions, created by the interaction of man and space over time.' (Art. 3, para. 1, point 1).
1089. Tangible cultural heritage is part of the cultural heritage forming immovable cultural heritage and movable cultural heritage (Art. 2, para. 1, point 2).
1090. Intangible cultural heritage shall be understood to mean practices, displays, expressions, knowledge, skills, as well as instruments, objects, artefacts and cultural spaces associated with them, which communities, groups and in certain cases individuals, recognize as part of their cultural heritage. It is transmitted from generation to generation, communities and groups recreate it depending on the environment, their interaction with nature and history, giving them a sense of identity and continuity. In this way, they promote respect for cultural diversity and human creativity (Art. 2, para. 1. point 8).

892. Article 17 of the Law on Cultural Heritage defines that a cultural monument is an individual immovable object of cultural, historical, architectural, archaeological, artistic, ethnological, technical, palaeontological, or other social significance (paragraph 1).[1091]

893. Besides the definition of the 'cultural monument', the Law defines, *inter alia*, the following notions:

- Cultural goods are objects and creations of material and spiritual culture of general interest, valued and established in accordance with the law, and forming an integral part of the tangible cultural heritage (Article 3, paragraph 1, point 5).[1092]
- Cultural landscape means an area created as a result of the interaction between culture and nature, that is, people and their natural environment. The cultural landscape reflects the evolution of human society and settlements over time, ways of sustainable land use conditioned by the limitations and characteristics of the natural environment, as well as successive social, economic, and cultural influences and a specific spiritual relationship to nature (Article 15).
- A spatial cultural-historical entity is an urban or rural settlement or a group of individual or connected buildings that, due to their architectural features, homogeneity, or position in space, possess special values from a cultural, historical, artistic, ethnological, anthropological, and scientific point of view (Article 16).
- A cultural monument is an individual immovable object of cultural, historical, architectural, archaeological, artistic, ethnological, technical, palaeontological, or other social significance (Article 17, paragraph 1).[1093]
- An archaeological site is a part of the space on the surface of the land and in the ground, in caves, and underwater, which contains the remains of individual buildings, complex building units and other objects, constructions, and their parts, burial units and necropolises, hoards, movable objects, anthropological, palaeontological and geological material, as well as the entire stratigraphic context in which they are located (Article 18).
- A famous place is an area related to an event of special importance for history, an area with pronounced elements of natural and work-created values as a unique

1091. A cultural monument can be: (1) architectural work, its remains, recognizable parts or belongings; (2) the building with the associated immovable property and belongings; (3) archaeological object or structure of archaeological character; (4) a work of applied art, painting or sculpture, an inscription, a geological site, a work or remnant of technical culture, old industry or infrastructure and other property that is permanently linked to a specific architectural object or place; (5) memorial or other memorial object (para. 2).

1092. Immovable cultural goods are cultural landscapes, spatial cultural and historical units, cultural monuments, archaeological sites and landmarks (point 6); Movable cultural goods are museum material, archival material, film and other audiovisual material, old and rare library material (point 7).

1093. A cultural monument can be: (1) architectural work, its remains, recognizable parts or belongings; (2) the building with the associated immovable property and belongings; (3) archaeological object or structure of archaeological character; (4) a work of applied art, painting or sculpture, an inscription, a geological site, a work or remnant of technical culture, old industry or infrastructure and other property that is permanently linked to a specific architectural object or place; (5) memorial or other memorial object (para. 2).

whole, as well as memorial graves or cemeteries and other memorials that were erected to permanently preserve the memory of significant events, personalities and places from national history, of special cultural and historical significance (Article 19).

894. Part Within Chapter IV of the Law (Articles 41–54: Determination of cultural goods), the following issues are regulated: Determination of Protection Measures, Determination of Immovable Cultural Goods, Determination of Movable Cultural Goods, Determination of Cultural Goods of Exceptional Importance, Preservation of Intangible Cultural Heritage, and Identification and Records of Intangible Cultural Heritage).

Central institutions of protection, in addition to other tasks, 'make nomination files for the entry of cultural heritage on the UNESCO lists' (Article 91, paragraph 1, point 5).[1094] The methods of the inscription of cultural properties in the Register of cultural properties and the competent institutions responsible for keeping the Register of immovable and movable cultural properties are prescribed by Articles 55–65.[1095]

895. The Law on Protection of Freedoms and Rights of National Minorities (OJ FRY, No. 11/2002, OJ S&M, No. 1/2003, OJ RS, Nos 72/2009 – other law 79/13 CC, 47/18) prescribes, in its Article 12, that in order to preserve and develop national and ethnic particularities, members of national minorities have the rights to establish special cultural, artistic and scientific institutions, societies and associations. The State is obliged to participate in financing of those societies and associations, in accordance with its possibilities. The museums, archives and institutions for protection of the cultural monuments, which are founded by the State, are obliged to ensure presentation and protection of the cultural and historical heritage of the national minorities on its territory.

896. The following sub-legal Acts regulating the protection of cultural goods are also relevant:

– Regulation on the detailed conditions and method of awarding recognition for outstanding contribution to national culture, i.e., the culture of national minorities (OJ RS, Nos 11/20, 11/23).

1094. To monitor and review the implementation of international obligations and ratified conventions, as well as cultural heritage registered and proposed for inclusion on UNESCO lists, the Ministry is establishing the National Committee for Tangible Cultural Heritage and the National Committee for Intangible Cultural Heritage (Art. 94). Cultural heritage inscribed on the UNESCO World Heritage List enjoys special access, protection, care and concern. Cultural heritage located on the territory of the Autonomous Province of Kosovo and Metohija enjoys special access, protection, care and concern (Art. 40).

1095. The Central Register is a public register of cultural goods for the territory of the Republic of Serbia run by central institutions for protection according to the types of cultural goods, unless otherwise stipulated by law (Art. 3, para. 1, point 22); 23) The National Register of Intangible Cultural Heritage is a public register run by the Centre for Intangible Cultural Heritage (point 22).

- Regulation on special award for contribution to the development of culture (OJ RS, No. 91/10).
- Rulebook on the detailed conditions, procedures, management, and way of working in the Unified Information Systems for individual areas of protection and preservation of cultural heritage, as well as on the obligations of protection institutions and employees (OJ RS, No. 5/23).
- Rulebook on the content and the way of keeping central records of the public cultural institutions located on the territory of the RS (OJ RS, No. 38/10).
- Rulebook on keeping records of persons who perform independent artistic or other activity in the field of culture (OJ RS, No. 41/10).
- Rulebook on the procedure of keeping the evidence of the immovable areas which are under prior protection (OJ RS, No. 19/95).
- Rulebook on labelling the immovable cultural goods (OJ RS, No. 51/96).
- Rulebook on the data which are to be entered into the Register, procedure of keeping the Register and the Central Register of the immovable cultural goods and the documentation concerning the cultural goods (OJ RS, Nos 30/95 and 37/95).
- Rulebook on the registers of archival material (OJ RS, No. 24/97).
- Rulebook on the registers of film material (OJ RS, No. 47/96).
- Rulebook on registers of artistic-historical works (OJ RS, No. 35/96), etc.

897. Serbia is a contracting party to the following international treaties regulating the protection of cultural heritage:

- European Convention on the Protection of Archaeological Heritage (1969) (OJ SFRY – IT, No. 9/90).
- Convention on Protection of Cultural Goods in Case of Armed Disputes (1954) (OJ FPRY – IT, No. 4/56).
- Convention on Measures for Banning and Preventing Illegal Import, Export and Transfer of Properties of Cultural Goods (1970) (OJ SFRY – IT, No. 50/73).
- Convention Concerning the Protection of the World Cultural and Natural Heritage (1972) (OJ SFRY – IT, No. 56/74).
- Convention for the Protection of the European Architectural Heritage (1985) (OJ SFRY – IN, No. 4/91).
- Convention on the Archaeological Heritage (Revised) (1992) (OJ RS – IT, No. 42/09).
- European Convention on Cinematographic Coproduction (1992) (OJ SM – IT, No. 204).
- Council of Europe Framework Convention on the Value of Cultural Heritage of Society (2005) (OJ RS – IT, No. 1/10).
- Convention on Protection and Promotion of Diversity of Cultural Expressions (UNESCO, 2005) (OJ RS – IT, No. 42/09).
- Convention for the Safeguarding of the Intangible Cultural Heritage (OJ RS – IT, No. 1/10).

– European Convention for the Protection of the Audiovisual Heritage (OJ RS – IT, No. 7/14), etc.[1096]

§3. Landscapes

898. According to the Law on Nature Protection (OJ RS, Nos 36/09, 88/10, 91/10 – corr., 14/16, 95/18 – other law, and 71/21), areas of exceptional geological, biological, ecosystem and/or landscape diversity can be declared as protected areas of general interest (Article 28). List of protected area in the RS includes sixteen landscapes of extraordinary characteristics (e.g., Klisura Reke Gradac, Dolina Pčinje, Ovčarsko-Kablarska klisura, Miruša, Lepterija-Sokograd, Subotičak pešćara, Veliko ratno ostrvo, Kosmaj, Vlasina, Vršačke planine, Avala).

§4. Legal Regulation

899. The basic legal Acts regulating protection of landscapes in Serbia are:

– *EPL* (OJ RS, Nos 135/04, 36/09, 36/09 – other law, 72/09 – other law, 43/11 CC, 14/16, 76/18 and 95/18 – other law).
– Law on Nature Protection (OJ RS, Nos 36/09, 88/10, 91/10 – corr., 14/16, 95/18 – other law, and 71/21).
– Law on National Parks (OJ RS, Nos 84/15 and 95/18 – other law).
– Law on Spatial Plan of the Republic of Serbia (OJ RS, No. 88/10), etc.

900. Protection of natural landscapes is mentioned in the EPL. In Article 3, point 4 of the Law, it is stated that protected natural good 'is a preserved part of nature with special values and characteristics (geodiversity, biodiversity, scenery, landscape, etc.), due to which they have permanent ecological, scientific, cultural, educational, health recreational, tourist and other significance and therefore as a public good it enjoys special protection'. In the same Article of the mentioned Law, there is a provision that public natural good is 'a cultivated or uncultivated part of natural wealth, that is, air, water goods, water-fronts, underground goods, forests, sceneries or landscapes equally accessible to all' (Article 3, point 5).

901. The EPL also prescribes that public natural goods 'shall be used in a way and under conditions which shall enable development and permanency of their natural, physical, health or aesthetic values in accordance with the regulations' (Article 18). Finally, the same Law prescribes that an action plan shall be made for 'Advancement of Spatial Planning and Landscaping' (Article 65, point 1).

1096. In the field of culture, RS has signed and confirmed a large number of bilateral agreements regulating various issues of importance for cooperation, including the protection of monuments.

902. Article 26 of the Law on Nature Protection of Landscapes shall imply planning and implementation of measures which prevent unwanted changes, disturbances or destruction of significant landscape characteristics, their diversity, uniqueness and aesthetical values and enable the traditional way of using the landscape.[1097] Conservation of significant and characteristic features of the landscape must be provided for when planning and organizing space and when planning and using natural resources.[1098]

I. Landscape of Exceptional Characteristics

903. The activities and operations which disturb primary natural and created values and landscape character shall be prohibited within the landscape of exceptional characteristics (Article 33, paragraph 5). Landscape of exceptional characteristics shall be an area of recognizable appearance with significant natural, biological-ecological, aesthetic and cultural-historical values, which developed in time as a result of interaction between nature, natural potentials of the area and the traditional way of life of the local population. Landscape of exceptional characteristics can be a natural landscape of exceptional characteristics[1099] and a cultural landscape of exceptional characteristics[1100] (Article 33, paragraphs 1 and 2). Protection measures, the mode for carrying out economic and traditional activities and use of natural and created values within the landscape of exceptional characteristics shall be closely established in the formal decision on proclamation of protected area (Article 33, paragraph 6).

904. Serbia ratified the European Landscape Convention (Florence, 2000) (OJ RS – IT, No. 4/11). In 2018, Serbia ratified the Protocol, amending the European Landscape Convention from 2016 (CETS No. 219).[1101] In addition, Serbia is a member of the Protocol on Conservation and Sustainable Use of Biological and Landscape Diversity to the Framework Convention on the Protection and Sustainable Development of the Carpathians done in Kiev on 22 May 2003 (OJ RS – IT, No. 1/13).

1097. Landscape is a certain territory whose character represents a specific joint of natural and created values characteristic for the given region (Art. 4, point 56).

1098. According to their natural and created characteristics, landscapes shall be divided into landscape types which express the diversity of natural and cultural heritage (Art. 26, para. 1).

1099. Natural landscape of exceptional characteristics shall be an area of significant biological-ecological and aesthetic value, in which the traditional way of life of the local population has not significantly disturbed the nature and natural ecosystems (Art. 33, para. 3).

1100. Cultural landscape of exceptional characteristics shall be an area of significant landscape, aesthetic and cultural-historical value, which developed in time as a result of interaction between the nature, natural potentials of the area and the traditional way of life of the local population (Art. 33, para. 4).

1101. *See* https://www.coe.int/en/web/conventions/full-list?module=signatures-by-treaty&treatynum=219 (8.2.2024). However, the Legal Information System of the RS (in the part that refers to international treaties) does not confirm this information. https://www.pravno-informacioni-sistem.rs/reg-overview# (8.2.2024).

Chapter 2. Parks and Reserves

§1. Physical Context

905. According to the Report on the state of the environment for 2018, during 2018, new 6,416 ha of the territory of the RS were protected, which is about 1% more than in 2017.[1102] The total area of protected natural resources in 2022 is 707,821 ha, which represents 8% of the territory of the RS. A total of 469 protected areas and properties are under state protection.[1103]

According to EPA data, the total number of protected natural assets is 474, and of these, 247 areas cover an area of about 536,000 ha, which represents 6.02% of the territory of Serbia. About 230 'point objects' (mainly trees) are under the protection of the State.[1104] The draft of the spatial plan until 2035 foresees that declared protected areas and areas proposed for protection will include in the planning period a total protected area of 909,530 ha (10.28% of the territory of Serbia), of which 40,880 ha are in the I degree protection regime (4.49%) and in regime II protection level 229,975 ha (25.28%).[1105]

906. The UNESCO preliminary list of natural assets of Serbia contains five assets ('Đerdap' National Park, 'Deliblatska Peščara' Special Nature Reserve, 'Tara' National Park with the Drina Canyon, 'Đavolja varoš' Nature Monument, 'Šar-Planina' National Park).[1106] The following sites have been registered based on the Convention Concerning the Protection of the World's Cultural and Natural Heritage under the MAB – Man and Biosphere Programme: Biosphere Reservation 'Golija – Studenica' with a surface area of 53,804 ha (0.61% of the territory of Serbia) and the Biosphere Reservation in Serbia – 'Bačko Podunavlje' with a surface area of 176,635 ha. Following the Convention on Wetlands of International Importance, Especially as Waterfowl Habitats (Ramsar Convention), eleven areas were entered on the List of Ramsar Sites (Peštersko polje, Gornje Podunavlje, Koviljsko – Petrovaradinsi-rit, Labudovo okno, Ludaško jezero, Obedska bara, Slano Kopovo, Stari Begej-Carska bara, Zasavica, Vlasina and Đerdap), with a total area of 130,411 ha.[1107]

§2. Legal Regulation

907. Legal protection of national parks and other specially protected zones has a relatively long tradition in Serbia (Yugoslavia). A decree regulating protection of national parks was, for example, enacted already in 1938. It should be stressed that legal regulation concerning parks and reserves is closely related not only to other

1102. EPA. 2019a, 173.
1103. EPA. 2023a, 179.
1104. http://indicator.sepa.gov.rs/pretrazivanje-indikatora/indikatorilat/allfindr/75bae269633f4ac1b63eb84fdd1b170f (19.1.2024). For a list of protected areas, *see* the Extract from the Central Register – protected areas, maintained by the Institute for Nature Protection. INCS. 2023.
1105. MCTI. 2021, 324.
1106. GOV RS. 2021a, 15.
1107. *Ibid.*, 14.

fields, in the first place, with wildlife protection but also with other fields, for example, water, forestry, fishing, hunting, mining, spatial planning, traffic, tourism, etc. So, in many cases, the same legal or sub-legal Act is relevant for two or more of the above-mentioned domains.

908. Presently, there are several basic legal Acts regulating protection of parks and reserves:

- The Law on Nature Protection (OJ RS, Nos 36/09, 88/10, 91/10 – corr., 14/16,95/18 – other law, and 71/21).
- The Law on National Parks (OJ RS, Nos 84/2015, 95/18 – other law).
- The Law on Forests (OJ RS, Nos 30/10, 93/12, 89/15 and 95/18 – other law).
- The Law on Protection and Sustainable Use of Fish Resources (OJ RS, Nos 128/14 and 95/18 – other law).
- The Law on Wild Game and Hunting (OJ RS, Nos 18/10, 95/18 – other law, and 92/23 – other law).

I. The Law on Nature Protection

909. The definition of 'protected area' is given in Article 28 of the Law on Nature Protection. It says that areas which have strong geological, biological, ecosystem and/or landscape diversity and are important as habitats of birds and other migratory species that are important in accordance with international regulations can be declared as protected areas of general interest.[1108] Protected areas can be associated with the transboundary protected areas of the neighbouring countries.[1109]

A. Strict and Special Natural Reserves

910. Article 29 gives definitions of strict and special natural reserve, as well as prescribes which operations and activities are prohibited within strict and special natural reserve. Strict natural reserve is an area of unchanged natural characteristics with representative natural ecosystems, intended solely to preserve the original nature, gene fund, ecologic equilibrium, monitoring of natural phenomena and processes, scientific research that does not affect the natural characteristics, values, phenomena and processes.[1110] Special natural reserve is an area of unchanged or

1108. There are three protection regimes prescribed to be established in protected area: (1) first degree – strict protection; (2) second degree – active protection and (3) third degree – proactive protection (Art. 35).

1109. The management plan and measures for protection of a protected area which has been connected in transboundary manner with a protected area in the neighbouring country shall be established by mutual consent with the competent authorities of that country, with consent of the Ministry.

1110. Within the strict and the special natural reserve it shall be prohibited to carry out operations and activities and perform actions which can impair the features due to which they have been declared as protected natural asset (picking and destroying of plants, disturbing, catching and killing of animals, introducing new biological species, melioration works, various forms of economical and

slightly changed nature, of particular importance due to its uniqueness, rareness or representativeness, which includes a habitat of endangered wild species of plants, animals and fungi, without settlements or with scarce settlements in which people live in harmony with the nature, and which are intended for conservation of the existing natural features, gene fund, ecological equilibrium, natural phenomena and processes, scientific research and education, controlled visits and preservation of traditional ways of life.

B. National Park

911. Article 30 contains definition of national park. It says that national park is an area with a large number of diverse natural ecosystems of national importance, with distinguished landscape characteristics and cultural heritage in which people live in harmony with nature, intended for conservation of the existing natural values and resources, with overall landscape, geological and biological diversity, as well as for meeting of scientific, educational, spiritual, aesthetical, cultural, touristic, health and recreational needs and other activities in accordance with the principles of nature protection and sustainable development.[1111] Activities and operations that do not disturb the original state of nature shall be allowed in the national park, as well as carrying out activities that have the function within education, health and recreational and touristic needs, continuation of the traditional way of life of local communities, and in the way that does not jeopardize the survival of species of the natural ecosystems and landscapes, in accordance with this Law and the management plan adopted by the manager (Article 30, paragraph 2).[1112]

C. Natural Monument

912. It is prescribed in Article 31 that natural monument is a less unchanged or partially changed natural spatial entity, object or phenomenon, physically clearly distinguished, recognizable and/or unique, with representative geomorphological, geological, hydrographical, botanical and/or other characteristics, as well as by human labour created value of botanical, aesthetic, cultural or educational significance. Any actions or activities on the natural monument that endanger its characteristics and values shall be prohibited.[1113]

---

other usage, etc.) (Art. 29, para. 4). All economic and other activities shall be prohibited in the strict natural reserve (Art. 29, para. 8). Measures for protection of strict and special natural reserve shall be closely determined by the decision on the proclamation of protected area (Art. 29, para. 6).

1111. The measures for protection of the national park and the manner of its use shall be determined in detail by a special Law (Art. 30, para. 6).

1112. The activities referred to in para. 2 of this Article can be limited with purpose of preserving the original state of nature in the national park (Art. 30, para. 3).

1113. Measures to protect the natural monument and the mode for its use shall be defined in detail by the Act on proclamation of protected area (Art. 31, para. 4).

D. Protected Habitat

913. Article 32 prescribes that protected habitat is an area which includes one or more types of natural habitats important for conservation of one or more populations of wild species and their communities. Also, Article 32 prescribes objectives of habitat protection (paragraph 2). The activities and operations which endanger or damage one or more habitat types shall be prohibited within the protected habitats.[1114]

E. Landscape of Exceptional Characteristics

914. Landscape of exceptional feature is an area of recognizable appearance with significant natural, biological-ecological, aesthetic and cultural-historical values that are developed over time as a result of interaction between nature, natural potentials of the area and the traditional way of life of the local population. Landscape of exceptional features can be a natural landscape[1115] and a cultural landscape of exceptional features[1116] (Article 33). The activities and operations which disturb primary natural and created values and landscape character shall be prohibited within the landscape of exceptional characteristics (Article 33, paragraph 5).[1117]

F. Natural Park

915. Natural park is an area of well-preserved natural values with mostly preserved natural ecosystems and picturesque landscapes, intended for conservation of the overall geological, biological and landscape diversity, as well as meeting of scientific, educational, spiritual, aesthetic, cultural, touristic, health-recreational needs and other activities harmonized with the traditional way of life and principles of sustainable development. Within the natural park, economic or other activities which threaten its substantial characteristics and values are not allowed (Article 34).[1118]

1114. The importance, purpose and protection measures are determined in an Act on proclamation of protected habitat (Art. 32, para. 4).
1115. Natural landscape of exceptional characteristics shall be an area of significant biological-ecological and aesthetic value, in which the traditional way of life of the local population has not significantly disturbed the nature and natural ecosystems (Art. 33, para. 3).
1116. Cultural landscape of exceptional characteristics shall be an area of significant landscape, aesthetic and cultural-historical value, which developed in time as a result of interaction between the nature, natural potentials of the area and the traditional way of life of the local population (Art. 33, para. 4).
1117. Protection measures, the mode for carrying out economic and traditional activities and use of natural and created values within the landscape of exceptional characteristics shall be closely established in the formal decision on proclamation of protected area (Art. 33, para. 6).
1118. Protection measures, the mode for carrying out economic activities and use of natural values within the natural park shall be closely established in the formal decision on proclamation of protected area (Art. 34, para. 3).

II. Law on National Parks

916. The basic legal Act regulating the field of national parks in the RS is the Law on National Parks (OJ RS, Nos 84/2015 and 95/18 – other law), adopted in 2015. It has the following six parts: Part I – General Provisions (Article 1); Part II – The Objective of the Law (Article 2); Part III – Values, size, boundaries and protection regimes (Articles 3–10); Part IV – Management and sustainable usage of national park (Articles 11–24); Part V – Supervision (Article 25) and Part VI – Transitory and final provisions (Articles 26–29).

This Law regulates the goals, values, size, boundaries and protection regimes, management and sustainable use of the National Park 'Fruška Gora' National Park 'Đerdap' National Park 'Tara' National Park 'Kopaonik' and the National Park 'Šar planina' (hereinafter 'the National park') (Article 1, paragraph 1).

917. The objectives to be achieved by this Law are: (1) the preservation and improvement of the value of biodiversity, geodiversity, as well as cultural and historical value; (2) the preservation and improvement of ecologically important areas and diversity of landscapes; (3) preservation of geological heritage facilities; (4) preservation and improvement of habitats, types of habitats and wild flora and fauna; (5) preservation and improvement of adequate quality of life in the National Park through the development of social, cultural and economic activity; (6) preservation of cultural and historical heritage; (7) preservation of traditional ways of life; (8) Preservation of natural processes and the balance between natural processes and human activities, i.e., sustainable development of the national park; and (9) formidable nature experience for visitors, education, research, sport and recreation (Article 2, paragraph 1).

918. Protection and sustainable use of the National Park is conducted in accordance with the National Park Management Plan for a period of ten years and other Acts adopted on the basis of this Law, regulating the protection of nature. In the area of the National Park shall be established regimes of protection of I, II and III grade, on which are applied prohibitions and restrictions on works and activities, identified in the Management Plan and regulations governing nature protection. The Management Plan and spatial plan of the special purpose areas must not be contrary (Article 10, paragraphs 1–3). The management plan includes measures, prohibitions and restrictions on works and activities in accordance with prescribed protection regimes (Article 12, paragraphs 1–2).

In the area of the National Park, the construction of buildings, which is contrary to the spatial plan for special purpose areas, is prohibited (Article 10, paragraph 4).

919. The Government gives approval on the Management Plan, after obtaining opinion of the competent ministries. The Management plan is implemented by an annual National Park Management Programme (hereinafter 'Programme Management') (Article 12, paragraphs 4–5).

The spatial plan for the special purpose area of the National Park will be developed with the protection regimes I, II and III prescribed by this Law. Urban development plans in the area of the National Park shall be adopted with prior approval of the Ministry (Article 19, paragraphs 1–2).

920. The Professional Council of the National Park is a professional and consultative body that monitors and analyses the programmes and projects in the field of nature conservation and sustainable use of natural resources, in particular: (1) National Park Management Plan; (2) National Park Management Programme; (3) programmes and projects to implement the measures and activities for protection and development of the National Park; and (4) consider other activities of the management relating to operations of protection and development of National park (Article 22, paragraph 1).

The Ministry shall supervise the implementation of the provisions of this Law (Article 25, paragraph 1).

III. Sub-legal Acts

921. In the field of nature protection, a large number of by-laws have been adopted, such as:

- Regulation on protection regimes (OJ RS, No. 31/12).
- Regulation on ecological network (OJ RS, No. 102/10).
- Decision on the establishment of the Institute for Nature Protection of Serbia (OJ RS, Nos 18/10, 9/17, 65/22).
- Statute of the Institute for Nature Protection of Serbia (OJ RS, No. 73/10).
- Rulebook on official clothing, i.e., the uniform of guards in national parks and protected areas (OJ RS, No. 105/20).
- Rulebook on criteria for the identification of landscapes and the method of assessing their significant and characteristic features (OJ RS, No. 119/17).
- Rulebook on the cost list for disposal of confiscated specimens of strictly protected, protected and non-native wild species (OJ RS, No. 63/17).
- Rulebook on evaluation criteria and the procedure for categorizing protected areas (OJ RS, No. 97/15).
- Rulebook on the form of national park supervisor official ID (OJ RS, Nos 117/14 and 97/15).
- Rulebook on internal order and guard service (OJ RS, No. 59/21).
- Rulebook on the procedure for proposing and appointing members of the Council of National Park Users (OJ RS, No. 46/18).

  Rulebook on the procedure for proposing and appointing members of the Expert Council of the National Park (OJ RS, No. 42/18).

922. It should be added that the regime of protection of specific locations is regulated by sub-legal Acts adopted for each individual protected area, for example:

- Regulation on the proclamation of the Nature Park 'Mali Bosut' (OJ RS, No. 8/24).
- Regulation on the proclamation of the Nature Park 'Radan' (OJ RS, No. 4/24).
- Regulation on the protection of landscapes of exceptional features 'Planina Cer' (OJ RS, No. 54/23).
- Regulation on the proclamation of the Special Nature Reserve 'Uvac' (OJ RS, No. 27/23).
- Regulation on the protection of landscapes of exceptional features 'Stolovi' (OJ RS, No. 84/22).
- Regulation on the protection of landscapes of exceptional features 'Maljen' (OJ RS, No. 83/21).
- Regulation on the proclamation of the Strict Nature Reserve 'Kalenić' (OJ RS, No. 84/20).
- Regulation on the proclamation of the Monument of Nature 'Tunnel Cave Prerast in the Zamna Canyon' (OJ RS, No. 81/20).
- Regulation on the proclamation of the Special Nature Reserve 'Zasavica' (OJ RS, No. 54/19).
- Regulation on the proclamation of the Special Nature Reserve 'Rtanj' (OJ RS, No. 18/19).
- Regulation on the proclamation of the Landscape of Outstanding Features 'Vlasina' (OJ RS, No. 25/18).
- Regulation on the proclamation of the Nature Park 'Zlatibor' (OJ RS, No. 91/17).
- Regulation on the Proclamation of the Special Nature Reserve 'Milesevka River Gorge' (OJ RS, No. 104/14).
- Regulation on the proclamation of the Special Nature Reserve 'Carska bara' (OJ RS, No. 46/11).
- Regulation on the protection of the Nature Park 'Stara planina' (OJ RS, No. 23/09).
- Regulation on the protection of the Special Nature Reserve 'Ludaško Lake' (OJ RS, No. 30/06).
- Regulation on the protection of the Special Nature Reserve 'Uvac' (OJ RS, Nos 25/06 and 110/06).
- Regulation on the protection of the Natural Monument 'Stopića pećina' (OJ RS, No. 75/05).
- Regulation on the protection of the Nature Park 'Shargan-Mokra Gora' (OJ RS, Nos 52/05, 105/05, 81/08 and 49/12 – CC).
- Regulation on the protection of the Special Nature Reserve 'Deliblatska peščara' (OJ RS Nos 3/02 and 81/08).
- Regulation on the protection of the Golija Nature Park (OJ RS, Nos 45/01 and 47/09).
- Regulation on the protection of the Special Nature Reserve of the Upper Danube (OJ RS, Nos 45/01, 81/08 and 107/09).
- Regulation on the protection of landscapes of exceptional features 'Ovčarsko – Kablarska klisura' (OJ RS, No. 16/00).
- Regulation on the protection of the Nature Park 'Sićevačka klisura' (OJ RS, No. 16/00).

- Regulation on the protection of natural monuments 'Danube Park' (OJ RS, No. 25/98).
- Regulation on the protection of the special nature reserve 'Selevenjske pustare' (OJ RS, No. 37/97).
- Regulation on the protection of the special nature reserve 'Karadjordjevo' (OJ RS, No. 37/97).
- Regulation on protection of a special nature reserve 'Stari Begej-Carska Bara Swamp' (OJ RS, No. 56/94).
- Regulation on protection of special reserve 'Ludasko Lake' (OJ RS, No. 56/94).
- Regulation on protection of special nature reserve 'Obedska swamp' (OJ RS, No. 56/94).
- Regulation on protection of general nature reserve 'Vitanovaca' (OJ RS, No. 9/95).
- Regulations on protection of special nature reserve 'Jelasnicka klisure gorge' (OJ RS, No. 9/95).
- Regulation on protection of natural monument 'Homoljska Potajnica' (OJ RS, No. 9/95).
- Regulation on protection of natural monument 'Risovaca' (OJ RS, No. 9/95).
- Regulation on protection of natural monument 'Vrelo Mlave' (OJ RS, No. 9/95).
- Regulation on protection of natural monument 'Resavska cave' (OJ RS, No. 9/95).
- Regulation on protection of natural monument 'Krupajsko vrelo' (OJ RS, No. 9/95).
- Regulation on protection of natural monument 'Lisine' (OJ RS, No. 9/95).
- Regulation on protection of natural monument 'Đavolja Varos' (OJ RS, No. 9/95).[1119]

IV. International Treaties and Harmonization with EU Legislation

923. Serbia is a contracting party to the following international treaties related to nature protection:

- International Plant Protection Convention (1951) (OJ FPRY – IT, No. 7/55).
- Ramsar Convention on Wetlands of International Importance Especially as Waterfowl Habitat (1971) (OJ SFRY – IT, No. 9/77).
- International Convention for the Protection of Birds (OJ SFRY – IT, No. 6/73).

1119. *See also* following regulations regarding:(1) natural monuments: 'Prerasti – Vratne' (OJ RS, No. 99/14), 'Promuklica' (OJ RS, No. 101/14); (2) special nature reserve: 'Goč – Gvozdac' (OJ RS, No. 99/14), 'Klisura reke Maleševke' (OJ RS, No. 104/14), 'Mala jasenova glava' (OJ RS, No. 116/14), 'Ritovi donjeg Potisja' (OJ RS, Nos 121/14 and 25/18), 'Suva planina' (OJ RS, No. 72/15), 'Iznad Tatalije' (OJ RS, No. 72/15), 'Tesne Jaruge' (OJ RS, No. 72/15), 'Zelenika' (OJ RS, No. 72/15) and 'Peštersko polje' (OJ RS, No. 114/15); and (3) strict nature reserves 'Mustava' (OJ RS, No. 99/14); 'Kukavica' (OJ RS, No. 107/14), 'Felješana' (OJ RS, No. 107/14), 'Dolina potoka Bigar' (OJ RS, No. 72/15); landscape of exceptional properties: 'Kamena gora' (OJ RS, No. 99/14), 'Ozren – Jadovnik' (OJ RS, No. 107/14). For the full list, *see* http://www.pravno-informacioni-sistem.rs/reg-overview# (6.1.2024).

- Convention on International Trade in Endangered Species of Wild Fauna and Flora (1979) (CITES) (OJ SFRY – IT, No. 11/01).
- Convention on Biological Diversity (OJ SFRY – IT, No. 11/01) and Cartagena Protocol on Biosafety (OJ SM – IT, No. 16/05).
- Convention on Conservation of Migratory Species of Wild Animals Bonn Convention (OJ RS – IT, No. 102/07).
- Convention on the Conservation of European Wildlife and Natural Habitats – Bern Convention (OJ RS – IT, No. 102/07).
- Convention on the Protection and Sustainable Development of the Carpathians – Carpathian Convention (OJ RS – IT, No. 102/07).[1120]
- United Nations Convention to Combat Desertification in Countries Experiencing Serious Drought and/or Desertification, Particularly in Africa (OJ RS – IT, No. 102/07).
- European Landscape Convention (OJ RS – IT, No. 4/2011).
- Convention of the European Forest Institute (OJ RS – IT, No. 2/17).
- Nagoya Protocol on Access to Genetic Resources and the Fair and Equitable Sharing of Benefits Arising From Their Utilization to the Convention on Biological Diversity (OJ RS – IT, No. 12/18).
- Agreement on the Conservation of Bats in Europe (OJ RS – IT, No. 13/18).
- Agreement on the Conservation of African – Eurasian Migratory Waterbirds (AEWA) (OJ RS – IT, No. 13/18).

924. ‘ Alignment with the EU acquis in the field of nature protection, in particular with the Habitats and Birds Directives, is moderate.’[1121]

1120. Serbia also ratified the following protocols: Protocol on Conservation and Sustainable Use of Biological and Landscape Diversity to the Framework Convention on the Protection and Sustainable Development of the Carpathians (OJ RS – IT, No. 1/13); Protocol on Sustainable Forest Management to the Framework Convention on the Protection and Sustainable Development of the Carpathians (OJ RS – IT, No. 5/15); and Protocol on Sustainable Tourism to the Framework Convention on the Protection and Sustainable Development of the Carpathians (OJ RS – IT, No. 5/15).

1121. EC 2023, 136. Illegal construction in national parks was reported by the inspectorate but no action was taken. *Ibid.* ‘It is easier to understand the identification of a great number of illegally built structures in the protected areas that have been put under protection just recently. But, it is alarming to notice that each spatial plan analysed here states the same problem even though some of the areas have been under protection and regulated by spatial and urban plans for decades.’ Pantić, et al., 2019, 184.

Chapter 3. Wildlife Protection

§1. INTRODUCTION

925. The RS is characterized by high genetic, species and ecosystem diversity. The highland and mountainous regions of the RS, as a part of the Balkan Peninsula, are one of the six European biodiversity centres. Moreover, in terms of the wealth of its flora, the RS is potentially one of the global centres of plant diversity. Although the RS's 88,361 km^2 represents only 2.1% of European territory, biodiversity of different groups of organisms remains high. The RS hosts: 39% of European vascular flora, 51% of European fish fauna, 49% of European reptile and amphibian fauna, 74% of European bird fauna and 67% of European mammal fauna.[1122] In the territory of the RS, 2,633 species are protected, out of which 1,783 are strictly protected.[1123]

926. Generally speaking, the MEP and the Nature Protection Institute are the main institutions competent in the field. Besides them, certain competences are also, as in the case of parks and reserves, given to the EPA (data collection and reporting on the status of biodiversity) and the Secretariat for Environmental Protection and Sustainable Development of the APV.

§2. LEGAL REGULATION

927. Wildlife protection is presently regulated by numerous legal and sub-legal Acts in Serbia. They are often the same as those regulating parks and reserves, as mentioned in the previous chapter. As already mentioned, Article 89 of the Constitution prescribes that everyone shall be obliged to protect natural rarities (scientific, cultural and historical heritage), as well as goods of public interest in accordance with the Law (the RS, APs and LSG units shall be held particularly accountable for the protection of heritage).

928. The following could be regarded as the most important legal regulations:

(1) *EPL* (OJ RS, Nos 135/04, 36/09 – other law, 72/09 – other law, 43/11CC, 14/16, 76/18 and 95/18 – other law).
(2) Law on Nature Protection (OJ RS, Nos 36/09, 88/10, 91/10 – corr., 14/16, 95/18 – other law, and 71/21).
(3) Law on National Parks (OJ RS, Nos 84/15 and 95/18 – other law).[1124]

1122. MESP. 2011, *supra*, para. 18. *See also* GOV RS. 2010a, 34–37.
1123. EPA. 2019a, 173.
1124. Several other laws could be relevant too. These are: Law on Game and Hunting (OJ RS, Nos 18/10, 95/18 – other law, and 92/23 – other law); Law on the Protection and Sustainable Use of Fish Stocks (OJ RS, Nos 128/14 and 95/18 – other law); Law on the Welfare of Animals (OJ RS, No. 41/09); Law on Forests (OJ RS, Nos 30/10, 93/12, 89/15 and 95/18 – other law); Law on Agriculture and Rural Development (OJ RS, Nos 41/09, 10/13 – other law and 101/16); Law on the

(4) The Law on Game and Hunting (OJ RS, Nos 18/10, 95/18 – other law, and 92/23 – other law).[1125]
(5) Regulation on the control of use and trade of wild flora and fauna (OJ RS, Nos 31/05, 45/05 – corr., 22/07, 38/08, 9/10, 69/11 and 95/18 – other law).
(6) Rulebook on transboundary movement and trade in protected species (OJ RS, Nos 99/09 and 6/14).[1126]

I. Law on Environmental Protection

929. The EPL (OJ RS, Nos 135/04, 36/09 – other law, 72/09 – other law, 43/11CC, 14/16, 76/18 and 95/18 – other law) has several provisions concerning biodiversity, which is defined as 'a diversity of organisms within a specie, among the species and ecosystems and it covers full genetic diversity, species and ecosystems diversity at local, national, regional and global level' (Article 3, point 7).

Spatial Plan of the Republic of Serbia from 2010 until 2020 (OJ RS, No. 88/10); Law on Food Safety (OJ RS, Nos 41/09 and 17/19); Law on Animal Husbandry (OJ RS, Nos 41/09, 93/12 and 14/16); Law on the Protection of Rights of Breeders of Plant Varieties (OJ RS, Nos 41/09 and 88/11); Law on GMOs (OJ RS, No. 41/09); Law on Tourism (OJ RS, No. 17/19), etc.

1125. *See* part devoted to Hunting and Fishery.

1126. Apart from that, list of relevant by-laws include, *inter alia*, the following: Rulebook on compensation for damage caused by strictly protected wild animal species (OJ RS, No. 118/23), Regulation on the ecological network (OJ RS, No. 102/10); Rulebook on criteria for identification of landscapes and manner of assessment of their significant and characteristic features (OJ RS, No. 119/17); Rulebook on the cost estimate for the disposal of confiscated specimens of strictly protected, protected and allochthonous wild species (OJ RS, No. 63/17); Rulebook on contents and operational methods of the protected areas' register (OJ RS, No. 81/10); Rulebook on conditions to be fulfilled by protected area managers (OJ RS, No. 85/09); Rulebook on protected area rangers' identity cards (OJ RS, Nos 117/14, 97/15); Rulebook on the appearance (look) of the nature protection logo and procedure and conditions for its use (OJ RS, No. 84/09); Rulebook on proclamation and protection of strictly protected and protected species of wild plants, animals and fungi (OJ RS, Nos 5/10, 47/11, 32/16 and 98/16); Rulebook on distinguishing criteria of habitat types, habitat types, sensitive, threatened, rare and priority habitats for protection, as well as protection measures for the conservation of habitat types (OJ RS, No. 35/10); Rulebook on compensation tariffs for determining compensation levels for damage caused through an unauthorized act in relation to strictly protected and protected wild species (OJ RS, No. 37/10); Rulebook on methods, tools and resources for commercial fishing, as well as methods, tools and resources for recreational fishing (OJ RS, Nos 9/17 and 34/18); Regulation on the method of determining costs and their amount for damage caused to fish stock (OJ RS, No. 3/16); Rulebook on conditions, programme and methods for fishing guard examinations and professional examinations for fishermen (OJ RS, Nos 60/15 and 96/16); Rulebook on categorization of fishing waters (OJ RS, No. 10/12); Rulebook on conditions and methods for organizing fishing guards, legitimization form for fishing guards and appearance (look) of the fishing guards badge (OJ RS, Nos 07/10 and 3/16 – other rulebook); Rulebook on entering into the production of GMOs and products of GMOs (OJ FRY, No. 62/02 and OJ RS, No. 29/09); Regulation on regimes of protection (OJ RS, No. 31/12), Regulation on compensatory measures (OJ RS, No. 20/10); Regulation on evaluation criteria and procedure for classification of protected areas (OJ RS, No. 97/15); Rulebook on fish warden uniforms, appearance of the warden badge and fish warden official ID form (OJ RS, Nos 39/16 and 38/17); Decision on protection of plant species as natural rarities (OJ RS, Nos 11/1990 and 49/1991); Decision on protection of animal species as natural rarities (OJ RS, Nos 11/1990 and 49/1991).

930. As already mentioned, the whole second part of the Law is devoted to 'management of natural values' (Articles 11–32). On the basis of the Law, a ten-year Strategy for the Sustainable Use of Natural Resources has been adopted (OJ RS, No. 33/12). It will be followed by specific plans for APs and LSGs. The nature protection law improves nature management.[1127] Article 26 of the EPL prescribes that:

> biodiversity protection, use of biological resources, genetically modified organism and biotechnology shall be executed on the basis of this Law and obligations taken through international agreements. Biodiversity and biological resources shall be protected and used in a way that shall enable their survival, diversity, renewal and improvement in case of misbalance.

931. Concrete measures to be taken in connection with protection and use of flora and fauna and trade with endangered and protected species of wild flora and fauna are indicated in Articles 27 and 28.

In order to protect biodiversity and biological resources, the Ministry and other competent bodies and organizations have obligations to control import and growth of plant and animal species of foreign origin (Article 27).[1128]

II. The Law on Nature Protection

932. The Law on Nature Protection (OJ RS, Nos 36/09, 88/10, 91/10 – corr., 14/16, 95/18 – other law, and 71/21) prescribes in Article 36 that wild species that are threatened or may become endangered, which have special significance from the genetic, ecological, ecosystem, scientific, health, economical and other aspects, shall be protected as strictly protected wild species or protected wild species (Article 36 paragraph 1).[1129] It is prescribed which wild species can be declared as strictly protected[1130] or protected.[1131]

1127. It is prescribed by the Art. 17 of the EPL, that the activities which threaten the environment, natural balance, biodiversity, hydrographic, geomorphologic, geological, cultural and landscape values, or which in any way degrade the quality and properties of the natural good, are not be allowed within a protected natural good (para. 2).

1128. It is prohibited to harass, abuse, hurt and destroy wild fauna and to demolish their habitats. Apart from that, it is also prohibited to destroy, tear or in any other way to desertification of wild flora or to destroy and demolish its habitats (Art. 27, paras 2 and 3).

1129. Wild species are all types of animals, plants and fungi that are naturally evolved, including hybrids and all specimens reproduced in captivity or under artificial conditions, with the exception of domesticated races on whose evolutionary process has affected the man for its own purposes (Art. 4, para. 13).

1130. The following wild species can be declared as strictly protected: (1) species extinct in the Republic of Serbia and return through a reintroduction programme; (2) extremely endangered wild species; (3) endangered wild species; (4) relict species; (5) local endemite; (6) stenoendemite; (7) wild species subject to a ratified international agreement; and (8) a species requiring strict protection for other reasons (Art. 36, para. 2).

1131. The following wild species can be declared as protected: (1) vulnerable wild species; (2) endemic species; (3) indicator, key and umbrella species; (4) relict species; (5) wild species subject to a ratified international agreement; (6) wild species not endangered, but, due to its appearance, can

933. Protected species, within the meaning of this Law, are determined on the basis of national and international red lists or red books, expert findings and scientific knowledge (Article 36, paragraph 3).[1132] The ecological network is established as a functionally and spatially connected entity in order to conserve habitat types of particular importance for the protection, renewal and/or improvement of degraded habitats and for the conservation of habitats of wild species of flora and fauna (Article 38).[1133]

934. On the basis of the estimate of endangerment for certain wild species and the obligations from the approved international agreements, as well as on the basis of the national and international red lists and/or red books and/or other professional documentation, the Minister shall, by mutual consent with the Minister competent for the agriculture, forestry and water management, and at the proposal of the Institute, and/or other authorized scientific or expert organizations, declare the wild species as strictly protected wildlife species or protected wildlife species (Article 48, paragraph 1).[1134] The Institute shall take care of the species, as well as holders of such species, protected areas managers, public enterprises for forest management, users of hunting areas and fishery areas who are obligated to plan and implement measures and activities of monitoring and management of strictly protected species and protected wild species populations within the management programmes and plans, in compliance with this and special laws (Article 48, paragraph 2).

935. Article 64 of the Law prescribes responsibility for damage caused by wild species. Namely, this Article defines that the RS is not responsible for damage caused by wild species, except in the cases laid down by this Law and other regulations. A legal entity, entrepreneur, or private entity to whom strictly protected or protected wild species may cause economic or any other damage shall be obliged to duly and at his/her on expense undertake all authorized actions and activities in

be easily confused with an endangered wild species; and (7) wild species of economic importance which can be endangered by uncontrolled exploitation or destruction of the habitat (Art. 36, para. 3).

1132. Strictly protected and protected wild species in terms of this Law are determined on the basis of national and international red lists or red books, ratified international treaties, expert findings and/ or scientific knowledge. Red List and Red Book of endangered wild species with places where they are located, population abundance and the level of vulnerability, are determined by the Ministry, at the proposal of the institution (Art. 36, paras 4 and 5).

1133. The ecological network shall be made up of important ecological areas and ecological corridors. Important ecological areas are: (1) areas of national importance which by their bio-geographic presence and representativeness contribute to the conservation of biological diversity in the Republic of Serbia; and (2) areas of international importance which by their bio-geographic presence and representativeness contribute to the conservation of habitat types and habitats of species including birds in accordance with ratified international agreements and common rules of international Law. The ecological network of the Republic of Serbia is established by the Government (Art. 38, paras 2, 3 and 4).

1134. *See* Rulebook on declaring and protection of the strictly protected and protected wild plants, animals and fungi (OJ RS, Nos 5/2010, 47/11, 36/16 and 98/16). There are a total of 1,760 strictly protected wild species of algae, plants, animals and fungi. *See* MESP. 2011, *supra*, 32.

order to prevent the occurrence of damage (Article 64 paragraph 2).[1135] However, the injured party has the right to reimbursement in the amount of the real damage induced by strictly protected and protected species if the injured party implements prescribed measures and activities.[1136]

A. Protection and Conservation of Wild Species

936. Prevention of all activities that contribute to disturbance of favourable state of wild species populations, destruction or damage to their habitats, nests, litters or disruption of their life cycle and/or favourable state[1137] shall be deemed as protection and conservation of wild species (Article 71). During the execution of work and activities in nature and use of natural values in the wild species' habitats, measures, methods and technical means that contribute to the conservation of favourable state of species and/or do not endanger wild species and/or disturb the habitats of their populations shall be applied, or these works and activities may be restricted in the period overlapping with significant stages of the life cycle of the species (Article 72).

B. Strictly Protected Wild Species

937. Strictly protected wild species can be protected in the entire territory of the RS or in individual parts thereof (Article 73, paragraph 1).[1138]

938. It shall be prohibited to use, destroy and execute other activities that could endanger strictly protected wild plants, animal including birds and fungi species and their habitats (Article 74, paragraph 1).[1139] The following shall be prohibited: (1) to

1135. Under the action or activity in terms of para. 2 of this Article the following shall be understood: fencing, safeguarding of goods and chasing out of strictly protected animal species, from the place wherein directly threaten the goods and in the manner not threatening for the survival of species.

1136. The amount of reimbursement for damage (in line with criteria for the estimation of damage prescribed by the Minister) is fixed in agreement between the Ministry, i.e., competent body of the AP and the injured party, while the court shall fix the amount of damage in the case of dispute (Art. 65, para. 5).

1137. The favourable state of wild species shall be provided by the protection of their habitats and protection measures for particular species in compliance with this Law (Art. 71, para. 2).

1138. If an area is the temporary habitat of a strictly protected wild species and its protection cannot be provided in some other way, the Ministry can, by a special decision, with prior opinion of the Ministry responsible for agriculture and forestry, declare that area or the part thereof is temporarily protected as long as the need for protection exists (Art. 73, para. 2).

1139. Notwithstanding the provisions of Art. 74 of this Law, when there is no other satisfactory solution and the exemption is not damaging the survival of populations of strictly protected wild species at a favourable conservation status in their natural habitat, i.e., when there is no other satisfactory solution for wild bird species, the Ministry may allow activities that aim at: (1) research and education, recolonization (repopulation), reintroduction and breeding operations in in-situ and ex-situ conditions; (2) prevention of serious damage to crops, livestock, forests, fishponds and water and other forms of property; (3) protection of public health and public safety and in case of birds the air safety as well, or for other reasons of predominant public interest, including reasons of social

destroy specimens of plant and fungi species and the development forms thereof by picking, collecting, cutting, or uprooting or digging in all stages of the biological cycle, and to endanger or destroy their habitats; (2) to keep and trade in strictly protected plant and fungi species growing in the wild and the development forms thereof; (3) capture, keep and/or kill strictly protected wild animal species in all stages of the biological cycle, damage or destroy the development forms thereof, eggs, nests and litters, as well as the area of their breeding sites and resting places and to endanger or destroy their habitats; (4) to significantly disturb these species, particularly during the period of breeding, rearing, hibernation and migration; (5) to cut off migratory routes; (6) to hide, keep, breed, trade in, export, transport and offer for sale or exchange or in any other way acquire or publicly expose animal species including all their derivatives and development forms (Article 74, paragraph 2).[1140]

C. Protected Wild Species

939. Protected wild species can be protected in the entire territory of the RS or in individual parts thereof (Article 76, paragraph 1).[1141] Protected wild species of fungi, lichens, plants, animals or their parts can be collected for the purpose of processing, trading, cross-boundary commerce, as well as cultivation and rearing, on the basis of a permit issued by the Ministry in accordance with law (paragraph 3).[1142]

D. The Use and Collecting of Protected Wild Species

940. Pursuant to Article 77, the use and collecting of protected wild species shall be allowed exclusively in a way that does not endanger favourable status of the population.[1143] The Institute for Nature Protection shall register the manner and

---

and economic nature and beneficial consequences of primary importance for the environment; (4) protection of wild plant and animal species and conservation of wild habitats; (5) allowing, under strictly controlled conditions and under limited scope, taking or keeping of certain specimens in limited quantity (Art. 75, para. 1). A permit for the situation referred to in para. 1 of this Article shall be issued by the Ministry upon previously obtained opinion of the Institute.

1140. Fine ranging between RSD 500,000 and 2,000,000 shall be imposed to legal entity for the offence if such legal entity undertakes actions which may endanger strictly protected species of plants, animals, fungi and their habitats (Art. 126, point 11).

1141. The management of populations of protected wild species that is not regulated by rules concerning hunting and fisheries shall be implemented on the basis of a permit issued by the Ministry in accordance with law (Art. 76, para. 2).

1142. The detailed conditions and protection measures for protected wild species and measures for the protection of their habitats shall be specified by the decision referred to in Art. 48 of this Law (para. 4).

1143. The Minister shall prescribe in more detail the conditions and measures for the protection of protected wild species including the following: (1) prohibition of use in terms of time; (2) quantitative and qualitative restrictions in their use; (3) prohibition of use in terms of space aiming at recovery of population to a satisfactory level (Art. 77, para. 2). Should it be established that due to usage a protected wild species is endangered, the Minister can prohibit or restrict the use of that species, previously acquiring the opinion of the Institute (Art. 77, para. 4).

scope of usage of protected wild species for the purpose of determining and following up population status including wild species whose usage is regulated by the Law on Hunting and the Law on Fishery.

E. Permit to Research Strictly Protected and Protected Wild Species

941. The Ministry shall issue the permit for scientific research and educational purposes for the research of strictly protected and protected wild species that is performed by methods that could endanger the species (such as capturing, collecting, marking, sampling, etc.), with previously obtained opinion from the Institute (Article 78, paragraph 1).[1144] The research reports referred to in paragraph 1 of this Article shall be submitted to the Ministry, the Institute and the Manager of the protected area by the end of the calendar year (Article 78, paragraph 3). Taking out of specimens of strictly protected and protected wild species and/or their parts and derivatives referred to in paragraph 1 of this Article for scientific and research purposes shall be carried out on the basis of a permit issued by the Ministry, pursuant to Article 94 of this Law (Article 78, paragraph 4).

F. Wild Animals

942. The use of certain means for capturing and killing wild animals that endanger or disturb their populations and/or habitats, affect their welfare and that can cause their local disappearance shall be prohibited. The prohibited means are prescribed in Article 79. The prohibited means shall be considered the following in particular: (1) traps; (2) adhesives; (3) chemical means like attractants; (4) live animals used as decoys in hunting of birds and game; (5) crossbows, bows, arrows and/or other weapons with strings, that can fling an arrow or other projectile by pulling the string or some other elastic; (6) bird hunting with nets; (7) lethal or stunning electrical devices; (8) luminous devices; (9) mirrors and other dazzling devices; (10) sound transmitters (tape recorders, cassette recorders, audio recorders and players, etc.) that emit sound of calling, crying or responding; (11) devices for illuminating targets; (12) sighting devices for night shooting comprising an electronic image magnifier or image converter; (13) explosives; (14) poisons or anaesthetic baits; (15) automatic weapons; (16) aircrafts; (17) motor-driven vehicles in motion used to hunt animals; and (18) other devices specified by other law and ratified international agreements (Article 79, paragraph 2).[1145]

1144. No complaint against the decision referred to in para. 1 shall be allowed, but administrative dispute may be instituted against it (Art. 78, para. 5).

1145. Certain means referred to in para. 2 of this Article can be used exceptionally and restrictively for scientific and research purposes. The permit to use the means referred to in para. 3 of this Article shall be issued by the Ministry by a ruling, with prior opinion of other competent authorities (Art. 79, para. 3). No complaint against the decision shall be allowed but administrative dispute may be instituted against it (Art. 79, para. 4).

G. Migratory Species

943. Public roads and other traffic routes, telecommunication and electric systems, waterworks and other buildings whose construction cuts off usual corridors for daily and seasonal migration of wild animals, cause habitat fragmentation, or in some other way disturb their normal life cycle shall be constructed so as to reduce negative impacts with the application of special construction and technical solutions on the buildings and around them, during the periods of both construction and exploitation (Article 80, paragraph 1).[1146] Special technological solutions enabling free and secure communication of wild animals shall be prescribed by the Minister (Article 80, paragraph 2).

H. Allochthonous Species

944. Introduction of allochthonous wild species and hybrids thereof into the wild on the territory of the RS shall be prohibited[1147] (Article 82, paragraph 1).[1148] Exceptionally, introduction referred to in paragraph 1 of the present Article shall be permitted if scientifically and professionally proven and acceptable from the aspect of nature protection and sustainable management, that is, if such introduction does not endanger populations or natural habitat of autochthonous wild species (Article 83, paragraph 2). In case of unintentional introduction of allochthonous wild species and hybrids thereof into the free nature on the territory of the RS, or if there is a reasonable doubt that such introduction will occur, the Minister shall stipulate actions to exterminate or prevent further spread of introduced allochthonous wild species and hybrids thereof (Article 83).

I. Relocation of Specimens of Autochthonous Species

945. Relocation of live specimens of autochthonous wild species in free nature on the territory of the RS can be carried out based on research and planning documents, in accordance with the present and other laws. Relocation referred to in the preceding paragraph can be carried out provided that research findings show that

---

1146. Towers and technical components of medium and high voltage ducts shall be so executed as to protect birds and bats against the electric shock and mechanical injury. Locations of wind powered generators (windmills) shall be so determined as to avoid important habitats and migration routes thereof (Art. 81, paras 1 and 2). Usage of strong light sources (advertising rotating reflectors, lasers and the like) pointed towards the sky shall not be allowed, unless when used for safety and air traffic control purposes (Art. 81, para. 5).

1147. An allochthonous species is a species that came into ecosystems on the territory of the Republic of Serbia by intentional or accidental introduction (Art. 4, para. 2).

1148. Fine ranging between RSD 500,000 and 2,000,000 shall be imposed to legal entity for the offence if such legal entity introduces allochthonous wild species and their hybrids into free nature contrary to Art. 82 of this Law (Art. 126, point 17).

such action would not endanger in any way the favourable status of species population, that is, the animal welfare, and in case of accidental occurrences (floods, fires, droughts, etc.) (Article 84, paragraphs 1 and 2).[1149]

J. Reintroduction of Wild Species

946. Reintroduction of wild species into the free nature on the territory of the RS can be carried out based on research, reintroduction programme and permit.[1150] Reintroduction of wild species can be carried out provided that research findings show that such action contributes to the favourable status of the species.[1151]

K. Wild Animal Species

947. Live specimens of wild animal species may be kept in captivity only if they are provided with living conditions in accordance with the law and well-suited for the type, breed, gender, age, physical and biological specificities and ethological needs of the species (Article 86, paragraph 1).[1152] The Minister shall prescribe conditions that must be fulfilled by zoos and other facilities and/or spaces for keeping animals in the sense of paragraph 1 of this Article, the conditions for keeping, prohibition or restriction on keeping certain species, training and educational programmes and the manner of marking and recording specimens of wild animal species referred to in paragraph 1 of this Article (paragraph 4). Amendments to the Law (2016) introduced, *inter alia*, new provisions related to the zoo (Article 86a).

948. A legal person, entrepreneur or natural person keeping a specimen of strictly protected or protected wild species in captivity shall submit an application to the Ministry for a certificate, in accordance with the regulation governing transboundary movement and trade in wild flora and fauna species, except in cases when for the concerned species there is already a valid certificate issued by the ministry or when an exemption has been stipulated (Article 88, paragraph 1). The certificate

1149. Relocation of live specimens of autochthonous wild species in free nature shall be approved by the Ministry upon obtaining the opinion of the Institute (Art. 84, para. 3).

1150. The permit referred to in para. 1 of the present Article shall be issued by the Ministry through the Resolution (Art. 85, para. 5).

1151. Feasibility Study and EIA Study should be done prior to any reintroduction (Art. 85, para. 2).

1152. Legal persons, entrepreneurs and natural persons keeping specimens of strictly protected and protected wild species shall keep evidence confirming that these are: (1) lawfully imported specimens; (2) lawfully acquired specimens before the species was protected by the Law; (3) specimens originating from breeding in accordance with this Law; (4) specimens or their offspring, that were in accordance with this Law reported to the Ministry by 1 Jun. 2011 (Art. 87, para. 1). The permits and certificates issued in accordance with this Law, the regulations adopted based on this Law or in accordance with the Law on the Ratification of the CITES (OJ FRY – IT, No. 11/01 – hereinafter 'CITES Convention'), as well as other substantiated evidence based on which the Ministry can determine the lawful acquisition of specimens, including the results of laboratory and other technical analysis carried out by institutions designated by the Ministry for determining the origin of specimens, shall be deemed proof of origin referred to in para. 1 of this Article (para. 2).

referred to in paragraph 1 of this Article shall be issued if the applicant proves that the conditions imposed by this Law and the regulation on transboundary movement and trade in wild flora and fauna species have been met (Article 88, paragraph 2).[1153]

949. A legal person, entrepreneur or natural person who intends to breed or artificially propagate specimens of strictly protected or protected wild species shall obtain a licence in accordance with this Law (Article 89, paragraph 1).[1154] If, during the validity of the licence referred to in paragraph 1 of this Article, an inspection procedure in accordance with this Law determines that breeding or artificial propagation is performed contrary to conditions based on which the licence was issued, the Ministry shall revoke the licence (Article 89, paragraph 3).[1155]

L. *Trade in Wild Animals*

950. A legal person, entrepreneur or natural person engaged in trade in specimens of strictly protected, i.e., protected wild animal species shall keep live animals in accordance with Article 86 of this Law, shall treat specimens in accordance with Article 87 of this Law and shall conduct trade in accordance with regulation governing transboundary movement and trade in specimens of wild species (Article 90, paragraph 1).[1156] When performing trade in specimens of strictly protected or protected wild animal species, the seller, i.e., owner shall provide the new owner with the proof of origin in accordance with Article 87 of this Law (paragraph 3).[1157]

951. For the purpose of temporary and/or permanent care of live specimens of wild animal species, the Ministry shall establish rescue centres, zoos or other legal or natural persons (Article 91, paragraph 1). The Minister, in consent with the minister responsible for veterinary activities, shall stipulate conditions to be met by the rescue centres referred to in paragraph 1 of the present Article (paragraph 2).[1158]

1153. The Ministry shall keep a register of specimens of strictly protected and protected wild animal species for which the certificates referred to in para. 1 of this Article have been issued (Art. 88, para. 3).
1154. The owner of specimens of strictly protected or protected wild animal species referred to in para. 1 of this Article shall ensure that those specimens do not escape into the wild and shall be responsible for damages caused by those animals if they escape (Art. 89, para.4).
1155. Breeding places of specimens of strictly protected or protected wild species, in accordance with the CITES Convention, can apply for permits for transboundary trade of these specimens for commercial purposes, only if the breeding place was registered with the CITES Secretariat (para. 5).
1156. The trade referred to in para. 1 of this Article shall cover the sale and purchase, acquisition for commercial purposes, presentation to the public for profit, use with the aim of acquiring profit, keeping for sale, offering for sale, requesting for purchase or transport for sale, rent, exchange or any other form of change in ownership (Art. 90, para. 2).
1157. Certificates and other documents issued on the basis of this Law for the purpose of trade in strictly protected or protected wild animal species shall be used only for the specimens to which they relate (Art. 90, para. 4).
1158. The rescue centre referred to in this Article shall be obliged to obtain an operating licence issued by the Ministry by virtue of a decision (Art. 91, para. 3).

952. Specimens of strictly protected, protected and allochthonous wild species that are handled contrary to provisions of this Law shall be confiscated in accordance with this Law, and a notice of confiscation containing data on the confiscated specimens shall be issued (Article 92, paragraph 1).[1159]

953. A person who finds a specimen of a strictly protected or protected wild animal species shall immediately notify the Ministry and the Institute of: (1) dead specimens found and (2) live specimens that are sick, injured or unable to survive in the wild by themselves (Article 93, paragraph 1).[1160]

III. Permit for Collection and Place on Market

954. In accordance with Article 27, paragraph 4 of the EPL, some protected species of wild flora and fauna, their developing forms and parts, may be collected and placed on the market only in the way and under conditions determined in the permit issued by the Ministry. Such a permit is issued after the Ministry obtains a positive opinion from the organization in charge of nature protection.

955. Legal or natural person that carries out the trade with wild flora and fauna is obliged to pay a charge.[1161]

956. According to Article 76 of the Law on Nature Protection, protected wild species of fungi, lichens, plants, animals or their parts can be collected for the purpose of processing, trading and cross-boundary commerce, as well as cultivation and rearing, on the basis of a permit issued by the Ministry in accordance with Law (paragraph 3). The detailed conditions and protection measures for protected wild species and measures for the protection of their habitats shall be specified by the decision referred to in Article 48 of this Law (paragraph 4).[1162] The management of

---

1159. The Ministry shall decide how the temporarily kept, temporarily confiscated, permanently confiscated and abandoned specimens of strictly protected, protected and allochthonous wild species are handled, in accordance with the regulation on transboundary movement and trade in wild flora and fauna species (para. 2).
1160. The Ministry may establish a special team of experts – natural and/or legal persons for cases requiring intervention on living specimens of wild animals in the wilderness or in captivity. Mutual rights and obligations shall be regulated by an agreement concluded between the Ministry and the persons referred to in para. 2 of this Article (Art. 93, paras 2 and 3).
1161. The amount of the charge from para. 5 of this Article shall be determined by the Act for putting under control the usage and trade of wild flora and fauna which shall be enacted by the Government (Art. 27, para. 6).
1162. On the basis of the estimate of certain endangered species and the obligations from the approved international agreements, as well as on the basis of the national and international red lists and/or red books and/or other professional documentation, the Minister shall, by mutual consent with the Minister competent for the agriculture, forestry and water management, and at the proposal of the Institute, declare wild species as strictly protected wildlife species or protected wildlife species. The decision referred to in para. 1 of this Article shall establish the protection measures for the strictly protected and protected wild plant, animal and fungi species, as well as the measures for protecting their habitats. The decision shall be published in the 'Official Journal of the Republic of Serbia' (Art. 48).

protected wild species population, which is not governed by the regulations from the field of hunting and fishing, is done on the basis of permits issued by the Ministry in accordance with the Law, on the base of previously obtained decision of the Institution (paragraphs 2 and 5).

957. The Regulation on the control of use and marketing of wild flora and fauna (OJ RS, Nos 31/05, 45/05, 22/07, 38/07 and 9/10) prescribes protection of endangered wild species of flora, fauna and fungi, their gathering from natural habitats, utilization, breeding and trade, and determines compensation for their exploitation (Article 1). In three Annexes are listed the species protected by this Regulation and sanctions are defined in Articles 21 and 23.[1163]

IV. Import and Export of Endangered and Protected Species

958. Export and import or transit of protected wild plant and animal species, their parts and derivatives are carried out in accordance with the Law on Ratification of the Convention on International Trade in Endangered Species of Wild Fauna and Flora (OJ FRY – IT, No. 11/01), EPL, Law on Nature Protection (OJ RS, Nos 36/09, 88/10, 91/10 – other law, 14/16, 95/18 – other law, and 71/21), and regulation on putting under control the use and trade of wild flora and fauna Rulebook on the Transboundary Movement and Trade in Protected Species (OJ RS, Nos 99/2009 and 6/2014).[1164]

General provisions concerning import and export of endangered and protected species of wild flora and fauna are contained in Article 28 of the EPL. These activities must be carried out in such a way that 'the exported quantity or the number of specimens of the endangered and protected species of wild flora and fauna shall not be detrimental to the survival of the species concerned in the Republic, as well as under other conditions regulated by law, on the basis of the permit issued by the Ministry'.

959. An import/export permit is needed for endangered and protected species of wild flora and fauna, as well as their different lifecycle forms and parts. An application for such a permit must be submitted[1165] with:

1163. The first control (State monitoring) started in 1993 through the by-law (Ordinance on collection of wild plant and animal species). Today, the Regulation covers 105 protected species, particularly: seventy-eight plant species, three lichen species, fifteen fungus species and nine animal species.

1164. *See also* Art. 14(1) and (3) of the Law on Foreign Trade (OJ RS, Nos 36/09 and 36/11 – other law, 88/11 and 89/15) and the Decision on determining goods subject to issuance of specific documents on importation, exportation and transit (OJ RS, Nos 59/22, 107/22, 3/23, 85/23, and 120/23).

1165. The competent Minister closely prescribes documentation that is to be submitted, contents and design of the permit and keeps the Register of issued permits. He/she also designates scientific and professional organizations authorized to give opinion concerning the export of wild.

(1) the opinion of a scientific and professional organization that exports the endangered or protected species of wild flora and fauna in the requested quantity or number of specimens shall not be detrimental to their survival;
(2) statement by the importer and/or exporter concerning the intended use of the specimen; and
(3) any other prescribed documentation.[1166]

960. On the base of opinion of the authorized scientific or professional organizations, the Ministry issues licences and other documents (certificates, opinions, information, etc.) approving the import, export, entry and carries out specimens of wild species, their parts and derivatives, protected under the Law and confirmed international treaties, as well as for the import of live specimens of allochthonous wild species that are not protected (Article 94).[1167] In the course of import, export, carrying in and out, or transit, living animals must be transported and kept in the way to avoid any injury or harm to their health and to avoid inhuman treatment, in line with the special regulations (Article 94, paragraph 9).

961. Transboundary transport of strictly protected and protected species, their parts and derivatives, as well as import or export or live spaces of allochthonous wild spaces, must be reported to customs service, in accordance with the provisions of the present Law and other regulations (Article 95, paragraph 1).[1168] Veterinary medical and phytosanitary inspection of consignments referred to in paragraph 1 of Article 95 which has jurisdiction over the border phytosanitary and veterinary inspection is carried out in accordance with special regulations. Minister sets the border crossings where import, export, carrying in and out and transit of strictly protected and protected wild species, their parts and derivatives can be performed, as well as the requirements in terms of their equipment and competence to carry out these tasks (Article 95, paragraphs 3 and 4).

962. The customs authority shall carry out checks of the import, export, carrying in and out, re-export and transit of specimens in terms of this Law, within its authority (Article 96, paragraph 1). For places mentioned in Article 95, paragraph 1 of this Law, the customs authority does special checks whether valid licences, certificates or other documents issued in accordance with the regulation referred to in Article 94 of this Law are submitted, and/or other prescribed licences of the other state-issued in accordance with the CITES (Article 96, paragraph 2). The customs authority with the permits and certificates referred to in paragraph 2 of this Article shall act in a manner prescribed by regulation on the transboundary movement of protected wildlife in Article 94 of this Law (Article 96, paragraph 3).

1166. Ministry is obliged to keep the Register of issued permits (Art. 28, para. 6).

1167. The permit referred to in para. 1 of the present Article shall be issued provided that: (1) the right to dispose of unit of wild animal, fungus and plant species is lawfully obtained; (2) the animals or consignment are duly marked; and (3) all measures for animal welfare in the course of transport are taken (Art. 94, para. 2).

1168. The customs service shall, in the course of import, export, carrying in and out, or transit of species examine the corresponding permits and verify crossing of the border in the dedicated column of the permit form (Art. 95, para. 3).

963. Rulebook on transboundary movement and trade in protected species (OJ RS, Nos 99/09 and 6/2014) prescribes the following: conditions for import, export, introduction, taking out or transit, trade and breeding of endangered and protected plant and animal species (hereinafter 'protected species'), parts and derivatives thereof; issuance of permits and other documents (verifications, certificates and opinions); documents that are submitted with permit application, contents and layout of the permit; list of species, parts and derivatives thereof, whose import or export is strictly forbidden, restricted or halted; exemptions from permitting obligations; methods of marking animals or deliveries; and implementation of inspection activities, maintenance of records and reporting.

964. It should be added that Serbia implements CITES.[1169]
'The implementation of CITES and the relevant national wildlife-trade-related legislation has improved in recent years, with a steady increase in the number of seizures, confiscations and convictions made regarding illegal transboundary and internal trade in protected species.'[1170] The EC Report (2019) explains the progress made in CITES more precisely: 'Enforcement capacities are insufficient, especially regarding wildlife trade and the Convention on International Trade in Endangered Species of Wild Fauna and Flora (CITES).'[1171] CITES is not specifically mentioned in the last four reports of the EC. However, all reports state that 'institutional and human resource capacity at national and local levels remains weak, in particular as regards enforcement and wildlife trade'.[1172]

V. Harmonization of National Legislation with EU Legislation

965. 'Alignment with the EU acquis in the field of nature protection, in particular with the Habitats and Birds Directives, is moderate. Serbia needs to address gaps in legislation, which currently allow the hunting of non-huntable birds, especially the goshawk and the turtle dove.'[1173]

1169. *See* MEP. 2018.
1170. The most frequent seizures are live reptiles and birds. In addition, seizures of other taxonomic groups were also recorded, as well as seizures of parts, derivatives and products of protected species. UNECE. 2015, 101.
1171. EC. 2019, 86.
1172. *See* EC. 2023, 136; EC. 2022, 122; EC. 2021, 115; EC, 2020, 106.
1173. EC 2023, 136. 'Serbia needs to fully incorporate EU standards on prohibited means of capturing and killing wild animals, including in its legislation on hunting.' Authorities need to address illegal hunting and illegal logging more effectively.

Chapter 4. Agricultural Resources

§1. Conditions for Agricultural Production

966. Generally speaking, conditions for agricultural production (natural characteristics of soil, climate, water resources, etc.) are favourable in Serbia, not only in the Northern AP of Vojvodina but also in many other parts.

One of the basic components of Serbian economic development is agriculture. Besides its economic importance, it is also exceptional in terms of social and ecological aspects. In comparison with EU countries, Serbian agriculture represents a relatively high percentage (15.3%), while industrial production participates with around 24.4% of gross domestic product in 2005, which is somewhat higher than the EU average.[1174] Since the beginning of the twenty-first st century, the contribution of agriculture to GDP has been declining, primarily as a consequence of the faster growth of activities in non-production sectors (primarily trade). However, the share of agriculture in the GDP structure of the economy of the RS is still very high.[1175] The area of central Serbia is dominated by soils with weakly acidic to acidic reaction, carbonate-free to weakly carbonate, weakly humus, with very low and low content of easily accessible phosphorus and soils with optimal and high content of easily accessible potassium. The area of AP Vojvodina is dominated by weakly alkaline soils, which are differently provided with carbonates and weakly humus, with varying content of easily accessible phosphorus and soils from optimal to high content of easily accessible potassium.[1176]

967. The participation of employees in agriculture and the food industry in the total number of employees in Serbia in 2022 was 18.8%, which is at the level of last year's participation.[1177] The participation of the export of agricultural and food products in the total export of goods from the RS amounted to 17.2% (the lowest participation recorded so far), while the participation in imports was at the level of 8.3%, which is at the level multi-year average.[1178] The structure of farms is very unsatisfactory, with an average size of only 3 ha and with only 5.5% farmers, out of the total number of 778,891, with estates over 10 ha.[1179]

1174. GOV RS. 2006b, 5.
1175. GOV RS. 2014b, point 2.1.2. Compared to the average of the EU countries (twenty-seven Member States), the Republic of Serbia has a significantly higher share of the GDP of the agriculture sector in the total GDP, and a significantly lower share of the services sector.
1176. EPA. 2019a, 173.
1177. MAFWM. 2023, 14 The high share of agriculture in the basic macroeconomic aggregates of the Republic of Serbia compared to other countries can be attributed to rich natural resources and favourable climatic conditions for agricultural production. In addition, the slower process of structural reforming of the rest of the economy and delays in that process also contribute to this. GOV RS. 2014b, point 2.1.2 ('Importance of agriculture in the national economy').
1178. MAFWM. 2023, 24
1179. GOV RS, 2005b, 9. *See also* GOV RS. 2008b, 101–103. However, a tendency of concentration and centralization of farms according to the size can be noted. According to the 2012 agriculture census, 3.1% of the total number of farms are over 20 ha, and this group of farmers use 44% of

968. During 2023, in the RS, 47,579 ha of agricultural land were irrigated, 12.9% less than in the previous year. Of the total irrigated area, arable land and gardens accounted for 93.4% of the irrigated area, followed by orchards (share of 6.0%) and other agricultural land (share of 0.6%).[1180]

969. Bearing in mind natural resources, favourable land and climate conditions, biodiversity, and relatively healthy agroecosystems, it can be said that in the RS, there are favourable conditions for the development of integral and organic production.[1181] One of the sectoral objectives in agriculture is 'increase areas under organic farming and other environmentally friendly farming production systems'.[1182] The total area with the organic production in 2014 amounted to 9,446.58 ha, which is 1,218.57 ha more than in 2013. These include surfaces which are in the process of conversion and surfaces that have an organic status. The share of agricultural land under organic agriculture in relation to the utilized agricultural area in 2014 was 0.27%.[1183] According to data of the MAFWM, the total area under organic production in 2017 was 13423.13 ha.[1184]

970. The main institution in Serbia dealing with agricultural policy is the MAFWM. Plant protection products and residues are regulated by following three ministries: MAFWM – Phytosanitary Directorate, Forest Directorate, Veterinary Directorate, Agricultural Land Directorate, Directorate for Agrarian Payments, etc.; MME, Ministry of Construction, Transport and Infrastructure; and Ministry of Health. The MAFWM is competent for fertilizers.[1185]

§2. Legislation

971. Due to the fact that agriculture is given high importance in Serbia, legal Acts regulating it are numerous.

---

the total used farmland. On the other hand, agricultural farms using up to 5 ha make up 77.7% of the total number of registered farms, which makes 25.2% of the used agricultural land. GOV RS. 2014b, 10.

1180. STAT. OFFICE RS. 2024a. During 2023, in the RS, 47 579 ha of agricultural land were irrigated, 12.9% less than in the previous year.

1181. GOV RS. 2014b, point 2.3.4 'Integral and organic production'.

1182. GOV RS. 2008b, 103.

1183. EPA. 2015, 61.

1184. MEP. 2019, 130. These areas include areas that are in the process of conversion and those with organic status.

1185. Agricultural Inspection Sector as an administrative body within the MAFWM conducts supervision of the implementation of the relevant laws including, *inter alia*, Law on Agricultural Land (OJ RS, Nos 62/06, 65/08 – other law, 41/09, 112/15, 80/17 and 95/18 – other law) Law on Plant Health (OJ RS, No. 41/09), Law on Food Safety (OJ RS, Nos 41/09 and 17/19), Law on Plant Protection Products (OJ RS, No. 41/09), Law on Plant Nutrition Products and Soil Enhancers (OJ RS, Nos 41/09 and 17/19), Law on GMOs (OJ RS, No. 41/09), Law on Organic Production (OJ RS, Nos 30/10 and 17/19 – other law), Law on Wine (OJ RS, Nos 41/09 and 93/12), Law on Agriculture and Rural Development (OJ RS, Nos 41/09 and 10/13 – other law, 101/16), and regulations adopted under these laws.

The Constitution of Serbia prescribes in Article 88 that utilization and management of agricultural land, forestland and municipal building land on private assets shall be permitted. The Law may restrict the models of utilization and management, by prescribing terms of utilization and management, in order to eliminate the danger to the environment, and in order to prevent violation of rights and legally based interests of other persons.

The Constitution prescribes that APs shall, in accordance with the Law, regulate following matters of provincial interest: agriculture, water economy, forestry, hunting, fishery, tourism, catering, spas and health resorts, environmental protection, industry and craftsmanship, road, river and railway transport and road repairs, organizing fairs and other economic events (Article 183, point 2). Municipalities are responsible for protection, improvement and use of agricultural land (Article 190, point 7).

I. General Legislation

972. The current basic framework of agricultural policy is contained in several documents, including the following: Agriculture and Rural Development Strategy of the RS for the period 2014–2024 (OJ RS, No. 85/14); EPL (OJ RS, Nos 135/04, 36/09, 72/09– other law, 43/11CC, 14/16, 76/18 and 95/18 – other law); Law on Agriculture and Rural Development (OJRS, Nos 41/09, 10/13 – other law and 101/16); Law on Agricultural Land (OJ RS, Nos 62/06, 65/08 – other law, 41/09, 112/15, 80/17 and 95/18); Law on Soil Protection (OJ RS, No. 112/15);[1186] Law on Public Health (OJRS, No. 15/16); Law on Plant Protection Products (OJRS, Nos 41/09 and 17/19); Law on Plant Nutrition Products and Soil Enhancers (OJRS, Nos 41/09 and 17/19); Law on Privatization OJ 2014 (OJ RS, Nos 83/14, 46/15, 112/15 and 20/16 – authentic interpretation); Law on Food Safety (OJRS, Nos 41/09 and 17/19); Law on Organic Production (OJRS, Nos 30/10 and 17/19 – other law); Law on Livestock (OJ RS, Nos 41/09, 93/12 and 14/16); Law on Wine (OJRS, Nos 41/09 and 93/12), etc.

973. The existing strategic document is the Agriculture and Rural Development Strategy of the RS (OJ RS, No. 85/14), in which one of the strategic goals, among other issues (the production growth and stability of the producers' income, competitiveness improvement with adjustments to requirements of the domestic and international markets and with technological and technical improvement of the sector, sustainable resources management, improvement of the quality of life in rural areas and poverty reduction, efficient public policy management and institutional framework improvement for agricultural and rural areas development), is environment protection. According to the Sustainable Development Strategy, the main objective of the Agricultural policy is development of sustainable, cost-effective and environment-friendly agriculture as the basis for rural development and competitiveness needed for access to the EU market.[1187]

1186. For more details, *see* chapter devoted to soil pollution.
1187. GOV RS. 2008b, 103.

974. EPL contains the following provisions relevant for agriculture: Article 22 (Protection of Land and Soil); Article 33 (Planning and Construction); Article 34 (Spatial and Urban Planning); Article 35 (SEA); Article 36 (EIA); and Article 124 (Transitional and Final Provisions).

975. The Law on Agriculture and Rural Development (OJ RS, Nos 41/09, 10/13 – other law and 101/16) regulates the following: objectives of agricultural policy and manner of achieving thereof; types of incentives in agriculture; conditions for exercising rights to incentives; incentive beneficiaries; Register of agricultural households, record keeping and reporting in agriculture; integrated agricultural information system and supervision over implementation of this Law (Article 1).[1188]

976. Agricultural policy and rural development policy of the RS shall include measures and activities undertaken by competent authorities with the objectives of, *inter alia*, protecting the environment from adverse effects of agricultural production (Article 3, point 5).

977. The Law lays down the duty to adopt a Strategy for Agriculture (Article 4) as well as two national programmes – for agriculture and rural development (Articles 5 and 6).

978. Pursuant to Article 12 (Forms of Structural Incentives), rural development measures shall be the type of incentives which support improvement of competitiveness in agriculture and forestry (investment in agriculture and forestry and introduction of new standards in production and circulation of agricultural products), improvement of environmental protection programmes, preservation of biodiversity and programme for rural economy diversification and upgradation of life quality in rural areas (paragraph 2).

979. Article 18 prescribes that incentive beneficiary shall be obliged to observe regulations governing environmental quality standards, public health protection, animal and plant health protection, protection of animal welfare and protection of agricultural land.[1189]

980. Law on Agricultural Land (OJ RS, Nos 62/06, 65/08 – other law, 41/09, 112/15, 80/17 and 95/18) regulates planning, protection and use of agricultural land. This Law stipulates that the State agricultural land can be leased on the basis of market principles or provide equal right to lease to all natural and legal persons.[1190] This

---

1188. This Law shall establish Administration for Agricultural Payments, as an administration authority within the ministry in charge of agriculture and shall govern its competences (Art. 1, para. 2).

1189. Under the conditions specified in this Law, right to incentives shall be given to agricultural households and family agricultural households that are entered in the Register of Agricultural Households, LSG units, as well as other persons and organizations (incentive beneficiaries) (Art. 15).

1190. The Law defines that the agricultural land cannot be alienated and that the owner of agricultural land cannot be a foreign natural or legal person, unless registered in the Republic of Serbia (Art. 1). However, Serbia agreed that it will adjust its legislation (by 1 Sep. 2017), so as to enable EU

Law establishes the Agricultural Land Administration as the administrative bodies within the Ministry responsible for agriculture affairs and regulates its scope (Article 1, paragraph 3, and Article 77a, 77b).

981. Law on Food Safety (OJ RS, Nos 41/09 and 17/19) governs general conditions for safety of food and feed, duties and responsibilities of food and feed business operators, rapid alert system, emergency measures and crisis management, food and feed hygiene and quality (Article 1).[1191] The objective of this Law is to ensure a high level of protection of human life and health and protection of consumer interests, including the principle of honesty and good faith in the food trade, taking into account protection of animal health and welfare and plant health and environmental protection, where appropriate (Article 3). The Law is based on the principle of risk analysis, precaution, protection of consumer interests and transparency in the procedures for selecting the appropriate measures in the field of food and feed safety (Articles 6–10).

II. Phytosanitary Policy

982. Legal framework in the field of phytosanitary policy is established on the basis of the following laws: Law on Plant Health (OJRS, No. 41/09), Law on Plant Protection Products (OJRS, No. 41/09), Law on Plant Nutrition Products and Soil Enhancers (OJRS, No. 41/09), Law on Seed (OJRS, Nos 45/05 and 30/10), Law on Planting Material of Fruit Trees, Vine and Hops (OJRS, No. 18/05), Law on Seed and Planting Material (OJRS, Nos 54/93, 67/93, 35/94 and 43/94 – corr., 135/2004, 18/2005, 45/2005 and 101/2005), Law on Protection of Plant Breeders Rights (OJRS, No. 41/09), Law on Plant Varieties Registration (OJRS, No. 30/10), Law on Genetically Modified Organisms (OJRS, No. 41/09), Law on Forest Reproductive Material (OJ RS), Nos 135/04, 8/05 and 41/09), Law on Forest (OJRS, Nos 30/10, 93/12, 89/15, and 95/18 – other law).

983. The Law on Plant Health regulate the protection and promotion of plant health; measures for preventing introduction of harmful organisms, for detecting them, preventing their spread and suppressing them; phytosanitary control; requirements for the production, processing, finishing, importation, storage and circulation of plants,[1192] plant products[1193] and regulated objects, as well as requirements for providing services in the sphere of the protection of plant health (Article 1).

---

nationals to acquire real estate in Serbia – under the same conditions as Serbian nationals. This includes, also, legislation governing the sale of agricultural land (Art. 63 of SAA).

1191. The provisions of this Law shall not apply to primary food production and preparation, handling and storage of food for private domestic use, as well as feed for non-food-producing animals (Art. 2).

1192. 'Plants' means living plants and ive plant segments, including seeds (Art. 4, point 2).

1193. 'Plant products' shall mean all products of plant origin, unprocessed or subjected to simple processing methods, on account of which they can no longer be regarded as plants, as well as wood, if it retains fully or partially its naturally rounded surface, with or without bark, or if it is in the form of chipboard, sawdust, small fragments or wood waste or if it is used in the form of sawn

984. According to Article 107 of the Law on Plant Health, the Law on the Protection of Plants (OJ FRY, Nos 24/98 and 26/98 and OJ RS, No. 101/05) and other laws shall cease to apply from the effective date of this Law, except for provisions referred to pesticides and fertilizers, while Articles 26 and 32 of that Law shall cease to apply from 1 January 2011.[1194]

985. The Law on Plant Protection Products governs the registration, control, circulation, importation, and application of plant protection products in agriculture and forestry, the tasks of public interest in the area of plant protection products, and other issues relevant for plant protection products[1195] (Article 1). This Law governs the establishment of maximum residue levels of plant protection products and their control in food and feed.

986. The Law on Plant Nutrition Products and Soil Enhancers governs classification, quality, labelling, phytosanitary control, sampling in the circulation, importation and use of plant nutrition products and soil enhancers and testing of plant nutrition products and soil enhancers, as well as other issues of significance for plant nutrition products and soil enhancers (Article 1).[1196] Plant nutrition products and soil enhancers which also contain plant protection products, namely the chemicals, may be produced, placed into circulation, and used in the territory of the RS if they are classified, packaged and labelled in accordance with this Law and the regulations adopted based on this Law and the regulations governing the plant protection products, namely the chemicals (Article 3).

987. Pursuant to *the Law on Plant Protection,* pesticides and fertilizers could be placed on market only, as prescribed by Article 47, on the basis of permit given by competent authority. The Law stipulates conditions for getting permanent and

---

timber, packaging, laths, pallets and packing materials in the transportation of consignments, and may be a risk for the plant health (Art. 4, point 3).

1194. Law on the Protection of Plants from Diseases and Pests (OJ SRS, Nos 14/84 and 6/89 – other law, OJ RS, Nos 53/93, 67/93, 48/94 and 101/05) also shall cease to apply from the effective date of the Law on Plant Health.

1195. Plant protection products, for the purpose of this Law, shall be: (1) plant protection products; (2) products of general use for plant protection; (3) ancillary plant protection products; (4) other plant protection products which contain one or more basic substances (hereinafter 'other products'). Plant protection products, for the purpose of this Law, shall be deemed to be also plant protection products which are used in organic production and the plant protection products which contain or are composed of GMOs, or which are obtained from them, provided that the intentional introduction into the environment, placement into circulation or transit of such organisms is allowed based on the assessment of risk to the environment and human health, in accordance with the law governing GMOs (Art. 2).

1196. On the day this Law comes into force, the provisions of the Law on Plant Protection (OJ FRY, Nos 24/98 and 26/98 – correction, and OJ RS, No. 101/05 – other law) shall cease to apply in the part governing fertilizers (Art. 51). According to Art. 50, the regulations adopted based on the authorizations from this Law shall be adopted within one year from the date this Law comes into force. Until the adoption of regulations referred to in para. 1 of this Article, the regulations adopted based on the Law on Plant Protection (OJ FRY, Nos 24/98 and 26/98 – corr., and OJRS, No. 101/05 – other law) shall apply, except for provisions of such regulations that are not in compliance with this Law.

temporary permits for pesticides (Article 48) and permanent permits for fertilizer (Article 49).[1197]

988. Articles 64–68 regulate import of the pesticides and fertilizers.[1198] Permit for import of already prepared pesticides and fertilizers is issued by the competent authority only when this kind of pesticides and fertilizers is not possible to produce in country or if the existing quantity is not enough to satisfy domestic needs.[1199] Article 67 prescribes conditions for import for scientific purposes and temporary import or import of elements for domestic production.[1200]

989. Plant Variety Protection (plant breeders' rights) in the RS is regulated by the *Law on Protection of Plant Breeders' Rights.*[1201] In March 2010, Serbia ratified the International Convention for the Protection of New Varieties of Plants (OJRS – IT, No. 19/10).

III. Veterinary Legislation

990. The Law on Veterinary Medicine (OJRS, Nos 91/05, 30/10, 93/12 and 17/19 – other law), Law on Animal Health Protection (OJ RS, Nos 37/91, 50/92, 33/93, 52/93, 53/93 – other law, 48/94 – other law, 53/95, 52/96, 25/20, 91/05 –

1197. Articles 51–54 of the Law regulate procedure for testing of the pesticides and fertilizers and procedure for registration of pesticides and fertilizers is regulated by Arts 55–59.

1198. Besides, it should be mentioned that several other laws are also relevant for foreign trade issues, like the Law on Foreign Trade (OJ RS, Nos 36/09 and 36/11 – other law, 88/11, 89/15 – other law), the Law on Customs Tariff (OJ RS, Nos 62/05, 61/2007 and 5/2009), Customs Law (OJ RS, Nos 18/10, 111/12, 29/15), etc.

1199. The Rulebook on Trade, Imports and Sampling of Pesticides (OJ FRY, No. 59/01 and OJ RS, No. 104/05) regulate trade, import and sampling of pesticides. Import permits for plant protection products must be obtained from the Serbian Ministry of Agriculture, Phytosanitary Departments. *See also* Decision on the amount of reimbursement for the conducted phytosanitary examination of plants and the control of pesticides and fertilizers in trade over the State border (OJ RS, No. 113/13).

1200. There is a specific ordinance, when the food safety is concerned, on residue limits for pesticides and other contaminants (e.g., hormones, antibiotics and mycotoxins) which can be found in food. The Rulebook on quantities of pesticides, metals and metalloids and other toxic substances, chemotherapeutics, anabolics and other substances that may be found in foodstuffs (OJ FRY, Nos 5/92 and 11/92 – corr. 32/02 and OJ RS, Nos 25/10 – other rulebook, and 28/11 – other rulebook). *See also* the Rulebook concerning the maximum residue limits on plant protection agents in food and feed and also concerning the food and feed to be checked for maximum residue limits on plant protection agents (OJ RS, Nos 29/14 and 37/14 – corr., 39/14, 72/14, 80/15, 84/15, 35/16 and 81/16), Rulebook on health safety of dietetic products (OJ RS, Nos 45/2010, 27/11, 50/12, 21/15 and 75/15) and Rulebook on pesticide testing methods (OJ FRY, Nos 63/2001 and 65/2001, OJ RS, No. 93/2005).

1201. So far three following regulations have been adopted based on the Law on Protection of Plant Breeders' Rights: Rulebook on content and manner of keeping the Register of applications for granting plant breeders' rights, Register of granted breeders' rights, Register of transferred rights and Register of licence agreement (OJRS, No. 70/09); Rulebook on form and content of the application for granting plant breeders' right, the required documentation, the amount and manner of delivery of reproductive material samples (OJRS, No. 82/2009) and Rulebook on the list of species of agricultural plants to which are related exceptions to the breeder's right and the elements for establishing small farmers (OJRS, No. 38/10), etc.

other law and 101/05 – other law), Law on Animal Welfare (OJRS, No. 41/09), Law on Livestock Production (OJ RS, Nos 41/09, 93/12 and 14/16), Law on Food Safety (OJRS, Nos 41/09 and 17/19) and Law on Drugs and Medical Products (OJRS, Nos 30/10, 107/12, 105/17 – other law, and 113/17 – other law) have established a legal framework in the field.

Law on Veterinary Medicine regulates the protection and promotion of animal health and welfare, determines the infectious animal diseases and measures to prevent the occurrence, detection, prevention of spreading, suppression and eradication of infectious animal diseases and diseases that can be transmitted from animals to humans, veterinary and sanitary control and conditions for production and trade of animals, animal products, feed of animal origin, animal feed and the requirements for performing veterinary practice.

991. Law on Animal Welfare regulates the welfare, rights, obligations and responsibilities of natural and legal persons, that is, entrepreneurs in animal welfare, treatment of animals and protection of animals from torture, protection of animal welfare at killing, during keeping, breeding, trade, transport, slaughtering and conducting experiments on animals, as well as other issues of importance for the protection of animal welfare.[1202]

992. Law on Livestock Production establishes objectives in livestock production; livestock entities and their organizational forms; breeding objectives and implementation of breeding programmes, control of productivity and preservation of characteristics of domestic animals; breeding of domestic animals, bee keeping, aquaculture, game raising, preservation of genetic reserves of domestic animals biodiversity in livestock production; production and trade of food of plant origin for domestic animals and products of animal origin; and trade in breeding material and other issues of importance for animal husbandry.[1203]

IV. Organic Agriculture

993. Since 2006, after the entry into force of the first Law on Organic Production and Organic Products (OJ RS, No. 62/06) and the introduction of incentives for the development of organic production, there has been a constant increase in the number of producers, areas where organic production methods are applied, as well as the number of individual species of animals in livestock production.[1204] The area

1202. The general requirements for keeping and handling of animals are prescribed by the Law on Animal Welfare, and one of the basic principles of this Law is the principle of responsibility referring to all owners and keepers of animals, regardless of business operations they perform in connection with animals and different animal species. The Law prescribes that all legal and natural persons are entitled to keep and breed animals if they meet the requirements for keeping and breeding the animals. For more information, *see* GOV RS. 2011d, 197–202.

1203. Provisions of this Law relate to breeding of cattle, buffalo, sheep, goats, horses, donkeys, pigs, poultry, fur animals, rabbits, bees, raising game, fish and other aquatic animals and other farmed animals.

1204. GOV RS. 2014b, point 2.3.4 ('Integral and organic production').

of organic farming increased from around 1,000 ha in 2009 to 7,000 ha of arable land in 2013. The main products are cereals, fruits, fodder plants and industrial plants. Organic animal production is limited to around 5,000 animals (of which ~ 70% are in the phase of conversion). Organic sheep (50%) and poultry (35%) production prevails. In 2012, 1,061 operators were registered as organic, including those in group production.[1205]

994. Organic production is regulated by the Law on Organic Production (OJ RS Nos 30/10 and 17/19 – other law), which has been in force since 1 January 2011.[1206] The Law regulates in detail the organic production of agricultural and other products; organic production aims and principles (Articles 1–6); subjects of organic production (Articles 7–9); control organizations (Articles 9–16); organic production methods (Articles 14–16); control and certification in organic production (Articles 17–25); processing, labelling, transportation, placing on the market, imports and exports of organic products (Articles 26–32); supervision of the performance of delegated tasks (Articles 33–39); and other matters relevant to organic production (Articles 40–51).

995. The 2013 Law on Incentives in Agriculture and Rural Development (OJ RS, Nos 10/13, 142/2014, 103/2015, 101/2016, 35/23 and 92/23) provides incentives for the implementation of agro-environmental measures, incentives for organic production and incentives, etc. (Articles 37 and 38). In February 2013, the Government adopted the Rulebook on Payment of Agriculture Subsides (OJ RS, No. 20/13). The Law envisions the following four groups of government incentives: (1) direct payments (i.e., production subsidies, compensation for agriculture inputs, credit support) (Articles 14–3); (2) rural development payments (i.e., incentives to improve agricultural competitiveness and investments in sustainable rural development) (Articles 34–40); (3) specific incentives (i.e., funds to develop a market-information system in agriculture, provide extension services and support science-based projects in agriculture) (Articles 41 and 42); and (4) credit support (Article 42a).

996. On the basis of the Law on Organic Productions (OJRS Nos 30/10 and 17/19 – other law), following sub-legal Acts have been adopted, *inter alia*:

- Rulebook on control and certification in organic farming and organic production methods (OJ RS, Nos 95/20, and 24/21).
- Rulebook on documents submitted to the authorized control organizations for the purpose of issuing certificates and the terms and conditions of sales of organic products (OJ RS, No. 88/16).
- The list of authorized inspection agency for controlling and certification of organic production for 2023 (OJ RS, No. 2/23).

1205. EC. 2015, p. 15.
1206. Before the implementation of this Law commenced, the provisions of the Law on Organic Agriculture and Organic Products (OJ RS No. 62/06) were applicable; the pertinent rulebooks, which still apply, were developed on the basis of this Law.

- Rulebook on the form of official identification card of the inspector for organic production (OJ RS, Nos 61/08 and 81/15 – other rulebooks).
- Rulebook on the form and content of the request form for obtaining a certificate that the product was produced by organic farming methods (OJ RS, No. 51/02).

997. In addition to the regulations mentioned above, several other regulations are relevant (or could be relevant) for organic production. Some of them are the following regulations:

- Law on Financing and Securing the Financing of Agricultural Production (OJ RS, No. 128/14).
- Law on the performance of advisory and expert work in the field of agriculture (OJ RS, No. 30/10).
- Regulation on the distribution of incentives in agriculture and rural development in 2024 (OJ RS, Nos 3/24, 6/24).
- Rulebook on the conditions and method of exercising the right to incentives for organic livestock production (OJ RS, No. 63/23).
- Rules on the use of incentives for organic plant production (OJ RS, No. 60/23).
- Rulebook on the use of incentives for organic production (OJ RS, Nos 52/14, 57/14, 71/14, 62/15, 33/16 and 41/17 – other rulebooks).
- Rulebook on incentives for the implementation of activities aimed at increasing competitiveness through certification of the quality system of food, organic products, and products with a geographical indication (OJ RS, Nos 39/18, 17/21, 132/21, 27/22, 23/23), etc.

V. Harmonization with EU Legislation and International Treaties

998. According to the last EC Report, ' Serbia has some level of preparation in agriculture and rural development. Limited progress was made, in particular on recruitment to the IPARD structures and efficiency of processing IPARD applications, and payment requests.'[1207] For organic farming, new legislation aligning with the EU acquis in the area of organics has been drafted and should be adopted without further delay.[1208]

999. Serbia is a contracting party to the following international treaties: Convention on Biological Diversity, Cartagena Protocol on Biosafety to the Convention on Biological Diversity, Convention on the Elaboration of a European Pharmacopeia, Revised Text of the International Plant Protection Convention, European Convention for the Protection of Animals for Slaughter (CETS No. 102); European Convention for the Protection of Animals kept for Farming Purposes (CETS No. 087); European Convention for the Protection of Vertebrate Animals used for

1207. EC. 2023, 139.
1208. *Ibid.*

Experimental and other Scientific Purposes (CETS No. 123) and European Convention for the Protection of Pet Animals (CETS No. 125),[1209] etc. Serbia ratified the Convention Concerning Safety and Health in Agriculture (ILO Convention 184) (OJ RS – IT, No. 2/19); Nagoya Protocol on Access to Genetic Resources and the Fair and Equitable Sharing of Benefits Arising From Their Utilization to the Convention on Biological Diversity (OJ RS – IT, No. 12/18); International Treaty on Plant Genetic Resources for Food and Agriculture (OJ RS – IT, No. 1/13); International Convention for the Protection of New Varieties of Plants of 2 December 1961, as Revised at Geneva on 10 November 1972, on 23 October 1978 and on 19 March 1991 (OJ RS – IT, No. 19/10); Convention on the Prior Informed Consent Procedure for Certain Hazardous Chemicals and Pesticides in International Trade (Rotterdam Convention) (OJ RS – IT, No. 38/09); and the Convention on POPs (Stockholm Convention) (OJ RS – IT, No. 42/09).

In addition, Serbia has concluded a number of bilateral agreements on cooperation in the fields of agriculture, veterinary medicine, plant protection, etc.

1209. Serbia is not a contracting party to the European Convention for the Protection of Animals during International Transport (CETS No. 065). *See*, https://www.coe.int/en/web/conventions/full-list?module=signatures-by-treaty&treatynum=065 (6.1.2024).

Chapter 5. Biotechnology

1000. Biotechnology is still not sufficiently developed activity in Serbia.[1210] There are no livestock clones or other genetically engineered (GE) animals (including fish, birds, insects, and mammals) or GE genetics used in Serbia's commercial production. In addition, there are no GE crops under development.[1211]

1001. Growing evidence suggests that GMOs may present threats to autochthonous biodiversity when deliberately or accidentally released into an environment. In some cases, such as endangered species, such threats could be significant. Risks are centred on possibilities of gene flow and hybridization between GMOs and autochthonous species, as well as impacts that GMOs may have on ecosystem food webs and human health. These impacts could in turn result in further chain reactions and negative overall impacts to conservation and the sustainable use of biological diversity.[1212] According to the sixth National report to the UN Convention on Biological Diversity 'introduction of invasive and allochthons species and genetically modified organisms' is one of the causes that lead to the reduction of biodiversity in Serbia (along with fragmentation and degradation of habitats, illegal hunting, fishing and collecting, illegal and inadequate forest cutting, and inadequate preservation of genetic diversity of autochthonous populations of plant and animal species).[1213]

1002. Biotechnology is in competence of the MAFWM. In the MAFWM, activities related to GMOs are carried out by the Plant Protection Directorate,[1214] General Inspectorate and Veterinary Directorate.[1215] Besides the Ministry, in the activities in the field of GMOs, participate the following bodies: Expert Council for Biosafety[1216] and accredited laboratories.[1217]

1210. UNEP, GEF, 2006, 6.

1211. For additional information, *see* Maslac, T. 2022.

1212. MESP. 2011, *supra*, 60.

1213. MEP. 2019, 194. The same statement was made in GOV RS. 2019b, (Special objective 1.1. 'Reduced negative impacts on biodiversity').

1214. Plant Protection Directorate, as an authority within the Ministry, in the field of GMO is in charge of receiving and reviewing applications for approval to work with GMOs in closed systems and the deliberate release of GMOs into the environment (field trials with GMOs) or for all expert and technical tasks related to biological protection in the use of GMOs. In accordance with Art. 61 of the Law on Food Safety, MAFWM is responsible for issuing permits for first placing of GMO foods and GMO feeds on the market, and on the basis of a prior opinion of the Expert Council for risk assessment in the field of Security of food, and in accordance with the regulation concerning the conditions of placing of GMOs on the market.

1215. General Inspectorate and the Veterinary Directorate (organizations within the Ministry) are responsible for the supervision and control of experimental work with GMOs. Pursuant to Art. 12 of the Law on Food Safety Veterinary Directorate controls GMO feed all stages of production, processing and placing on the market. General Inspectorate, control GMO food through all stages of food production, processing and transport of GMOs.

1216. According to Art. 6 of the Law on GMO, for the considerations of expert issues and providing expert opinion related to GMOs, Expert Council for Biosafety has been established, consisting of eighteen members chosen among outstanding scientists and experts in the fields that are relevant for biosafety (biologists, geneticists, entomologists, ecologists, veterinarians, agronomists, nutritionists, toxicologists, allergists and other professions).

§1. LEGAL REGULATION

1003. The Agriculture and Rural Development Strategy of the RS for the period 2014–2024 (OJ RS, No. 85/14) does not define specific targets for GMOs.[1218]

1004. EPL prescribes that 'biodiversity protection, use of biological resources, genetically modified organism and biotechnology shall be executed on the basis of this Law and obligations taken through international agreements' (Article 26, paragraph 3).

1005. The matter of GMOs in the RS is regulated by the Law on GMO (OJRS, No. 41/09) and the Law on Food Safety (OJRS, Nos 41/09 and 17/19).

1006. The RS ratified the Cartagena Protocol on Biosafety to the Convention on Biological Diversity, with annexes (OJ SMN – IT, No. 16/05), and became a member of the Cartagena Protocol on Biosafety.

1007. The basic legal Act regulating biotechnology in Serbia is the Law on Genetically Modified Organisms (Law on GMO) (OJ RS, No. 41/09). It prescribes the general framework for handling and use of GMOs, and detailed conditions are defined in sub-legal Acts. The Law comprises fifty-three Articles in eight following parts: I Basic Provisions (Articles 1–8); II Permitting Procedure (Articles 9–18); III Requirements for use in close systems and for deliberate release into the environment of the GMOs (Articles 19–27); IV Handling, packaging and transport of GMO and GMO products (Articles 28–31); V Register of GMO and GMO products and licence Register (Articles 32–36); VI Supervision (Articles 37–44); VII Penal provisions (Articles 45–49); VII Transitional and final provisions (Articles 50–53).

1008. The Law on GMO prescribes the procedure for issuing approvals for use in closed systems, for deliberate release into the environment, for placing on the market or for transit of GMOs[1219] and products containing GMOs, conditions for use in closed systems and for deliberate release into the environment of GMOs, handling,

1217. Testing of GMOs and GMO products for the purpose of identification and quantification of genetic modification is carried out by laboratory accredited by the Ministry. At this point, the four laboratories are accredited for GMO analyses. These are the following: SP Laboratory, Novi Bečej; Institute of Molecular Genetics and Genetic Engineering – Laboratory of Molecular Biology, Belgrade; Institute of Field and Vegetable Crops, Novi Sad; A Bio Tech Lab, Sremska Kamenica. GOV RS. 2018, 661. *See also* UNECE. 2015, 15.

1218. GOV RS. 2014b, point 3.1.3v, ('external challenges').

1219. Genetic material shall mean part of a plant, animal, fungus, microorganism, virus or viroid containing hereditary information (Art. 4, point 1). Pursuant to Art. 3 of the Law agriculture products of non-animal origin are not considered GMOs if they contain up to 0.9% threshold of GMOs and impurities of GMOs. Apart from that, seed and reproductive material are not considered GMOs if they contain up to 0.1% threshold of GMOs and impurities of GMOs.

packaging and transport of GMOs and products containing GMOs, as well as other issues of importance for GMOs and products containing GMOs (Article 1).[1220]

1009. No GMOs or products containing GMOs can be traded or grown for commercial use in the territory of the RS (Article 2).[1221] So, 'in Serbia, production of GM plants is prohibited. However, contamination of the environment can come as a result of an act with disrespect to the prohibition, by an owner or user of agricultural land.'[1222]

1010. The Law on Food Safety (OJ RS, Nos 41/09 and 17/19) stipulates the first marketing of GMO foods and genetically modified feed (GMO animal feed), the method of issuing permits for the first placement on the market of GMO food and GMO feed records of licences issued, traceability and labelling of GMOs in particular GMO food and feed, and inspections in these fields. For the first placement on the market of genetically modified food and genetically modified feed in the RS, business operator that is distributing food or feed must be licensed.[1223]

1011. The Law on General Product Safety (OJ RS, Nos 41/09, and 77/19) regulates issues related to 'general product safety, criteria for evaluating product compliance with general safety requirements, obligations of manufacturers and distributors, conditions and methods informing and exchanging information regarding the risks that the product poses to the health and safety of consumers and other users, as well as conducting supervision to ensure that the products placed on the market are safe' (Article 1, paragraph 1).[1224]

1012. The following by-laws are applied:

– Rulebook on the content and the application form for use of GMO in closed systems, manner of protection of confidential data from the application, as well as

1220. The provisions of this Law shall not apply to the product containing GMO product which is not a Living Modified Organism (LMO) and is not used as food, feed, medicine or auxiliary medicine. The provisions of this Law shall not apply to GMOs and to GMO products which are not LMOs, if they are intended for medical use and if their use is governed entirely by other regulations (Art. 5).

1221. The person that, contrary to the provisions of this Law, commences the use of GMOs and GMO products in closed systems, deliberate release into the environment, placing on the market or transit, or disposes of them into the environment and thus causes harmful consequences for human health and the environment, shall be punished for a criminal offence by imprisonment of up to three years. The GMOs and GMO products referred to in para. 1 of this Article shall be confiscated and destroyed at the expense of the person having committed the criminal offence (Art. 45).

1222. *See*, Nikolić, Gajinov. 2014, 105. Such a situatiion 'opens an array of questions, to which traditional institutes of civil law are not capable of giving complete and precise answers.'

1223. Permit is issued by the Minister, based on the prior opinion of the expert scientific advice, in accordance with the regulation concerning the conditions for the marketing of genetically modified food and genetically modified feed.

1224. In addition, this law regulates the ban on the production, import, export, and circulation of misleading products, which, with their deceptive appearance, endanger the health and safety of consumers (Art. 1). There are no specific indications about GMOs.

on the content of the application for renewal of approval for use in closed systems (OJ RS, Nos 69/12, and 44/18 – other), which is partially harmonized with Directive 2009/41/EC.

- Rulebook on limited usage of GMO (OJ of FRY, No. 62/02, and OJ RS, No. 69/12 – other rulebooks)[1225] only Appendix 1 is used), which is harmonized with Directive 90/219/EC.
- Rulebook on the introduction of GMO and GMO products to production (OJFRY, No. 62/02) – harmonized with Directive 2001/18/EC (only the part of the Rulebook relating to the knowingly deliberate release of GMOs to the environment for any purpose except for placing on the market is used).
- Rulebook on the content and data of the Registry of GMO and GMO products (OJ FRY, No. 66/02).

1013. Serbia made no progress in aligning its legislation on GMO with the EU acquis to regulate this area more transparently and safely. 'This is crucial for further progress in negotiations for membership of the World Trade Organisation and is a prerequisite for opening this chapter.'[1226] In addition, Serbia has not ratified the GMO amendment to the AC (Almaty 2005).[1227] According to the NPAA, for the period 2022–2025, the adoption of a new Law on GMO is planned. The deadline for the Government to adopt the law is the end of 2024.[1228]

1225. These are regulations that were adopted based on the old Law on Genetically Modified Organisms (OJ FRY, No. 21/01, and OJ RS, No. 101/05 – other law), which are applied until the adoption of by-laws based on the Law on Genetically Modified Organisms organisms (OJ RS, No. 41/09) if they do not contradict this law.

1226. EC. 2023, 141.

1227. *See*: https://treaties.un.org/pages/ViewDetails.aspx?src=TREATY&mtdsg_no=XXVII-13-b&chapter=27&clang=_en (25.1.2023). For additional information *see*: AC. 2023.

1228. GOV RS. 2022f, 385.

Chapter 6. Forests

1014. Serbia is considered a medium-forested country. The situation with the exploitation of forests in Serbia is generally speaking positive (wood volume is increasing faster than the annual cut),[1229] but the forests are endangered by different causes and especially by illicit cutting, other damage caused by man including pollution, damage caused by insects, damage by natural catastrophes and storms, damage caused by plant diseases, damage by fire, etc.[1230] The total area of forests in Serbia is 2,360,400 ha, and the percentage of forest cover is 26.7%, which is somewhat lower than the average percentage of forest cover in Europe. The area of state-owned forests managed by the State Enterprises amounts to 1,375,553 ha, which is 51.4% of the area of forests and other wooded land in Serbia. The remaining forest area is managed by private owners, other social enterprises, and National Parks.[1231]

Forestry traditionally plays an important role in economic development of Serbia,[1232] and it also has a long tradition of legal regulation.[1233] Forests are both State and privately owned. State-owned forests are mostly managed by the State-founded public enterprise 'Srbijašume' (85%) and in the APV by the enterprise 'Vojvodinašume' (7.5%), national parks (6.5%) and educational and research institutions (1%).[1234]

1015. The MAFWM is the main institution competent in the field of forestry. Its Forestry Department is responsible for all activities concerning forests, including the inspection. State forests are managed by public companies whose founder is the State – 'Srbijašume' (Serbia Forests) and 'Vojvodinasume' (Vojvodina Forests), while five public enterprises are managed by national parks. Scientific institutions also play an important role, especially the Forestry Institute in Belgrade and the Research and Development Institute for lowland forestry and the environment in

1229. 'The proportion of annual volume increase (about 9 million m3) and annual logging (about 3.2 million m3) is about 3:1. Together with the structure of forest roads and the certification process, it can be said that forest resources are being sustainably used.' EPA. 2019c, 10.
1230. Most severe damages to forests in 2011 and 2012 were caused by human activities, while over the past years, the greatest damages have been caused by natural disasters and insects. In 2017, 11,415 cubic metres of timber burned down, which is about 70% less than in 2016. EPA. 2019c, 30. For general data, *see* Glavonjić et al., 2005;Jović, Glavonjić. 2020, 235.
1231. GOV RS. 2006a, 14. According to the STAT. OFFICE – total forest by area (2020) is 2,262,386 ha, STAT. YEARB. SERB. 2023, 234. 'In the period 1953–2012, there was an increase in the area under forest by over one million hectares, an increase of 75% compared to 1953.' EPA. 2019c, 10.
1232. 'The overall significance of the wood industry sector, which has an important role in Serbia's gross domestic product, employment, and foreign trade, is considerably lower than its potential.' GOV RS. 2006a (Ch. 4.6: Wood Industry and Market). The forest sector contributed 1.3% to the national GDP in 2019, including the value added by forestry and logging and the manufacture of wood and wood products. Over 1,498,000 hectares of forests are used for productive purposes. Cuchietti, et al., 2023, 4.
1233. For example, Duke Milos's decree on prohibition of uncontrolled wood cutting from 1821. *See* GOV RS. 2006a, 4; *see also* Veličković, 2003.
1234. EPA. 2007, *supra*, 41. PE 'Srbijašume' manages state forests and forest land on a total area of 897,118.20 ha (state of the growing stock as of 1 Mar. 2023). https://srbijasume.rs/en/gazdovanje-sumama/sumski-fond/podaci-o-sumskom-fondu/ (21.2.2024).

Novi Sad. The Statistical Office makes a survey on areas under forests, once in three years, and annual surveys on planting, growing and exploitation of forests, forest damages and surveys on forest roads, transportation and mechanization. Surveys on the production and sale of forest products are done on a monthly basis, and surveys on hunting biannually.

1016. Forestry Development Strategy of the Republic of Serbia was adopted in 2006 (OJ RS, No. 59/06) and defines current conditions in forestry and developmental goals. The Strategy is guided by the principle of sustainable use of forests and their protection, according to obligations stemming from the acceptance of the Ministerial Conference on the Protection of Forests in Europe (MCPFE). Complete inventory of the forests in the Republic was conducted between 2004 and 2007.[1235]

§1. Legal Regulation

1017. The Serbian Constitution contains provisions in its Article 88 relevant for forests, and Article 183 prescribes that competence is given to APs too, 'in accordance with the Law', for regulating matters of provincial interest in different fields, including forestry.

1018. Provisions concerning forest policy and the framework for specific legal regulation are also contained in the Law on Spatial Plan of the RS (OJ RS, No. 88/10).

1019. EPL (OJRS, Nos 135/04, 36/09, 72/09 – other law, 43/2011 – CC, 14/2016, 76/18 and 95/18 – other law) also contains some basic provisions concerning protection of forests. Article 25, for example, prescribes that:

> In order to preserve and enhance forest ecosystems, forests shall be managed in a way that shall ensure rational forest management, genetic fund preservation, enhancement of the structure and realization of forests priority function. State authorities, forests owners and users are obliged to undertake necessary measures for preservation and sustainable use of forests, measures of renewal, afforest ration and improvement, as well as control and protection of forests in case of transboundary pollution.

1020. The Law on Forests (OJ RS, 30/2010, 93/2012, 89/2015 and 95/18 – other law) is the main legal Act concerning protection of forests in Serbia.

It has the following fourteen parts: Part I – General Provisions (Articles 1–8), Part II – Forest conservation (Articles 9–16), Part III – Planning (Articles 17–38), Part

1235. *See* MAFWM, 2009. – Within the project 'Contribution of sustainable forest management to low emissions and adaptive development' which was implemented in the period 2018–2023 and financed by the GEF, the Second National Forest Inventory of the RS was carried out. The FAO, as the implementing agency of the project, submitted the final data on the results of the Second National Forest Inventory to the MAFWM – Forestry Administration. https://upravazasume.gov.rs/ (21.2.2024).

IV – Forest Management (Articles 39–66), Part V – Forest inventory and forest information system (Articles 67 and 68), Part VI – Organization of forest management (Articles 69–75), Part VII – Financing (Articles 76–89), Part VIII – Forest value (Article 90), Part IX – The Chamber of forestry engineers (Articles 91–96), Part X – Performing the activities in forestry (Article 97), Part XI – Property rights (Articles 98–103), Part XII – Supervision (Articles 104–110), Part XIII – Penalty provisions (Articles 111–113), and Part XIV – Transitional and final provisions (Articles 114–121). Also, inventory of forests and forestlands of forest areas is attached to this Law making it an integral part.

1021. This Law regulates conservation, protection, planning, cultivation and usage of forests, management of forests[1236] and forestland,[1237] monitoring implementation of this Law and other issues relevant to the forests and forestland (Article 1). Provisions of this Law relate to forests and forestland in all forms of property (Article 2).

1022. The Law provides conditions for sustainable forest management[1238] and forestland as a resource of common interest, in the manner and to the extent to which they permanently maintain and enhance their productive capacity, biological diversity, as well as the capacity of renewal and vitality. Also, it enhances their potential to mitigate climate change, as well as their economic, ecological and social functions, and it does not harm the surrounding ecosystems (Article 3).

1023. Conservation, protection and improvement of forest conditions, the use of forest resources and their functions and planting of new forests in order to achieve optimal forest cover, spatial distribution and structure of forest fund in the RS are the activities of common interest (Article 4, paragraph 1).[1239] Protection of public interest from paragraph 1 of this Article is provided by (Article 4, paragraph 2): (1) permanent prohibition of forest areas reduction; (2) increasing of total forest fund, as well as the share of State ownership of forests in the RS, especially in forests with special purpose; (3) funding of the conservation, protection and improvement of the existing state and the establishment of new forests, preparation of plans and

1236. *Forest*, in terms of this Law, means a land area covered by forest trees, a minimum area of 5 acres, the minimum coverage area of the crowns of the trees 30%. Under forest are considered forest nurseries in complex of forest and seed plantations, as well as protective belts of trees larger than 5 acres. Under forest are not considered, parks in urban areas, as well as trees under power lines and in corridor of transmission lines, regardless of the surface (Art. 5, paras 1–4).

1237. *Forestland* is land on which forest is grown, land on which is, due to its natural characteristics, more rational to grow forest, land on which facilities for forest and wild life management are built, as well as realization of forest functions and which cannot be used for other purposes except in cases and under conditions specified by this Law (Art. 5, para. 4).

1238. *Forest management* is a set of agreed professionally scientific, technical and technological, economic, organizational and social activities undertaken in a certain period in the forest for its protection, maintenance, improvement and usage (Art. 8, point 7).

1239. Activities of common interest referred to in Art. 4 of this Law shall be financed from: (1) funds for the renovation-reproduction of forests; (2) Budget of the Republic of Serbia or AP; (3) Budget Fund or Budget Provincial Fund. Activities of public interest referred to in Art. 4 of this Law may be financed from the budget of local government units, in accordance with this Law (Art. 76, paras 1 and 2).

programmes of forest management through the Forest Budget Fund of the RS (hereinafter 'Budget Fund'), that is, funding of the conservation, protection and improvement of the existing state and building of new forest, development plans and programmes of forest management through the Forest Budget Fund of the AP (hereinafter 'the Provincial Budget Fund'); (4) adoption of the programme for development of forestry, forest management plans and their implementation; (5) setting up of legal entities for the management of State-owned forests; (6) establishment, maintenance and usage of national information system in forestry; (7) providing financial, technical and advisory support to the owners of forests; (8) prohibition of alienation of State-owned forests, except in cases stipulated by this Law; (9) preservation and protection of forests as environmental factors; and (10) performing other tasks in accordance with this Law and regulations adopted pursuant to the Law.

I. Forest Conservation, Monitoring and Sanation

1024. In order to preserve forests, except when otherwise provided by this Law, following is prohibited: (1) devastation[1240] and deforestation;[1241] (2) total deforestation[1242] which is not planned as a regular form of reforestation; (3) cutting, which is inconsistent with the forest management plans; (4) felling of protected trees and strictly protected species; (5) whitening of trees; (6) pasture, cattle browsing and acorning in the woods; (7) the collection of other forest products (mushrooms, fruits, herbs, snails and others); (8) cutting of seed stands and seed trees which is not prescribed by forest management plans; (9) use of stone, gravel, sand, humus, soil and peat, except for the construction of infrastructure facilities for forest management; (10) arbitrary seizure of forests, destruction or damage of forest plantations, marking and boundary signs, as well as construction of buildings that are not intended for forest management; (11) disposal of waste, harmful substances and hazardous materials and waste, as well as noise pollution in any way; and (12) taking other actions which might yield weak forests or that might endanger forest functions (Article 9, paragraph 1).

1025. Change of purpose of forests and forestland can be made: (1) when it is determined by the development plan of the forest area; (2) if it is required by public interest established by Law or special Act of the Government; (3) for construction of buildings for protection of people and property from natural disasters and for national defence; (4) in the process of regrouping and consolidation of agricultural land and forests; (5) for the construction of economic and residential buildings of forest owners on an area of up to 10 acres; (6) for the purpose of construction of

1240. *Forest devastations* are illegal operations which endanger or prevent the durability of forest production or cultivation of forests on the land and threaten the survival of forests and their socially useful functions (large-scale felling similar to total cutting, any action that may cause taking roots, rinsing and removal of soil by wind or water, etc.) (Art. 8, point 15).

1241. *Forest clearing* involves the removal of forest tree species in a particular area for conversion of forestland (Art. 8, point 8).

1242. *Total deforestation* is the removal of all or nearly all trees in a particular area (Art. 8, point 2).

facilities for the use of other RES of small capacity (small power stations and other similar facilities, in terms of regulations governing the energy sector) and the exploitation of mineral resources, if the area of forests and forestlands for these purposes is less than 15 hectares (Article 10, paragraph 1).[1243]

1026. It is prohibited to cut trees, destroy young trees and collect seeds from strictly protected forest tree species identified by a special regulation governing the protection of nature, unless they are a source of infection from diseases and pests, that is, if they threaten people and facilities (Article 13, paragraph 1).[1244] In order to preserve and use genetic resources, species directed in paragraph 1 of this Article, forest management plans include measures for the protection, use and expanding of area of these species (Article 13, paragraph 3).

1027. Monitoring the impact of transboundary air pollution is a system of continuous monitoring and analysis of the overall situation of forest ecosystems caused by the impact of transboundary air pollution, in accordance with internationally accepted methodology. These activities are performed by the Ministry or by the organization appointed by the Ministry and financed from the RS budget (Article 15, paragraphs 1–4).

1028. The owner, that is, user of forest[1245] is required to carry out sanation as follows: bare surface effect resulting from natural disasters (fire, wind, snow, etc.), the surface on which the rejuvenation and afforestation have failed; areas where the devastation was committed – illegal total cutting or deforestation or illegal cutting of trees of rare species (Article 16, paragraph 1).

II. Forests, Forestland and Forest Planning

1029. The forest areas are established with the aim of providing conditions for balanced and sustainable development of forests, the rational implementation of forest management measures and other forest resources in a particular territory (Article 17, paragraph 1).[1246] Forests and forestland included in forest areas and national parks are determined in the inventory of forests and forestlands of forest areas, which is attached to this Law making its integral part (Article 17, paragraph 4).

1243. Change of purpose of forests in para. 1, items (4)–(6) of this Article shall be made with the consent of the Ministry (Art. 10, para. 2).

1244. The species referred to in para. 1 of this Article may be used with the consent of the Ministry, but at the territory of AP with the consent of the competent authorities of the AP (Art. 13, para. 2).

1245. *Forest user* is a legal entity that manages the State-owned forests in accordance with this Law and other regulations (Art. 8, point 9).

1246. The forest area is planned geographic and natural entity that includes forests and forestland of forest area and of national parks (Art. 17, para. 2). Forest area covers forests in all forms of ownership and for all purposes, other than forest in national parks (Art. 17, para. 5).

1030. Management units,[1247] as the basic unit of planning, are established by the development plan of the forest area, according to the needs of the organization of forest management and according to criteria for the division of forest areas (Article 18, paragraph 1).

1031. Forestry Development Programme in the RS is the strategic planning document which sets out the directions for development of forests and forestry with an action plan for their implementation.[1248]

1032. Forest management plans are: (1) forest area development plan, that is, forest area development plan in a national park; (2) the basis for forest management; and (3) programme for forest management (Article 20, paragraph 1).

1033. National Forest Inventory is carried out to determine the condition of forests for the purpose of strategic planning, other State agencies, other branches of economy, defence, and scientific research, as a rule every ten years (Article 38, paragraph 1).[1249]

III. Forest Protection and Management

1034. Protection of forests from unlawful appropriation, usage, destruction and other illegal activities (disposal of waste and toxic pollutants, forest pollution, destruction of border signs and labels, etc.) is provided by the user, that is, owner of the forest[1250] (Article 39, paragraph 1).

1035. The owner and beneficiary of forest is required to monitor the impact of biotic and abiotic factors on the health of forests and promptly take measures to protect forests and forestlands[1251] (Article 42, paragraph 1).

1036. In cases of significant disturbance of biological balance and serious damage of forest ecosystems caused by the effect of natural disasters, the Ministry shall determine the measures for protection and rehabilitation of forests carried out by owners, that is, users of forests and provide financial resources (Article 45, paragraph 1).

1247. Management Unit, as a rule makes territorial integrity of forests and forestlands, except forest owner – a natural person, and includes the entire complex or just part of it (Art. 18, para. 2). Management unit includes forests and forestland of the same type of ownership, in the forest area of 5,000 acres (Art. 18, para. 3).
1248. Forestry Development Programme on territory of the Republic of Serbia adopts the Government for a period of ten years (Art. 19, para. 3).
1249. National Forest Inventory is to be performed by the Ministry or it can be delegated by the advertisement published in the OJ of the Republic of Serbia (Art. 38, paras 2 and 3).
1250. Forest owner is a natural or legal persons (company, cooperatives, churches and religious communities, association), owning the forests (Art. 8, point 18).
1251. If owner, i.e., user of the forest does not act in accordance with para. 1 this Article, the Ministry, i.e., the competent authority of the AP at the territory of AP, shall ensure the enforcement of these obligations at the expense of owners, i.e., users of the forest (Art. 42, para. 2).

1037. Forest user is obliged to issue a plan for forest protection from fire in the forest area for all forests regardless of ownership, for a period of five years (Article 46, paragraph 1). Ignition of open fire is forbidden in the forest and on land in proximity to the forest, at a distance less than 200 m from the woods edge (Article 47, paragraph 1).[1252]

1038. Natural and legal persons which caused the damage are obliged to compensate for the damage to the owner, that is, to the forest user (Article 48).

1039. Waste disposal is forbidden in the forest, on forestland at a distance less than 200 m from the edge of the forest, of toxic substances and other hazardous wastes, as well as construction of facilities for storage, processing or destruction of waste, toxic substances and other hazardous waste (Article 49, paragraph 1).[1253]

1040. The owner, that is, user of forest is required to prevent dumping of waste, toxic substances and other hazardous waste, as well as without delay notify the Ministry, at the territory of AP, the competent authority of AP (Article 49, paragraph 2).

1041. It is forbidden to drain and perform work which changes the water regime in the forest which threatens the survival and vitality of the forest (Article 50, paragraph 1).[1254]

1042. The following are forbidden in the forest without agreement of owners, that is, user of forest: (1) setting up of temporary buildings, tents and camping establishment; (2) organizing a mass meeting which might be detrimental to the forest; (3) setting up the board and signs which damage the tree; (4) setting up the fences; (5) movement of motor vehicles off roads intended for that purpose, except for official purposes; (6) the movement in closed and restricted areas, roads, fenced hunting grounds, experimental and business buildings; (7) moving in the areas where the following works are carried out – forest works and afforestation, logging, building construction, hunting, etc. (Article 51, paragraph 1).

1043. The citizens have free access to the forest for the purpose of enjoyment, relaxation and recreation, on their own responsibility for their safety and with

---

1252. Notwithstanding para. 1 this Article, the fire can be stoked in the forest and on forestland, at a place specified just for that purpose, settled up and clearly marked, implementing of measures stipulated in Art. 61 of this Law (Art. 47, para. 2).
1253. The owner, i.e., the user of forest is required to prevent the actions specified in para. 1 of this Article, remove garbage, toxic substances and other hazardous waste, as well as to undertake all measures for rehabilitation of damaged forests (Art. 49, para. 3).
1254. The elaboration and implementation of the projects of headwater management in forest ecosystems, enacted in accordance with special regulations, shall ensure a sufficient quantity of free water (the biological minimum) to meet the needs of plants and animals in the forest (Art. 50, para. 2).

obligation not to harm the forest (Article 51, paragraph 2). Free access can be restricted in protected forest areas or in forest areas where people's security might be threatened (Article 51, paragraph 3).[1255]

1044. Pasture, browsing in the forest can be done only with the permission of owners that is, user of the forest, which can issue the licence only if pasture, browsing or acornation is allowed in forest management plans, and if forest is not in process of renewing (Article 52, paragraph 1).[1256]

1045. Legal entities entrusted to manage the game, in accordance with the regulations governing wildlife and hunting, are obliged to number the types of game and maintain them at a level that does not disrupt the biological balance of forest ecosystems and does not prevent the implementation of forest management objectives (Article 53, paragraph 1).

IV. Forest Management Organization and Inventory of Forests and Forestland

1046. Management of forests as a natural resource is under the jurisdiction of the RS (Article 69, paragraph 1). The Ministry is in charge of forest management at the RS level, and at the territory of AP, the competent authorities of the AP are in charge. Also, forest management is performed through State-owned legal entities for forest management and through legal entities for management of forest owners (Article 69, paragraph 2).

1047. State-owned forests in the area covered by forest, that is, national park area, are managed by a public company or a company founded by the RS or AP, which meets the requirements established by this Law and by special regulations (Article 70, paragraph 1).

1048. Forest users managing forest and forestland shall keep and maintain records of these items (the Forests Cadastre) (Article 67, paragraph 1).[1257] The authority responsible for keeping records of real estate is required to enable the Ministry to use data on forests and forestland for production of forest management plans (Article 67, paragraph 3) free of charge.[1258]

1049. The Ministry establishes and maintains a single information system for forests and forestry of the RS (Article 68, paragraph 1).

1255. The owner, i.e., user of the forest is required to mark with visible warning signs part of the forest where access is forbidden (Art. 51, para. 4).
1256. Pasture is allowed on forestland until its afforestation (Art. 52, para. 2). Live stockholders can use the forest for pasture, browse or acornation, only under the supervision of shepherd (Art. 52, para. 3).
1257. Forest users are obliged to apply to the State agency responsible for keeping records of real estate to record changes made in the previous year, not later than 31 March of current year (Art. 67, para. 2).
1258. The Minister shall prescribe the content and manner of forest cadastre (Art. 67, para. 4).

1050. Based on the Law on Forests, eighteen by-laws were adopted. This includes, *inter alia,* the following:

- Rulebook on the method and time of remittance, assigning a remittance stamp, the method of marking the stumps of illegally cut trees, and the method of recording these trees and stumps in the remittance books (OJ RS, No. 110/21).
- Regulation on establishing the Annual Program for the use of funds for the sustainable development and improvement of forestry in 2023 (OJ RS, Nos 23/23, 58/23, 87/23).
- Rulebook on the content, management, maintenance, and use of the information system in forestry (OJ RS, No. 49/21).
- Rulebook on the programme and method of passing the professional exam for obtaining a license to perform professional tasks in forest management (OJ RS, No. 57/17).
- Rulebook for work and conduct in the performance of professional and advisory work in the owner's forests (OJ RS, Nos 40/17, 8/21).
- Rulebook on the use of forest roads of the Public Enterprise for Forest Management 'Srbijašume' (OJ RS, Nos 93/16, 95/18).
- Rulebook on the form and content of the forest stamp, the form of the accompanying note, that is, the delivery note, the conditions and method of stamping felled wood, the method of keeping records and the method of stamping, that is, the marking of conifer trees intended for New Year's and other holidays (OJ RS, No. 93/16).
- Rulebook on the identification form of forest guards (OJ RS, No. 82/16).
- Rulebook on the content of the forest area development plan, i.e., the forest development plan in the national park (OJ RS, No. 145/14).
- Rulebook on the form and content of official identification and the appearance of the official uniform of the forestry inspector, as well as the method of keeping records of issued official identification cards (OJ RS, Nos 19/13, 81/15 – other rulebooks).
- Rulebook on forest reproductive materials (OJ RS, No. 46/11), etc.

1051. A large number of regulations in other areas may refer to various issues in the field of forest management. These are, for example, the following:

- Law on Game and Hunting (OJ RS, Nos 18/10, 95/18 – other law, and 92/23 – other law).
- Law on public property (OJ RS, Nos 72/11, 88/13, 105/14, 104/16 – other law, 108/16, 113/17, 95/18, and 153/20).
- Law on Public Enterprises and Performing Activities of General Interest (OJ RS, Nos 15/16, 88/19).
- Law on Nature Protection (OJ RS, Nos 39/09, 88/10 – corr., 14/16, 95/18 – other law, and 71/21).
- Law on Environmental Protection (OJ RS, Nos 135/04, 36/09- other law, 72/09- other law, 43/11-CC, 76/18, 95/18 – other law, and 95/2018 – other law), etc.

1052. Serbia has ratified the United Nations Convention to Combat Desertification in Countries Experiencing Serious Drought and/or Desertification, particularly in Africa (1994).

Chapter 7. Hunting and Fishery

1053. Hunting and fishery in Serbia are not too important from an economic point of view, although both activities contribute to overall food production and the tourist industry to a certain extent.

Total hunting area in Serbia is 8,828,588 ha (73.6% hunting grounds and 26.4% non-hunting grounds).[1259] In about 360 hunting grounds, in addition to 44 breeding grounds (41 in 2021), 82,416 hunters hunted during 2022, which is about 3% more than in 2021.[1260] The catch of all game species was reduced during the 2022–2023 hunting year. The catch of the following species decreased the most: wild ducks (76%), quail (65%), pheasant (35%), fallow deer (46%), roe deer (43%), rabbit (39%), wild boar (36%) and foxes (30%).[1261]

1054. When diversity of fishing species in fishing waters is concerned, situation in Serbia is more or less similar to the situation in other countries in the region, but in spite of favourable natural potential, number of registered fishermen and the productivity in fish production are among the lowest in Europe,[1262] due to the fact that until recently the sector of fishery has not been given adequate priority. Out of seven endemic fish species of the Danube basin, five live in the RS.[1263] Since 2003, a mild growth of catch has been generally recorded for all fish species of ecosystem of inland waters that are target catch of recreational and commercial fishing, while the increase in catch recorded for carp, catfish, pikeperch and somewhat pike has been markedly high due to the increase in demand of these species on the Serbian market.[1264] 'The catch of fish decreased, after several years of increase. Freshwater habitats are more endangered than forest habitats, especially due to fragmentation of river habitats. Production in carp ponds increased by about 17%, but catch from carp ponds increased by about 31% compared to 2017.'[1265]

1055. MAFWM – Forestry Department (Hunting) have certain competencies and responsibilities. The affairs in fishing are conducted by the MAFWM (Veterinary Directorate).

MAFWM is competent in managing fishing resources in fishing waters, which entails preservation and protection, catch and use of fish and farming all species and age categories of fish. Fishing resource management is done in accordance with the principle of sustainable use, which contributes to preservation of ichtiofaunistic

---

1259. GOV RS. 2010a, 82.
1260. EPA. 2023a, 131. 'Population trend of the most important hunting species was stable in the period 2014–2016.' *Ibid.*, 130.
1261. *Ibid.*
1262. GOV RS. 2008b, 104. In 2022, the number of professional fishermen (393) decreased by about 9% compared to 2021. The total number of licences issued for recreational fishing was 94,568, which is about 14% less than in 2021. The intensity of sport and commercial fishing is almost identical as in 2021. EPA. 2023a, 132.
1263. GOV RS. 2010a, 83.
1264. GOV RS. 2011c, 11.
1265. EPA. 2019c, 10. During 2022, a total of 2380 t of fish was caught, which is almost the same as in 2021. EPA. 2023a. 132.

diversity and ecological integrity of water ecosystems. Fish farming covers production of spawn, young fish and fish in fisheries, in confined parts of fishing waters and fishing water cages.

§1. Legal Regulation

I. General Regulations

1056. The Constitution of Serbia explicitly mentions 'hunting and fishery' only once in Article 183, that prescribes that APs shall, in accordance with the Law, regulate the matters of provincial interest in various fields, including hunting and fishery.

1057. EPL (OJ RS, Nos 135/04, 36/09 and 36/09 – other law, 72/09 – other law, 43/11CC, 14/16, 76/18 and 95/18 – other law) contains provisions on hunting and fishing in Article 33 (Planning and Construction) and in Article 35 (Strategic EIA).

1058. The Law on SEA (OJ RS, Nos 135/04 and 88/10) prescribes in Article 5 that strategic assessment shall be carried out for all plans, programmes bases and strategies (hereinafter 'plans and programmes') in the areas of spatial and urban planning or land-use planning, agriculture, forestry, fishery, *hunting,* energy, industry, transport, waste management, water management, telecommunications, tourism, conservation of natural habitats and wild flora and fauna, that set the frameworks for granting the approval for future development projects defined by the EIA related regulations.

II. Law on Game and Hunting

1059. The Law on Game and Hunting (OJ RS, Nos 18/10, 95/18 – other law, and 92/23 – other law) is the main legal Act regulating protection of wild game and hunting in Serbia. It consists of 115 Articles divided into eleven parts as follows: I. Basic Provisions (Articles 1–4); II. Organization of the Hunting (Articles 5–8); III. Chamber of Hunting (Articles 9–19); IV. Protection of Wild Game (Articles 20–30); V. The Hunting Grounds and Hunting Area (Articles 31–37); VI. Management of the Hunting Ground and Wild Game (Articles 38–77); VII. Financing (Articles 78–86); VIII. Damages and Compensation of Damages (Articles 87–91); IX. Monitoring (Articles 92–101); X. Penal Provisions (Articles 102–105); and XI. Transitional and Final Provisions (Articles 106–115).

1060. The basic aim of the Law is described in first three Articles. It is stated that wild game is a natural resource of Serbia (Article 1) and that protection, breeding, hunting and usage of wild game are activities of public interest (Article 3). It should also be added that Article 4 contains precise definitions of some notions used in the Law. Organization of hunting is mainly regulated by Articles 5–8. Article 5, paragraph 1 prescribes that the competent organ for hunting in the RS is the Ministry for hunting (the Ministry). According to paragraph 2 of the same Article, AP regulates the hunting in matters of provincial interest on its territory. The matters are enumerated in Article 6.

1061. The Law also prescribes certain managerial responsibilities to public enterprises, business associations and the Serbian Hunting Association (Articles 7 and 8) which are obliged to cooperate with each other in matters concerning hunting and to exchange relevant information (Article 8, paragraph 4).[1266]

1062. Articles 9–19 of the Law regulate establishment, composition, activities, structure, statute, financing, issuance of licences, evaluation of professional work and some other issues of the Chamber of Hunting. The institution has been established with the task of 'realization and protection of rights and interests of persons engaged in activities concerning hunting, as well as improvement of hunting in accordance with management of population of wild game, public interest and universally accepted international standards … '(Article 9).

1063. The Law prescribes protection of wild game by dividing it into two categories: (1) game species protected by a permanent hunting ban and (2) species of game that are prohibited from hunting during a certain period (Article 20). Procedure of declaring seasonal hunting periods is regulated by Article 21, according to the game species, obligations of hunters concerning animal welfare, and hunting grounds management. A number of prohibitions are prescribed by Article 22 (e.g., to catch protected game; to keep it in closed or fenced spaces, to destruct wild game lairs, nests and eggs; to collect eggs of protected birds, etc.), as well as exceptional cases when these prohibitions do not apply (Article 23). It does not apply to the organized catching of injured game or game which is endangered by natural catastrophes or to implementing measures regarding their breeding and populating. The Law also regulates introduction of new wild game into existing hunting grounds (Articles 24 and 25), measures of wild game health protection (Article 26), measures regarding their breeding and populating (Article 27), measures regarding protection of wild game outside hunting grounds (Article 28), protection of wild game from stray dogs and cats (Article 29) and entrance to the hunting grounds which is allowed only to 'persons armed with hunting rifles and other means prescribed for hunting, if they have hunting card and hunting license' (Article 30).

1064. Establishment of hunting territory and hunting grounds is regulated by Articles 31–37. While the whole territory of Serbia is regarded as one hunting territory (Article 31), hunting grounds are divided into open and fenced ones (Article

1266. According to Art. 7, public enterprises and business associations are responsible for protection, breeding, hunting and sustainable usage of wild game as a natural resource, for hunting grounds management, distribution of hunting maps, etc. Pursuant to Art. 8, Serbian Hunting Association is the institution responsible for establishing various commissions (for evaluation of wild game trophies, for exhibition of the trophies, for passing hunting examination, etc.) issuance of hunting licences, publishing activities, etc.

32). Rules of establishment of hunting grounds are regulated in detail (Articles 33–35 and 37) and definition of non-hunting grounds is given (Article 36).

1065. A large part of the Law contains provisions dealing with management of the hunting ground and wild game (Articles 38–77). It is prescribed in detail how a legal person obtains the right to use a hunting ground, how long the contract lasts, what are the exceptions, etc. (Articles 38–43). The Minister prescribes, besides other matters, procedure for establishment of hunting areas and hunting grounds, conditions for hunting management, public procedure for obtaining the right to use a hunting ground, contents of the contract and the amount of guarantee to be given by the legal person who wants to obtain the right for hunting management (Article 44).

1066. Several articles of the Law are devoted to planning documents. The basic document is the Strategy of Developing Hunting in the RS adopted by the Government for a period of fifteen years (Article 45). Another planning document prescribed by the Law is the Programme of development of a hunting area (Article 46). There must also be the so-called hunting basics prepared for every hunting ground – a document which regulates protection, breeding, hunting, usage of wild game and management of hunting grounds (Article 47). The user of a hunting ground is also obliged to prepare an annual plan for management of his/her ground based on the above-mentioned hunting basics (Article 48).[1267]

1067. Articles 54–58 of the Law regulate position and duties of game wardens and management of the hunting grounds. Articles 59–77 regulate various aspects of hunting (hunting examination, hunting card, prescribe hunting periods seasonally, according to the game species, the right to hunting, licence to hunt big game, use of hunting dogs, battle against poachers, hunting tourism, exception when it is possible to hunt protected game, etc.) game trophies, export of game and other uses of hunted game.[1268]

1068. Other legal Acts relevant to hunting in Serbia are, *inter alia*, following:

- Law on Forests (OJ RS, Nos 30/10, 93/12, 89/15 and 95/18 – other law).
- Law on Animal Welfare (OJ RS, No. 41/09).
- Law on Veterinary Medicine (OJ RS, Nos 91/05, 30/10, 93/12 and 17/19 – other law).
- *EPL* (OJ RS, Nos 135/04, 36/09, 72/09, 43/11 CC, 14/16, 76/18 and 95/18 – other law).
- Law on National Parks (OJ RS, Nos 84/15 and 95/18 – other law).
- Law on Tourism (OJ RS, No. 17/19).

1267. Articles 50–52 regulate rights and duties of users of neighbouring hunting grounds, users and owners of land, waters and forests, and users (i.e., managers) of protected natural resources. Article 53 deals with the cadastre of hunting grounds and central database, kept by the Ministry.

1268. Financing is regulated by Arts 78–86. Damages and Compensation of Damages by Arts 87–91. Monitoring is regulated by Part IX of the Law (Arts 92–101), while penal provisions are contained in Part X (Arts 102–105). Transitional and final provisions are contained in Arts 106–115.

- Law on Weapons and Ammunition (OJ RS Nos 20/15, 10/19, 20/20, and 14/22).
- Law on Associations (OJ RS, Nos 51/10, 99/11 – other law and 44/18 – other law).

Based on the Law on Game and Hunting (OJ RS, Nos 18/10, 95/18 – other law, and 92/23 – other law), several by-laws were adopted. Some of the more significant ones are the following:

- Regulation on the establishment of hunting areas in the RS (OJ RS, No. 88/20).
- Rulebook on cadastre of hunting ground and central database (OJ RS, No. 40/12).
- Rulebook on measures for preventing damages from wild animals and damage to wildlife and the procedure and method of determining damages (OJ RS, No. 2/12).
- Rulebook on the format and content of the official identity card and official badge of hunting inspector, as well as the manner of use of protective equipment (OJ RS, Nos 60/11 and 81/15 – other rulebooks).
- Rulebook on professional examination for obtaining a licence to perform certain hunting activities (OJ RS, No. 65/11).
- Rulebook on the manner of marking and labelling of boundaries and hunting-technical facilities in the hunting areas (OJ RS, No. 76/11).
- Rulebook on the security measures in the hunting areas (OJ RS, Nos 76/11, and 41/21).
- Rulebook on hunting dogs (OJ RS, No. 80/11).
- Rulebook on the game warden service (OJ RS, Nos 84/11 and 56/15).
- Order on game closed season (OJ RS, 55/06).
- Rulebook on proclamation of closed season for protected wild species (OJ RS, Nos 9/12, 31/13, 55/15 and 67/15, 75/16, and 92/21), etc.

III. Law on Conservation and Sustainable Use of Fish Resources

1069. Law on Conservation and Sustainable Use of Fish Resources (OJ RS, Nos 128/14 and 95/18 – other law) contains following eight chapters: Basic provisions (Articles 1 and 2); fishing areas (Articles 3–21); conservation and protection of the fish stock (Articles 22–31); fishing (Articles 32–49); turnover of fishes (Articles 50 and 51); supervision (Articles 53–57); penal provisions (Articles 58–63); and transitional and final provisions (Articles 64–68).[1269]

1269. On the date of enactment of this Law, the Law on Fishery (OJ RS, Nos 36/09 and 32/13 CC) shall cease to be effective (Art. 67). The secondary legislation to be adopted on the base of this Law shall be issued within one year from the date of entry into force of this Law. Until issuing the regulations referred to in para. 1 of Art. 66, the Decision on the determination of fishing areas (OJ RS, Nos 115/07, 49/10 and 60/12) and regulations adopted pursuant to the Law on the protection and sustainable use of fish stocks (OJ RS, Nos 36/09 and 32/13 – US), except for provisions of these regulations that are not in accordance with the Law (Art. 66, paras 1–2).

1070. The Law regulates management of the fish stock in fishing waters that includes protection and sustainable use of the fish stock in public interest. Management of fish resources shall be done according to the principle of sustainable use that contributes to the protection of ichthyofauna diversity and ecological integrity of aquatic ecosystems (Article 1).[1270]

A. Fishing Areas

1071. Fishing areas are established for the purpose of sustainable use of fish resources[1271] in fishing waters. Fishing area is established by the Minister responsible for the fishing stock issues (Minister) (Article 3 paragraph 1).[1272] Fishing area in the protected area is declared and used by controller of the protected area, with prior approval of the Minister and the controller is user of the fishing area (Article 3, paragraph 2).

1072. For the fishing waters that are at the same time the State border, border fishing areas are determined according to the State border. Water fishing in fishing areas and the prescribed measures for the Protection and Sustainable Use of fish resources are entered in the fishing water cadastre kept by the Ministry responsible for environmental protection and sustainable utilization of the fish stock (hereinafter 'the Ministry') (Article 3, paragraphs 5–6).

The fishing area may be conceded for use to a commercial entity or public enterprise (hereinafter 'user') satisfying the following requirements: (1) it is registered by the competent authority and entered in the appropriate register; (2) they shall be technically and professionally equipped for performing the activity, that is, they have an employee in continuous employment with minimum university degree of the second grade (master academic studies, specialized academic studies and specialized professional studies), or on the basic studies of at least four years, biological, environmental, veterinary, or livestock (zoo technical) orientation, with attended, and passed the course(s) from the field of fishery or ichthyology (hereinafter 'a specialist'); (3) that, within two years prior to announcement of the competition for concession of the fishing area for use, they were not sanctioned for corporate offences or corporate minor offences, etc. (Article 6, paragraph 1, points 1–3).

1073. The Law defines that fishing area may be granted for use to a company or public company or user fulfilling certain conditions and that fishing area shall be granted for use for a certain charge (Article 7).[1273]

1270. The fish resources in fishing waters are owned by the State (Art. 1, para. 4).
1271. The fish resources include all kinds of fish, mollusks, crabs and other aquatic organisms which are protected and sustainably used (Art. 2, point 25).
1272. The Act referred to in paras 2 and 3 of this Article regulates boundaries and purpose of the fishing area with regard to the type of fishing performed therein (commercial and/or recreational) (Art. 3, para. 4).
1273. Charges for the use of fishing area are revenue in the budget of the Republic of Serbia, while charges for the use of fishing area in the territory of AP are revenue in the budget of the AP.

The contract on the use of fishing area is negotiated by the Minister, or the competent organ of the province, with the user of fishing area (Article 8). It is prescribed that the user is obliged to organize protection of the fishing area (Article 11).

1074. Fish watchman licence is issued by the competent ministry to the person who has passed professional exam for a fish watchman; his/her authority as an official person has been prescribed by the Law (Articles 13 and 14).

Legal person, entrepreneur or physical person, who is by practising fishing breaking provisions of this Law, or in some other way causes harm to fish resources, is obliged to recompense the damage to the user of fishing area (Article 16, paragraph 1).[1274]

1075. The user is obliged to have the programme of management of fishing area and to obtain approval for it (Article 17, paragraph 1).[1275] Manager of the protected areas is required to harmonize programme management fishing area with management plans (Article 20, paragraph 1). For fishing waters for which consent for declaration of fishing area is not given, controller prescribes protective measures and usage of fish stock in the Protected Area Management plan (Article 20, paragraph 3).[1276]

B. Preservation and Protection of Fish Resources

1076. Actions forbidden in the fishing area are prescribed in Article 22, paragraph 1. To preserve and protect fish stocks, a closed season is established for all or certain types of fish in the fishing area, and hunting fish that do not have the required size is prohibited. The Minister shall prescribe measures for the conservation and protection of fish stocks (Article 23, paragraphs 1–2).

1077. It is not allowed to introduce allochthonous (non-native) types of fish into fishing waters (Article 30). Apart from that, it is not allowed to introduce fish species from regionally remote geographic areas, as well as species that originate from geographically close but mutually isolated basins.

Amount of charges that are revenue for Republic of Serbia budget shall be 15% from fees paid for licence issuance for commercial fishing and 10% from fees paid for licence issuance for recreational fishing (annual, daily, for more days) (Art. 7, paras 2–4).

1274. The Minister prescribes the Regulation on the amount of charges for damage done to fish resources and Regulation on categorization of fishing waters (Art. 16, para. 4).

1275. In accordance with the fishing area management programme, the user shall enact the annual fishing area management programme at the latest by the end of the current year for the following year (Art. 17, para. 2).

1276. The user of the fishing area is required to prepare an annual report on the use of fishing area and submit it to the competent ministry or the provincial authority and the Agency for Environmental Protection, not later than 1 March of the current year for the previous year (Art. 21).

C. Fishing

1078. Commercial fishing in a fishing area can be done by a commercial society or an entrepreneur who fulfils conditions prescribed by this Law (Article 32, paragraph 1).[1277] Commercial fishing is practised by entrepreneur and commercial society in accordance with the contract with the user of fishing area and the annual permit for commercial fishing, according to the programme of management of fishing area and annual programme of management of fishing area, as well as the temporary programme of management of fishing area and categorization of fishing waters (Article 32, paragraph 4).[1278]

1079. Register of commercial fishers is kept by the Ministry (Article 34).[1279]

1080. Annual permit for commercial fishing is issued by the user of fishing area on request by a commercial society or an entrepreneur (Article 35).[1280] The user of the fishing area, for the purpose of preservation of fish resource as a natural resource, shall issue the number of annual commercial fishing permits specified by the fishing area management programme and categorization of fishing waters (Article 35). A commercial entity and entrepreneur shall perform commercial fishing by means of fishing hooks, fishing nets and traps not jeopardizing the juvenile fish species and animals eaten by the fish (Article 37).[1281] The commercial entity or entrepreneur performing commercial fishing shall be obliged to keep daily records on fish catching, prepare a monthly and annual report and submit them to the user of the fishing area at the end of current month, that is, year (Article 39, paragraph 1).[1282]

1277. Commercial society can practice commercial fishing provided that it has only employed persons with VII degree of professional education (or master studies), in biology, ecology or cattle breeding; they should be enlisted in the Register of commercial fishers (Art. 30, para. 2). An entrepreneur can practice commercial fishing if he is entered in the Register of Commercial Fishermen (Art. 32, para. 3).
1278. 'Commercial fishing is carried out on the Danube, the Sava and the Tisa rivers. Although these are the largest rivers flowing through Serbia, their geographic contribution in relation to the entire territory is reduced to one-third of the country's territory. In accordance with the Regional Strategy for Conservation and Sustainable Management of Sturgeon Population of the North-West Black Sea and Lower Danube River in accordance with CITES, 26 Nov. 2003, Tulcea, Romania, the fishing on the Danube River from 863 km to 860 km (Hydroelectric Power Plant "Đerdap II") is prohibited.' GOV RS. 2011c,14.
1279. The Minister shall prescribe in detail the contents and method of keeping the Register of commercial fishers (Art. 34, para. 2).
1280. For issuing of the annual permit referred to in para. 1 of this Article, the commercial entity or entrepreneur shall pay the costs of permit issuance established by the user (Art. 33, para. 2).
1281. The user of the fishing area intended for commercial fishing may, through the fishing area management programme, restrict or ban use of certain tools used for commercial fishing. For the purpose of protection of fish resources, the user of the fishing area may, with the consent of the Minister, i.e., competent provincial authority, temporarily and maximum for a period of one year, ban commercial fishing in a certain part of the fishing area (Art. 38, paras 1 and 2).
1282. The user may not issue a commercial fishing permit in the current year to the commercial entity or entrepreneur which failed to submit the annual report for the previous year (Art. 39, para. 2).

1081. Recreative and sport fishing can be done by persons with the permit for recreative fishing.[1283]

1082. Fishing for scientific research purposes shall be performed in the presence of the inspector in charge of activities of protection and sustainable use of fish resources based on permit issued by the Minister and on the territory of the AP, the competent provincial body (Article 47, paragraph 1).[1284]

Fishing for scientific research purposes may be performed by means of any fishing hooks, fishing nets and traps and electrofishing device to the extent and scope which does not disturb the composition of ichthyofauna or significantly reduce the existing fish resources (Article 48, paragraph 1).[1285]

1083. Electrofishing is done with the permit issued by the Minister, i.e., competent body of the AP and supervised by an inspector. In exceptional cases, electrofishing can be done by fish stocking and saving fish in a flooded area with the permit issued by the Minister (Article 49).

D. Trade in Fish

1084. Trade in fish can be done by legal persons and entrepreneurs registered for fish trade, as well as companies and entrepreneurs engaged in commercial fishing, in accordance with special regulations (Article 50, paragraph 1).[1286]

It shall be prohibited to place on the market the fish under the prescribed size or fish caught during the closed season (Article 51, paragraph 1).[1287] Apart from that, it is prohibited to place on the market prepared trophy fish or their parts without consent of the Ministry (Article 51, paragraph 4). Fish caught in fishing waters before closed fishing season cannot be put on the market after twenty-four hours from commencement of closed fishing season (Article 51, paragraph 2).

E. Supervision

1085. The inspection of enforcement of provisions of this Law and regulations enacted on the basis of this Law shall be performed by the Ministry through competent

---

1283. Persons younger than 14 years can practice recreative fishing without the permit with one fishing rod if they are in company of persons with the permit for recreative fishing (Art. 40, para. 2).

1284. The holder of the permit shall be obliged to notify the user and the Ministry, i.e., competent body of the AP of the time when fishing for scientific research purposes is to be performed and to prepare a report on performed fishing and submit it to the Ministry (Art. 47, para. 3).

1285. Fishing for scientific research purposes may be performed by organizations registered for expert and scientific research from the field of fishing fishery, ichthyology, fish biology or ecology of continental waters (Art. 48, para. 2).

1286. Associations, recreative fishing and other persons cannot put in the market caught fish (Art. 50, para. 3).

1287. When traded during the time of closed seasons or traded of fishes which do not have prescribed size, the legal person and the entrepreneur must have documentation to prove the origin of the fish, the species and the quantity of fish (Art. 51, para. 4).

inspector (Article 54, paragraph 1). The Ministry, in supervising the work of the relevant Provincial authority, users and managers of protected area, may require the submission of reports and information on the performance of delegated tasks, to give the required instructions and warn of failure to perform the delegated tasks in accordance with the Law (Article 53, paragraphs 2–3).[1288]

1086. The Law on animal husbandry (OJ RS, Nos 41/2009, 93/2012 and 14/2016) regulates the goals of animal husbandry; agents in livestock production and their organizational forms; breeding objectives and the implementation of breeding programmes; control of productivity and maintenance of properties of domestic animals; breeding of domestic animals; beekeeping; aquaculture; breeding of wild animals; conservation of genetic reserves of domestic animals and biological diversity in livestock; fishery products; primary production of food for domestic animals and animal products; transport breeding material, as well as other issues of importance to animal husbandry (Article 1). Conditions for conducting aquaculture are regulated by Articles 65 and 66 of the Act. The Law also regulates the import, export and transit of fishery products (Article 66b).

1087. Besides the Law on fishing and the Law on animal husbandry, a number of specific by-laws regulate protection of fish. They are, *inter alia*, following:

- Rulebook on the value of daily, multi-day, and annual permits for recreational fishing for the year 2024 (OJ RS, No. 77/23).
- Rulebook on the form, content and scope of final report on the use of fishing area (OJ RS, No. 52/17).
- Rulebook on the categorization of fishing waters (OJ RS, No. 10/12).
- Rulebook on conditions and manner of organizing fish warden service, warden ID forms and appearance of the warden badge (OJ RS, Nos 07/10 and 3/16 – other rulebooks).
- Rulebook on the manner of determining and the amount of compensation of damage caused to fish resources (OJ RS, No. 03/2016).
- Rulebook on the monitoring programme for monitoring the status of fish resources in fishing waters (OJ RS, No. 71/10).
- Rulebook on the content of the annual commercial fishing permit form (OJ RS, No. 56/2015).
- Rulebook on the appearance and content of the form of records of fishermen catch and the manner of keeping records of fish catch (OJ RS, No. 34/15).
- Rulebook on the appearance and content of the form of records of commercial fishermen catch and the manner of keeping records of fish catch (OJ RS, No. 37/15).
- Rulebook on conditions, programmed and manner of going for an examination for fish warden and professional fisherman examination (OJ RS, Nos 60/15 and 96/16).

1288. The Ministry shall perform supervision over the work of the competent authority of the AP in performing the entrusted activities (Art. 50, para. 2).

- Rulebook on the content of form of one-day, multi-day and annual permit for recreational fishing, and one-day, multi-day and annual permit for recreational fishing in protected area (OJ RS, No. 15/15).
- Rulebook on conditions to be fulfilled by ranching materials (OJ RS, No. 86/15).
- Rulebook on conditions and procedure for the issuance and withdrawal of fish warden licences and the manner of keeping the register of issued fish warden licences (OJ RS, Nos 02/16, and 112/17 – CC).
- Rulebook on the content and manner of keeping the fishing water cadastre (OJ RS, No. 03/2016).
- Rulebook on conditions and manner of organizing fish warden service and the form of keeping records of daily activities of fish warden service (OJ RS, No. 03/2016).
- Rulebook on the scope and content of the recreational fishermen educational programme (OJ RS, No. 03/2016).
- Rulebook on fish warden uniforms, appearance of the warden badge and fish warden official ID form (OJ RS, No. 39/2016).

IV. International Treaties and Harmonization with EU Legislation

1088. The RS is a party to the following agreements:

- Agreement on fisheries in the Danube River waters (Bucharest 1958) between the Government of the Federative People's Republic of Yugoslavia, the People's Republic of Bulgaria, the People's Republic of Romania and the Union of Soviet Socialist Republics.
- Agreement on fisheries in border waters (Timisoara, 1961) signed between the Government of the Federative People's Republic of Yugoslavia and the People's Republic of Romania governing fishing and fisheries in boundary waters.
- Agreement on boundary waters fishing (Belgrade, 1961) signed between the Government of the Federative People's Republic of Yugoslavia and the People's Republic of Bulgaria, governing fishing and fisheries in boundary waters.
- Regional Strategy for Conservation and Sustainable Management of Sturgeon Population of the North-West Black Sea and Lower Danube River in accordance with CITES, 26 November 2003, Tulcea, Romania.

1089. Serious steps have been undertaken towards improvement of legal regulation in the fields of hunting and fishery.[1289]

The Serbian fishing industry is very small and consists of inland fishing, which is not covered by the EU *acquis*. The administrative body for the fisheries sector needs to be adapted to the needs of the CFP, while the capacity of the administration to deal with management and control of fishing activities needs to be enhanced and

1289. The most frequently committed environmental crimes are devastation of forests, illegal logging, poaching game, illegal fishing, and killing and cruelty to animals, while the number of charges filed for the criminal offences related to environmental pollution, failure to undertake environmental protection measures or damaging the environment is much smaller. UNECE. 2015, 56

brought into line with CFP obligations. Overall, Serbia should be able to align with the EU *acquis* in the fisheries chapter and implement it effectively in the medium term.[1290] According to the last EC report, 'Serbia is moderately prepared in the area of fisheries and aquaculture. No progress was made during the reporting period.'[1291]

1290. EC. 2011, 80.

1291. EC. 2023, 141. In the coming year, Serbia should: (1) adopt an action plan for full compliance with the requirements of the EU acquis by the date of accession, in particular regarding the organization of markets, aquaculture, data collection and control measures, and illegal, unreported, and unregulated fishing; (2) address the severe understaffing of authorities responsible for policy formulation and antifraud controls for fisheries (including border controls). *Ibid.*

Chapter 8. Subsoil and Minerals

§1. Mineral Resources in Serbia

1090. Serbia has numerous deposits of mineral resources. In terms of diversity, an important place is occupied by energy mineral raw materials, primarily coal, oil, and gas.[1292] The problem is that the resources are used unsustainably; there is no complete analysis of the state and level of exploration of natural resources and goods by types, spatial distribution, variety, volume, and quality. There are not enough reserves of medium and high-calorie coal.[1293]

Almost 90% of energy mineral resources of Serbia are low-quality lignite and oil and gas account for less than 10%. Reserves of coal are insufficient what may be a limiting factor to the development of the energy sector.

Deposits of metallic mineral resources are not very rich. Copper is the most important mineral resource with significant economic potential.[1294]

There are numerous sources (more than 1,000) of mineral, thermal and thermal mineral water. Their total yields are more than 1,000 l/s.[1295]

1091. The MME is competent for the activities concerning mining. Article 8 of the Law on Ministries (OJ RS, Nos 128/20, 116/22, and 92/23 – other law) prescribes that the MME is responsible for carrying out work in this area. This includes, among other things, tasks related to the strategy and policy of mining development; the creation of a balance of mineral raw materials; geological research related to the exploitation of mineral raw materials; creating a programme of research works in the field of basic geological research related to the sustainable use of resources; creation of annual and medium-term programs of detailed investigative works in the field of geological research related to the exploitation of mineral raw materials and provision of material and other conditions for the realization of these programs; exploitation of all types of mineral raw materials and geological resources; inspection supervision in the field of mining, as well as other tasks specified by law. Another institution established as an independent regulatory body is the AERS.

§2. Legislation

1092. Article 87 of the Constitution of Serbia prescribes that 'Natural resources shall be utilized under the terms and in a manner stipulated by the Law.' Natural and legal persons may obtain particular rights on particular goods in public use,

1292. 'The volume of geological research in RS has increased significantly in the past ten years, and in that period dozens of exploration permits were issued mostly for sites in the east country.' At https://serbia-business.eu/what-influenced-the-expansion-of-geological-research-in-serbia/ (19.2.2024).
1293. NA. 2010, (Ch. 2. General assessment).
1294. GOV RS. 2008b, 84–89. *See also* UNECE. 2007, 7. For more details, *see* NA. 2011, 4–11.
1295. UNECE. 2007, 81.

under the terms and in a manner stipulated by Law. Article 22 prescribes that protection, utilization and arrangement of land, agricultural and forest soil and goods of general interest shall comprise preservation of productivity, structure, layers, rocks and mineral formation, as well as their natural and transitive shapes and processes. Throughout project realization as well as before its execution (constructing, mineral raw material exploiting, etc.), the protection of land and soil shall be ensured.

1093. According to Article 34, spatial and urban plans shall ensure measures and conditions of environmental protection and, in particular, determine special regimes for preservation and use of the areas of protected natural goods, water springs, thermal and mineral springs, forests, agricultural land, public green areas, recreation areas and spas.

1094. The proposal for the Strategy for the Management of Mineral Resources of the RS until 2030 was prepared in 2011. During 2012, the document was the subject of discussion in the NA.[1296] However, the adoption of the Strategy was not published in the OJ. At the beginning of 2024, the MME announced a tender for the development of the Strategy for the Management of Mineral and Other Geological Resources of Serbia and the Action Plan for the implementation of this strategy. The strategy proposal should refer to the period from 2025 to 2040, with a projection until 2050.[1297]

1095. The main laws regulating geological exploration and exploitation of mineral raw materials are:

- Law on Mining and Geological Explorations (OJ RS, Nos 101/15, 95/18 – other law, and 40/21).
- Law on Public-Private Partnership and Concessions (OJ RS, Nos 88/11, 15/16 and 104/16).[1298]

1096. The Law on Mining and Geological Explorations regulates measures and activities of the mineral policy and the manner of implementation thereof, conditions and manner of execution of geological explorations of mineral and other geological resources, researching of geological environment, as well as geological explorations for the purpose of spatial and urban planning, designing, construction of buildings and remediation of site, manner of classification of resources and reserves of mineral raw materials and ground waters, exploitations of reserves of mineral raw materials and geothermal resources, construction, use and maintenance of mining facilities, plants, machines and equipment, execution of mining works, mining waste management, remediation and recultivation of abandoned mining

1296. *See*: http://www.parlament.gov.rs/Pedeset_tre%C4%87a_sednica_Odbora_za_industriju_.15090.941.html (19.2.2024). *See* NA. 2011.
1297. At https://www.tanjug.rs/srbija/politika/68081/ministarstvo-rudarstva-i-energetike-raspisalo-je-tender-za-izradu-strategije-o-upravljanju-mineralnim-resursima/vest (19.2.2024).
1298. Energy Law (OJ RS, Nos 145/14 and 95/18 – other law, 40/21, 35/23 – other law, and 62/23) also deserves mentioning. For more details, *see* chapter devoted to 'rational use of energy'.

facilities, as well as inspection over the implementation of the present Law (Article 1). The legal Act is divided into the following chapters: Basic Provisions (Articles 1–10); Mineral policy and development plan of geological explorations and mining industry of the RS (Articles 11–13); Geological institute of the RS (Articles 14 and 15); Geological explorations (Articles 16–82); Investment-Technical documentation for conducting the mining works (Articles 83–125); Licences for performing the specific activities in geological explorations and exploitations (Articles 126–128); Protective measures (Articles 129–143); Other provisions on exploitations (Articles 144–156); Royalties for geological explorations of mineral resources and geothermal resources (Articles 157–160); Cadastre and information system in the field of geological explorations and mining (Articles 161–167); Inspection supervision (Articles 168–176); Penalty provisions (Articles 177–186); and Transitional and final provisions (Articles 187–195).

1097. According to Article 3, geological explorations shall be a complex process and a set of activities comprising the application of adequate methods and technical means, which are performed in order to look into the development, composition and structure of the Earth's crust to find, test and assess the mineral and other geological resources in geological-economic terms, to prospect and determine the reserves of mineral raw materials[1299] and the possibility of their mining, to determine and assess the geological, engineering-geological and hydrogeological properties of the site being explored, particularly from the standpoint of spatial and town planning, design and construction of facilities, and to identify and eliminate the harmful impacts of geological and technogenic processes on geological and living environment, and cultural assets and assets enjoying prior protection (point 12).

1098. Geological explorations can be conducted by the branches of foreign legal entities under conditions and in the manner prescribed by this Law and the law which establishes the rights of foreign persons in respect of the use of assets of the public interest and in accordance with the laws governing the area of defence and the confidentiality of data (Article 22, paragraph 5).

1099. Mineral resources, ground water resources, geothermal resources as well as other geological resources shall be the natural assets in the ownership of the RS, which may be used under the conditions and in the manner set forth by this Law. Mineral resources or mineral raw materials of strategic importance for the RS are: (1) Oil and natural gas; (2) Coal; (3) Copper and gold ore; (4) Lead and zinc ore;

1299. *Mineral raw materials* shall be the concentrations of mineral substances, of the organic and inorganic origin, which may be used cost-effectively at a certain level of technical and technological development, either in their natural form or upon adequate processing. They shall include all types of coal and oil shale (slates), liquid and gaseous hydrocarbons (oil and gas) and other natural gases, radioactive mineral raw materials, metallic mineral raw materials, including precious and rare metals, non-metallic mineral raw materials, including raw materials for the supply of construction materials, precious and semiprecious stones, all types of salts and solvents, groundwater from which useful mineral raw materials are obtained, groundwater related to mining technology and accompanying gases, technogenic mineral raw materials and secondary mineral raw materials (Art. 3, para. 8).

(5) Boron and lithium ore; (6) Oil slates (oil shales or shales); and (7) other mineral resources, as determined by a separate Act of the Serbian Government on a proposal of the Ministry responsible for geological explorations and/or mining (Article 4, paragraphs 1 and 2).[1300]

Mineral policy and development plan of geological explorations and mining is pursued through the implementation strategy for managing the mineral resources and other geological resources of the RS (Article 11, paragraph 3). The Strategy shall be enacted by the NA at the proposal of the Government for a period of a minimum of ten years (Article 12, paragraph 4).[1301]

1100. The Government adopts an action plan and, if necessary, programmes to implement the strategy, upon the proposal of the Ministry (Article 13, paragraph 1).[1302] The action plan for the implementation of the Strategy determines the dynamics of implementing measures for the implementation of the Strategy, following the law governing the planning system (Article 13, paragraph 3).

1101. For the purposes of this Law, geological explorations are basic and applied (Article 16). The basic geological explorations shall be performed by the Institute according to the Long-term Basic Geological Prospecting Development Programme (the Long-Term Programme) and the Annual Basic Geological Explorations Programme (the Annual Programme) (Article 19). The applied geological explorations of mineral and other geological resources are carried out on own and/or other people's land (in private or public property) within the framework of the research area on the basis of Decision on approval for geological explorations issued by the Ministry, at the request of the company, or other legal entities and entrepreneurs (Article 30, paragraph 1). The applied engineering-geological-geotechnical explorations for the needs of construction of the infrastructure facilities (high dams, hydropower plants, thermal power plants, regional roads and railways, oil pipelines, gas pipelines, airports, etc.) of strategic importance for the RS, as well as the engineering-geological-geotechnical explorations for the needs of construction and rehabilitation of the facilities of mining infrastructure shall be performed on the basis of the Decision on approval of geological explorations issued by the Ministry, at the request of a company or other legal entity (Article 30, paragraph 2).

1102. The holder of the research has the right to exclusive use and disposal of geological data and things and documents resulting from applied geological research (reports and studies on the results of geological research and other geological documentation, as well as the core of research wells, samples and analyses

1300. Geological research and exploitation of mineral resources are in the public interest (para. 3). As an exception to para. 3 of this article, if exploitation is carried out in a protected area or an area of an ecological network, the public interest and significance are determined following the law regulating nature protection (para. 4).
1301. The strategy contains elements prescribed by the law regulating the planning system of the Republic of Serbia (para. 2).
1302. Certain special goals established by the Strategy can be developed through programs (para. 2).

from all research works, etc.), following this law (Article 49, paragraph 1).[1303] After the cessation of applied geological research, the RS may use the results of such research in a way that does not endanger the interests of the data owner, respecting the regulations governing data protection, and only in the following cases: defending the country and raising the level of general safety of the population, remediating the consequences of geological hazards (earthquakes, floods, landslides, landslides, etc.), making strategic studies to determine and evaluate the total mineral potential of the geological environment or other geological resources, as well as the needs of spatial planning and other long-term strategic documents of general interest (Article 49, paragraph 3).[1304]

1103. The approval for exploration of hydrocarbons in liquid and gaseous state (oil and gas) and other natural gases shall be given to a company or other legal entity or entrepreneur, selected on the basis of conducting a public tender procedure (Article 54). Decision on conducting a public tender for the exploration of hydrocarbons in liquid and gaseous state (oil and gas) and other natural gases shall be made by the Ministry or the competent provincial authority if the raw material is on the territory of the AP, if it assesses that there is a need for establishing the same mineral raw materials in a certain area or on the basis of a proposal by a company or another legal entity and entrepreneur registered for the exploration of mineral raw materials (Article 55).

1104. The holder of the certificate of reserves and resources can obtain a decision on approval for exploitation and/or exploitation field, following this law (Article 65, paragraph 1). Mining of mineral raw material reserves may also be performed by foreign legal entities under the conditions and in the manner prescribed by this Law and the law setting the rights of foreign persons with respect to utilization of the assets of public interest (Article 65, paragraph 2).

1105. Exploitation of the reserves of mineral resources and exploitation of nonmetallic mineral resources for obtaining the construction materials (hereinafter

1303. The holder of the research is obliged to keep the reports and studies on the results of geological research and other geological documentation in the prescribed manner, as well as the core of exploratory wells and samples and analyses from all exploratory works and to make them available for inspection by the ministry, i.e., the competent body of the autonomous province for checking the research results (para. 2). If the results of geological research and the documents from para. 1 of this article contain information that is considered secret information following the applicable regulations that determine the protection of secret information, the holder of the research may transfer such information to third parties only in the manner and under the conditions established by those regulations (para. 6). If the holder of the research is no longer known or no longer exists and the right of ownership of the results cannot be determined, the ministry responsible for mining and geological research can dispose of the results of geological research as well as documents containing geological results (para. 7).

1304. Mining objects created in the process of geological research that are not registered as the property of the holder of the research are not considered the results of the research from para. 1 of this article and upon completion of the research become the property of the Republic of Serbia and can be used by the holder of the research permit or the holder of the exploitation permit, on which these facilities are located in the exploration or exploitation field (para. 4).

'exploitation') is done on the basis of the decision, which shall issue: (1) approval for exploitation field or approval for exploitation; (2) approval for the construction of mining facilities and/or conducting the mining operations; and (3) approval for the use of mining facilities (Article 68, paragraph 1).

Manual washing of precious metals from alluvial sediments and collecting other minerals from the earth's surface may be granted to a natural person. The holder of approval shall offer the washed quantities of metal to the National Bank of Serbia at market prices, submit the report for washed precious metals and collect other minerals to the Ministry on quantities and places where they are washed or collected (Article 75).

1106. Exploitation of the non-metallic mineral raw materials for obtaining the construction materials and exploitation of mineral resources for obtaining the natural construction materials is carried out on the basis of the decision on approval for exploitation issued by the Ministry, i.e., the competent authority of AP if the exploitation is carried out on the territory of the AP (Article 77, paragraph 1).

1107. The exploitation of reserves and resources of mineral resources is carried out according to the investment-technical documentation for construction of the mining facilities and/or conducting the mining works, exploitation of the non-metallic resources for obtaining the construction materials and exploitation of the mineral resources for obtaining the natural construction materials (Article 83, paragraph 1). For the purposes of this Law, the investment-technical documentation shall mean: (1) pre-feasibility study; (2) feasibility study of mining the deposits of mineral raw materials; (3) long-term mining programme; (4) mining projects; and (5) annual operating plan (Article 84, paragraph 1).

Technical control shall be performed for mining projects from Article 84, paragraph 2, points (1)–(5) of this Law (Article 97, paragraph 1). Technical control includes control of the project in terms of compliance with the law and other regulations in the field of mining, application of modern achievements and methods of the mining profession and science, as well as compliance with valid regulations on safety and health at work, the safety of people and facilities and environmental protection and protection cultural goods and goods that enjoy prior protection, as well as compliance with conditions issued following special regulations on environmental protection, water management, and cultural monuments (paragraph 2).

1108. In order to protect water and the environment, the company shall have to: (1) plan measures that prevent endangering the water regime and environment, or remediation and rehabilitation measures, and ensure implementation of the prescribed measures; (2) keep data on types and quantities of dangerous and harmful matters used in performing its activities, or keep data on types and quantities of dangerous, harmful and waste matters emitted or disposed in the environment; and (3) implement the measures and conditions which prevent endangering the water regimes and environment, contained in the analysis of the activity impact on the environment and water regime in accordance to the special Law (Article 130).

1109. The Minister shall prescribe special measures and the manner of controlling the application of measures for protection against fire and explosions in the underground mining facilities. In other mining facilities, the regulations in force shall be applied in the area of protection against fire and explosion. The Minister shall prescribe special measures and the manner of controlling occupational safety and health measures in performing the works of geological explorations and exploitation of mineral resources. In terms of measures for occupational safety and health, environment protection against fire and explosions and other measures of protection relating to performing the mining works that are not regulated by this Law, the provisions of special regulations shall be applied governing such measures of protection (Article 143).

1110. The holder of exploitation shall, in the course and upon finalization of exploitation works no later than one year from the date of finalization of works in the areas where mining works were completed, carry out reclamation of the land fully in accordance with the technical project of technical and biological reclamation, that is a constituent part of the main or supplementary mining design. The Ministry or competent authority of AP and the Ministry responsible for agriculture and water management or the Ministry shall be notified of measures referred to in paragraph 1 of this Article (Article 153, paragraphs 1 and 2).

1111. The Geological Institute of Serbia (hereinafter 'the Institute'), as a special organization with the status of a legal entity, shall perform the basic geological explorations pursuant to Articles 17 and 18 of this Law and other geological explorations included in the annual programme referred to in Article 20 of this Law, as well as the activities of applied geological explorations of importance for the RS, on the basis of a special decision by the Government on the proposal of Ministry. The Institute shall also perform other activities of interest for the RS, such as: elaboration and printing of geological maps at a scale of 1:25,000 and more detailed and elaboration of specialized and thematic geological maps (metallogenetic or mineralgenetic, geomagnetic, gravimetric, radiogravimetric, geochemical, hydrogeological, engineering-geological, structural-tectonic, seismic, geoecologic, etc.) (Article 14).

1112. Inspection supervision over the application of the provisions of this law and the regulations adopted for its implementation is carried out by the Ministry, through geological and mining inspectors, within the scope established by this law (Article 168, paragraph 1). The AP is entrusted with the inspection supervision referred to in paragraph 1 of this article on the territory of the AP (Article 168, paragraph 2).

1113. Articles 177–186 prescribe three kinds of penalty: criminal offences, corporate (commercial) offences and offences.

1114. The Law on Public-Private Partnership and Concessions (OF RS, Nos 88/11, 15/16 and 104/16),[1305] as well as the corresponding provisions of laws and other regulations governing public property and the budget system, apply to all investments of funds in public property in a joint venture with a private partner solely to implement public-private partnership projects (Article 2, paragraph 1).[1306]

1115. Following sub-legal Acts, *inter alia*, have also been adopted:

(1) Regulation on determining the value of mined mineral raw materials or other geological resources without necessary approvals (OJ RS, No. 83/21).
(2) Regulation on the conditions and procedure for issuing a permit for waste management, as well as criteria, characterization, classification, and reporting on mining waste (OJ RS, No. 53/17).
(3) Decision on the termination of the Geological Institute of Serbia d.o.o. Belgrade (OJ RS, No. 119/13).
(4) Rulebook on establishing the Annual Program of Basic Geological Research for 2023 (OJ RS, No. 39/23).
(5) Rulebook on determining the conditions and working methods of the Commission for verification of resources and reserves of mineral raw materials, underground water, and geothermal resources (OJ RS, Nos 46/22, 21/23).
(6) Rulebook on the content and method of exchanging documents and submissions that are submitted electronically during the implementation of procedures related to administrative procedures conducted within the MME, or the competent provincial body (OJ RS, No. 109/21).
(7) Rulebook on the content and form of the professional supervision diary (OJ RS, No. 74/21).
(8) Rulebook on the content of the Final Report and the Annual Report on the results of geological research (OJ RS, No. 88/19).
(9) Rulebook on conditions, criteria and content of projects for all types of geological research (OJ RS, Nos 45/19, 72/21).
(10) Rulebook on conditions and manner of performing technical control of geological research projects (OJ RS, No. 41/19).
(11) Rulebook on the content, form and manner of submitting the annual operational plan and annual business report (OJ RS, No. 7/19).

1305. The Law regulates, *inter alia*, conditions and method of concession awarding, subject matter of concession, entities competent, i.e., authorized to conduct concession award procedure, termination of concession, protection of rights of the participants in public contract award procedures, form and content of contracts on public-private partnership with or without elements of concession (the public contract) and legal protection in public contract award procedures, conditions and method of drawing up, proposing and approval of public-private partnership projects, specify the entities competent, i.e., authorized to propose and realize the public-private partnership projects, rights and obligations of public and private partners, etc (Art. 1).

1306. The provisions of this law apply to public-private partnerships that are implemented following the special rules of procedure of international organizations, except for the provisions related to the procedure for awarding public contracts (para. 2).

(12) Rulebook on the content of the study on the conditions of exploitation of groundwater or hydrogeothermal resources, i.e., petrogeothermal resources and the conditions and manner of performing technical control of the study (OJ RS, No. 7/18).
(13) Rulebook on the conditions, criteria, content and method of classifying petrogeothermal resources and the method of presentation in the report (OJ RS, No. 7/18).
(14) Rulebook on the form of official identification card, appearance and content of the mark and type of equipment of geological and mining inspectors (OJ RS, Nos 81/13 and 81/15 – other rulebooks).
(15) Rulebook on the content of the feasibility study for the exploitation of mineral raw materials deposits (OJ RS, No. 108/2006).
(16) Rulebook on conditions performing certain professional tasks on exploitation mineral (OJ RS, Nos 40/97 and 32/98).
(17) Rulebook on the method for mining measures performance (OJ RS, No. 40/1997).
(18) Rulebook on conditions and manner of conducting technical review of mining facilities (OJ RS, No. 40/97).
(19) Rulebook on the contents of mining projects (OJ RS, No. 27/97).
(20) Rulebook on the content of the long-term programme for exploitation of mineral raw materials deposits and annual plans for mining works (OJ RS, Nos 27/1997 and 7/19).
(21) Rulebook on the criteria for determination of potentiality of areas concerning mineral raw materials occurrences (OJ RS, No. 51/1996).
(22) Rulebook on the criteria for the award of geological exploration works and of associated funds (OJ RS, No. 51/1996).
(23) Rulebook on the classification and categorization of replenishing solid mineral resources and maintenance of records about them (OJ RS, No. 53/79).
(24) Rulebook on the classification and categorization of groundwater and maintenance of records about them (OJ SFRJ, No. 34/79), etc.[1307]

1116. Priorities for further development in various domains, including the mining sector, are defined in several strategic documents – Energy Development Strategy of the RS until 2025, with projection until 2030, National Strategy for Sustainable Use of Natural Resources and Goods, Mineral Resources Management

1307. The list of these regulations also includes regulations that were adopted based on the previously valid Law on the Uniform Method of Determining, Recording and Collecting Data on Reserves of Mineral Raw Materials and Groundwater and on the Balance of These Reserves (OJ SFRJ, No. 53/77): :1) Rulebook on classification and categorization of oil, condensate, and natural gas reserves and on keeping records about them (OJ RS, No. 80/87); (2) Rulebook on classification and categorization of reserves of solid mineral raw materials and keeping records on them (OJ RS, No. 53/79); (3) Rulebook on the classification and categorization of underground water reserves and record keeping (OJ RS, No. 34/79). These regulations are applied based on authorization from the Law on Mining and Geological Explorations (OJ RS, No. 101/15), until the adoption of regulations based on that law.

Strategy of the RS until 2030, Waste management programme of the RS for the period 2022–2031, National Plan for the Adoption of Acquis for the period 2022–2025, etc.

Part III. Zoning and Land-Use Planning

§1. Introduction

1117. Serbia has a relatively long tradition in legal regulation concerning zoning and land-use planning. Already in the first part of the nineteenth century, there were some Acts enacted regulating this field, for instance, the 1837 Decree on village street planning.

1118. The process of urbanization in Serbia has been quite fast. According to the population census of 1948, percentage of urban population was 20.7%, and in 2002, it reached 56.4% and is still growing.[1308] Urbanization has caused, among other things, environmental problems, especially in large cities, and depopulation of rural areas. The increase in inhabitants has not been followed by adequate measures in different sectors including the environment (air pollution, sewerage, waste management, illegal construction,[1309] etc.), what contributed to the violation of spatial plans and threatened rational use of space. The strategy of sustainable urban development of the RS is being adopted for the first time in the RS in 2019, following the needs of planning the urban space, solving the problems of urban development, and the potential that urban settlements carry as generators of development activities.[1310]

The recent Spatial Plan of the RS 2021–2035 is currently in the draft stage (has passed the procedure of the public insight).[1311] Similar to previous spatial plans of RS (1996 and 2010), 'this plan through planning regions organizes the space of Serbia at the level of urban areas which in perspective should have the role of more even and rational regional development instruments'.[1312]

1308. GOV RS. 2008b, 69.
1309. 'There has been enormous illegal construction which started in the late 1960s, and culminated in the 1990s, under the circumstances of a widespread societal anomie … . Responsible authorities were estimating that the total number of illegal building in Serbia surpassed one million. However, more reliable are estimates pitching at the interval between 400,000 and 500,000 illegal constructions.'Vujošević & Spasić, 2007, 14.
1310. *See* GOV RS. 2019b. Analysing statistical data, it was observed that the development of urban and other settlements in terms of population did not take place gradually or uniformly. The share of the total population living in urban settlements increased: from 44% in 1971, to 59.4% in 2011. *Ibid.*, Ch. 4.1.4.1. Demographic changes in urban settlements.
1311. *See*: https://www.mgsi.gov.rs/lat/dokumenti/javni-uvid-u-nacrt-prostornog-plana-republike-srbije-od-2021-do-2035-godine-i-izvestaj-o (18.2.2024).
1312. Jeftić, et al., 2021, 198.

§2. General Environmental Legislations

1119. The Serbian Constitution regulates spatial planning and land use in several provisions. It prescribes that the NA shall adopt a development plan and spatial plan (Article 99, paragraph 1, point 10). In accordance with Article 183, 'autonomous provinces shall, in accordance with the Law, regulate the matters of provincial interest in … , *inter alia*, urban planning and development … '.

1120. Article 88 prescribes that:

> Utilisation and management of agricultural land, forest land and municipal building land on private assets shall be permitted. The Law may restrict the models of utilisation and management that is stipulate terms of utilisation and management, in order to eliminate the danger of causing damage to environment or prevent violation of rights and legally based interests of other persons.

According to Article 190, point 7, the municipality shall, through its bodies and in accordance with the Law, provide for the protection, improvement and use of agricultural land. Besides that, the Municipal Assembly shall pass general Acts within its competences, *inter alia*, and adopt the development plan and the municipal spatial plan (Article 191).

1121. According to Article 7 of the Law on Ministries (OJ RS, Nos 128/20, 116/22, and 92/23 – other law), the Ministry of Construction, Transport and Infrastructure is the focal point for activities in the field of spatial planning. Several other ministries and institutions also have some competence in this field.

1122. The EPL has a number of provisions concerning spatial planning. Besides the definition provisions, the following Articles should be mentioned: 12, 19, 20, 33–36, 64–66, 68, 74, 81, 105, 120 (point 4) and 124 (point 2).

1123. The following provisions deserve special attention: according to Article 12, sustainable use and protection of natural values shall be provided by, *inter alia*, the Strategy for spatial development of the Republic, besides the National Strategy of Sustainable Use of Natural Resources and Goods. In the same subchapter (devoted to 'planning and utilization of natural values'), Article 19 prescribes that the developing and spatial plan shall determine the construction zones depending on the environmental capacity, the degree of load and objectives of the construction.[1313]

1124. The 'planning and construction' and 'spatial and urban planning' are regulated by Articles 33 and 34. Article 33 prescribes that:

1313. In certain zones, in which protected distance or area have been established, it shall be allowed to carry out the activities in a way determined by special regulations in accordance with natural load of the environment.

spatial planning, use of natural resources and goods established by spatial and urban plans and other plans (plans of spatial arranging and agricultural land basis, forests, water-system, hunting basis and programs of enhancement of fishery in fishing areas as well as other plans) must be regulated by the obligation to (1) preserve and enhance natural resources and goods at greatest possible extent, and if they are not renewable, to use them rationally; (2) ensure protection and smooth realization of functions of protected natural values with their protected environment and to preserve wild plant and animal species habitats and communities at greatest possible extent; (3) ensure preservation of built-up areas; (4) ensure conditions for human relaxation and leisure; (5) establish measures of environmental protection; (6) show existent status following the elements from points 1–4 of this Article and planned status with measures needed for the fulfilment of those plans.[1314]

1125. Article 34 of the EPL prescribes second important authorization for the competent authorities in the environmental. According to this article, 'spatial and urban plans must ensure measures and conditions of environmental protection'[1315] and conditions for this measure will be issued by the Ministry, AP body or self-governance units at request of the authority in charge of plan preparation and its passing in, and on the basis of conditions and measures of competent authorities.

1126. Article 65 of the EPL prescribes adoption of the action plan for advancement of spatial planning and landscaping as an obligation.[1316]

1127. The Law on SEA prescribes that strategic assessment shall be carried out for all plans, programmes and sectoral master-plans in the following fields: town planning, land use, agriculture planning, forestry, fishing industry, hunting, energy, industry, transport, waste management, water management, telecommunications, tourism, preservation of natural habitats and wildlife (flora and fauna). It means that all national plans and programmes, as well as municipal spatial and land-use plans, should undergo an assessment.[1317]

1314. The Ministry, competent authority of the AP or local self-governance unit participates in the procedure of preparation and planning in a way established by law.

1315. These measures and conditions of environmental protection relate, 'in particular: (1) to determination of special regimes for preservation and use of the areas of protected natural goods, water springs, thermal and mineral springs, forests, agricultural land, public green areas, recreation areas and spas; (2) to determination of areas of threatened parts of the environment (polluted areas, areas endangered with erosion and torrents, exploitation of mineral raw materials, flooded areas and so on) and determination of measures for these areas rehabilitation; (3) to determination of measures and conditions of environmental protection according to which space intended to be exploited for minerals shall be utilized, or according to which industrial and energetic plants shall be constructed, as well as facilities for waste treatment and disposal, infrastructure and other facilities whose construction or utilization may threaten the environment'.

1316. Action and rehabilitation plans are prepared by the Ministry in cooperation with other ministries in charge of certain areas (Art. 67, para. 2). The AP and local self-governance units are in charge to adopt local action and rehabilitation plans for their territory and in accordance with the National Programme and plans (Art. 68).

1317. The SEA reports have mostly been issued for spatial and urban plans. In 2005 and 2006, the Directorate for Environmental Protection issued eleven opinions on decisions to develop SEA at the

§3. Legislation on Spatial Organization and Construction

1128. In the field of spatial planning and construction, the following two laws are of key importance.

- Law on Spatial Plan of the Republic of Serbia (OJ RS, No. 88/10).[1318]
- Law on Planning and Building (OJ RS, Nos 72/09, 81/09 – corr., 64/10 – CC, 24/11, 121/12, 42/13 – CC, 50/13 – CC, 98/13 – CC, 132/14, 145/14, 83/18, 31/19, 37/19 – other law, 9/20, 52/21, and 62/23).[1319]

1129. The Law on Spatial Plan of the RS from 2010 to 2020 (OJ RS, No. 88/10) was adopted by the Serbian Parliament at the meeting held on 23 November 2010. The spatial plan sets the long-term basis for organization, development, protection and use of space in Serbia, in order to coordinate the economic and social development of natural, ecological and cultural resources and restrictions on the territory of the RS. In the field of protection and improvement of the quality of environment, strategic priorities until 2014 were continuation and further systematic development of the campaign 'Cleaning Serbia', along with the engagement of all actors and LSGs; rehabilitation of all polluted industrial and mining-energy sites; reduction of air pollution which originates from energy production and other industries; improvement of the quality of surface and underground water; prevention of further deprivation of land and preserving and improving its quality; reducing the level of noise along roads and industries that endanger housing; harmonizing national regulations in the field of environmental protection with EU legislature, along with strengthening institutional capacity; establishing and extending monitoring and further development of an integrated cadastre of polluters; improving public access to information on the quality of environment and developing public awareness; promoting rational use of natural resources and maximum use of secondary raw materials; and reducing emission of polluted materials and introducing cleaner production technologies.

---

national level, two consents on SEA reports and 137 opinions on draft decisions to implement SEA at the local level. The Secretariat for environmental protection of the city of Belgrade has issued eighty-three SEA opinions on draft decisions on SEA and four consents on SEA reports. UNECE. 2007, 25.

1318. The draft spatial plan of the Republic of Serbia was prepared in 2021 (for the period until 2035), but it has not yet been adopted. *See*: https://www.mgsi.gov.rs/sites/default/files/PPRS%20 Nacrt.pdf (24.1.2024).

1319. The latest amendments to the Law (2023) refer, *inter alia*, to the following issues: Green Building Incentives, Incentives for Green Building Certification, Waste Management Requirements for Building Permits, Energy Passport at Notary Offices, Studies for Cultural Heritage Protection, Abolishing Land Conversion, Introduction of Chief State Urbanist, Conditions Outside Unified Procedure, Permit Choice for Large Projects, Reinstating the Engineering Chamber's Authority, etc.

I. The Law on Planning and Building

1130. The Law consists of the following chapters: I Basic provisions (Articles 1–9); II Spatial and urban planning (Articles 10–70); III Spatial Planning Agency of the Republic (Articles 71–81); IV Buildable land (Articles 82–109); V Construction of facilities (Articles 110–132); VI Building permit (Articles 133–147); VII Construction (Articles 148–153); VIII Usage permit (Articles 154–160); IX Professional exam and licenses for the responsible planner, the urban planner, the designer and contractor (Articles 161 and 162); X Engineering Chamber of Serbia (Articles 163–166); XI Removal of facilities (Articles 167–171); XII Supervision (Articles 172–184); XIII Legalization of facilities (Articles 185–200); XIV Authorization for introducing by-laws (Article 201); XV Penalty provisions (Articles 202–212); and XVI Transitional and final provisions (Articles 213–223).

1131. The Law regulates the conditions and modalities of spatial planning and development; the development and use of buildable land and the construction of facilities; carrying out supervision over the application of this Law and supervisory inspections; other issues of significance in the development of space, landscaping and use of buildable land, and the construction of facilities (Article 1, paragraph 1).[1320]

II. Principles of Development and Use of Space

1132. Pursuant to Article 3 of the Law the development and use of space is based on several principles including the following: (1) sustainable development through an integrated approach to the planning; (2) balanced territorial development; (3) rational use of soil encouraging measures urban and rural renovation and reconstruction; (4) rational and sustainable utilization of non-renewable resources and the optimal use of the renewable resources; (5) protection and sustainable use of natural resources and immovable cultural assets; (6) Prevention of technical and technological accidents, fire and explosion protection from the elements, eliminating the causes for climate changes; (7) planning and development of space for defence purposes; (8) compliance with European regulations and standards in the field of spatial planning; (9) improvement and use of information technologies that contribute to better efficiency and effectiveness of public administration in the construction business; (10) public participation; (11) preservation of customs and traditions; (12) the preservation of specificity of the compartment; and (13) horizontal and vertical coordination.[1321]

1320. The provisions of this Law do not apply to the construction of facilities which, in terms of the Law governing affairs of defence, are considered military facilities, as well as the construction of facilities which in terms of the Law governing mining are considered as mining facilities, plants and equipment (Art. 1, para. 2).

1321. It should be noticed that the Law does not contain explanations of the meaning of these principles. Therefore, it is not quite clear what elements they comprise and what are their real consequences.

1133. The latest amendments to the Law (2023) introduce the concept of green infrastructure (Article 3, paragraph 5).[1322] In addition, a green building certificate is introduced. A green building certificate shall be obtained with the aim of reducing greenhouse gas emissions, using ecologically certified building materials and equipment, reducing waste production, and using RES, for all new buildings over 10,000 m2 gross building area, upon issuance of occupancy permit (paragraph 6).[1323] Facilities must be designed, built, and maintained in such a way that the use of natural resources is sustainable, and in particular that: (1) it is possible to reuse or recycle the building, parts of the building, or construction material after removal and (2) use environmentally friendly raw materials or secondary materials in buildings (Article 3a, paragraph 2).

III. Energy Properties of Facilities

1134. In accordance with Article 4, improving energy efficiency means reducing consumption of all types of energy, reducing energy savings and ensuring sustainable construction by applying technical measures, standards, and requirements for planning, design, construction and use of buildings and spaces.[1324] The building in which the functioning involves consumption of energy must be designed, built, used and maintained in a manner that provides the prescribed energy performance of buildings (Article 4, paragraphs 1–2).[1325]

IV. Documents of Spatial and Urban Planning

1135. Documents of spatial and urban planning are as follows: (1) Planning Documents;[1326] (2) Documents for the Implementation of Spatial Plans;[1327] (3)

1322. Green infrastructure shall be a strategically planned network of functionally connected natural and near-natural elements, the design, construction, use, and maintenance of which is carried out in a way that provides ecological, economic, and social benefits through natural, biodiversity-based solutions.
1323. At the proposal of the ministry responsible for construction, the government adopts measures to encourage green construction of the existing national building fund (Art. 3, para. 7).
1324. Energy properties of facilities are consumed or calculated amount of energy to meet the different needs related to the standardized use relate in particular to energy for heating, hot water, cooling, ventilation and lighting. Energy properties certificates shall be determined by the release of the Energy Properties of Facility issued by an authorized organization that meets the requirements for certification of energy performance of buildings. The fulfilment of the conditions shall be determined by special decision of the Minister in charge for construction affairs (Art. 4, paras 3–4 and 6).
1325. The government, at the proposal of the ministry in charge of construction, adopts a Long-term strategy for encouraging investment in the renovation of the national building fund, as well as the National methodology for calculating the energy characteristics of buildings (Art. 4, para. 15).
1326. Planning documents are Spatial and Urban Plans. Spatial plans are as follows: (1) Spatial Plan of the Republic of Serbia; (2) Regional Spatial Plan; (3) Spatial Plan of the unit of local administration; and (4) Spatial Plan of the region of special use. Urban plans are as follows: (1) General Urban Plan; (2) General Regulation Plan; and (3) Detailed Regulation Plan (Art. 11).

Urban Technical Plans;[1328] (4) Sustainable Urban Development Strategy of the RS; and (5) National Architectural Strategy (Article 10).

1136. Documents of spatial and urban planning must be reconciled, so that documents of a smaller region are in compliance with documents of wider region (Article 33, paragraph 1).[1329]

V. Content of the Planning Documents

1137. Relevant Planning documents have to contain environmental protection measures. The Law prescribes that environmental protection measures and SEA are an integral part of following planning documents: the Spatial Plan of the RS (Article 15, paragraph 1, point 10[1330] and paragraph 2); the Regional Spatial Plan (Article 18, paragraph 1, point 12 and paragraph 2); the Spatial Plan of LSG units (Article 20, paragraph 2); and the Spatial Plan for a Special Purpose Area (Article 22, paragraph 1, point 13 and paragraph 2). Integral parts of the spatial plan for special purpose, spatial plan of the LSG unit and urban plans are: (1) the rules of organization; (2) the rules of construction; and (3) the graphical part (Article 29).

1138. Planning rules contained in the land-use plan of special purpose, spatial plan of the local government and urban plans include, in particular, conditions and measures for the protection of natural resources and immovable cultural property and the protection of natural and cultural heritage, the environment and human life and the health; and building energy efficiency measures (Article 30, paragraph 1, points 4 and 7).[1331]

1327. Implementation programmes of spatial plans are as follows: (1) Implementation programme for the Spatial Plan of the Republic of Serbia; and (2) Implementation programme for the Regional Spatial Plan (Art. 12).

1328. Urban and technical documents for the implementation of planning documents are as follows: (1) urban design project; (2) design project of reallotment and allotment; and (3) design project of correction of borders of adjoining lots and merge two adjacent allotments of the same owner (Art. 13).

1329. Planning documents must be in compliance with the Spatial Plan of the Republic of Serbia. Urban plans must be in compliance with spatial plans (Art. 33, para. 2).

1330. Apart from the following: (1) starting points for the production of the plan; (2) assessment of the existing situation; (3) goals and principles of spatial planning; (4) principles and proposals for the protection, landscaping and development of nature and natural systems; (5) spatial development and distribution of the population; (6) networks of settlements and public services; (7) spatial development of traffic and infrastructural systems of significance for the Republic of Serbia; (8) concept and proposals for spatial development of industry; (9) measures of protection, landscaping and improving natural and cultural property; (11) definition of inter-regional and intra-regional functional networks; (12) planned entities of common spatial and developmental characteristics, for which spatial plans of a lower order will be drawn up; (13) measures for the implementation of Spatial Plan; and (14) long-term developmental strategies of the Republic of Serbia. Report on SEA is an integral part of the documentation basis of the planning document (Art. 15).

1331. Reconstruction shall be understood to mean the execution of construction and other works on an existing facility in unchanged size and volume affecting the fulfilment of the basic requirements

1139. The graphic part[1332] of the spatial plan shows solutions in accordance with the contents of the plan.

VI. Procedure for Adoption of Planning Documents

1140. According to Article 46, the decision[1333] to draw up a planning document is brought by the organ authorized to pass it, upon prior securing of the opinion of the organ responsible for professional control, that is, the committee for plans. Competencies for drawing up planning documents are regulated by Article 35. A holder of the drafting of a planning document during the early public inspection submits to the competent authorities, special organizations and holders of public authorizations, which in accordance with this Act and special regulations determine the conditions for planning and spatial development, the requests for issuing these conditions (Article 47b, paragraph 1).[1334]

1141. The presentation of the planning document for public insight is made after the professional verification is completed (Article 49). The presentation of the planning document for public insight is announced in daily and local newspapers and lasts thirty days from the date of announcement (Article 50, paragraph 1).[1335] The presentation of the planning document for public insight is overseen by the Ministry responsible for spatial planning affairs, that is, the organ of the unit of local administration with jurisdiction over affairs of spatial and urban planning (Article 50, paragraph 1).[1336]

---

for the facility, changing the technological process; changing the outside appearance of the facility, or increasing the number of functional units; replacing devices, plant, equipment, and installation with increased capacity (Art. 2, point 61).

1332. Graphic part of the Spatial Plan is made on topographic maps (Art. 32, para. 2).

1333. Prior to rendering of a decision on drawing up a planning document, the holder of the plan preparation obtains an opinion of the authority competent for tasks of environmental protection on the need for preparation of the SEA (para. 6). In addition, before deciding on the preparation of the planning document, the holder of the plan obtains the opinion of the organization for the protection of immovable cultural property on the need to prepare a study on the protection of immovable cultural property (para. 7). The decision to go forward is announced in the appropriate official newspaper, and the Central Registry of Planning Documents.

1334. The competent authority, a special organization, i.e., holder of public authority, is obliged to act upon the request referred to in para. 1 of this Article, within fifteen days from the day of receipt of the request. Exceptionally, it can also act within thirty days from the day of receipt of the request, with an explanation of the competent authority, i.e., organization for failure to act within the stated time limit (para. 2).

1335. Planning documents with their supplements must be accessible to the public at the premises of the entity which passed them, except a specific annex referring to special preparatory measures of territory for defence purposes (Art. 41).

1336. The responsible organ, i.e., the committee for plans, writes a report on the completed public insight into the planning document, which includes data on the completed public insight, with all remarks and decisions for each remark. The report from para. 3 of this Article is submitted to the bearer of the preparation of the planning document, who is obliged to act on the decisions included in para. 3 of this Article within thirty days from the day of delivery of the report (Art. 50, paras 3 and 4).

VII. Location Permit

1142. Articles 53a–57 regulate location permit's relevant issues. Pursuant to Article 53a, location permits are issued for facilities for which building permits are issued by this Law, as well as for the objects that are connected to the utility and other infrastructure and which fulfil all the conditions and data required for preparing the technical documents, in compliance with the valid planning document.[1337] The location permit for facilities from Article 133 of this Law is issued by the Ministry with jurisdiction over affairs of urbanism, that is, by the AP (Article 53a, paragraph 4).[1338] The location permit for facilities not determined in Article 133 of this Law is issued by the authorized organ of the unit of local administration (Article 53a, paragraph 5).

1337. A location permit can also anticipate building in stages (Art. 53a, para. 7).

1338. In accordance with Art. 133 of the Law the building permit for the construction of a facility is issued by the ministry authorized for the tasks in construction (Ministry), unless otherwise determined by this Law. The Ministry issues the building permit for facilities as follows: (1) high dams and accumulations filled with water, waste and ashes for which is prescribed technical surveillance; (2) nuclear and other facilities which are used for the production of nuclear power, radio isotopes, radiation, storage of radioactive waste materials for scientific research purposes; (3) facilities for processing crude oil and gas, international and pole delivery lines, gas and crude oil pipelines for transport, gas pipelines of nominal working pressure of over sixteen bar, if they cross over at least two municipalities, storage of crude oil, gas and crude oil derivatives with capacity over 500 tons; (4) facilities for the basic chemical and manufacturing industries, black and non-ferrous metallurgy, facilities for the treatment of rubber, facilities for the production of cellulose and paper, and facilities for the processing of non-metal mineral raw materials, except facilities for the primary processing of decorative and precious stones; (4a) seveso plants and seveso complex; (5) stadiums for 20,000 or more viewers, facilities of construction range of 50 m or more, facilities of height of 50 m or more, silos with capacity over 20,000 m^3, facilities of penal and correctional institutions, etc.; (6) thermoelectric power stations of power 10 and more MW and thermoelectric power stations and heating stations of power 10 and more MW and power lines and transformer stations of 110 and more kV; (7) inter-regional and regional facilities for water supply and sewage, drinking water production plants of capacity over 200 l/s and plants for the purification of waste water capacity over 200 l/s; (8) regulation jobs for the protection of city and rural areas greater than 300 ha from floods; (9) facilities within the boundaries of immovable cultural property of exceptional importance and cultural property registered at the UNESCO list of World Cultural and Natural Heritage, facilities in the protected surroundings of cultural property of great importance to certain borders of land plots and buildings in the protected surroundings of cultural assets registered in the UNESCO list of World Cultural and Natural Heritage, facilities in the protected areas in accordance with the Act on the protection of cultural property (except the transformation of common premises into a flat or business premises in the protected surroundings of cultural property of outstanding significance and cultural assets registered in the world heritage list), as well as facilities within national parks and facilities within the boundaries of protected natural goods of great importance (except for family houses, agricultural and economic facilities and their infrastructure facilities that are being built in the villages), in accordance with the Law; 9a) facilities within the boundaries of the protected natural area of the first and second category declared by the Government act, in the sense of the provisions of the law governing the protection of nature (except for family residential buildings, agricultural and economic buildings, with associated infrastructure, which are built in villages); (10) plants for the treatment of non-dangerous waste by incineration or chemical treatment, capacity of more than 70 tons per day; (11) plant for the treatment of hazardous waste by incineration, thermal and/or physical, physicochemical and chemical treatments, as well as the central storage and/or landfill for hazardous waste disposal; (12) airports intended for public air transport; (13) passenger ports, harbours, landing places and marines – I category; (14) State-owned roads of the first and second class, travelling facilities and

1143. Before submitting a request for issuing a location permit, a buildable lot is formed in compliance with this Law, except in cases anticipated in Article 69, paragraphs 1, 3, 5 and 6 of this Law (Article 54, paragraph 10).[1339]

1144. Location permit for facilities referred to in Article 133 of this Law is issued by the Ministry in charge of urban planning or a competent authority of the AP of the facilities referred to in Article 134 of this Law.[1340] Location permit for

---

traffic connections to these roads and border crossings; (15) public railroad infrastructure with connections and the underground railway; (16) telecommunication facilities and network, systems or resources which are of international or trunk importance and those which are being constructed on the territory of two or more municipalities; (17) hydroconstruction facilities on waterways; (18) waterway canals and ship locks which are not part of the hydro-energy system; (19) regional dumps and dumps for the storage of non-dangerous waste for zones with over 200,000 inhabitants; (20) facilities for the production of energy out of renewable sources with power of 10 or more MW; (21) facilities intended for the production of weapons and military equipment in the sense of the law regulating the field of production of weapons and military equipment, as well as facilities for the production and storage of explosive materials; (22) facilities for health care that have accommodation capacities of over 500 beds; (23) facilities built on the territory of two or more units of local self-government; (24) facilities for the storage of state commodity reserves; and 25) scientific and research campuses.

1339. Article 69 relates to the 'separate cases of construction lot formation'. For construction or building of electro-energy and telecommunication facilities or appliances a construction lot of area with different size or location than the one prescribed by the planning document for this zone can be formed on condition that there is access to the facility or appliances for the purpose of maintenance and removal of defects or damage (para. 1). When provisions about formation of construction lots prescribed by this Law do not apply for construction of pole transformer stations 10/04 kV and 20/04 kV (para. 2). If the overhead line infrastructural facility covers the territory of two or more cadastral municipalities, prior to issuing the occupancy permit, forming one or more building lots, so that a building plot represents the sum of the parts of individual cadastral parcels within the cadastral boundaries of municipalities, except in the case as evidence of resolved property-legal relations in the process of issuing building permits filed an objection about the right, in accordance with this Law (para. 5). If the overland line infrastructural facility covers the territories before issue of the usage permit one or more construction lots are formed so that one construction lot represents the sum of parts of separate land registry lots within the borders of the land registry municipality, except in the case when as proof of resolved ownership and legal relations during the procedure of issue of location and building permits was used, the contract about the right of usage, in accordance with this Law (para. 6).

1340. The building permit is issued to the investor. Together with the request for issuing of a building permit must be submitted the project for building permit. The investor must have the appropriate rights to the land or premises, and it needs to submit the evidence required by Law that regulates the specific content and method of issuing the building permit and paid the corresponding administrative fees. An integral part of the application is a copy of the project for issuing of the building permit signed and stamped with personal licence stamp by the chief designer (Art. 135, para. 1). For the construction of line infrastructural facilities, proof of appropriate Law serves as the legally binding or final decision about expropriation concluding a contract on the right of easement in accordance with this Law and concluding a lease agreement on the land in private ownership, as well as other evidence set forth in Art. 69 of this Law. For the construction or performance of work on construction land or facility owned by more than one person, as proof of proper Law, it is also necessary to enclose the certified agreement of these persons, while if or of adding floors to a residential building, it is also necessary to enclose the contract concluded in accordance with a separate Law. For the construction of energy facilities, prior to the issuance of the construction permit, it is also necessary to enclose the energy permit in accordance with a separate Law (Art. 135, paras 4, 6 and 9).

facilities that are not specified in Articles 133 and 134 of this Law will be issued by the competent authority of the LSG unit. Together with a request for the issuance of location permit shall be submitted the conceptual design of the future building or part thereof (sketch, drawing, graphic, etc.) (Article 53a, paragraphs 4–6). If a planning document, or separate document, does not contain possibilities, limitations and conditions for the construction of buildings, and all the conditions for accession to the utility, transport and other infrastructure, the competent authority that conditions shall obtain ex officio, at the expense of the applicant in amount of actual costs of issuance. Holders of public authority shall make such requirements at the request of the competent authority within a period of fifteen days from the date of receipt of the request (Article 54, paragraph 1).

1145. Location conditions contain all the urban, technical and other conditions and data necessary for the preparation of idea project, project for a building permit and the project for execution (Article 55).[1341] The competent authority shall issue the location conditions within five working days of obtaining all necessary conditions and other data from the holder of public authority (Article 56, paragraph 1).

1146. The location permit is issued on the basis of the spatial plan of an area of special purposes and the spatial plan of a unit of local administration, for parts of the territory within the catchment area of the plan for which no preparation of an urban plan is anticipated; on the basis of the general regulation plan, for parts of the territory within the catchment area of the plan for which no preparation of a detailed regulation plan is anticipated; and on the basis of the detailed regulation plan (Article 57, paragraphs 1–3).[1342]

VIII. Buildable Land

1147. Buildable land can be held in all forms of ownership (Article 84, paragraph 1).[1343] Buildable land is marketable. The right of ownership of buildable land

1341. This includes *inter alia*, data on whether, in connection with the construction of the facility or the execution of works following the issued location conditions, it is necessary to initiate the procedure of obtaining consent for the EIA study or the decision that the preparation of this study is not necessary, and which the competent authority obtains through a unified procedure from the ministry responsible for environmental affairs (Art. 55, point 4a).

1342. If the planning documents anticipate the preparation of an urban plan or the urban project is made at request of the investor, the location permit is issued on the basis of that planning document and the urban design project. The conditions of the holder of public authority, contained in the valid planning document (and obtained in the process of creating and confirming the urban project), are at the same time the conditions used when issuing location conditions if a confirmed urban project is submitted (Art. 57, para. 4).

1343. Buildable land is a land designated by Law and planning documents for the construction and use of buildings, as well as land on which buildings are constructed in accordance to the Law (Art. 82).

in public ownership[1344] can be held by the RS, the AP, that is, a unit of local administration (Article 84, paragraph 2).

1148. Pursuant to Article 87, buildable land can be: (1) developed and undeveloped (built and unbuilt); and (2) arranged and unarranged.

IX. Construction of Facilities

1149. In the part related to the construction of facilities,[1345] the Law in Article 112 prescribes that previous work, depending on the type and characteristics of the facility, comprises conditions for fire protection and the protection of the *environment* as well as the investigation and preparation of analyses and projects, and other expert material; procurement of information which analyse and elaborate geological engineering, technical, hydrological, meteorological, urban, technical, technological, economic, energy, seismic, water supply and traffic conditions; and other conditions which affect the construction and use of a certain facility.

X. Previous Feasibility Study

1150. The previous feasibility study enables the determination especially of the spatial, *ecological,* social financial, market and economic justification of the investment for various solutions defined by the general project, based on which the planning document is prepared and the decision made on the feasibility of investing into previous work for the preliminary design and feasibility study (Article 113, paragraph 1). The previous feasibility study contains the general project referred to in Article 117 of this Law (Article 113, paragraph 2).

XI. Feasibility Study

1151. The feasibility study particularly determines the spatial, *ecological*, social, financial, market and economic justification of the investment into the chosen solution, elaborated by the preliminary design, based on which the feasibility of the investment is decided (Article 114, paragraph 1). The feasibility study contains the preliminary design referred to in Article 118 of this Law (Article 114, paragraph 2).

1344. Buildable land in public ownership is marketable, under conditions set forth in this and other Laws (Art. 85, paras 1 and 2).

1345. 'Construction of the facility' is the sum of operations which include the following: preliminary works, the production and control of the technical documents, preparatory works for construction, the construction of the facility and professional supervision during the construction of facility (Art. 2, point 30). The construction of facilities is carried out based on the building permit and technical documentation, under the conditions and in the way which is determined by this Law (Art. 110).

XII. The General Project

1152. The general project contains particularly the data about the macro location of the facility, general disposition of the facility, technical and technological concept of the facility, the method of providing the infrastructure, the possible options for the spatial and technical solutions, from the point of fitting into the space, the natural conditions, the EIA, geological engineering and technical characteristics of the land from the aspect of determining the general concept and justifiability construction of the facility, investigation work made for the preparation of preliminary project, the protection of natural and immovable cultural property, and the functionality and rationality of the project (Article 117).

XIII. The Preliminary Project and Preliminary Design

1153. The preliminary design is made for the purpose of obtaining location requirements and can be part of the urban project for the needs of urban-architectural elaboration of location (Article 117a). The preliminary project is made for the construction of facilities and performing works from Article 145 of this Law, as well as for facilities referred to in Article 133 of this Law, when subject to professional scrutiny by the review committee (Article 118).[1346]

XIV. Technical Inspection

1154. The technical inspection of the main project can be performed by a company, other legal entity or contractor which fulfils the conditions for the preparation of technical documentation prescribed by the Law and determined by the investor (Article 129, paragraph 2).[1347]

1155. The technical inspection of the main project specially comprises the control of compatibility with all the conditions and regulations contained in the location permit, with the Law and other regulations, with the technical norms, standards and quality norms, as well as with all parts of the technical documentation; compatibility of the project with the results of the previous studies; assessment of the appropriate soil for founding of the facility; check the validity and accuracy of the technical and technological solutions and the construction solution of the facility;

1346. The project for the building permit is made for the purpose of obtaining the decision on the building permit (Art. 118a, para. 1). The project for execution is to be prepared for the purpose of execution of the works on the building (Art. 123, para. 1). The project of built facility is prepared for the purposes of obtaining of use permit, use and maintenance of the facility. The project of the built facility is to be prepared for all objects for which building permit is to be obtained, according to the provisions of this Law (Art. 124, paras 1 and 2).

1347. The technical inspection of the main project cannot be performed by the authorized designer who prepared the project, or who is employed in the company which prepared the project, or in the company which is the investor (Art. 129, para. 3).

stability and safety; rationality of the project materials; effect on the *environment* and adjacent facilities (Article 129, paragraph 4).

XV. Review of the Project

1156. The general project and the preliminary project, the previous feasibility study and the feasibility study for facilities referred to in Article 133 of this Law are subject to review (professional inspection) by a commission formed by the minister authorized for tasks in construction (review commission) (Article 131, paragraph 1).[1348]

XVI. Building Permit

1157. According to Article 133, the building permit for the construction of a facility is issued by the ministry authorized for the tasks in construction (Ministry), if it is not otherwise determined by this Law.[1349] The issue of the building permit is entrusted to the AP for the construction of facilities determined by Article 133 of this Law, which is completely built on the territory of AP. The issue of the building permit is entrusted to the local government units for the construction of facilities which are not determined in Article 133 of this Law (Article 134).[1350] The building permit shall lapse if the construction of the facility, or execution of the work, is not started within three years from the validity date of the decision by which the building permit was issued, i.e., within three years from the date of the decision to amend the decision on the building permit (Article 140).[1351]

1348. The professional inspection is concerned with the concept of the facility, particularly from the aspect of adequacy of the location in view of the type and use of the facility; the conditions for construction of the facility in view of the application of measures for the protection of the *environment*; the seismic, geological and technical, traffic and other conditions; the provision of energy conditions in comparison with the type of planned energy sources; the technical and technological properties of the facility; the technical, technological and organizational solutions for construction of the facility; updatedness of the technical solutions and compatibility with the development programs in this field, as well as other prescribed conditions for the construction of the facility (Art. 132, para. 1).

1349. *See* explanations for 'location permit' (Arts 53a–57).

1350. Appeals on the decision about the building permit issued by the LSG unit are solved by the ministry authorized for tasks in construction. The AP is entrusted with the solution of appeals against the first-degree decision about the building permit issued by the LSG unit, made for the construction of facilities which are built on the territory of the AP. The city of Belgrade is entrusted with the solution of appeals against the first-degree decision for the building permit issued for construction or reconstruction of facilities up to 800 m^2 of gross developed construction area and the first instance decision on the approval of the works referred to in Art. 145 of this Law, on the territory of the city of Belgrade (Art. 139, paras 1–3).

1351. In December 2023, the number of 2,510 building permits was issued, presenting a decrease of 2.0% when compared to December 2022. Out of the total number of permits issued in December 2023, 83.9% related to buildings, and 16.1% to civil engineering constructions. STAT. OFFICE RS. 2024b.

XVII. Construction of Facilities and Execution of Work for Which the Building Permit Is Not Issued

1158. A special type of facilities may be built, i.e., certain works carried out even without obtaining the decision of the competent authority, in accordance with the special regulation referred to in Article 201, paragraph 7, item 13a) of this Act (Article 144).[1352]

1159. Upon the request of the investor for the construction of certain types of facilities, i.e., the execution of certain works that are more precisely determined by the regulation referred to in Article 201, paragraph 7, item 13a) of this Act, the authority in charge of issuing the building permit issues a decree to approve the execution of works (Article 145, paragraph 1).[1353] The competent authority renders a decree upon the request referred to in paragraph 1 of this Article within five working days from the day of submission of the request (paragraph 6).[1354]

XVIII. Temporary Building Permit

1160. The temporary building permit is issued, *inter alia*, for the construction of: asphalt plants, aggregate separators, concrete factories; independent anchored meteorological anemometric poles as well as poles for other purposes; temporary roads and connectors, connectors to the utility network for the needs of the construction or operation of facilities; temporary roads, as well as for performance of exploration work on the location, for the purpose of determining special conditions for the preparation of the main project and for the removal of existing installations, etc. (Article 147, paragraph 1).

1161. Depending on the type of facility and works, the temporary building permit is issued for the precisely determined period in which the facility can be used

---

1352. The minister prescribes in more detail: A special type of facilities and a special type of works for which it is not necessary to obtain a decision of the competent authority, as well as the type of facilities being built, i.e., the type of work being carried out, based on the decision on the approval, as well as the scope and content and control of the technical documentation enclosed with the request and the procedure carried out by the competent authority (Arts. 144 and 145), (Art. 201, para. 7, item 13a).

1353. The requests for issuing a decree on approval to execute works on the facilities, i.e., areas referred to in Art. 2, items 24), 24a), 24c and 24d) of this Law, public drinking fountains and fountains, as well as for the investment maintenance and adaptation of facilities *within the boundaries of the national park* and *facilities within the boundaries of protection of protected natural assets of exceptional importance*, as well as for carrying out works on investment maintenance and adaptation *in the protected environment of cultural assets of exceptional significance and cultural assets registered in the List of World Cultural Heritage*, are decided by the competent authority of the local self-government unit in whose territory the actual facility is located (Art. 145, para. 4).

1354. The setting up and removal of smaller temporary pre-fabricated facilities on public purpose areas (booths, summer and winter gardens, stalls and other moveable furniture), bubble halls for sport, shelters for people in public transport, facilities for depositing and separation of river aggregates and floating plants on wetlands, is provided by and managed by the local government unit (Art. 146, para. 1).

or the works carried out, and it cannot be longer than three years from the date of the decision about the temporary building permit (Article 147, paragraph 7).[1355] At the investor's request, the decree on temporary building permit may be extended once for another three years (paragraph 11).

XIX. Usage Permit

1162. The suitability of the building for use is determined by the technical inspection (Article 154, paragraph 1).[1356] In performing the technical inspection, for facilities for which a study was made about the effect on the *environment*, a person who is an expert in the field which is the subject of the study and who has acquired the academic diploma of master in the appropriate profession, on the second degree studies, on the specialized academic studies, or on the basic studies for the duration of at least five years must participate (Article 156, paragraph 2).[1357]

1163. The facility can be used after previously obtaining the usage permit (Article 158, paragraph 1).[1358] The organ authorized for issuing the building permit issues, by decision, will issue the usage permit, within five days from the date of submission of the application for issuance of usage permits (Article 158, paragraph 2).[1359] The usage permit is issued for the whole facility or part of a facility which represents a technical

1355. In case the investor himself does not remove the temporary facility in the determined term, the authority which made the decision about the temporary building permit, will ex officio, submit a request to the construction inspection for the removal. The appeal to the decision of the construction inspector does not delay execution of the decision (Art. 147, paras 7 and 8).

1356. Technical inspection of the facility shall be made upon completion of the facility, or part thereof, which represents a technical-technological unity and can as such be used independently, in accordance to this Law. Technical inspection may be conducted in parallel with the execution of the works (Art. 154, paras 2 and 3).

1357. In performing the technical inspection persons who cannot participate are those who are employed in the company or other legal entity who has prepared the technical documentation, or was the contractor with the investor, persons who have participated in the preparation of the technical documentation and the study about the effect on the environment, or in execution of the work with the investor, persons who performed the professional supervision, persons who are performing inspection supervision, as well as persons who work on the job of issuing building permits in the agency authorized for issuing building permits (Art. 156, para. 3).

1358. The usage permit is issued when it is determined that the facility, or part of it, is suitable for use. The usage permit contains the warranty period for the facility and certain types of work determined by special regulation (Art. 158, paras 4 and 5).

1359. The authority responsible for issuing the building permit shall issue a permit for use within five working days from the date of submission of the application for the issuance of the use permit (Art. 158, para. 2). An appeal can be made to the decision mentioned in para. 2 of this Article within eight days from the date of delivery. When the decision is made by the ministry authorized for tasks in construction, or the agency of the AP, then appeal cannot be made to the decision mentioned in para. 2 of this Article, but it is possible to start a lawsuit within thirty days from the delivery date (Art. 158, paras 8 and 9).

and technological unity and can, as such, be used independently (Article 158, paragraph 4).[1360]

1164. If, for the purpose of determining the suitability of the facility for use, it is necessary to carry out previous examinations and inspection of the installations, appliances, plants, stability and safety of the facility, appliances and plants for the protection of the *environment*, appliances for protection against fire, or other examinations, or if it is prescribed by the technical documentation, the commission for the technical examination, a company or other legal entity which is entrusted to carry out the technical examination can propose to the authorized organ to allow the trial operation of the facility, if they determine that conditions are fulfilled for it and shall immediately inform the competent authority on it (Article 157, paragraph 1).[1361]

XX. Permit for the Removal of Facility

1165. Removal of a facility or part thereof, except in the case of execution of a decision by the inspection, can be carried out only based on the permission for the removal of the facility or part thereof (Article 168, paragraph 1).[1362] Together with the request for permission for the removal of the facility, or part thereof, it is also necessary to submit: (1) the main project for the removal with technical inspection; (2) proof of ownership of the facility; (3) special conditions, in case of a facility whose removal would endanger the public interest (protection of existing and other infrastructure, protection of cultural goods, protection of *the environment*, etc.) (Article 168, paragraph 2).

1166. The permission for the removal of the facility, or part thereof, is issued within eight days from submission of adequate documentation (Article 168, paragraph 3).[1363]

1360. The owner of the facility for which is issued the usage permit enables execution of work on capital and current maintenance of the facility, as well as the regular, exceptional and specialized examinations of the facility, in accordance with separate regulations (Art. 159).

1361. Trial operation cannot last more than one year. It is the responsibility of investors to monitor the results of the trial operation (Art. 157, para. 2).

1362. A body of the local government unit responsible for construction will approve, by decision, ex officio, or upon request by an interested party, the removal of a facility, or a part thereof, when it is determined that its stability is endangered due to deterioration or major damage and that it represents imminent threat to the life and health of people, nearby facilities and safety in traffic (Art. 167, para. 1).

1363. An appeal can be submitted against the resolution referred to in para. 3 of this Article within fifteen days from delivery of the resolution. When the resolution is issued by the ministry responsible for construction, or the appropriate body of the AP, an appeal cannot be submitted, but an administrative dispute can be started by filing a lawsuit within thirty days from the delivery of the resolution (Art. 168, paras 4 and 5).

XXI. Rights and Duties of the Building Inspector

1167. Pursuant to Article 175, the building inspector has the right and duty to check, *inter alia*, 'whether the contractor has undertaken the necessary measures for the safety of the facility, the surrounding facilities, traffic and the *environment*;' (Article 175, paragraph 1, point 7).[1364]

1168. It is the duty of the building inspector to provide expert assistance in fulfilling the entrusted jobs in the field of inspection and to give expert explanations and opinions, as well as to participate in the inspection when necessary. When the building inspector during inspection determines that during construction, measures were not taken for the safety of the facility, the traffic, the surroundings and for the protection of the *environment*, he/she will order the investor or contractor to remove noted deficiencies, set the term for compliance, as well as suspend further work until these measures are performed, under threat of forced execution which will be charged to the investor or contractor (Article 177, paragraph 1, point 1). If the building inspector during inspection determines that use of the facility represents a threat to the life and health of people, the safety of neighbouring facilities, or the surroundings, or is a threat to the *environment*, he/she will order that necessary work is done, or he/she will forbid the use of the facility, or part thereof (Article 178, paragraph 1, point 5).

A. *Other Relevant Legislation*

1169. Many other legal and sub-legal acts are relevant (or may be relevant) for spatial organization and construction in Serbia, for example, the following:

- Law on special procedures for the realization of the international specialized exhibition EXPO BELGRADE 2027 (OJ RS, No. 92/23).
- Law on Republic Administrative Fees (OJ RS, Nos 43/03, 51/03 – correction, 53/04, 42/05, 61/05, 101/05 – other law, 42/06, 47/07, 54/08, 5/09, 54/09, 35/10, 50/11, 70/11, 55/12, 93/12, 47/13, 65/13 – other law, 57/14, 45/ 15, 83/15, 112/ 15, 50/16, 61/17, 113/17, 3/18 – correction, 50/18, 95/18, 38/19, 86/19, 90/19 – correction and 98/20, 62/21).
- Law on construction products (OJ RS, No. 83/18).
- Law on Legalization of Buildings (OJ RS, Nos 96/15, 83/18, 81/20–81 – CC, 1/23 – US, 62/23).
- Law on State Survey and Cadastre (OJ RS, Nos 72/09, 18/10, 65/13, 15/15 CC, 96/15, 47/17 – Authentic Interpretation, 113/17 – other law, 27/18 – other law, 41/18 – other law, 9/20 – other law, and 92/23).
- Law on the National Spatial Data Infrastructure (OJ RS, No. 27/18).

1364. The building inspector is authorized to supervise the use of the facility and to take action if he/she determines that use of the facility endangers the life and health of people, the safety of the surroundings, *the environment*, and if inappropriately used affects the stability and safety of the facility (Art. 175, para. 2).

- Law on Public Property (OJ RS, Nos 72/11, 88/13, 105/14, 104/16 – other law, 108/16, 113/17, 95/18, and 153/20).
- Law on Expropriation (OJ RS, Nos 53/95, 16/01, 23/01, 20/09, 55/13 CC and 106/16 – Authentic interpretation).
- Law on Legalization of Buildings (OJ RS, Nos 96/2015, 83/18, 81/20 CC, 1/23 CC, and 6/23).
- Law on Conversion of the Right of Use to the Right of Ownership over Construction Land for a Fee (OJ RS, Nos 64/201 and 9/20).
- Law on Returning of Seized Property and Indemnification (OJ RS, Nos 72/11, 108/13, 142/14, 88/15 – CC, 95/18, and 153/20).
- Law on Transfer of Real Property (OJ RS, Nos 93/14, 121/14 and 6/15).
- Mortgage Law (OJ RS, Nos 115/05, 60/15, 63/15 CC and 83/15).
- Law on Agriculture Land (OJ RS, Nos 62/06, 65/08 – other law, 41/09, 112/15, 80/17 and 95/18 – other law).
- Law on Housing and Building Maintenance (OJ RS, Nos 104/16 and 9/20 – other law).
- Law on Communal Activities (OJ RS, Nos 88/11, 104/16 and 95/18).

1170. In the field of spatial planning and construction, a large number of by-laws are applied. Among them are the following:

- Regulation on the conditions, criteria, and content of documentation for determining projects for the construction of buildings of importance, that is, of special importance for the RS (OJ RS, No. 93/23).
- Regulation on Location Conditions (OJ RS, No. 87/ 23).
- Regulation on conditions, manner and procedure under which buildable land in public ownership can alienate or lease for less than the market price, or rent, or free of charge, and the conditions, manner and procedure of the property exchange (OJ RS, Nos 61/15, 88/15, 46/17, 30/18, and 53/21).
- Rulebook on the appearance and content of the official sign, as well as the procedure for closing the construction site (OJ RS, No. 97/23).
- Rulebook on the appearance, content, and location of the construction site sign (OJ RS, No. 97/23).
- Rulebook on the content and method of keeping the inspection book, construction diary, and construction book (OJ RS, No. 96/23).
- Rulebook on the content, method, and procedure of preparation and the method of control of technical documentation according to the class and purpose of facilities (OJ RS, No. 96/23).
- Rulebook on the conditions to be met by legal entities and entrepreneurs for the performance of technical documentation work, i.e., the construction of buildings, for buildings for which the building permit is issued by the ministry, i.e., the competent authority of the AP (OJ RS, Nos 41/22, 77/22).
- Rulebook on the conditions of professional liability insurance (OJ RS, No. 81/23).
- Rulebook on special types of buildings and special types of works for which it is not necessary to obtain an act of the competent authority, as well as the type of buildings that are built, that is, the type of works that are performed, based on the

decision on approval for the execution of works, as well as the scope, content, and control of technical documentation that is attached to the request and the procedure carried out by the competent authority (OJ RS, No. 87/23).
- Rulebook on technical requirements for concrete (OJ RS, No. 48/23).
- Rulebook on the method of expressing the performance of construction products and building elements concerning essential characteristics – reaction to fire, resistance to fire, and behaviour in the event of an external fire (OJ RS, No. 21/22).
- Rulebook with a list of Serbian standards that have adopted harmonized standards that are applied following the law regulating construction products and a list of adopted Serbian documents for evaluation (OJ RS, Nos 120/21, 139/22).
- Rulebook on the classification of buildings (OJ RS, No. 22/2015).
- Rulebook on general rules for the parcelling, regulation and construction (OJ RS, No. 22/2015).
- Rulebook of procedure for implementation of a unified procedure electronically (OJ RS, No. 96/23).
- Rulebook on the Content, Method and Procedure for Drafting Physical and Urban Planning Documents (OJ RS, No. 32/19).
- Rulebook on an identity card and type of equipment of urban planning and construction inspector (OJ RS, Nos 30/15, 81/15 – other rulebooks and 97/23).
- Rulebook on taking a professional exam in the field of spatial and urban planning, preparation of technical documentation, construction, and energy efficiency, as well as licenses for spatial planners, urban planners, urban architects, engineers, architects, landscape architects, and contractors, as well as registers of licensed persons (OJ RS, No. 2/21).
- Rulebook on the content and manner for conducting of professional supervision (OJ RS, Nos 22/15 and 24/17).
- Rulebook on the content of information on the location and content of location permit (OJ RS, No. 3/10).
- Rulebook on the content and manner of issuing building permits (OJ RS, Nos 93/11 and 103/13 – CC).
- Rulebook on energy efficiency of buildings (OJ RS, No. 61/11).
- Rulebook on the conditions, content and method of issuance of certificate on energy performance of buildings (OJ RS, Nos 69/ 12 and 44/18 – other law, and 111/22).
- Rulebook on general rules of parcelling out, regulation and building (OJ RS, No. 22/15), etc.[1365]

1365. For more information, *see* https://www.mgsi.gov.rs/lat/dokumenti-list/6/179; https://www.mgsi.gov.rs/lat/dokumenti-list/7/180 (6.1.2024).

Part IV. Liability Questions

1171. Liability for environmental damage is doubtlessly one of the most complex and most important problems of contemporary environmental law. The fact that the definition of environment is steadily being widened and that there is still not enough legal practice in applying the existing legal regulation on liability makes things even more complex.[1366]

There are grounds in Serbian law for liability for actions contrary to the prescribed environmental standards, as well as in civil law, criminal law and administrative law.[1367]

1172. Serbia has not yet ratified the Convention on Civil Liability for Damage resulting from Activities Dangerous to the Environment (CETS No. 150) nor the Convention on the Protection of Environment through Criminal Law (CETS No. 172). According to the available information, those conventions are still not on the priority list for ratification.

1366. On this subject, *see also* Stojanović, Zindović, 2015, 50–55.

1367. In 2022, environmental protection inspectors submitted a total of 68 requests to initiate misdemeanour proceedings, 15 applications to initiate proceedings for economic offences. In 13 cases, the inspectors were called by the acting judicial authorities to the court to give statements as witnesses. During the year, thirty-eight verdicts were passed, and the inspectors filed an appeal against one verdict. MEP. 2023b, 31.

Chapter 1. Civil Liability

1173. Civil law protection of the environment is essentially based on principles of prevention and restitution or on combination of these two principles. Important is also the regulating principle. The application in civil law of the principle of prevention, which is one of the most important principles in environmental law, means, besides other things, that the court can prohibit some activity which could endanger the environment above the permitted levels of pollution.

§1. Law on Environmental Protection

1174. EPL regulates environmental liability in a rather general way. Article 5 prescribes that subjects of liabilities are 'the Republic, Autonomous Province, and local self-governance body, legal and natural entities'. All of them are responsible for every activity by which environmental status and conditions could be changed. The following formulation in paragraph 2 of the mentioned Article has a special importance:

> In performing their activities, legal and natural entities are obliged to provide: rational use of natural resources, calculation of environmental protection expenditures in their investment and running costs, implement regulations, namely take environmental protection measures in compliance with the law.

1175. Article 9, paragraph 5 of the same Law also deserves mentioning. It prescribes that 'Any legal or natural entity who shall be involved in environmental pollution by its illegal or improper activities shall be liable in compliance with the law.' In the case of liquidation or bankruptcy of a company or other legal person, the polluter is liable for environmental pollution. The polluter, or its legal successor, is also obliged to eliminate the cause of pollution and the consequences of direct or indirect environmental pollution.

1176. One of the basic principles of environmental protection is, according to the Law, the principle of subsidiary liability. It is defined by Article 9, paragraph 8 which prescribes that 'state authorities, within their financial abilities, shall eliminate the consequences of environmental pollution and reduce damages when the polluter is unknown, and when pollution originates from the sources outside the territory of the Republic'.

1177. Chapter VII (Articles 102–108) of the EPL is devoted to questions of responsibility for environmental pollution.

1178. Article 102 of the Law prescribes general measures and activities that are obligatory for legal and private entities. These are: (1) applying and implementing regulations on environmental protection; (2) sustainable use of natural resources, goods and energy; (3) introducing energy efficient technologies and use of renewable natural resources; (4) using products, processes, technologies and practice less harmful to the environment; (5) undertaking preventive measures or eliminating the consequences of threat and damage to the environment; (6) keeping records in a prescribed way on raw materials and energy consumption, polluting matters and energy release, classification, characteristics and quantities of waste, as well as on other data and their submission to competent authorities; (7) controlling the activities and operation of plants that may represent risk or that may cause danger towards human health and environment; and (8) other measures in compliance with law. 'Legal and private entity shall implement measures of environmental protection from paragraph 1 of this Article on their own or via authorized organization.'

1179. Principle of objective responsibility, as a basic for polluter responsibilities, has been formulated in Article 103.

1180. Polluters have obligation to undertake measures determined by rehabilitation and plan of protection from accident,[1368] namely to undertake necessary measures in order to reduce damage in the environment or eliminate further risks, hazards or rehabilitation of the damage in the environment. If the damage made to the environment cannot be rehabilitated through adequate measures, the person who has caused it shall be responsible for paying a charge equivalent to the value of the destroyed good (Article 104).[1369]

1181. The polluter is liable for the damage made to the environment. He/she is obliged to cover expenditures for the evaluation of damage and elimination of it. In particular, it includes: (1) costs of urgent interventions undertaken at the moment of the damage occurrence which is necessary for organizing and preventing the effects of damage towards the environment, space and human health; (2) direct and indirect costs of rehabilitation, establishment of new or recovery of the previous environmental and spatial status, as well as monitoring of rehabilitation and environmental damage effects; (3) costs for prevention of the occurrence of the same or similar damage towards the environment and space; and (4) charge costs which are to be paid to persons directly threatened by environmental and spatial damage. The polluter is obliged to ensure financial or other warranties in order to

---

1368. Article 63 (Rehabilitation Measures and Subsidiary Liability) prescribes, when 'handling with dangerous substances' is concerned, that 'to prevent further spread of pollution caused by an accident, legal and natural entity shall immediately take rehabilitation measures planned for protection at its own cost'. If the polluter responsible for the accident is found subsequently, the authority that paid the cost of elimination of the consequences of environmental pollution shall claim the reimbursement.

1369. Generally speaking, the rehabilitation plan shall be made whenever pollution in the given area exceeds the effects of the measures taken, namely when the capacity of the environment is at risk or there is a risk of permanent degradation of the quality or damage in the environment. The Government is, according to the Art. 66, responsible for rehabilitation plans in following cases: (1) when the level and the scope of degradation of the environment exceeds the rehabilitation possibilities of the AP, namely local self-governance unit; (2) when the responsible polluter is unknown and the environmental pollution causes harmful consequences across the borders of the Republic; (3) when the responsible polluter is beyond the jurisdiction of the Republic, and the environmental pollution causes harmful effects in its territory; (4) when the environmental pollution endangers an area of extraordinary relevance for the Republic or causes harmful effects; and (5) when it is necessary to take urgent and intervention measures in emergency cases.

ensure the payment of the charge from paragraph 1 of this Article during and after performance of the activity. The Government shall prescribe types of warranty from paragraph 2 of this Article, the amount of the means and validity period of the warranty supplied by the polluters (Article 105).

1182. Every person affected by damage shall have right to reimbursement. The request for reimbursement may be submitted directly to the polluter or insurer (financial guarantee)[1370] of the polluter, if such insurer of financial guarantee exists.

1183. If several polluters are responsible for the environmental damage, and if it is not possible to determine share of certain polluters, the costs shall be borne jointly and individually.

1184. The procedure for reimbursement shall be out-of-date in three years from the date when the damaged party found out about the damage and the damage maker. However, this claim shall be out-of-date in twenty years after the occurrence of the damage. Court procedure for reimbursement shall be urgent. The Republic shall keep the right to reimburse the means if there are no other persons with such right (Article 107).

1185. Article 108 of the EPL prescribes that 'to the issues regarding liability for damage to the environment which have not been particularly regulated by this Law, general rules of the Law on Obligations shall be applied'.

§2. Law on Obligation Relations

1186. Liability for causing the danger of damage is prescribed by the Law on Obligation Relations (OJ SFRY, Nos 29/78, 39/85, 45/89, 57/89, OJ SRY, Nos 31/93, 22/99, 23/99, 35/99, 44/99, and OJ SCG, No. 1/2003). That means that in some cases, a person could be responsible even when actual damage is not done, for instance, for activities that are potentially dangerous for the environment. One who causes such a danger is always the potential polluter; his/her responsibility is objective and his/her guilt is not necessary to prove. The potential victim is the person (or persons) who are in danger of suffering damage if the pollution occurs.

1187. There are different forms of court actions in cases of environmental damage. The court can decide on:

- compensation for the damage (pecuniary or non-pecuniary);
- prohibition of activities which cause or can cause the damage;
- socially justified measures for removing the danger to the environment.

1370. It is prescribed by Art. 106 of the Law that polluter, whose installation or activity represent threat towards human health and environment is obliged to insure him against liability for possible damage caused to third party in an accident.

1188. When it comes to compensation, there are two situations. If the damage is a result of activities licensed as activities of public importance, then the polluter pays only for the damage above the permitted level of pollution. In another situation, when the polluter is not licensed, he/she is obliged to compensate (in kind or pecuniary, depending on the courts' decision) for the whole damage. The court can also prohibit further activity that endangers the environment. Such a prohibition can be the only sanction, or it may be combined with compensation.

Socially justified measures for removing the cause of the environmental danger can also be ordered by the court, especially in cases in which a larger number of people is in potential danger of serious pollution.

1189. Socially justified measures for removing the cause of the environmental danger (pollution of air, water, soil, etc.) are usually based, in Serbian judicial practice, upon Article 156 of the Law of Obligations (*actio popularis*).[1371]

1190. The mentioned Article establishes the so-called ecological claim prescribing the right to demand removal of the danger from damage or disturbance:

(1) Everybody can claim from other persons to remove the source of danger which could cause more considerable damage to the claimant or indefinite number of other persons, as well as to abstinence from activities which causes disturbance or danger from damage, if the disturbance or damage cannot be prevented by adequate measures.
(2) The court, reacting to the claim of interested person, will order undertaking adequate measures for preventing the damage or disturbance, or removing the source of danger. This will be done at the expense of the owner of the source of danger, if he/she himself does not do it.
(3) If the damage is caused in the course of activity which has general interest which is authorized by competent authority, only compensation for damage which overpasses normal thresholds could be demanded.
(4) But, even in that case, it is possible to demand undertaking of socially acceptable measures for prevention of the damage or its minimizing.

§3. Law on Basic Proprietary Relations

1191. The Law on Basic Proprietary Relations (OJs of SFRY, Nos 6/80 and 36/90 and of SRY, No. 29/96, OJ RS, No. 115/2005) is another important legal Act to be mentioned. Article 5[1372] of the Law prescribes two elements of key importance:

(1) It is the duty of the owner of the real estate to, while using his/her real estate, avoid activities:

1371. On this subject, *see* Rakić-Vodinelić, 89; Petrušić, 2003; Radonjić, Stjelja, 2018.
1372. Everybody is obliged to restrain from infringing the ownership rights of others (Art. 3, para. 2).

- by which usage of other real estate is made harder (transmission of smoke, unpleasant smelt, heat, soot, vibrations, noise, outlet of wastewater, etc.) above the measure which is usual (common) regarding to the nature and purpose of real estate as well as local circumstance; or
- by which more considerable damage is caused.

(2) Duty of the owner of the real estate to remove causes which originated from his/her real estate and – by which usage of other real estate is made harder (transmission of smoke, unpleasant smelt, heat, soot, vibrations, noise, outlet of wastewater, etc.) above the measure which is usual (common) regarding to the nature and purpose of real estate as well as local circumstance, or by which is caused more considerable damage.

§4. Law on Privatization

1192. The Law on Privatization[1373] (OJ RS, Nos 83/14, 46/15, 112/15 and 20/16) comprises the following eighteen Chapters: I Basic provisions (Articles 1–17); II Preparation for privatization (Articles 18–22); III Methods of privatization (Articles 23–35); IV Sale of Capital (Articles 36–47);. V Sale of Property (Articles 48–56); VI Control Procedure and Method of Performance of Obligations from Sale Contract of Capital or Property (Article 57); VII Sale of shares and stakes (Articles 58–60); VIII Transfer of Capital Free of Charge (Articles 61–65); IX Strategic Partnership (Articles 66–74); X Measures for Preparation and Discharge of Privatization Subjects' Obligations (Articles 75–78); XI Privatization of State Capital from Succession (Article 79); XII Pronouncing Bankruptcy to End the Privatization (Article 80); XIII Privatization of Privatization Subjects with Minority Capital (Article 81); XIV Special Provisions (Articles 82 and 83); XV Supervision over Implementation of the Law (Article 84); XVI Criminal Act (Article 85); XVII Appropriate Application of the Laws and Suspension of Proceedings (Articles 86 and 87); and XVIII Transitional and Final Provisions (Articles 88–95).

The Law on Privatization regulates the conditions and procedure for change of ownership of social and public capital[1374] and property (Article 1, paragraph 1).

1193. In the process of privatization property or part of the property, the subject to privatization can be sold. The sale of property is organized and conducted by the Ministry in charge of economic affairs (Article 48, paragraphs 1 and 2). The Programme for sell of property is issued by the competent authority of the privatization entity (Article 49, paragraph 1). The Programme includes, in particular, data about the business entity to be privatized, property values, social programme, i.e., obligations to employees, a programme of environmental protection, as well as other data of importance for the sale of property of the privatization entity (Article 50, paragraph 1).

1373. *Privatization,* in terms of this Law, means changing of capital and property ownership of legal entities that operate with social and public capital (Art. 2, para. 1, point 1).

1374. *Public capital* is the capital of the Republic of Serbia, APs and local self-government (Art. 2, para. 1, point 2).

1194. The funds[1375] for repairing the damage which is the subject of privatization caused to the environment prior to the conclusion of the sales contract, i.e., a contract on the recapitalization provided to the budget of the RS (Article 83, paragraph 1).

1375. The Government shall prescribe the manner and conditions of use of the funds (Art. 83, para. 2).

Chapter 2. Criminal Liability

1195. Most criminal acts concerning the environment are prescribed by the Criminal Code, but several other laws also contain provision on criminal responsibilities.[1376]

§1. Criminal Code

1196. The Criminal Code (OJ RS, Nos 85/05, 88/05 – corr., 107/05 – corr., 72/09, 111/09, 121/12, 104/13, 108/14, 94/16, 35/19) contains a separate chapter (Chapter XXIV) devoted to criminal acts against the environment and besides that several other provisions of the Code are related to the environment. The Code contains following eighteen criminal acts against the environment:[1377]

(1) Environmental pollution (Article 260).
(2) Omission to apply measures of environmental protection (Article 261).
(3) Illegal building and use of objects and installations which pollute environment (Article 262).
(4) Damage of objects and installations for environmental protection (Article 263).
(5) Impairment of environment (Article 264).
(6) Destroying, damaging and taking abroad a protected natural asset (Article 265).
(7) Bringing dangerous substances into Serbia and unlawful processing, depositing and stockpiling of dangerous substances (Article 266).
(8) Illegal construction of nuclear plants (Article 267).
(9) Endangerment of right to information on the state of the environment (Article 268).
(10) Killing and wanton cruelty to animals (Article 269).
(11) Transmitting of contagious animal and plant diseases (Article 270).
(12) Malpractice in Veterinary Services (Article 271).
(13) Producing harmful products for treating animals (Article 272).
(14) Pollution of livestock fodder and water (Article 273).
(15) Devastation of forests (Article 274).
(16) Forest theft (Article 275).
(17) Poaching game (Article 276).
(18) Poaching fish (Article 277).

1197. Article 260 deserves special attention. It prescribes that:

1376. 'The most frequently committed environmental crimes are devastation of forests, illegal logging, poaching game, illegal fishing, and killing and cruelty to animals, while the number of charges filed for the criminal offences related to environmental pollution, failure to undertake environmental protection measures or damaging the environment is much smaller.' UNECE. 2015, 56.

1377. For judicial practice based on the old Criminal Code, *see* Joldžic, Jovašević, 2013; Jovašević, 2014.

(1) persons who by breaking rules on protection, conservation and improvement of environment, pollute air, water or soil in considerable measure or in wider space shall be punished by imprisonment up to three years;
(2) if the act from paragraph 1 of this Article is done by negligence, the perpetrator will be fined or punished by prison for up to one year;
(3) if the act from paragraph 1 of this Article caused destruction or damage of the animal or plant life to a greater extent or to environmental pollution which is so intensive that its rehabilitation needs longer time and considerable expenditure, the perpetrator will be punished in prison from one to eight years;
(4) if the act from paragraph 2 of this Article caused destruction or damage of the animal or plant life to a greater extent or to environmental pollution which is so intensive that its rehabilitation needs longer time and considerable expenditure, the perpetrator will be punished by prison from six months to five years;
(5) if the conditional verdict for acts from paragraphs 1 to 4 of this Article is decided, the court could prescribe the obligation for the perpetrator to undertake certain measures aimed at protection, conservation and improvement of the environment.

1198. Article 268 deals with endangerment of right to environmental information on the state of the environment. It prescribes that 'whoever contrary to regulations withholds information or gives false information on the state of the environment and events that is required for evaluation of environmental hazard and undertaking measures for protection of human life and health, shall be punished by fine or imprisonment up to one year'.[1378]

§2. Law on the Liability of Legal Persons for Criminal Offences

1199. Liability of legal persons for criminal acts, as well as the sanctions of legal persons for criminal acts, is regulated by the Law on the Liability of Legal Persons for Criminal Acts (OJ RS, No. 97/08). The Law regulates conditions governing the liability of legal entities for criminal offences, penal sanctions that may be imposed on legal entities, as well as procedural rules when ruling on the liability of legal entities,[1379] on imposing penal sanctions, passing a decision on rehabilitation, termination of security measures or legal consequences of the conviction, and on enforcement of court decisions (Article 1).

1378. Previous EPL (OJ RS, No. 66/91) contained provisions concerning the right to information to a certain extent different from those in the new EPL. 'Whosoever proclaims as confidential information essential for assessing dangers to the human environment and for taking up action and measures aimed at protecting the life and health of person shall be fined and punished by imprisonment of up to five years for a criminal offence committed. An attempt that is made to this effect shall be punished' (Art. 109).

1379. A legal person is a national or a foreign entity considered as a legal person under positive legislation of the Republic. A liable person is a natural person legally or de facto entrusted with certain duties within a legal entity, as well as a person authorized, that is, a person who may reasonably be considered as authorized to act on behalf of a legal entity (Art. 5).

1200. This Law shall be applicable to the following: to national and foreign legal persons held accountable for a criminal offence committed in the territory of the Republic; to foreign legal entities held accountable for criminal offences committed abroad to the detriment of the Republic, nationals thereof or national legal persons; and to national legal entities held accountable for criminal offences committed abroad (Article 4, paragraphs 1–3).[1380]

1201. A legal entity may be liable for criminal offences constituted under a special part of the Criminal Code and under other laws if the conditions governing the liability of legal entities provided for by this Law are satisfied (Article 2).[1381]

1202. Conditions for establishing liability of legal entities for criminal offences are prescribed in the general part of the Law (Second part: Articles 6–11 with sanctions in Articles 12–26). Elements of the criminal proceedings are defined in the second part of the Law (Articles 35–54)[1382] as well as enforcement of court decision in Articles 55–71.

§3. Other Sources of Law

1203. The four basic laws on environmental protection (EPL, Law on EIA, Law on Strategic EIA, Law on Integrated Prevention and Pollution Control) do not contain provisions on criminal responsibility.

1204. Several other laws contain provisions against environmental crimes such as the Law on Water (OJ RS, Nos 30/2010, 93/12, 101/16 and 95/18), the Law on Prohibition to Build Nuclear Power Plants (OJ FRY, No. 12/1995), the Law on Mining and Geological Explorations (OJ RS, Nos 101/15, 95/18 – other law, and 40/21), and others, etc.

1205. The Law on Water has provisions for the following criminal acts:

– Unauthorized charging or use of a reservoir (Article 209).[1383]

1380. In cases referred to in paras 2 and 3 of this Article, this Law shall not apply if special conditions governing criminal prosecution referred to in Art. 10, para. 1 of the Criminal Code are fulfilled (Art. 4, para. 4).

1381. The Republic of Serbia (the Republic), the AP and the local self-government unit, that is, government authorities and authorities of the AP and LSG unit cannot be liable for criminal offences. Other legal entities vested with public powers by virtue of law cannot be liable for criminal offences committed when exercising such public powers (Art. 3).

1382. Unless otherwise stipulated by this Law, the provisions of the Criminal Procedural Code shall be applicable by analogy in the criminal proceedings conducted against an accused legal entity (Art. 54).

1383. Any person who has charged a reservoir or used water from a reservoir, and thereby caused a threat to human life or health or property, shall be charged with a criminal offence and sentenced to a prison term of six months to five years.

– Damage during extraction of river deposits (Article 210).[1384]

1206. Law on Prohibition on Building Nuclear Plants in FRY in Article 3 sanctions as a criminal act 'preparation, permitting of building or commencement of building of nuclear power plants, installations of production of nuclear fuel or installations for processing of used nuclear fuel' in the territory of FRY.

1384. Any person who has damaged a channel, bank, or control construction as a result of extraction of river deposits from the channel of watercourse, shall be charged with a criminal offence and sentenced to a prison term of six months to five years, or assessed a fine. In addition to the penalty for a criminal offence per para. 1 of this Article, any object used in committing the criminal offence shall be confiscated from the perpetrator.

Chapter 3. Other Forms of Liability

§1. Law on Economic Offences

1207. According to the definition taken from the Law on Economic Offences (OJ SFRY, Nos 4/1977, 36/1977 – correction, 14/1985, 74/1987, 57/1989 and 3/1990, OJ FRY, Nos 27/1992, 16/93 – other law, 31/93 – other law, 41/93 – other law, 50/93 – other law, 24/1994, 28/1996 and 64/2001, and OJ RS, No. 101/05 – other law), an economic offence is a socially harmful violation of regulations on economic or financial business which causes or may cause serious consequences, and which is qualified as a commercial offence by the competent authority (Article 2).

1208. Responsible for an offence can be a legal person (and responsible person in legal person), an entrepreneur and a physical person. State authorities and authorities of local governments cannot be responsible for offences but responsible persons in these authorities can be. Enterprises and other legal entities can be held responsible for a criminal act.

1209. Each of the environmental laws in force provides a penalty for economic (commercial) offences (the EPL, the Law on Environment Protection Fund, the Law on EIA, the Law on IPPC, the Law on SEA, the Law on Waste Management, the Law on Packaging and Packaging Waste, the Law on Biocidal Products, the Law on Chemicals, the Law on Nature Protection, the Law on National Parks, the Law on Prohibition of Development, Production, Storage and Use of Chemical Weapons and its Destruction, the Law on Protection and Sustainable Use of Fishing Resources, the Law on Environmental Noise, the Law on Radiation and Nuclear Safety and Security, the Law on Non-ionizing Radiation Protection, the Law on Air Protection, the Law on Waters).

§2. Law on Offences

1210. Offences are illegal acts defined in Article 2 of the Law on Offences (OJ RS, Nos 65/13, 13/16, 98/16 – CC, 91/19 – other law, 91/19, and 112/22 – CC). They may be prescribed by laws, decrees of the Government and municipal, city or AP's authorities (Article 4). They cover activities of enterprises or other legal entities, entrepreneurs and natural persons, as defined by the Law.

1211. Sanctions for offences have been prescribed by all environmental laws, for example:

- *EPL* prescribes offences of the legal entity, responsible person within legal entity, natural entity and responsible person within competent authority or organization carrying out public authorizations (Articles 117–121).
- Law on EIA (Articles 42 and 43).
- Law on SEA (Article 25).

– Law on Integrated Environmental Pollution, Prevention and Control (Articles 30–32).[1385]

1212. It could be added, as a concluding remark, that there are many systematic problems concerning environmental liability in Serbia. Provisions related to competencies and to instruments for implementation in some basic sources of Serbian environmental law are still not sufficiently harmonized. Enforcement of environmental legislation in Serbia is not always efficient enough and suffers from serious drawbacks, especially because of weak monitoring system, lack of certain environmental standards, insufficient coordination between environmental laws and other laws defining other responsibilities of institutions at the national and sub-national levels, the insufficient capacity of municipal-level environmental inspection bodies, charges and sanctions envisaged by legal provisions are not properly enforced and are not high enough to be real deterrents, the generally low awareness of and compliance with the law, etc.

1213. Serbian judiciary system is still not efficient enough, when imposing sanctions for environmental offences is concerned. It usually takes time for a court proceeding to result in a court order and an adequate sanction, which are sometimes inadequate or largely symbolic. Judges, as well as prosecutors and police bodies, need more training in environmental law. Due to the fact that there is no sufficient data regarding the relation between lawsuits (both administrative and criminal) and the sanctions imposed, it is presently not possible to assess the effectiveness of enforcement.[1386]

1214. Sector for control and surveillance (MEMSP) organized training for judges and public prosecutors (2008) and for magistrates and environmental protection inspectors (2009) in cooperation with the Organization for Security and Co-operation in Europe (OSCE) and the Ministry of Justice. The aim of these trainings was to increase penalties in the field of environmental protection, to speed up processing of inspector complaints and to help inspectors learn how to compile claims for instituting infringement procedures.[1387]

1385. Besides the above-mentioned and in relation with 'administrative responsibility', it should be mentioned that there are several relevant sources of law. Law on Civil Servants (OJ RS, Nos 79/05, 81/05 – corr., 83/05 – corr., 64/07, 67707 – corr., 116/08, 104/09 and 99/14) contains several provisions of general character in Ch. IX (civil servants liability) and Arts 121–126 deal with 'liability for damage'.

1386. UNECE. 2007, 27–32.

1387. GOV RS. 2011a, p. 70.

Part V. Juridical Actions of Individuals

§1. Introduction: Constitution of Serbia

1215. Articles 22 and 36 of the Constitution of Serbia (OJ RS, Nos 83/06, 115/21, 16/22) guarantee the right to an effective legal remedy. Article 22 prescribes that 'judicial protection when any of their human or minority rights guaranteed by the Constitution have been violated or denied. They also have the right to elimination of consequences arising from the violation. The citizens have the right to address international institutions in order to protect their freedoms and rights guaranteed by the Constitution'.

1216. In Article 36, it is stated that 'Equal protection of rights before courts and other State bodies, entities exercising public powers and bodies of the AP or LSG shall be guaranteed. Everyone shall have the right to an appeal or other legal remedy against any decision on his/her rights, obligations or lawful interests.'

1217. Article 97, p. 2 of the Constitution prescribes that the RS shall organize and provide for:

> exercise and protection of freedoms and rights of citizens; constitutionality and legality; proceedings before courts and other state bodies; liabilities and sanctions for violation of freedoms and rights of citizens stipulated by the Constitution and for violation of laws, other regulations and general acts; amnesty and pardon for criminal offences.

1218. The CC has been established by Article 168. According to the mentioned Article, the Court is competent to decide, *inter alia*, on compliance of laws and other general Acts with the Constitution, generally accepted rules of the international law and ratified international treaties, compliance of ratified international treaties with the Constitution, compliance of other general Acts with the Law, compliance of the Statute and general acts of APs and LSG units with the Constitution and the Law, etc.

1219. The basis for 'constitutional appeal' has been established by Article 170 of the Constitution. The appeal may be lodged against individual general acts or actions performed by State bodies or organizations exercising delegated public powers which violate or deny human or minority rights and freedoms guaranteed by the Constitution, if other legal remedies for their protection have already been applied or not specified.[1388]

1220. Individuals can realize constitutional right to a healthy environment (Article 74 of the Constitution)[1389] and above-mentioned rights in different procedures: administrative and juridical (civil, criminal, etc.). Which procedure will be started depends on rights that are violated, on the way by which they were violated and on the choice of the individual who lodges the appeal. Administrative and judicial procedures can be started parallel and independently, if legally prescribed conditions are fulfilled.

1388. 'A high number of cases (29 672) are pending before the Constitutional Court, 99.13% of which are constitutional appeals and only 227 related to normative control.' EC. 2023, 28. In 2022, the CC worked on 16 249 cases: 16 075 were constitutional appeals and 116 cases of normative control. The CC resolved 14 203 cases, of which 13 969 constitutional appeals and 175 normative control cases. *Ibid.*

1389. *See* title 'constitutional provisions', Introduction (Ch. 2).

Chapter 1. Administrative Remedies

1221. There are many questions in the field of environment that could be involved in administrative procedures (for instance, issuing various permits, asking for opinions, decisions of inspection, etc.). The Law on General Administrative Procedure is the basic source of Law (OJ RS, Nos 18/16, 9/18 – authentic interpretation, and 2/23 – CC), although several other laws and by-laws are also relevant to a certain extent.

§1. Law on General Administrative Procedure

1222. It is prescribed by Article 90 of the Law on General Administrative Procedure that the procedure is initiated at the request of the party or ex officio. A 'party' to administrative proceedings is a natural or legal person whose administrative matter is the subject of administrative proceedings and any other natural or legal person whose rights, obligations or legal interests may be affected by the outcome of administrative proceedings (Article 44).

1223. According to Article 13, one of the basic principles of the Law is the 'Right to appeal and objection'. Parts VI and VII of the Law are devoted to the 'legal remedies' (Articles 147–189). General time limit for lodging an appeal is fifteen days (Article 153) unless otherwise prescribed by law.[1390]

1224. An objection may be filed due to non-fulfilment of obligations from the administrative contract (Article 25 of this Law), due to administrative action (Article 28 of this Law) and due to the manner of providing public services (Article 32 of this Law), if it cannot declare another legal remedy in the administrative procedure (Article 147, paragraph 1).[1391]

1225. According to Article 176, the procedure which has ended with a decision against which no appeal can be lodged (final decision) shall be repeated, *inter alia*, if new facts become known or new evidence is acquired that could, alone or in connection with previously stated facts or presented evidence, lead to a different solution; if the decision favourable to the party is based on untrue claims of the party by which the authorized official was misled; if the decision was made by an unauthorized person, or the procedure was conducted or decided by an unauthorized person or a person who had to be exempted; if the party was not represented in accordance with the law, etc.

1390. When the competent authority does not issue a decision within the legally prescribed time limit, an appeal may be filed after the expiration of that time limit, and no later than within one year from the expiration of that time limit (para. 2).

1391. The objection shall be declared within: (1) six months from the failure of the body to fulfil the obligation from the administrative contract; (2) fifteen days from undertaking an administrative action or from failing to undertake an administrative action; (3) when the public service is not provided in such a way as to ensure orderly and quality, under equal conditions, realization of rights and satisfaction of user's needs – fifteen days (para. 2).

1226. The Law also regulates the rules related to:

- annulment of the final decision (Article 183);
- revocation of the decision (Article 184);
- annulment, revocation or change of the final decision on the recommendation of the Protector of Citizens (Article 185).

§2. Law on State Administration

1227. According to the Law on State Administration (OJ RS, Nos 79/05, 101/07, 95/10, 99/14, 30/18 – other law and 47/18), natural and legal persons have several rights. Article 80 of this Law prescribes that State administration authorities are obliged to, upon the request, give opinions on interpretation of provision of laws and other general Acts within the time limit of thirty days. The authorities are also obliged to enable everyone adequate ways for the submission of complaints about their work and about improper conduct of employees. In the case of a submitted complaint, the authorities have to respond within fifteen days from the date the complaint was filed (Article 81).

§3. Law on Environmental Protection

1228. The EPL (OJ RS, Nos 135/04, 36/09, 72/09 – other law, 43/11 – CC, 14/16, 76/18 and 95/18 – other law) regulates, among other things, administrative procedure in cases of appeals lodged against administrative decisions in the field of environmental protection (i.e., competence issues).

Pursuant to Article 81a, the interested public, in the process of exercising right to a healthy environment, shall have the right as a party to initiate the decision-review procedure before the responsible authority or court, in accordance with the law.

1229. According to Article 114 of the Law, the Minister shall decide on the appeal against the first instance decision of the responsible municipal and/or city authority or authority of the city of Belgrade that was adopted in the course of performing delegated tasks (paragraph 1). The responsible authority of the AP shall decide on the appeal against first instance decision of the responsible municipal, namely city authority from the territory of the AP, adopted in the course of performing delegated tasks (paragraph 2). The Minister shall decide on the appeal against the first instance decision of the regional unit of the Ministry and on the appeal against the first instance decision of the responsible authority of the AP (paragraphs 3 and 4).

1230. The appeal against first-degree ruling of the Ministry shall be decided by the Government (paragraph 5).

§4. LAW ON ENVIRONMENTAL IMPACT ASSESSMENT

1231. According to Article 11 of the Law on EIA, the project developer[1392] and the public concerned[1393] are entitled to file a complaint against the decision of the competent authority concerning the application for a decision on the need for an impact assessment. The complaint referred to in paragraph 1 of this Article 'shall be submitted to the competent authority of the second instance in accordance with the law regulating environmental protection. The competent authority of the second instance shall decide on the complaint within twenty days from the date of receipt of the complaint'.

1232. The right to appeal against the decision made on the application for a decision on the scope and content of the EIA Study is established by Article 15 of the Law. Public concerned and the project developer are entitled to file a complaint against the decision of the competent authority on the application for a decision on the scope and content of the EIA Study.[1394]

1233. The complaint against the decision of the inspector, referred to in Article 37, paragraph 1, points 1–5, may be submitted to the Minister within fifteen days from the date of receipt of the decision. The same period is prescribed for the complaint against the decision of the inspector of the AP and the LSG unit (Article 39, paragraph 2).[1395]

§5. LAW ON INTEGRATED ENVIRONMENTAL POLLUTION PREVENTION AND CONTROL

1234. Article 15 of the Law on Integrated Environmental Pollution Prevention and Control prescribes when the decision on permit[1396] granting is concerned, that 'no complaints can be filed against the decision of the competent authority[1397] ... while administrative court proceeding can be instigated'.

1392. 'Project developer' means the applicant for a permit or an approval for construction or reconstruction of structures or for other interventions in nature and the environment (Arts 2, 3).
1393. Public concerned includes the public affected by or likely to be affected by the project, including NGOs that promote environmental protection and are registered with the competent authority (Arts 2 and 7).
1394. The complaint shall be submitted to the competent authority of the second instance in accordance with the law regulating environmental protection. The competent authority of the second instance shall decide on the complaint within twenty days from the date of receipt of the complaint.
1395. The AP and the LSG unit are entrusted with the inspection supervision tasks relating to the enforcement of the provisions of this Law for projects that are under the responsibility of the competent authority of the AP and of the LSG with respect to the impact assessment procedure.
1396. Integrated permit means the decision of the competent authority adopted in the written form, approving the start-up of the whole or a part of installation, or the execution of the activity, the integral part of which is the documentation containing the set conditions which guarantee that such installation or activity is in compliance with the requirements prescribed by this Law (Arts 2 and 10).
1397. The competent authority can issue the decision on permit granting or refuse the permit granting application.

1235. It is prescribed by Article 22 of the Law that the competent authority shall adopt conclusion initiating the permit, revoke procedure and inform the operator within five days from the date of procedure initiating and submitting evidence for initiating it. The operator is entitled to file the complaint against the conclusion within eight days of its receipt.

Complaint against the inspector's decision can be submitted to the Minister within fifteen days from the date of its receipt (Article 28).[1398]

1398. The complaint does not postpone the execution of the decision and Minister's decisions are final.

Chapter 2. Judicial Remedies

1236. Judicial system is regulated by the relevant provisions of the Constitution of the RS (Articles 142–152) and by following laws:

- Law on Organization of Courts (OJ RS, No. 10/23).
- Law on Constitutional Court (CC) (OJ RS, Nos 109/07, 99/11, 18/13 CC, 40/15 – other law, 103/15, 10/23, and 92/23).
- Law on the Seats and Territories of Courts and Public Prosecutions (OJ RS, No. 101/13).
- Law on Public Prosecution (OJ RS, No. 10/23).
- Law on High Judicial Council (OJ RS, No. 10/23).
- Law on Judges (OJ RS, No. 10/23).

1237. In 2006, two important documents were adopted: the National Judicial Reform Strategy (OJ RS, No. 44/2006) and the Action Plan for Strategy Implementation. According to the Strategy, effective judiciary relies on four basic principles: independence, transparency, accountability and efficiency.[1399]

On 1 July 2013, the NA of the RS adopted the National Strategy of Judicial Reform for the period 2013–2018 (OJ RS, No. 57/13). In July 2020, the Government adopted the Judiciary Development Strategy for the period 2020–2025 years (OJ RS, Nos 101/20, and 18/22.[1400]

1238. The kind of judicial remedy depends on the character of the procedure. In principle, there are regular and irregular judicial remedies. The regular ones are used in cases of decisions that have not come into force yet and the second ones are used in cases of decisions which have come into force.

Most common judicial remedy in all three procedures (criminal, civil and administrative) is an appeal. As a rule, the upper court decides about the appeal and the procedure, both in criminal and civil procedures and postpones implementation of the contested decision of the lower court. The right to lodge appeals is vested with the parties, attorneys, and prosecutor and, of course, those persons who suffered damage which depends on concrete case.

§1. Criminal Procedure

1239. According to the Criminal Procedure Code (OJ RS, 72/11, 101/11, 121/12, 32/13, 45/13, 55/14, 35/19, 27/21 – CC, 62/21 – CC), 'prosecutor' can be a public prosecutor, private prosecutor and subsidiary prosecutor (Article 2, point 5). The

1399. A number of laws were adopted as part of the National Judicial Reform leading to the establishment of a new organization of the judiciary and the prosecution, namely, the Law on High Judicial Council, Law on State Prosecutorial Council, Law on Judges, Law on Public Prosecution, Law on Organization of Courts and Law on the Seats and Territorial Jurisdiction of Courts and Public Prosecutor's Office. MESP, 2010b, 63.

1400. *See* https://www.pravno-informacioni-sistem.rs/SlGlasnikPortal/eli/rep/sgrs/vlada/strategija/2020/101/1/reg (16.1.2024).

public prosecutor is the authorized prosecutor for criminal offences which are prosecuted ex officio, and the private prosecutor is the authorized prosecutor for criminal offences prosecutable by private prosecution (Article 5).[1401]

1240. In accordance with Article 280, State and other bodies, legal and natural persons report criminal offences which are prosecutable ex officios about which they were informed or learned in another manner, under the conditions stipulated by law or other regulations (paragraph 1).[1402]

1241. The motion for criminal prosecution is submitted within three months of the date when the injured party learnt about the criminal offence and the suspect (Article 53, paragraph 2).[1403] Private lawsuit is filed within three months of the date the injured party learnt about the criminal offence and the suspect (Article 65).

1242. A motion for prosecuting criminal offences which are prosecuted on the basis of a motion by an injured party is submitted to the competent public prosecutor (Article 53, paragraph 1). Private lawsuit is filed with the competent court (Article 65, paragraph 1).[1404]

1243. Regular legal remedies are appeals against first instance court judgments (Articles 432–462),[1405] appeals against judgments of courts of second instance (Articles 463 and 464)[1406] and appeals against rulings (Articles 465–469).[1407]

1401. Criminal prosecution is initiated: (1) by the first action of the public prosecutor, or authorized police personnel based on a request of a public prosecutor, undertaken in accordance with this Code for the purpose of investigating the grounds for suspicion that a criminal offence has been committed or a certain person has committed a criminal offence; and (2) by the submission of private prosecution where a public prosecutor declares that he is abandoning prosecution (Art. 52), or he may be replaced by a subsidiary prosecutor, under the conditions prescribed by this Code (Art. 5, paras 2 and 3).

1402. The cases in which failure to report a criminal offence represents a criminal offence are prescribed by the Criminal Code (Art. 280, para. 2).

1403. An injured party as a subsidiary prosecutor is entitled to: (1) represent the prosecution in accordance with the provisions of this Code; (2) submit a motion and evidence for realizing a restitution claim and a motion for interim measures to secure it; (3) retain a proxy from among attorneys; (4) request the appointment of a proxy; (5) perform other actions provided for by this Code. Besides the rights referred to in para. 1 of this Article, a subsidiary prosecutor also exercises the rights of the public prosecutor, except those that the public prosecutor has in his capacity as a public authority (Art. 58).

1404. Private prosecutors are entitled to: (1) bring and represent a private lawsuit; (2) submit a motion and evidence for realizing a restitution claim and a motion for interim measures to secure it; (3) retain a proxy from among attorneys; and (4) perform other actions provided for by this Code (Art. 64).

1405. Authorized persons may file an appeal against a judgment issued in the first instance within fifteen days of the date of delivery of a copy of the judgment. Especially in complex cases, the parties and the defence counsel may immediately after the judgment is proclaimed request an extension of the time limit for filing an appeal. A timely and admissible appeal against a judgment stays execution of the judgment (Art. 432, paras 1, 2 and 4). The parties, the defence counsel and the injured party may file an appeal (Art. 433, para. 1).

1406. An appeal may only be filed against a judgment by which the court of second instance reversed a first instance judgment, which acquitted the defendant of the charges, and pronounced a judgment finding of the defendant guilty (Art. 463). An appellate court adjudicates an appeal against

1244. Extraordinary legal remedies are reopening for criminal proceedings (Articles 470–481)[1408] and motions for the Protection of Legality (Articles 482–494).[1409]

1245. Serbia is a contracting party to the following conventions of the Council of Europe relating to legal cooperation in criminal matters:

- European Convention on Extradition (ETS 24).
- European Convention on Mutual Assistance in Criminal Matters (ETS 30).
- European Convention on the Supervision of Conditionally Sentenced or Conditionally Released Offenders (ETS 51).
- European Convention on the International Validity of Criminal Judgments (ETS 70).
- European Convention on the Transfer of Proceedings in Criminal Matters (ETS 73).
- European Convention on the Non-Applicability of Statutory Limitation to Crimes against Humanity and War Crimes (ETS 82).
- Additional Protocol to the European Convention on Extradition (ETS 86).
- European Convention on the International Effects of Deprivation of the Right to Drive Motor Vehicles (ETS 88).
- European Convention on the Suppression of Terrorism (ETS 90).
- Additional Protocol to the European Convention on Information on Foreign Law (ETS 97).
- Second Additional Protocol to the European Convention on Extradition (ETS 98).
- Additional Protocol to the European Convention on Mutual Assistance in Criminal Matters (ETS 99).
- Convention on the Transfer of Sentenced Persons (ETS 112).

---

a judgment of a court of second instance pursuant to the provisions of this Code applicable to second instance proceedings. The provisions of Art. 454 of this Code will also be applied to a co-defendant who was not entitled to file an appeal against a second instance judgment (Art. 464).

1407. The parties and persons whose rights are violated may appeal against rulings of the investigating judge and other rulings issued by courts in the first instance at all times, except where explicitly specified in this Code on which no appeal is permitted (Art. 465, para. 1). A ruling of the panel issued during the investigation and the indicting procedure is not appealable, unless otherwise specified by this Code. Rulings issued for the purpose of preparing and conducting the trial may only be challenged in the appeal against the judgment. Rulings of the second instance court are not appealable, unless otherwise specified by this Code. Rulings of the Supreme Court of Cassation are not appealable (Art. 465, paras 2–5).

1408. Criminal proceedings concluded by a final ruling or a final judgment may at the request of an authorized person be reopened in the cases and under the conditions prescribed by this Code (Art. 470).

1409. A request for the protection of legality may be submitted by the Republic Public Prosecutor, the defendant and his defence counsel (Art. 483). An authorized person may submit in accordance with conditions prescribed in this Code a request for the protection of legality against a final decision of the public prosecutor or the court or for violation of provisions of the procedure which preceded its issuance. A request for the protection of legality is not allowed against a decision on the protection of legality or violation of provisions of the procedure before the Supreme Court of Cassation which preceded its issuance (Art. 482).

- European Convention on the Compensation of Victims of Violent Crimes (ETS 116).
- Convention on Laundering, Search, Seizure and Confiscation of the Proceeds from Crime (ETS 141).
- Additional Protocol to the Convention on the Transfer of Sentenced Persons (ETS 167).
- Criminal Law Convention on Corruption (CETS No. 173).
- Second Additional Protocol to the European Convention on Mutual Assistance in Criminal Matters 182).
- Convention on Cybercrime (ETS 185).
- Additional Protocol to the Convention on Cybercrime concerning the criminalization of acts of a racist and xenophobic nature committed through computer systems (ETS 189).
- Protocol amending the European Convention on the Suppression of Terrorism (ETS 190).
- Additional Protocol to the Criminal Law Convention on Corruption (ETS 191).
- Council of Europe Convention on the Prevention of Terrorism (ETS 196).
- Council of Europe Convention on Action against Trafficking in Human Beings (ETS 197).
- Council of Europe Convention on Laundering, Search, Seizure and Confiscation of the Proceeds from Crime and on the Financing of Terrorism (ETS 198).
- Third Additional Protocol to the European Convention on Extradition (ETS 209).
- Fourth Additional Protocol to the European Convention on Extradition (ETS 212).
- Protocol No. 15 amending the Convention for the Protection of Human Rights and Fundamental Freedoms (ETS 213).
- Protocol amending the European Landscape Convention (ETS 219).[1410]

§2. Civil Procedure

1246. Article 191 of the Civil Procedure Law (OJ RS, Nos 72/11, 49/13 CC, 74/13 – CC, 55/14, 87/18,18/20, and 10/23 – other law) prescribes that a civil action is initiated by filing a complaint.

1247. Any natural or legal person may be a party to the proceedings (Article 74). Exceptionally, a litigation court may recognize attributes of a party to associations that do not have litigant competence in terms of provisions of this Article. In such a case, they essentially fulfil the vital prerequisites for acquiring litigant competence, especially if they possess property on which enforcement may be conducted (Article 74, paragraph 4).

1410. *See* https://www.coe.int/en/web/conventions/by-member-states-of-the-council-of-europe?module=treaties-full-list-signature&CodePays=SAM&CodeSignatureEnum=&DateStatus=01-06-2024&CodeMatieres= (6.1.2024).

1248. Two kinds of legal remedies have been established by the Civil Procedure Law: ordinary legal remedies and extraordinary legal remedies.

I. Ordinary Legal Remedies

1249. Ordinary legal remedies are appeals against judgments and against decisions. Article 367 of the Civil Procedure Law prescribes that parties may file an appeal against the first instance judgment within fifteen days from the day when judgment transcript is delivered to them, unless otherwise regulated by this Law. Time limit to file an appeal is eight days in litigations concerning bills of exchange and checks.

A timely filed appeal prevents the judgment from becoming enforceable in the part challenged by the appeal (Article 367, paragraph 2).

1250. It is prescribed by Article 373 that a judgment may be challenged in the following cases: (1) in case of significant violation of civil procedure rules; (2) due to an incorrect or incomplete fact finding; and (3) due to incorrect application of material law.

1251. According to Article 377, the appeal is submitted to the court which rendered the first instance judgment in a sufficient number of copies for the court and for the other party. Article 399 prescribes that decision of the first instance court may be appealed unless otherwise provided in this Law. If this Law specifically provides that no special appeal is allowed, a decision of the first instance court can be challenged only in the appeal against the final decision (Article 399, paragraph 2).

II. The Extraordinary Legal Remedies

1252. The extraordinary legal remedies are:

- revision (403–420);
- a request for review of a final judgment (Articles 421–425);
- repeated trial (Articles 426–435).

1253. According to provisions of Article 389, parties may file an appeal against a first instance judgment to the Supreme Court of Serbia within fifteen days of the delivery, if a party requests that the Supreme Court adjudicate the appeal and the other party agrees. This legal remedy may be invoked in civil actions, where review is allowed, only in case of an incorrect application of substantive law and a significant violation of civil procedure rules specified under Article 361, paragraph 2, item 5.[1411]

1411. A significant violation of civil procedure provisions exists if the court does not apply, or improperly applies certain provision of this Law in the course of the proceedings, which affected or might have affected rendering of a lawful and proper judgment. Significant violations of civil procedure

1254. According to Article 394, parties may file a request for review of a final second instance judgment in all civil action proceedings within thirty days of the delivery of the judgment. Review is not allowed in litigations concerning property where the claim is related to pecuniary value or handing over of things or performance of another obligation, if the value of the subject of litigation, in regard to the challenged part of a final judgment, does not exceed RSD 500,000.

1255. Review is not allowed in property-related litigation where the claim is not related to pecuniary value or handing over of things or performance of another obligation, if the value of the subject of litigation does not exceed RSD 500,000. Exceptions are prescribed by this Article too.[1412]

1256. The Supreme Court of Serbia rules on a motion for review (Article 396).

1257. The Motion for the Protection of Legality is defined by Article 413. The public prosecutor may file a motion for the protection of legality against a final court decision or upon the proposal of a party within three months. The time limit for the Motion for the Protection of Legality starts to run:

- In case of a first instance decision which has not been appealed – as of the day when such decision may not be appealed any more.
- In case of a second instance decision against which a motion for review has not been filed – as of the day when such decision is delivered to the party who last received such decision.

1258. Article 422 prescribes that the trial completed by a final court decision may be repeated upon the request of a party in following cases:

(1) if a party did not have an opportunity to argue before the court due to an illegal action, and in particular due to the failure of the court to effect service;
(2) if a person who cannot be a party to the proceedings took part in the proceedings as the plaintiff or defendant;
(3) if a party who is a legal entity was not represented by an authorized person;
(4) if a party incompetent for litigation was not represented by a legal representative;
(5) if a legal representative or attorney of a party was not properly authorized to participate in the proceedings or as regards certain actions in the proceedings,

provisions occur, *inter alia*, if contrary to the provisions of this Law, the Court made a decision on a claim that the parties could not dispose with (Art. 3, para. 3).

1412. Review of the final second instance court judgment that cannot be reviewed according to the provisions of Art. 394 is exceptionally allowed, if appellate court rules that it is necessary to interpret a legal issue of general interest or ensure uniform case law or when new interpretation of the law is necessary.

unless their participation in the proceedings or certain actions was later approved;
(6) if a decision of the court was founded on a false testimony of a witness or expert witness;
(7) if a decision of the court was based on a counterfeited document or document certifying false contents;
(8) if a decision of the court was made through a criminal offence of the judge, or lay judge, legal representative or attorney of a party, the other party or third party;
(9) if a party gains a possibility to use a final decision of the court made earlier between the same parties about the same claim;
(10) if a decision of the court is based on another decision of the court or another body, and such decisions are subsequently reversed, set aside or annulled;
(11) if an interlocutory issue (Article 12) was subsequently decided before the competent body and the decision was based on the decision about such issue;
(12) if a party learns about new facts or finds or obtains a possibility to use new evidence, which could have resulted in a more favourable decision for such party had it been used in the previous proceedings;
(13) if the European Court for Human Rights, after final decision of the national court, passed a decision about the same or similar legal relation against Serbia and Montenegro.[1413]

§3. Administrative Dispute

1259. It is prescribed by Article 14 of the Law on Administrative Disputes (OJ RS, No. 111/09) that an administrative dispute[1414] can be initiated against an administrative Act which was passed in the second degree and against the first instance administrative Act against which no appeal is allowed in administrative procedure.[1415]

1413. Repeated procedure may not be requested due to reasons referred to in Art. 422, points 1–3 of this Law if such reasons were presented unsuccessfully in the course of previous proceedings. Trial may be repeated due to circumstances stipulated in Art. 422, points 1, 7, 8 and 9 of this Law only if a party was unable, through no fault of his/her own, to present such circumstances before the previous proceedings were finished by a final court decision (Art. 423).

1414. In an administrative dispute the court decides about the legality of final administrative Acts, except those for which another kind of judicial protection was prescribed. The court also decides about the legality of final individual acts dealing with right, obligation, or on the law-based interest, for which is not prescribed other kinds of judicial protection. The court also decides about the legality of other final individual Acts when it is prescribed by law. Provisions of this Law concerning the administrative Act are applied to other Acts against which an administrative dispute could be initiated (Art. 3).

1415. Administrative disputes may be initiated when the competent authority on the application, or a party's appeal, has not brought an administrative Act, under the conditions stipulated by this law (Art. 15).

1260. Administrative dispute is initiated by a lawsuit (Article 17). The lawsuit shall be filed within thirty days of receipt of the administrative Act to the party that filed the lawsuit or by law required shorter period (Article 18, paragraph 1).[1416]

1261. Extraordinary legal remedies are request for review of court decisions (Articles 49–55) and repetition of the procedure (Articles 56–65). In accordance with Article 49 of the Law against a final decision of the Administrative Court, the party and the competent public prosecutor may file a request for review of the Court's decision to the Supreme Court of Cassation.[1417]

1262. Pursuant to Article 56 procedure completed by a final verdict or decision of the Court shall be reopened by the party's lawsuit in following cases: (1) if the party finds new facts, or finds and acquires the ability to use new evidences, which would resolve the dispute better if presented or used in earlier proceedings; (2) if the Court's decision has resulted from criminal acts of a judge or Court employee, or the decision was obtained by making fraudulent act of the agent or representative of a party, his/her opponent or the opponent's attorney or representative, and if such action constitutes a criminal offence; (3) if the Court's decision was based on the adopted verdict in criminal or civil matters, and such Act was later repealed by another final Court decision; (4) if the documents underlying the Court's decision were false or fraudulently altered, or if the witness, expert or party at the hearing before the court, gave false testimony, and the court decision was based on that testimony; (5) if the party finds or acquires the ability to use an earlier court decision made in the same dispute; (6) if an interested person was not allowed to participate in the administrative proceedings; and (7) if the subsequent attitude of the decision of the European Court of Human Rights, in the same case, affects the legality of validly completed court trial.

1416. The term referred to in para. 1 of this Article applies to the authority authorized to file an action if it is an administrative document (Art. 18, para. 2). If the authority authorized to file the lawsuit, or interested party, has not been submitted to an administrative Act, the authority or interested person may file a lawsuit, within sixty days from receipt of the administrative Act to the party (Art. 18, para. 3).

1417. The request may also be submitted in the following cases: (1) when the law approves it; (2) in cases where the court had the jurisdiction to decide in full; (3) in matters in which an administrative appeal procedure was excluded (Art. 49, para. 2). The request may be filed for violation of the Law, other regulation or general Act, or violation of rules of procedure that could have affected the decision (Art. 49, para. 3).

Chapter 3. Other Forms of Juridical Actions of Individuals

§1. The Protector of Citizens (Ombudsman)

1263. The Protector of Citizens (Ombudsman) is a public authority established in 2007 by the Law on the Protector of Citizens (OJ RS, Nos 79/2005 and 54/2007).[1418] According to Article 3 of the Law on the Protector of Citizens (OJ RS, No. 105/2021),[1419] 'the Protector of Citizens shall be independent and autonomous in the performance of his/her duties provided for in this Law and no one shall have the right to influence his/her work and activities'.

1264. The Protector of Citizens shall also ensure that human and minority rights and freedoms are protected and promoted (Article 1, paragraph 2). In addition, the Protector of Citizens performs other duties. The Protector shall perform the duties of the National Preventive Mechanism, following the Law on Ratification of the Optional Protocol to the Convention against Torture and Other Cruel, Inhuman or Degrading Treatment or Punishment (OJ S&M – International Treaties, Nos 16/05 and 2/06 and OJ RS – International Treaties, No. 7/11) (Article 2, paragraph 1); The Protector shall perform the tasks of the National Independent Mechanism for monitoring the implementation of the Convention on the Rights of Persons with Disabilities, according to the Law on Ratification of the Convention on the Rights of Persons with Disabilities (OJ RS – International Agreements, No. 42/09); The Protector of Citizens shall perform the duties of a National Rapporteur on Trafficking in Human Beings, following the Law on Ratification of the Council of Europe Convention on Action against Trafficking in Human Beings (OJ RS – International Agreements No. 19/09); The Protector of Citizens shall hold the position of a special body that protects, promotes, and improves the rights of the child.

1265. The Protector of Citizens shall have the power to control the legality and regularity of work of administrative authorities to determine whether their acts, actions or failure to act resulted in violations of citizens' rights guaranteed by the Constitution, ratified international treaties, generally accepted rules of international law, laws, other regulations and general acts of the RS (Article 19, paragraphs 1 and 2).[1420] The Protector of Citizens shall not have the power to control the work of the NA, the President, the Government, the CC, courts and public prosecutor's offices.

1418. The Provincial Ombudsman was established in 2002 by virtue of the decision of Provincial Assembly on Provincial Ombudsman. *See* OJ AVP, No. 37/14. The Law on Local Self-government (OJ RS, Nos 129/07, 83/14 – other law, 101/16 – other law, 47/18, and 111/21 – other law) envisages the institution of ombudsman at the local level.

1419. This law hereby regulates the position, mandate and investigation before the Protector of Citizens as an independent state authority that shall protect the rights of citizens and control the work of government agencies, the body authorized for legal protection of property rights and interests of the Republic of Serbia and other bodies and organizations, enterprises and institutions vested with public powers (hereinafter 'administrative authorities') (Art. 1).

1420. The Protector of Citizens shall be entitled to propose laws within his/her mandate (Art. 20, para. 1).

The Protector of Citizens may undertake procedural and other actions in proceedings before state and other bodies and organizations, when he/she is authorized to do so by special regulations (Article 19, paragraphs 2 and 3).

1266. The Protector of Citizens shall initiate investigations pursuant to citizens' complaints or on own initiative (Article 27, paragraph 1).[1421] The Protector of Citizens may initiate investigation on his/her own initiative, when on the basis of his/her own knowledge or information received from other sources, including only exceptionally anonymous complaints, he/she estimates that an act, action or failure to act of an administrative authority caused a violation of human rights or freedoms (Article 38, paragraph 1).

1267. Any natural person or legal entity, whether local or foreign, who considers that their human or minority rights and freedoms have been violated by an act, action or failure to act of an administrative authority may file a complaint with the Protector of Citizens (Article 28, paragraph 1). Prior to filing a complaint, the complainant shall endeavour to protect his/her rights in appropriate legal proceedings before an administrative authority (Article 28, paragraph 7).[1422] By way of exception, the Protector of Citizens may initiate investigation even before all available legal remedies before the competent administrative bodies have been exhausted if the complainant would sustain irreparable damage or if the complaint concerns a violation of the good governance principle, including in particular unfair treatment of the complainant by administrative bodies, untimely acting or other violations of the code of ethics for employees of administrative authorities (Article 28, paragraph 9).

1268. The Protector of Citizens shall not proceed on anonymous complaints (Article 28, paragraph 10).[1423]

1269. Complaints shall be filed in writing or orally for the record and shall not require the payment of any fees or other charges. A complaint may be filed not later than three year from the day the violation of the right of citizen occurred, and/or from the date of the last action undertaken by the administrative authority in respect of the violation (Article 29).[1424]

1421. In addition to the right to initiate and conduct investigations, the Protector of Citizens shall have the right to act preventively by providing good services, mediation and giving advice and opinions on issues within his/her sphere of competence, with a view to improving the work of administrative bodies and protection of human rights and freedoms (Art. 32, para. 1).

1422. The Protector of Citizens shall instruct the complainant to initiate relevant legal proceedings where such proceedings are available, and shall not initiate the investigation until all available legal remedies before the competent administrative authorities have been exhausted (Art. 28, para. 8).

1423. By way of exception, if the Protector of Citizens considers that an anonymous complaint provides grounds for his/her acting, he/she may initiate own initiative investigation (Art. 28, para. 11).

1424. The Protector of Citizens shall pass a Conclusion dismissing a complaint: (1) If the subject matter of the complaint is not within the mandate of the Protector of Citizens; (2) If the complaint is filed after the expiry of the statutory time limit; (3) If the complaint is filed before exhausting all available legal remedies before administrative authorities, and the requirements specified under Art. 29

1270. The Protector of Citizens shall submit to the complainant and the relevant administrative authority the Conclusion on initiating the investigation procedure and shall demand the administrative authority to provide its opinion on the complaint in writing and to submit necessary notifications and documents within a time limit determined by the Protector of Citizens, which cannot be longer than fifteen days (Article 34, paragraph 1).[1425]

1271. Upon completing the investigation procedure, the Protector of Citizens shall compile a case report in writing, which he/she shall submit to the competent authority and the complainant and publish it on his/her official website (Article 37, paragraph 1). In the report on the case, the Protector of Citizens shall determine whether there were illegalities and irregularities in the acts, actions, or omissions of the administrative authority, which violated the human or minority rights and freedoms of citizens (Article 37, paragraphs 1, and 2). If they find irregularities and illegalities in the work of administrative bodies, the Protector of Citizens shall make a recommendation in the case report on how irregularities and illegalities in work should be rectified, i.e., the manner of improving the work of authorities (paragraph 3).[1426]

1272. If the administrative authority fails to submit the notification referred to in paragraph 5 of this Article to the Protector of Citizens within the set deadline, if fails to comply or only partially complies with the recommendation, as well as if it fails to comply with the recommendation on the dismissal of an official responsible for the violation of the right or initiation of disciplinary proceedings against an employee responsible for the violation of the right, the Protector of Citizens shall notify the immediately superior authority the NA, the Government and the public thereof (Article 37, paragraph 7).[1427]

---

para. 9 of this Law have not been met; (4) If the complaint is anonymous or insulting or if a decision on its merits has already been made; (5) If the complaint does not contain the information required for acting on it, and the complainant has not rectified such shortcomings within the additional period of five working days determined for supplementing the complaint, or sought the assistance of the Secretariat of the Protector of Citizens in rectifying such shortcomings (Art. 32, para. 1). A complaint filed by a child cannot be dismissed in the cases referred to in para. 1, items 3) and 5) of this Article.

1425. The administrative authority to which a complaint relates shall grant the Protector of Citizens access to its official premises. All officials and employees in the administrative authority shall accept a request of the Protector of Citizens to participate in the investigation procedure and provide necessary explanations(Art. 34, para. 4, and 5).

1426. The administrative authority, within the deadline determined by the Protector of Citizens in the case report, which cannot be shorter than fifteen or longer than ninety days from the day of receiving the case report, shall notify the Protector of Citizens whether and in what way it acted on the recommendation referred to in para. 3 of this Article, i.e., on the reasons for which it may not have acted on the recommendation (Art. 37, para. 5).

1427. The Protector of Citizens shall submit a regular annual report on his/her work and the state of human rights in the Republic of Serbia to the National Assembly, which shall include the following: information on activities in the preceding year, information on identified irregularities in the work of administrative authorities, recommendations for improvement of the practice and the normative regulation of individual fields, proposals for improvement of the status of citizens about administrative bodies, as well as data on the implementation of recommendations and proposals

§2. The Commissioner for the Information of Public Importance and the Protection of Personal Data

1273. The Commissioner for the Information of Public Importance and the Protection of Personal data (CIPIPDP) was established by Article 1, paragraph 2 of Law on Free Access to the Information of Public Importance (OJ RS, Nos 120/04, 54/07, 104/09, 36/10, and 105/21) as an autonomous and independent State authority.

1274. Pursuant to Article 16, if a public authority does not respond to a request within the specified deadline, an applicant may lodge a complaint with the CIPIPDP, except in cases where this Law provides otherwise (paragraph 4).

1275. An applicant may lodge a complaint with the CIPIPDP if: (1) a public authority rejects or denies an applicant's request, within fifteen days of service of the relevant decision or other document; (2) a public authority, in contravention of Article 16, paragraph 2 of this Law, failed to reply to a submitted request within the statutory time limit; (3) a public authority, in contravention of Article 17, paragraph 2 of this Law, made the issuance of a copy of a document containing the requested information conditional on the payment of a fee exceeding the necessary reproduction costs; (4) a public authority does not grant access to a document containing the requested information in the manner set forth in Article 18, paragraph 1 of this Law; (5) a public authority does not grant access to a document containing the requested information and/or does not issue a copy of the document in the manner set out in Article 18, paragraph 4 of this Law; or (6) a public authority otherwise obstructs or prevents an applicant from exercising his/her freedom of access to information of public importance, in contravention to the provisions of this Law (Article 22, paragraph 1). However, complaints shall be inadmissible if lodged against decisions of the NA, the President of the Republic, the Government of the RS, the Supreme Court of Serbia, the CC and the Republic Public Prosecutor (Article 22, paragraph 2).[1428]

§3. The Commissioner for the Protection of Equality

1276. The Law on Prohibition of Discrimination (OJ RS, Nos 22/09, and 52/21)[1429] established the Commissioner for the Protection of Equality appointed by the NA (Article 28).

---

from previous reports (Art. 39, para. 1). For the annual reports (2008–2019), *see* http://www.ombudsman.org.rs/index.php?option=com_content&view=category&layout=blog&id=11&Itemid=13 (6.1.2024).

1428. An administrative dispute complaint may be lodged against the decision in para. 2 of this Article, in accordance with Law, which fact shall be notified to the Commissioner by the relevant court ex officio (Art. 22, para. 3).

1429. *See* http://ravnopravnost.gov.rs/en/ (6.1.2024). For the information about activities of the Commissioner for the Protection of Equality (2010–2019), *see* http://ravnopravnost.gov.rs/en/reports/ (6.1.2024).

1277. According to Article 33 of the Law the Commissioner: (1) shall receive and review complaints pertaining to violations of provisions of this Law, provide opinions and recommendations in specific cases, and pass measures in accordance with the provisions of Article 40 of this Law; (2) shall provide information to the person lodging a complaint concerning his/her rights and the possibility of initiating court proceedings or some other proceedings for the purpose of protection, or recommend reconciliation; (3) shall file charges in accordance with Article 43 of this Law, pertaining to violations of rights guaranteed by this Law, in his/her own name, and with the agreement and on behalf of the person discriminated against, unless proceedings before a court of law have already been initiated or concluded by passing an enforceable decision; (4) shall submit misdemeanour notices on account of violations of rights guaranteed by this Law; (5) shall submit an annual report and special reports to the NA about the situation concerning the protection of equality; (6) shall warn the public of the most frequent, typical and severe cases of discrimination; (7) shall monitor the implementation of laws and other regulations, initiate the passing or amending of regulations for the purpose of implementing and developing protection against discrimination, and provide opinions concerning the provisions of draft laws and other regulations pertaining to the prohibition of discrimination; (8) shall establish and maintain cooperation with organs authorized to ensure equality and the protection of human rights on the territory of an AP or a local government; and (9) shall recommend measures to public administration organs and other persons aimed at ensuring equality.

1278. Pursuant to Article 17, discrimination in the provision of public services shall be considered to occur if a legal or physical entity, within the framework of its/his/her activities or profession, refuses to provide a service on the grounds of a personal characteristic of an individual or a group of persons, or if the said entity, in order to provide the service in question, requires the fulfilment of some condition that is not required of other individuals or group of persons, or if the said entity unwarrantedly gives priority to another individual or a group of persons when it comes to providing a service.[1430]

§4. Mediation

1279. In relation to judicial and administrative proceedings, mediation (conciliation) represents an alternative mechanism for settling of disputes.[1431]

1430. Everyone shall have the right to equal access to objects in public use (objects where the head offices of public administration organs are located, objects used in the sphere of education, health care, social welfare, culture, sports, tourism, objects used for the purpose of *environmental protection*, protection against natural disasters and the like), as well as public spaces (parks, squares, streets, pedestrian crossings and other public transport routes and the like), in accordance with the Law (Art. 17, para. 2).

1431. Mediation is any procedure, notwithstanding its name, whereby the parties wish to settle their dispute through one or more mediators assisting the parties to reach an agreement (Art. 2). For more information on mediation, *see* https://www.mpravde.gov.rs/en/sekcija/28482/mediation.php (6.1. 2024).

1280. According to Article 1 of the Law on Mediation in Dispute Resolution (OJ RS, No. 55/14), this Law regulates the notion, principles, procedure and legal effect of mediation in dispute settlement, conditions for mediation, the rights and duties of intermediaries and the training programme of mediators.[1432] Mediation is applied in disputed relationships where the parties may freely dispose of their claims, unless another law prescribes exclusive jurisdiction of a court or another authority, regardless of whether mediation is carried out before or after the initiation of judicial or other proceedings (Article 3, paragraph 1). Mediation is possible especially in the following disputes: property-related disputes concerning the fulfilment of the obligation to act, other property disputes, disputes relating to environmental protection issues, consumer disputes, family, commercial disputes, administrative matters, and all other contentious relations where mediation is appropriate to the nature of the contentious relations and can aid in their resolution (Article 3, paragraph 2). The Law shall also apply to mediation in criminal and misdemeanour proceedings with respect to property claims and claims for damages, as well as in labour disputes unless otherwise stipulated by a special law (Article 3, paragraph 2).[1433]

1281. The mediation process is initiated by the conclusion of an agreement on mediation (Article 18, paragraph 1), i.e., mediation procedure is initiated by submission of the mediation agreement to the court or other authority conducting the proceedings.[1434]

1282. Relationships between mediation and judicial or other proceedings are regulated by Chapter V (Articles 30–32).[1435]

1432. Key novelties of the Law includes, *inter alia*, following: introduction of a Registry of Mediators kept by the Ministry of Justice as a public central electronic database (Art. 42); licensing system for mediators (Ch. VII); power of an enforceable document if agreement on dispute resolution contains enforceability clause, or if the signatures of the parties and the mediator are certified by a court or a notary; establishing system of training for mediators (Ch. VIII); non-compulsory Tariff on Mediation Fees enacted by the Minister of Justice; possibility of court tax exemption incentive (Art. 31), etc.
1433. The provisions of this Act shall not apply to the settlement of disputes relating to the determination and collection of public revenues (Art.3, para. 4).
1434. In this case, stay of judicial proceedings is no longer than sixty days (Art. 18, para. 3).
1435. Mediation procedure may be initiated before or after the judicial proceedings have been initiated, during the proceedings on legal remedies or in the course of enforcement proceedings. The Civil Procedure Law (OJ RS, Nos 72/2011, 49/2013 – CC, 74/2013 – CC, 55/2014, 87/18, 18/20, and 10/23 – other law), in Art. 11 proscribes that the court will refer parties to mediation or to an informative hearing regarding mediation, in accordance with the law, as well as that the court will indicate to the parties the possibility that they can reach an out-of-court settlement through mediation or in another suitable way. The court will stay the proceedings and refer parties to mediation, if it is so proscribed in the law, or when the parties themselves willingly propose to settle the dispute through mediation (The Civil Procedure Law, Art. 340). Guidelines for enhancing the use of mediation in the Republic of Serbia, Supreme Court of Cassation, High Court Council, Ministry of Justice, 2017, 2, https://www.mpravde.gov.rs/files/20170628%20Joint%20Guidelines%20for%20Enhancing%20the%20Use%20of%20Mediation%20SCC%20MoJ%20HCC.PDF (6.1.2024).

Selected Bibliography

Books and Articles

Arsić, M. (2016). Dugoročne posledice ekonomskog sloma privrede Srbije tokom tokom 90-ih godina 20-og veka [Long Run Consequences of Collapse of Serbian Economy During the Nineties of the 20th Century]. *Ekonomske ideje i praksa*, 22, 23–41.

Bakrač, T.S., Klem, E., Milanović, M. (2018). Ekološke posledice NATO bombardovanja Republike Srbije 1999. godine [Environmental Consequences of the NATO Bombing of the Republic of Serbia in 1999]. *Vojno delo*, 7, 475–492.

Birnie, P.W., Boyle, A.E. (2002). *International Law and Environment.* Oxford University Press.

Bjegovic-Mikanovic, V., Vasic, M, Vukovic, D., Jankovic, J., Jovic-Vranes, A., Santric-Milicevic, M., Terzic-Supic, Z., Hernández-Quevedo, C. (2019). *Serbia: Health system review. Health Systems in Transition*, 21(3), WHO.

Bobić, M. & Todić, D. (2015). Usklađivanje nacionalnih propisa Republike Srbije sa propisima EU i učešće javnosti [Harmonisation of National Regulations of the Republic of Serbia with EU Regulations and Public Participation], in G. Marković (Ed.) Collection of Papers, *Relationship Between the EU Law and the Law in the Region*, Istočno Sarajevo: Pravni fakultet, 458–472.

Bogdanović, S. (Ed.). (2008). *Zaštita životne sredine Republike Srbije – između politike i prakse približivanja EU* [*Protection of the Environment of the Republic of Serbia – Between Policy and Practice of Association with the EU*]. Novi Sad: Jugoslovensko udruženje za vodno pravo.

Cuchietti, A., Morales-Hidalgo, D., García, J. (2023). *Complementary document to the results of the Serbian Second National Forest Inventory – Land Cover Change assessment using the FAO Collect Earth tool – From 2000 to 2019.* FAO, MAFWM, GEF.

Čalić, M.Z. (2004). *Socijalna istorija Srbije 1815–1941: usporeni napredak u industrijalizaciji* [Social History of Serbia 1815–1941: Slow Progress in Industrialization]. Belgrade: Clio.

Čavoški, A. (2010). Transposition of Acquis – Challenges and Difficulties Facing the Serbian Administration. *European Review of Public Law* 22, No. 4, 1179–1197.

Čavoški, K. (Ur). (2020). *Secesija sa stanovišta unutrašnjeg i međunarodnog prava i njene političke posledice* [Secession Through the Eyes of Domestic and International Law and its Political Consequences]. Beograd: Srpska akademija nauka i umetnosti.

Čok, V. (1998). Legal Grounds of Environmental Protection in Yugoslavia. *Yugoslav Law*, 3, 159–174, Belgrade: Institute of Comparative Law.

Dimić, LJ. (2001). *Istorija srpske drzavnosti*, knjiga III, Srbija u Jugoslaviji 1918–1990 [*History of the Serbian Statehood, Book III, Serbia in Yugoslavia*]. Beseda, Novi Sad: SANU.

Drenovak – Ivanović – M. (2016). Environmental Impact Assessment in Serbian Legal System: Current Issues and Prospects for Revision, *Anali Pravnog fakulteta u Beograd*, Vol. 64, No. 3, 126–139.

Djurdjević, V. (2020). *Drought Initiative – Republic of Serbia Recommendations for development of the National Drought Plan of the Republic of Serbia*. UN Convention to Combat Desertification, Ministry of Environmental Protection.

Đurđević, V., Vuković, A., Vujadinović Mandić, M. (2018). *Climate Change Observed in Serbia and Future Climate Projections Based on Different Scenarios of Future Emissions*. UNDP Serbia.

Etinski, R. (2013a). Specifične osobine ljudskih prava zajemčenih Arhuskom konvencijom [Specific Features of Human Rights Guaranteed by the Aarhus Convention]. *Zbornik radova Pravnog fakulteta*, Novi Sad, 47(2), 79–92.

Etinski, R. (2013b). Neposredna primena međunarodnog ugovora u pravnom poretku Republike Srbije, in Novaković, M. (Ed). *Basic Concepts of Public International Law – Monism & Dualism*. Belgrade. 729–756.

Gazzini, T. (2001). NATO Coercive Military Activities in the Yugoslav Crisis (1992–1999), *European Journal of International Law*, 12(3), 391–436, https://doi.org/10.1093/ejil/12.3.391.

Glavonjić, B. et al. (2005). *Forest and Forest Products Country Profile: Serbia and Montenegro*. Geneva Timber and Forest Discussion Paper 40, Geneva: UNECE/FAO.

Grbić, V. & Todić, D. (2011). Ekonomski instrumenti za upravljanje otpadom u ruralnim regionima jugoistične Evrope [Economic Instruments for Waste Management in Rural Regions of South East Europe]. *Ekonomika poljoprivrede*, 2, 55–61.

Ignjatić, M., Todić, D. (2014). *Rezultati i problemi u sprovođenju IPA programa prekogranične saradnje od značaja za oblast životne sredine i Poglavlje 27* [Results and Problems in the Implementation of the IPA Cross Border Cooperation Program Relevant for Environmental Field and Chapter 27]. in A. Mihajlov (ur). Collection of Papers, *Poglavlje 27- Životna sredina i klimatske promene*, Beograd: Ambasadori održivog razvoja i životne sredine, 16–21.

Ignjatović, J. & S. Đorđević. (2006). *Priručnik za predstavnike javne vlasti o pristupu informacijama od javnog znacaja u oblasti voda i životne sredine* [*Guide of Public Authorities on Access to Information of Public Importance in the Field of Water and Environment*]. Beograd: Reginalni centrar za zivotnu sredinu za centralnu i istocnu Evropu [REC – Regional Environmental Centre for Central and East Europe].

Janković, M.M. (1996). Razvoj ekološke misli u Srbiji [*Development of Ecological Thought in Serbia*]. Beograd: Ekocentar.

Jeftić, M., Šećerov, V., Tošić, D. (2021). Development of the urban systems in Serbia – towards new spatial plan of the Republic of Serbia, in Grčić, M. *et. al.* (Eds). *Innovative Approach and Perspectives of the Applied Geography*, Collection of Papers of the 5th Serbian Congress of Geographers, 9–11 September 2021, Novi Sad. – Novi Sad: Faculty of Sciences, Department of Geography, Tourism and Hotel Management.

Joldžić, V., Jovašević, D. (2013). *Ekološki prekršaji u pravnom sistemu Republike Srbije: teorijsko-praktični pristup* [Environmental offences in the legal system of the Republic of Serbia: a theoretical-practical approach]. Beograd: Institut za kriminološka i sociološka istraživanja.

Josimović, B., Stefanović, N., Bezbradica, Lj. (2017). Transponovanje evropske directive o proceni uticaja planova i programa na životnu sredinu u planiranju u Srbiji [Transposition of European Directive on the Assessment of the Effects of Plans and Programmes on the Environment in Planning in Serbia]. *Arhitektura i urbanizam*, 44, 31–35.

Jovašević, D. (2014). Sistem ekoloških delikata u Srbiji [System of Environmental Delicts in Serbia]. *Teme*, 38(2), 621–639.

Jović, D., Glavonjić, B. (2020). Serbia, in *FOREST EUROPE, 2020: State of Europe's Forests*, 235–236.

Lepotić Kovačević, B. (2021). Energetska efikasnost – posebna oblast prava energetike ili princip prava energetike [Energy Efficency – Special Part of the Energy Law or Principle of the Energy Law], in J. S.Perović Vujačić (Ed). *Primena prava i pravna sigurnost.* Zbornik radova 34. Susreta Kopaoničke škole prirodnog prava – Slobodan Perović, Proceedings of the 34th Meeting of Kopaonik School of Natural Law – Slobodan Perović, Tom I/Vol. I, 259–273.

Lilić, S. (2011). Instruments of Environmental Justice. *Facta universitatis – series: Law and Politics*, 9(1), 35–52.

Lilić, S., Drenovak, M. (2009). *Upravna i upravno-sudska zaštita prava na učešće javnosti u stvarima od značaja za životnu sredinu u Srbiji.* [The Right to Public Participation in the Matters of Environmental Protection]. *Anali Pravnog fakulteta u Beogradu*, 57(1), 217–231.

Maslac, T. (2022). *Agricultural Biotechnology Annual – Serbia.* United States Department of Agriculture (USDA), Global Agricultural Information Network. https://apps.fas.usda.gov/newgainapi/api/Report/DownloadReportByFileName?fileName=Agricultural%20Biotechnology%20Annual_Belgrade_Serbia_RB2022-0009.pdf (25.1.2024).

Milenković, M. (2014). *Javne agencije i zaštita životne sredine u pravu Evropske unije i u pravu Srbije – doktorska disertacija* [Public Agencies and the Protection of the Environment in European Union Law and Serbia Law – Ph.D. thesis]. Beograd: Univerzitet u Beogradu, Pravni fakultet.

Mladenov, M. (2017). *Pravo na odgovarajuću životnu sredinu kao osnovno ljudsko pravo – doktorska disertacija* [The Right to an Adequate Environment as Fundamental Human Right Ph.D. Thesis]. Novi Sad: Univerzitet u Novom Sadu, Pravni fakultet.

Nikolić, D., Gajinov, T. (2014). Konvencionalna upotreba poljoprivrednog zemljišta i imisije genetski modifikovanih organizama [Conventional Agricultural

Land Use and Immissions of Genetically Modified Organisms]. *Zbornik radova Pravnog fakulteta Novi Sad*, 48(3), 81–105.

Pantić, M., Živanović Miljkovć, J., Milijić, S. (2019). Land use and building regulations: the case of spatial plans for protected natural areas (Serbia). *Facta Univesitatis*, 17(2), 173–187. https://doi.org/10.2298/FUACE190315010P.

Pavlović, S.K. (2004). *Srbija: istorija iza imena* [Serbia: The History Behind the Name] Beograd: Clio.

Petković, G. (2021). Nezakonit promet opasnih otpada u pravu i praksi [Illegal Traffic of Hazardous Waste in Law and Practice]. u Perović, J.S. (Ed). *Primena prava i pravna sigurnost*: zbornik radova 34. susreta Kopaoničke škole prirodnog prava – Slobodan Perović, Tom 1. Beograd. 213–228.

Petković, G. (2014). Pravni aspekt borbe protiv korupcije u oblasti zaštite životne sredine [The Legal Aspect of the Fight Against Corruption in the Field of Environmental Protection]. *Pravni život*, 9.

Petković, G. (2005). Novo zakonodavstvo u oblasti upravljanja zaštitom životne sredine [New Legislation on Environmental Management], *Pravni život*, No. 9, 551–572.

Petrušić, N. 2003). Zaštita od imisija u građanskom sudskom postupku [Protection from Imission in Court Procedure], *Pravni život*, 12.

Pokuševski, D. (Ed.). (2022). *Human Rights in Serbia 2021: Law, Practice, and Interranational Human Rigths Standards.* Belgrade: The Belgrade Centre for Human Rights, 238–247.

Račić, A.J. (2019). Hemijske i biološke posledice NATO bombardovanja Srbije [Chemical and Biological Consequences of the NATO Bombing of Serbia]. *Tehnika*, 74(3), 478–481.

Radonjić, A., Stjelja, I. (2018). *Ekološka tužba – pravo svih nas da zaštitimo životnu sredinu: priručnik sa preporukama* [Environmental Lawsuit – the Right of All of us to Protect the Environment: a Handbook with Recommendations]. Beograd: Beogradski centar za ljudska prava.

Rakić-Vodinelić, V. (1989). Ekoloska tužba, *Pravni život*, No. 4.

Sharman N. (2023). Objectives of public participation in international environmental decision-making. *International and Comparative Law Quarterly*. 72(2), 333–360. doi:10.1017/S0020589323000088.

Slavnić, Lj. (2013). Pravo na zaštitu zdravlja: skromni dometi ustava Srbija [The Right to Protection of Health: Modest Achievements of the Constitution of Serbia]. *Pravo – teorija i praksa*. 30(1–3), 28–41.

Smailagić, J., et al. (2013). *Climate characteristics of Serbia.* Belgrade: Republic Hydrometeorological Service of Serbia.

Stojanović, P., Zindović, I. (2015). Pravna odgovornost za razvoj i zaštitu životne sredine [Legal Liability for Sustainable Development and Environmental Protection]. *Anali Pravnog fakulteta u Beogradu*, LXIII, 1, 41–57.

Šolak, Z. (2007). Pravo na zdravlje i ekonomska osnova njegovog ostvarenja [Right to Health and Economic Bases of Its Realization], *Pravni život*, godina LVI, 9, 277–308.

Tintor, Lj. (2022). Pravo na čistu i zdravu životnu sredinu: dometi i ograničenja ljudskog prava u nastajanju [The Right to a Clean and Healty Environment:

Achievemnts and Limits of Human Rights in Making]. *Harmonius-Journal of Legal and Social Studies in South East Europe,* 313–334.

Todić, D. (2023a). Zakoni o klimatskim promenama: potreba ili normativno pomodarstvo (primer Srbije i Hrvatske) [Climate Change Laws: A Necessity or a Normative Newfangledness (examples of Serbia and Croatia)]. *Strani pravni život,* 1, 75–89.

Todić, D. (2023b). The Global Pact for the Environment: Elements of Codification or/and a new International Agreement. *Zbornik radova Pravnog fakulteta u Nišu,* 99, 169–187.

Todić, D. (2021. Conditions and Effects of Environmental Legislation Changes: Twenty years from the beginning of the Europeanization process in the Republic of Serbia. *Zbornik radova Pravnog fakulteta u Nišu,* 91, 51–74.

Todić, D. (2019). Multilateral Environmental Agreements and EU Integration of Western Balkan States (Status of Bosnia and Herzegovina, Montenegro, Serbia and Croatia in Multilateral Environmental Agreements), *European Energy and Environmental Law Review,* 28(1), 17–27.

Todić, D. (2018a). *Ujedinjene nacije, međunarodni ugovori i životna sredina* [*United Nations, International Treaties and Environment*], Beograd: Institut za međunarodnu politiku i privredu.

Todić, D. (2018b). Status Republike Srbije u savremenim međunarodnim ugovorima u oblasti životne sredine i ustavi (1974–2006) [The Status of the Republic of Seriba in Contemporary International Environmental Agreements and Constitutions (1974–2006)]. *Zbornik radova Pravnog fakulteta u Nišu,* 77, 1–16.

Todić, D. (2017a). 'Europeanisation' of law of the Republic of Serbia: Between (un)clear goals and (in)appropriate indicators, In: B. Milisavljević, T. Jevremović Petrović, M. Živković (Eds). *Law and Transition*, Belgrade: University of Belgrade, Faculty of Law, 45–56.

Todić, D. (2017b). Savremeno zakonodavstvo Republike Srbije u oblasti životne sredine: od 'integralnog sistema' ka hiperprodukciji propisa [Contemporary Environmental Legislation of the Republic of Serbia: From the 'integral system' to the Hyperproduction of Regulations], *Collection of Papers, Faculty of Law Niš*, 56(77), 1–16.

Todić, D. (2016). Pariski sporazum o klimi u sistemu međunarodnih ugovora od značaja za EU integracije Republike Srbije [Paris Agreement on Climate in the System of International Agreements relevant for the EU Integration of the Republic of Seriba], *Evropsko zakonodavstvo*, 58, 111–129.

Todić, D., Dimitrijević, D. (2014). Priority goals in international co-operation of the Republic of Serbia in the field of environment and sustainable development, *International Environmental Agreements: Politics, Law and Economics*: 14(2), 163–179. DOI: 10.1007/s10784-013-9207-4.

Todić, D., Todić, J. (2022). Transboundary issues and cooperation in the domain of environmental protection in the legislation of Croatia, Serbia, Montenegro and Bosnia and Herzegovina. *Glasnik Advokatske komore Vojvodine*, 94(4), 1130–1178.

Todić, D. & Vukasović, V. (2002). *Ekološka kriza u svetu i odgovor međunarodne zajednice – izbor najznačajnijih međunarodnih dokumenata i jugoslovenskih propisa* [*Environmental Crises and Responses of International Community*].

Beograd: Savezni sekretarijat za rad, zdravstvo i socijalno staranje, Institut za međunarodnu politiku i privredu.

Todić, D., Zlatić, M. (2018). Transboundary Cooperation of Western Balkan States in the field of water resources management: Between the existing treaties and a new international treaties, *Environmental Science & Policy*, 89, 67–72.

Tubić, B. (2012). Pravo na informisanje o životnoj sredini u međunarodnim pravinim aktima [The Right to Environmental Information in International Legal Documents]. *Zbornik radova Pravnog fakulteta u Novom Sadu,* 3, 343–363.

Veličković, N. (2003). Razvoj zakonodavstva o šumarstvu od 1836 do 1990 [Development of Forest Legislation from 1836 to 1990], *Peščanik I*, Niš: Istorijski arhiv grada Niša.

Vučić, M. (2016). Procena uticaja na životnu sredinu u praksi Medunarodnog suda pravde [Environmental Impact Assessment in the Practice of the International Court of Justice]. *Medunarodni problemi*, 68(1), 72–94.

Vujošević, M. & N. Spasić. (2007). The Transition Changes and Their Impact on Sustainable Spatial, Urban and Rural Development of Serbia. In Vujošević, M. (Ed). *Sustainable Spatial Development on Towns and Cities*. Belgrade: International Scientific Conference, 25–26 January 2008. Conference Proceedings, Book I, Institute of Architecture and Civil Engineering in Belgrade, 1–45.

Vukasović, V. (2006). Međunarodnopravno regulisanje zaštite i održivog korišćenja vodnih lresursa sa posebnim osvrtom na sliv reke Save [International Legal Regulation of Protection and Sustainable use of Water Courses]. *Međunarodni problemi*, 1–2, 157–183.

Vukasović, V. & D. Todić. (2002). *Serbia and Montenegro, Environmental Law, International Encyclopaedia of Laws*, Supplement 37. The Hague, London, New York: Kluwer Law International.

Documents and Reports

A) Documents and Reports – International institutions

AC. (2023). *Overview of Implementation of the Aarhus Convention with regards to GMOs*. Aarhus Convention secretariat (AC/GRT_LMO-GMO/2023/Inf.1). Economic Commission for Europe. Geneva.

EC. (2023). *Serbia 2023 Report*, European Commission, SWD(2023) 695 final, Brussels, 8.11.2023. https://www.mei.gov.rs/upload/documents/eu_dokumenta/godisnji_izvestaji_ek_o_napretku/ec_report_serbia_2023.pdf (6.1.2024).

EC. (2022). *Serbia 2022 Report*, European Commission, SWD(2022) 338 final, Brussels, 12.10.2022. https://www.mei.gov.rs/upload/documents/eu_dokumenta/godisnji_izvestaji_ek_o_napretku/ec-report-2022.pdf (24.10.2022).

EC. (2019). *Serbia 2019 Report*, European Commission, SWD(2019) 219 final, Brussels, 29.5.2019. https://neighbourhood-enlargement.ec.europa.eu/system/files/2019-05/20190529-serbia-report.pdf (18.1.2024).

EC. (2016a). *Serbia 2016 Report*. European Commission. SWD(2016) 361 final. Brussels. https://neighbourhood-enlargement.ec.europa.eu/system/files/2018-12/20161109_report_serbia.pdf (29.1.2024).

EC. (2016b). *Screening report Serbia, Chapter 27 – Environment*, WP Enlargement + Countries Negotiating Accession to EU MD 114/16. 8.6.16. https://

neighbourhood-enlargement.ec.europa.eu/system/files/2018-12/screening_report_serbia_-_chapter_27_-_environment.pdf (6.1.2024).

EC. (2015). *Screening report Serbia, Chapter 11* – Agriculture and Rural Development. WP Enlargement + Countries Negotiating Accession to EU MD 29/15. 24.2.15. https://www.mei.gov.rs/upload/documents/eu_dokumenta/Skrining/screening_report_ch_11.pdf (19.1.2024).

EC. (2011). *Commission opinion on Serbia's application for membership of the European Union.* {SEC(2011) 1208 final}. Brussels, 12.10.2011 COM(2011) 668 final. https://mei.gov.rs/upload/documents/eu_dokumenta/misljenje_kandidatura/sr_rapport_2011_en.pdf (22.2.2024).

EEA. (2023). *Waste prevention country profile – Serbia*. European Environment Agency. Copenhagen.

HRW. (2004). *Failure to Protect: Anti-Minority Violence in Kosovo, March 2004*. Human Right Watch, July 2004, Vol. 16 No. 6(D).

IAEA – Annual Report 2007. International Atomic Energy Agency. https://www.iaea.org/publications/reports/annual-report-2007 (5.1.2024).

REC. (2001). *International Law and the Baia Mare Cyanide Spill*. Regional Environmental Centre for Central and Eastern Europe, with the support of the Government of the United Kingdom.

UN. (2023). Report of the Secretary-General, S/2023/735, 5 Oct. 2023, points 92–101. https://unmik.unmissions.org/sites/default/files/s2023735.pdf (23.11.2023).

UN. (2020). Report of the Secretary-General, S/2020/255, 31 March 2020, points 17–23, https://unmik.unmissions.org/sites/default/files/s-2020-255.pdf (6.1.2024).

UN. (1999). Resolution 1244 of the UN Security Council (1999), S/RES/1244 (1999), 10 Jun. 1999; https://peacemaker.un.org/kosovo-resolution1244 (15.04.2024); *see also* https://www.srbija.gov.rs/kosovo-metohija/en/8919 (22.11.2023).

UNDP. (2022). *Serbia National Human Development Report 2022*. United Nations Development Programme. New York.

UNDP. (2005). *Poverty Reduction in Serbia – The Role of Civil Society*. Belgrade: UNDP, 162–180.

UNECE. (2015). *Environmental Performance Reviews, Serbia*, Third Review, New York and Geneva: United Nations, 2015.

UNECE. (2007). *Environmental Performance Reviews, Republic of Serbia*. Second Review, New York and Geneva: United Nations, 2007.

UNECE. (2003). *Environmental Performance Reviews, Yugoslavia*. New York and Geneva: United Nations, 2003.

UNEP. (2004). *From Conflict to Sustainable Development: Assessment of Environmental Hot Spots – Serbia and Montenegro*, UNEP, Ministry of Science and Environmental Protection of the Republic of Serbia, Ministry of Environmental Protection and Physical Planning of the Republic of Montenegro.

UNEP. (2001). *Depleted Uranium in Kosovo, Post-Conflict Environmental Assessment*. United Nations Environment Program, Nairobi. https://wedocs.unep.org/handle/20.500.11822/8647 (16.1.2024).

UNEP. (1999). *The Kosovo Conflict. Consequences for the Environment & Human Settlements*. Switzerland.

UNEP, GEF. (2006). *Development of National Biosafety Framework for Serbia and Montenegro*. Belgrade and Novi Sad: UNEP, GEF, 6. http://www.gmo-free-regions.org/fileadmin/files/gmo-free-regions/Montenegro/Development_of_National_Biosafety_Framework.pdf (6.1.2024).

UNEP, OCHA. (2000). *Cyanide Spill at Baia Mare, Romania*. UNEP/OCHA Assessment Mission, Report. https://reliefweb.int/report/romania/cyanide-spill-baia-mare-romania-unepocha-assessment-mission-advance-copy (14.2.2024).

UNESCO. (2004). *Cultural Heritage in South-East Europe*, Kosovo Protection and Conservation: A Multi-ethnic Heritage in Danger, Mission Report 26–30 April 2004. http://unesdoc.unesco.org/images/0013/001389/138966eb.pdf (6.1.2024).

UNMIK Regulation 032/2000, https://unmik.unmissions.org/sites/default/files/regulations/04serbian/SC2000regs/RSC2000_32.pdf (4.1.2024).

WB. (2023). *Toward Sustainable Growth*. Western Balkans Regular Economic Report No. 24, Fall 2023. World Bank Group. Washington DC.

WHO. (2019). *Health impact of ambient air pollution in Serbia: A call to action*, World Health Organisation, Regional office for Europe, Ministry of Health, Ministry of Environmental Protection, Institut of Public Health of Serbia. https://serbia.un.org/sites/default/files/2019-10/Health-impact-pollution-Serbia_0.pdf (6. 1.2024).

B) Documents and Reports: Republic of Serbia

CIPIPDP. (2023). *Report on the Work for 2022*. Belgrade: Commissioner for Information of Public Importance and Personal Data Protection. https://www.poverenik.rs/en/o-nama/annual-reports.html (14.2.2024).

EPA. (2023a). *Izveštaj o stanju životne sredine u Republici Srbiji za 2022 godinu*. [Report on the State of Environment in the Republic of Serbia for the 2022]. Beograd: Ministarstvo zaštite životne sredine, Agencija za zaštitu životne sredine [Belgrade: Ministry of Environmental Protection, Environmental Protection Agency].

EPA. (2023b). *Godišnji izveštaj o stanju kvaliteta vazduha u Republici Srbiji 2022 godine*. [Annual Report on the State of Air Quality in the Republic of Serbia in 2022]. Beograd: Ministarstvo zaštite životne sredine, Agencija za zaštitu životne sredine.

EPA. (2023c). *Rezultati ispitivanja kvaliteta površinskih i podzemnih voda 2022 [Results of Surface and Underground Water Quality Testing: 2022*]. Beograd: Ministarstvo zaštite životne sredine, Agencija za zaštitu životne sredine.

EPA. (2023d). *Upravljanje otpadom u Republici Srbiji u periodu 2011–2022. godine. [Waste Management in the Republic of Serbia in the period 2011–2022. years]*. Beograd: Ministarstvo zaštite životne sredine, Agencija za zaštitu životne sredine.

EPA. (2022). *Privredni potencijali i aktivnosti od značaja za životnu sredinu Republike Srbije 2020 godine [Economic Potentials and Activities of Importance for the Environment in the Republic of Serba in 2020*]. Beograd: Ministarstvo zaštite životne sredine, Agencija za zaštitu životne sredine.

EPA. (2021). *Report on economic instruments for environmental protection 2019: Indicators Review*. Belgrade: Ministry of Environmental Protection, Environmental Protection Agency.

EPA. (2020). *Izveštaj o stanju zemljišta u Republici Srbiji – Indikatorski prikaz 2018–2019 [The Report on the State of Land in the Republic of Serbia for 2018 and 2019*]. Beograd: Ministarstvo zaštite životne sredine, Agencija za zaštitu životne sredine.

EPA. (2019a). *Izveštaj o stanju životne sredine u Republici Srbiji za 2018. godinu [Report on the State of the Environment in Serbia for 2018*]. Beograd: Ministarstvo zaštite životne sredine, Agencija za zaštitu životne sredine.

EPA. (2019b). *Životna sredina u Srbiji 2004–2019. [Environment in Serbia 2004–2019].* Beograd: Ministarstvo zaštite životne sredine, Agencija za zaštitu životne sredine.

EPA. (2019c). *Environment in Serbia 2004–2019.* Extended Summary. Belgrade: Ministry of Environmental Protection, Environmental Protection Agency. http://www.sepa.gov.rs/download/ENG_FIN_JubilarnaPublikacija.pdf (13.2.2024).

EPA. (2015). *Poljoprivreda i životna sredina u Republici Srbiji – indikatorski prikaz [Agriculture and the Environment in Serbia]*, Beograd: MAEP, EPA.

EPA. (2007). *Environment in Serbia: An Indicator-Based Review.* Belgrade: Ministry of Science and Environmental Protection of the Republic of Serbia; Environmental Protection Agency. https://wedocs.unep.org/bitstream/handle/20.500.11822/9619/-Environment_in_Serbia_an_indicator_%e2%80%93_based_review-2007Serbia_Environment_2007.pdf.pdf?sequence=3&isAllowed=y (10.2.2024).

FMDSE. (2000). *The Consequences of NATO Bombing for the Environment in FR Yugoslavia.* Belgrade: Federal Ministry for Development, Science and the Environment.

GOV RS. (2023a). *Strategija niskougljeničnog razvoja Republike Srbije za period od 2023. do 2030. godine sa projekcijama do 2050. godine.* [The Low-carbon Development Strategy of the Republic of Serbia for the period from 2023 to 2030 with Projections until 2050]. Beograd: Vlada Republike Srbije [Belgrade: Government of the Republic of Serbia]. (OJ RS, No. 46/23).

GOV RS. (2023b). Program prilagođavanja na izmenjene klimatske uslove za period od 2023. do 2030. godine sa akcionim planom [Program for Adaptation to Changed Climate Conditions for the period from 2023 to 2030 with Action Plan]. (OJ RS, No. 119/23).

GOV RS. (2O23c). *Plan upravljanja vodama na teritoriji Republike Srbije do 2027. godine* [Water Management Plan on the Territory of the Republic of Serbia until 2027]. (OJ RS, No. 33/23).

GOV RS. (2022a). *Program zaštite vazduha u Republici Srbiji od 2022. do 2030. godine sa akcionim planom* [Air Quality Programme of the Republic of Serbia for the period 2022–2030 with an Action Plan]. (OJ RS, No. 140/22).

GOV RS. (2022b). *Program upravljanja otpadom u Republici Srbiji za period 2022–2031* [Waste Management Program of the Republic of Serbia for the period 2022–2031]. (OJ RS, No. 12/22).

GOV RS. (2022c). *Strategija za stvaranje podsticajnog okruženja za razvoj civilnog društva u Republici Srbiji za period od 2022–2030. godine.* [Strategy for Creating a Stimulating Environment for the Development of Civil Society in the Republic of Serbia for the period from 2022–2030. years]. OJ RS, No. 23/22).

GOV RS. (2022d). *Odluka o utvrđivanju Energetskog bilansa Republike Srbije za 2023. godinu* [Decision on Determining the Energy Balance of the Republic of Serbia for the year 2023]. (OJ RS, No. 144/22).

GOV RS. (2022e). *Migration profil of the Republic of Serbia for 2021*. Government of the Republic of Serbia. https://kirs.gov.rs/media/uploads/Migracije/Publikacije/Eng/Migration%20Profile%20of%20the%20Republic%20of%20Serbia%20for%202021.pdf (12.2.2024).

GOV RS. (2022f). *National Programme for the Adoption of the EU Acquis 2022–2025, NPAA IV.* Belgrade: Government of the Republic of Serbia, Ministry of European Integration. https://www.mei.gov.rs/upload/documents/nacionalna_dokumenta/npaa/NPAA_2022-2025_EN.pdf (6.1.2024).

GOV RS. (2021a). *Program zaštite prirode Republike Srbije za period od 2021. do 2023. godine [Nature Protection Program of the Republic of Serbia for the period from 2021 to 2023].* (OJ RS, No. 53/21).

GOV RS. (2021b). *Strategija reforme javne uprave u Republici Srbiji za period od 2021. do 2030. godine [Strategy for Public Administration Reform in the Republic of Serbia for the period 2021–2030].* (OJ RS, No. 42/21, 9/22).

GOV RS. (2020). *Nacionalni plan za smanjenje emisija glavnih zagađujućih materija koje potiču iz starih velikih postrojenja za sagorevanje.* [National Plan to Reduce Emissions of Major Pollutants Originating from Old Large Combustion Plants]. (OJ RS, No. 10/20).

GOV RS. (2019a). *Pregovaračka pozicija Republike Srbije za Međuvladinu konferenciju o pristupanju Republike Srbije Evropskoj uniji za Poglavlje 27 – Životna sredina i klimatske promene* [Negotiating Position of the Republic of Serbia for the Intergovernmental Conference on the Accession of the Republic of Serbia to the European Union for Chapter 27 – Environment and Climate Change]. Beograd: Vlada Republike Srbije.

GOV RS. (2019b). *Strategija održivog urbanog razvoja Republike Srbije do 2030. godine* [Sustainable Urban Development Strategy of the Republic of Serbia until 2030]. (OJ RS, No. 47/19).

GOV RS. (2019c). *Opšti plan za odbranu od poplava* [General Plan for Flood Protection]. Beograd: Vlada Republike Srbije. (OJ RS, No. 18/19).

GOV RS. (2018). *National Programme for the Adoption of the EU Acquis, Third Revision, NPAA III.* Belgrade: Government of the Republic of Serbia, Ministry of European Integration. https://www.mei.gov.rs/upload/documents/nacionalna_dokumenta/npaa/third_revision_npaa_18.pdf (6.1.2024).

GOV RS. (2017). *Strategija upravljanja vodama na teritoriji Republike Srbije do 2034.* [Water Management Strategy in the Republic of Serbia for the period up to 2034]. (OJ RS, No. 3/17).

GOV RS. (2016). *Nacionalni program za usvajanje pravnih tekovina Evropske unije: druga revizija* [National Programme for the Adoption of the EU Acquis: NPAA II, Second Revision], Belgrade: Government of the Republic of Serbia, European Integration Office. https://www.mei.gov.rs/upload/documents/nacionalna_dokumenta/npaa/NPAA_2016_revizija_srp.pdf (6.1.2024).

GOV RS. (2015a). *Nacionalna strategija za rešavanje pitanja izbeglica i interno raseljenih lica za period od 2015. do 2020. godine* [The National Strategy for

Resolving the Problems of Refugees and Internally Displaced Persons for the period 2015–2020]. (OJ RS, No. 62/15).
GOV RS. (2015b). *Migration Profile of the Republic of Serbia for 2015*. Belgrade. http://www.kirs.gov.rs/media/uploads/Migracije/Publikacije/Eng/Migration_profile_of_the_Republic_of_Serbia_for_2015.pdf (23.11.2023).
GOV RS. (2014a). *Nacionalni program za usvajanje pravnih tekovina Evropske unije* [National Programme for the Adoption of the EU Acquis: NPAA]. Belgrade: Government of the Republic of Serbia, European Integration Office, Belgrade. https://www.mei.gov.rs/upload/documents/nacionalna_dokumenta/npaa/npaa_2014_2018.pdf (17.1.2024).
GOV RS. (2014b). *Strategija poljoprivrede i ruralnog razvoja RS za period 2014–2024* [Strategy for Agriculture and Rural Development for the period 2014–2024]. (OJ RS, No. 85/14).
GOV RS. (2011a). *Answers to the European Commission's Questionnaire, Chapter 27 (Environment)*, Government of the Republic of Serbia, Belgrade, 2011. https://www.mei.gov.rs/eng/documents/national-documents/answer-to-the-european-commisions-questionnaire (6.1.2024).
GOV RS. (2011b). Answers to the European Commission's Questionnaire, Chapter 15 (Energy), Government of the Republic of Serbia, Belgrade, 2011. https://www.mei.gov.rs/eng/documents/national-documents/answer-to-the-european-commisions-questionnaire (6.1.2024).
GOV RS. (2011c). Answers to the European Commission's Questionnaire, Chapter 13 (Fisheries), Government of the Republic of Serbia, Belgrade, 2011. https://www.mei.gov.rs/eng/documents/national-documents/answer-to-the-european-commisions-questionnaire (6.1.2024).
GOV RS. (2011d). Answers to the European Commission's Questionnaire, Chapter 12 (Food safety, veterinary and phytosanitary policy), Government of the Republic of Serbia, Belgrade, 2011. https://www.mei.gov.rs/eng/documents/national-documents/answer-to-the-european-commisions-questionnaire (6.1.2024).
GOV RS. (2011e). *Nacionalna strategija za aproksimaciju u oblasti životne sredine* (National Environmental Approximation Strategy for the Republic of Serbia), Beograd: Vlada Republike Srbije.
GOV RS. (2010a). *Nacionalni program zaštite životne sredine* [National Environmental Protection Programme]. (OJ RS, No. 12/10).
GOV RS. (2010b). *Strategija upravljanja otpadom za period 2010–2019. godine [Waste Management Strategy 2010–2019*] (OJ RS, No. 29/10).
GOV RS. (2008a). *National Programme for Integration with European Union*. Belgrade: The Republic of Serbia, the Government. https://www.mei.gov.rs/upload/documents/NPI/npi_2009-10_incl_annexes_eng.pdf (27.1.2024).
GOV RS. (2008b). *Nacionalna strategija održivog razvoja* [National Sustainable Development Strategy]. (OJ RS, No. 57/08).
GOV RS. (2008c). *Odluka Vlade Republike Srbije o poništavanju protivpravnih akata privremenih organa samouprave na Kosovu i Metohiji o proglašenju jednostrane nezavisnosti* [Decision on the Annulment of the Illegitimate Acts of the Provisional Institutions of Self-government in Kosovo and Metohija on their Declaration of Unilateral Independence]. (OJ RS, No. 19/08) http://www.srbija.gov.rs/kosovo-metohija/index.php?id=43159 (4.1.2024).

GOV RS. (2006a). *Strategija razvoja šumarstva Republike Srbije* [Forestry Development Strategy of the Republic of Serbia]. (OJ RS, No. 59/06).

GOV RS. (2006b). *Nacionalna strategija privrednog razvoja Republike Srbije od 2006. do 2012. godine* [National Strategy on Economic Development of the Republic of Serbia from 2006 to 2012]. Beograd: Government of the Republic of Serbia.

GOV RS. (2002). *Vodoprivredna osnova Republike Srbije* [Water Management Basis of the Republic of Serbia]. (OJ RS, No. 11/02).

INCS. (2023). Izvod iz Centralnog registra: zaštićena područja. Zavod za zaštitu prirode Srbije [Extract from the Central Register: Protected Areas, Institute for Nature Conservation of Serbia].

MAEP. (2016). *First Biennial Update Report of the Republic of Serbia under the United Nations Framework Convention on Climate Change*. Belgrade: Ministry of Agriculture and Environmental Protection. https://unfccc.int/files/national_reports/non-annex_i_parties/biennial_update_reports/application/pdf/serbur1e.pdf (6.1.2024).

MAFWM. (2023). *Izveštaj o stanju u poljoprivredi u Republici Srbiji u 2022. godini. Knjiga I – horizontalni pregled [*Report on the state of agriculture in the Republic of Serbia in 2022. Book I – horizontal overview*]*. Beograd: Ministarstvo poljoprivrede, šumarstva i vodoprivrede. Ministry of Agriculture, Forest and Water Management.

MAFWM. (2019). *Sava and Drina River Corridors Integrated Development Program. Environmental and Social Management Framework for Serbia.* Draft Document. https://rdvode.gov.rs/doc/Environmental-and-Social-Management-Framework-for-Serbia.pdf (27.1.2024).

MAFWM. (2009). *The National Forest Inventory of the Republic of Serbia*. Belgrade: MAFWM, Forest Directorate. https://upravazasume.gov.rs/wp-content/uploads/2015/12/The-national-forest-inventory-of-the-Republic-of-Serbia-1.pdf (21.2.2024).

MCTI. (2021). *Prostorni plan Republike Srbije od 2021. do 2035. godine – Draft.* [*Spatial Plan of the Republic of Serbia from 2021 to 2035 – Draft*]. Ministry of Construction, Transport and Infrastructure. https://www.mgsi.gov.rs/sites/default/files/PPRS%20Nacrt.pdf (19.1.2024).

MEDEP. (2013). *Aarhus Convention Implementation Report*, Republic of Serbia, Ministry of Energy, Development and Environmental Protection. https://www.unece.org/env/pp/reports_trc_implementation_2014.html (6.1.2024).

MEP. (2023a). *Second Biennial Update Report of the Republic of Serbia to the UN Framework Convention on Climate Change. BUR 2*. https://unfccc.int/documents/636126 (8.2.2024).

MEP. (2023b. *Izveštaj o radu 2022 – Inspekcija za zaštitu životne sredine* [Work Report 2021, Environmental Protection Inspection]. Beograd: Ministarstvo zaštite životne sredine.

MEP. (2022). *Izveštaj o radu 2021 – Inspekcija za zaštitu životne sredine* [Work Report 2021, Environmental Protection Inspection]. Beograd: Ministarstvo zaštite životne sredine. https://www.ekologija.gov.rs/sites/default/files/inline-files/Inspekcija%20za%20zastitu%20zivotne%20sredine%20godisnji%20izvestaj%202021_0.pdf (14.2.2024).

MEP. (2019). *Sixth National Report to the United Nations Convention on Biological Diversity.* Belgrade: Ministry of Environmental Protection.

MEP. (2018). *CITES Republic of Serbia Implementation Report (2015–2017).* Ministry of Environmental Protection. https://cites.org/sites/default/files/reports/15-17Serbia.pdf (20.1.2024).

MEP. (2012). *Aarhus Convention Implementation Report*, Republic of Serbia. Ministry of Environmental Protection.. https://aarhusclearinghouse.unece.org/national-reports/reports?field_nr_report_language_aux_2_value=en&field_nr_report_language_aux_value=en&field_nr_q_year_target_id_verf%5B%5D=18900&field_nr_party_target_id_verf%5B%5D=17621&combine= (6.1.2024).

MESP. (2011). *Biodiversity Strategy of the Republic of Serbia for the period 2001–2018.* Belgrade: Ministry of Environment and Spatial Planning.

MESP. (2010a). *Initial National Communication of the Republic of Serbia under the United Nations Framework Convention on Climate Change.* Belgrade: The Ministry of Environment and Spatial Planning. https://unfccc.int/sites/default/files/resource/srbnc1.pdf (6.1.2024).

MESP. (2010b). *Aarhus Convention Implementation Report*, Republic of Serbia, Belgrade: Ministry of Environment and Spatial Planning. http://www.unece.org/fileadmin/DAM/env/pp/reporting/NIRs%202011/Serbia_NIR_2011_e.pdf (6.1.2024).

MESP. (2010c). *First National Report of the Republic of Serbia to the United Nations Convention on Biological Diversity, Republic of Serbia,* Belgrade: Ministry of Environment and Spatial Planning, July 2010. http://www.cbd.int/doc/world/cs/cs-nr-01-en.pdf (6.1.2024).

MME. (2023a). *Integrated Energy and Climate Plan of the Republic of Serbia for the period 2030 with the projections up to 2050 (Draft).* Belgrade: Ministry of Mining and Energy. https://www.energy-community.org/dam/jcr:01992fc5-4981-4ee3-84f8-f1f96830b4ba/INECP_Serbia_ENG_13.06.23%20.pdf (21.1.2024).

MME. (2023b). *Početna osnova plana razvoja energetske infrastrukture i mera energetske efikasnosti za period od 2028. sa projekcijama do 2030. godine* [The Initial Basis of the Energy Infrastructure Development Plan and Energy Efficiency Measures for the Period up to 2028 with Projections up to 2030]. Beograd: Ministarstvo rudarstva i energetike. https://www.mre.gov.rs/sektori/sr/60/1/5/0 (5.2.2024).

NA. (2015). *Strategija razvoja energetike Republike Srbije do 2025, godine sa projekcijama do 2030.* Narodna skupština. [Energy Development Strategy of the Republic of Serbia until 2025, with projection until 2030, National Assembly]. (OJ RS, 101/15).

NA. 2013. *Nacionalna strategija za borbu protiv korupcije u Republici Srbiji za period od 2013. do 2018. godine*. Narodna skupština. [National Strategy for the Fight Against Corruption in the Republic of Serbia for the period from 2013 to 2018. National Assembly]. OJ RS, No. 57/13).

NA. (2011). *Strategija upravljanja mineralnim resursima Republike Srbije do 2030* (Predlog). Narodna skupština. [Mineral Resources Management Strategy of the Republic of Serbia until 2030 (Proposal), National Assembly] http://www.ekoregistar.sepa.gov.rs/strategija-upravljanja-mineralnim-resursima-republike-srbije-do-2030-godine (6.1.2024).

Selected Bibliography

NA. (2010). *Prostorni plan Republike Srbije od 2010. do 2020. godine.* Narodna skupština. [Spatial Plan of the Republic of Serbia from 2010 to 2020, National Assembly]. OJ RS, No. 88/2010.

NA. (2005). *Nacionalna strategija za borbu protiv korupcije u Republici Srbiji.* Narodna skupština. [National Strategy for the Fight Against Corruption in the Republic of Serbia, National Assembly]. (OJ RS, No. 109/05).

NBS. 2024. *Macroeconomic Developments in Serbia.* Belgrade: National Bank of Serbia.

PDA. (2022). *Public Debt Management Strategy 2022–2024.* Belgrade: Public Debt Administration. https://javnidug.gov.rs/en/strategija (13.2.2024).

SRBATOM. (2023). *Izveštaj o izlaganju stanovništva jonizujućem zračenju u 2022. godini.* [Report on the Level of Exposure of the Population to Ionizing Radiation from the Environment in the Republic of Serbia in 2022]. Serbian Radiation and Nuclear Safety Directorate, Beograd, 2023. https://www.srbatom.gov.rs/srbatomm/monitoring-radioaktivnosti/?lang=bs (19.1.2024).

SRBATOM. (2020). *Izveštaj o izlaganju stanovništva jonizujućem zračenju u 2019. godini* [Report on the Level of Exposure of the Population to Ionizing Radiation from the Environment in the Republic of Serbia in 2019]. Beograd: Direktorat za radijacionu i nuklearnu sigurnost i bezbednost Srbije. http://www.srbatom.gov.rs/srbatomm/wp-content/uploads/2020/07/Izvestaj-Monitoring-2019-20200713.pdf (5.1.2024).

SRBATOM. (2018). *First National Report: Joint Convention on the Safety of Spent Fuel Management and on the Safety of Radioactive Waste Management.* Belgrade: Serbian Radiation Protection and Nuclear Safety Agency. https://www.srbatom.gov.rs/srbatomm/wp-content/uploads/2019/10/SERBIA-Joint-Convention-First-National-Report.pdf (19.2.2024).

STAT. OFFICE RS. (2024a). *Irrigation, 2023.* Statistical Release, Number 006 – Year LXXIV. https://publikacije.stat.gov.rs/G2024/PdfE/G20241006.pdf (16.2.2024).

STAT. OFFICE RS. (2024b). *Issued building permits*, Statistical Release, https://publikacije.stat.gov.rs/G2024/HtmlE/G20241032.html (18.2.2024).

STAT. OFFICE RS. (2023a). *Eco – bulletin 2022.* Statistical Office of the Republic of Serbia. Belgrade. https://publikacije.stat.gov.rs/G2023/Pdf/G20235701.pdf (26.1.2024).

STAT. OFFICE RS. (2023b). *Progress Report on the Implementation of Sustainable Development Goals by 2030 in the Republic of Serbia*, Report for 2022. Belgrade: Statistical Office of the RS.

STAT. OFFICE RS. (2022a). *Progress in monitoring of environment related SDG indicators in the Republic of Serbia – 2021.* Belgrade: Statistical Office of the RS. https://www.stat.gov.rs/en-US/publikacije/publication/?p=13661 (29.2.2024).

STAT. OFFICE RS. (2022b). *Poverty and Social Inequality*, 2021. Belgrade: Statistical Office of the Republic of Serbia. https://www.stat.gov.rs/en-US/vesti/statisticalrelease/?p=8870&a=01&s=0102?s=0102 (14.2.2024).

STAT. OFFICE RS. (2021). *The 2019 Serbian National Health Survey.* Belgrade: Statistical Office of the Republic of Serbia.

STAT. OFFICE RS. (2020). Statistical Release, No. 182, Year LXX, 2.7.2020.

STAT. YEARB. SERB. (2023). *Statistical Yearbook of the Republic of Serbia 2023*. Belgrade: Statistical Office of the Republic of Serbia, 2023, https://www.stat.gov.rs/en-us/publikacije/publication/?p=15431 (6.1.2024).

STAT. YEARB.SERB. (2019). *Statistical Yearbook of the Republic of Serbia 2019*. Belgrade: Statistical Office of the Republic of Serbia, 2019, https://publikacije.stat.gov.rs/G2019/PdfE/G20192052.pdf (6.1.2024).

STAT. YEARB. SERB. (2015). *Statistical Yearbook of the Republic of Serbia*, Belgrade: Statistical Office of the Republic of Serbia, https://publikacije.stat.gov.rs/G2015/PdfE/G20152016.pdf (6.1.2024).

STAT.YEARB.SERB. (2007). *Statistical Yearbook of the Republic Serbia*. Belgrade: Statistical Office of the Republic of Serbia. https://www.stat.gov.rs/en-US/publikacije/?d=2&r= (6.1.2024).

Young Researchers of Serbia. (2023). *A Green Agenda with No Agenda: shadow report on Chapter 27 – Environment and Climate Change: April 2022 – April 2023*. Belgrade. https://www.koalicija27.org/wp-content/uploads/2023/10/K27-izvestaj-2023-EN-web.pdf (27.1.2024).

Young Researchers of Serbia. (2022). *One step forward, two steps back: Shadow Report on Chapter 27: Environment and Climate Change: January 2021 – March 2022*. Belgrade. https://www.koalicija27.org/wp-content/uploads/2022/10/Shadow-_Report_Coalition-27_2022.pdf (19.2.2024).

Official Journals

Official Journal of the Autonomous Province of Vojvodina (Službeni list Autonomne Pokrajine Vojvodine).

Official Journal of the City of Belgrade (Službeni list grada Beograda).

Official Journal of the Federal Republic of Yugoslavia: OJ FRY (Službeni list Savezne Republike Jugoslavije).

Official Journal of the Federal People's Republic of Yugoslavia– OJ FNRY (Službeni list Federativne Narodne Republike Jugoslavije).

Official Journal of the Republic of Montenegro– OJ RM (Službeni list Republike Crne Gore).

Official Journal of the Republic of Serbia– OJ RS (Službeni glasnik Republike Srbije).

Official Journal of the Serbia and Montenegro– OJ S&M (Službeni list Srbije i Crne Gore).

Official Journal of the Socialist Autonomous Province of Kosovo-Metohija– OJ SAP KM (Službeni list Socijalističke autonomne pokrajine Kosova i Metohije).

Official Journal of the Socialist Autonomous Province of Vojvodina– OJ SAP V(Službeni list Socijalističke autonomne pokrajine Vojvodine).

Official Journal of the Socialist Federal Republic of Yugoslavia– OJ SFRY (Službeni list Socijalističke Federativne Republike Jugoslavije).

Official Journal of the Socialist Republic of Montenegro– OJ SRM (Službeni list Socijalističke Republike Crne Gore).

Official Journal of the Socialist Republic of Serbia– OJ SRS (Službeni glasnik Socijalističke Republike Srbije).

Selected Bibliography

Instead of a footnote: All the Republics and Provinces in the former Yugoslavia (Socialist Federal Republic of Yugoslavia) had in their name the attribute 'Socialist'. Due to that, all official journals had to change their titles after disintegration of the former Yugoslavia.

UNMIK. Official Gazette. https://unmik.unmissions.org/sites/default/files/regulations/index.htm (8.9.2020).

Index

The numbers here refer to paragraph numbers.

Index